The MMPI-2 / MMPI:
An Interpretive Manual

The MMPI-2 / MMPI:
An Interpretive Manual

ROGER L. GREENE

Texas Tech University

ALLYN AND BACON

Boston   London   Toronto   Sydney   Tokyo   Singapore

Copyright © 1991 by Allyn and Bacon
A Division of Simon & Schuster, Inc.
160 Gould Street
Needham Heights, Massachusetts 02194

Portions of this text appeared in *The MMPI: An Interpretive Manual* © 1980 by
The Psychological Corporation.

Library of Congress Cataloging-in-Publication Data

Greene, Roger L.
    The MMPI-2/MMPI : an interpretive manual / Roger L. Greene.
      p.   cm.
    "Portions of this text appeared in the MMPI: an interpretive
manual. c 1980"– –T.p. verso.
    Includes bibliographical references and index.
    ISBN 0-205-12525-5
    1. Minnesota Multiphasic Personality Inventory.   I. Title.
II. Title: MMPI-two/MMPI.
    [DNLM: 1. MMPI.   WM 145 G799ma]
BF698.8.M5B75   1991
DNLM/DLC
for Library of Congress   91-13934
                                 CIP

Printed in the United States of America
10 9 8 7 6 5 4 3 2 1 95 94 93 92 91

To Grant and Leona Dahlstrom

for their professionalism,

scholarliness, and personal warmth

Contents

Preface

The restandardization of the MMPI that resulted in the MMPI-2 has opened a whole new era of clinical use and research on this venerable instrument. Although some anguish has been aired about specific issues in the use of the MMPI-2, most of this concern reflects how central the MMPI has been to personality assessment for almost fifty years. It will be exciting to watch the empirical data amass as we make the transition to the MMPI-2.

This revision of my *MMPI Manual* is intended to provide clinicians who have used the MMPI for years the necessary information for making the transition to the MMPI-2. Consequently, this book contains the most current summary of the research on the MMPI and the available information on the MMPI-2. This "dual" coverage sometimes results in awkward referencing to the MMPI-2 or the MMPI within the same section. MMPI-2 or MMPI will be used as most appropriate to the specific material that is being discussed. Any reference to the use of the instrument prior to 1989 is to the original MMPI.

This revision also will serve as an introduction to the MMPI-2 for clinicians with no prior experience with the test. As with the original *MMPI Manual,* this revision is intended to provide a summary of the extant research on the instrument and a step-by-step procedure for profile interpretation.

The chapters have been reorganized slightly from my original *MMPI Manual.* The examples of clinical case interpretation have been moved to Chapter 7 to make it explicit that the information on the Supplementary and Content Scales now in Chapter 5 is to be included in profile interpretation.

PREFACE TO THE ORIGINAL *MMPI MANUAL*

This book arose out of the frustrations of trying to find a single source that would contain all the information needed by a clinician learning to interpret the MMPI (the Minnesota Multiphasic Personality Inventory). Some texts were too advanced and detailed for a clinician's first exposure to the MMPI, and often they omitted basic issues. Others were too elementary to provide any instruction on how to interpret and use the results of the MMPI. Combining these two types of information often resulted in a hodgepodge of material that was difficult for the clinician to organize and integrate.

In addition there was the difficulty of trying to make the process of interpreting psychological tests explicit for clinicians, who have often remarked that the basis for specific statements or inferences in interpretations of MMPI profiles was not clear. Despite the empirical basis of the MMPI, there sometimes was not a demonstrable correlate underlying an inference that was nevertheless frequently used by clinicians.

In a single source this book provides an introduction to some basic issues in the development and administration of the MMPI, as well as a step-by-step procedure for interpreting it. In addition, it discusses the use of the MMPI with such special groups as adolescents, the aged, and minorities, and it reviews the use and interpretation of critical items, special scales, and short forms. Although the text was written for the clinician with little prior exposure to the MMPI, experienced clinicians should find it helpful as a review of MMPI interpretation and as an update on the research in this rapidly growing area.

The behaviorial or personality correlates of each validity and clinical scale and all high-point pairs are included to make the process of profile interpretation more explicit. The two examples in Chapter 6 include a step-by-step description of the procedure to be followed by the clinician. With the process of profile interpretation made more explicit, clinicians can direct their research toward ascertaining which inferences are accurate and which need to be revised or eliminated.

Acknowledgments

I wish to express my appreciation to five anonymous reviewers who provided valuable feedback on an earlier draft of the manuscript. Their comments and insights helped me to elucidate many issues and to clarify the content. Of course, I accept the ultimate responsibility for any inadequacies that may remain.

I specifically would like to thank Dr. James Hedlund and Drs. Robert C. Colligan and Kenneth P. Offord who generously provided access to huge MMPI datasets that are cited frequently throughout the text. I also would like to thank countless clinicians and clients who have provided numerous insights on the nuances of the MMPI-2 and MMPI.

Finally, I wish to thank the many individuals who gave me permission to reproduce copyrighted materials. Specific citations occur whenever such material is used in the book.

Note about the Text

The terms *clinician* and *client* are used throughout this book as generic labels to describe the person interpreting and the person taking the MMPI-2. Since the MMPI-2 is employed in a variety of professional settings and administered to an equally large variety of persons, these terms were adopted to provide continuity. Occasionally, when the specific content being discussed requires it, another term will be used to describe the person taking the MMPI-2.

All research published in major psychological journals on the MMPI-2 and MMPI through December 1990 were reviewed for inclusion in the book. This review focused on the years since 1980 to provide an update of the recent research. Because of space limita-tions, numerous studies that were reviewed could not be included. To the best of my knowledge, however, no major substantive article on MMPI-2 or MMPI has been omit-ted.

In order to avoid the expression MMPI-2/MMPI, either MMPI-2 or MMPI will be used when a statement is appropriate to only one version of the test, and MMPI-2 will be used when the information is known or as-sumed to be relevant to both versions. Clini-cians should realize that the correlates re-ported are almost entirely based on the MMPI and their application to the MMPI-2 awaits empirical validation, although it is probably safe to assume that most of these correlates will generalize to the MMPI-2.

CHAPTER 1

The Evolution of the MMPI

The Minnesota Multiphasic Personality Inventory (MMPI) is currently the most widely used and researched objective personality inventory. Dahlstrom, Welsh, and Dahlstrom (1975) include almost 6,000 references on the clinical and research applications of the MMPI in *An MMPI Handbook*; Buros' (1978) *The Eighth Mental Measurements Yearbook* contains more than 5,000 citations on the MMPI; and Lubin, Larsen, Matarazzo, and Seever (1985) report that the MMPI is the most frequently used test in professional settings. Originally devised by Hathaway and McKinley in 1940, the MMPI provides an objective means of assessing abnormal behavior. A person taking the MMPI sorts 550 statements into one of three categories: "true," "false," or "cannot say." The person's responses to these statements are then scored on 10 clinical scales that assess major categories of abnormal behavior. In addition, 4 validity scales assess the person's test-taking attitudes. Table 1–1 illustrates the scale names and numbers of the 10 clinical and 4 validity scales. A standard profile sheet (see Profile 1–1) is used for plotting the person's scores on these 14 scales.

After a brief review of the history of objective personality inventories, this chapter will describe the rationale underlying the development of the MMPI and the methods used for item selection and scale construction. Problems associated with interpreting the content of individual items as well as assessing test-taking attitudes will be discussed. The chapter will conclude with a discussion of the appropriateness of the original norms for the MMPI for contemporary use (cf. Colligan, Osborne, Swenson, & Offord, 1983, 1989) and the development of the MMPI-2 (Butcher, Dahlstrom, Graham, Tellegen, & Kaemmer, 1989), the current revision of the MMPI.

THE EARLY HISTORY OF OBJECTIVE PERSONALITY INVENTORIES

Personality assessment, like intellectual assessment, received its first major impetus during World War I when a need arose for assessment procedures to screen large numbers of individuals. In response to this demand, Woodworth and Poffenberger developed the Woodworth Personal Data Sheet (Wood-

TABLE 1-1 MMPI Validity and Clinical Scales

Scale Name	Number	Abbre-viation	Number of Items
Validity			
Cannot Say		?	
Lie		L	15
F (Infrequency)		F	64
K (Correction)		K	30
Clinical			
Hypochondriasis	1	Hs	33
Depression	2	D	60
Hysteria	3	Hy	60
Psychopathic Deviate	4	Pd	50
Masculinity-Femininity	5	Mf	60
Paranoia	6	Pa	40
Psychasthenia	7	Pt	48
Schizophrenia	8	Sc	78
Hypomania	9	Ma	46
Social Introversion	0	Si	70

worth, 1920), a self-rating scale for detecting neurotic individuals. They assembled 116 items reflecting neurotic symptoms to which a person answered "yes" or "no." The total number of positive answers resulted in a score that indicated whether the person should be interviewed individually by a psychiatrist. Some items were considered so pathognomonic that a "yes" response to any of them prompted an individual interview. The items were heterogeneous in content since they tapped every symptom of psychological nervousness that Woodworth and Poffenberger could identify. The items were chosen because Woodworth and Poffenberger thought that they assessed psychological maladjustment; no empirical or theoretical perspective was employed in selecting items to be included on the test. Although the Personal Data Sheet was developed too late to be very useful in selecting recruits, since the United States was already involved in World War I,

it did identify those recruits who were emotionally unsuitable for service in the army under wartime conditions.

The success of psychological testing during World War I stimulated the development in the next decade of several personality inventories similar to the Personal Data Sheet. Probably the best known of these instruments is the Bernreuter Personality Inventory (Bernreuter, 1933), which measures neuroticism, dominance, introversion, and self-sufficiency. Like other personality inventories of this era, the Bernreuter Personality Inventory was constructed on a rational rather than an empirical basis. That is, the test developer would include items on a particular scale that, on the basis of clinical experience, were thought to measure a specific trait or construct. Likewise, the test developer would determine the scoring direction for any particular item on a rational basis. For example, if the test developer felt that a "yes" response to the item "Do you daydream a lot?" indicated neuroticism, that item would be added to the neuroticism scale with "yes" as the "deviant" response. The total number of these "deviant" responses, responses that the test developer felt tapped the specific trait or construct being assessed, became the score on the scale.

Strong critiques (cf. Landis & Katz, 1934; Super, 1942) devastated the Bernreuter Personality Inventory and other rationally derived personality inventories of this era. For example, to investigate how certain groups would perform on the Bernreuter Personality Inventory, Landis and Katz (1934) administered the inventory to 224 patients with a known clinical diagnosis and examined their scores. On the neuroticism scale 39 percent of the neurotic patients scored above the 90th percentile; 23 percent of the schizophrenic patients and 21 percent of the manic-depressive patients, however, also scored above the 90th percentile. Thus, this scale is inadequate since in addition to identifying some

PROFILE 1-1

MINNESOTA MULTIPHASIC™
PERSONALITY INVENTORY
S.R. Hathaway and J.C. McKinley

PROFILE

Name **Tim Smith**

Address **547 Geneva Avenue**

Occupation **Clerk**   Date Tested **5/ 6/89**

Education **12th**   Age **47**

Marital Status **Married**   Referred by **Dr. Clark**

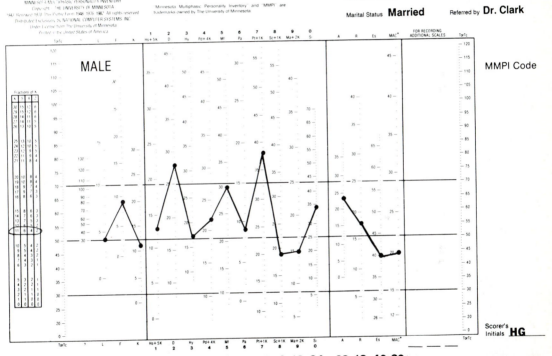

MALE

MMPI Code

Scorer's Initials **HG**

27309

Raw Score __0__ __4__ __9__ __11__ __7__ __28__ __17__ __18__ __30__ __9__ __27__ __8__ __13__ __34__   __23__ __18__ __40__ __20__ __ __ __ __ __ __ __ __

K to be added __6__   __4__   __11__ __11__ __2__

Raw Score with K __13__   __22__   __38__ __19__ __15__

*49 item version

neurotic patients correctly, it also misclassified several groups of psychotic patients as neurotic.

Furthermore, analyzing responses to individual items revealed additional problems. Bernreuter weighted a positive response to the items in the neurotic direction; however, Landis and Katz (1934) found that other groups endorsed some items as much or more frequently than neurotics. For example, the item "Are you critical of others?" elicited a "yes" response from 69 percent of the normal sample as compared with 32 percent of the neurotic sample and 39 percent of the psychotic sample. Similarly, the item "Do you daydream frequently?" was answered "yes" by 43 percent of the normal sample, 40 percent of the neurotic sample, and 31 percent of the psychotic sample.

Other studies (cf. Page, Landis, & Katz, 1934) demonstrated that identifying psychotic individuals with a rationally derived scale is also difficult. Page and associates constructed a rationally based scale by selecting 100 commonly accepted schizophrenic symptoms and traits from the psychiatric literature. The 50 traits considered schizophrenic by at least 10 of the 12 psychiatrists who reviewed the list were combined into a questionnaire. Page and colleagues administered the questionnaire to 125 schizophrenic patients, 100 manic-depressive patients, and 240 normal individuals, who were matched for intelligence and social status. They found little difference in the average number of the "schizophrenic" traits reported by the three groups: schizophrenics ($M = 17.60$; $SD = 7.50$), manic-depressives ($M = 14.00$; $SD = 7.35$), and normals ($M = 18.00$; $SD = 6.35$). The normal individuals, in fact, actually acknowledged having more of the "schizophrenic" traits than the schizophrenic patients did.

In examining responses to individual items, Page and associates (1934) also found inadequacies. Only 14 of the 50 traits reliably differentiated one group from the other two

groups. Even more striking, the normal individuals endorsed 11 of the 50 items more frequently than the schizophrenics did. Some of these 11 items were: "Are you often occupied with your own thoughts?" "Do you think it is possible for other people to influence your actions?" "Do your emotions change frequently without cause?"

Thus, the early personality inventories constructed on a rational basis were unsuccessful outside of a wartime setting. This should not be interpreted as an indictment of the general procedure, however. In the last three decades several widely used personality tests have been developed at least partly on a rational basis, such as the Edwards Personal Preference Schedule (Edwards, 1959) and the Personality Research Form (Jackson, 1968). Wiggins (1966) also successfully constructed 13 content scales for the MMPI on a rational basis, which have been validated as veridical self-reports of psychopathology (Jarnecke & Chambers, 1977; Lachar & Alexander, 1978). Chapter 5 provides further information on Wiggins' content scales and the new content scales for the MMPI-2 (Butcher, Graham, Williams, & Ben-Porath, 1989). Wiggins (1973) provides an excellent, in-depth analysis of the relative merits of empirically and rationally derived scales.

CONSTRUCTION OF THE MMPI

Out of the psychometric wilderness of the early 1930s appeared two men, Starke Hathaway and J. C. McKinley, who, under the banner of empiricism, waged a new battle for the scientific advancement of personality assessment. They sought to develop a multifaceted or multiphasic personality inventory, now known as the MMPI, that would surmount the shortcomings of the previous personality inventories, some of which were described above. Instead of using independent sets of tests, each with a special purpose, Hathaway and McKinley included in a single inventory a wide sampling of behavior of significance to psychologists. They wanted to create a large pool of items from which various scales could be constructed, in the hope of evolving a greater variety of valid personality descriptions than was currently available.

To this end, Hathaway and McKinley (1940) assembled more than 1,000 items from psychiatric textbooks, other personality inventories, and clinical experience. After deleting duplicate items and items that they considered relatively insignificant for their purposes, they arrived at a sample of 504[1] items. The items were written as declarative statements in the first-person singular, and most were phrased in the affirmative. Hathaway and McKinley (1940) arbitrarily classified the items under 25 headings as a convenience in handling and in an effort to avoid duplication (see Table 1–2). However, they did not attempt to obtain any particular number of items for a category or to insure that an item was actually properly classified in a category. Table 1–2 shows that some categories are heavily overrepresented and other categories are underrepresented.

Using the 504 items, Hathaway and Mc-Kinley (1940) next constructed a series of quantitative scales that could be used to diagnose abnormal behavior. In selecting items for a specific scale (e.g., Hypochondriasis), they used an empirical approach. The items had to be answered differently by the criterion group (e.g., hypochondriacal patients) as compared with normal groups. Since their approach was strictly empirical and no theoretical rationale was posited as the basis for accepting or rejecting items on a specific scale, it is not always possible to discern why a particular item distinguishes the criterion group from normal groups. Rather, items were selected solely because the criterion group answered them differently than other groups.

Scale *1* (Hypochondriasis) was constructed first (McKinley & Hathaway, 1940).[2] This choice was not simply fortuitous. Hypochondriasis is one of the simpler, more defi-

TABLE 1–2 Content Categories for MMPI Items

Content Category	Number of Items
Social attitudes	72
Political attitudes, law and order	46
Morale	33
Affect, depressive	32
Delusions, hallucinations, illusions, ideas of reference	31
Family and marital	29
Phobias	29
Affect, manic	24
Habits	20
Religious attitudes	20
General neurologic	19
Sexual attitudes	19
Occupational	18
Lie	15
Obsessive, compulsive	15
Educational	12
Cranial nerves	11
Gastrointestinal	11
Vasomotor, trophic, speech, secretory	10
General health	9
Sadistic, masochistic	7
Genitourinary	6
Motility and coordination	6
Cardiorespiratory	5
Sensibility	5
TOTAL	504

Note: The category names and sizes are from Hathaway and McKinley (1940).

nite diagnostic categories, and hypochondriacs also were one of the largest groups of patients available to McKinley and Hathaway. Since the procedure for developing Scale *1* typifies the procedure for most of the clinical scales, it will be described in detail. Later, the development of the other clinical scales will be described only in cases where the procedure differs.

The first step in developing Scale *1* was to select an appropriate criterion group. Using a diagnostic classification as the basis for the criterion group selection was logical since McKinley and Hathaway's intent was to develop an inventory to aid in differential diagnosis. They defined hypochondriasis as an abnormal neurotic concern over bodily health, excluding the symptomatic occurrence of hypochondriacal features in psychotic individuals. Using this definition, they selected 50 cases of pure, uncomplicated hypochondriasis as their criterion group.

The next step was to select groups of normal individuals. The primary normative group, which served as the reference group for determining the standard MMPI profile for over 40 years, consisted of 724 individuals who were friends or relatives of patients in the University Hospitals in Minneapolis. The only criterion for exclusion was if an individual was currently receiving treatment from a physician. This group reflected a fairly representative cross section for sex and marital status of the Minnesota population aged 16 to 55 in the late 1930s. Dahlstrom and colleagues (1975) reported that all of the persons in the primary normative group were white since very few members of any ethnic minority other than American Indian resided in Minnesota at that time. The current normative groups for the MMPI-2 will be described at the end of Chapters 1 and 2, and the use of the MMPI with minority individuals will be described in Chapter 8.

Four additional normative groups were used in the development of Scale *1* and other clinical scales on the MMPI. Two groups were formed to assess whether "nuisance" variables such as age, socioeconomic class, or education were influencing differential item endorsement by members of the criterion group and the primary normative group. One group consisted of 265 precollege high-school graduates who came to the University of Minnesota Testing Bureau for precollege guidance. The other was composed of 265 skilled workers from local Works Progress Administration projects. A third normative group consisted of 254 patients who were hospitalized for some form of physical disease in the general wards of the University Hospitals. None of the patients had obvious psychiatric symptomatology. The fourth general normative group consisted of 221 patients in the psychopathic unit of the University Hospitals, regardless of diagnosis.

Once the criterion group and the other reference groups were established, the process of item selection began. For the criterion group and each of the normal groups, the frequency of "true" and "false" responses was calculated for each item. An item was considered significant and was tentatively selected for a scale if the difference in frequency of response between the criterion group and the normative or reference groups was at least twice the standard error of the proportions of "true/false" responses of the two groups being compared. For example, the response frequencies for two potential items for Scale *1* are provided in Table 1–3. In this example, only two groups, the criterion group of hypochondriacs and the original normative group, are compared; before any items were finally selected, the criterion group was compared with the other normative groups as well.

The following (Ferguson, 1971) was used for the test of the significance of the difference between two independent proportions:

$$Z = \frac{p_1 - p_2}{\sqrt{pq[(1/n_1) + (1/n_2)]}}$$

where

p = the proportion of "true" responses in the total group
p_1 = the proportion of "true" responses in the first sample
p_2 = the proportion of "true" responses in the second sample
q = $1 - p$
n_1 = the number of persons in the first sample
n_2 = the number of persons in the second sample

TABLE 1–3 Frequency of Response by Group for Two Possible Items for Scale *1* (Hypochondriasis)

| | Group | | | |
| | Normals[a] | | Hypochondriacs[b] | |
Item	True	False	True	False
1. I have few or no pains	211(81%)	51(19%)	17(34%)	33(66%)
2. Much of the time my head seems to hurt all over.	10(4%)	252(96%)	5(10%)	45(90%)

[a] $n = 262$
[b] $n = 50$

Thus, the values of p and q for the first item would be the following:

$$p = \frac{211 + 17}{262 + 50} = \frac{228}{312} = .73$$

$$q = 1 - p = 1.0 - .73 = .27$$

Substituting these values in the above formula results in the following:

$$Z = \frac{.81 - .34}{\sqrt{(.73)\,(.27)\,[(1/262) + (1/50)]}}$$

$$= \frac{.47}{.069} = 6.81$$

Checking a standard table of Z values shows that this Z value would result in a probability less than .001. Hathaway and McKinley considered significant any percentage difference of at least twice the standard error of the independent proportions, or any Z equal to or greater than $+2$. Since a Z of $+2$ has a probability slightly less than .05 using a two-tailed test, they essentially selected only items that were significant beyond the .05 level. Thus, the first item in the preceding example would be tentatively included in Scale *1*, and a "false" response would be the "deviant" answer since the hypochondriacal patients responded more frequently in the "false" direction. If this item also differentiated the hypochondriacal group from the other normative groups using an identical procedure, it would then be included on Scale *1*.

Using the same procedure for the second sample item would result in substituting the following values in the formula:

$$Z = \frac{.04 - .10}{\sqrt{(.048)\,(.952)\,[(1/262) + (1/50)]}}$$

$$= \frac{-.06}{.033} = -1.82$$

This item would not be included on Scale *1* since the proportions of endorsement are not significantly different between the two groups.

Having selected items according to this procedure, Hathaway and McKinley then eliminated some of them for various reasons. First, the frequency of the criterion group's response was required to be greater than 10 percent for nearly all items; those items that yielded infrequent "deviant" response rates from the criterion group were excluded even if they were highly significant statistically since they represented so few criterion cases. Additionally, items whose responses appeared to reflect biases on variables such as marital status or attitudes toward one's children were excluded.

Finally, Hathaway and McKinley rejected a few more of the tentatively selected items that, after a rational inspection of the list, they concluded were not germane to the construct of hypochondriasis. Interitem correlations were not calculated nor were any other psychometric bases used in selecting items. The psychometric problems that later were discovered with some of the validity and clinical scales arose because these issues were not considered when each scale was constructed. These problems will be discussed below as appropriate when each scale is reviewed.

The preliminary Scale *1* consisted of 55 items that had been identified by this procedure. The next step was weighting or combining them into a scale. Evaluation of several methods of weighting individual items showed no advantage over using unweighted items. Therefore, each item simply received a weight of "one" in deriving a total score. In other words, a person's score on Scale *1* is equal to the total number of items that the individual answers as the criterion group did.

The responses of the normative group consisting of psychiatric patients helped to refine Scale *1*. A fair number of psychiatric patients obtained high scores on this scale although the psychiatric staff had not noted the presence of hypochondriasis. To eliminate this potential source of bias, the responses of 50 patients who had no hypochondriacal symptoms but who obtained the highest scale scores on the preliminary Scale *1* were contrasted with the original criterion group of 50 hypochondriacal patients. Items showing a significant difference in frequency of endorsement between these two groups were located and combined into a separate grouping, known as the correction of Scale *1*. (This correction of Scale *1* should not be confused with the *K*-correction of Scale *1*, which will be discussed later.) For each of these correction items that an individual answered in the nonhypochondriacal direction, one point was subtracted from the total score on Scale *1*. Cross-validation revealed that the corrected score on Scale *1* was more effective in differentiating the groups than the original uncorrected score.

The normative group with physical disease also was used in developing Scale *1*. This group scored more like the normal group than like the hypochondriacal group on the corrected Scale *1*. Thus, their actual physical symptoms appeared to alter their total scores only moderately in the direction of hypochondriasis.

More recently, Scale *1* was modified again. In order to differentiate Scale *1* more clearly from Scale *3* (Hysteria), McKinley and Hathaway (1944) eliminated from Scale *1* those correction items that also appeared on Scale *3*, thus arbitrarily making Scale *1* into a somatic complaints scale. They also eliminated some of the original items from Scale *1* that did not separate hypochondriacs from normals under subsequent analyses. This final step resulted in the 33 items that are currently used on Scale *1*.

Soon after the development of Scale *1* (McKinley & Hathaway, 1940), five other clinical scales were developed: *2* (Depression) (Hathaway & McKinley, 1942); *7* (Psychasthenia) (McKinley & Hathaway, 1942); and *3* (Hysteria), *4* (Psychopathic Deviate), and *9* (Hypomania) (McKinley & Hathaway, 1944). The description of the construction of three other clinical scales—*5* (Masculinity-Femininity), *6* (Paranoia), and *8* (Schizophrenia)—was not published until 1956 (Hathaway, 1956), although these three scales had been used routinely for more than a decade. (More detailed information on each of these scales will be provided in Chapter 4.)

Scale *5* (Masculinity-Femininity) was developed somewhat differently than the other clinical scales. Some 55 items, mostly related to sexual orientation, were added to the MMPI item pool after the data already had been collected from the original normative sample.[3] Thus, the criterion group of male homosexuals who were used in developing Scale *5* could not be contrasted with the original normative group on these 55 items. Consequently, 54 male soldiers were used as one of the normative groups for this scale, and items that distinguished them from the male homosexuals were included on Scale 5. In addition, items that differentiated males from females within the normative sample were included on this scale. The effects of these different construction procedures for Scale 5 will be explored more fully in Chapter 4.

In 1946 Scale 0 (Social Introversion) was added to the MMPI (Drake, 1946), completing the standard MMPI clinical profile. Scale 0 also was constructed differently from the other clinical scales. Drake selected MMPI items that differentiated 50 college students who scored above the 65th percentile on the Minnesota T-S-E Inventory (Evans & McConnell, 1941) from 50 students who scored below the 35th percentile.

The Minnesota T-S-E Inventory assesses introversion-extroversion in three areas: thinking (T), social (S), and emotional (E). Drake limited his initial work to the social introversion-extroversion area, or, more specifically, he investigated introversion-extroversion only in the social area as assessed by the Minnesota T-S-E Inventory. Although Drake conducted his analysis on males and females separately, their norms were so similar that he combined the normative data for the two sexes into a single group before finally incorporating it into the standard MMPI profile. (This issue will be explored more fully in Chapter 4.)

INTERPRETATION OF INDIVIDUAL ITEM CONTENT

Individuals sometimes fail to provide a veridical self-report (one that accurately reflects how others perceive their behavior) in responding to personality inventory items. There are several possible reasons for their inaccurate self-description. First, although persons constructing test items generally assume that each item has essentially the same meaning to all persons taking the test, this is not always the case. For example, for a test item such as "I have headaches frequently," persons may interpret "frequently" to mean once a day, once a week, or once a month and respond "true" or "false" accordingly. One client might endorse this item as being "true" since he has headaches at least once a month; another might endorse this item as being "false" since she has headaches only once a week. The ambiguity inherent in any test item makes it extremely difficult to obtain a veridical self-description since the person answering a specific test item and an observer rating the person on that item's content may each interpret the item somewhat differently.

Second, although self-ratings provided through item responses can be useful since direct observations of behavior are often impractical, impossible, or inefficient, individuals vary in their self-awareness and in their ability or willingness to report the appropriate behaviors. Third, the rational method of test construction also requires that the test developer be knowledgeable about the relationship between persons' responses to individual items and the construct being assessed. The fallacies and errors in earlier rationally derived personality inventories suggest that it is difficult if not impossible for the test developer to have this depth of understanding of the dynamics of a personality inventory.

These problems can be demonstrated by the response of psychopaths to the MMPI item "I have been quite independent and free from family rule." A test developer would likely make the a priori assumption that psychopaths would respond "true" to this item. In fact, psychopaths answered this item "false" more often than the normative groups. This response does not mean that this specific behavior is actually characteristic of psychopaths; rather it means that psychopaths say it is characteristic of them. As such it can be treated like any other statement an individual makes. It indicates how the person interprets the statement and how the person thinks, perceives, and feels even though it may actually be untrue. Although this statement is untrue, it still provides useful diagnostic information about the individual.

Another example is the response of hypochondriacs to the MMPI item "I have few or no pains." They answered this item "false" more often than the normative group. Such a response does not necessarily mean that hypochondriacs actually experience more pain than other persons, but it does show that they are more willing to say that it is true about themselves.

Although these issues unquestionably exist in the interpretation of item content on the MMPI, they do not invalidate it. The empirical approach to item selection used by Hathaway and McKinley, in fact, freed the test developers of these problems since it assumes that the client's self-report is just that and makes no a priori assumptions about the relationships between the client's self-report and the client's behavior. Items are selected for inclusion in a specific scale only because the criterion group answered the items differently than the normative groups irrespective of whether the item content is actually an accurate description of the criterion group. Any correlates between clients' responses to a given item or scale and their behavior must be demonstrated empirically. The interested reader should consult Meehl's (1945) article, which explores this issue in greater depth, and the section on critical items in Chapter 5.

ASSESSMENT OF TEST-TAKING ATTITUDES

In addition to the accuracy of the self-report in reflecting a client's actual behavior, the honesty or frankness with which the client attempts to respond to the items is also important. It is possible that a client might adopt a test-taking attitude other than that desired by the test developer. A client may decide, for whatever reason, to overreport (exaggerate)

or underreport (deny) the behavior being assessed by the test instrument, or a client may respond randomly to the test items because of an unwillingness or inability to respond appropriately. In either case it is important for the interpreter of the test inventory to be aware of the possibility that the client has responded inappropriately. Previous test developers often paid lip service to the importance of appropriate test-taking attitudes, but they did not provide specific directions on how to develop or maintain those attitudes. More important, they did not provide a means of assessing whether those attitudes were actually present. In the development of the MMPI this problem was directly assessed through what are now called the validity scales.

Meehl and Hathaway (1946) were convinced of the necessity of assessing two dichotomous categories of test-taking attitudes: defensiveness ("faking-good") and plus-getting ("faking-bad").[4] (These two categories will be called "underreporting" and "overreporting" of psychopathology, respectively, throughout later sections of this book to avoid the connotations inherent in the terms of "faking-good" and "faking-bad," since it is not always clear whether the person's motivation for distorting responses is conscious or unconscious.)

To assess these two categories of test-taking attitudes, Meehl and Hathaway considered three possible approaches. First, they could give the client an opportunity to distort the responses in a specific way and observe the extent to which the client did so. One way of implementing this approach would be to repeat items within the MMPI, phrased either identically or in the negative rather than the affirmative. A large number of inconsistent responses would suggest that the client was either unable or unwilling to respond consistently. Although Meehl and Hathaway rejected this solution, the old MMPI group booklet form included 16 identically repeated items that could be used to detect inconsistent responding (see the *TR* [Test-Retest] Index section in Chapter 3); however, these 16 items have been deleted in the MMPI-2 (see below).

Second, Meehl and Hathaway considered providing an opportunity for the client to answer favorably when a favorable response would almost certainly be untrue. This solution would involve developing a list of extremely desirable but very rare human qualities. If a client endorsed a large number of these items, it is highly probable that the responses would be dishonest. The *L* (Lie) scale was developed specifically for this purpose. Items for the *L* scale, based on the work of Hartshorne and May (1928), reflect behaviors that, although socially desirable, are all rarely true of a given individual. A large number of responses in the deviant direction on the *L* scale indicates response distortion.

The *F* scale was developed according to a variant of this second approach for assessing test-taking attitudes. Items for the *F* scale were selected primarily because they were answered with a relatively low frequency by a majority of the original normative group. In other words, if a client endorsed a large number of the *F* scale items, that person would be responding in a manner that was atypical of most people in the normative group. In addition, the items include a variety of content areas so that any specific set of experiences or interests for a particular individual would be unlikely to influence the person to answer many of the items in the deviant direction. The *F* scale effectively identified individuals who were intentionally faking pathology; however, schizoid individuals and persons who were overly pessimistic about themselves also obtained high scores. Therefore, additional procedures were needed to separate these two groups of persons from those who faked their pathology or misunderstood the items. Meehl and Hathaway thought the *L* scale would serve this function, which pro-

vided another reason for its use as a validity scale.

Third, Meehl and Hathaway considered using an empirical procedure to identify items that elicit different responses from persons taking the test in an appropriate fashion and those who have been instructed to "fake" psychopathology. Gough's Dissimulation scale (Gough, 1954, 1957), which was based on this procedure, will be described in Chapter 3.

Meehl and Hathaway adopted a variant of this third approach in developing a third validity scale, the *K* scale. Their task was to differentiate abnormal persons who were hospitalized and yet obtained normal profiles from normal individuals who for some reason obtained abnormal profiles. They selected 25 male and 25 female patients diagnosed as having psychopathic personalities, alcoholism, and other behavior disorders who (1) had a T score of 60 or higher on the *L* scale, which would indicate some form of response distortion, and (2) had diagnoses indicating that they should have abnormal profiles, but (3) had actual profiles in the normal range. Based on a comparison of this group with the original normative sample on all items, 22 items were selected that showed at least a 30 percent difference in the response rates of the two groups.

It was later found that these 22 items generally did an adequate job of identifying defensiveness in most patients; however, depressed and schizophrenic patients tended to score low. To counteract this tendency, 8 items were added and scored to differentiate these two groups from the original normative group. This final step resulted in the 30-item *K* scale, which is currently used. Meehl and Hathaway also empirically determined the proportions of *K* that when added to a clinical scale would maximize the discrimination between the criterion group and the normative group. Since Meehl and Hathaway determined the optimal weights of *K* to be added to each clinical scale in a psychiatric inpatient population, they warned that with maladjusted normal populations and other clinical populations, other weights of K might serve to maximize the identification of pathological individuals. This issue of the optimal weights to be added to each clinical scale in different populations will be discussed in Chapter 3 when the K scale is examined in more depth.

CURRENT DEVELOPMENTS

The issue of whether the items and norms for the MMPI developed in the early 1940s are appropriate for contemporary use has been raised repeatedly and debated widely (cf. Butcher, 1972; Colligan et al., 1983; Faschingbauer, 1979). Since the typical individual in the original Minnesota normative group was "about thirty-five years old, was married, lived in a small town or rural area, had had eight years of general schooling, and worked at a skilled or semiskilled trade (or was married to a man with such an occupation level)" (Dahlstrom, Welsh, & Dahlstrom, 1972, p. 8), it seems apparent that there have been numerous changes in our society over the ensuing five decades.

Pancoast and Archer (1989) collated the existing literature on the performance of normal individuals on the MMPI to assess the adequacy of the norms based on the original Minnesota normative group. The mean MMPI profile for these normal men (Profile 1-2) and women (Profile 1-3) showed T scores near 55 for Scales K, 3 (Hysteria), 4 (Psychopathic Deviate), and 9 (Hypomania). Only on Scales L and 1 (Hypochondriasis) did the mean T scores approach 50. Pancoast and Archer found that studies as early as 1949 demonstrated that normal individuals showed generally small, but consistent variations from the mean scores of the original Minnesota normative group. Two conclusions can be drawn from the data summarized by Pancoast and Archer. First, the scores of normal individuals may have been slightly different from the original Minnesota normative group on the standard validity and clinical scales since the MMPI was first developed. Second, there have been only small changes in normal individuals across five decades as reflected by their mean T scores on the standard validity and clinical scales.

Greene (1990) examined the changes in the standard validity and clinical scales on the MMPI within four frequently occurring codetypes (Spike *4*, *2-4/4-2*, *2-7/7-2*, and *6-8/8-6*) in samples of psychiatric patients over a span of 40 years. The mean and median profiles were virtually identical within all four codetypes for all four samples as can be seen in Table 1-4. The range in scores across all of the clinical scales in all four samples was 2 T points for the Spike *4* codetypes, 4 T points in the *2-4/4-2* codetypes, 5 T points in the *2-7/7-2* codetypes, and 9 T points in the *6-8/8-6* codetypes. The average difference between the highest and lowest score on all of the clinical scales was 2.2, 3.0, 2.5, and 5.5 T points for these four codetypes, respectively. It appears that the MMPI scale scores of psychiatric patients have been very stable over this time span. Greene's data did not address whether the empirical correlates of these codetypes remained unchanged across the 40 years that the MMPI has been in use. However, the stability of the MMPI scale scores across these years would at least suggest that the correlates probably have not changed. Of course, empirical data are needed to address this question.

The finding that normal individuals and psychiatric patients have shown only minimal changes on the standard validity and clinical scales of the MMPI across 40 years is very surprising, and would suggest that the MMPI may not be as outdated as many people have thought. The recent work of Colligan and associates (1983) in developing contemporary

PROFILE 1–2

MMPI™

MINNESOTA MULTIPHASIC™
PERSONALITY INVENTORY
S.R. Hathaway and J.C. McKinley

PROFILE

NAME_____

ADDRESS_____

OCCUPATION_____ DATE TESTED __ / __ / __

EDUCATION_____ AGE_____

MARITAL STATUS_____ REFERRED BY _____

MALE

Various MMPI Normal Samples
Pancoast and Archer (1989)

T score __ 49 53 56 53 54 57 57 59 54 54 53 56 50 __ __ __ __

PROFILE 1–3

MMPI™

MINNESOTA MULTIPHASIC ™
PERSONALITY INVENTORY
S.R. Hathaway and J.C. McKinley

PROFILE

MINNESOTA MULTIPHASIC PERSONALITY INVENTORY
Copyright © THE UNIVERSITY OF MINNESOTA
1943. Renewed 1970. This Profile Form 1948, 1976, 1982. All rights reserved.
Distributed Exclusively by NATIONAL COMPUTER SYSTEMS, INC.
Under License from The University of Minnesota
Printed in the United States of America

"Minnesota Multiphasic Personality Inventory" and "MMPI" are
trademarks owned by The University of Minnesota.

NAME_____

ADDRESS_____

OCCUPATION_____ DATE TESTED __ / / __

EDUCATION_____ AGE_____

MARITAL STATUS_____ REFERRED BY _____

FEMALE

Various MMPI Normal Samples

Pancoast and Archer (1989)

T score __ **50 52 56 51 53 55 54 47 55 53 53 51 55** __ __ __ __

*49 item version

NATIONAL COMPUTER SYSTEMS

27309

TABLE 1–4 MMPI Performance within Four Codetypes Across Four Decades

Sample	N	(%)	Age	Gender	L	F	K	1(Hs)	2(D)	3(Hy)	4(Pd)	5(Mf)	6(Pa)	7(Pt)	8(Sc)	9(Ma)	O(Si)
2-4/4-2																	
Minnesota 1950	68	(2.71%)	35.1	53%F													
Mean				47%M	53	63	53	66	84	70	84	53	66	71	70	56	60
Median					50	60	53	66	82	72	81	51	65	69	69	55	61
Minnesota 1960	245	(4.11%)	32.3	64%F													
Mean				36%M	51	65	53	63	83	69	84	54	66	71	66	57	64
Median					46	62	51	64	80	69	83	53	65	71	66	55	64
Missouri 1970	607	(5.77%)	38.1	22%F													
Mean				78%M	51	62	51	61	82	66	83	56	64	68	66	58	60
Median					46	60	49	59	80	65	81	55	62	68	65	58	60
Texas 1980	241	(5.29%)	33.0	50%F													
Mean				50%M	50	64	51	63	82	67	84	53	66	70	70	58	62
Median					46	62	49	62	80	67	81	51	65	69	69	55	63
Spike 4																	
Minnesota 1950	70	(2.79%)	28.6	53%F													
Mean				47%M	52	54	61	52	55	58	75	53	56	56	59	57	49
Median					50	53	59	52	55	59	71	53	56	56	60	58	48
Minnesota 1960	208	(3.49%)	26.5	51%F													
Mean				49%M	51	56	60	54	57	60	77	51	56	58	57	56	50
Median					50	53	59	54	58	60	74	51	56	58	55	55	49
Missouri 1970	752	(7.15%)	34.0	25%F													
Mean				75%M	53	55	58	53	57	58	77	52	56	55	57	58	49
Median					50	53	57	52	57	58	74	51	53	55	57	58	48
Texas 1980	201	(4.42%)	29.8	61%F													
Mean				39%M	52	55	58	52	57	59	76	50	57	56	58	58	52
Median					50	53	57	52	56	59	74	49	56	55	57	58	51

continued

15

TABLE 1–4 *continued*

Sample	N	(%)	Age	Gender	L	F	K	1(Hs)	2(D)	3(Hy)	4(Pd)	5(Mf)	6(Pa)	7(Pt)	8(Sc)	9(Ma)	0(Si)
2-7/7-2																	
Minnesota 1950	157	(6.26%)	37.8	55%F													
Mean				45%M	51	58	52	68	90	71	67	52	65	85	74	53	67
Median					50	55	51	68	88	70	67	51	65	83	73	53	68
Minnesota 1960	381	(6.39%)	37.9	47%F													
Mean				53%M	50	61	52	68	90	71	69	55	65	86	71	53	68
Median					46	60	51	67	88	71	67	53	65	84	71	53	69
Missouri 1970	392	(3.72%)	40.3	25%F													
Mean				75%M	50	63	49	66	90	68	70	58	66	85	74	54	69
Median					46	60	48	65	88	67	69	57	65	83	73	53	69
Texas 1980	180	(3.95%)	33.6	44%F													
Mean				56%M	49	63	50	66	89	69	70	56	67	85	75	54	69
Median					46	60	49	65	89	67	69	55	65	83	73	53	69
6-8/8-6																	
Minnesota 1950	121	(4.83%)	32.9	69%F													
Mean				31%M	51	89	44	63	70	62	72	60	90	75	95	73	65
Median					46	88	42	60	69	58	71	59	88	74	94	73	64
Minnesota 1960	137	(2.30%)	32.1	71%F													
Mean				29%M	53	94	46	69	70	65	74	61	89	74	91	72	65
Median					50	96	46	67	70	64	71	59	88	75	90	70	64
Missouri 1970	686	(6.52%)	30.4	36%F													
Mean				64%M	49	93	43	70	76	67	79	60	95	81	101	75	65
Median					46	92	40	68	76	66	79	59	94	79	101	73	65
Texas 1980	225	(4.94%)	28.3	52%F													
Mean				48%M	49	92	45	70	73	67	77	58	92	79	99	73	64
Median					46	94	42	68	72	64	74	57	91	79	99	73	63

norms for the MMPI and the current restandardization of the MMPI that has resulted in the MMPI-2 also have examined the changes that have occurred since the MMPI was developed originally.

A Contemporary Normative Study of the MMPI

Colligan and colleagues (Colligan et al., 1983, 1989; Colligan, Osborne, Swenson, & Offord, 1984) investigated whether the original MMPI norms were appropriate for contemporary use. They essentially replicated the data-collection procedures employed by McKinley and Hathaway (1940) and gathered a representative sample of individuals living within 50 miles of the Mayo Clinic in Rochester, Minnesota. "Persons having chronic diseases (for example, diabetes) were excluded from the study, as were patients receiving cancer treatment, those with rheumatoid or other types of arthritis, those described as being chemically dependent, having a learning disability, or being mentally retarded, and persons undergoing psychotherapy" (Colligan et al., 1983, pp. 74–75).

Their final sample consisted of 1,408 white individuals (646 men and 762 women), whose mean age was in their mid–40s and who had a mean of 13 years of education. Nearly three-fourths of them were married. These individuals were somewhat older and better educated than the original Minnesota normative sample that has been described above. Colligan and associates also selected a subset of these individuals "in proportion to the age and sex in the general population of adult whites in the United States, as determined by the 1980 census" (1983, p. 87) so that they could make more direct comparisons with the original normative group since the population of the United States had increased in age and become better educated in the ensuing four decades.

Profiles 1–4 and 1–5 provide the mean profile (and the profile for the mean plus two standard deviations [i.e., the profile equivalent to a T score of 70]) for these contemporary men and women plotted on the *original* MMPI norms. As can be seen in these two profiles, the men average 3 to 8 T score points higher on the clinical scales and the women average 1 to 6 T score points higher (except on Scale *5* [Masculinity-Femininity] where they are 4 points lower) on the clinical scales than the original Minnesota normative group. The men's profile equivalent to a T score of 70 averages 2 to 7 T points higher on the clinical scales, whereas the women's profile equivalent to a T score of 70 is fairly similar to the original Minnesota normative group.

Two basic points can be made based on the data presented in Profiles 1–4 and 1–5. First, there are some differences in MMPI performance across the five decades that the MMPI has been in use, although these differences are not as substantial as might have been expected, given the changes in our society in the last 50 years. If Profiles 1–4 and 1–5 are compared with the data reported by Pancoast and Archer (1989) in Profiles 1–2 and 1–3, respectively, further support can be provided for the statement that the scores of normal individuals may have been slightly different from the original Minnesota normative group on the standard validity and clinical scales since the MMPI was first developed. Second, it appears that these changes average less than one-half standard deviation (5 T points) and these small changes in profile elevation are not likely to have major impact on the clinical interpretation of the MMPI.

Colligan and colleagues (1983) continued the procedure of using *K*-corrected scores and they used the same correction weights on the same clinical scales (Scales *1* [Hypochondriasis], *4* [Psychopathic Deviate], *7* [Psychasthenia], *8* [Schizophrenia], and *9* [Hypomania]) that had been suggested by Meehl and Hathaway (1946). However, they made one

PROFILE 1–4

MMPI™

MINNESOTA MULTIPHASIC ™
PERSONALITY INVENTORY
S.R. Hathaway and J.C. McKinley

PROFILE

NAME_____

ADDRESS_____

OCCUPATION_____ DATE TESTED __/__/__

EDUCATION_____ AGE_____

MARITAL STATUS_____ REFERRED BY _____

MALE

Contemporary Normative Sample

Colligan and Associates (1983)

Mean (T 50)
———

Mean + 2 SD (T 70)
- - - - - -

T score __ 49 54 54 54 54 57 54 58 55 54 53 55 53 __ __ __ __

NATIONAL
COMPUTER
SYSTEMS

*49 item version

27309

PROFILE 1–5

MMPI™

MINNESOTA MULTIPHASIC ™
PERSONALITY INVENTORY
S.R. Hathaway and J.C. McKinley

PROFILE

MINNESOTA MULTIPHASIC PERSONALITY INVENTORY
Copyright © THE UNIVERSITY OF MINNESOTA
1943. Renewed 1970. This Profile Form 1948, 1976, 1982. All rights reserved.
Distributed Exclusively by NATIONAL COMPUTER SYSTEMS, INC.
Under License from The University of Minnesota
Printed in the United States of America

"Minnesota Multiphasic Personality Inventory" and "MMPI" are
trademarks owned by The University of Minnesota

NAME_____

ADDRESS_____

OCCUPATION_____DATE TESTED__/__/__

EDUCATION_____AGE_____

MARITAL STATUS_____REFERRED BY_____

FEMALE

Contemporary Normative Sample

Colligan and Associates (1983)

Mean (T 50)
———

Mean + 2 SD (T 70)

T score __ **50 52 55 51 54 53 53 46 56 53 54 51 56** __ __ __ __ .

NATIONAL
COMPUTER
SYSTEMS

* 49 item version

27309

major change when they decided to employ normalized T scores. The linear transformations of raw scores into T scores that are used on the standard MMPI profile sheet assume an underlying normal distribution that is not typical for most of the scales since T scores greater than 69 occur quite frequently. The normalized T scores that were developed by Colligan and colleagues produced a normal distribution for each scale in their normative sample. The issue of linear versus normalized T scores will be explored further in the next chapter.

There has been only limited research with the Colligan and associates (1983) norms. Colligan, Osborne, Swenson, and Offord (1985) reported the frequency with which codetypes occurred in four clinical samples, and the concordance between their contemporary norms and the original MMPI norms. Concordance of codetypes between the two sets of norms ranged from 40 to 60 percent for women and from 50 to 70 percent for men, whereas agreement on single scales ranged from 66 to 79 percent for women and from 69 to 79 percent for men.

Miller and Streiner (1986) reported the concordance between profiles generated by contemporary norms and the original MMPI norms in a large sample of psychiatric patients. They found that 48.4 percent of the profiles showed no changes in the two highest clinical scales, and another 15.1 percent of the profiles had the two highest clinical scales reversed. Thus, 63.5 percent of the profiles had the same codetype using the two sets of norms. In 23.6 percent of the profiles, the highest clinical scale remained the same while another clinical scale became the second highest scale. A totally unique codetype was produced in 9.4 percent of the profiles. Although it is important to know the concordance between codetypes generated by the two sets of norms, the primary issue remains whether the original or contemporary norms more accurately reflect external correlates.

Over the ensuing years Colligan and colleagues have provided contemporary norms for Barron's (1953) Ego Strength scale (Colligan & Offord, 1987a), Welsh's (1956) Anxiety and Repression scales (Colligan & Offord, 1988a), Wiggins' (1966) Content scales (Colligan & Offord, 1988b), and the $F - K$ index (Osborne, Colligan, & Offord, 1986).

Tables for converting raw scores into T scores so that the clinician can compare a client's performance with a *contemporary* adult sample are available in Colligan and associates (1983). Hsu and Betman (1986) have provided tables for converting the T scores for the original MMPI normative group into Colligan and colleagues' (1983) contemporary norms and vice versa. Colligan and colleagues (1983) also illustrate a standard profile sheet for use with their contemporary norms (p. 421).

The MMPI-2

The MMPI-2 (Butcher et al., 1989) represents the restandardization of the MMPI that marks the advent of a new era of clinical usage and research of this venerable inventory. Restandardization of the MMPI was needed to provide current norms for the inventory, develop a nationally representative and larger normative sample, provide appropriate representation of minority groups, and update item content where needed. Continuity between the MMPI and the MMPI-2 has been maintained since new criterion groups and item derivation procedures were *not* used on the standard validity and clinical scales. Thus, the items on the validity and clinical scales of the MMPI are essentially unchanged on the MMPI-2 except for the elimination of 13 items based on item content (see Table 1–5) and the rewording of 68 items.

The profile forms for the original MMPI

TABLE 1–5 Thirteen Items Dropped from the Standard Validity and Clinical Scales

---

F Scale

14. I have looseness in my bowels (diarrhea) once a month or more.
53. A minister can cure disease by praying and putting his hand on your head.
206. I am very religious (more than most people).
258. I believe there is a God.

Scale *1* (*Hs*)
63. I have had no difficulty in starting or holding my bowel movements.

Scale *2* (*D*)
58. Everything is turning out just as the prophets of the Bible said it would.
95. I attend religious services almost every week.
98. I believe in the second coming of Christ.

Scale *5* (*Mf*)
69. I am very strongly attracted by members of my own sex.
70. I used to like drop-the-handkerchief.
249. I believe there is a Devil and a Hell in afterlife.
295. I liked "Alice in Wonderland" by Lewis Carroll.

Scale *0* (*Si*)
462. I have had no difficulty starting or holding my urine.

Note: Reproduced from the MMPI by permission. Copyright © 1943, renewed 1970 by the University of Minnesota. Published by the University of Minnesota Press. All rights reserved.

(Profile 1–1) and the MMPI-2 (Profile 1–6) also are virtually identical. A quick comparison of Profile 1–1 and 1–6 will not reveal any readily apparent differences between the two forms. Only on closer examination are any differences seen on the MMPI-2 profile form: the Cannot Say (*?*) scale has been moved to the bottom of the page, T scores of 65 are considered to be clinically significant instead of T scores of 70, and the T score distributions have been truncated at 30 so that T scores below 30 do not occur.

In the development of the MMPI-2, the Restandardization Committee (Butcher et al., 1989) started with the 550 items on the original MMPI. They reworded 141 of these 550 items to eliminate outdated and sexist language and to make these items more easily understood. Rewording these items did not change their item-scale correlations in most cases (Ben-Porath & Butcher, 1989). The Restandardization Committee then added 154 provisional items that resulted in the 704 items in Form AX, which was used to collect the normative data for the MMPI-2.

When finalizing the items to be included on the MMPI-2, the Restandardization Committee deleted 77 items from the original MMPI in addition to the 13 items deleted from the standard validity and clinical scales and the 16 repeated items. Consequently, most special and research scales that have been developed on the MMPI are still capable of being scored unless the scale has an emphasis on religious content or the items are drawn predominantly from the last 100 items on the original MMPI. The content areas for these 77 items that were not retained plus the

PROFILE 1–6

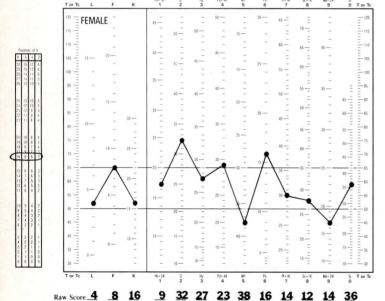

MMPI-2 S.R. Hathaway and J.C. McKinley
*Minnesota Multiphasic
Personality Inventory -2*

Profile for Basic Scales

Name **Cherie Jones**

Address **2894 Albion Way**

Occupation **Secretary**   Date Tested **3/ 4/91**

Education **13th** Age **27** Marital Status Single

Referred by **Dr. Smiley**

MMPI-2 Code **26'43-1078/59 F-KL**

Scorer's Initials **HG**

Raw Score **4 8 16 9 32 27 23 38 16 14 12 14 36**

? Raw Score **0**

K to be Added **8   6   16 16 3**

Raw Score with K **17   29   30 28 17**

13 items deleted from the standard validity and clinical scales can be seen in Table 1–6. Levitt (1990) also has grouped these 77 items into logical content categories and provided the actual items within each category.

The Restandardization Committee included 68 of the 141 items that had been rewritten, and they incorporated 107 of the provisional items to assess major content areas that were not covered in the original MMPI item pool. The rationale for including and dropping items from Form AX that resulted in the 567 items on the MMPI-2 has not been made explicit to date. Table 1–7 illustrates the changes that were made in the transition from the 566 items on the MMPI to the 567 items on the MMPI-2.

The MMPI-2 was standardized on a sample of 2,600 individuals who were selected from seven different states (California, Minnesota, North Carolina, Ohio, Pennsylvania, Virginia, and Washington) to reflect national census parameters on age, marital status, ethnicity, and so on. The demographic characteristics of this sample can be seen in Table 1–8.

The normative sample for the MMPI-2 varies significantly from the original normative sample for the MMPI in a number of areas: years of education, representation of

TABLE 1–7 Changes in Items from the MMPI to the MMPI-2

	Number of Items
MMPI	566
Drop 16 repeated items	−16
Drop 13 items from the standard validity and clinical scales	−13
Drop 77 items from the last 167 items	−77
TOTAL	460
Add 89 items for the new content scales	+89
Add 18 unscored items	+18
MMPI-2	567

minority individuals, and occupational status. The individuals in the normative sample for the MMPI-2 also are more representative of the United States as a whole since national census parameters were utilized in their collection. However, they still varied from the census parameters on years of education and occupational status. The potential impact of the relatively high level of education and occupational status characteristic of the MMPI-2 normative group on the standard validity and clinical scales and codetype interpretation remains to be determined empirically.

Profiles 1–7 and 1–8 illustrate the average scores for men and women on the standard validity and clinical scales in the MMPI-2 normative sample when plotted on the *original* MMPI norms. The MMPI-2 normative sample scores about 3 to 5 T points higher on most of these scales. Only on Scales *L*, *1* (Hypochondriasis), and *0* (Social Introversion) are their scores nearly identical. Thus, the transition to the MMPI-2 norms will mean that the new profiles are slightly less elevated when compared to the original MMPI norms. It also should be noted that the average scores for the standard validity and clinical scales for the MMPI-2 correspond very closely to those reported by Col-

TABLE 1–6 Content Areas of MMPI Items *Not* Retained on the MMPI-2

Content Area	Number of Items
Interests/hobbies	17
Religion	16
Interpersonal relationships	14
Negative affects	12
Bodily functions	9
Miscellaneous	5
Sexuality	5
Sensory functions	4
Substance abuse	3
Blushing	3
Dreaming	2
TOTAL	90

PROFILE 1–7

MMPI™

MINNESOTA MULTIPHASIC
PERSONALITY INVENTORY
S.R. Hathaway and J.C. McKinley

PROFILE

NAME_____

ADDRESS_____

OCCUPATION_____ DATE TESTED ___/___/___

EDUCATION_____ AGE_____

MARITAL STATUS_____ REFERRED BY _____

MALE

MMPI-2 Normative Sample

Butcher and Associates (1989)

| T score | | 48 | 56 | 56 | 54 | 58 | 58 | 58 | 64 | 56 | 57 | 58 | 58 | 52 | | | | |

NATIONAL
COMPUTER
SYSTEMS   NCS

* 49 item version   27309

PROFILE 1–8

MMPI™

MINNESOTA MULTIPHASIC ™
PERSONALITY INVENTORY
S.R. Hathaway and J.C. McKinley

PROFILE

MINNESOTA MULTIPHASIC PERSONALITY INVENTORY
Copyright ⓒ THE UNIVERSITY OF MINNESOTA
1943. Renewed 1970. This Profile Form 1948, 1976, 1982. All rights reserved.
Distributed Exclusively by NATIONAL COMPUTER SYSTEMS, INC.
Under License from The University of Minnesota
Printed in the United States of America

"Minnesota Multiphasic Personality Inventory" and "MMPI" are
trademarks owned by The University of Minnesota

NAME_____

ADDRESS_____

OCCUPATION_____ DATE TESTED _/_/_

EDUCATION_____ AGE_____

MARITAL STATUS_____ REFERRED BY _____

FEMALE

MMPI-2 Normative Sample

Butcher and Associates (1989)

T score __ 48 54 55 52 54 55 57 46 57 54 56 55 54 __ __ __ __

NATIONAL
COMPUTER
SYSTEMS

*49 item version

27309

TABLE 1–8 Demographic Variables for the MMPI-2 Normative Sample

Variable	N	Percentage	Census	Variable	N	Percentage	Census
Gender				**Education**			
Female	1462	56.2%		Part high school	129	5.0%	33.5%
Male	1138	43.8		High school	640	24.6	34.4
				Part college	651	25.0	15.7
				College graduate	700	26.9	8.7
Ethnicity				Postgraduate	480	18.5	7.8
White	2117	81.4%	85.0%				
Black	314	12.1	10.5				
Native-American	77	3.0	0.5	**Marital Status**			
Hispanic	73	2.8	—	Married	1717	66.0%	59.0%
Asian-American	19	.7	1.5	Never married	518	19.9	25.9
Other			2.5	Divorced	220	8.5	5.7
				Widowed	89	3.4	7.2
				Separated	56	2.2	2.3
Age							
18–19	50	1.9%	5.4%				
20–29	641	24.7	25.2	**Occupation**			
30–39	769	29.6	19.3	Professional	1060	40.8%	15.6%
40–49	401	15.4	14.0	Managerial	277	10.7	11.2
50–59	321	12.3	14.3	Skilled	215	8.3	2 5.5
60–69	277	10.7	11.5	Clerical	365	14.0	27.2
70–79	120	4.6	7.5	Laborer	205	7.9	20.6
80–89	21	.8	3.1	None of the above	463	17.8	—
				(Missing data)	15	.6	—

Note: Adapted from Butcher et al. (1989).

ligan and associates (1983). (Profile 1–4 should be compared to Profile 1–7 and Profile 1–5 to Profile 1–8.)

It also is possible to compare the average scores of the MMPI-2 normative group on the Wiener and Harmon (Wiener, 1948) Obvious and Subtle subscales (see Chapter 3 for a discussion of these subscales) with the original Minnesota normative group (see Profiles 1–9 and 1–10). It is readily apparent in Profiles 1–9 and 1–10 that the MMPI-2 normative group and the original Minnesota normative group have almost identical scores on the obvious subscales (excluding *Ma-O*), whereas their scores are very different on the subtle subscales (excluding *D-S*). Thus, the differences between the MMPI-2 normative group and the original Minnesota group in Profiles 1–7 and 1–8 predominantly reflect the influence of the subtle items on these five sub-

scales. It does not appear that the relatively high level of education and occupational status characteristic of the MMPI-2 normative group adversely affected scores on the obvious subscales since these scores are very similar to the original Minnesota normative group. Again, it can be noted that the scores of the MMPI-2 normative group on the Wiener and Harmon Obvious and Subtle subscales correspond very closely to those reported by Colligan and associates (1983).

The *K*-correction procedure, which will be described in detail in Chapters 2 and 3, will continue to be used with the MMPI-2 with the same *K*-weights being used on the same clinical scales. However, in a major departure from the MMPI, the MMPI-2 will have raw scores converted to uniform T scores for all clinical scales except Scales 5 (Masculinity-

PROFILE 1–9

MMPI™

MINNESOTA MULTIPHASIC™
PERSONALITY INVENTORY
S.R. Hathaway and J.C. McKinley

WIENER-HARMON SUBTLE-OBVIOUS
SUBSCALES PROFILE

MINNESOTA MULTIPHASIC PERSONALITY INVENTORY
Copyright ☆ THE UNIVERSITY OF MINNESOTA
1943. Renewed 1970. This Profile Form 1948, 1976, 1982, 1986. All rights reserved.
Distributed Exclusively by NATIONAL COMPUTER SYSTEMS, INC.
Under License from The University of Minnesota
Printed in the United States of America

"Minnesota Multiphasic Personality Inventory" and "MMPI" are
trademarks owned by The University of Minnesota.

NAME **MMPI-2 Normative Sample**

ADDRESS

OCCUPATION _____ DATE TESTED __ / __ / __

EDUCATION _____ AGE _____

MARITAL STATUS _____ REFERRED BY _____

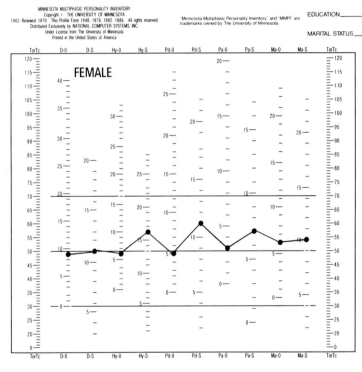

FEMALE

MMPI-2 Normative Sample

Butcher and Associates (1989)

Scorer's Initials _____

Raw Score   9   11   6   16   5   11   3   7   6   10

NATIONAL
COMPUTER
SYSTEMS
27212

PROFILE 1–10

MMPI™

MINNESOTA MULTIPHASIC™
PERSONALITY INVENTORY
S.R. Hathaway and J.C. McKinley

WIENER-HARMON SUBTLE-OBVIOUS
SUBSCALES PROFILE

MINNESOTA MULTIPHASIC PERSONALITY INVENTORY
Copyright · THE UNIVERSITY OF MINNESOTA
1943. Renewed 1970. This Profile Form 1948, 1976, 1982, 1986. All rights reserved.
Distributed Exclusively by NATIONAL COMPUTER SYSTEMS, INC.
Under License from The University of Minnesota
Printed in the United States of America

"Minnesota Multiphasic Personality Inventory" and "MMPI" are
trademarks owned by The University of Minnesota

NAME _____

ADDRESS _____

OCCUPATION _____ DATE TESTED __/__/__

EDUCATION _____ AGE _____

MARITAL STATUS _____ REFERRED BY _____

MALE

MMPI-2 Normative Sample

Butcher and Associates (1989)

Scorer's
Initials _____

Raw Score   **8   11   5   16   6   10   3   8   7   10**

NATIONAL
COMPUTER
SYSTEMS

Femininity) and *0* (Social Introversion). Scales *5* and *0* will retain their linear T scores. The uniform T scores for the clinical scales were developed based on the composite distribution for each clinical scale by gender so that the percentiles will be equivalent across the scales. Thus, a uniform T score of 75 on Scale *2* (Depression) will be equivalent to a T score of 75 on Scale *6* (Paranoia). The issues involved in the change to uniform T scores will be discussed in Chapter 2.

A number of supplementary scales are available to assist the clinician in interpreting the standard validity and clinical scales on the MMPI-2. Most of these supplementary scales will be familiar to the clinician who has used the MMPI: Barron's (1953) Ego Strength scale; Gough, McClosky, and Meehl's (1951) Dominance scale; Gough, McClosky, and Meehl's (1952) Social Responsibility scale; Kleinmuntz's (1961a) College Maladjustment scale; MacAndrew's (1965) Alcoholism scale; Megargee, Cook, and Mendelson's (1967) Overcontrolled Hostility scale; and Welsh's (1956) Anxiety and Repression scales. These scales have had a few minor changes made in them at the item level. Seven new scales are represented in the supplementary scales: two gender-role scales (Gender Role-Femininine; Gender Role-Masculine), two Post-traumatic Stress Disorder scales (Post-Traumatic Stress Disorder—Keane; Post-Traumatic Stress Disorder—Schlenger), and three validity scales (Back *F*; True Response Inconsistency; Variable Response Inconsistency). The three new validity scales will be discussed in Chapter 3; the remainder of the supplementary scales will be reviewed in Chapter 5.

A total of 15 new content scales have been developed for the MMPI-2 (Butcher et al., 1989). These scales are: Anxiety, Fears, Obsessiveness, Depression, Health Concerns, Bizarre Mentation, Anger, Cynicism, Antisocial Practices, Type A, Low Self-Esteem, Social Discomfort, Family Problems, Work Interference, and Negative Treatment Indica-

tors. These new content scales will be described in Chapter 5.

Since uniform T scores change the relationships among the clinical scales, the relative frequencies with which high-point scales and codetypes occur will be changed. Concordance rates for codetypes between the MMPI-2 and MMPI are reported to range from 57 to 70 percent in clinical samples (Butcher et al., 1989), and appear to be similar to those reported for the Colligan and associates (1983) norms when compared to the original MMPI norms. This issue will be explored in more depth in Chapter 6, which also will report the specific codetype concordance rates between the MMPI-2 and MMPI.

An important question about the MMPI-2 will involve whether the correlates of the individual scales and the codetypes that were derived on the MMPI can be applied to the MMPI-2. For example, if a client has a *2-4/4-2* codetype on the MMPI-2, can the clinician use the correlates of a *2-4/4-2* codetype that were developed on the MMPI for interpreting the profile? An associated question is even more difficult to answer. If the client has a *2-8/8-2* codetype and would have had a *2-4/4-2* codetype if linear rather than uniform T scores had been used, are correlates of the former or latter codetype, or even some other codetype, more appropriate for this client? Clearly such questions require an empirical answer. Studies of the correlates of the MMPI-2 will begin to appear over the next few years once it becomes readily available to clinicians. In the interim, clinicians will need to be very cautious in using MMPI correlates to interpret MMPI-2 profiles.

At this time *the MMPI-2 is to be used only with adults 18 years of age and older*, since normative data do not exist for persons under 18 years of age. Adolescents are still to be tested with the original MMPI. Work is currently underway to develop a restandardized version of the MMPI for use with adolescents, the MMPI-A, which should be available in late 1991 or 1992. The MMPI-A will be a new form designed specifically for adolescents, although it will retain the standard validity and clinical scales of the original MMPI.

A Note on Research with the MMPI-2

The advent of the MMPI-2 may have a quick appeal to researchers who would like to report the relationships among the new MMPI-2 norms, the Colligan and associates (1983) norms, and the original MMPI norms (Hathaway & Briggs, 1957). The important issue with these three sets of norms is not whether they produce different elevations on the various scales and/or codetypes, since such differences would be expected or there would be no reason for their publication. Rather, the issue is whether the behavioral and clinical correlates are more related to any specific set of norms. Unfortunately, the latter research is more difficult and time-consuming than the former, which requires only that the researcher calculates three sets of norms for a given MMPI-2 and reports their concordance rates. Hopefully, researchers and journal editors will realize that a careful investigation of the clinical correlates of these various sets of norms within specific codetypes is needed to address this critical issue.

ENDNOTES

1. Hathaway and McKinley did not provide a rationale for deleting insignificant items. Although potentially useful items may have been discarded, this procedure was acceptable at the time since they used an empirical method of item selection. The issue of their rationale for deletion of items, however, has become more relevant since item content is sometimes important in current usage of the MMPI. Wiggins' (1966) content scales are an example.

2. It is now customary to identify each scale by its number rather than its name. The use of the scale number reduces the emphasis placed on diagnostic labels like hypochondriasis, schizophrenia, and so on, and encourages the clinician to be aware of the empirical correlates of specific scores on each scale.

3. The addition of 55 items to the original 504 items on the MMPI would produce an item pool of 559 items. Since the MMPI contains only 550 items, it is not clear what happened to the other 9 items (W. G. Dahlstrom, personal communication, 1979).

4. The term *plus-getting* describes the procedure of making a deviant response to an item on a scale, thus adding plus one to the total score on the scale.

CHAPTER 2

Administration and Scoring

Administering and scoring the MMPI-2 are usually straightforward procedures that can be handled by a competent psychometrician. The apparent ease of MMPI-2 administration sometimes leads clinicians to underestimate the importance of establishing appropriate conditions for taking the MMPI-2, clarifying the test instructions if necessary, and unobtrusively monitoring the client's progress. Occasionally clinicians inappropriately relegate the task of MMPI-2 administration to a secretary or clerk, who may administer the test incorrectly. The ease of MMPI-2 administration does not absolve the clinician of the responsibility for insuring that it is handled properly.

Before administering the inventory for the first time, the clinician should read the *MMPI-2 Manual* (Butcher, Dahlstrom, Graham, Tellegen, & Kaemmer, 1989) and Chapter 1 of *An MMPI Handbook* (Dahlstrom, Welsh, & Dahlstrom, 1972). The *Handbook*, the definitive reference on the MMPI, is particularly useful when the clinician anticipates any unusual circumstance in administration or whenever a more general text omits answering any question. Although the *Hand-*

book addresses issues in the administration of the MMPI, the clinician should realize that the suggestions also are appropriate for the MMPI-2.

Once administered, the MMPI-2 can be scored either by hand or by computer. This chapter will describe the procedures for scoring and profiling the MMPI-2; examples of a clinician's interpretation of the MMPI-2 profile and several computer interpretive services will be provided in Chapter 7. This chapter also will address several related issues, such as the various forms of the MMPI-2; T score derivation; linear, normalized, and uniform T scores; and the effects of various demographic variables on MMPI performance.

ADMINISTRATION

Reading level is a crucial factor in determining whether or not a person can complete the MMPI-2; inadequate reading ability is a major cause of inconsistent patterns of item endorsement. Butcher and colleagues (1989) suggest that most clients who have had at least *eight* years of formal education can take the MMPI-2 with little or no difficulty since the items are written on an eighth-grade level or less. The clinician should note this eighth-grade reading level on the MMPI-2 since the MMPI was considered to have a sixth-grade reading level. However, Ward and Ward (1980) found that readability for some MMPI scales reached the seventh-grade level, and Blanchard (1981) reported that nine years of education was necessary for a criterion of 90 percent comprehension of the MMPI items.

This issue of the reading level required to complete the MMPI-2 becomes more serious when it is realized that most freshman-level college texts are written at the ninth-grade level. Despite the increased years of education of most people, reading level can still be a potential problem. Clients with less education may be able to take the MMPI-2 if their reading level is adequate. If there is any reason to suspect that a person's reading level may be deficient, the clinician should ascertain the person's reading level, administering a brief reading test such as the Gray Oral Reading Test (Gray & Robinson, 1963) if necessary. Reading level becomes especially important among minority individuals who, despite their fluency in speaking English, may be unable to read English. Anyone who cannot read may be defensive about revealing this deficiency; at times persons have responded to all 567 items even though they were unable to read them.

Although less important than reading level, a person's age and intelligence also affect ability to complete the MMPI-2. The *Manual* (Butcher et al., 1989) states that the MMPI-2 can be given to clients *18 years and older.* Presently, only the original MMPI should be administered to adolescents 17 years of age and younger. There is no upper age limit for the MMPI-2 as long as the reading level is adequate. Persons who score below a Wechsler Adult Intelligence Scale—Revised (Wechsler, 1980) IQ of 70 probably will be unable to complete the MMPI-2.

Even when a person has inadequate reading skills or an IQ below 70, the clinician need not automatically abandon the idea of administering the MMPI-2, since such persons sometimes can complete the inventory if it is presented orally. An audiotaped version of the MMPI-2, available from National Computer Systems (NCS), P.O. Box 1416, Minneapolis, MN 55440 (800–627–7271), serves this purpose. Dahlstrom and associates (1972) reported that taped administrations of the MMPI were effective with IQs as low as 65 and reading levels as low as the third grade.

Few explicit guidelines exist regarding how much assistance the clinician can provide for a client who has marginal reading skills. It seems reasonable to give standard dictionary definitions of terms if the client asks. The clinician should refrain, however, from administering the MMPI-2 by reading the items aloud since this practice is a significant change from standardized administration and its effects are unknown. Hopefully, future research will compare the responses obtained when the clinician reads items aloud with responses obtained in the standard administration. Until such research is conducted, the clinician should consider administering some other personality instrument to persons with limited intelligence or reading ability unless standard definitions provide adequate clarification or the taped version can be used.

Psychiatric impairment rarely precludes taking the MMPI-2 unless the client is agitated and unable to sit still long enough to complete the test. Clients who are severely depressed or noncommunicative frequently can complete the MMPI-2, providing the clinician with valuable information that might otherwise be unavailable. Such clients usually feel pleased that they can complete the task and relieved that other clients have had experiences similar to their own, as evidenced by items referring to such experiences on the MMPI-2.

After determining that the person is capable of completing the MMPI-2, the clinician should insure that the individual is seated comfortably and provided with a pencil for taking the test. If a pencil is used in taking the MMPI-2, the client can easily change any responses if so desired. Since few problems generally occur in administration, the MMPI-2 can be given to small groups of individuals as long as there is sufficient room so that each person's privacy can be respected.

Giving a brief explanation of why the test is being administered and what uses will be made of the results, as well as answering any other questions that the client may have about testing, will pay tremendous dividends in avoiding invalid profiles. Clients also should be told whether they will be provided with feedback on their results. In most, if not all, instances, clients should be provided with such feedback which will enhance their motivation to complete the MMPI-2 appropriately. Friedman, Webb, and Lewak (1989, pp. 43–47) provide illustrations of common questions asked about taking the MMPI with their suggested answers. The client should read the instructions, the clinician should answer any questions about them, and then the client should proceed at his or her own pace in completing the test. More than 90 percent of the persons taking the MMPI-2 will not need any explanation of the instructions, and they will complete the test in 60 to 90 minutes.

One common question asked by clients is whether they should report prior feelings or current ones. The clinician should clarify that *the client should report current feelings and experiences.* Clients also occasionally question the appropriateness of the content of some MMPI items, particularly those related to gender, bodily functions such as elimination, and religion (Butcher & Tellegen, 1966; Walker & Ward, 1969). Most of these objectional items have been deleted from the MMPI-2, so there should be few objections to item content. Clients who raise objections to item content frequently can be reassured by being told that their answers will remain confidential and that their answers to groups of items, rather than individual items, are what is important. If this reassurance is insufficient, the client may be allowed to omit an objectionable item. The number of such omissions must be minimized, however, since the validity of the entire test becomes an issue if the client omits more than 10 items (see Chapter 3).

If the client still objects to many items, the clinician may need to use some other personality instrument. Exploring more fully the reasons for the client's reluctance to complete the MMPI-2 also might be useful. Clients are more likely to object to item content when the MMPI-2 is being used for personnel selection; they may have legitimate questions about the relevance of such items to job performance. In such situations, the clinician should explain how the results from the MMPI-2 will be used and how they are relevant to personnel selection.

Once or twice during the test session, the clinician should unobtrusively check on the client's progress. If possible, and particularly if the client appears confused, the clinician should verify that the client is placing the answers correctly on the answer sheet. The clinician should be available throughout the test session in case any questions arise.

Although it is preferable to have the client complete the MMPI-2 in a single session, it is *not* mandatory to do so. In such a case the client should be encouraged to complete the MMPI-2 within a few days at most in order to minimize the possibility of any significant changes in the client's current status during the testing period. Some clients are relieved to know that they may complete the MMPI-2 across several days since its length may appear formidable if it is to be completed in one session. Awareness of the client's need to complete the MMPI-2 across several days will increase the likelihood of obtaining a valid MMPI-2.

Computer Administration

The MMPI-2 can also be administered by computer wherein the client sits in front of a terminal and responds to the items as they are presented on the screen. Because the MMPI-2 items are copyrighted, clinicians must lease the software to be used on the computer from the test distributor. At this time the only authorized distributor of the software for computer administration of the MMPI-2 is NCS (P.O. Box 1416, Minneapolis, MN 55440, 800–627–7271).

Honaker (1988) has provided a critical review of the comparability of hand and computer MMPI administrations and concluded that (1) computer administration is generally viewed in a more positive light and takes less time to complete, (2) individuals are ranked similarly across the two procedures, and (3) computer administration may produce lower overall profiles. Honaker describes a number of methodologic issues that must be addressed before clinicians can assume that hand- and computer-administered MMPIs or MMPI-2s yield equivalent scores. Honaker (1988; Honaker, Harrell, & Buffaloe, 1989) and Butcher (1987) provide excellent overviews of the issues that are involved in the use of computers with the MMPI that should be consulted by the clinician interested in this topic.

TEST FORMS

The MMPI-2 exists in many different forms: softcover, hardcover, audiotape, and computer. All of these forms have the items in the same order with the same item numbers. All MMPI-2 test forms, answer sheets, and profile sheets are available from NCS, P.O. Box 1416, Minneapolis, MN 55440 (800–627–

7271). Since the MMPI-2 is a restricted test, only professionals with appropriate training may purchase the test materials. The qualifications for ordering the test materials are outlined in the NCS catalog of tests or can be obtained directly from NCS.

MMPI-2 booklets are available in either softcover or hardcover. Both MMPI-2 booklets have the 567 items in the same item order, unlike the MMPI where the Group Booklet form (softcover) and Form R (hardcover) have the last 200 items in different orders. The softcover booklet of the MMPI-2 is preferable in situations where clients may mark on or otherwise deface the booklet, since it is less expensive than the hardcover booklet. The hardcover booklet is useful in situations such as a hospital where the client may not have a desk or table readily available on which to work.

Several answer sheets can be used with the MMPI-2 booklets, some of which are designed for hand or computer scoring and others which are designed to be read by optical scanners. When purchasing MMPI-2 test materials for the first time, the clinician should insure that the answer sheet is appropriate for the test booklet and hand or computer scoring as desired.

Once the client has completed the MMPI-2, the clinician should inspect the answer sheet for any problems, such as an omitted item, an item marked both "true" and "false," marking all or most of the items as "true" or "false," or an item for which the client changed the response but failed to show clearly which answer was intended. Occasionally, a client will even omit an entire column of items. Usually the client can readily correct these problems; then scoring of the responses can begin.

Hand Scoring

Scoring can be accomplished either by computer (discussed later in this chapter) or by hand. The first step in hand scoring is to examine the answer sheet carefully and indicate omitted items and double-marked items by drawing a line through both the "true" and "false" responses to these items with a brightly colored ink pen. Also, cleaning up the answer sheet is helpful and facilitates scoring. Responses that were changed need to be erased completely if possible, or clearly marked with an "X" so that the clinician is aware that the item has not been endorsed by the client.

There is one scale that must always be scored without a template: The *?* (Cannot Say) scale score is the total number of items not marked and double marked. All of the validity and clinical scales on all hand-scored answer sheets are scored by placing a plastic template over the answer sheet with a small box drawn at the scored (deviant) response—either "true" or "false"—for each item on the scale. The total number of such items marked equals the client's raw score for that scale; this score is recorded in the proper space on the answer sheet. One scale—Scale *5* (Masculinity-Femininity)—is scored differently for males and females, and unusually high or low scores on this scale might indicate that the wrong template was used. Among females, for example, a raw score of less than 30 is unusual, and such raw scores should at least arouse a suspicion that the wrong template was used in scoring the scale. All scoring templates are made of plastic and they must be kept away from heat.

Plotting the profile is the next step in the scoring process. In essence, the clinician transfers all the raw scores from the answer sheet to the appropriate column of the profile sheet (see Profile 2–1). Some precautions must be taken and data calculations performed. First, separate profile sheets are used for males and females, as with the scoring templates for Scale *5*; an unusually high or low score plotted for Scale *5* should alert the clinician to the possibility that the wrong profile sheet was selected.

Second, each column on the profile sheet is used to represent the raw scores for a specific scale. Each dash represents a raw score of 1 with the larger dashes marking increments of 5. Thus, the clinician notes the client's raw score on the scale being plotted and makes a point or dot at the appropriate dash. Since the client has a raw score of 7 on the *L* (Lie) scale (see Profile 2–1), the clinician finds the dark dash marked 5 on this scale and then counts up 2 more dashes and makes a point or dot at 7. A similar procedure is followed for the other two validity scales. Once the clinician has plotted the client's scores on the three validity scales, a solid line is drawn to connect them. The raw score on the *?* (Cannot Say) scale is merely recorded in the proper space in the lower left-hand corner of the profile sheet.

A similar procedure is followed to plot the ten clinical scales except that five of the clinical scales (*1* [Hypochondriasis], *4* [Psychopathic Deviate], *7* [Psychasthenia], *8* [Schizophrenia], and *9* [Hypomania]) are *K*-corrected and a fraction of *K* is added to the raw score before the client's score is plotted. (The rationale and procedure for the *K*-correction will be described in the next section.) For these five scales that are *K*-corrected, the clinician plots the raw score on the scale with *K* added. Thus, on Scale *1* the client's *raw score plus one-half (.5) of the raw score of K* is 15 (see Profile 2–1), so the clinician finds the dark dash marked 15 and makes a point or dot there. Once the clinician has plotted the client's scores on the ten clinical scales, another solid line is drawn to connect them. The clinician should note that the validity and clinical scales are *not* connected, since the determination of the validity of the MMPI-2 is independent of or precedes the evaluation of the clinical scales.

The left and right columns of the profile for basic scales provide the T score equivalents for the raw scores on each scale (see Profile 2–1). For example, the client's raw

PROFILE 2-1

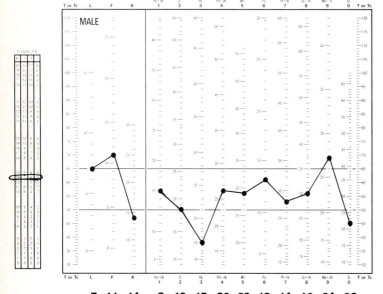

MMPI-2

S.R. Hathaway and J.C. McKinley
Minnesota Multiphasic
Personality Inventory - 2

Profile for Basic Scales

Minnesota Multiphasic Personality Inventory-2
Copyright © by THE REGENTS OF THE UNIVERSITY OF MINNESOTA
1942, 1943 (renewed 1970), 1989. This Profile Form 1989.
All rights reserved. Distributed exclusively by NATIONAL COMPUTER SYSTEMS, INC.
under license from The University of Minnesota.

"MMPI-2" and "Minnesota Multiphasic Personality Inventory-2" are trademarks owned by
The University of Minnesota. Printed in the United States of America.

Name **John Brown**

Address **6411 Chicago Street**

Occupation **Janitor**   Date Tested **4/ 8/91**

Education **9th** Age **47** Marital Status **Married**

Referred by **Dr. Nichols**

MMPI-2 Code **96-145872/0:3 F'L-K**

Scorer's Initials **HG**

MALE

	L	F	K	Hs+.5k 1	D 2	Hy 3	Pd+.4k 4	Mf 5	Pa 6	Pt+1k 7	Sc+1k 8	Ma+.2k 9	Si 0	
Raw Score	7	11	14	8	18	15	20	29	13	14	16	24	22	
? Raw Score 0														
K to be Added			7			6				14	14	3		
Raw Score with K			15			26				28	30	27		

score of 7 on the *L* (Lie) scale is equivalent to a T score of 65. Similarly, the client's raw score with *K* of 15 on Scale *1* (Hypochondriasis) is equivalent to a T score of 57. The profile form for the basic scales provides a direct means of converting the raw scores on the standard validity and clinical scores into the appropriate T scores. The development and use of T scores will be described below.

K-CORRECTION

As noted in Chapter 1, Meehl and Hathaway (1946) developed the *K* scale to identify individuals who were defensive in endorsing the MMPI items. They determined that the raw scores on five scales, when transformed into *K*-corrected form, enhanced the ability of these scales to discriminate their respective criterion groups from other groups of respondents (see Chapter 3). This *K*-correction process is a standard step in plotting the MMPI and it was *not* changed in the restandardization of the MMPI-2.

The standard profile sheet can be used only to plot directly *K*-corrected profiles. In order to use this profile sheet correctly, the clinician must add to five of the clinical scales the proper fractions of the client's raw score on the *K* scale. The five clinical scales in question and their *K*-corrections are *1* (Hypochondriasis) + .5*K*; *4* (Psychopathic Deviate) + .4*K*; *7* (Psychasthenia) + 1*K*; *8* (Schizophrenia) + 1*K*; and *9* (Hypomania) + .2*K*. Thus, in Profile 2–1 where *K* = 14, the following amounts were added to Scales *1*, *4*, *7*, *8*, and *9*, respectively: 7, 6, 14, 14, and 3.

The clinician need not calculate the values of the *K*-correction since a table on the left side of the profile sheet provides all needed fractions of *K* for all possible raw scores on the *K* scale. Circling the raw score of the *K* scale and the other numbers on this same row in the table on the profile sheet facilitates locating the appropriate fractions of *K* to be added to each of the *K*-corrected scales (see Profile 2–1).

LINEAR T SCORES

Inspection of the completed profile sheet provides the clinician with a standard score (T score) as well as a raw score for each scale. T scores among normals have a mean of 50 and a standard deviation of 10. Thus, a T score of 70 indicates that a score is two standard deviations above the mean, and a T score of 30 is two standard deviations below the mean. Knowing the client's T score on a scale is important for two reasons. First, it shows how the client scored compared to the group of normals on whom the MMPI-2 was standardized. For example, knowing that a male client has a raw score of 26 on Scale *5* (Masculinity-Femininity) means virtually nothing, but the fact that the client has a T score of 50 on this scale tells the clinician that the client is no different on this scale than the MMPI-2 normative group.

Second, T scores enable the clinician to compare the client's scores on the various scales with one another. For example, knowing that a male client has a raw score of 26 on Scale *5* and 39 on Scale *0* (Social Introversion) means very little; knowing that the client has a T score of 50 on Scale *5* and 65 on Scale *0*, however, allows the clinician to determine the relative deviation and the interpretive importance of these two scales in this specific client.

Since the T score equivalent of each raw score can be read directly from the profile sheet when the raw score is plotted, the clinician need not perform any calculations to convert raw scores to T scores. The following equation was used to obtain the linear T score equivalents of each raw score:

$$T = 50 + 10 \left(\frac{X - M}{SD} \right)$$

where:

X = the client's raw score
M = the mean score on the scale in normals
SD = the standard deviation on the scale in normals

In converting raw scores to T scores, fractions were rounded to the nearest whole number. For example, if a male answered 35 items on Scale *5* (Masculinity-Femininity) of the MMPI-2 in the deviant direction or like the criterion group on whom the scale was constructed, substituting 35 in the above formula would produce a T score of 68 (see Profile 2–1):

$$T = 50 + 10 \left(\frac{35 - 26.01}{5.08} \right)$$
$$= 50 + 10(1.8) = 50 + 18 = 68$$

Similarly, if a male answered 21 items on Scale *5* in the deviant direction, substituting this raw score in this formula would produce a T score of 40:

$$T = 50 + 10 \left(\frac{21 - 26.01}{5.08} \right)$$
$$= 50 + 10(-1.0) = 50 - 10 = 40$$

The above described procedure was used to develop T scores for all of the validity and clinical scales on the original MMPI. These T scores are known as linear T scores since they are linear transformations of the raw scores that maintain the underlying distributions of the raw scores. The MMPI-2 retained linear T scores for the standard validity scales, Scales *5* (Masculinity-Femininity) and *0* (Social Introversion), and the Supplementary scales (see Chapter 5). However, the remainder of the clinical scales on the MMPI-2 and all of the content scales (see Chapter 5) are uniform T scores.

The original T scores for the MMPI clinical scales were developed using a linear transformation of the raw scores. (The T scores for the validity scales were assigned arbitrarily so it is not clear what transformation of these scores was involved [Hathaway & McKinley, 1983].) As noted above, the transformation of raw scores to T scores allows clinicians to know how much a client's score on a specific clinical scale deviates from the mean of the original Minnesota normative group and to compare a client's scores on the various scales with one another.

Inherent in the use of T scores on the MMPI is the assumption that they have similar meanings from one clinical scale to the next (i.e., a T score of 75 on Scale *4* (Psychopathic Deviate) has the same probability of occurrence as a T score of 75 on Scale *8* [Schizophrenia]). This assumption is valid, however, only if the scales involved have similar distributions. If the underlying raw score distributions for each scale are not similar, then a T score of 70 will not be equivalent to the 97.7 percentile.

Colligan, Osborne, and Offord (1980) examined the raw score distributions of the standard validity and clinical scales in the Hathaway and Briggs (1957) "purified" sample of the original Minnesota normative group that was used to derive the T scores on the standard profile sheet for the MMPI. They found that most of these scales showed significant skewness to the right, with from 4.8 to 8.0 percent of these normal individuals scoring above a T score of 70 instead of the 2.3 percent that would be expected with a normal distribution. Colligan and colleagues recommended that Scales *1* (Hypochondriasis), *2* (Depression), *7* (Psychasthenia), *8* (Schizophrenia), and *9* (Hypomania) in women and Scales *1* (Hypochondriasis), *2* (Depression), *4* (Psychopathic Deviate), *7* (Psychasthenia), *8* (Schizophrenia), and *9* (Hypomania) in men should be interpreted more conservatively because of the increased frequency with which elevations occurred in normal individuals.

NORMALIZED T SCORES

Colligan and associates (1980) suggested that normalized transformations of the raw scores on each MMPI scale should replace linear transformations to insure that the same T score elevation would have similar meaning across scales. However, no further research was generated on this issue until Colligan, Osborne, Swenson, and Offord (1983, 1984, 1989) developed normalized T scores for their contemporary normal sample, described in Chapter 1. These normalized T scores were developed by determining the transformation of the raw scores on each validity and clinical scale of the MMPI that would result in a normal distribution. They found that square root and log transformations of the raw scores were necessary to produce these normal distributions.

The interested clinician can see Table 39 (Colligan et al., 1983, pp. 206–207) or Table 24 (Colligan et al., 1989, pp. 60–61) for the specific transformation used on each scale. These transformations resulted in 0.6 to 3.6 percent of the normalized T scores of their census-matched samples on the MMPI validity and clinical scales being greater than 70 compared with the expected percent of 2.3. The more recent publications of Colligan and colleagues seemed to spur further interest in this issue that continues unabated.

Hsu (1984) presented five reasons for questioning Colligan and colleagues' (1983) recommendation to use normalized transformations of the raw scores on the MMPI. First, he questioned whether the underlying dimensions of psychopathology were normally distributed that would justify a normalized transformation of the raw scores measuring the dimension. Second, he argued that the differences in skewness and kurtosis of the normalized as compared to the linear

transformation could result in different groups of clients with extreme scores on a given scale. Third, Hsu wondered whether the normalized transformations of Colligan and associates (1983) were tested to see whether significant skewness and/or kurtosis was present. Fourth, he questioned the assumption that equality of percentile ranks for normalized T scores was a more valid indicator of psychopathology than equality of linear T scores since no empirical data were presented. Finally, he noted that all of the existing literature on the MMPI is based on linear T scores and switching to normalized T scores would make these data irrelevant since the elevations of the individual scales and the rank ordering of the scales would differ.

Colligan, Osborne, and Offord (1984) provided a point-by-point rebuttal to Hsu (1984). First, Colligan and colleagues stated that the assumption of a normal distribution for dimensions of personality are accepted widely in the social sciences and Hsu did not present any data to indicate that the assumption was untenable. Second, they agreed with Hsu that skewness and kurtosis did differ from scale to scale and as a result they used different transformations as appropriate. Third, they did not state specifically whether they tested the kurtosis of their normalized transformations, although they presented data on the skewness of each transformation. Fourth, they believed that the more reliable scores produced by normalized transformations would enable clinicians to realize that true differences were being reflected when two scales were being compared, not some artifact of skewness. Finally, they suggested that the possible invalidation of existing MMPI research is a serious problem that needed to be evaluated empirically. If this empirical research were to demonstrate that contemporary norms were more appropriate, then clinicians will need to consider utilizing current methodology rather than rely on an aging database no matter how extensive it might be.

Since some clinicians may prefer using T scores based on linear transformations of the raw scores, Osborne and Colligan (1986) provided equations for computing linear T scores for the Colligan and associates' (1983) contemporary normative sample. These linear T scores tended to vary less than four points from the normalized T scores for this contemporary sample except on the *F* scale, which differed by 9 points in men and 11 points in women.

UNIFORM T SCORES

The MMPI-2 Restandardization Committee (Butcher et al., 1989) realized the importance of insuring that the same T score elevation would have similar meaning or equal probability of occurring across scales, and they developed uniform T scores to meet this need. Uniform T scores were developed for all clinical scales on the MMPI-2 (except Scales *5* [Masculinity-Femininity] and *0* [Social Introversion], which retained linear T scores) and the new content scales (see Chapter 5). Linear T scores were retained on Scales *5* and *0* because these two scales were derived in a different manner than the other clinical scales and the distribution of raw scores was less skewed (Butcher et al., 1989). These uniform T scores were developed in a three-step process.

First, non-*K*-corrected linear T score distributions were determined by gender for each of the eight clinical scales. This step resulted in 16 distributions of linear T scores. Second, the associated linear T score was determined for each percentile in each of the 16 distributions. Finally, composite or average T scores were determined for each percentile. These composite T scores were then used to create uniform T scores for each of the eight clinical scales. Uniform T scores result in a similar probability of occurrence of a particular T score across these eight clinical scales while maintaining the underlying positive skew in the distribution. A easy means of understanding uniform T scores is to realize that they are equivalent percentiles across these scales.

Table 2–1 provides an illustration of the process of creating uniform T scores for two scales. In this illustration, the composite or average T score for the 92nd percentile was 65, which would become the uniform T score for the 92nd percentile on both scales. Similarly, the composite T score for the 96th percentile was 70, which would become the uniform T score for that percentile.

These uniform T scores produce slight changes in the overall elevation of the profile and may alter the rank ordering of the clinical scales, which would result in a different code-type than would be obtained with linear T

TABLE 2–1   Illustration of the Process of Creating Uniform T Scores

Uniform T Score	Percentile	Scale *1* (Hypochondriasis)		Scale *2* (Depression)	
		Men	Women	Men	Women
80	99	82	79	81	80
75	98	76	74	75	74
70	96	70	69	72	68
65	92	66	67	64	64
60	85	60	61	59	61

scores. Since all of the interpretive issues raised about normalized T scores also are applicable to uniform T scores, they will not be reiterated here.

Table 2–2 illustrates the relationship among linear, normalized, and uniform T scores. Linear and uniform T scores are very similar throughout the distribution on Scale *1* (Hypochondriasis), whereas uniform T scores are four or more points lower above T scores of 70 on Scale *2* (Depression). Normalized and uniform T scores are virtually identical until a T score of about 65 on both scales; the uniform transformation produces slightly to significantly higher T scores above that point.

These comparisons among these three procedures for transforming raw scores into T scores illustrate the points that were made above: (1) normalized and uniform transformations reduce the overall profile eleva-

tion, (2) normalized transformations will result in fewer scores above a T score of 65 than uniform transformations, and (3) the relationships among any pair or set of scales will be altered substantially by these changes in relative elevation and distribution of the T scores. Again, clinicians are cautioned against casually assuming that correlates of scales from the MMPI will generalize directly to the MMPI-2. Such generalizations need to be verified empirically. It would appear that there are sufficient research opportunities with the MMPI-2 to keep clinicians busy for several decades.

COMPUTER SCORING

Computer scoring of the MMPI-2 eliminates the need for the clinician to go through all of the above steps for scoring and plotting the

TABLE 2–2 Comparisons among Linear, Normalized, and Uniform T Scores for a Male Client

	Scale 1 (Hypochondriasis)			Scale 2 (Depression)		
	T Score			T Score		
Raw Score	Linear	Normalized	Uniform	Linear	Normalized	Uniform
10	47	43	42	34	26	32
12	51	49	48	39	33	36
14	56	54	54	43	39	40
16	60	59	59	48	44	45
18	64	63	64	52	49	50
20	69	66	68	56	53	54
22	73	69	73	61	57	59
24	78	72	77	65	61	62
26	82	75	81	70	64	66
28	87	78	86	74	67	70
30	91	80	90	78	70	74
32	96	82	94	83	73	78
34	100	85	99	87	75	81
36	105	86	103	92	77	85
38	109	88	108	96	80	89
40	114	90	112	100	82	93

Note: Raw scores on Scale *1* are *K*-corrected. The uniform and linear T scores may be found in Appendices A and K of Butcher et al. (1989), respectively. The normalized T scores may be found in Table 44 (p. 227) of Colligan et al. (1983) or Appendix C (p. 116) of Colligan et al. (1989).

profile. Computer scoring also encourages the clinician to use the content and supplementary scales (see Chapter 5) since no extra time is required. Various computer scoring services are available through NCS, P.O. Box 1416, Minneapolis, MN 55440 (800–627–7271); clinicians will need to determine which service is most appropriate for their clinical setting. There are three basic types of computer scoring services: the MMPI-2 can be administered, scored, and interpreted (if desired) on a personal computer in the clinician's office; the clinician can use a personal computer and a modem to transmit the client's responses to the MMPI-2 to NCS and have the results transmitted back to the clinician's personal computer; or the clinician can mail the answer sheet to NCS for computer scoring. Clinicians need to insure that they are using an answer sheet for the MMPI-2 that is compatible with whatever computer scoring service is to be used, since different answer sheets are employed.

ERRORS IN SCORING

Few if any errors in scoring generally occur with the MMPI. Occasionally, the clinician miscounts the number of deviant responses on a specific scale. Greene (1980) reported that at least 70 percent of the hand-scored answer sheets for two samples of MMPI clients—Clinic Clients and University Students—had no errors on any of the 14 validity and clinical scales, and another 12 to 14 percent had errors on only one scale (see Table 2–3). For a third group—Medical Patients—whose answer sheets were computer scored, 100 percent of the answer sheets were scored perfectly. The computer is not always 100 percent accurate, however; Dahlstrom and associates (1972) and Fowler and Coyle (1968b) have reported errors in computer-scoring services. Nevertheless, errors occur infrequently in hand scoring the MMPI and even more rarely in computer scoring.

When an error did occur, in the above two samples, it was most likely a result of the clinician counting only one fewer deviant item than the client actually answered (see Table 2–4). Consequently, errors in scoring should have a negligible effect on the interpretation of the profile. This statement is not meant to suggest that clinicians do not need to be concerned about scoring the MMPI or the MMPI-2; when clinicians exercise reasonable care, however, few substantial errors in scoring occur.

Other than miscounting the number of deviant responses, the other likely source of error, as already mentioned, is using the template for the opposite gender in scoring Scale

TABLE 2–3 Percentage of Answer Sheets Scored Incorrectly

Number of Scales Scored Incorrectly	Group[a]		
	Clinic Clients	University Students	Medical Patients
0	70%	82%	100%
1	14	12	0
2	6	2	0
3	6	4	0
4+	4	0	0

Note: See Greene (1980, pp. 22–25) for a more complete description of these groups.
[a]$n = 50$ for each group.

TABLE 2–4 Percentage of Answer Sheets
Scored Incorrectly with Errors
of Varying Magnitude

Magnitude of Error[a]	Group	
	Clinic Clients	University Students
−3	2.6%	0.0%
−2	7.7	7.1
−1	82.1	85.7
+1	2.6	7.1
+2	5.1	0.0

[a]A negative magnitude indicates that the clinician counted fewer deviant items than the client actually answered.

5 (Masculinity-Femininity). Unusually high or low scores on Scale 5 should alert the clinician to the possibility that the wrong template was used, particularly if such a score seems inappropriate for the individual being tested.

INTERPRETING THE PROFILE

Once the MMPI-2 has been scored and plotted on the standard profile sheet, the process of interpreting the profile can begin. The first step involves translating the T scores on each scale into more usable information. The next two chapters will present interpretations of various T score elevations on each of the validity and clinical scales both individually and in some combinations with each other. Chapter 6 will provide the correlates of the two clinical scales with the highest elevation at or above a T score of 65 (i.e., the codetype or high-point pair of the profile). The correlates of the codetype are the core of the process of interpreting the profile. Finally, Chapter 7 will present illustrations of integrating all of this information to complete the process of profile interpretation.

Before turning to the interpretations of the various validity and clinical scales in the next two chapters, the effects of demographic variables such as age, gender, and education on MMPI profiles will be discussed.

EFFECTS OF DEMOGRAPHIC VARIABLES ON MMPI PROFILES

Clinicians generally are aware that a number of demographic variables such as age, gender, education, ethnicity, and environmental setting may have an potential effect on MMPI scores. However, there is little systematic research that has investigated the influence of any single demographic variable on MMPI profiles, let alone combinations of these variables. Only the variables of age in the comparison of adolescents and adults, and ethnicity in the comparison of blacks and whites have been explored in any real depth. The research in these two specific areas will be summarized in Chapter 8. This section will be limited to a more general discussion of the effects of single demographic variables on MMPI profiles. Gynther (1983) has provided a recent review of this area. Little empirical research exists at this time to know whether similar results would be found on MMPI-2 profiles, although it would be expected that these results should generalize directly to the MMPI-2.

Age

The primary interest in the effects of age on MMPI profiles has involved the comparison of adolescents and adults, as was noted earlier. Little interest has been focused on the effects of age across the adult life span. Colligan and colleagues (1983, 1989) and Swenson, Pearson, and Osborne (1973) have provided data on the effects of age on MMPI profiles in adults. Table 2–5 provides the mean scores for the standard validity and clinical scales for six age groups in the Colligan and colleagues' contemporary normative sample of adults. Increases in mean

TABLE 2–5   Effects of Age on MMPI Scale Scores in the Colligan et al. (1983) Contemporary Normative Sample

Age	N	L	F	K	1(Hs)	2(D)	3(Hy)	4(Pd)	5(Mf)	6(Pa)	7(Pt)	8(Sc)	9(Ma)	0(Si)
Men														
20–29	75	45.3	55.9	52.7	50.7	51.7	54.4	56.0	58.6	56.1	54.8	55.6	60.0	52.1
30–39	61	47.1	55.1	54.5	51.7	54.6	57.9	57.3	59.3	57.4	55.0	53.9	56.0	52.6
40–49	44	48.3	53.1	56.8	52.7	53.2	56.7	54.3	58.7	54.3	52.4	51.4	53.4	51.8
50–59	45	49.9	53.6	54.8	55.7	55.7	59.0	52.3	58.0	54.4	52.8	50.6	49.8	54.1
60–69	35	53.0	53.3	55.5	55.4	57.5	56.7	50.8	55.7	52.3	52.8	50.3	49.4	54.3
70+	27	56.4	53.9	55.5	59.1	59.5	56.8	49.8	52.8	52.9	51.9	51.4	48.7	55.2
Women														
20–29	77	46.1	51.9	55.0	48.8	52.0	52.0	55.0	45.6	56.4	54.3	54.4	54.1	53.7
30–39	62	47.0	51.3	56.1	49.0	51.9	53.0	54.8	44.8	56.5	52.8	53.3	51.7	53.8
40–49	44	48.6	51.7	55.4	50.9	52.4	52.9	52.7	45.4	56.7	52.9	53.2	51.0	56.0
50–59	49	50.7	52.4	55.7	53.2	54.4	54.6	52.9	47.1	54.2	52.6	53.2	49.6	55.9
60–69	42	53.7	51.5	56.3	52.3	54.6	52.7	49.4	49.1	52.3	52.1	52.5	46.1	58.7
70+	44	56.1	54.4	52.1	55.7	57.6	54.4	48.5	51.6	53.9	53.8	53.3	48.8	57.7

Note: Data are adapted from Colligan et al. (1983), Appendix J, pp. 340–352. These data are expressed as means of the linear T scores based on the original Minnesota normative group.

scores as a function of age occurred frequently and were five T points or more on Scales *L, 1* (Hypochondriasis), and *2* (Depression) in both men and women, and on Scale *5* (Masculinity-Femininity) in women. Decreases in mean scores of 5 T points or more occurred only on Scales *4* (Psychopathic Deviate) and *9* (Hypomania) in men and women, and on Scale *5* in men. These changes in mean scores were nearly 10 T points (one standard deviation) on Scales *L, 1,* and *9* (men only).

Swenson and associates (1973) reported the MMPI data from 50,000 medical outpatients, and Table 2–6 summarizes the mean profiles on the standard validity and clinical scales for six age groups. They found systematic effects as a function of age, with most scales showing consistent small decreases in elevation. The decreases in elevation across these age groups were five T points or larger on Scales *3* (Hysteria), *4* (Psychopathic Deviate), *7* (Psychasthenia), *8* (Schizophrenia), and *9* (Hypomania) in both men and women. Only the *L* scale increased in elevation in both men and women, and Scale *5* (Masculinity-

Femininity) increased in women. Five scales were relatively unaffected by age: Scales *F, K, 1* (Hypochondriasis), *2* (Depression), and *0* (Social Introversion). These small decreases in elevation would mean that there was a slightly smaller probability of a clinical scale being elevated above a T score of 70 with increasing age in these medical outpatients.

Both Colligan and associates (1983, 1989) and Swenson and associates (1973) found that mean scores decrease consistently with increasing age on Scales *4* and *9*, and increase on the *L* scale. There also was a tendency for scores to decrease on Scales *7* and *8* with increasing age, although these decreases were smaller in the normal sample than in the medical sample. Since both studies used a cross-sectional design (i.e., they sampled their individuals at one point in time rather than following a single group of individuals across time), it is not possible to know for sure whether the prevalence of psychopathology actually decreases with age or whether older individuals with less psychopathology are simply more likely to participate in studies such as these. Regardless of the explana-

TABLE 2–6   Effects of Age on MMPI Scale Scores in Medical Patients

Age	N	L	F	K	1(Hs)	2(D)	3(Hy)	4(Pd)	5(Mf)	6(Pa)	7(Pt)	8(Sc)	9(Ma)	0(Si)
Men														
20–29	1298	48.7	53.7	57.1	60.9	60.2	63.1	60.2	57.2	55.6	59.6	56.3	57.8	51.3
30–39	2905	48.7	52.6	57.6	62.4	60.8	63.6	58.4	56.7	55.5	57.8	53.7	55.2	51.0
40–49	5379	49.1	52.3	57.0	63.0	60.9	63.2	57.1	56.2	54.8	56.0	52.2	53.3	51.3
50–59	7097	50.0	52.3	55.9	62.4	61.5	61.7	55.7	55.6	54.0	54.7	51.1	51.9	52.3
60–69	5315	51.9	52.4	55.6	60.7	61.1	59.2	53.6	54.7	52.6	53.1	50.5	50.0	53.1
70+	1733	53.4	52.8	55.1	60.5	61.3	58.1	52.0	54.3	52.1	52.8	50.7	48.8	53.6
Women														
20–29	1690	49.7	53.3	57.1	59.4	58.7	61.4	58.6	48.2	57.1	58.6	57.8	54.6	53.7
30–39	3474	50.5	52.4	57.4	62.0	60.6	63.3	57.4	48.4	56.9	58.4	56.8	51.9	54.0
40–49	5955	51.2	51.9	56.7	62.0	60.0	62.5	55.5	49.4	55.4	56.4	55.4	51.1	54.2
50–59	7209	52.4	51.4	56.5	60.7	59.4	60.3	54.0	50.0	54.2	55.2	54.3	50.5	54.1
60–69	5229	54.3	51.3	55.7	59.3	59.0	58.0	51.8	52.2	53.3	53.7	52.8	49.0	54.4
70+	1471	56.3	52.0	55.2	58.7	58.7	56.4	50.3	54.2	52.7	53.1	52.3	48.2	55.1

Note: Data are adapted from Swenson et al. (1973), Table I, p. 13. These data are expressed as means of the linear T scores based on the original Minnesota normative group.

tion of these differences, however, these changes in mean scores as a function of age reveal that the probability of obtaining a profile with a clinical scale elevated at a T score of 70 or higher will decrease slightly as the client's age increases.

There have been few studies of the effects of age on MMPI profiles in psychiatric settings. Aaronson (1958) reported the changes in the highest clinical scale by age for the cases in Hathaway and Meehl's *An Atlas for Clinical Use of the MMPI* (1951). Peaks on Scales *1* (Hypochondriasis) and *2* (Depression) were more likely in the older patients and peaks on Scales *4* (Psychopathic Deviate)

and *8* (Schizophrenia) in the younger patients. Newmark and Hutchins (1980) found that a discriminant function developed on younger schizophrenics could identify only 22 percent of older (age 44–54) schizophrenics.

Hedlund and Won Cho (1979) and Schenkenberg, Gottfredson, and Christensen (1984) have provided T scores for the standard validity and clinical scales by decade (see Tables 2–7 and 2–8). These patients showed consistent decreases in T scores across the decades on Scales *F*, *4* (Psychopathic Deviate), *6* (Paranoia), *8* (Schizophrenia), and *9* (Hypomania). These decreases

TABLE 2–7   Effects of Age on MMPI Scale Scores in Psychiatric Patients

Age	N	L	F	K	1(Hs)	2(D)	3(Hy)	4(Pd)	5(Mf)	6(Pa)	7(Pt)	8(Sc)	9(Ma)	0(Si)
20–29	2956	50.9	68.5	50.5	60.5	67.8	62.6	75.2	57.6	68.4	68.6	74.8	66.1	57.6
30–39	2359	51.0	65.1	50.8	61.9	69.0	63.3	73.5	57.1	66.3	66.9	70.7	63.3	57.8
40–49	2006	51.1	62.3	51.1	63.2	69.5	64.0	70.7	55.7	63.6	65.1	66.6	60.9	57.7
50–59	1481	51.5	61.1	51.3	64.9	69.5	64.3	68.4	55.0	62.8	63.8	65.0	59.8	57.0
60–69	566	53.3	60.7	51.5	65.2	69.8	63.3	65.9	55.5	62.4	63.3	64.0	57.8	58.1
70+	60	52.8	64.0	52.2	65.1	69.7	62.5	68.1	52.0	62.7	65.1	68.5	59.8	59.1

Note: Data are from Hedlund and Won Cho (1979). These data are expressed as linear T scores based on the original Minnesota normative group.

TABLE 2-8   Effects of Age on MMPI Scale Scores in Psychiatric Patients

Age	N	L	F	K	1(Hs)	2(D)	3(Hy)	4(Pd)	5(Mf)	6(Pa)	7(Pt)	8(Sc)	9(Ma)	0(Si)
20–29	245	49.2	64.3	48.3	59.3	68.0	62.7	76.4	63.7	65.3	63.8	66.3	64.8	58.8
30–39	264	48.4	64.9	48.2	62.1	70.7	65.4	77.2	63.2	64.4	64.4	66.6	62.6	60.2
40–49	225	48.2	60.8	48.6	63.4	71.8	66.4	75.5	62.1	62.1	62.9	63.7	61.4	58.8
50–59	192	48.6	59.3	48.2	66.8	70.8	67.6	70.3	60.9	60.3	61.3	61.7	59.1	58.2
60+	63	50.3	59.0	50.0	66.7	69.2	66.4	64.4	59.8	60.5	59.1	60.9	57.3	58.3

Note: Data are adapted from Schenkenberg et al. (1984), p. 1421. These data are expressed as linear T scores based on the original Minnesota normative group.

were particularly notable on Scales *4* and *9* where they were approximately 10 and 8 T score points, respectively. Only on Scale *1* (Hypochondriasis) did these patients show an increase in T scores with increasing age.

Several trends are evident in these psychiatric patients with increasing age that were noted in the normal individuals and the medical patients: (1) the decreases in scores on a number of clinical scales will result in fewer profiles reaching or exceeding a T score of 70, (2) Scales *4* and *9* decreased, and (3) only Scale *K* was unaffected by age.

There also were age effects in one sample that was not evident in other samples: (1) the *L* scale increased in the normal and medical samples, but it did not change in the psychiatric samples, (2) Scale *2* increased in the normal sample but it did not change in either the medical or psychiatric samples, (3) Scale *7* decreased in medical patients but it did not change in the normal or psychiatric samples, (4) Scale *1* increased in both the normal and psychiatric samples but it did not change in the medical sample, and (5) the *F* scale decreased in the psychiatric samples but it did not change in the medical or normal samples.

Several investigators have examined the effects of age on individual clinical scales of the MMPI or special scales. Dye, Bohm, Anderten, and Won Cho (1983) factor-analyzed Scale *2* (Depression) and identified significant differences in the expression of depression in three age groups (20–39, 40–59, and 60+). The youngest group of patients emphasized the intrapsychic nature of depression, the middle-aged group felt vulnerable in interpersonal relationships and approached stresses in a less active manner, and the oldest group of patients highlighted frustration and anger in their relationships.

Probably their most important finding was that the oldest group of patients did not express concern over declining physical well-being which has been conjectured to produce elevations on Scales *1* (Hypochondriasis) and *2* (Depression) (cf. Swenson, 1961). Hyer, Harkey, and Harrison (1986) reported that older patients tended to respond more conservatively and to show less pathology on a number of the 77 supplementary scales that they examined.

It is apparent that age does affect MMPI profiles, although these effects are a function of the sample and more complex than might be expected. The next question is what can be done about these effects. Colligan and associates (1983, 1989) suggested one solution when they provided age-specific normalized T scores for all of the standard validity and clinical scales. Another solution would be to provide adjustments to only those scales that are most affected by increasing age. For example, 5 to 10 T points could be added to Scales such as *4* (Psychopathic Deviate) and *9* (Hypomania) that consistently decrease with age. Graham (1979) suggested such a solution for a variety of demographic variables but to date there has not been a single study of such a correction process.

Both of these solutions also will change the relationships among the clinical scales and the resulting codetypes. These potential changes in codetype may leave the clinician without any empirical basis on which to decide which codetype and what correlates are most appropriate for a specific profile.

Until empirical data are available to suggest what scales should be adjusted and by what amount, clinicians will need to remain aware of the potential effects of age on MMPI and MMPI-2 scores.

Gender

Hathaway and McKinley (1983) were aware of the effects of gender on MMPI profiles since they developed separate norms for all of the clinical scales except Scales *6* (Paranoia), *9* (Hypomania), and *0* (Social Introversion). They did not develop separate norms for any of the validity scales, although males score slightly higher on Scale *F* and *K*, and lower on Scale *L* (see Appendix D).

Because separate T score norms are used for men and women, gender is less likely to have any appreciable effect on MMPI or MMPI-2 profiles. In fact, if gender does affect MMPI or MMPI-2 profiles, that would be one basis for arguing that the T score conversions are somehow inappropriate. Clinicians who are reporting research on mixed samples of men and women should be sure to use non-*K*-corrected T scores in analyzing their data to minimize any potential effects of gender. However, raw scores are preferable for analyzing data when *only* men or women are being studied (Butcher & Tellegen, 1978).

Clinicians will need to be aware of the potential effects of gender when raw scores are reported, as is typical for some supplementary scales such as the MacAndrew

(1965) Alcoholism scale where men score about two raw-score points higher than women (see Chapter 5; Greene & Garvin, 1988).

Aaronson (1958) and Webb (1971) reported that men were more likely to have high-points on Scales *1* (Hypochondriasis) and *7* (Psychasthenia), whereas women were more likely to have high-points on Scales *3* (Hysteria) and *6* (Paranoia). Gender differences also occur in the frequency with which MMPI codetypes are found (see Chapter 6, Tables 6–1, 6–2, 6–3, and 6–4). Some codetypes (*2-0/0-2, 3-8/8-3, 4-6/6-4*) are more frequent in women; others (*1-2/2-1, 4-9/9-4*) are more frequent in men. There has been little published research on whether gender differences occur in the empirical correlates of codetypes. This dearth of research could reflect that gender differences are rarely found and hence are considered unimportant to report or the absence of research.

Gynther, Altman, and Sletten (1973) found gender differences in the empirical correlates of only 1 (*2-4/4-2*) of 14 codetypes, which would support the former position. However, Kelley and King (1978, 1979a, 1979b) reported consistent patterns of gender differences in their studies of codetypes in an university mental health setting, which would support the latter position. This issue of whether demographic variables such as gender affect the empirical correlates of a scale or codetype needs to be investigated further. Hopefully, the ensuing years will see more research on demographic variables being published.

Ethnicity

As noted above, the effects of ethnicity on MMPI profiles will be covered in Chapter 8.

Education/Intelligence/Social Class

The demographic variables of education, intelligence, and social class tend to be reported as if they were interchangeable in MMPI research despite their different referents. Typically a researcher will use one of these three variables because the information is readily available.

Several studies have indicated that this set of demographic variables can have a significant effect on MMPI profiles. For example, ethnic effects on MMPI profiles can be accentuated or eliminated depending on whether or not these variables are controlled (cf. Cowan, Watkins, & Davis, 1975; Penk, Roberts, Robinowitz, Dolan, Atkins, & Woodward, 1982; Penk, Robinowitz, Roberts, Dolan, & Atkins, 1981; Rosenblatt & Pritchard, 1978). Similarly, Heilbrun (1979) found that an index of psychopathy based in part on the raw score on Scale 4 (Psychopathic Deviate) was directly related to the frequency of violent crimes in a sample of white prisoners, but only in those prisoners with an IQ less than 95.

As noted in Chapter 1, the MMPI-2 normative group averaged nearly 15 years of education, while the original MMPI normative group averaged around 8 years of education. This difference in level of education between the MMPI and the MMPI-2 has been a source of concern (cf., Caldwell, 1990). Butcher (1990) categorized the MMPI-2 normative group into five groups based on years of education and concluded that the MMPI-2 T scores showed minimal impact from education. Most of the mean scale scores for all five levels of education fell at or very near a T score of 50. Only Scale K in men and women

and Scale 5 (Masculinity-Femininity) in men were significantly correlated with years of education. Butcher did suggest that the interpretation of scores on Scale 5 in men with less than a high school education or with postgraduate training should be adjusted slightly to account for the small effects of education.

Summary

It is clear that some demographic variables do affect MMPI profiles, and may have similar effects on MMPI-2 profiles. However, there is not a simple, direct relationship between any single variable and scores on a given scale. It also appears that the more data that are available on a single variable, the more complex are the relationships that are identified. Research in this area is still in the preliminary stages where single variables are examined at a time. Research that looks at the potential interaction of two or more of these variables simply is nonexistent. It also is necessary for researchers to progress beyond merely reporting mean T scores as a function of some demographic variable and begin to examine whether the correlates of a given MMPI-2 scale or codetype change as a function of the demographic variable.

Stated simply, the question is whether a man with an eighth-grade education and an IQ of 90 will have the same correlates of a 2-7/7-2 codetype as a woman with a college degree and an IQ of 120. It is time to begin to look for empirical answers to basic questions such as these.

CHAPTER 3

Validity Indexes and Validity Configurations

The MMPI was one of the first personality tests to offer a means of directly assessing a client's test-taking attitudes. Thus, the first step in interpreting an MMPI-2 profile is to examine the various validity scales and indexes to determine the client's test-taking attitude. If these validity indexes reveal an inappropriate attitude, the entire profile may be invalid and the interpretation of the profile should be tentative at best.

In this chapter the process for assessing the validity of an MMPI-2 profile will be described, which will emphasize additional MMPI-2 measures of test-taking attitudes such as the Variable Response Inconsistency (*VRIN*) scale (Butcher, Dahlstrom, Graham, Tellegen, & Kaemmer, 1989), and the Wiener and Harmon (Wiener, 1948) Obvious and Subtle subscales. Several MMPI measures of test-taking attitudes, such as the Test-Retest (*TR*) index (Dahlstrom, Welsh, & Dahlstrom, 1972), the Carelessness scale (*CLS*: Greene, 1978a), the Gough Dissimulation scale (*Ds-r*: Gough, 1954, 1957), and the Positive Malingering (*Mp*) scale (Cofer, Chance, & Judson, 1949), also will be reviewed even though they are not available on the MMPI-2. The corre-

lates of each traditional validity scale also will be provided. Finally, the research on simulation of psychopathology, detection of response sets, and subtle and obvious items on the MMPI will be reviewed.

A NOTE ON THE CONCEPT OF VALIDITY ON THE MMPI-2

The concept of validity traditionally has meant the degree to which a test actually measures what it purports to measure (Anastasi, 1968). For example, a graduate-school aptitude test is valid to the extent that it can identify students who will succeed in graduate school. The test's validity would be assessed by the relationship between scores on the test and some index of success in graduate school, such as grade point average or completion of a graduate degree. Similarly with the MMPI-2, the overall relationship of the test to some external criterion (i.e., the accuracy with which the MMPI-2 can predict some other variable such as length of hospitalization or psychiatric diagnosis) would be a measure of its validity.

The concept of validity on the MMPI-2 also has a second, somewhat different meaning. It describes the test-taking attitudes of an individual client, that is, whether or not the client has endorsed the test items in some distorted manner. If the client has provided a consistent and accurate self-appraisal when responding to the MMPI-2 items, the profile is considered to be valid. Consequently, it is possible for a client to provide a valid MMPI-2 on one occasion, an invalid MMPI-2 at another time, and a valid MMPI-2 on a third testing. Because in this second sense validity actually can refer to the consistency with which the client has endorsed the items, as well as the accuracy with which the client has described himself or herself, the clinician needs to be aware of the multiple meanings of the concept of validity on the MMPI-2.

The usage of the concept of validity to refer to the consistency of item endorsement within a single administration of the MMPI-2 would be described more appropriately by the term of reliability. Specifically, one type of reliability—internal consistency—has been used traditionally to refer to the extent to which a person responds in a consistent manner throughout a test or scale.

The usage of the concept of validity also to refer to the accuracy of the self-appraisal by the client further complicates this issue, since a client can provide a consistent pattern of item endorsement that is distorted in some manner so as to make himself or herself look more or less psychopathologic. The term validity of the MMPI-2, however, has a long history of usage, and attempting to convince several generations of clinicians to use more appropriate terms is probably unrealistic. Therefore, the clinician needs to understand the multiple meanings of the concept of validity on the MMPI-2.

STEPS IN ASSESSING MMPI-2 VALIDITY

Assessing the validity of a specific administration of the MMPI-2 to a client is a process that involves multiple steps, which need to be carried out in a sequential manner.[1] An overview of these steps is provided in Figure 3-1. The clinician will see the various meanings of the concept of validity that are raised at each of these steps and their differential effects on overall profile validity as they are explained below.

The clinician also may be surprised that the traditional validity scales of the MMPI-2 (Scales L, F, and K) are introduced at a very late stage in this process. Hopefully, the rationale for this revised process for determining the validity of an individual administration of the MMPI-2 will become clearer in the next few pages. The first step in assessing the validity of this specific administration of the MMPI-2 is to evaluate the number of items omitted (see Figure 3-1), which is discussed in the next section.

ITEM OMISSIONS

Cannot Say (?) Scale

The ? scale consists of the total number of items that the client omits, that is, fails to answer or answers both "true" and "false." Therefore, the ? scale is *not* composed of a specific set of items as the other validity and clinical scales are; the client potentially can omit any one or combination of the 567 items. Thus, the term *scale* is a misnomer since it comprises no specific items.

In standard scoring procedures omitted items are considered to be answered in the nondeviant direction since only items answered in the deviant direction are counted. Thus, the effect of omitted items is potentially to lower the elevation of the overall profile and of any scale on which the items were omitted, since if the client had answered the item a deviant response might have been given.

Clopton and Neuringer (1977b) pro-

FIGURE 3–1   Steps in Assessing MMPI-2 Validity

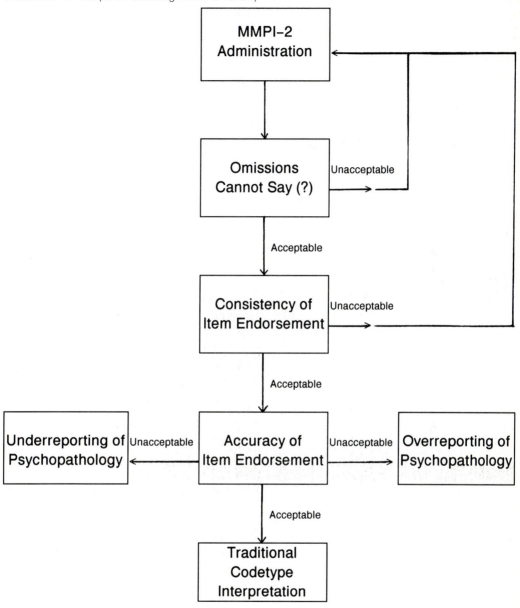

vided data to show how randomly omitting six different numbers of items (5, 30, 55, 80, 105, and 130) affects MMPI profile elevation and distorts profile configuration. The clinical scales dropped an average of .45, 2.74, 5.61, 7.70, 9.09, and 11.54 T score points, re-spectively, when these six quantities of random items were omitted. More important, the codetype of the profile (the two highest elevated clinical scales) changed in 1, 8, 4, 8, 10, and 17 profiles, respectively, from a group of 30 profiles at each level of item omission. Thus, omitting only 30 items changed the codetype for more than 25 percent of their profiles, and when 130 items were omitted, more than half of the codetypes changed. Consequently, profile distortion seems possible when 30 or more items are omitted, even though profile elevation may be reduced only slightly.

It is clearly preferable to minimize the number of omitted items. Initially explaining to the client the reasons for and importance of completing the MMPI-2 will help obtain the client's full cooperation in completing the test. If the client omits an excessive number of items (11 or more), the clinician can ask the client to review the omitted items and respond to them based on whether each is *mostly true* or *mostly false*. If the client still omits an excessive number of items, the clinician can question the client about the reasons for not responding. A final solution is to construct an augmented profile (discussed later in this chapter).

A major issue concerning omitted items is the client's motivation for doing so. Is the client *unwilling* to answer the omitted items or is the client *unable* to answer them? Distinguishing these two categories of omitted items would be useful (Brown, 1950). In the former instance the client probably would have given a deviant response if he or she had actually answered the items; when this assumption is tenable, construction of an augmented profile might be considered. In the latter instance ignoring the omitted items seems preferable since they are probably irrelevant for this particular client. Unfortunately, no one, including Brown (1950), has provided criteria by which these two categories of omitted items can be distinguished. A clinician may be able to make this distinction by interviewing the client extensively. This procedure, however, is time-consuming and often impractical or impossible. Fortunately, most clients omit few items, and so the problem rarely occurs.

The number of MMPI items omitted by specific clients has not been extensively examined. Clopton and Neuringer (1977b) reported the mean number of item omissions in three different populations: psychiatric patients at a large Veterans Administration (VA) hospital, outpatients of a regional mental health center, and applicants for jobs as police officers and firefighters. The percentage of persons who omitted five or fewer items from these three populations was 85.6, 88.9, and 93.7, respectively, and the corresponding mean number of omitted items was 4.68, 2.24, and 2.45. Clopton and Neuringer did not report the specific items that were omitted.

Rosen (1958) and Tamkin and Scherer (1957) also reported median *?* scale scores of less than 4 in two other VA male psychiatric samples. Rosen noted that only 15 of his 307 patients (4.9 percent) omitted more than 30 items. Ball and Carroll (1960) analyzed the *?* scale scores in groups of high-school freshmen and adolescent delinquents. The mean *?* scale scores for these adolescent populations ranged from 1.07 to 6.74 and were significantly lower for girls than boys.

Tables 3–1 and 3–2 present the number of MMPI items omitted in normal individuals and psychiatric patients, respectively. As can be seen in Table 3–1, 5 or fewer items were omitted in 76 to 98 percent of these normal individuals, and more than 30 items were omitted by less than 1 percent, except for Greene's (1986) sample of adult males. There is a consistent trend for men to omit slightly more items than women in all samples except Colligan, Osborne, Swenson, and Offord (1983). The modal number of items omitted in these normal individuals was 0, and the average number of omitted items was less than 4.

The psychiatric samples reported in Table 3–2 omitted slightly more MMPI items than the normal individuals. Five or fewer items were omitted in 58 to 62 percent of

TABLE 3–1 Frequency of Omitted Items on the MMPI in Normal Samples by Gender

Number of Omitted Items	Colligan et al. (1983) Adults		Lavin (1984) Adults		Greene (1986) Adults		Greene (1986) College Students	
	Male (N = 646)	Female (N = 762)	Male (N = 1031)	Female (N = 146)	Male (N = 163)	Female (N = 238)	Male (N = 208)	Female (N = 224)
0	46.0%	45.0%	65.7%	75.3%	55.2%	56.3%	77.9%	77.7%
1–5	35.3%	36.1	24.4	17.8	20.9	29.4	17.8	20.1
Cumulative %	81.3%	81.1%	90.1%	93.1%	76.1%	85.7%	95.7%	97.8%
6–10	5.0	4.9	4.1	2.1	11.6	5.9	1.4	1.8
Cumulative %	86.3	86.0	94.2	95.2	87.7	91.6	97.1	99.6
11–30	10.2	10.2	4.8	4.1	4.9	8.4	2.4	0.4
Cumulative %	96.5	96.2	99.0	99.3	92.6	100.0	99.5	100.0
30+	3.5	3.8	1.0	0.7	7.4	0.0	0.5	0.0
M	4.9	5.1	2.5	1.5	3.7	2.5	1.1	0.5
SD	11.1	11.4	9.7	4.8	3.6	4.4	5.6	1.5

Note: Lavin (1984) administered only the first 399 items of Form R to job applicants in the nuclear power industry.

TABLE 3-2   Frequency of Omitted Items on the MMPI in Psychiatric Patients by Gender

Number of Omitted Items	Psychiatric Patients (Hedlund & Won Cho, 1979)							
	Adults				Adolescents			
	Male (N = 8,646)		Female (N = 3,743)		Male (N = 693)		Female (N = 290)	
0	29.8%		28.4%		28.0%		27.9%	
1-5	32.3		30.4		31.0		30.8	
Cumulative %		62.1%		58.8%		59.0%		58.7%
6-10	16.8		17.2		21.1		21.7	
Cumulative %		78.9		76.0		80.1		80.4
11-30	14.7		17.4		14.6		13.1	
Cumulative %		93.6		93.4		94.7		93.5
31+	6.4		6.6		5.3		6.5	
M	8.7		9.3		7.7		8.4	
SD	18.1		19.2		13.1		15.1	

these patients, and more than 30 items were omitted by 5 to 6 percent. There do not appear to be any gender or age (adult versus adolescent) differences in the number of items omitted in this psychiatric sample. The finding that psychiatric patients omit slightly more items than normal individuals highlights the importance of assessing item omissions in clinical populations.

Although high ? scale scores occur infrequently, research is needed to establish the causes of excessive omissions when they do occur. The work in this area to date has resulted in conflicting findings. Dahlstrom and colleagues (1972) suggested that defensive procedures are one significant cause of elevated ? scale scores. In an empirical study, however, Tamkin and Scherer (1957) found that high ? scale scores did not seem to represent a defensive, evasive attitude in their psychiatric sample. Moreover, Eaddy (1962) found that intolerance of ambiguity and desire for uncertainty were not related to level of item omission on the ? scale among college sophomores. Although the relative infrequency with which most clients omit items makes this area of research slow and time-consuming, more research is sorely needed in a variety of clinical populations.

In addition to the number of items omitted, the specific items most frequently omitted also are of interest. Dahlstrom, Welsh, and Dahlstrom (1975) have summarized in Appendix A of their *Handbook* the frequency with which each MMPI item was omitted by the purified Minnesota adult sample and three different samples of college students. Gravitz (1967) reported the frequency with which specific items were omitted by normal men and women taking the MMPI as preemployment screening for vocational positions. Gravitz concluded that the omitted items were those that probed personal and private feelings. Ball and Carroll (1960) found that items omitted by adolescents fell into four content areas: items not applicable to adolescents, religion, sexual and bodily functions, and unwillingness or inability of the adolescents to make a positive decision about themselves.

Gravitz (1967) reported that men omitted 25 different MMPI items and women omitted 16 different items 5 percent of the time or more from the standard validity and clinical scales. The Scales from which items were omitted most frequently were *2* (Depression), *5* (Masculinity-Femininity), and *0* (Social Introversion).

MMPI items that are omitted frequently in normal and psychiatric samples are presented in Tables 3–3 and 3–4, respectively. If items omitted over 5.0 percent of the time are used as a criterion, normal individuals are slightly more likely to omit items than psychiatric patients. The actual MMPI items that are omitted appear to be similar in the normal

and psychiatric samples: Group Booklet items 17, 53, 58, 70, 98, 168, 232, 295, 400, 476, 483, 513, and 558. The content of these items is provided in Table 3–5. There is a religious content to five of these items (53, 58, 98, 476, and 483), all of which were eliminated from the MMPI-2; the remainder appear to reflect a variety of content areas. It should be noted that item 17 has been reworded on the MMPI-2 (item 6), which may make this item more understandable. Most of the other frequently omitted items on

TABLE 3–3   MMPI Group Booklet Items Frequently Omitted in Normal Samples by Gender

Normal Adults (Greene, 1986)				Normal Adults (Gravitz, 1967)			
Male (N = 163)		Female (N = 238)		Male (N = 7,149)		Female (N = 4,816)	
Item	%	Item	%	Item	%	Item	%
70	35.6	58	24.4	70	12.8	58	18.4
58	19.6	70	19.3	295	9.9	70	17.6
483	15.3	441	15.5	400	9.8	255	14.8
513	14.1	513	13.4	127	8.9	287	8.5
471	13.5	483	13.0	564	8.7	310	8.4
115	10.4	115	11.3	255	8.2	20	7.9
295	10.4	98	10.9	502	7.3	295	7.4
258	9.2	249	10.9	547	7.0	297	6.7
65	8.0	17	9.2	549	7.0	237	6.4
249	8.0	558	9.2	98	6.9	306	6.2
566	8.0	255	8.8	415	6.7	98	6.1
98	7.4	471	8.8	232	6.5	400	5.9
17	6.7	65	7.6	115	6.4	17	5.5
220	6.1	168	7.6	249	6.4	289	5.5
387	6.1	295	7.6	451	6.2	127	5.3
19	5.5	476	7.6	455	5.9	564	5.3
231	5.5	11	7.1	287	5.4	302	5.0
239	5.5	19	7.1	306	5.4		
255	5.5	53	6.7	521	5.3		
		101	6.7	58	5.1		
		20	6.3	299	5.1		
		52	6.3	297	5.1		
		310	6.3	101	5.1		
		232	5.9				
		236	5.9				
		220	5.5				
		258	5.5				

Note: Gravitz (1967) only reported omissions for items on the standard validity and clinical scales.

TABLE 3-4   MMPI Group Booklet Items Frequently Omitted in Psychiatric Samples by Gender

Psychiatric Patients (Hedlund & Won Cho, 1979)							
Adults				Adolescents			
Male (N = 8,646)		Female (N = 3,743)		Male (N = 693)		Female (N = 290)	
Item	%	Item	%	Item	%	Item	%
513	15.5	513	13.1	58	14.3	513	14.8
58	12.7	58	11.7	255	11.7	58	12.1
483	8.7	558	9.3	513	10.2	255	11.0
558	7.9	441	8.7	483	9.2	441	9.3
287	7.6	476	6.1	70	8.2	42	8.6
295	7.0	287	6.0	558	6.9	98	6.9
400	7.0	483	5.8	53	6.8	483	6.9
53	6.8	400	5.7	57	6.3	17	6.6
415	6.6	485	5.7	98	6.1	558	6.6
98	6.4	42	5.6	236	6.1	115	6.2
70	6.3	232	5.5	42	5.8	133	6.2
249	6.2	295	5.4	306	5.8	476	5.9
232	5.6	168	5.2	476	5.8	19	5.5
168	5.5	53	5.2	232	5.6	57	5.5
476	5.4	415	5.2	17	5.2	232	5.5
373	5.3	98	5.0	168	5.2	249	5.5
364	5.1			400	5.2	65	5.2
413	5.1			415	5.1	168	5.2
299	5.0					209	5.2
562	5.0					295	5.2
						485	5.2
						519	5.2

the MMPI have been eliminated: 70, 400, 476, 483, and 513. However, several of these items are still found on the MMPI-2 (168[180], 232[211], 400[345], and 558[470]). It would be expected that clients will omit slightly fewer items on the MMPI-2, since a number of the objectionable MMPI items have been dropped.

In scoring a client's MMPI, the clinician should ascertain how many of the omitted items are among those commonly omitted items from Tables 3-3 or 3-4. These items probably have no particular significance for this client and can be ignored as long as they are not excessive (<11). Clients who omit idiosyncratic items, that is, those items that are *not* omitted commonly, should be inter-

viewed, if possible, to evaluate their inability to endorse these specific items since most clients are capable of doing so.

For example, suppose that a male psychiatric patient omitted the following 22 MMPI items: 4, 17, 53, 58, 61, 70, 73, 77, 87, 98, 115, 116, 135, 168, 173, 232, 295, 318, 400, 513, 558, and 562. Since 78.9 percent (see Table 3-2) of male psychiatric patients omit 10 or fewer items, this patient has omitted more items than most male psychiatric patients. When Table 3-4 is consulted, he omitted 11 items that male psychiatric patients commonly omit (53, 58, 70, 98, 168, 232, 295, 400, 513, 558, and 562). (Item 17 also could be included in this category since it is omitted commonly in other samples.) He

TABLE 3–5   Content of Frequently Omitted MMPI Items

MMPI Item Number	Item Content
17	My father was a good man. [My father is a good man, (if your father is dead) my father was a good man.]
53	A minister can cure disease by praying and putting his hand on your head. [A minister or priest can cure disease by praying and putting a hand on your head.]
58	Everything is turning out just like the prophets of the Bible said it would.
70	I used to like drop-the-handker-chief.
98	I believe in the second coming of Christ.
168	There is something wrong with my mind.
232	I have been inspired to a program of life based on duty which I have since carefully followed.
295	I liked "Alice in Wonderland" by Lewis Carroll.
400	If given the chance I could do some things that would be of great benefit to the world.
476	I am a special agent of God.
483	Christ performed miracles such as changing water into wine.
513	I think Lincoln was greater than Washington.
558	A large number of people are guilty of bad sexual conduct.

also omitted 10 idiosyncratic items: 4, 61, 73, 77, 87, 115, 116, 135, 173, and 318. The clinician could interview the patient about his inability to endorse these latter 10 items.

Data will need to be collected to determine what items are commonly omitted on the MMPI. It does appear that several MMPI-2 items (180, 211, 345, and 470) would be expected to fall into the category of commonly omitted items.

Hathaway and McKinley (1967) arbitrarily converted raw scores on the *?* scale of the MMPI to T scores. They assigned a raw score of 30 on the *?* scale to a T score of 50; thus 30 omitted items should be an average score for the reference population. Assuming that a client could omit 1 item in 5 (110 items total) and still have an interpretable profile, Hathaway and McKinley assigned a raw score of 110 to a T score of 70.

In light of the findings reported above, Hathaway and McKinley's estimate of the number of items a client could omit without distorting the profile is extremely high. The findings reported above suggest that a raw score of 30 on the *?* scale occurs about 5 percent of the time; this means that a raw score of 30 is nearly a T score of 70, not a T score of 50 as Hathaway and McKinley (1967) assumed. Similarly, the research reported indicates that a raw score of 100 on the *?* scale occurs about .5 percent of the time; this is approximately a T score of 80, not 70 as Hathaway and McKinley suggested. Thus, the *?* scale T score equivalents on the standard profile sheet of the MMPI are of questionable accuracy, and the clinician should consider using the T score equivalents previously described that are more accurate estimates of the frequency with which items are omitted.

There are two small changes on the MMPI-2 that may affect the *?* scale. First, the *?* scale is not included on the standard profile sheet for the MMPI-2 (see Profile 2–1); instead the number of omitted items is simply noted at the lower lefthand corner of the sheet. Second, the instructions for administering the MMPI-2 discourage clients from omitting items. These two changes may cause clinicians to underestimate the importance of checking for item omissions. Consequently, clinicians will need to be more intentional in checking each client's answer sheet to determine the exact number of item omissions.

No reliability data on the *?* scale have been reported. The interpretation of four levels of elevation of the *?* scale are summarized in Table 3–6.

The first step in determining the validity of this specific administration of the MMPI-2 involves ascertaining the number of omitted items, as outlined in Figure 3–1. Tables 3–45 (MMPI-2) and 3–46 (MMPI) (pages 100–101) provide a summary of the quantitative data that are needed to use the flowchart for the first step. If only the first 370 items of the MMPI-2 are administered because the clinician is only interested in obtaining a client's scores on the standard validity and clinical scales, the clinician should *not* count the non-administered items as being omitted.

A summary of the potential causes of excessive item omissions is presented in Table 3–7 as well as some possible solutions for these problems. Most of these solutions allow for the client to correct the problem of omissions on the MMPI-2 so that the clinician then can proceed with the assessment of the consistency of item endorsement. Consequently, this step ensures that an excessive number of items have not been omitted once any reasons that the client might have for omitting items have been identified and corrected.

Constructing an Augmented Profile

A clinician occasionally will be faced with a situation in which a client omitted a sizable number of items and it is not possible to have the client complete these items. For example,

TABLE 3–6 Interpretations of Cannot Say (*?*) Scale Elevations

Raw Score	Interpretation
0	1. *Low.* These clients are able and willing to respond to all of the items. This is the expected score for most samples.
1–5	2. *Normal.* Scores in this range indicate clients who are omitting a few items characteristically omitted by the individual's reference group or omitting a few items that have idiographic significance. The specific items omitted and their content should be scanned. There is little probability of profile distortion unless all omitted items are from a single scale.
6–30	3. *Moderate.* Scores in this range indicate clients who have omitted more items than is typical of most individuals. The scales from which the items have been omitted should be checked. There is a distinct possibility as the number of omitted items approaches 30 that the profile may be distorted as to configuration or codetype. Constructing an augmented profile might be considered. The profile may be of questionable validity as the number of omitted items approaches 30.
31 +	4. *Marked.* THE PROFILE IS VERY LIKELY TO BE INVALID. These clients are unwilling or unable to complete the MMPI-2 in an appropriate manner. They may be overly cautious in trying not to reveal any significant information about themselves, obsessionally unable to come to any decision about numerous items, or simply so defiant and uncooperative that they will not answer the items. If possible, the clinician should have the client complete the omitted items or retake the entire test. A client who fails to complete the MMPI-2 does not automatically fall into this category.

TABLE 3–7 Potential Causes of and Solutions for Excessive Item Omissions

Cause	Solution
1. Client is unsure of frequency of occurrence of item content.	1. Emphasize to client that item responses indicate "mostly" true and "mostly" false.
2. Client has been careless in completing the test.	2. Encourage the client to take sufficient time to respond to all items.
3. Client is very defensive and unwilling to endorse any items that might be "controversial."	3. Explain that answers to individual items are less important than scores on scales; reassure client that responses to items are confidential.
4. Client is not familiar with item content.	4. None; actually very few of such items for most people.

when the MMPI-2 is administered as a screening procedure, it may not be possible to interview the client again or have the client retake the omitted items. One way of handling such circumstances is to augment the obtained profile. There are no well-defined criteria as to when a profile should be augmented. Augmenting is probably unnecessary if fewer than 5 items have been omitted, and probably inappropriate if more than 30 items have been omitted. Consequently, augmenting the profile may be considered between these two extremes if it is not possible to have the client retake the omitted items, *although clinicians should be well aware that there are no empirical data to justify this procedure.*

There are two methods of augmenting

the profile. The first is based on the assumption that the client systematically avoided answering the omitted items and that, if the client had responded to them, the response would have been in the deviant direction. The process basically involves determining which items were omitted from which scales and adding one point for each omitted item to the raw score on the appropriate scale. (Appendix E of this book lists the scales on which each MMPI-2 item is scored. Karol [1985] has provided this same information in tabular form for the MMPI that may facilitate determining the scales on which each item is scored.)

Since some items are scored on more than one scale and may even be scored in the opposite direction from one scale to the next, it is possible for the omitted items to be scored as if the client responded both "true" and "false" to them. This "double" scoring of items is a logical inconsistency in this method of constructing an augmented profile; however, if it appears that the client systematically avoided the omitted items, this method represents an appropriate attempt to salvage as much clinical data as possible from an otherwise lost cause.

An example of this method of augmenting the profile might be that a male client omitted 10 items when taking the MMPI-2 (see Table 3–8). By checking Appendix H, the clinician can determine which scales contained these items. To construct the augmented profile, the clinician would then add one point for each omitted item to the raw score of the appropriate scale. For example, two points would be added to the raw score for Scale 7 (Psychasthenia) since 2 omitted items (9 and 242) appear on this scale. A similar procedure would be followed for the other items and scales (see Table 3–8). The clinician would then plot the augmented profile on the standard profile sheet. If the *K* scale has been augmented, all the *K*-corrected scales (*1, 4, 7, 8,* and *9*) also would have to be

TABLE 3–8 Example of the Procedure for Constructing an Augmented Profile

Items	MMPI-2 Item Number	Scale True	Scale False
1.	9		2, 7
2.	42	F, 8	
3.	65	3	
4.	95		2
5.	134		2
6.	148		2
7.	167	0	3, 4
8.	177	5	8
9.	189		2
10.	242	7, 8, 9	

augmented if a *K*-corrected profile is being plotted.

In addition, the clinician should indicate on the profile sheet that the profile has been augmented using standard procedures. In this example, in which only 10 items were omitted, augmenting the profile changed the two highest clinical scales from Scales 7 (Psychasthenia) and 0 (Social Introversion) to Scales 2 (Depression) and 7 (see Table 3–9). Since the codetype based on which clinical scales are most elevated in the profile is a central feature of MMPI-2 interpretation, a shift such as this in the codetype can have a significant effect on the interpretation of the profile.

The second method of augmenting the profile is based on the assumption that the client did not systematically avoid the omitted items and would not have answered all the omitted items in the deviant direction. This method would be appropriate if, for example, the client had insufficient time to complete the MMPI-2 and omitted a number of the later items.

After determining, in the fashion described above, which scales contained the omitted items, the clinician would calculate the proportion of items on each of these scales that the client answered in the deviant direction. Then for each scale the clinician would multiply this proportion times the number of omitted items, assuming that the client would answer the same proportion of the omitted items in the deviant direction.

Using the same example as above (see Tables 3–8 and 3–9), the client answered 27 of the 57 items on Scale 2 (Depression) in the deviant direction and omitted 5 items. Thus, the client answered 27/52, or .519 of the items in the deviant direction. Multiplying .519 times the number of omitted items (5) yields 2.60; this figure, which would be rounded to the nearest whole number (3), would be added to the raw score for Scale 2. A similar process would be followed for each scale on which items were omitted. As with the first method of augmenting the profile, the clinician would then plot the augmented profile, adjusting the *K*-corrections if the *K* scale was augmented and noting on the profile sheet that the profile was augmented by this procedure.

TABLE 3–9 Standard and Augmented Scale Scores

Scale	Standard Profile Raw score (with *K*)	Standard Profile T score	Augmented Profile Raw score (with *K*)	Augmented Profile T score
L	1	39	1	39
F	7	58	8	61
K	11	41	11	41
1 (*Hs*)	17	62	17	62
2 (*D*)	27	68	32	78
3 (*Hy*)	22	52	24	57
4 (*Pd*)	28	62	29	64
5 (*Mf*)	31	60	32	62
6 (*Pa*)	13	61	13	61
7 (*Pt*)	39	77	41	81
8 (*Sc*)	37	69	40	74
9 (*Ma*)	16	41	17	43
0 (*Si*)	45	72	46	73

CONSISTENCY OF ITEM ENDORSEMENT

After the number of items omitted has been checked and found to be in the acceptable range or corrected in one of the manners described above, the next step in the process of assessing the validity of this administration of the MMPI-2 is to verify the consistency of item endorsement (see Figure 3–1). Consistency of item endorsement verifies that the client has endorsed the items in a reliable manner. It is necessary to insure that the client has endorsed the items consistently before it is appropriate to determine the accuracy with which the client has endorsed the items.

Another way of understanding the difference between the consistency and accuracy of item endorsement, which may clarify why they are distinct steps in this process of assessing the validity of an individual profile, is helpful. Conceptualize the assessment of consistency of item endorsement as being independent of or irrelevant to item content, and the assessment of accuracy of item endorsement as being dependent on or relevant to item content. Thus, measures of the consistency of item endorsement assess whether the individual has provided a reliable pattern of responding to the items throughout the test regardless of their content, whereas measures of the accuracy of item endorsement assess whether the individual has attempted to distort his or her responses to the items in some specific manner.

The consistency of item endorsement on the MMPI-2 is assessed by the Variable Response Inconsistency (*VRIN*) and True Response Inconsistency (*TRIN*) scales. The consistency of item endorsement on the MMPI is assessed by the Test-Retest (*TR*) Index (Dahlstrom et al., 1972) and the Carelessness scale (*CLS*: Greene, 1978a).

Since the function of measures of the consistency of item endorsement on the MMPI-2 will be clearer after exploring the use of these measures on the MMPI, this section will begin with a review of the measures of the consistency of item endorsement on the MMPI. The clinician who is already familiar with this information can proceed directly to the discussion of *VRIN* and *TRIN* (pages 68–76).

Test-Retest (*TR*) Index (MMPI)

One measure of the consistency of item endorsement on the MMPI is the Test-Retest (*TR*) index (Dahlstrom et al., 1972). This Index is the total number of the 16 repeated items on the MMPI that the client has endorsed inconsistently. These 16 repeated items from Scales *6*, *7*, *8*, and *0* were added to the MMPI to facilitate scoring of the IBM answer sheet. The *Group Booklet* form numbers for these MMPI items are provided in Table 3–10. These 16 repeated items were omitted from the MMPI-2, presumably to shorten the test, so the *TR* index cannot be scored on the MMPI-2.

Buechley and Ball (1952) reported that the *TR* index was helpful in discriminating between adolescents with a T score of 70 or higher on the *F* scale who were unable or unwilling to respond consistently to the MMPI, and adolescents whose responses were consistent. They concluded that a score of three or more on the *TR* index indicated an invalid profile. Dahlstrom and associates (1972) suggested that four or more inconsistent responses indicate questionable response reliability, although they did not provide a basis for this decision rule.

Greene (1979) investigated response consistency on the *TR* index in four samples: psychiatric patients at a large VA hospital, clients at a university psychology clinic, young adolescents seen at a juvenile probation office, and university students enrolled in introductory psychology. The frequency of inconsistent responses varied substantially, both

TABLE 3–10 Percentage of Inconsistent Responses for the Test-Retest (*TR*) Index Items by Sample

MMPI Group Booklet Item Numbers		Percentage of Inconsistent Responses by Sample[a]			
		VA	Psychology Clinic	College Students	Juvenile Probation
1.	8–318	20%	8%	12%	42%
2.	13–290	6	6	16	18
3.	15–314	28	20	28	34
4.	16–315	2	12	16	26
5.	20–310	12	6	6	20
6.	21–308	6	2	20	14
7.	22–326	10	14	18	18
8.	23–288	4	14	0	14
9.	24–333	20	14	14	34
10.	32–328	12	14	16	30
11.	33–323	16	10	14	28
12.	35–331	8	14	0	28
13.	37–302	10	16	6	28
14.	38–311	4	4	2	32
15.	305–366	8	8	4	28
16.	317–362	12	12	12	22

Note: From ''Response consistency on the MMPI: The TR index,'' by R. L. Greene, *Journal of Personality Assessment,* 1979, *43,* p. 70. Copyright © 1979 by the Society for Personality Assessment, Inc. Reprinted by permission.

[a]*n* = 50 for each sample.

within and among samples. The mean number of inconsistent responses by each sample was 1.86 (*SD* = 1.97) for VA psychiatric patients, 1.90 (*SD* = 1.71) for psychology clinic clients, 1.86 (*SD* = 1.78) for college students, and 4.14 (*SD* = 2.84) for juvenile probation adolescents.

The high frequency of inconsistent responses in the juvenile probation sample probably reflected the general uncooperativeness and poor motivation of these adolescents since they had an appropriate reading level to take the MMPI. The juvenile probation sample also had more invalid profiles than the other three groups. When a cutting score of four or more inconsistent responses was used, 52 percent of the juvenile probation profiles would be classified as invalid.

The more stringent cutting score of three or more inconsistent responses would classify 68 percent of their profiles as invalid.

Comparing *TR* index scores with other validity indicators such as the *F* scale yielded mixed results in these four samples (Greene, 1979). Among profiles in all four samples ruled invalid by a T score greater than 80 on the *F* scale, approximately 4 to 14 percent of them were valid according to the *TR* index, using a cutting score of four or more inconsistent responses. More importantly, among profiles that would be considered valid because of a T score less than 70 on the *F* scale, which has been a traditional criterion for calling a profile valid, 8 to 16 percent were invalid according to the *TR* index. Thus, the *TR* index seems to identify some invalid profiles that would go undetected by the *F* scale alone, and it identifies some profiles as valid that the *F* scale alone would consider to be invalid.

The frequency with which normal and psychiatric samples endorsed the items inconsistently on the *TR* index are provided in Tables 3–11 and 3–12, respectively. Normal samples were very consistent in their endorsement of the *TR* items, with 95 percent of these individuals making four or fewer inconsistent responses. Males made slightly more inconsistent responses than females. Gravitz and Gerton (1976) reported similar levels of inconsistent responses in their 2,000 normal individuals undergoing preemployment screening; however, they found that women made slightly more inconsistent responses than men.

Psychiatric samples also were very consistent with 85 percent of the patients making four or fewer inconsistent responses. Adult and adolescent psychiatric patients scored in a very similar manner on the *TR* index, which is somewhat unexpected since adolescents generally are seen as being less compliant. The presence of psychopathology did not preclude these patients from being able to endorse the items on the *TR* index in a consistent manner.

One of the advantages of the *TR* index compared to the *F* scale in the assessment of the consistency of item endorsement is that the *TR* index is *not* affected by the presence of psychopathology as the *F* scale is. The similarity among Greene's (1979) three samples (excluding juvenile probation) in frequency of inconsistent responses to individual items and in the distribution of total scores suggests that the *TR* index is relatively independent of the type or degree of psychopathology (see Tables 3–10 and 3–12). This contention is

TABLE 3–11   Frequency of Inconsistent Responses on the Test-Retest (*TR*) Index for Normal Samples by Gender

Number of Inconsistent Responses	Colligan et al. (1983) Adults		Greene (1986) Adults		College Students	
	Male (N = 646)	Female (N = 762)	Male (N = 163)	Female (N = 238)	Male (N = 208)	Female (N = 224)
0	32.2%	40.3%	27.6%	42.9%	25.5%	36.6%
1	29.7	29.5	41.7	36.6	32.2	33.0
2	19.4	14.1	16.0	8.8	20.2	17.9
3	9.7	7.6	3.1	7.6	14.4	6.7
4	4.2	3.9	6.1	2.9	4.3	4.0
Cumulative % (0–4)	95.2%	95.4%	94.5%	98.8%	96.6%	98.2%
Cumulative % (5+)	4.8	4.6	5.5	1.2	3.4	1.8
5	1.1	1.7	3.1	0.8	1.9	1.3
6	1.7	0.9	0.0	0.4	0.5	0.5
7	0.6	0.4	0.0	0.0	0.5	0.0
8+	1.4	1.6	2.4	0.0	0.5	0.0
M	1.48	1.28	1.47	0.95	1.53	1.14
SD	1.76	1.72	1.84	1.15	1.43	1.22

TABLE 3–12 Frequency of Inconsistent Responses on the Test-Retest (*TR*) Index for Psychiatric Patients by Gender and for Stimulus Avoidant Patterns

Number of Inconsistent Responses	Psychiatric Patients (Hedlund & Won Cho, 1979)				Stimulus Avoidant Patterns	
	Adults		Adolescents			
	Male (N = 8,646)	*Female* (N = 3,743)	*Male* (N = 693)	*Female* (N = 290)	*Random* (N = 100)	*Stimulus Avoidant* (N = 436)
0	18.9%	15.0%	17.7%	22.1%	0.0%	0.0%
1	23.9	21.9	21.9	26.2	0.0	0.0
2	19.7	20.1	18.0	19.0	0.0	1.4
3	13.6	15.6	16.5	11.0	0.0	0.9
4	9.0	9.9	8.7	8.3	1.0	6.2
Cumulative % (0–4)	85.1%	82.5%	82.8%	86.6%	1.0%	8.5%
Cumulative % (5+)	14.9	17.5	17.2	13.4	99.0	91.5
5	6.0	6.9	4.9	4.1	3.0	17.0
6	3.3	4.3	4.2	3.4	6.0	13.8
7	2.4	2.7	3.3	2.8	12.0	17.9
8+	3.2	3.6	4.8	3.1	78.0	42.9
M	2.40	2.67	2.79	2.64	8.06	7.24
SD	1.74	1.77	1.85	1.78	2.00	2.20

Note: Stimulus avoidance patterns were defined as sequences of responses such as TFTF, TTFTTF, FFTFFT, and so on. See Nichols, Greene, and Schmolck (1989) for a complete description.

supported by the findings of Jones, Neuringer, and Patterson (1976) and Coché and Steer (1974), who reported small mean differences between various diagnostic groups.

Although elevations on the *F* scale can represent inconsistent patterns of item endorsement, *or* the client's acknowledgment of the presence of psychopathology, *or* the client's overreporting of psychopathology (see Accuracy of Item Endorsement below), the *TR* index is relatively unaffected by the type and severity of psychopathology, so it can provide an independent estimate of the consistency of item endorsement on the MMPI.

The *TR* index is useful in identifying inconsistent patterns of item endorsement, but the clinician should keep in mind that an acceptable score on the *TR* index indicates only that the client has endorsed the items consistently and not necessarily accurately, since the client could consistently overreport or underreport psychopathology (see Accuracy of Item Endorsement later in this chapter). Moreover, since the *TR* index assesses only the consistency of the client's responses, it will not detect "all true" or "all false" response sets, which are consistent but nonveridical test-taking sets. The Carelessness scale (Greene, 1978a), which will be discussed in the next section, is more sensitive to these response sets on the MMPI. The *TR* index will easily detect "random" response sets that would yield a score of approximately 8 (see Table 3–12; Rogers, Dolmetsch, & Cavanaugh, 1983; Rogers, Harris, & Thatcher, 1983).

The *TR* index will detect some MMPI

profiles with inconsistent responses that would be considered valid by traditional validity indicators such as the *F* scale, and it can demonstrate that the client has been endorsing the items consistently despite elevated scores on the *F* scale (Evans & Dinning, 1983; Maloney, Duvall, & Friesen, 1980). These findings indicate that the *TR* index and the traditional validity indicators are *not* measuring identical processes in test-taking attitudes (Fekken & Holden, 1987).

An interesting issue that has not yet been examined is the elevation and configuration of the clinical scales in those persons who achieve a T score of 70 or below on the *F* scale (i.e., a valid profile) and who have six or more inconsistent responses on the *TR* index (i.e., an invalid profile). Research also is needed to examine the effects of various levels of inconsistency of item endorsement on profile validity using independent or nontest validity criteria.

The 16 pairs of items on the *TR* index are a potential source of discrepancies in scoring the standard MMPI validity and clinical scales, since historically there was no consistent convention on whether the first or second occurrence of each pair of items was to be scored. Some scoring templates and computer scoring services used the first occurrence of each pair of items, whereas others used the second occurrence (McGrath, O'Malley, & Dura, 1986). Any time the *TR* index for a client does not equal zero, there is the possibility of a discrepancy in scoring when different MMPI templates or computer scoring services are compared. These potential discrepancies will be most serious on Scale *8* (Schizophrenia) since 13 pairs of *TR* items are scored on that scale.

The current *Manual for Administration and Scoring of the MMPI* (Hathaway & McKinley, 1983) states that any templates marked with a 1983 copyright or later score the first occurrence of each pair of *TR* items. The *Manual* also states that scoring the second occurrence is in error (p. 13). Clinicians should check their MMPI scoring templates to insure that the first occurrence of each pair of *TR* items is being scored.

Carelessness Scale (*CLS*) (MMPI)

The Carelessness scale (*CLS:* Greene, 1978a) has been developed as an alternative indicator of consistency of item endorsement on the MMPI. Prior development of a carelessness scale for the Addiction Research Center Inventory (Haertzen & Hill, 1963) indicated that psychologically opposite items are more sensitive than repeated items in detecting the inability or unwillingness of a client to complete the inventory appropriately.

Greene's (1978a) *CLS* scale on the MMPI consists of 12 pairs of empirically selected items that were judged to be psychologically opposite in content. Greene provided normative data for three samples: VA psychiatric inpatients, clients at a university psychology clinic, and college students. The MMPI *Group Booklet* item numbers for these 12 pairs of items, the direction of scoring for a deviant response, and the frequency of deviant responses by sample are presented in Table 3-13.

The maximum total score on the *CLS* scale is 12 if the client answers all 12 pairs of items inconsistently. Greene suggested that a cutting score of four or more deviant responses is optimal in identifying invalid profiles; however, he did not use any external criteria to validate this cutting score. The mean number of inconsistent responses by each sample was 1.76 (*SD* = 1.45) for VA psychiatric patients, 2.20 (*SD* = 1.28) for psychology clinic clients, and 1.48 (*SD* = 1.34) for university students.

The more subtle nature of the *CLS* scale—based on items that are not simply repeated but are psychologically opposite— should enable the clinician to detect a pattern of inconsistent item endorsement on the

TABLE 3–13 Item Composition, Direction of Scoring, and Frequency of Deviant Responses by Sample for the Carelessness (*CLS*) Scale

Item Pair	MMPI Group Booklet Item Numbers	Deviant Responses	Frequency of Deviant Responses[a]		
			VA	College	Psychology Clinic
1.	10–405	Same	22%	8%	18%
2.	17– 65	Different	4	8	26
3.	18– 63	Different	26	34	20
4.	49–113	Same	2	6	6
5.	76–107	Same	12	12	34
6.	88–526	Same	12	8	24
7.	137–216	Same	20	14	30
8.	177–220	Different	4	6	8
9.	178–342	Same	22	20	16
10.	286–312	Different	18	12	10
11.	329–425	Same	24	12	18
12.	388–480	Different	10	8	14

Note: From "An empirically derived MMPI Carelessness scale," by R. L. Greene, *Journal of Clinical Psychology,* 1978, *34,* p. 408. Copyright ©1978 by the *Journal of Clinical Psychology.* Reprinted by permission.

[a]*n* = 50 for each sample.

MMPI in sophisticated clients who might recognize the existence of identical repeated items and consequently go undetected by the *TR* index. The *CLS* scale also is useful in detecting "all true" and "all false" response sets since either response set would result in a total score of seven deviant responses (see Table 3–13). In addition to detecting clients who are unwilling to answer the MMPI appropriately, the *CLS* scale also seems to detect clients who are psychologically confused and unable to answer the MMPI appropriately. In such a case, an interview with the client usually enables the clinician to recognize the client's mental confusion.

Bond (1986) and Fekken and Holden (1987) have noted that carelessness is *not* the primary cause of inconsistent responding to the *CLS* items in normal students. It may be more appropriate to call the *CLS* scale an inconsistency scale, which does not imply any motivation by the client for his or her inconsistent responses. This point will be even clearer when the potential causes of inconsistent responding are summarized in Table 3–23 (page 76).

The frequency with which normal and psychiatric patients endorsed the *CLS* items are provided in Tables 3–14 and 3–15, respectively. Normal samples were very consistent in their endorsement of the *CLS* items, with 97 percent of these individuals making four or fewer inconsistent responses. There did not appear to be any gender differences in the endorsement of the *CLS* items. Psychiatric samples also were very consistent, with 85 percent of the patients making four or fewer inconsistent responses. Adult and adolescent psychiatric patients scored in a very similar manner on the *CLS* scale. It appears that the *CLS* scale performs in a very similar manner as the *TR* index in assessing consistency of item endorsement.

As with the *TR* index, further research is

TABLE 3-14 Frequency of Inconsistent Responses on the Carelessness (*CLS*) Scale for Normal Samples by Gender

Number of Inconsistent Responses	Colligan et al. (1983) Adults		Greene (1986) Adults		Greene (1986) College Students	
	Male (N = 646)	Female (N = 762)	Male (N = 163)	Female (N = 238)	Male (N = 208)	Female (N = 224)
0	27.4%	31.9%	40.5%	43.3%	26.4%	35.3%
1	35.8	31.5	25.2	30.7	30.8	31.7
2	19.6	22.8	18.2	19.3	24.5	20.1
3	11.6	8.4	9.2	4.6	9.6	9.8
4	3.6	4.0	4.4	1.3	6.3	2.2
Cumulative % (0–4)	98.0%	98.6%	97.5%	99.2%	97.6%	99.1%
Cumulative % (5+)	2.0	1.4	2.5	0.8	2.4	0.9
5	1.2	0.6	2.5	0.8	1.4	0.9
6	0.6	0.8	0.0	0.0	1.0	0.0
7	0.2	0.0	0.0	0.0	0.0	0.0
8+	0.0	0.0	0.0	0.0	0.0	0.0
M	1.35	1.26	1.19	0.92	1.47	1.15
SD	1.24	1.21	1.31	1.03	1.31	1.13

needed on the *CLS* scale to validate it externally. Information is needed on how frequently "inconsistent profiles" detected by each of these measures are, indeed, invalid. Meanwhile, both the *TR* index and the *CLS* scale can be used to identify some MMPI profiles that should be interpreted cautiously, if at all.

Since the *TR* index and the *CLS* scale are both relatively short scales with 16 and 12 items, respectively, their reliability as a measure of the consistency of item endorsement can be enhanced by summing the score on the two scales. The frequency with which normal and psychiatric samples made inconsistent responses on the sum of the *TR* index and the *CLS* scale are provided in Tables 3–16 and 3–17.

Normal samples were very consistent in their endorsement of the sum of the *TR* index and *CLS* scale, with 97 percent of these individuals making eight or fewer inconsistent responses and most of them making five or fewer inconsistent responses. There did not appear to be any gender differences. Psychiatric samples also were very consistent, with 85 percent of the patients making eight or fewer inconsistent responses. Adult and adolescent psychiatric patients scored in a very similar manner on the sum of the *TR* index and the *CLS* scale.

Nichols, Greene, and Schmolck (1989) have developed a set of decision rules based on the *TR* index and the *CLS* scale to identify inconsistent patterns of item endorsement on the MMPI. They also compared the use of these rules with more traditional measures of validity such as the *F* and *K* scales and found that their rules were generally superior. They recommended that their decision rules be used

TABLE 3–15 Frequency of Inconsistent Responses on the Carelessness (*CLS*) Scale for Psychiatric Patients by Gender and for Stimulus Avoidant Patterns

Number of Inconsistent Responses	Psychiatric Patients (Hedlund & Won Cho, 1979)				Stimulus Avoidant Patterns	
	Adults		Adolescents			
	Male (N = 8,646)	*Female* (N = 3,743)	*Male* (N = 693)	*Female* (N = 290)	*Random* (N = 100)	*Stimulus Avoidant* (N = 436)
0	12.6%	8.8%	9.7%	10.0%	0.0%	0.0%
1	22.1	19.7	16.9	19.0	0.0	0.5
2	23.5	22.8	21.9	24.1	0.0	1.8
3	17.8	19.0	20.6	16.9	2.0	5.5
4	11.8	14.9	12.7	14.1	4.0	10.6
Cumulative % (0–4)	87.8%	85.2%	81.8%	84.1%	6.0%	18.4%
Cumulative % (5+)	12.2	14.8	18.2	15.9	94.0	81.6
5	6.4	8.0	9.1	9.0	16.0	13.1
6	3.4	3.9	5.2	3.8	16.0	28.9
7	1.7	1.8	2.9	2.8	28.0	19.0
8+	0.7	1.1	1.0	0.3	34.0	20.4
M	2.40	2.67	2.79	2.64	5.90	6.08
SD	1.74	1.77	1.85	1.78	1.71	1.71

Note: Stimulus avoidance profiles were defined as sequences of responses such as TFTF, TTFTTF, FFTFFT, and so on. See Nichols, Greene, and Schmolck (1989) for a complete description.

in clinical and research settings to identify inconsistent patterns of item endorsement.

Variable Response Inconsistency Scale (*VRIN*) (MMPI-2)

The Variable Response Inconsistency scale (*VRIN*) consists of 67 pairs of items that have similar or opposite item content. These pairs of items are scored if the client is inconsistent in his or her responses. Table 3–18 provides two examples of pairs of *VRIN* items and the inconsistent response(s). For example, if a client endorses item 99 "false" and 138 "true," it is scored as an inconsistent response.

Table 3–18 also shows that few normal individuals or clients endorse this particular pair of items inconsistently. If a client en-

dorses item 6 "true" and item 90 "false" or item 6 "false" and item 90 "true," it is scored as an inconsistent response. Slightly more normal individuals and clients are likely to endorse this pair of items inconsistently. *VRIN* actually consists of 49 pairs of unique items, since two separate response patterns are scored for 18 of these 67 item pairs, as with items 6 and 90.

The first three columns of Table 3–19 illustrate the distribution of scores on *VRIN* if the client randomly "endorsed" the MMPI-2 items. Since only one of the four possible combinations of "true" and "false" response patterns are scored on each of the 67 pairs of items on *VRIN*, the average score in such random sorts is 16.75 (67/4). Some 15.3 percent of these random sorts are at or below the recommended cutting score of 13 (T score

TABLE 3-16   Frequency of Inconsistent Responses on the Sum of the Test-Retest (*TR*) Index and the Carelessness (*CLS*) Scale for Normal Samples by Gender

| | Colligan et al. (1983) | | Greene (1986) | | | |
| | Adults | | Adults | | College Students | |
Number of Inconsistent Responses	*Male* *(N = 646)*	*Female* *(N = 762)*	*Male* *(N = 163)*	*Female* *(N = 238)*	*Male* *(N = 208)*	*Female* *(N = 224)*
0	11.5%	16.8%	13.5%	24.8%	9.1%	13.8%
1	20.6	21.5	28.2	24.8	18.3	25.0
2	22.8	22.4	15.3	19.7	18.3	21.0
3	14.4	14.4	15.3	16.0	18.3	17.4
4	10.5	8.3	12.3	6.7	16.8	12.5
5	9.4	6.2	6.1	5.0	10.1	7.1
6	4.2	4.3	1.8	0.4	2.4	0.9
7	2.2	2.4	3.1	0.8	2.4	0.9
8	1.1	1.0	1.8	0.8	1.4	0.4
Cumulative % (0-8)	96.7%	97.3%	97.5%	99.2%	97.1%	99.1%
Cumulative % (9+)	3.4	2.7	2.5	0.8	2.9	0.9
9	1.5	0.5	0.0	0.4	1.0	0.0
10	0.5	0.8	0.0	0.0	0.5	0.9
11	0.6	0.4	0.0	0.4	1.0	0.0
12+	0.7	1.0	2.5	0.0	0.4	0.0
M	2.8	2.5	2.7	1.9	3.0	2.3
SD	2.4	2.4	2.6	1.8	2.2	1.8

of 80 on *VRIN*). However, it has been noted clinically that clients with scores on *VRIN* as high as 13 or 14 appear to have endorsed the items consistently. As can be seen in Table 3-19, 24.4 percent of random sorts are at or below a score of 14.

Research is needed to determine empirically whether the suggested cutting score of 13 or higher on *VRIN* to indicate an inconsistent pattern of item endorsement is appropriate. Until such data are available, clinicians are urged to use the following guidelines: (1) when the scores on *VRIN* are 7 or lower, or 16 and higher, there is a high probability that the client has endorsed the items consistently or inconsistently, respectively; and (2) when scores on *VRIN* are in the intermediate range of 8 to 15, it is not clear whether the client has endorsed the items consistently or inconsis-

tently. In this latter case, the clinician is encouraged to examine the indexes described in the next section. It also may be useful to examine these indexes even in cases where *VRIN* is 7 or lower to insure that the items have been endorsed consistently.

$|F - F_B|$ (MMPI-2)

The *F* scale and the Back *F* (*FB*) scale are composed of items that were endorsed less than 10 percent of the time by the normative sample on the MMPI and MMPI-2, respectively. Each of these scales will be described in more detail below when the traditional validity scales of the MMPI-2 are discussed. Since the items on both scales are infrequently endorsed, clients would be expected to endorse approximately the same number

TABLE 3–17 Frequency of Inconsistent Responses on the Sum of the Test-Retest (*TR*) Index and the Carelessness (*CLS*) Scale for Psychiatric Patients and for Stimulus Avoidant Patterns

Number of Inconsistent Responses	Psychiatric Patients (Hedlund & Won Cho, 1979)				Stimulus Avoidant Patterns	
	Adults		Adolescents			
	Male (N = 8,646)	*Female* (N = 3,743)	*Male* (N = 693)	*Female* (N = 290)	*Random* (N = 100)	*Stimulus Avoidant* (N = 436)
0	4.2%	2.4%	2.7%	4.1%	0.0%	0.0%
1	9.6	7.3	7.2	7.9	0.0	0.0
2	12.5	10.5	11.0	12.8	0.0	0.0
3	14.8	13.1	14.3	15.2	0.0	0.0
4	14.2	13.8	11.8	16.2	0.0	0.0
5	11.1	12.5	13.0	9.3	0.0	0.0
6	9.3	10.8	11.0	9.7	1.0	0.0
7	6.5	7.8	6.8	7.2	2.0	1.4
8	5.1	6.3	4.9	4.5	0.0	1.8
Cumulative % (0–8)	87.3%	84.5%	82.7%	86.9%	3.0%	3.6%
Cumulative % (9+)	12.7	15.5	17.3	13.1	97.0	96.4
9	3.6	4.8	4.3	3.4	1.0	7.3
10	2.6	3.3	2.3	2.4	3.0	5.0
11	2.1	2.3	3.3	2.4	10.0	10.1
12+	4.4	5.1	7.4	4.9	83.0	74.4
M	4.76	5.27	5.38	4.83	13.96	20.63
SD	3.29	3.28	3.58	3.30	2.68	2.79

Note: Stimulus avoidance profiles were defined as sequences of responses such as TFTF, TTFTTF, FFTFFT, and so on. See Nichols, Greene, and Schmolck (1989) for a complete description.

of items on each scale. Consequently, the *absolute* value of the difference between the number of items that the client has endorsed on each scale can be used as a measure of the consistency of item endorsement.

Table 3–19 provides the distribution of this measure of the consistency of item endorsement for randomly endorsed MMPI-2s. Exactly 75 percent of these random sorts have a score of 7 or higher on this index, and the mean is approximately 10. Less than 26 percent of these random sorts with *VRIN* scores in the intermediate range (8 to 15) had scores of 6 or lower on this index. Thus, the clinician can be fairly confident

that the client has endorsed the items consistently if this index is 6 or lower when *VRIN* is in the intermediate range of 8 to 15.

The clinician also can add the score on *VRIN* to the absolute value of $F - F_B$ to provide a second measure of consistency of item endorsement for scores in the intermediate range of 8 to 15. Less than 15 percent of the random sorts had scores of 20 or less on this index (see Table 3–19). Only 31.1 percent of the scores in the intermediate range on *VRIN* had scores of 20 or lower. Consequently, the clinician can use scores of 20 or lower on this index (*VRIN* plus the absolute

TABLE 3–18 Examples of Scored Responses on VRIN with Frequency of Response by Sample

	138. I believe that I am being plotted against.			
	Normal Individuals		**Clients**	
99. Someone has it in for me.	*True*	*False*	*True*	*False*
True	2.0%	3.7%	14.8%	9.7%
False	0.0	94.3	4.8	70.7
Deviant Response: 99F–138T.				

	90. I love my father or (if your father is dead) I loved my father.			
	Normal Individuals		**Clients**	
6. My father is a good man.	*True*	*False*	*True*	*False*
True	91.2%	1.3%	85.3%	3.3%
False	5.5	2.0	5.5	5.9
Deviant Responses: 6T–90F; 6F–90T.				

Note: $N = 401$ normal individuals; $N = 1,500$ clients.

value of $F - F_B$) to indicate that the client has endorsed the items consistently.

Finally, the clinician can add the raw scores on the F and F_B scales to the absolute value of $F - F_B$ to provide a third measure of consistency of item endorsement for scores in the intermediate range on *VRIN*. None of these random sorts had scores lower than 36 on this index (see Table 3–19), which the clinician could use as another means of assessing consistency of item endorsement for these intermediate scores on *VRIN*.

Table 3–20 provides data for 31 clients who obtained intermediate scores (8 to 15) on *VRIN*. These 31 cases were identified in a sample of 90 MMPI-2s collected on an inpatient alcohol treatment program and a state psychiatric hospital. Over one-third (34.4 percent) of these clients scored in the intermediate range on *VRIN*, although approximately 14 percent would be expected to have scored in this range based on a T score of 61 for a raw score of 8 on *VRIN* in men. Five of these 31 cases, marked with asterisks in Table 3–20, have very questionable consistency of item endorsement, and one case (#27) is

clearly inconsistent. Conversely, almost two-thirds of these clients with scores in the intermediate ranges on *VRIN*, and most of the cases (#25, 26, 28, 29, 30) with the highest scores within this range, appear to have endorsed the items consistently. Hopefully, the clinician realizes the necessity of routinely checking the consistency of item endorsement with these additional measures for clients who have intermediate scores on *VRIN*.

In discussing the consistency of item endorsement, it has been assumed that the client has followed the same pattern of item endorsement for all 567 items. This assumption may not always be appropriate, since clients' motivation may change as they go through the test. For example, a client could endorse the first 400 items consistently and then endorse the remainder of the items inconsistently. Since all of the items on the standard validity and clinical scales on the MMPI-2 occur in the first 370 items, if the client started endorsing the items randomly after item 370, the clinician could still score and interpret these scales. If it were possible to assess the clients' patterns of item endorsement

TABLE 3–19 Assessing Random Responses on the MMPI-2 with *VRIN*, *F*, and Back *F* Scales

	VRIN		$|F - F_B|$			$VRIN + |F - F_B|$			$F + F_B + |F - F_B|$	
Raw Score	Frequency	Cumulative Percent	Frequency	Cumulative Percent	Raw Score	Frequency	Cumulative Percent	Raw Score	Frequency	Cumulative Percent
0			27	1.1	8	2	0.1	36	1	0.0
1			58	3.4	9	1	0.1	38	4	0.2
2			62	5.9	10	4	0.3	40	7	0.5
3			86	9.3	11	3	0.4	42	15	1.1
4			108	13.6	12	5	0.6	44	24	2.0
5			124	18.6	13	6	0.8	46	50	4.0
6	1	0.0	159	25.0	14	13	1.4	48	81	7.3
7	3	0.2	157	31.2	15	15	2.0	50	111	11.7
8	7	0.4	181	38.5	16	41	3.6	52	154	17.9
9	20	1.2	210	46.9	17	57	5.9	54	192	25.6
10	27	2.3	156	53.1	18	55	8.1	56	253	35.7
11	57	4.6	207	61.4	19	78	11.2	58	253	45.8
12	96	8.4	188	68.9	20	90	14.8	60	265	56.4
13	172	15.3	179	76.1	21	90	18.4	62	254	66.6
14	228	24.4	144	81.8	22	131	23.6	64	198	74.5
15	283	35.8	121	86.7	23	140	29.2	66	186	81.9
16	315	48.4	101	90.7	24	163	35.8	68	160	88.3
17	286	59.8	73	93.6	25	177	42.8	70	110	92.7
18	275	70.8	54	95.8	26	164	49.4	72	77	95.8
19	254	81.0	34	97.2	27	165	56.0	74	35	97.2
20	188	88.5	30	98.4	28	161	62.4	76	32	98.5
21	109	92.8	14	98.9	29	148	68.4	78	20	99.3
22	78	96.0	13	99.4	30	130	73.6	80	14	99.8
23	50	98.0	5	99.6	31	108	77.9	82	2	99.9
24	26	99.0	3	99.8	32	114	82.4	86	1	100.0
25	16	99.6	2	99.8	33	94	86.2	88	1	100.0
26	7	99.9	2	99.9	34	84	89.6			
28	2	100.0	2	100.0	35	61	92.0			
					36	65	94.6			
					37	47	96.5			
					38	29	97.6			
					39	15	98.2			
					40+	43	100.0			
	$M = 16.74$		$M = 10.05$			$M = 29.8$			$M = 59.95$	
	$SD = 2.44$		$SD = 4.83$			$SD = 8.6$			$SD = 7.58$	

Note: $N = 2,500$ for each comparison.

TABLE 3–20   Assessing Consistency of Item Endorsement for Intermediate Scores (8 to 15) on *VRIN* with *F* and Back *F* Scales

Client	Raw Scores			$|F - F_B|$	$VRIN + |F - F_B|$	$F + F_B + |F - F_B|$
	VRIN	*F*	F_B			
1	8	10	7	3	11	20
2	8	6	8	2	10	16
3	8	3	4	1	9	8
4	8	11	12	1	9	24
5	8	14	13	1	9	28
6	8	10	9	1	9	20
7	8	7	11	4	12	22
8	8	7	4	3	11	14
9	8	10	7	3	11	20
10	8	8	10	2	10	20
11	8	17	19	2	10	38
12	8	24	22	2	10	48
13**	8	21	12	9	17	42
14	9	4	2	2	11	8
15	9	13	7	6	15	26
16	9	5	2	3	12	10
17	9	15	9	6	15	30
18	9	11	10	1	10	22
19	9	14	16	2	11	32
20	9	6	7	1	10	14
21	9	12	5	7	16	24
22**	9	10	19	9	18	38
23**	10	14	19	5	15	38
24**	10	13	19	6	16	38
25	11	17	18	1	12	36
26	11	5	3	2	13	10
27**	11	25	7	18	29	50
28	12	8	8	0	12	16
29	13	6	4	2	15	12
30	13	11	13	2	15	26
31**	15	17	15	2	17	34

Note: These 31 cases were obtained from a sample of 90 alcoholic and psychiatric inpatients. Those clients marked with double asterisks have questionable consistency of item endorsement by one or more of the indexes discussed in the text.

in blocks or groups of items rather than for the entire 567 items, it might be possible to score those items up to the point where the client started responding randomly.

As shown in Table 3–21, the *VRIN*, *F*, and F_B items are fairly evenly distributed throughout the MMPI-2 so clinicians could determine when clients start to make inconsistent responses. This approach might be particularly appropriate for intermediate scores on *VRIN* where it is more difficult to make an assessment of the consistency of item endorsement. Research that addresses the consistency of item endorsement as the

TABLE 3–21   Distribution of *F*, *F_B*, and *VRIN* Items by Blocks of 100 and an Example of a Client Who Endorsed the Items Inconsistently

	Number of Items on Scale			Number of Items Endorsed by Client			
Item Numbers	*F*	*F_B*	*VRIN*	*F*	*F_B*	*VRIN*	Total
1–100	16	0	4	1	0	0	1
101–200	17	0	6	1	0	1	2
201–300	17	2	9	4	0	1	5
301–400	10	13	9	0	5	3	8
401–500	0	11	10	0	6	2	8
501–567	0	14	11	0	7	0	7
Total	60	40	49	6	18	7	

Note: There are only 49 unique item pairs on *VRIN*, since two response patterns are scored on 18 item pairs.

client goes through the MMPI-2 clearly is needed.

Clinicians should realize that *VRIN* may be insensitive to cases in which the client begins to endorse the items inconsistently part way through the MMPI-2 for the same reasons that *VRIN* is insensitive to random response patterns. Since only one of the four possible combinations of "true" and "false" response patterns are scored on each of the 67 pairs of items on *VRIN*, the probability of a client endorsing any single pair of items is .25, not .50. Consequently, a client may have a low score on *VRIN* since the first item in a pair may have been endorsed appropriately. It would seem that the relationship between the number of *F* and *F_B* items endorsed may be more sensitive to this type of inconsistency than *VRIN*.

Table 3–21 also shows the pattern of item endorsement on *VRIN*, *F*, and *F_B* for a 33-year-old alcoholic inpatient. It is apparent that the patient started to endorse the items inconsistently somewhere between items 300 and 400, since she endorsed almost one-half of the *F_B* items in each block of 100 items after endorsing very few of the *F* items. When asked about her performance on the MMPI-2, she related that she became "tired" as she went through the items and responded in a "hurry" toward the end of the test. The stan-

dard validity and clinical scales still appeared to provide a good description of her since they are based on the first 370 items. The MMPI-2 content scales, which tend to be concentrated in the last 150 items (see Chapter 5), were elevated rather significantly and did not fit her clinical picture at all.

True Response Inconsistency Scale (*TRIN*) (MMPI-2)

The True Response Inconsistency scale (*TRIN*) consists of 23 pairs of items. *TRIN* is very similar to *VRIN* except that the scored response is either "true" or "false" to both items in each pair. Table 3–22 provides two examples of pairs of *TRIN* items and the inconsistent response(s). For example, if a client endorses both items 40 and 176 "true," it is scored as an inconsistent response. Similarly, if a client endorses both items 125 and 195 either "true" or "false," it is scored as an inconsistent response. Table 3–22 also shows that few normal individuals or clients endorse either of these pairs of items inconsistently.

TRIN has 14 pairs of items to which the inconsistent response is "true" and 9 pairs to which the inconsistent response is "false." Scoring *TRIN* is somewhat complicated. One point is *added* to the client's score for each of the 14 item pairs that are scored if endorsed

TABLE 3–22 Examples of Scored Responses on *TRIN*

	176. I have very few headaches.			
	Normal Individuals		**Clients**	
40. Much of the time my head seems to hurt all over.	True	False	True	False
True	.5%	7.2%	4.5%	11.4%
False	72.1	20.2	68.6	15.5

Deviant Response: 40T–176T.

	195. There is very little love and companionship in my family as compared to other homes.			
	Normal Individuals		**Clients**	
125. I believe that my home life is as pleasant as that of most people I know.	True	False	True	False
True	2.7%	84.1%	11.3%	51.6%
False	3.7	9.5	20.4	16.7

Deviant Responses: 125T–195T; 125F–195F.

Note: N = 401 normal individuals; *N* = 1,500 clients.

"true," whereas one point is *subtracted* for each of the 9 item pairs that are scored if endorsed "false." Then 9 points are added to this score. (Nine points are added to the score so that it is not possible to obtain a negative score on *TRIN*. If a client endorsed none of the 14 "true" item pairs and all 9 of the "false" item pairs, a score of –9 would be obtained. Adding 9 points avoids this problem.)

For example, if a client endorsed three of the "true" item pairs on *TRIN*, and six of the "false" item pairs, the score would be 6 (3 − 6 + 9). If a client endorsed eight of the "true" item pairs on *TRIN*, and two of the "false" item pairs, the score would be 15 (8 − 2 + 9). The former client with a relatively low score of 6 on *TRIN* has a propensity to say "false" to the items regardless of their content, whereas the latter client with a score of 15 is tending to say "true" to the items.

Scores on TRIN should *not* be used to determine whether a client has endorsed the items consistently. High scores on *TRIN* re-

flect that clients tend to be "yea-sayers," low scores are obtained by clients who are "nay-sayers," regardless of the item content. The empirical correlates of high and low scores on *TRIN* will need to be determined.

A final comment about *TRIN* needs to be made for those clinicians who use the computer scoring of the MMPI-2 provided by National Computer Systems. The Extended Score Report for the MMPI-2 indicates a score of 9 on *TRIN* by placing an asterisk at a T score of 50. Otherwise, a "T" or "F" is plotted at the appropriate T score based on the client's raw score. Since only T scores above 50 are possible on *TRIN*, there needs to be a mechanism whereby high and low scores are differentiated. Scores from 9 to 19 are indicated by placing a "T" at the appropriate T score.

For example, if a woman's raw score on *TRIN* was 15, a "T" would be plotted at a T score of 95. Scores from 0 to 8 are indicated by placing a "F" at the appropriate T score.

Thus, if a man's raw score was 3, a ''F'' would be plotted at a T score of 92. This procedure may be clearer if the standard profile form for the Supplementary Scales is examined (see Profile 7–3, page 298).

Summary

Now that *VRIN* and the relationship between F and F_B as measures of the consistency of item endorsement on the MMPI-2, and the *TR* index and the *CLS* scale have been described as measures of the consistency of item endorsement on the MMPI, the next step in the implementation of the flowchart in Figure 3–1 can be described. The criteria, summarized in Table 3–45 for the MMPI-2 and Table 3–46 for the MMPI, provide the quantitative data necessary to determine whether the items have been endorsed in a consistent manner. Once it has been determined that the items have been endorsed consistently, the clinician then can proceed to the next step to assess the accuracy of item endorsement. If the items have not been endorsed consistently, the clinician will need to ascertain the reasons for the inconsistency in item endorsement.

A summary of the potential causes of inconsistency in item endorsement is presented in Table 3–23 as well as some possible solutions for these problems. Most of these solutions allow for the MMPI-2 to be readministered so that a consistent pattern of item endorsement can be obtained and the clinician then can proceed with the assessment of the accuracy of item endorsement. Consequently, this step insures that the items have been endorsed consistently once any problems have been identified and corrected.

ACCURACY OF ITEM ENDORSEMENT

After item omissions and consistency of item endorsement have been checked, the next step in the process of assessing the validity of

TABLE 3–23 Potential Causes of and Solutions for Inconsistent Item Endorsement

Cause	Solution
1. Client has not been told why the MMPI-2 is being administered.	1. Explain why the MMPI-2 is being administered and how the data are to be used.
2. Inadequate reading ability or comprehension; inadequate educational opportunity.	2. Present the MMPI-2 orally by tape administration (see Chapter 2). Dahlstrom and colleagues (1972) reported that tape administrations are effective with reading/education levels as low as the third grade.
3. Limited intellectual ability.	3. Present the MMPI-2 orally by tape administration (see Chapter 2). Dahlstrom and colleagues (1972) reported that tape administrations are effective with IQs as low as 65.
4. Too confused psychiatrically or neuropsychologically.	4. Readminister the MMPI-2 when the client is less confused.
5. Still toxic from substance abuse.	5. Readminister the MMPI-2 when the client is detoxified.
6. Noncompliant or uncooperative.	6. Be sure client understands the importance of the MMPI-2 for treatment/intervention and readminister the MMPI-2. If the client is still noncompliant, that issue becomes the focus of treatment.

the MMPI-2 is to verify the accuracy of item endorsement (see Figure 3–1). Accuracy of item endorsement verifies whether the client has adopted a response set either to over-report ("fake-bad," malinger, make socially undesirable responses, etc.) or underreport ("fake-good," defensiveness, make socially desirable responses, etc.) either the presence or severity of psychopathology.

As noted in Chapter 1, the terms *over-reporting* and *underreporting* of psychopathology will be used throughout this book rather than the terms indicated parentheti-cally since a client's motivation for over-reporting or underreporting may range from being very conscious and intentional to being out of awareness and unconscious. Since the client's test data reveal only that the items have been endorsed inaccurately, it is neces-sary to determine the client's motivation for inaccurate item endorsement from a clinical interview and a review of the client's reasons for taking the MMPI-2.

Several issues about overreporting and underreporting of psychopathology must be made explicit before the scales and indexes for assessing accuracy of item endorsement are discussed. First, it will be assumed that overreporting and underreporting represent an unitary dimension that is characterized by the overreporting of psychopathology at one

end of the dimension and underreporting at the other (see Figure 3–2). Consequently, ac-curate patterns of item endorsement grad-ually will shade into overreporting or under-reporting of psychopathology as one moves up or down this dimension; there is no exact point at which the client's performance sud-denly reflects either overreporting or under-reporting of psychopathology. Instead, a probability statement can be made that this client's performance has a particular likeli-hood of reflecting either overreporting or un-derreporting of psychopathology.

Second, it will be assumed that clients who are endorsing the items inaccurately will overreport or underreport psychopathology in general rather than a specific mental disor-der or a set of symptoms. It is very difficult for clients to take the MMPI-2 in an accurate manner as if they have a specific mental dis-order, that has been documented frequently (see Gough Dissimulation Scale and Simula-tion as Role Playing below). The interested clinician is encouraged to take the MMPI-2 with a specific mental disorder in mind and see how well the scales and indexes designed to assess accuracy of item endorsement detect it.

Third, the presence of overreporting or underreporting of psychopathology *cannot* be taken as evidence that the client does or

FIGURE 3–2

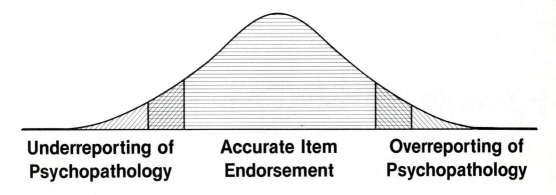

Underreporting of Psychopathology   Accurate Item Endorsement   Overreporting of Psychopathology

does not have actual psychopathology, since a client who actually has some specific mental disorder can overreport or underreport psychopathology. The scales and indexes to assess accuracy of item endorsement *cannot* determine whether the client actually has psychopathology—only whether the client has provided an accurate self-description.

Finally, the scales used to assess the consistency of item endorsement (*TR* index and *CLS* on the MMPI; *VRIN*, *F*, and F_B on the MMPI-2) are *not* appropriate to assess the accuracy of item endorsement (Gallucci, 1984), and the scales/indexes used to assess the accuracy of item endorsement are *not* appropriate to assess the consistency of item endorsement (Rogers, 1983). These two steps in assessing the validity of an specific administration of the MMPI-2 need to be understood as independent events using the scales/indexes that are appropriate at each step.

In assessing the accuracy of item endorsement, it is more efficient to discuss procedures for assessing overreporting of psychopathology and then underreporting since the same scales and indexes do not always work for both response sets.

Overreporting of psychopathology on the MMPI-2 can be assessed by the Wiener and Harmon (Wiener, 1948) Obvious and Subtle subscales, critical items (cf. Lachar & Wrobel, 1979), the *F* and F_B scales, and the *F-K* Dissimulation index. In addition to these measures, the Gough Dissimulation Scale (Gough, 1954, 1957) can be used to assess overreporting of psychopathology on the MMPI. All of these methods for assessing overreporting of psychopathology except for the *F* and F_B scale will be discussed within this section. The *F* and F_B scale will be reviewed below in the section on the standard validity scales.

Underreporting of psychopathology can be assessed by the Wiener and Harmon (Wiener, 1948) Obvious and Subtle subscales, critical items (cf. Lachar & Wrobel, 1979), the *L*

scale, the *K* scale, and the *F-K* index. In addition to these measures, the Positive Malingering Scale (Cofer et al., 1949) can be used to assess underreporting of psychopathology on the MMPI. Only the additional measures for assessing underreporting of psychopathology will be discussed here. The *L* scale and the *K* scale will be reviewed below in the section on the standard validity scales.

The reader should realize that it is *not* necessary to score all of these methods for assessing overreporting and underreporting of psychopathology for every client. Several methods will be illustrated within each response set and the relative advantages and disadvantages of each will be provided. The reader will need to decide which method is most appropriate for his or her specific treatment setting and clients. Overreporting and underreporting of psychopathology will be examined in turn.

Overreporting of Psychopathology

Wiener and Harmon Obvious and Subtle Subscales (MMPI-2 and MMPI)

Examining endorsements to obvious versus subtle items has shown some promise in detecting overreporting and underreporting of psychopathology. In the early research in this area, Wiener and Harmon (Wiener, 1948) performed a rational inspection of MMPI items, identifying obvious items as those that they thought were easy to detect as indicating emotional disturbance, and subtle items as those that were relatively difficult to detect as reflecting emotional disturbance. This procedure resulted in the identification of 146 obvious and 110 subtle items.

The empirically determined deviant response for 65 (59 percent) of these subtle items was in the opposite direction from what would be expected by merely inspecting item content, whereas only 8 (5 percent) of these obvious items were scored in the opposite direction. These findings substantiate the subtle and obvious nature of these two groups of items, respectively. Although Wiener and Harmon had intended to develop obvious and subtle subscales for each clinical scale, it was possible to do so for only five scales: Scales 2(*D*), 3(*Hy*), 4(*Pd*), 6(*Pa*), and 9(*Ma*). Thus, the total score on each of these five scales can be divided into an obvious score and a subtle score, which could be evaluated as to their respective contributions to the total score. The items on the obvious and subtle subscales for each of these five scales appear in Appendix A of this text.

The other clinical scales were composed primarily of obvious items so it was not possible to develop obvious and subtle subscales. These clinical scales include the scales that require the most *K*-correction (Scales 1[*Hs*], 7[*Pt*], and 8[*Sc*]). Wiener and Harmon's preliminary work also suggested that elevation of the obvious scales tended to predict failure in school or vocational training, whereas the subtle scales were not significantly related to these criteria.

Research on the Wiener and Harmon Obvious and Subtle subscales (Wiener, 1948) has demonstrated their usefulness in identifying both overreporting and underreporting of psychopathology (Anthony, 1971; Greene, 1988b; Harvey & Sipprelle, 1976; Hyer et al., 1988; Walters, 1988a; Walters, White, & Greene, 1988). A general pattern for the obvious scales to be more elevated than the subtle scales when the clients were overreporting psychopathology was apparent in these studies. It is difficult, however, to integrate the results into any type of decision rule since no more than any two of these studies used the same index of overreporting.

The available research does not suggest explicit criteria for defining an overreporting response set based on the obvious and subtle subscales as was noted above. It probably is safe to assume that a client who achieves T scores of 80 or more on all five obvious scales

and T scores near 50 on all five subtle scales is trying to overreport. The converse relationship between scores on the obvious and subtle subscales should arouse the suspicion of a underreporting response set. Since it will be assumed that overreporting and underreporting of psychopathology are a general process, one method for creating a criterion to assess these response sets would be to sum the differences between the obvious and subtle subscales. This procedure is illustrated in Table 3–24.

The T scores for each of the obvious and subtle subscales has been calculated, their difference determined on each clinical scale, and these differences have been totaled into a single overall measure. The first client has a total T score difference of +207, which strongly suggests that overreporting of psychopathology has occurred. The second client has a total T score difference of –99, which strongly suggests that underreporting of psychopathology has occurred.

Before the use of this total T score difference to assess accuracy of item endorsement is explored, several issues must be addressed. First, there are a number of obvious and subtle subscales that could be used to assess accuracy of item endorsement (see the section on Obvious and Subtle subscales later in this chapter). The Wiener and Harmon (Wiener, 1948) Obvious and Subtle subscales were selected because they have the longest history of usage in the MMPI field. The high degree of item overlap among the various obvious and subtle subscales and their high correlations suggest that any of these obvious and subtle subscales would work equally well.

Second, the question of whether large T score differences on the individual clinical scales have any significance has not been explored (e.g., it is not clear whether a T score difference of +30 points on Scale 2 [Depression] has the same meaning as +30 points on Scale 9 [Hypomania].

TABLE 3–24 Assessing Accuracy of Item Endorsement by the Total T Score Difference on the Obvious and Subtle Subscales

Scale	Client 1		Client 2	
	T Score	Difference	T Score	Difference
2 (D)				
Obvious	98		50	
Subtle	28	+70	74	−24
3 (Hy)				
Obvious	95		41	
Subtle	45	+50	64	−23
4 (Pd)				
Obvious	98		45	
Subtle	55	+43	66	−21
6 (Pa)				
Obvious	83		48	
Subtle	52	+31	67	−19
9 (Ma)				
Obvious	82		37	
Subtle	69	+13	49	−12
Total T Score Difference		+207		−99

Note: Wiener and Harmon's (Wiener, 1948) Obvious and Subtle subscales were used in these examples.

Finally, it must be explicit that these obvious and subtle subscales are *not* being used to predict specific external criteria since it is reasonably well-known that the obvious scales are better predictors of most criteria than subtle scales (see the section on Obvious and Subtle subscales later in this chapter). Instead the total T score difference between the obvious and subtle subscales is being used as an index of the accuracy of item endorsement. This usage of the difference between the obvious and subtle subscales is in the same vein as the first approach to assess test-taking attitudes outlined by Meehl and Hathaway (1946), which was described in Chapter 1.

Tables 3–25 and 3–26 present the distribution of this total T score difference on the Wiener and Harmon (Wiener, 1948) Obvious and Subtle subscales for normal and psychiatric samples by gender, respectively. The mean total T score difference in normal samples is in the range of 0 to –30, whereas in psychiatric samples it is in the range of 50 to 60. Psychiatric samples do score slightly higher on this index than normals, which is to be expected since they should be acknowledging the presence of some form of psychopathology that will increase their score on the obvious subscales. The psychiatric samples also are more variable on this index with their standard deviations about 50 percent larger than the normal samples. The distributions appear to be relatively normal in all of the various samples. There appear to be few gender or age (adolescent versus adult) differences in any of the samples.

It must be understood that a total T score difference above whatever criterion is used to identify overreporting of psychopathology must be used as *presumptive* rather

TABLE 3–25 Distribution of the Total T Score Difference between Obvious and Subtle Subscales on the MMPI for Normal Samples by Gender

| Total T Score Differences | Greene (1986) | | | |
| | Adults | | College Students | |
	Male (N = 163)	Female (N = 238)	Male (N = 208)	Female (N = 224)
276– 300	0.0%	0.0%	0.0%	0.0%
251– 275	0.0	0.0	0.0	0.0
226– 250	0.0	0.0	0.0	0.0
201– 225	0.0	0.0	0.5	0.0
176– 200	0.0	0.0	0.9	0.0
151– 175	0.0	0.0	1.0	0.9
126– 150	0.6	1.3	3.9	1.3
101– 125	2.5	1.6	3.8	3.6
76– 100	6.1	2.6	7.2	4.0
51– 75	8.6	3.3	12.0	9.4
26– 50	10.4	8.8	12.0	12.5
1– 25	10.5	6.8	16.9	17.0
−24– 0	12.8	17.6	17.8	13.8
−49– −25	14.8	16.0	12.5	18.8
−74– −50	22.0	18.2	7.2	11.6
−99– −75	6.8	14.7	2.9	3.5
−124––100	4.9	8.8	1.4	3.6
−149––125	0.0	0.4	0.0	0.0
M	−11.9	−30.5	19.1	0.2
SD	59.1	56.4	61.7	56.8

than definitive evidence of this overreporting response set. It always is necessary to verify that the client is overreporting psychopathology rather than actually experiencing severe psychopathology (cf. Schretlen, 1990). When the total T score difference exceeds +200, it should be readily apparent by an interview whether the client is overreporting psychopathology, since if the client's responses were accurate, there is severe psychopathology. Occasionally in an inpatient setting, total T score differences above +200 will be seen in a client who is endorsing the items accurately. In an outpatient setting, it is much less likely for difference scores in this range to reflect actual psychopathology since the client should be so devastated that he or she would be unable to function.

The setting in which the client is taking the MMPI will have a significant effect on the range of scores that are seen on this index. Table 3–27 summarizes the percentile equivalents for this index in several different populations. It appears that normal adults obtain slightly higher scores on this index than persons taking the MMPI as part of a job application process, and neither group is likely to report psychopathologic symptoms. In fact, the job applicants are less likely to report any form of psychopathology since it might reduce the probability of their obtaining a position.

For example, a total T score difference of +80 is at the 95th percentile in normal adults and the 99th percentile in the job applicants, whereas it is between the 50th and

TABLE 3-26 Distribution of the Total T Score Difference between Obvious and Subtle Subscales on the MMPI for Psychiatric Samples by Gender

| Total T Score Differences | Psychiatric Patients (Hedlund & Won Cho, 1979) | | | |
| | Adults | | Adolescents | |
	Male (N = 8,646)	Female (N = 3,743)	Male (N = 693)	Female (N = 290)
276– 300	0.3%	0.1%	0.1%	0.0%
251– 275	0.7	0.2	0.9	0.0
226– 250	1.7	1.0	1.5	1.0
201– 225	2.8	1.9	2.7	2.4
176– 200	3.9	3.4	4.3	4.2
151– 175	5.3	5.2	4.8	6.9
126– 150	6.9	7.0	6.9	7.9
101– 125	8.9	9.1	10.1	13.8
76– 100	10.2	11.4	10.3	8.3
51– 75	10.9	10.9	8.6	9.6
26– 50	10.8	11.6	11.1	10.0
1– 25	9.7	10.7	12.6	4.2
−24– 0	8.8	9.2	11.1	10.0
−49– −25	7.8	7.1	7.2	8.9
−74– −50	5.7	5.7	3.9	6.2
−99– −75	3.4	3.6	2.3	3.2
−124–−100	1.8	1.3	1.5	2.7
−149–−125	0.4	0.6	0.1	0.7
M	56.5	51.8	58.4	55.5
SD	85.1	79.7	81.8	85.7

75th percentile in psychiatric samples (see Table 3-27). Thus, higher scores on this index occur more frequently in psychiatric samples who both are more likely to have significant psychopathology and have some potential motivation to report it. The reader also should note the large number of patients who achieve negative numbers on this index that suggest the underreporting of psychopathology. This issue will be explored later.

In order to emphasize the statement that accuracy of item endorsement can be independent of whether the client actually has psychopathology, Table 3-28 reports the scores on this index for a sample of schizophrenic patients (Davies, Nichols, & Greene,

1985), bipolar disorder, manic patients (Davies et al., 1985), and a general sample of psychiatric patients (Hedlund & Won Cho, 1979). It should be evident that these groups of patients have very similar distributions on this index. Even though the first two groups of patients met all DSM-III criteria for their respective diagnoses, a substantial number of them can be considered to have endorsed the items inaccurately either by overreporting or underreporting psychopathology.

When a client's responses have been identified as reflecting the overreporting of psychopathology, the standard profile is no longer interpretable since it reflects an overreporting response set. The clinician should

TABLE 3–27 Percentile Equivalents for the Total T Score Difference between Obvious and Subtle Subscales on the MMPI by Population

Percentile	Nuclear Power Plant Personnel (Lavin, 1984)		Normal Adults (Greene, 1986)		Psychiatric Patients (Hedlund & Won Cho, 1979)	
	Male (N = 1,031)	Female (N = 146)	Male (N = 163)	Female (N = 238)	Male (N = 8,646)	Female (N = 3,760)
99	80	80	128	133	250	229
95	42	28	80	84	203	184
90	25	12	70	47	172	158
75	−9	−20	33	−4	115	107
50	−45	−53	−22	−33	53	50
25	−80	−86	−58	−74	−8	−7
10	−114	−117	−77	−102	−55	−55
5	−132	−134	−100	−103	−79	−79
1	−140	−140	−122	−116	−111	−115

describe the client's style of overreporting psychopathology, determine the potential causes for this response set, and assess the implications for treatment/intervention; the clinician should *not* attempt to interpret the codetype or any of the individual scales.

Table 3-29 summarizes the relative advantages and disadvantages for using this index of the total T score difference between the obvious and subtle subscales as a means of assessing the accuracy of item endorsement. The reader will need to compare the advantages and disadvantages of this index with the other means of assessing accuracy of item endorsement described below to deter-

TABLE 3–28 Percentile Equivalents for the Total T Score Difference between Obvious and Subtle Subscales on the MMPI by Diagnostic Group

Percentile	Psychiatric Patients (Hedlund & Won Cho, 1979)		Schizophrenic Patients (Davies et al., 1985)	Bipolar Disorder, Manic Type, Patients (Davies et al., 1985)
	Male (N = 8,646)	Female (N = 3,760)	(N = 85)	(N = 83)
99	250	229	239	204
95	203	184	195	157
90	172	158	185	144
75	115	107	133	96
50	53	50	81	41
25	−8	−7	11	−23
10	−55	−55	−51	−75
5	−79	−79	−96	−87
1	−111	−115	−122	−116

TABLE 3–29 Relative Advantages and Disadvantages of the Total T Score Difference between Obvious and Subtle Subscales to Assess Accuracy of Item Endorsement

Advantages	Disadvantages
1. Sensitive to extent or degree of overreporting and underreporting of psychopathology so a single index can be used to assess the accuracy of item endorsement.	1. Too complex to score by hand because of large number of scoring templates required and transforming raw scores to T scores and obtaining difference score.
2. Some research data that supports sensitivity of obvious and subtle subscales to inaccuracy of item endorsement.	2. Cannot check for inaccuracy past item 361 since the last 206 items are *not* scored on these scales.
3. Relatively easy to separate genuine psychopathology from overreporting.	

mine the usefulness of this measure in his or her particular setting.

Lachar and Wrobel (1979) Critical Items (MMPI-2 and MMPI)

Despite the inherent difficulties in understanding responses to individual MMPI items (difficulties that provided the original impetus for the empirical selection of items on the MMPI), clinicians have been unwilling to ignore the information that might be contained in those responses. The original set of "critical" items, which were thought to require careful scrutiny if answered in the deviant direction, was rationally or intuitively selected by Grayson (1951). Grayson's early work on critical items has since been followed by the development of other sets of critical items (see Chapter 5). Since these critical items have obvious or face valid item content (Wrobel & Lachar, 1982), they provide another means of assessing the accuracy of item endorsement.

The Lachar and Wrobel (1979) critical items will be used to illustrate this procedure;

any critical item set could be used to assess accuracy of item endorsement, and the clinician may prefer to use another set of these items that are described in Chapter 5. Regardless of the set of critical items that are used, the rationale for assessing accuracy of item endorsement will remain the same.

Lachar and Wrobel (1979) developed their critical items to be face-valid (obvious) descriptors of psychological concerns. They first identified 14 categories of symptoms that summarized problems that motivate people to seek psychological treatment and that help the clinician make diagnostic decisions. Then 14 clinical psychologists read each MMPI item and nominated items that would be face-valid indicators of psychopathology in one of these 14 categories. These items were empirically validated by contrasting item response frequencies for normals and psychiatric samples matched for gender and race. Lachar and Wrobel were able to validate 130 of the 177 items nominated.

After eliminating 19 items that were highly duplicative of item content in other items on the list, they arrived at a final list of

111 (20.2 percent) critical items out of a possible 550 MMPI items.

The total number of Lachar and Wrobel critical items that are endorsed by the client can become another index of the accuracy of item endorsement. A client who is trying to overreport psychopathology would be expected to endorse a large number of these items, whereas a client who is trying to underreport psychopathology would be expected to endorse few of them. Tables 3–30 and 3–31 summarize the total number of Lachar and Wrobel critical items that are endorsed by normal individuals and psychiatric patients, respectively.

The normal individuals endorse 17 to 26 (16 to 23 percent) of these items on the average, whereas the psychiatric patients endorse 36 to 40 (32 to 36 percent). There do not appear to be any gender or age (adolescent versus adult) differences in the endorsement of these critical items. The psychiatric patients endorse more of these items, as would be expected. They also are more variable in endorsing these items, with standard deviations almost twice as large as the normal individuals. It is interesting to note that almost 20 percent of these psychiatric patients endorse fewer total critical items than the average normal individual. Again, it should go without saying that overreporting and underreporting of psychopathology do *not* indicate whether a person has psychopathology, only that the person does not endorse the items accurately.

Table 3–32 summarizes the relative advantages and disadvantages of using the total number of Lachar and Wrobel (1978) critical items endorsed as a means of assessing the accuracy of item endorsement. Again, the reader will need to decide which of these various indexes of the accuracy of item endorse-

TABLE 3–30   Distribution of Total Number of Lachar and Wrobel (1979) Critical Items Endorsed in Normal Samples by Gender

Total Critical Items	Colligan et al. (1983)		Greene (1986)			
	Adults		Adults		College Students	
	Male (N = 646)	*Female (N = 762)*	*Male (N = 163)*	*Female (N = 238)*	*Male (N = 208)*	*Female (N = 224)*
91+	0.0%	0.0%	0.0%	0.0%	0.0%	0.0%
81–90	0.0	0.0	0.0	0.0	0.0	0.0
71–80	0.0	0.0	0.0	0.0	0.5	0.4
61–70	0.3	0.2	0.0	0.0	0.9	0.0
51–60	0.6	0.4	2.5	2.1	6.8	2.3
41–50	1.7	2.4	6.1	1.3	8.6	5.8
31–40	6.5	6.7	8.0	13.4	17.8	17.4
21–30	21.2	18.0	20.8	18.5	22.1	26.8
11–20	40.7	40.5	33.8	40.8	35.1	37.0
0–10	29.0	31.8	28.8	23.9	8.2	10.3
M	16.9	16.5	19.4	18.6	26.4	23.4
SD	9.9	10.1	12.5	10.9	14.1	11.9

Note: These are the total number of critical items endorsed, *not* T scores.

TABLE 3–31   Distribution of Total Number of Lachar and Wrobel (1979) Critical Items Endorsed in Psychiatric Samples by Gender

| | Psychiatric Patients (Hedlund & Won Cho, 1979) | | | |
| | Adults | | Adolescents | |
Total Critical Items	Male (N = 8,646)	Female (N = 3,743)	Male (N = 693)	Female (N = 290)
91+	0.3%	0.3%	0.7%	0.0%
81–90	1.8	1.4	2.6	1.7
71–80	3.9	3.2	4.8	4.2
61–70	6.9	7.3	6.6	11.7
51–60	10.7	12.7	13.0	13.8
41–50	14.3	18.0	16.2	19.3
31–40	18.6	18.7	16.7	15.2
21–30	20.3	19.3	21.7	14.4
11–20	17.3	14.1	13.9	16.9
0–10	5.9	5.0	3.8	2.8
M	36.5	38.0	39.2	40.5
SD	19.3	18.3	19.5	19.3

Note: These are the total number of critical items endorsed, *not* T scores.

ment is most appropriate for his or her specific clients and treatment setting.

F-K Index (Gough Dissimulation Index) (MMPI-2 and MMPI)

Another validity indicator, the *F-K* index (Gough Dissimulation index), has been devel-oped by combining two of the three tradi-tional validity scales. The reader is cautioned *not* to confuse the *F-K* index (Gough Dissim-ulation index) with the Gough Dissimulation scale (*Ds*: Gough, 1954), which will be de-scribed in the next section. The *Ds* is a set of empirically derived items designed to assess overreporting of psychopathology, whereas the *F-K* index utilizes the relationship be-

TABLE 3–32   Relative Advantages and Disadvantages of the Lachar and Wrobel Critical Items to Assess Accuracy of Item Endorsement

Advantages	Disadvantages
1. Easy to score by hand.	1. Limited research to evaluate how clients with actual psychopathology endorse these items.
2. Assesses accuracy of item endorsement throughout the test (last item scored is #466).	2. Requires administration of all 567 items.
3. Can be used to assess overreporting and underreporting of psychopathology.	

tween the standard validity scales of F and K to assess overreporting.

Gough (1947, 1950) suggested that this index—the *raw* score of the F scale minus the *raw* score of the K scale—would be useful in screening MMPI profiles for accuracy of item endorsement. If the F-K index was greater than +9, the profile was designated as overreporting (i.e., the client was trying to feign the presence of psychopathology). If the F-K index was less than 0, the profile was classified as underreporting (i.e., the client was trying to deny the existence of any form of psychopathology). Intermediate scores on the F-K index (0 to 9) indicated accurate item endorsement (i.e., valid profiles). Gough (1950) reported that the F-K index readily detected overreporting profiles; in one sample it accurately classified 97 percent of the authentic profiles and 75 percent of the overreporting profiles.

Most studies of the F-K index in identifying overreporting profiles on the MMPI have utilized normal persons who were instructed to feign psychopathology. Numerous investigators working with students (Cofer et al., 1949; Exner, McDowell, Pabst, Stackman, & Kirk, 1963; Hunt, 1948) have confirmed the ability of the F-K index to identify students who are instructed to overreport psychopathology; some of these investigators (Exner et al., 1963; Hunt, 1948), however, also noted that the F scale alone identified overreporting profiles even more efficiently than the F-K index.

Gallucci (1984) found that scores on the F-K index corresponded directly with the presumed motivation of veterans who were undergoing psychiatric evaluations to determine their eligibility for disability benefits. These veterans also seemed to dissimulate psychopathology in general rather than any specific psychiatric diagnosis.

Working with clients referred for psychological evaluation, Anthony (1971) found the F-K index to have limited success. He in-

structed 40 male nonpsychotic clients to exaggerate their presenting psychopathology when they took the MMPI a second time. Using the cutoff points on this index suggested by Gough (1947), Anthony reported that fewer than half (16) of the 40 exaggerated profiles were identified by the F-K index. Almost one-half (17) of the exaggerated profiles had a raw score on the F scale of less than 15, which would directly account for the limited success of the F-K index in identifying the exaggerated profiles since the raw score on the F scale is close to 9 even before the raw score on the K scale is subtracted.

Anthony (1971) found that even with using different cutoff scores on the F-K index, he could only correctly classify 75 percent of the profiles. Thus, the usefulness of the F-K index seems to be more limited with clients who are exaggerating their psychopathology than with students. Since the former problem is the one faced in a clinical situation, the F-K index at best may screen a few such clients.

Tables 3–33 and 3–34 summarize the distribution of scores for the F-K index (Gough Dissimulation index) in normal individuals and psychiatric patients, respectively. The normal individuals achieve mean scores of nearly –10 on this index, whereas the psychiatric patients achieve mean scores near 0. If F-K scores greater than +10 are said to be overreporting psychopathology, almost 25 percent of the adolescent psychiatric patients and 16 percent of the adult psychiatric patients would be so classified.

Since the F scale also may reflect the presence of actual psychopathology, it would be expected that this index would have a high false positive rate (clients who are said to be overreporting psychopathology who are actually experiencing significant psychopathology). A cutting score much higher than +9 would need to be used on the F-K index to decrease the number of false positives; it is not

TABLE 3–33   Distribution of Difference Scores on the *F-K* Index (Gough Dissimulation Index) in Normal Samples by Gender

| F-K Difference Score | Greene (1986) | | | |
| | Adults | | College Students | |
	Male (N = 163)	Female (N = 238)	Male (N = 208)	Female (N = 224)
16+	0.0%	0.0%	0.0%	0.0%
11– 15	0.0	0.4	4.3	1.3
6– 10	5.5	1.7	3.9	2.3
1– 5	1.2	2.9	13.4	7.6
–4– 0	10.5	13.1	18.8	18.7
–9– – 5	33.7	26.0	25.0	31.7
–14– –10	12.9	23.5	23.1	27.2
–19– –15	32.5	29.9	10.5	8.5
– –20	3.7	2.5	1.0	2.7
M	–10.0	–10.3	–5.6	–7.2
SD	7.0	6.1	7.6	6.5

TABLE 3–34   Distribution of Difference Scores for the *F-K* Index (Gough Dissimulation Index) in Psychiatric Samples by Gender

| F-K Difference Score | Psychiatric Patients (Hedlund & Won Cho, 1979) | | | |
| | Adults | | Adolescents | |
	Male (N = 8,646)	Female (N = 3,743)	Male (N = 693)	Female (N = 290)
36+	0.5%	0.3%	1.0%	0.0%
31– 35	0.9	0.7	1.3	0.3
26– 30	1.6	1.2	2.3	1.1
21– 25	2.4	2.4	5.5	4.1
16– 20	4.3	4.3	5.8	6.6
11– 15	6.3	6.3	7.3	12.4
6– 10	8.8	10.0	11.4	11.0
1– 5	13.4	12.9	14.5	15.9
–4– 0	17.8	18.6	14.5	13.4
–9– – 5	18.2	18.6	17.1	14.2
–14– –10	14.5	15.1	12.5	12.0
–19– –15	8.3	7.1	4.8	7.3
–20	3.0	2.5	2.0	1.7
M	–1.3	–1.3	1.8	1.1
SD	11.8	11.3	12.7	11.5

clear whether a more appropriate cutting score can be identified for this index since the *F* scale also is elevated by actual psychopathology.

Table 3–35 summarizes the relative advantages and disadvantages of using the *F-K* index as a means of assessing the accuracy of item endorsement. The *F-K* index is likely to be the least desirable of the various scales/indexes that have been described to assess overreporting of psychopathology because of the high false positive rate.

Gough Dissimulation Scale (Ds-r) (MMPI)

The Gough Dissimulation (*Ds*) scale (Gough, 1954) consists of 74 items, later revised to 40 items (*Ds-r*: Gough, 1957), that significantly differentiated a group of neurotic patients from groups of college students and professional psychologists instructed to simulate the responses of neurotic patients in taking the MMPI. The items on the *Ds-r* scale may be found in Appendix D. The items pertain not to neuroticism but to the prevailing stereotypes about neuroticism.

The psychologists and students scored three to four times higher than neurotic patients on the *Ds* scale. The professional psychologists were only slightly better at simulating neurosis than the students, and both groups were easily identified by the *Ds* scale. Gough's results suggest that professional psychologists endorse the same erroneous stereotypes about neuroticism that students without any training in psychopathology endorse. Apparently, formal training in psychopathology does not eliminate common stereotypes about neuroticism. Gough's findings underscore the advantage of empirically selecting items or empirically validating items selected to assess a specific behavior.

The interested reader can demonstrate this result by taking the MMPI as a client with a specific neurotic disorder and then scoring the *Ds-r* scale. After scoring the *Ds-r* scale, the reader should examine the content of the items on the scale to gain an appreciation of the types of items that are stereotypically thought to reflect neuroticism.

A study by Mehlman and Rand (1960) offers general support for Gough's findings that persons attempting to simulate psychopathology on the MMPI can be identified readily by their responses to the test items.

TABLE 3–35   Relative Advantages and Disadvantages of the *F-K* Index (Gough Dissimulation Index) to Assess Accuracy of Item Endorsement

Advantages	Disadvantages
1. No special scales need to be scored since the *F* and *K* scales are scored routinely.	1. Requires separate scale/index to assess underreporting since *F-K* index is very insensitive to underreporting of psychopathology.
2. Requires administration of only first 365 items to score.	2. Cannot assess accuracy of item endorsement past first 365 items.
	3. A number of valid profiles are labeled to be overreporting because the elevation on the *F* scale also can reflect the severity of psychopathology.
	4. Elevated by inconsistent patterns of item endorsement since the *F* scale will be elevated.

They presented 45 MMPI items to clinical psychologists, graduate students in psychology, and undergraduates, and asked them to indicate the clinical scale on which each item was found. There were no differences between the groups in their ability to indicate the scale on which the item appeared, and all groups could accurately identify only about four or five items.

These results are not surprising, since MMPI scales were formed empirically, not rationally. Because these persons could not guess which scales contained various items, the implication is that they also would be unable to distort their responses to simulate accurately those of a client who actually had a specific form of psychopathology and achieve an elevated score on the appropriate scale.

In investigating the *Ds* scale, Anthony (1971) reported that it had an optimum hit rate of 86 percent in identifying male clients with nonpsychotic diagnoses referred for psychological testing who were instructed to exaggerate their presenting symptoms. The *Ds* scale had a higher hit rate in identifying these clients who were overreporting psychopathology than did either the raw score on the *F* scale or the *F-K* index, although the differences in hit rate were not statistically significant. Thus, the *Ds* scale appears to deserve serious attention in its utility to identify overreporting of psychopathology on the MMPI.

Tables 3–36 and 3–37 summarize the range of scores that are seen on *Ds-r* for normal individuals and psychiatric patients on the MMPI, respectively. T scores of 70 or higher occur in about 10 percent of the normal individuals, 30 percent of the adult psychiatric patients, and 40 percent of the adolescent psychiatric patients. If a T score of 90 or higher on the *Ds-r* scale were used to indicate overreporting of psychopathology, 6 to 9 percent of the psychiatric patients would be classified as endorsing the items inaccurately with little difference between the adult and adolescent patients, whereas none of the normal adults and 0.5 percent of the college students would be so classified. The reader can see what would happen if other cutting scores

TABLE 3–36   Distribution of T Scores for the MMPI Gough Dissimulation Scale—Revised (*Ds-r*) in Normal Samples by Gender

	Colligan et al. (1983)[a]		Greene (1986)			
	Adults		Adults		College Students	
T Score Range	*Male (N = 646)*	*Female (N = 762)*	*Male (N = 163)*	*Female (N = 238)*	*Male (N = 208)*	*Female (N = 224)*
90+	0.3%	0.3%	0.0%	0.0%	0.5%	0.4%
80–89	1.0	0.6	0.0	0.4	5.8	0.8
70–79	3.6	4.8	9.2	6.6	9.6	8.4
60–69	16.4	15.8	11.0	18.5	18.2	23.7
50–59	35.1	30.4	32.5	21.3	30.8	28.2
40–49	39.3	42.4	43.6	45.7	34.6	33.9
0–39	4.3	5.7	3.7	7.1	0.5	4.5
M	51.5	51.6	52.8	52.2	56.7	55.0
SD	9.7	9.8	10.3	10.2	11.4	10.4

[a]Colligan et al. (1983) scored the original Gough Dissimulation Scale.

TABLE 3–37 Distribution of T Scores for the MMPI Gough Dissimulation Scale—Revised (*Ds-r*) in Psychiatric Samples by Gender

| T Score Range | Psychiatric Patients (Hedlund & Won Cho, 1979) | | | |
| | Adults | | Adolescents | |
	Male *(N = 8,646)*	*Female* *(N = 3,743)*	*Male* *(N = 693)*	*Female* *(N = 290)*
110+	0.2%	0.1%	0.2%	0.0%
100–109	2.1	1.6	3.5	0.6
90– 99	5.0	4.7	5.8	5.8
80– 89	7.7	8.4	11.6	12.1
70– 79	15.8	16.9	18.0	24.5
60– 69	17.9	22.6	20.2	22.1
50– 59	22.7	20.5	24.7	16.9
40– 49	26.1	21.9	15.3	16.2
0– 39	2.4	3.7	0.7	1.7
M	61.8	62.4	65.9	65.8
SD	16.3	15.4	16.1	14.8

were used to identify inaccurate patterns of item endorsement.

At this time, there is not an empirically derived scale on the MMPI-2 to detect over-reporting of psychopathology. The development of such a scale is strongly encouraged.

Summary

Four different indexes to assess overreporting of psychopathology have been described above and two additional methods (the *F* and F_B scales) will be described below. After reviewing the relative advantages and disadvantages of each of these indexes, the reader should select the index that is most appropriate for his or her specific clients and treatment setting. It is *not* necessary to use several of these indexes simultaneously since they are correlated highly and consequently are very redundant. For example, the correlations for the MMPI among the total T score difference on the Wiener and Harmon (Wiener, 1948) Obvious and Subtle subscales, the *Ds-r* scale (Gough Dissimulation Scale: Gough, 1957),

and the Lachar and Wrobel (1979) critical items range between .88 and .92 in Hedlund and Won Cho's (1979) psychiatric samples, whereas the correlations between the *F* scale and the *F-K* index (Gough Dissimulation Index: Gough, 1947) and these three scales/indexes range from .70 to .86 in these same samples.

The lower correlations with the *F* scale and the *F-K* index may reflect that these two measures are influenced by the consistency of item endorsement and the presence of actual psychopathology, which was conjectured above. These lower correlations would suggest that one of the two earlier mentioned measures (the total T score difference on the Wiener and Harmon Obvious and Subtle subscales or the Lachar and Wrobel critical items) may be a more "pure" estimate of overreporting of psychopathology. Research that evaluates this hypothesis with independent estimates of overreporting of psychopathology is clearly needed.

Table 3–38 provides the percentile equivalents for these five scales/indexes on the

TABLE 3–38 Percentile Equivalents for Five Scales/Indexes of Overreporting Psychopathology in Adult Psychiatric Patients (Hedlund & Won Cho, 1979) by Gender

Percentile	Total T Score Difference[a]		Ds-r Scale (T Score)		Total Critical Items Endorsed[b]		F Scale (Raw Score)		F-K Index	
	Male (N = 8,646)	Female (N = 3,743)	Male (N = 8,646)	Female (N = 3,743)	Male (N = 8,646)	Female (N = 3,743)	Male (N = 8,646)	Female (N = 3,743)	Male (N = 8,646)	Female (N = 3,743)
99	250	229	104	100	85	84	39	37	32	30
95	203	184	93	90	72	70	30	28	21	19
90	172	158	86	83	64	63	23	22	15	14
75	115	107	72	73	49	50	14	15	5	5
50	53	50	58	60	33	36	8	8	−3	−3
25	−8	−7	47	49	21	23	4	4	−10	−10
10	−55	−55	42	43	13	14	3	2	−16	−15
5	−79	−79	40	39	9	10	2	1	−18	−18
1	−111	−115	35	37	5	5	0	0	−23	−22

[a]See Table 3–24 for the procedure for calculating this total T score difference.
[b]The Lachar and Wrobel (1979) critical items are used in this example.

MMPI to assess the overreporting of psychopathology so that they can be compared directly. A total T score difference of 172 (the 90th percentile) on the Wiener and Harmon (Wiener, 1948) Obvious and Subtle subscales in these adult male psychiatric patients is equivalent to a T score of 86 on the Ds-r scale (Gough, 1957), a total of 64 of the Lachar and Wrobel (1979) critical items endorsed, a raw score of 23 on the F scale, and a F-K index (Gough, 1947) of +15.

It is important that the reader understand that once a profile has been defined as reflecting the overreporting of psychopathology, it cannot be interpreted as a valid profile. The client's specific reasons for overreporting psychopathology should be ascertained by a clinical interview, and the profile can be described as reflecting such a process; however, neither the codetype nor the individual scales can be interpreted.

The reader also should note that in Figure 3–1 once an MMPI-2 is said to be characterized by overreporting of psychopathology the interpretive process stops. The client could have the MMPI-2 readministered, although such a procedure rarely results in a valid profile. It seems that once a client is motivated for whatever reason to overreport psychopathology, it is very difficult for him or her to endorse the items accurately in this administration. It is not known whether overreporting of psychopathology would persist across treatment settings for a particular client.

Although the codetype from an overreported profile cannot be interpreted, it is possible to ascertain whether there are empirical correlates of such profiles in a similar manner to Marks, Seeman, and Haller's (1974) description of a K+ profile, which is described below. Only a few studies have reported explicitly the correlates of overreported profiles. Both Greene (1988b) and Hale, Zimostrad, Duckworth, and Nicholas (1986) found that clients who overreported psychopathology were very likely to terminate treatment within the first few sessions; frequently they did not return after the initial session. This finding that these clients terminate treatment quickly is almost exactly the opposite of what might be anticipated, since these clients are sometimes described as "crying for help" and they would be expected to remain in treatment longer than most clients. Additional research is needed to determine whether there are other correlates of overreported profiles.

Once these various scales and indexes to identify overreporting of psychopathology have been described, the next step in the implementation of the flowchart in Figure 3–1 can be made. The criteria, summarized in Table 3–45 for the MMPI-2 and in Table 3–46 for the MMPI, give the quantitative data necessary to determine whether the items have been endorsed inaccurately (i.e., to overreport psychopathology). Once it has been determined that the client has overreported psychopathology, the clinician will need to ascertain the reasons for the inaccurate item endorsement by a clinical interview.

A summary of the potential causes of overreporting of psychopathology are presented in Table 3–39, as well as some possible solutions for these problems. It remains to be determined whether it is possible to readminister the MMPI-2 to a client who has overreported psychopathology and obtain an accurate pattern of item endorsement. In any event the clinician must remember that neither the codetype nor the individual scales in an overreported profile can be interpreted.

Underreporting of Psychopathology

Wiener and Harmon Obvious and Subtle Subscales (MMPI-2 and MMPI)

The use of the total T score difference on the Wiener and Harmon Obvious and Subtle subscales to assess overreporting of psychopathology was described earlier. These scales also can be used to assess underreporting of psychopathology. The procedure for calculating the differences between the T scores for the obvious and subtle subscales and summing these difference scores to create an

TABLE 3–39   Potential Causes of and Solutions for Overreporting of Psychopathology

Cause	Solution
1. Client is making a "plea for help."	1. Explain to the client that treatment/services will be provided.
2. Client has a phenomenologic style to overreact and to be traumatized; frequently seen in Dependent and Histrionic Personality Disorders and Depressive Mood Disorders.	2. May not be any solution short of long-term treatment.
3. Client is trying to look psychopathologic because litigation, compensation, etc., are involved.	3. May not be any solution.

index of overreporting and underreporting of psychopathology was outlined in Table 3–24. In the situation where the client is trying to underreport psychopathology, the T scores on the subtle scales will be larger than on the obvious scales. Consequently, the total T score difference will be negative, reflecting that the client has endorsed more subtle than obvious items.

Tables 3–25 and 3–26 presented the distribution of this total T score difference on the Wiener and Harmon (Wiener, 1948) Obvious and Subtle subscales by gender for normal and psychiatric samples, respectively. Clearly, total T score differences in the range of –75 to –150 are strongly suggestive of underreporting. If total T score differences of

−75 or lower are deemed to be suggestive of underreporting, 5.6 percent of the adult male patients (3.4 percent + 1.8 + 0.4) and 5.5 percent of the adult female patients (3.6 percent + 1.3 + 0.6) exceed this criterion. Some 3.9 percent of the adolescent male patients and 6.6 percent of the adolescent female patients exceed this same criterion which suggests that age per se has little effect on whether a client will underreport psychopathology.

The clinician may decide that a different criterion should be used to identify underreporting of psychopathology in a clinical setting. Unless there is some reason to believe that "normal" individuals may be evaluated in this specific setting, clients that underreport psychopathology should be relatively unusual since they would be expected to have some form of psychological problem if they are in the clinical setting.

The fact that a sizable proportion of clients achieve negative numbers on this index (see Table 3–26) suggests that underreporting is not very unusual. Since normal adults' mean score on this index is about −25 (see Table 3–25), a clinician could decide that any client who scores less than −25 is underreporting psychopathology. By this criterion, 19.1 percent of the adult male patients (7.8 percent + 5.7 + 3.4 + 1.8 + 0.4) and 18.3 percent of the adult female patients (7.1 percent + 5.7 + 3.6 + 1.3 + 0.6) would be classified as underreporting. Almost 20 percent of these psychiatric patients would be defined as underreporting psychopathology!

The reader should not conclude that this high percentage of psychiatric patients who underreport psychopathology necessarily reflects some inherent flaw in this index; instead it simply reflects the large number of clients who are evaluated in a clinical setting and yet underreport psychopathology. As the other indexes and scales to assess underreporting of psychopathology are described

below, the reader will see that a similar percentage of clients are identified.

The reader is cautioned to remember that the setting in which the client is taking the MMPI-2 will have a significant effect on this index. As was shown in Table 3–27, individuals who are taking the MMPI in a personnel setting will have large negative numbers on this index since they realize that underreporting of any form of psychological problem may facilitate their selection.

Since the relative advantages and disadvantages of using this index of the total T score difference between the Obvious and Subtle subscales as an means of assessing the accuracy of item endorsement were presented in Table 3–29, they will not be repeated here.

Lachar and Wrobel (1979) Critical Items (MMPI-2 and MMPI)

The total number of the Lachar and Wrobel (1979) critical items that are endorsed can be used as another index of the accuracy of item endorsement. A client who is trying to underreport psychopathology would be expected to endorse few of these items since their item content is obvious (face valid) and reflective of psychopathology. Tables 3–30 and 3–31 summarized the total number of critical items that were endorsed by normal individuals and psychiatric patients, respectively. Almost 20 percent of the psychiatric patients endorsed fewer total critical items than the normal individuals who endorsed 17 to 26 (16 to 23 percent) of these items on the average. That is, nearly 20 percent of these psychiatric patients endorsed fewer total critical items than normal individuals despite their presence in a clinical setting. Again, the reader should note the similar percentage of patients who are identified as underreporting by this index.

Since Table 3–32 summarized the relative advantages and disadvantages for using the total number of Lachar and Wrobel (1979) critical items as a means of assessing the accuracy of item endorsement, they will not be repeated here. The reader will need to determine which of these indexes/scales to assess the accuracy of item endorsement is most appropriate for his or her specific clients and clinical setting.

F-K Index (Gough Dissimulation Index) (MMPI-2 and MMPI)

Gough's initial reservations about the efficiency of the *F-K* index in detecting underreporting of psychopathology have been corroborated by numerous investigators. Most studies (Cofer et al., 1949; Exner et al., 1963; Hunt, 1948; McAnulty, Rappaport, & McAnulty, 1985) have found extensive overlap in the distributions of the *F-K* index in students who took the MMPI normally and then retook the MMPI under underreporting instructions. Consequently, it has been difficult to find any specific score on the *F-K* index that reliably distinguishes normal student profiles from their underreporting profiles.

Another problem with the *F-K* index in identifying underreporting profiles is that anyone who is acknowledging the capability to handle his or her own problems, who is well-adjusted (high raw score on *K*), and who is not experiencing stress or conflict simultaneously (low raw score on *F*) will most likely be defined as underreporting rather than normal by this index. Thus, normal persons taking the MMPI-2 often will be inappropriately classified as producing underreporting profiles.

Several studies have examined the ability of the *F-K* index to detect underreporting profiles in pathologic populations. Hunt (1948) reported that a score lower than –11 on the *F-K* index correctly classified 62 percent of his prison sample who were instructed to underreport psychopathology. Grayson and Olinger (1957) and Johnson, Klingler, and Williams (1977), however, found that their

psychiatric patients instructed to underreport psychopathology could not be detected by the *F-K* index. Thus, the *F-K* index appears to be even more limited in detecting underreporting profiles among psychiatric clients than in identifying overreporting profiles in such clients; in either case its utility is questionable.

Several investigators have noted that some psychiatric clients have a difficult time in trying to underreport psychopathology. For example, Grayson and Olinger (1957) discovered that rather than producing a normal or a underreported profile with underreporting instructions, their patients merely changed the degree of severity or the nature of their behavior disorder.

Similarly, Lawton and Kleban (1965) found that their prison sample could not produce a normal profile when instructed to take the MMPI as a person not in trouble with the law. Although their prisoners were able to lower significantly seven of the clinical scales, they could not alter their high-point scales. Grayson and Olinger (1957) did find that those patients in their sample who were able to simulate a normal profile with underreporting instructions were more likely to receive an early discharge from the hospital. Thus, additional research is needed to investigate whether normal profiles produced by clients given underreporting instructions are a favorable prognostic sign in other settings.

If scores of –10 or lower on the *F-K* index are used a criterion of underreporting of psychopathology, nearly 25 percent of Hedlund and Won Cho's (1979) adult psychiatric patients and 20 percent of the adolescent psychiatric patients would be so classified (see Table 3–34). Again, there is the sizable percentage of psychiatric patients who are evaluated in a clinical setting that underreport psychopathology. Since normal individuals routinely achieve negative scores on this index (see Table 3–33), the *F-K* index will *not* distinguish between normal individuals who should score in this range and psychiatric patients who are underreporting psychopathology. However, if it is known that this client should be reporting psychopathology because of his or her presence in a treatment setting, the *F-K* index can alert the clinician to the possibility of underreporting of psychopathology.

Since the relative advantages and disadvantages of using the *F-K* index to assess accuracy of item endorsement were summarized in Table 3–35, they will not be repeated here.

Positive Malingering Scale (Mp) (MMPI)

The Positive Malingering Scale (*Mp*: Cofer et al., 1949) was developed to identify underreporting of psychopathology. Cofer and associates asked groups of college students to endorse the MMPI items like an emotionally disturbed person (overreport) or as to make the best possible impression (underreport). They then identified 34 items that were insensitive to overreporting (negative malingering) and yet susceptible to underreporting (posi-

tive malingering). They found that a cutting score of 20 or higher correctly identified 96 percent of the accurate MMPIs and 86 percent of the underreported MMPIs. A cutting score of 20 is equivalent to a T score of 69 in males and 73 in females in the original Minnesota normative group. They also noted that scores on the *Mp* scale tended to be related positively to scores on the Wiener (1948) Subtle subscales. Six of the 34 items on the *Mp* scale overlap with the *L* scale.

There has been little research reported on the *Mp* scale (Cofer et al., 1949). Otto, Lang, Megargee, and Rosenblatt (1988) reported that the *Mp* scale was able to identify nearly 80 percent of alcoholics who were instructed to hide any problems or shortcomings.

Tables 3–40 and 3–41 summarize the range of scores that were found on the *Mp* scale in normal individuals and psychiatric patients, respectively. T scores of 70 or higher were found in 2 to 6 percent of the normal individuals and 5 to 8 percent of the psychiatric patients. If a T score of 60 or higher was used to identify underreporting of psychopathol-

TABLE 3–40 Distribution of T Scores for the MMPI Positive Malingering (*Mp*) Scale in Normal Samples by Gender

	Colligan et al. (1983)		Greene (1986)			
	Adults		Adults		College Students	
T Score Range	Male (N = 305)	Female (N = 335)	Male (N = 163)	Female (N = 238)	Male (N = 208)	Female (N = 224)
80+	0.0%	0.3%	0.0%	0.0%	0.0%	0.4%
70–79	4.6	5.7	1.8	2.5	4.3	1.8
60–69	15.5	21.8	12.9	9.7	12.5	7.6
50–59	36.6	23.5	46.6	24.4	33.7	32.6
40–49	34.4	37.0	31.3	41.6	38.0	37.1
30–39	8.2	10.2	7.4	17.2	11.0	16.9
0–29	0.7	1.5	0.0	4.6	0.5	3.6
M	52.2	51.5	51.7	46.8	50.6	47.6
SD	9.9	10.7	8.3	10.8	9.5	10.1

TABLE 3–41 Distribution of T Scores for the MMPI Positive Malingering (*Mp*) Scale in Psychiatric Samples by Gender

| T Score Range | Psychiatric Patients (Hedlund & Won Cho, 1979) | | | |
| | Adults | | Adolescents | |
	Male (N = 8,646)	*Female (N = 3,743)*	*Male (N = 693)*	*Female (N = 290)*
80–89	0.6%	1.4%	0.3%	1.0%
70–79	4.4	6.4	5.9	5.9
60–69	16.8	15.2	21.8	9.7
50–59	31.7	30.0	38.5	33.1
40–49	31.8	31.5	27.6	37.2
30–39	13.6	12.9	5.8	11.7
0–29	1.1	2.6	0.1	1.4
M	51.3	51.2	54.3	50.4
SD	11.1	12.1	9.8	11.0

ogy, 17 to 27 percent of the psychiatric patients would be classified as endorsing the items inaccurately. The reader should recall how a similar percentage of patients were classified as underreporting by the total T score difference on between the Wiener and Harmon (Wiener, 1948) Obvious and Subtle subscales.

Table 3–42 summarizes the relative advantages and disadvantages of using the *Mp* scale (Cofer et al., 1949) to assess the accuracy of item endorsement on the MMPI. The reader will need to compare and contrast these advantages and disadvantages with the other indexes and scales described in this section to assess underreporting of psychopathology.

Summary

Four different means of assessing the underreporting of psychopathology have been described above, and two additional methods (the *L* scale and the *K* scale) will be described below in the section on the traditional valid-

TABLE 3–42 Relative Advantages and Disadvantages of the MMPI Positive Malingering (*Mp*) Scale to Detect Underreporting of Psychopathology

Advantages	Disadvantages
1. Easy to score by hand.	1. Requires use of a separate scale/index to identify overreporting of psychopathology.
2. Empirically derived with some research to document its use.	2. Requires administration of all 566 items.
3. Uses all of the items (#556 is last item scored).	

ity scales. After reviewing the relative advantages and disadvantages of each of these indexes, the reader should select the index that is most appropriate for his or her specific clients and treatment setting. The selection of one of these scales/indexes of underreporting is more difficult than for overreporting, since they appear to be measuring slightly different aspects of underreporting as indicated by their relatively low intercorrelations.

For example, the correlations between the Wiener and Harmon (Wiener, 1948) Obvious and Subtle subscales and the Lachar and Wrobel (1979) critical items and the *Mp* scale (Cofer et al., 1949) in Hedlund and Won Cho's (1979) psychiatric samples ranged between $-.30$ and $-.36$. The correlations between the *Mp* scale and the *F-K* index (Gough, 1947) also were very low, ranging between $-.18$ and $-.26$ in these same samples of patients. Research is needed that examines which of these scales/indexes of underreporting of psychopathology is most appropriate in a particular clinical setting and which validates these

scales/indexes with independent measures of underreporting.

Table 3–43 provides the percentile equivalents among these four scales/indexes of underreporting of psychopathology so that the reader can compare them directly. A total T score difference of –55 on the Wiener and Harmon (Wiener, 1948) Obvious and Subtle subscales in female psychiatric patients is equivalent to a T score of 65 on the *Mp* scale (Cofer et al., 1949), a total of 14 Lachar and Wrobel (1979) critical items endorsed, and a –15 on the *F-K* index (Gough, 1947).

When a client's responses have been identified as being endorsed inaccurately because of underreporting of psychopathology, the standard profile is no longer interpretable since it reflects an underreporting response set. The clinician will have little reason to try to interpret such a profile, however, since extreme underreporting results in no clinical scales being elevated over a T score of 65 (T score of 70 on the MMPI) and frequently no clinical scales are above a T score of 60. The clinician should describe the client's style of

TABLE 3–43 Percentile Equivalents for Four Scales/Indexes of Underreporting Psychopathology in Adult Psychiatric Patients (Hedlund & Won Cho, 1979) by Gender

Percentile	Total T Score Difference[a]		*Mp* Scale (T Score)		Total Critical Items Endorsed[b]		*F-K* Index	
	Male (N = 8,646)	Female (N = 3,743)	Male (N = 8,646)	Female (N = 3,743)	Male (N = 8,646)	Female (N = 3,743)	Male (N = 8,646)	Female (N = 3,743)
99	−111	−115	77	81	5	5	−23	−22
95	−79	−79	69	70	9	10	−18	−18
90	−55	−55	64	65	13	14	−16	−15
75	−8	−7	59	59	21	23	−10	−10
50	53	50	48	48	33	36	−3	−3
25	115	107	41	40	49	50	5	5
10	172	158	36	34	64	63	15	14
5	203	184	33	32	72	70	21	19
1	250	229	28	26	85	84	32	30

[a]See Table 3–24 for the procedure for calculating this total T score difference.
[b]The Lachar and Wrobel (1979) critical items are used in this example.

underreporting psychopathology, determine the potential causes for this response set, and assess the implications for treatment/intervention. If the clinician can appreciate that an underreported profile is not interpretable because of a response set since no clinical scales are elevated, the parallel situation that overreported profiles are equally uninterpretable because of a response set since most or all clinical scales are elevated may become more apparent.

Once these various scales and indexes to identify underreporting of psychopathology have been described, the next step in the implementation of the flowchart in Figure 3–1 can be made. The criteria, summarized in Table 3–45 for the MMPI-2 and in Table 3–46 for the MMPI, provide the quantitative data necessary to determine whether the items have been endorsed inaccurately (i.e., to underrreport psychopathology). Once it has been determined that the client has underreported psychopathology, the clinician will need to ascertain the reasons for the inaccurate item endorsement by a clinical interview.

A summary of the potential causes of underreporting of psychopathology as well as some possible solutions for these problems are presented in Table 3–44.

Once clinicians realize that underreporting of psychopathology is encountered frequently in a clinical setting, the empirical correlates of such a response set can be studied. It may be that clients who underreport psychopathology see their problems as less troubling to themselves and hence are less motivated to change. Their problems also may be more chronic in nature and consequently they may be more difficult to treat if they remain in treatment. Duckworth and Barley (1988) have provided a summary of the correlates of clients who produce such underreported profiles, which should be consulted by the interested reader. The reader also should review the discussion of $K+$ profiles below,

TABLE 3–44 Potential Causes of and Solutions for Underreporting of Psychopathology

Cause	Solution
1. Client is not the identified patient (i.e., the client's spouse or another family member is the identified patient) and wants to convince the clinician that he or she does not have any problems.	1. If the client can begin to trust the clinician it may be possible to readminister the MMPI-2.
2. Client believes that underreporting symptoms is necessary to obtain some desired outcome such as a personnel position, transfer to another agency or institution, and so on.	2. May be no solution.
3. Client believes that he or she does not have any problems, which is encountered frequently in Antisocial and Narcissistic Personality Disorders, Manic Mood Disorders, and many Substance Dependence Disorders.	3. Clients with Substance Dependence Disorders sometimes can be encouraged to be more rigorously honest and have the MMPI-2 readministered.

which is one form of underreporting psycho-pathology.

CUTTING SCORES FOR ASSESSING VALIDITY IN *PSYCHIATRIC* SETTINGS

Table 3–45 summarizes the cutting scores that can be used to assess overreporting and underreporting of psychopathology in psychiatric settings on the MMPI-2, and Table 3–46 provides similar information for the MMPI. The discussion in this section will be limited to the MMPI-2, since the only differences between the two tables are in the specific cutting scores used on a scale and less frequently the scale that is used. For example, total T score differences on the Wiener and

TABLE 3–45   Cutting Scores for Assessing MMPI-2 Validity

	Acceptable	Marginal	Unacceptable
I. *Item Omissions*			
Cannot Say (?)	0– 10	11– 30	31+
II. *Consistency of Item Endorsement*			
Variable Response Inconsistency Scale (*VRIN*)	0– 7	8– 15	16+
$|F - F_B|$ (raw scores)	0– 6	7– 10	11+
$VRIN + |F - F_B|$	0– 16	17– 20	21+
$F + F_B + |F - F_B|$	0– 36	37– 49	50+
III. *Accuracy of Item Endorsement*			
A. *Overreporting of Psychopathology*			
Total T Score Difference on Wiener and Harmon Obvious and Subtle subscales	4–130	131–230	231+
Total Lachar and Wrobel critical items endorsed	21– 48	49– 68	69+
B. *Underreporting of Psychopathology*			
Total T Score Difference on Wiener and Harmon Obvious and Subtle subscales	+130– –4	–5– –65	< –65
Total Lachar and Wrobel critical items endorsed	48– 21	20– 9	<9

Note: These cutting scores are set so that approximately the 75th percentile separates the acceptable and marginal categories, and approximately the 95th percentile separates the marginal and unacceptable categories in *psychiatric patients*. Clinicians may consider adjusting these cutting scores based on the specific base rates in their clients and the relative cost of identifying a certain percentage of clients' MMPI-2s as unacceptable. In other settings where the MMPI-2 is administered, such as *personnel selection*, appropriate cutting scores will need to be derived.

It is *not* intended for the clinician to score all of the scales/indexes within a given section of this table. The clinician should select the scale/index that is most appropriate for his or her clinical setting.

These MMPI-2 cutting scores were developed using Hedlund and Won Cho's (1979) MMPI data. These MMPI data were rescored after eliminating the 13 items that were dropped from the standard validity and clinical scales on the MMPI-2 and these raw scores were converted to MMPI-2 T scores. Thus, the cutting scores in this table need to be understood as being only close approximations to actual MMPI-2 data, although there is little reason to expect for them to be significantly different.

TABLE 3-46   Cutting Scores for Assessing MMPI Validity

	Acceptable	Marginal	Unacceptable
I. *Item Omissions*			
Cannot Say (*?*)	0- 10	11- 30	31+
II. *Consistency of Item Endorsement*			
Test-Retest (*TR*) Index	0- 4	- 5	6+
Carelessness (*CLS*) Scale	0- 4	- 5	6+
Sum of *TR* + *CLS*	0- 8	- 9	10+
III. *Accuracy of Item Endorsement*			
A. *Overreporting of Psychopathology*			
Total T Score Difference on Wiener and Harmon Obvious and Subtle subscales	-7-110	111-190	191+
Ds-r Scale (T score)	<70	70- 90	91+
Total Lachar and Wrobel critical items endorsed	23- 50	51- 70	71+
F Scale (T score)	<78	78-104	105+
B. *Underreporting of Psychopathology*			
Total T Score Difference on Wiener and Harmon Obvious and Subtle subscales	+110-- 7	-8--79	<-79
Mp Scale (T score)	<59	59- 70	71+
Total Lachar and Wrobel critical items endorsed	23- 50	22- 11	<11

Note: These cutting scores are set so that approximately the 75th percentile separates the acceptable and marginal categories, and approximately the 95th percentile separates the marginal and unacceptable categories in *psychiatric patients.* Clinicians may consider adjusting these cutting scores based on the specific base rates in their clients and the relative cost of identifying a certain percentage of clients' MMPIs as unacceptable. In other settings where the MMPI is administered, such as *personnel selection,* appropriate cutting scores will need to be derived.

It is *not* intended for the clinician to score all of the scales/indexes within a given section of this table. The clinician should select the scale/index that is most appropriate for his or her clinical setting.

Harmon (Wiener, 1948) Obvious and Subtle subscales between 131 and 230 are in the marginal range, and total T score differences of 231 and higher are in the unacceptable range for the overreporting of psychopathology.

The cutting scores for all indexes (Wiener and Harmon Obvious and Subtle subscales, total number of Lachar and Wrobel critical items endorsed, and *F* scale) have been set at the 75th and 95th percentiles for *psychiatric* patients (Hedlund & Won Cho,

1979). These cutting scores have been established very conservatively based on clinical experience since limited empirical data are available at this time. Consequently, scores in the unacceptable range should be considered as *presumptive* evidence of the overreporting of psychopathology. It should be readily apparent in a clinical interview if a patient's responses were accurate since pervasive and severe psychopathology should be present. Empirical research is needed to determine further correlates of the overreporting of psychopathology and whether these cutting scores should be raised or lowered.

Similarly, Tables 3–45 and 3–46 summarize the cutting scores that can be used to assess underreporting of psychopathology on the MMPI-2 and MMPI, respectively. For example, total T score differences on the Wiener and Harmon (Wiener, 1948) Obvious and Subtle subscales between –8 and –79 are in the marginal range, and total T score differences of –80 and lower are in the unacceptable range. The cutting scores for all indexes (Wiener and Harmon Obvious and Subtle subscales and total number of Lachar and Wrobel critical items endorsed) have been set at the 25th and 5th percentiles for psychiatric patients. Since normal individuals average around –25 on the total T score difference on the Wiener and Harmon Obvious and Subtle subscales, it seems plausible to assume that psychiatric patients who score below –25 are underreporting psychopathology. This example illustrates how conservatively the present cutting scores have been set. Research is needed to establish more precisely the cutting scores that should be used to indicate the underreporting of psychopathology.

Research is also needed to determine whether a specific scale or index of overreporting and underreporting is the most appropriate for a given clinical setting, and whether raising or lowering these proposed cutting scores would facilitate the identification of overreporting or underreporting. The establishment of the base rates with which overreporting and underreporting are encountered in a specific clinical setting is mandatory in any research that examines these cutting scores. Clinicians need to be aware of the frequency with which overreporting and underreporting occur in their clinical setting and begin to establish the empirical correlates of these response sets so that better assessments, treatments, and interventions can be made.

Table 3–47 provides the frequency with which inconsistent, overreported, and underreported profiles are encountered by codetype on the MMPI. A client's profile was defined as being inconsistent in Table 3–47 if the sum of the *TR* index and the *CLS* scale exceeded nine.

Some MMPI codetypes could be very likely to reflect inconsistent patterns of item endorsement. For example, 43.0 percent of *6-8/8-6* codetypes could result from inconsistent patterns of item endorsement! In fact, most codetypes that include Scale *8* (Schizophrenia) frequently could result from inconsistency. Some codetypes rarely result from inconsistent patterns of item endorsement (i.e., most Spike codetypes and codetypes that include Scale *3* [Hysteria]). Table 3–47 shows that 16 of the 55 codetypes (29.1 percent) could result from inconsistency 10 percent or more of the time.

Table 3–47 also indicates the frequency with which overreported and underreported profiles occur by MMPI codetype. A client's profile was defined as reflecting overreporting of psychopathology in Table 3–47 if the total T score difference on the Wiener and Harmon (Wiener, 1948) Obvious and Subtle subscales exceeded 110 (75th percentile), and as underreporting if this same index was less than –7 (25th percentile). Both of these cutting scores reflect the boundaries between acceptable and marginal accuracy of item endorsement in Table 3–46. Although these cutting scores have been selected somewhat arbitrarily, they do allow comparisons among the codetypes as to the frequency with which overreporting and underreporting psychopathology could occur.

Some MMPI codetypes could be very likely to reflect overreporting of psychopathology with four codetypes (*1-8/8-1, 2-8/8-2, 6-8/8-6,* and *7-8/8-7*) exceeding the cutting score over 40 percent of the time. An additional six codetypes (*1-6/6-1, 1-7/7-1, 2-7/7-2, 4-8/8-4, 6-7/7-6,* and *8-0/0-8*) exceed the cutting score over 20 percent of the time. Un-

TABLE 3–47 Frequency of Inconsistent and Inaccurate Profiles on the MMPI by Codetype

			Inaccurate					
	Inconsistent[a]		Underreporting[b]		Overreporting[c]		Total	
Codetype	Number	Percent	Number	Percent	Number	Percent	Number	Percent
6–8/8–6	535	43.0	14	1.1	511	41.1	1243	85.3
1–8/8–1	114	36.8	16	5.2	128	41.3	310	83.2
7–8/8–7	178	27.5	12	1.9	288	44.5	647	73.9
Spike 4	0	0.0	537	71.4	1	0.1	752	71.5
2–8/8–2	142	22.2	21	3.3	289	45.2	639	70.7
Spike 3	0	0.0	31	70.5	0	0.0	44	70.5
3–5/5–3	1	1.4	46	64.8	0	0.0	71	66.2
Spike 5	0	0.0	74	65.5	0	0.0	113	65.5
3–9/9–3	0	0.0	44	62.0	0	0.0	71	62.0
4–8/8–4	198	19.3	145	14.1	266	25.9	1026	59.4
8–9/9–8	191	32.8	37	6.3	109	18.7	582	57.9
3–6/6–3	4	6.3	26	41.3	4	6.3	63	54.0
3–4/4–3	13	2.7	242	50.2	3	0.6	482	53.5
1–7/7–1	7	17.1	3	7.3	11	26.8	41	51.2
4–5/5–4	4	1.3	146	48.5	2	0.7	301	50.5
3–8/8–3	11	15.7	17	24.3	7	10.0	70	50.0
2–3/3–2	20	7.3	98	35.6	16	5.8	275	48.7
2–6/6–2	18	10.5	27	15.8	33	19.3	171	45.6
3–0/0–3	0	0.0	5	45.5	0	0.0	11	45.5
6–7/7–6	7	12.5	5	8.9	13	23.2	56	44.6
1–2/2–1	66	12.2	46	8.5	96	17.7	485	42.9
1–4/4–1	27	10.0	81	30.1	7	2.6	269	42.8
1–3/3–1	22	6.5	114	33.7	8	2.4	338	42.6
5–6/6–5	5	8.2	19	31.1	2	3.3	61	42.6
Spike 7	0	0.0	12	36.4	2	6.1	33	42.4
1–6/6–1	6	14.6	2	4.9	9	22.0	41	41.5
Spike 6	0	0.0	39	38.2	2	2.0	102	40.2
Spike 9	0	0.0	135	38.9	3	0.9	347	39.8
8–0/0–8	3	6.3	4	8.3	12	25.0	48	39.6
Spike 8	0	0.0	18	33.3	3	5.6	54	38.9
6–9/9–6	37	13.9	32	12.0	34	12.7	267	38.6
3–7/7–3	1	3.8	9	34.6	0	0.0	26	38.5
4–6/6–4	52	8.8	125	21.2	50	8.5	590	38.5
5–9/9–5	3	1.7	61	35.3	1	0.6	173	37.6
5–8/8–5	11	16.2	5	7.4	9	13.2	68	36.8
2–7/7–2	49	10.1	23	4.7	104	21.4	487	36.1
Spike 1	0	0.0	26	34.2	1	1.3	76	35.5
2–9/9–2	8	8.8	22	24.2	2	2.2	91	35.2
2–4/4–2	68	6.3	245	22.8	63	5.9	1074	35.0
4–9/9–4	33	3.0	307	28.3	29	2.7	1083	34.1
2–5/5–2	1	1.1	24	25.5	7	7.4	94	34.0
5–0/0–5	0	0.0	12	27.9	1	2.3	43	30.2
4–7/7–4	20	7.4	44	16.3	17	6.3	270	30.0
1–9/9–1	4	4.2	12	12.6	12	12.6	95	29.5
Spike 2	0	0.0	61	26.8	4	1.8	228	28.5
7–0/0–7	0	0.0	4	10.5	5	13.2	38	23.7
7–9/9–7	7	8.8	6	7.5	5	6.3	80	22.5
Spike 0	0	0.0	11	20.4	1	1.9	54	22.2
6–0/0–6	1	1.8	10	17.5	1	1.8	57	21.1
9–0/0–9	2	5.3	6	15.8	0	0.0	38	21.1
5–7/7–5	0	0.0	4	16.0	1	4.0	25	20.0
4–0/0–4	1	0.8	21	16.5	2	1.6	127	18.9
1–0/0–1	0	0.0	2	10.5	1	5.3	19	15.8
2–0/0–2	4	1.4	23	8.3	14	5.1	276	14.9
1–5/5–1	0	0.0	3	12.5	0	0.0	24	12.5
Total	1874	13.2	3114	22.0	2189	15.5	14,149	

[a]*Inconsistent* was defined as the sum of *TR and CLS* greater than 9.

[b]*Underreporting* was defined as the total T score difference on the Wiener and Harmon (Wiener, 1948) Obvious and Subtle subscales less than − 7 (25th percentile).

[c]*Overreporting* was defined as the total T score difference on the Wiener and Harmon (Wiener, 1948) Obvious and Subtle subscales greater than +110 (75th percentile).

derreporting of psychopathology could even be more frequent with five codetypes (Spike *3*, *3-5/5-3*, *3-9/9-3*, Spike *4*, and Spike *5*) exceeding the cutting score over 60 percent of the time. An additional 15 codetypes exceed the cutting score over 30 percent of the time.

Finally, Table 3–47 summarizes the frequency with which invalid profiles (i.e., both inconsistent and inaccurate patterns of item endorsement) occur by MMPI codetype. Since the codetypes are ranked by the total percentage of invalid profiles, it is easily seen that 16 codetypes are invalid by these criteria over 50 percent of the time and 6 codetypes are invalid over 70 percent of the time. The lowest ranked codetype (*1-5/5-1*) is still invalid 12.5 percent of the time. The necessity for checking the consistency and accuracy of item endorsement for all clients should be readily apparent.

Table 3–48 provides the relative ranking of all codetypes by the total T score difference on the Wiener and Harmon (Wiener, 1948) Obvious and Subtle subscales for the MMPI-2 and the MMPI. It is apparent that the rankings of the codetypes are very similar on the MMPI-2 and the MMPI. If overreporting and underreporting of psychopathology are an unitary dimension, as was assumed earlier (see page 77), Table 3–48 illustrates how the various codetypes distribute themselves along this dimension.

Clinicians probably will not be surprised to see that clients with Spike *4* codetypes are among the farthest toward underreporting of psychopathology and *6-8/8-6* codetypes are the farthest toward overreporting. It is interesting, however, to see how the other codetypes rank relative to each other. For example, it seems somewhat unexpected for *2-4/4-2* codetypes to be ranked so low and for *1-6/6-1*, *1-7/7-1*, and *1-8/8-1* codetypes to be ranked so high. This information on the relative elevation of a number of validity and supplementary scales within each codetype will be explored further in Chapter 6 where pro-

totypic scores for each codetype are discussed.

IMPRESSION MANAGEMENT AND SELF-DECEPTION

Paulhus (1984, 1986) has proposed a two-factor model of socially desirable responding in self-reports of personality that provides another means of looking at how clients may produce inaccurate patterns of item endorsement. His model distinguishes between self-deception (where clients believe their positive self-reports) and impression management (where clients consciously dissemble to create a favorable impression in others).

Paulhus (1986) hypothesized that *self-deception* refers to a motivated unawareness of one of two conflicting cognitions, whereas *impression management* can be conceptualized as a strategic simulation, a motive, or as a skill. Paulhus (1986) suggested that Edwards' Social Desirability Scale (*ESD*: Edwards & Diers, 1962) assessed self-deception on the MMPI, whereas the *L* (Lie) Scale, the Positive Malingering Scale (*Mp*: Cofer et al., 1949), and Wiggins' Social Desirability Scale (*Wsd*: Wiggins, 1959) assessed impression management.

Only one study has examined Paulhus' model to date (Greene, Davis, & Welch, 1988). Greene and associates generated means and standard deviations on *ESD* ($M = 25.1$; $SD = 7.4$) and *Wsd* ($M = 17.4$; $SD = 5.3$) on a large sample ($N = 958$) of psychiatric inpatients. Patients who scored one standard deviation above their respective means were defined as high self-deception or impression management, and patients who scored one standard deviation below their means were defined as low self-deception or impression management.

Greene and colleagues (1988) reported that there was a trend for more male (70 percent) patients to be included in the high self-deception groups and for more female pa-

TABLE 3–48 Ranking by Codetype for the Total T Scale Difference for Obvious and Subtle Subscales

	MMPI			MMPI-2	
Codetype	M	SD	Codetype	M	SD
6–8/8–6	153.7	73.3	6–8/8–6	202.0	71.0
7–8/8–7	131.0	67.7	7–8/8–7	164.4	63.6
2–8/8–2	128.1	74.8	1–8/8–1	155.1	73.2
1–8/8–1	127.2	78.4	2–8/8–2	155.0	73.0
1–7/7–1	80.6	66.9	8–0/0–8	140.4	46.6
1–6/6–1	79.3	74.5	6–7/7–6	139.0	61.7
8–9/9–8	76.5	67.1	1–6/6–1	128.3	63.1
2–7/7–2	75.2	54.0	1–7/7–1	126.9	62.6
8–0/0–8	72.5	59.5	6–0/0–6	124.3	49.4
1–2/2–1	67.7	62.5	3–8/8–3	123.5	86.8
6–7/7–6	62.6	65.7	8–9/9–8	121.9	63.1
4–8/8–4	58.2	90.8	2–6/6–2	119.8	63.2
2–6/6–2	57.2	70.6	6–9/9–6	115.0	62.5
7–9/9–7	52.6	51.0	2–7/7–2	111.2	55.0
5–8/8–5	47.4	58.7	7–0/0–7	106.3	49.6
6–9/9–6	46.5	61.2	4–8/8–4	104.7	77.8
7–0/0–7	44.3	52.3	9–0/0–9	104.7	48.3
1–0/0–1	44.0	47.0	1–2/2–1	98.1	64.8
1–9/9–1	43.0	57.0	7–9/9–7	94.6	54.4
2–0/0–2	42.9	44.6	2–0/0–2	93.1	46.1
5–7/7–5	34.0	50.7	1–9/9–1	88.0	61.0
1–5/5–1	33.0	54.0	2–9/9–2	86.1	49.7
Spike 0	30.3	43.1	3–6/6–3	85.9	74.2
9–0/0–9	29.6	44.3	1–0/0–1	85.7	41.9
6–0/0–6	28.8	51.6	3–7/7–3	85.1	57.8
Spike 7	28.5	52.7	5–8/8–5	83.4	44.2
4–7/7–4	26.5	61.1	5–7/7–5	83.1	59.4
3–8/8–3	26.3	70.8	4–6/6–4	82.6	68.7
2–9/9–2	25.5	53.1	4–0/0–4	77.8	46.5
Spike 2	23.0	47.5	4–7/7–4	77.3	60.8
4–6/6–4	22.9	68.7	2–5/5–2	71.3	55.2
4–0/0–4	21.4	47.8	5–6/6–5	70.5	70.9
5–0/0–5	21.4	44.8	2–3/3–2	68.4	67.9
2–5/5–2	18.9	58.7	2–4/4–2	68.3	62.3
2–4/4–2	16.5	62.2	Spike 0	62.7	44.0
3–7/7–3	16.0	60.2	1–5/5–1	58.3	60.7
Spike 8	15.9	62.1	1–3/3–1	55.4	71.0
Spike 1	12.9	54.1	Spike 7	50.2	57.2
Spike 6	12.8	52.7	3–0/0–3	49.5	109.6
Spike 9	12.6	48.2	5–0/0–5	47.1	40.0
2–3/3–2	7.6	61.2	4–9/9–4	46.6	60.0
1–3/3–1	7.1	59.8	3–9/9–3	42.7	46.0
4–9/9–4	1.7	55.7	1–4/4–1	40.4	67.9
5–6/6–5	1.1	53.6	Spike 2	36.6	50.8
1–4/4–1	0.2	58.4	Spike 9	35.4	50.6
3–0/0–3	0.1	65.0	Spike 6	34.7	55.4
5–9/9–5	−14.4	47.6	Spike 8	33.4	62.2
3–6/6–3	−15.6	68.1	5–9/9–5	30.1	58.5
Spike 5	−23.9	53.6	Spike 1	24.6	53.3
3–9/9–3	−28.4	52.6	3–4/4–3	18.7	66.0
4–5/5–4	−30.5	52.8	Spike 5	0.8	54.3
Spike 4	−36.0	52.2	4–5/5–4	−2.0	53.8
Spike 3	−39.4	41.4	3–5/5–3	−7.6	49.9
3–5/5–3	−44.4	39.6	Spike 4	−15.0	54.4
3–4/4–3	−51.3	54.5	Spike 3	−18.3	51.4

tients (62 percent) in the low self-deception groups. MMPI codetypes including Scale *4* (Psychopathic Deviant) were particularly prominent in the high self-deception groups, and Scale *8* (Schizophrenia) was more likely to be elevated in the low self-deception groups. They noted that *4-6* codetypes, which are a fairly infrequent codetype, were the most frequent (38.5 percent) in the High Self-Deception and Low Impression Management Group.

Patients in the High Impression Management Groups scored lower consistently on group measures of intelligence. Patients in the Low Impression Management Groups were much more likely to receive some form of depressive diagnosis and patients in the High Impression Management Groups were more likely to receive a schizophrenic or manic diagnosis. There were fewer differences seen among these groups on Axis II (Personality Disorder) diagnoses. Patients in the Low Self-Deception and Low Impression Management Group were much more likely to receive a diagnosis in the Avoidant, Dependent, Compulsive, or Passive-Aggressive cluster than any of the other three groups.

Paulhus' model seems to produce interesting correlates in an inpatient psychiatric setting that need to be replicated and extended to other clinical settings.

TRADITIONAL VALIDITY SCALES

Lie (L) Scale

The *L* scale includes 15 items that were selected on a rational basis to identify persons who are deliberately trying to avoid answering the MMPI frankly and honestly (Dahlstrom et al., 1972). The scale assesses attitudes and practices that are culturally laudable but actually found only in the most conscientious persons. Content areas within the *L* scale include denial of minor, personal dishonesties and denial of aggression, bad thoughts, and weakness of character. Examples of *L* scale items with the deviant answer indicated in parentheses are:

> "At times I feel I like swearing." (false)
>
> "I get angry sometimes." (false)
>
> "Sometimes when I am not feeling well I am irritable." (false)[2]

The original Minnesota normative group answered most of the *L* scale items in the nondeviant direction; only three items—15, 135, and 165—were answered in the deviant direction by a majority of this sample. In Gravitz's (1970) sample of job applicants, these three items plus two more—45 and 255—were endorsed in the deviant direction by nearly a majority or more of the respondents. A majority of the MMPI-2 normative group also endorsed these same three items (16[15], 123[135], and 153[165]) in the deviant direction.

Gravitz (1970) also noted small but consistent gender differences in responding to the *L* scale items; this pattern would suggest the need for separate T scores by gender, which are not available on the MMPI. The T scores for the *L* scale as well as the other three validity scales (*?*, *F*, and *K*) provided by Hathaway and McKinley (1967) for the MMPI are identical for males and females. Separate T scores by gender are available for all of the validity scales on the MMPI-2 (Butcher et al., 1989). T scores on the *L* scale tend to vary by only one to three T points between men and women on the MMPI-2, similar to those reported by Gravitz (1970) for the MMPI.

Most adults respond to all *L* scale items (Gravitz, 1971); if any items are omitted, they are most likely to be 255 or 285 (Gravitz, 1967). Dahlstrom and associates (1972) have suggested that college students and adolescents are likely to omit a few of the *L* scale items (e.g., items 15, 135, 165, and 255) since they may not have had experience with the item content. As yet, no reported research has studied this issue, and similar information is not available for the MMPI-2.

Since "false" is the deviant answer to all *L* scale items, the *L* scale is extremely susceptible to unsophisticated deviant test-taking sets, such as the set to answer all items "false." Unusually high (7 or above) raw scores on the *L* scale, particularly in persons for whom such a score is unexpected, should at least raise the suspicion of a deviant test-taking set. The effects of such test-taking attitudes on the various validity indicators and methods of detection of these attitudes will be examined later in this chapter.

More sophisticated deviant response sets may go undetected by the *L* scale. Inspection of the *L* scale items reveals that it is readily apparent which responses are the deviant ones. Numerous studies have shown that the *L* scale does not detect sophisticated persons who were given instructions to falsify their answers to the MMPI (Dahlstrom et al., 1972; Vincent, Linsz, & Greene, 1966). These persons apparently realized that it would be unconvincing to give distorted responses to *L* scale items.

Thus, the *L* scale can be construed as a measure of psychological sophistication with high scores indicating a lack of such sophistication. College-educated persons and persons of higher socioeconomic classes rarely score above a raw score of 4. Conversely, persons who are not psychologically minded (including some persons from minority groups and lower socioeconomic classes) tend to score higher. Thus, a person's education level and socioeconomic class must be kept in mind when interpreting the *L* scale. Persons with a college education who score high on the *L* scale are likely to display deficiencies in judgment and lack of insight into their own behavior. Coyle and Heap (1965) have questioned whether such persons might have

paranoid trends. Fjordbak (1985) reported that hospitalized male forensic patients who had raw scores greater than 6 on the *L* scale and no clinical scales elevated had some type of psychotic disorder with prominent paranoid features.

The higher the elevation on the *L* scale, the lower will be the elevation of most clinical scales. Denial is characteristic of high scores on *L*; denial also results in refusing to acknowledge the presence of any form of psychopathology, thus lowering the elevation of the clinical scales. Elevations on the *L* scale are occasionally accompanied by elevations on Scale *1* (Hypochondriasis) and Scale *3* (Hysteria), which appear to tap the similar personality dynamics of denial and a lack of psychological mindedness. Elevations on the *L* scale sometimes also are associated with an elevation on Scale *9* (Hypomania) in which the client displays a grandiose self-concept centered around a pervasive denial of psychopathology.

Although few researchers have directly investigated the *L* scale, Burish and Houston (1976) have provided some validational evidence for it. In 66 male college students, they found that *L* correlated significantly (+.55) with the Denial (*Dn*) scale (see Chapter 4, page 145) and was unrelated to Scale *1* (Hypochondriasis) and Scale *8* (Schizophrenia). Hence, the *L* scale was significantly related to a construct (denial) that the *L* scale is intended to measure (convergent validity) and unrelated to two constructs (hypochondriasis and schizophrenia) from which the scale is intended to differ (discriminant validity).

Burish and Houston (1976) also found that students with high *L* scale scores performed better in a stressful situation than those with low scores. The high *L* scale students appeared to use their defensive strategies across different kinds of potentially threatening situations. Similarly, Matarazzo (1955) found that male medical students who scored high on the *L* scale were less anxious (as measured by the Taylor Manifest Anxiety scale) than those who scored low.

Test-retest reliability coefficients for the L scale on the MMPI tend to be slightly lower than those reported for Scales F and K (Dahlstrom et al., 1975). Reliability coefficients for intervals up to one week range from .70 to .85, and for intervals of one year or more range from .35 to .60. Little information is available for test-retest reliability on the MMPI-2. Test-retest reliability coefficients for the L scale on the MMPI-2 are .77 for men and .81 for women over a one-week interval (Butcher et al., 1989)

Hathaway and McKinley (1951) originally arbitrarily assigned T scores to the raw scores for the L scale on the MMPI. Inspection of Profile 1–1 will show that they assigned a raw score of 10 on the L scale to a T score of 70 and a raw score of 7 to a T score of 60. On the basis of their clinical experience of the frequency with which the various raw scores on the L scale occur, Hathaway and McKinley (1967) have suggested that a raw score of 7 on the L scale should equal a T score of 70, and Rosen (1952) has indicated that a raw score of 10 should equal a T score of 80. T scores for the L scale on the MMPI-2 were computed in the standard manner; they correspond reasonably well with those suggested by Hathaway and McKinley (1967) for the MMPI (1967) L scale.

The levels of L scale elevation and their interpretation are summarized in Table 3–49.

F Scale

The F scale consists of 60 items (64 items on the MMPI) that were selected to detect unusual or atypical ways of answering the test items. Unlike most of the other scales, the F scale was not derived by comparing item endorsements between criterion and normal groups; it is made up of items that no more than 10 percent of an early subsample of the Minnesota normative sample answered in the deviant direction.

The F scale is sometimes called the *frequency* or *infrequency* scale, but the exact derivation of the label "F" is unknown. The scale taps a wide variety of obvious and unambiguous content areas, including bizarre sensations, strange thoughts, peculiar experiences, feelings of isolation and alienation, and a number of unlikely or contradictory beliefs, expectations, and self-descriptions (Dahlstrom et al., 1972). Examples of F scale items with the deviant answer indicated in parentheses are:

"When I am with people, I am bothered by hearing very strange things." (true)

"No one cares much what happens to you." (true)

"I believe in law enforcement." (false)[3]

Most of the F scale items (35 of 60) on the MMPI-2 are scored only on the F scale; 15 items overlap with Scale 8 (Schizophrenia) and 9 items with Scale 6 (Paranoia). Eight of the F scale items (12, 48, 120, 132, 204, 222, 264, and 288) do not meet the 10 percent or below criterion for either males or females in the MMPI-2 normative sample, and an additional 4 items for males do not meet this criterion (Butcher et al., 1989). There also are 69 more items on the MMPI-2 that meet the 10 percent or below criterion; 37 of these items are found on the F_B scale (see below).

Five of the F scale items (20, 54, 112, 115, and 185) on the MMPI do not meet the 10 percent or below criterion for either males or females in the original Minnesota normative sample, and an additional 11 items for males and 3 for females do not meet this criterion (Dahlstrom et al., 1975). Most of these items, however, exceeded the criterion by only a few percentage points. There also are 38 more items that meet the 10 percent or below criterion that could have been included in the F scale but were not for unknown reasons.

TABLE 3-49   Interpretations of Lie (*L*) Scale Elevation

MMPI-2 T Score	MMPI Raw Score[a]	Interpretation
44 and below	0-2	1. *Low.* A set to endorse all items as "true" is possible. The other validity indicators should be evaluated. Clients may be attempting to create an extremely pathologic picture of themselves. Normal persons who are relatively independent or self-reliant are generally willing to admit these minor social faults.
45-55	3-5	2. *Normal.* Scores in this range indicate clients who are able to achieve an appropriate balance between admitting and denying minor social faults. These clients may be sophisticated persons who are attempting to create a favorable self-image.
56-64	6-7	3. *Moderate.* A random sort may have occurred. The other validity indicators should be evaluated. Scores in this range may indicate normal persons who are slightly more conforming than usual or clients who have a tendency to resort to denial mechanisms.
65 and above	8-15	4. *Marked.* An error in scoring may have occurred on the MMPI when this scale is scored without a template (i.e. "true" responses were counted instead of the "false" responses). Scores in this range may indicate: normal persons who are very self-controlled and who lack insight into their own behavior, persons with religious and moralistic training or occupations that deny even the most common human faults, unsophisticated persons who are trying to create an unusually favorable impression of themselves as in personnel selection, clients whose dynamics revolve around denial (frequently encountered in histrionic and somatization disorders), or psychiatric inpatients who may be overtly psychotic when all the clinical scales are *not* elevated (T scores <65 on the MMPI-2; T scores <70 on the MMPI).

[a]Since the raw scores arbitrarily assigned by Hathaway and McKinley (1967) to the T scores on the *L* scale on the MMPI are too low, in this table the raw scores have been adjusted based on clinical judgment to reflect more accurately the frequency with which specific raw scores are obtained.

Gravitz (1987) reported that normal job applicants endorsed a number of the MMPI *F* scale items more frequently than the 10 percent criterion of the original normative sample. More than 10 percent of the men and women endorsed MMPI Group Booklet items 112, 115, 199, and 206 in the deviant direction. The men also endorsed item 215 more than 10 percent of the time. Gravitz concluded that these changes in the frequency of item endorsement indicate that it may be necessary to renorm the MMPI. These same items also were endorsed more than 10 percent of the time by the MMPI-2 normative sample except for item 206, which was dropped.

Researchers have investigated the relationship between *F* scale elevations, validity of the profile, and extent of psychopathology. Hathaway and McKinley (1951) originally recommended that MMPI profiles should be ruled invalid if the T score on the *F* scale exceeds 70 (raw score >12). Researchers quickly showed, however, that all profiles with a T score greater than 70 on the *F* scale were not invalid. Kazan and Sheinberg (1945) reported that 35 of 37 male mental hygiene clinic patients with a T score greater than 70 on the *F* scale were providing valid self-descriptions on the MMPI. Similarly, Schneck (1948) believed that 10 of 17 male prisoners with a T score on the *F* scale greater than 70 were providing accurate responses, and their elevation on the *F* scale appeared to reflect the severity of their personality disturbance.

The next flurry of research investigated whether profiles with a T score on the *F* scale greater than 80 (raw score >16) should be considered invalid. Preliminary research in this area indicated that persons with a T score greater than 80 were likely to be diagnosed as having behavior disorders (Gynther, 1961; Gynther & Shimkunas, 1965a) in court-referred cases and as being psychotic in psychiatric samples (Blumberg, 1967; Gauron, Severson, & Englehart, 1962; Gynther & Shimkunas, 1965b).

Again, it appears that a specific raw score on the *F* scale cannot be used to consider profiles routinely as invalid since a majority of the persons in these studies were accurately classified. Instead, significant psychopathology tends to be correlated with T scores greater than 80 on the *F* scale, although the exact correlates differ as a function of the setting in which the MMPI is given.

Finally, Gynther, Altman, and Warbin (1973b) examined the correlates of *F* scale scores greater than a T score of 98 (raw scores >25) in white and black hospital patients. They identified and cross-validated seven descriptors of the white patients: they were un-

able to understand proverbs, were monosyllabic, had delusions of reference, had auditory hallucinations, were disoriented for place, had short attention spans, and did not know why they were hospitalized.

Essentially the white patients with a T score greater than 98 on the *F* scale could be described as confused psychotics, and their extreme profile elevations reflected the severity of their psychopathology. No descriptors could be cross-validated among the black patients (i.e., there were no replicable differences between black patients with a T score greater than 98 versus those with a T score equal to or less than 98). Obviously, the *F* scale was tapping different dimensions in black as compared to white patients. More information on the performance of blacks and other minority groups on the MMPI will be provided in Chapter 8.

Gynther, Lachar, and Dahlstrom (1978) have developed a new *F* scale for blacks that is designed to serve the same validity function as the standard *F* scale (i.e., to identify persons who endorse items that members of a normal population infrequently endorse). This new *F* scale for blacks also will be described in Chapter 8.

Other studies have investigated clients' responses to individual *F* scale items. Gynther and Petzel (1967) observed that psychotics and persons with behavior disorders were not differentiated by their raw scores on the *F* scale; they hypothesized that this occurred because these persons endorsed different subsets of items within the scale. They found, however, only one item that discriminated the two groups; therefore, their hypothesis was not supported.

McKegney (1965) observed that delinquent adolescents have elevated *F* scale scores and hypothesized that this occurred because some of the *F* scale items are accurate responses for them. Hence, McKegney thought that delinquent adolescents were consistently endorsing only certain *F* scale items that are meaningful for them. Three professionals and three nonprofessionals familiar with adolescents identified 21 F scale items that they felt could be answered truthfully by delinquent adolescents.

McKegney (1965) also found that 21 F scale items were answered more frequently by delinquent adolescents than by normal adolescents. These items dealt with such content as stealing, misbehaving in school, and injuring others; the items directly tap the behaviors and attitudes that caused the adolescents to be labeled delinquent. McKegney reported that these two sets of 21 items were positively correlated, but he did not report how many or which items overlapped between the two sets.

Thus, it appears that high F scale scores among delinquent adolescents may result at least partially from the fact that some items are genuinely more applicable to juveniles than to the original normative group. Archer (1984, 1987) has noted that most adolescents have higher scores on the F scale items than adults, which also suggests that a number of these items may not be infrequent items for adolescents.

Test-retest reliability coefficients for the MMPI F scale range from .80 to .97 for an interval up to two weeks and range from .45 to .76 for intervals from eight months up to three years (Dahlstrom et al., 1975). Test-retest reliability coefficients for the F scale on the MMPI-2 are .78 for men and .69 for women over a one-week interval (Butcher et al., 1989).

Elevation of the F scale is positively correlated with the overall elevation of the entire clinical portion of the profile and particularly Scales 6 (Paranoia) and 8 (Schizophrenia), both in adult psychiatric patients and in adolescents (Dahlstrom et al., 1972). Elevation of the F scale also is a rough index of the severity of the psychological distress that the client is experiencing; higher scores indicate more severe distress. Clinicians should keep

in mind, however, that the content of the F scale items is obvious, and clients may lower or raise their F scale scores virtually as desired. Such overreporting of psychopathology, however, can be detected easily by the indexes and scales described above.

Hathaway and McKinley (1951) also arbitrarily assigned the T scores to the raw scores on the F scale as they did on the ? and L scales. They assigned a T score of 70 to a raw score of 12 and a T-score of 80 to a raw score of 16 (see Profile 1–1, page 3). Again, clinical experience has shown that these T scores do not properly reflect the frequency with which the specific raw scores occur on the F scale. Based on clinical experience, Hathaway and McKinley (1967) later suggested that a raw score of 16 should equal a T score of 70.

T scores for the F scale on the MMPI-2 were computed in the standard manner; surprisingly, the raw scores do not appear to correspond to the scores that would be expected based on clinical experience. For example, a raw score of 16 on the MMPI-2 F scale is a T score of 85 in men and 92 in women rather than approximately a T score of 70, as suggested by Hathaway and McKinley (1967) on the MMPI.

The levels of F scale elevation and their interpretation are summarized in Table 3–50. Since it is not clear whether the T scores on the MMPI-2 accurately reflect the frequency with which raw scores will be seen in clinical settings, the levels of elevation in Table 3–50 have been based on *raw* scores rather than T scores.

Back F (F_B) Scale

The F_B scale consists of 40 items on the MMPI-2 that no more than 10 percent of the MMPI-2 normative sample answered in the deviant direction. This scale is analogous to the standard F scale except that the items are placed in the last half of the test. Item 281 is

TABLE 3–50 Interpretations of F and Back F (F_B) Scale Elevations

MMPI-2 Raw Score[a]	MMPI Raw Score[a]	Interpretation
0– 2	0– 2	1. *Low.* These clients have systematically avoided acknowledging the socially unacceptable or disturbing content represented in the scale. They may be trying to deny serious psychopathology (underreporting). Or they may be normal persons who are very conventional, unassuming, and unpretentious.
3– 7	3– 7	2. *Normal.* These clients are willing to acknowledge a typical number of unusual experiences.
8–15	8–15	3. *Moderate.* These clients are acknowledging the unusual experiences represented in this scale more than the typical person. The elevation reflects the extent and severity of the client's psychopathology, and how the client has adjusted to his or her psychopathology (i.e., an intact psychotic patient frequently falls in the middle of this range).
16–22	16–22	4. *Marked.* The profile may be invalid; other validity indicators should be checked. The elevation reflects the severity of distress and extent of psychopathology that the client is experiencing. Patients are likely to be diagnosed as having behavior disorders or being psychotics, depending on their age and type of treatment facility. Adolescents may be honestly acknowledging the deviant behaviors that caused them to be labeled delinquent.
23 and above	23 and above	5. *Extreme.* THE PROFILE IS PROBABLY INVALID. Other validity indicators should be checked. These clients are likely to be severely disorganized and psychotic; these characteristics are readily apparent in an interview. Scores in this range may indicate adolescents going through an identity crisis.

[a]Since the raw scores arbitrarily assigned by Hathaway and McKinley (1967) to the T scores on the F scale on the MMPI are known to be too high, and the T scores seem too low on the F scale and too high on the F_B scale on the MMPI-2, in this table the raw scores have been adjusted based on clinical judgment to reflect more accurately the frequency with which specific raw scores are obtained.

the first item on the F_B scale, whereas item 361 is the last item on the standard F scale (see Appendix A).

There are large differences between raw scores and their corresponding T scores on the F_B and F scales on the MMPI-2 (compare Profile 7–1, page 296, and Profile 7–3, page 298). For men a raw score of 16 is a T score of 108 on the F_B scale and a T score of 85 on the F scale, whereas for women a raw score of 12 is a T score of 89 on the F_B scale and a T score of 79 on the F scale. These T scores also are significantly higher than clinical experience suggested was appropriate on the F scale on the MMPI (Hathaway & McKinley, 1967).

Since items on both the F_B and F scales were endorsed by no more than 10 percent of the normative sample, it is surprising that there should be such large differences in T scores between these two scales. If clients were more likely to endorse the items randomly on the last half of the MMPI-2, higher raw scores, and hence lower T scores, would be expected on F_B rather than F; however, the opposite pattern was found in the MMPI-2 normative sample. Clearly, research is needed that examines the relationship between raw scores on F_B and F in clinical samples.

The clinician should recall the use of the relationship between the raw scores on the F and F_B scales as a measure of consistency of item endorsement (see page 69).

Test-retest reliability coefficients for the F_B scale on the MMPI-2 are .86 for men and .71 for women over a one-week interval (Butcher et al., 1989). These coefficients are slightly higher than those reported for the F scale.

The levels of F_B scale elevation and their interpretation should be very similar to the standard F scale since the items were selected by the same criterion. Consequently, the same interpretive statements are suggested for both F_B and F scales (see Table 3–50).

K Scale

The K scale consists of 30 items that were empirically selected to assist in identifying persons who displayed significant psychopathology yet had profiles within the normal range. Since the derivation of the K scale was described in Chapter 1, it will not be repeated here.

Most of the K scale items also are scored on other clinical scales and are fairly equally dispersed across these scales; only five items are unique to the K scale. The items usually are scored in the same direction when they appear on another clinical scale except that six of the seven items also found on Scale *0* (Social Introversion) are scored in the opposite direction. Item content on the K scale is heterogeneous and covers self-control and family and interpersonal relationships. Examples of K scale items with the deviant answer indicated in parentheses are:

"I like to let people know where I stand on things." (false)

"I have very few quarrels with members of my family." (true)

"People often disappoint me." (false)[4]

A K-corrected profile is automatically plotted if the standard profile sheet is used (see Profile 2–1). The K-corrected profile was developed by determining the proportion of K that, when added to the raw score on the clinical scale, would maximize the discrimination between the normative groups and the criterion group. McKinley, Hathaway, and Meehl (1948) determined that the discriminations could be improved on five of the clinical scales by the addition of a proportion of K. Thus, Scales *7* (Psychasthenia) and *8* (Schizophrenia) are corrected by the addition of the whole raw score of K, whereas Scales *1* (Hypochondriasis), *4* (Psychopathic Deviate), and *9* (Hypomania) are corrected by the addition of a fractional value of K (.5, .4, and .2, respectively). McKinley and associates found that the addition of K to the other clinical scales (Scales *2* [Depression], *3* [Hysteria], *5* [Masculinity-Femininity], and *6* [Paranoia]) actually reduced their discriminability; so these scales were not K-corrected.

Adolescent profiles on the MMPI are *not* K-corrected (see Chapter 8; Archer, 1987) so the standard profile sheet cannot be used directly. Special adolescent profile sheets are available for the MMPI so that clinicians can plot the profile without looking up the non-K-corrected T scores in a table.

The K-correction procedure was *not* examined in the restandardization of the MMPI, and the same K-weights are added to the same scales on the MMPI-2. Consequently, any critiques of the K scale on the MMPI should apply directly to the MMPI-2.

Despite urgings for investigators to cross-validate these K-corrections (Dahlstrom et al., 1972; McKinley et al., 1948; Meehl & Hathaway, 1946), almost no research has been published on the issue. The few published studies on K-correction weights (Heilbrun, 1963; Tyler & Michaelis, 1953; Yonge, 1966) found discouraging results.

Heilbrun investigated the K-corrections that would maximize the discrimination between normal college students and maladjusted students who either sought treatment at a university counseling center or were hospitalized. Heilbrun determined that only three scales separated normal from maladjusted college students better when K-corrected than when not K-corrected. He found that the following weights, different in some cases for males than for females, worked best: Scale 3 (Hysteria), $-.7K$ males, $-.5K$ females; Scale 7 (Psychasthenia), $1.0K$ males, $.8K$ females; and Scale 8 (Schizophrenia), $.7$ K males and females. Heilbrun did cross-validate these weights in his student sample; since no additional research has been conducted in other student samples, the generalizability of his results remains open to question.

Both Tyler and Michaelis (1953) and Yonge (1966) reported that adding K to the five K-corrected scales in their college student samples actually reduced the reliability and validity of these scales. Clearly, any clinician using the MMPI-2 or MMPI in a college setting needs to examine the usage of the traditional K-correction procedures. Using Heilbrun's proposed K-corrections, determining another more appropriate set of K-corrections, or avoiding the use of K-corrections altogether might be preferable. The need for additional research in other settings cannot be overemphasized.

Two recent studies (Jenkins, 1984; Wooten, 1984) have evaluated the effective of the K-correction procedure in clinical samples. Jenkins found virtually no change in the accuracy of identifying pain patients with Scale 1 (Hypochondriasis) or schizophrenic patients with Scale 8 (Schizophrenia) using K-weights that ranged from -1.0 to $+1.5$. Essentially, the K-correction procedure had no effect on the accuracy of classifying these groups of patients. However, Wooten found a slight improvement in hit rate using the K-correction procedure in Air Force trainees.

Wooten (1984) also noted that there were frequent changes in codetype when non-K-corrected profiles were compared with the standard K-corrected profile. He concluded that his data favored the use of the K-correction procedure. More than 40 years of using the MMPI without investigation of the appropriateness of the K-correction procedure defies explanation. Hopefully, researchers will begin to investigate the K-correction procedure on the MMPI-2.

Researchers have examined other aspects of the K scale than the K-corrections themselves. Several investigators (Heilbrun, 1961; Smith, 1959; Sweetland & Quay, 1953) examined the appropriateness of the scale as a measure of defensiveness and reported that the K scale in a normal population is a measure not of defensiveness but of personality integration and healthy adjustment, with high scores reflecting healthy adjustment.

Similarly, both Tyler and Michaelis (1953) and Yonge (1966) reported that in a normal college student sample the K scale was significantly negatively related to the five K-corrected scales on which high scores do indicate psychopathology. Working with maladjusted college students, Heilbrun (1961) and Nakamura (1960) found, however, that the K scale was measure of defensiveness. Consequently, it appears that the appropriateness of interpreting K as a measure of defensiveness varies according to the type of client. In a normal population high scores on the K scale do not indicate defensiveness; in a maladjusted population, however, high *K* scores do suggest defensiveness.

Research on the *K* scale in other settings also has yielded dismal results. Hunt, Carp, Cass, Winder, and Kantor (1948), Schmidt (1948), and Wooten (1984) reported that the *K*-correction contributed little to diagnostic efficiency for patients in a military setting. Silver and Sines (1962) also found that the *K*-correction did not increase the accuracy of predicting diagnostic classification in state hospital patients; the *K* scale was essentially unrelated to diagnostic classifications. Ruch and Ruch (1967) found that non-*K*-corrected clinical scales discriminated better between good and poor salesmen; the *K*-corrections actually decreased the discriminability of the two groups.

The one positive outcome in this area was provided by Ries (1966), who compared state hospital patients who scored higher than a raw score of 15 (T score greater than 55) on the *K* scale with patients who scored 15 or lower. For patients with raw scores of 16 or higher, 19 of 22 were rated as being unimproved after 60 days of hospitalization and 7 of 19 were rehospitalized within 12 months. For patients scoring 15 or lower, 25 of 31 were rated as being improved after the same time interval, and only 2 of 25 were rehospitalized within 12 months.

Clearly, in Ries' study the *K* scale was significantly related to an external criterion. In general, however, little research justifies the continued widespread use of the *K*-correction of the clinical scales. Hopefully, future research will investigate this area more thoroughly. Meanwhile, clinicians probably need to avoid using *K*-corrections in settings in which normal persons are being evaluated with the MMPI-2, but they should use the *K*-corrections in settings in which psychopathology is suspected, keeping in mind the potential inaccuracies that *K*-corrections may introduce.

Another consideration that clinicians need to keep in mind is that clients can achieve a high score on a clinical scale that is *K*-corrected in different ways. They can either endorse a large number of items in the deviant direction on the clinical scale or have a large *K*-correction added.

For example, a female client can achieve a total *K*-corrected raw score of 40 on Scale *8* (Schizophrenia) of the MMPI-2 in a variety of ways, including endorsing 15 Scale *8* items and 25 *K* scale items or 35 Scale *8* items and 5 *K* scale items. The non-*K*-corrected T scores for these two raw scores on Scale *8* are 56 and 78, respectively (see Appendix B). It should go without saying that in the latter case she is more likely to be overtly schizophrenic than in the former. This is not to suggest that either the *K*-corrected or non-*K*-corrected score is more accurate. The point is that clients achieving such scores will be very different both behaviorally and clinically, and clinicians need to be aware of these differences.

Low scores on the *K* scale (the client consistently admits problems) are accompanied by more frequent elevations of the clinical profile, especially in the psychotic tetrad (Scales *6*, *7*, *8*, and *9*). High *K* scale scores are associated with lower profile elevations and peaks on the neurotic triad (Scales *1*, *2*, and *3*) both in adult psychiatric and in adolescent populations (Dahlstrom et al., 1972).

The *K* scale is the only validity scale on the MMPI for which the T scores were derived in a standard manner. The *K* scale also is the only validity scale for which there is no specific score that indicates that the profile is invalid. The clinician, however, should be sensitive to *K* scores that are atypical of clients taking the MMPI-2 or the MMPI in a specific setting.

For example, in personnel selection very low *K* scores would be unusual, and clinicians should review such scores closely. Conversely, in psychiatric settings very high *K* scores would be unusual. When a client with known or suspected psychopathology has a highly elevated score on *K*, the client is likely being defensive about some form of psychological distress; the cause of the distress may not be discernible from the profile. In this situation it is usually recommended that the client be evaluated carefully for an underlying psychotic process, particularly if the clinical scales are within the normal range (see Normal *K* + profiles, page 121).

The interpretation of the *K* scale changes dramatically depending on the socioeconomic class and education level of the client and the setting in which the MMPI-2 is administered (e.g., personnel selection, state hospital, university). The potential impact of these factors on the *K* scale becomes even more noteworthy on the MMPI-2 because of the relatively high socioeconomic class and years of education that characterized the MMPI-2 normative group. Consequently, clinicians should be aware that the T scores on the *K* scale on the MMPI-2 may have been affected by these factors (cf. Caldwell, 1990). These factors appear to have minimal effect on the standard clinical scales that are *K*-corrected (Butcher, 1990).

Clinicians should be cautious in interpreting scores on the *K* scale in clients whose occupation or education level is subtantially lower than the MMPI-2 normative group until further research has addressed the potential impact of these factors. Levels of *K* scale elevation and their interpretation for persons with known or suspected psychopathology are summarized in Table 3–51. Similar information for "normal" persons is summarized in Table 3–52. Test-retest reliability coefficients for the *K* scale on the MMPI range from .78 to .92 for an interval up to two weeks and range from .52 to .67 for intervals from eight months to three years (Dahlstrom et al., 1975). Test-retest reliability coefficients for the *K* scale on the MMPI-2 are .84 for men and .81 for women

over a one-week interval (Butcher et al., 1989).

VALIDITY SCALE CONFIGURATIONS

Four validity scale configurations occur frequently in most clinical and normal populations. This limited number of common validity scale configurations is surprising since 27 possible configurations exist if each of the three validity scales is classified as average, above average, or below average.

The most frequently encountered validity scale configuration in most clinical settings is illustrated in Figure 3–3 (solid line). The frequency with which this configuration occurred in four samples of clients is presented in Table 3–53.

The essential characteristics of this configuration are that the *L* scale and the *K* scale are below a T score of 50 and the *F* scale is above a T score of 60. The client is admitting to personal and emotional difficulties, is requesting assistance with these problems, and is unsure of her own capabilities for dealing with these problems. As the *F* scale score increases, the client is either experiencing more problems and hence feeling worse, exaggerating the symptomatology in order to get help sooner, or simulating psychopathology. The clinician can use the other validity indexes described earlier in this chapter to distinguish which of these various causes of the *F* scale elevation is appropriate.

Under most conditions, this validity scale configuration is most desirable for any form of psychological intervention or treatment. There are two reservations, though: The *F* scale should not be above a T score of 90–100, and the *K* scale should not be below a T score of 35. In the former case the client may be experiencing so much stress and conflict that a psychotherapeutic intervention should not be initiated until some of the stress and conflict can be alleviated. In the latter case the client may not have the necessary

TABLE 3–51   Interpretations of *K* Scale Elevations for Clients with Suspected or Known Psychopathology

MMPI-2 T Score	MMPI T Score	Interpretation
30–34	27–35	1. *Markedly Low.* These clients probably have either fabricated or greatly exaggerated their problems to create the impression of a severe emotional disturbance (over-reporting). They may be experiencing acute psychotic distress, which may require hospitalization. The clinician should consider plotting a non-*K*-corrected profile because of the lack of contribution of the *K* score to those scales that are *K*-corrected. The prognosis for a psychological intervention is guarded.
35–40	36–45	2. *Low.* In this range are clients with limited personal resources who are experiencing severe distress that is being openly acknowledged. Such clients have poor self-concepts and are strongly self-dissatisfied but lack either the interpersonal skills or techniques necessary to alter the situation. These scores also may indicate persons who tend to be excessively open and revealing and who may be masochistic confessors. In lower-class clients this elevation reflects a moderate disturbance, whereas in higher-class clients it reflects low ego strength and more serious distress. The prognosis for a psychological intervention is guarded.
41–55	46–55	3. *Normal.* Scores in this range indicate clients who have a proper balance between self-disclosure and self-protection. Such persons have sufficient personal resources to desire and tolerate a psychological intervention. In higher-class clients a moderate level of personal distress would be expected. The prognosis for a psychological intervention is good.
56–64	56–69	4. *Moderate.* Scores in this range indicate clients who are being defensive and unwilling to acknowledge psychological distress. This defensiveness may be characterized by denial and hysteroid defenses, particularly in lower-class clients. The clinician should consider plotting a non-*K*-corrected profile because of the excessive contribution of the high *K* score to those scales that are *K*-corrected. The prognosis is guarded.
65 and above	70 and above	5. *Marked.* Scores in this range indicate clients who are consistently trying to maintain a facade of adequacy and control and are admitting no problems or weaknesses despite their presence in a mental health setting. Such persons have a serious lack of insight into and understanding of their own behavior. These clients are being extremely defensive about some kind of inadequacy, which may not be directly discernible from the profile. The clinician should examine the reasons that the client might be denying psychopathology and should plot a non-*K*-corrected profile. The prognosis for any form of psychological intervention is very poor because of the client's lack of insight into his or her own behavior.

TABLE 3–52 Interpretations of *K* Scale Elevations for Normal Persons

MMPI-2 T Score	MMPI T Score	Interpretation
30–40	27–45	1. *Low.* These clients are acknowledging limited resources for dealing with problems. The clinician should investigate whether the clients actually have some form of psychopathology that they are willing to report.
41–55	46–55	2. *Normal.* Scores in this range indicate clients from lower socioeconomic classes or with limited education levels who have an appropriate balance between self-disclosure and self-protection.
56–64	56–69	3. *Moderate.* Scores in this range indicate college-educated and upper-class persons who are well adjusted, insightful, self-reliant, and easily capable of dealing with their everyday problems. When under stress, such persons may be unwilling to seek help with their problems.
65 and above	70 and above	4. *Marked.* These clients' professed adjustment and self-adequacy are likely to reflect a defensive facade. These persons probably have little interest in examining the appropriateness of this facade.

personal resources for working on her problems.

In an inpatient setting clients with this validity scale configuration are likely to evidence poorer impulse control and a greater frequency of inappropriate and destructive behavior than clients with other types of validity scale configurations (Post & Gasparikova-Krasnec, 1979). As the client begins to improve, the *F* scale elevation should decrease and the *K* scale elevation should increase.

There are two variants of this validity scale configuration. In the first variant the *L* scale and the *K* scale are between a T score of 50 and 60, and the *F* scale is elevated above a T score of 65 (see Figure 3–3, dashed line). This client is admitting problems, which are of increasing severity as the *F* scale increases in elevation and simultaneously is trying to defend himself against these problems.

This pattern of ineffective defenses with the simultaneous admission of fairly severe problems is typical of chronically malad-justed clients (Gross, 1959). Such a client is hardly an optimal candidate for most forms of psychological intervention, and little change in this configuration occurs over time.

In the second variant of this validity scale configuration the *L* scale is below a T score of 50, the *F* scale is equal to or greater than the *K* scale, and the *K* scale is above a T score of 55 (see Figure 3–3, dotted line). The *F* scale in this configuration will not typically exceed a T score of 75.

This client has long-standing problems to which she has become so well adjusted that she can feel good about herself while at the same time admitting problems. As the *F* scale increases in elevation, the client still feels secure about herself despite the number and severity of problems. This client simply wants help in dealing with her current problems and will be satisfied when these current stresses are alleviated. The only change in this configuration with the alleviation of stress will likely be a decrease in elevation of the *F* scale.

FIGURE 3–3   Validity Scale Configuration:Caret

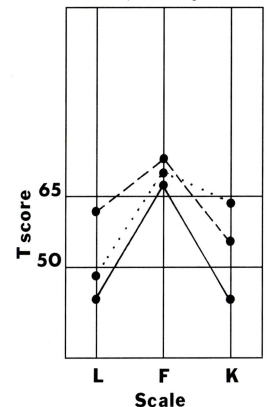

L   F   K

Scale

The second of the four commonly encountered validity scale configurations is illustrated in Figure 3–4. The frequency with which this configuration occurred in the four samples is presented in Table 3–53.

In this configuration the *L* scale and the *K* scale are elevated above a T score of at least 60, and may approach a T score of 65, and the *F* scale is near to or below a T score of 50. This client is attempting to avoid or deny unacceptable feelings, impulses, and problems. That is, the client is trying to present himself in the best possible light. This client tends to be simplistic and views the world in terms of the extremes of good and bad. The client will have an adequate social adjustment or, at worst, a mild behavioral disturbance (Gross, 1959).

In inpatient settings, clients with this validity scale configuration are likely to be psychotic, particularly if the clinical scales also suggest the presence of a psychotic condition (Sines, Baucom, & Gruba, 1979). This type of validity scale configuration occurs most frequently among defensive normals (e.g., unsophisticated job applicants), hysterics, and hypochondriacs.

TABLE 3–53   Frequency of Validity Scale Configurations by Sample

Validity Scale Configuration	Sample			
	Clinic Clients	Medical Patients	Prison Inmates	University Students
Figure 3–3 (solid line)	46.8%	19.5%	25.5%	38.8%
Figure 3–3 (dashed line)	17.4	11.2	21.0	10.5
Figure 3–3 (dotted line)	3.8	0.1	1.5	1.4
Figure 3–4	10.0	35.3	21.5	7.2
Figure 3–5	14.0	19.9	24.5	27.8
Figure 3–6	7.2	4.1	1.5	0.5
None of these[a]	0.8	9.9	4.5	13.9

[a]Most of these configurations were characterized by the *L, F,* and *K* scales being approximately equal to a T score of 50. See Greene (1980) for a more complete description of these samples of clients.

FIGURE 3–4   Validity Scale Configuration: Inverted Caret

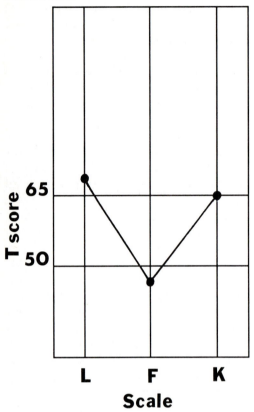

FIGURE 3–5   Validity Scale Configuration: Ascending Slope

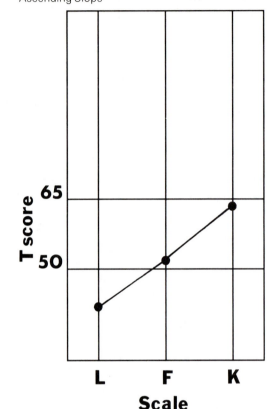

This configuration is often accompanied by elevations on Scales *1* (Hypochondriasis) and *3* (Hysteria) and average scores on the rest of the profile. Deliberate defensiveness and denial of psychopathology may be suspected, if there is a legitimate reason for evaluating the client. Typically these clients neither are referred for nor seek treatment. College students instructed to endorse the MMPI items in terms of their "ideal self" produce this validity scale configuration (Hiner, Ogren, & Baxter, 1969).

The third of the four validity scale configurations is illustrated in Figure 3–5, and the frequency of its occurrence in the four samples is presented in Table 3–53. The es-

sential features of this configuration are that the three validity scales have a positive slope in which the *L* scale is less than the *F* scale and the *F* scale is less than the *K* scale. Generally, the *L* scale is about a T score of 40, the *F* scale is about a T score of 50 to 55, and the *K* scale is in the T score range of 60 to 70.

This configuration is typical of a normal individual who has the appropriate resources for dealing with problems and who is not experiencing any stress or conflict at the present time. The *K* scale elevation in this configuration will move up or down depending on the person's reference group. For example, a normal college student will score at the upper end of this range, whereas the normal lower-class individual will score at the lower end of this range. A job applicant or a prison inmate who is trying to look "good" may have this validity scale configuration.

Lanyon and Lutz (1984) found that this validity scale configuration was characteristic of felony sex offenders who denied any sexual deviant behavior. It is unusual for a self-referred individual in a mental health setting to have this configuration; however, it can occur among (1) "normal" persons involved in marital conflict or (2) upper-class or college-educated persons who show sophisticated defensiveness. In these cases the clinical scales all will be submerged (within the average range) except for Scale *5* (Masculinity-Femininity) among males.

The last commonly encountered validity scale configuration is illustrated in Figure 3–6, and the frequency of occurrence of this configuration in the four samples is presented in Table 3–53. In this configuration the three validity scales have a negative slope in which the *L* scale is greater than the *F* scale, which is greater than the *K* scale. The *L* scale is elevated to a T score of 65, the *F* scale is about a T score of 50, and the *K* scale is equal to a T score of 40 to 45.

This client is naive and unsophisticated but is trying to look "good." Such clients usually have little education and come from the lower socioeconomic classes. Their attempt to look good usually is ineffective, and the neurotic triad (Scales *1*, *2*, and *3*) generally is elevated. For males, Scale *5* will be low. Even when the *F* scale is elevated, it usually will not exceed a T score of 65; the client is still trying to maintain a facade of looking good despite the admission of some problems.

These clients are poor candidates for any form of psychological intervention. They are unlikely to admit their problems, and when they do, they lack both the resources for and the interest in psychological interventions. This configuration changes little over time, except that the *F* scale will likely decrease if it is elevated higher than a T score of 50.

FIGURE 3–6   Validity Scale Configuration: Descending Slope

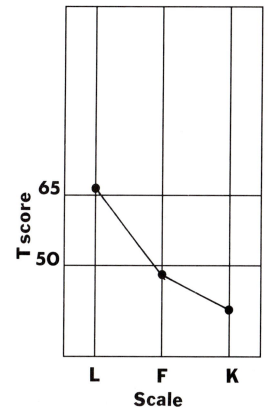

NORMAL *K*⁺ PROFILES

Occasionally a profile will be encountered in which the only significant validity or clinical scale elevation is on the *K* scale. Marks and Seeman (1963) identified such a profile as a Normal *K*⁺ profile. This profile is basically an elaboration of the second commonly encountered validity scale configuration already described (see Figure 3-4). A Normal *K*⁺ profile (Marks & Seeman, 1963; Marks,

Seeman, & Haller, 1974) has the following specific characteristics:

1. Psychiatric inpatients only
2. All clinical scales below a T score of 70
3. Six or more clinical scales less than or equal to a T score of 60
4. Scales *L* and *K* higher than the *F* scale with the *F* scale below a T score of 60
5. The *K* scale *5* or more T score points higher than the *F* scale

(Clinicians should note that no specific elevation on the *K* scale is specified by these criteria, only the relationship between the *K* scale and Scales *L* and *F*.) Marks and colleagues described these clients as shy, anxious, inhibited, and defensive about admitting that their problems could be psychological. They avoided close interpersonal relationships and were passively resistant. Their personality structure had a schizoid component, their stream of thought was often incoherent, and they frequently appeared perplexed. They also displayed paranoid features: they were suspicious, fearful, and sensitive to anything that might be construed as a demand.

Almost half of the patients with this profile were diagnosed as psychotic, and almost a quarter of them were diagnosed as having a chronic brain syndrome. As a group, the clients were significantly above average in intelligence, and more than 60 percent were educated beyond the high school level.

A number of investigators have reported the frequency with which the Normal K^+ profile is encountered. Gynther and Brilliant (1968) found that 3.6 percent of the clients referred for testing at a mental health center met all the preceding criteria for a Normal K^+ profile. Newmark, Gentry, Simpson, and Jones (1978) found that 4.7 percent of an inpatient population who were diagnosed schizophrenic produced a Normal K^+ profile.

Two recent studies (Barley, Sabo, & Greene, 1986; Winters, Newmark, Lumry, Leach, & Weintraub, 1985) reported similar frequency of occurrence of the Normal K^+ profiles. However, Craig (1984) found no Normal K^+ profiles among his male heroin addicts. It appears that the Normal K^+ profile occurs in 3 to 5 percent of clients in most clinical settings other than possibly substance abuse/dependence.

There has been limited research on the actual correlates of the Normal K^+ profile. It should be remembered that the original correlates of this profile were derived on female psychiatric inpatients (Marks et al., 1974). Gynther and Brilliant (1968) reported no reliable psychological or behavioral differences between the clients with a Normal K^+ profile and other clients. They did find that 45 percent of their patients had psychotic diagnoses.

Barley and colleagues (1986) found that their patients with a Normal K^+ profile were less likely to have had chronic illnesses, to have attempted suicide prior to hospitalization, and to have somatic complaints. Their behavior and emotional state was more likely to be overactive, and their current hospitalization was shorter in length. They found that 47 percent of these patients had a psychotic diagnosis, but none had a brain disorder diagnosis.

These studies suggest that clients with a Normal K^+ profile are likely to have a psychotic diagnosis about 50 percent of the time. It is much less clear whether they will have a neuropsychological disorder and what specific behavioral and psychological correlates will be found. Duckworth and Barley (1988) have a comprehensive review of this profile that should be consulted by the interested reader.

SIMULATION AS ROLE PLAYING

The ability to detect clients who are simulating psychopathology has been mentioned as a benefit of several of the validity indicators. Most investigations of the ability to simulate psychopathology have not provided the individual with an explicit description of the actual behavior to be simulated. The typical instructions vaguely request that the individual answer the items as a "neurotic" or "psychotic" person would. Under these conditions the traditional validity indicators generally are able to detect at least some cases of simulation. When a specific description of the role to be simulated is given to the individual, two consistent results have occurred: (1) the persons are better able to simulate a role than when less specific instructions are provided and (2) the traditional validity indicators are unlikely to detect this form of simulation.

Lanyon (1967) asked well-adjusted male college students (no clinical scales greater than a T score of 69) and maladjusted students (at least three clinical scales greater than a T score of 69 that included at least two scales other than Scales 5 or 9) to simulate "very good adjustment" and "psychopathic personality." The students were given a description of a psychopathic personality. Both groups of students could simulate good adjustment, but the well-adjusted students simulated psychopathic personality better than the maladjusted students. When simulating good adjustment, approximately one-third of the students in both groups were able to escape detection by the traditional validity indicators.

In a similar study Wilcox and Dawson (1977) found that college students who were given a description of a paranoid individual while under hypnosis could simulate a paranoid profile without being detected by the validity scales. Students who were given the description without being hypnotized, however, produced deviant profiles that were easily detected by the validity scales. Rather than using an external criterion to assess whether their students actually simulated a paranoid

profile, Wilcox and Dawson noted that both groups significantly elevated Scale 6 (Paranoia), which suggests that their manipulation was effective. Their results indicate that some students can simulate deviant profiles without being detected by the validity scales.

Anthony (1976) asked inpatients, outpatients, and nonprofessional employees of a state hospital to simulate various codetypes on the MMPI when they were given a personality description and case study of that profile type. He rated the degree of similarity between the simulated and criteria profiles. His results, which are difficult to interpret, suggest that ability to simulate a psychopathologic role reflects a complex relationship among the client's actual psychopathology, race, gender, and the role to be simulated. He did not find a general negative relationship between psychopathology and the ability to simulate psychopathologic roles as he had anticipated. Thus, the hypothesis that psychopathologic individuals are generally deficient in role-playing skills could not be supported.

Kroger and Turnbull (1975) asked male college students to take the MMPI either as an Air Force officer or as a creative artist, without providing a more explicit description of these two roles. They found that the students could simulate the profile of Air Force officers, and the traditional validity indicators, including the *F-K* index, were unable to detect this simulation.

The students produced a simulated profile for the artists that was similar in configuration but more elevated or deviant than the actual artist profile. To investigate this latter result further, they asked two more groups of students to take the MMPI as a creative artist and provided an extensive role description of artists. One group received an accurate role description and the other received an inaccurate one. The students with the accurate role description produced a simulated profile that was nearly identical to the profile of actual artists except for Scale 5; the traditional validity indicators did not detect this simulation.

Thus, students apparently are capable of simulating profiles of both deviant and nondeviant roles without being detected by the traditional validity indicators. Deviant roles appear to be more difficult to simulate. Gough's (1954, 1957) findings that both students and professionals were unable to simulate neurosis also suggest that deviant roles are more difficult to simulate, particularly if a specific role description is not provided.

Additional research seems necessary to furnish a clearer understanding of role simulation and its detection with the MMPI-2. In addition, research on the ability of pathologic groups to simulate specific deviant and nondeviant roles also is needed to clarify whether role simulation is likely to be a problem when clients take the MMPI-2.

DETECTION OF RESPONSE SETS

Another potential problem that the validity indicators attempt to address is detecting any inappropriate response sets that might be utilized by the client. Clients sometimes take the MMPI-2 by using some response set other than accurately endorsing the items. For example, a client with limited but adequate reading ability and intelligence may complete the MMPI-2 in a half hour or less, which would arouse legitimate concern about the authenticity of the item endorsements. Or a client may be unable or unwilling to take the MMPI-2, but instead of directly refusing to complete the task, he may endorse all items "true" or "false" or alternate "true" and "false" responses. Or a client may try to make herself look better or worse by over-reporting or underreporting psychopathology; both of these response sets have been discussed previously.

Clinicians should try to prevent these situations by enlisting the client's full cooperation before starting the test. As mentioned, various validity indicators can help detect these inappropriate response sets when either the profile configuration or other circumstances suggest their possible influence.

The two most blatant of these response sets are "all true" (see Profile 3–1) and "all false" (see Profile 3–2). Such sets are easy to detect by examining either the answer sheet or the profile sheet. The validity scale configuration is highly suspect in both instances. In the "all true" response set, the T scores of the L and K scales are 35 and 30, respectively, and the F scale is greater than a T score of 120. The psychotic tetrad (Scales 6, 7, 8, and 9) is extremely elevated, and the neurotic triad (Scales 1, 2, and 3) is around a T score of 50.

In the "all false" response set, all three validity scales are elevated between T scores of 80 and 100. The elevation of the L and K scales within this range never occurs in a valid profile. The neurotic triad is extremely elevated along with a moderate elevation on the psychotic tetrad. Most persons using an "all true" or "all false" response set will include a few answers in the other category, and this alters the profile somewhat. Even in these somewhat more sophisticated attempts at simulation, however, a "mostly true" or "mostly false" response set still is readily apparent merely with a casual examination of the validity scales and indexes.

A response set that is slightly more difficult to detect is a random response set (Profile 3–3). Frequently, this response set is identified as a *random sort*, a term that reflects the early history of the MMPI where the client sorted the items on the card form into "true" and "false" categories.

In random sorts or random response sets, the client endorses the items by randomly marking each item "true" or "false." This set may be suspected when a client completes the MMPI-2 much too quickly. It is important in these cases to confirm that the client has the appropriate intellectual level and

PROFILE 3-1

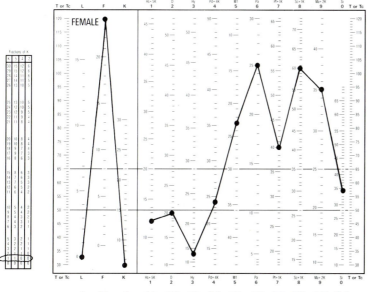

MMPI-2
S.R. Hathaway and J.C. McKinley
*Minnesota Multiphasic
Personality Inventory -2*

Profile for Basic Scales

Minnesota Multiphasic Personality Inventory-2
Copyright © by THE REGENTS OF THE UNIVERSITY OF MINNESOTA
1942, 1943 (renewed 1970), 1989. This Profile Form 1989.
All rights reserved. Distributed exclusively by NATIONAL COMPUTER SYSTEMS, INC.
under license from The University of Minnesota.

"MMPI-2" and "Minnesota Multiphasic Personality Inventory-2" are trademarks owned by
The University of Minnesota. Printed in the United States of America.

Name _____
Address _____
Occupation _____ Date Tested __/__/__
Education _____ Age _____ Marital Status _____
Referred By _____
MMPI-2 Code _____
Scorer's Initials _____

FEMALE

"All True" Response Set

	L	F	K	Hs+.5K 1	D 2	Hy 3	Pd+.4K 4	Mf 5	Pa 6	Pt+1K 7	Sc+1K 8	Ma+.2K 9	Si 0
Raw Score	0	41	1	11	20	13	24	23	25	39	59	35	34
K to be Added				1			0			1	1	0	
Raw Score with K				12			24			40	60	35	

? Raw Score **0**

PROFILE 3-2

MMPI-2

S.R. Hathaway and J.C. McKinley

Minnesota Multiphasic
Personality Inventory -2

Profile for Basic Scales

Name _____

Address _____

Occupation _____ Date Tested _/_/_

Education _____ Age _____ Marital Status _____

Referred By _____

MMPI-2 Code _____

Scorer's Initials _____

MALE

"All False" Response Set

	L	F	K	Hs+.5K 1	D 2	Hy 3	Pd+.4K 4	Mf 5	Pa 6	Pt+1K 7	Sc+1K 8	Ma+.2K 9	Si 0
Raw Score	15	19	29	21	37	47	26	31	15	9	19	11	35
? Raw Score 0													
K to be Added			15			12				29	29	6	
Raw Score with K			36			38				38	48	17	

PROFILE 3-3

Profile for Basic Scales

Minnesota Multiphasic Personality Inventory-2
Copyright © by THE REGENTS OF THE UNIVERSITY OF MINNESOTA
1942, 1943 (renewed 1970), 1989. This Profile Form 1989.
All rights reserved. Distributed exclusively by NATIONAL COMPUTER SYSTEMS, INC.
under license from The University of Minnesota.

"MMPI-2" and "Minnesota Multiphasic Personality Inventory-2" are trademarks owned by
The University of Minnesota. Printed in the United States of America.

Name _____

Address _____

Occupation _____ Date Tested __/__/__

Education _____ Age _____ Marital Status _____

Referred By _____

MMPI-2 Code _____

Scorer's Initials _____

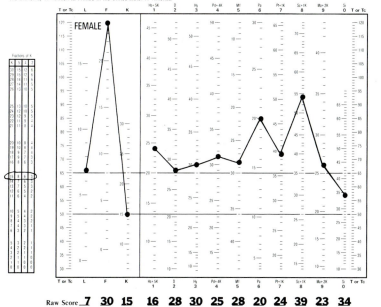

**"Random" Response Set
in Adults**

Raw Score **7 30 15 16 28 30 25 28 20 24 39 23 34**

? Raw Score **0**

K to be Added **8   6   15 15 3**

Raw Score with K **24   31   39 54 26**

NATIONAL
COMPUTER
SYSTEMS

24001

reading ability to complete the MMPI-2. Frequently, clients who are deficient in either area are reluctant to acknowledge their deficiency and instead respond randomly. The most apparent aspects of a random sort are the *F* scale elevation that approaches a T score of 120 and the Scale *8* (Schizophrenia) elevation that approaches a T score of 90. The *L* scale also is elevated higher than would be anticipated with this clinical scale configuration.

Measures of the consistency of item endorsement can be used to assess whether the client has responded randomly. In addition, a clinical interview will readily identify clients with genuine psychopathology who have profiles that appear similar to a random response set. Such clients will be experiencing an acute personality disorganization if they are not overtly psychotic. Frequently, they are so distressed that they are unable to complete the MMPI-2.

Archer, Gordon, and Kirchner (1987) examined the first three MMPI response sets in adolescents and concluded that the "all true" and "all false" responses were very similar to those produced by adults. However, the random response set differed in both shape and elevation (see Profile 3–4). Consequently, it will be even more important to check measures of the consistency of item endorsement with adolescents since the profile produced by a random reponse set is not as clearly deviant as with adults.

Two other response sets are the "all deviant" and "all nondeviant" response sets (see Profile 3–5). These response sets would require the client to answer either all or none of the items like the criterion group for each scale. Both produce theoretical profiles since each procedure requires that items be answered both "true" and "false" when the item is scored "true" on one scale and "false" on another. This double scoring of items occurs more often than might be expected since numerous items are scored on more than one scale

and occasionally with opposite responses as deviant. Although these two profiles are theoretical, they do illustrate the range in which each scale on the MMPI-2 can vary.

OBVIOUS AND SUBTLE ITEMS

Numerous investigators have examined obvious and subtle items on the MMPI (see review by Dubinsky, Gamble, & Rogers, 1985), and there is a tendency for each investigator to define *obvious* and *subtle* somewhat differently (cf. Hryckowian & Gynther, 1988; Ward, 1986). Since the Wiener and Harmon (Wiener, 1948) Obvious and Subtle subscales were reviewed earlier, they will not be covered in this section.

Seeman and associates (Vesprani & Seeman, 1974; Wales & Seeman, 1968, 1972) noted that many of the subtle items are also Zero items, items that are scored for abnormality even though a majority of the normative group endorsed the item in the deviant direction. For example, 57.9 percent of the original normative group endorsed the following item as "true": "At times my thoughts have raced ahead faster than I could speak them." Yet a "true" response to this item is scored both on Scales *5* and *9*. Thus, on these scales the deviant response for this item is "true" despite the fact that a majority of the normative group endorsed this item as "true," since a higher proportion of the criterion groups for these scales answered it in the same direction.

There are 84 Zero items that meet this criterion (see Appendix B in Dahlstrom et al., 1972). Seeman and colleagues further noted that obvious items tended to be X items, which were endorsed by a minority of the original normative group. Consequently, the Zero and X items are roughly comparable the to Wiener and Harmon (Wiener, 1948) Subtle and Obvious items, respectively.

Wales and Seeman (1968) found that subtracting the total number of deviant re-

PROFILE 3-4

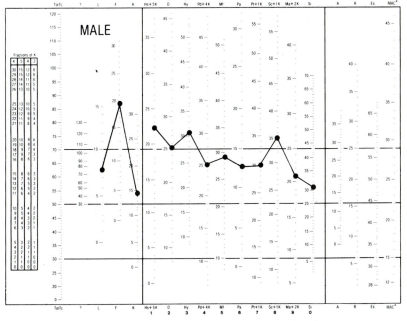

"Random" Response Set

in Adolescents

(Adolescent Norms)

Raw Score 0 7 30 15 16 28 30 25 28 20 24 39 23 34 __ __ __ __

K to be added __   __   __ __ __

Raw Score with K __   __   __ __ __   *49 item version

PROFILE 3-5

Name _____

Address _____

Occupation _____ Date Tested __/__/__

Education _____ Age _____ Marital Status _____

Referred By _____

MMPI-2 Code _____

Scorer's Initials _____

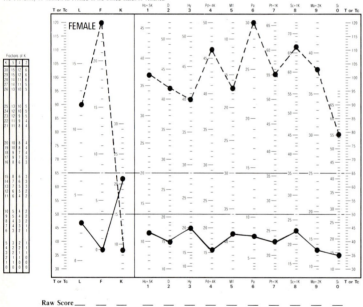

"All Deviant" and "All Nondeviant"
Response Sets

"All Deviant"

"All Nondeviant"
—

Raw Score ___   ___   ___   ___   ___   ___

? Raw Score ___

K to be Added ___   ___   ___   ___

Raw Score with K ___   ___   ___   ___   ___

sponses to the X items from the total number of deviant responses to the Zero items provides a useful index for identifying underreporting of psychopathology. Using 84 Zero and 315 X items, they found that college students instructed to underreport could successfully avoid endorsing the X (obvious) items, but they increased their score on the Zero (subtle) items in the direction of increased psychopathology. Wales and Seeman determined that a cutting score of – 4 for the Zero minus X difference score correctly identified 100 percent of the underreported profiles and 70 percent of the real student profiles.

In extending the investigation of Zero and X items to a psychiatric outpatient sample, Vesprani and Seeman (1974) found a similar pattern. When instructed to endorse the items as their "ideal self," the outpatients decreased their scores on the X (obvious) items and increased their scores on the Zero (subtle) items.

A third method of defining obvious and subtle items on the MMPI was devised by Christian, Burkhart, and Gynther (1978). They asked college students to rate on a 5-point scale from very obvious (5) to very subtle (1) how clearly each item indicated a psychological problem. Mean ratings for each item were used to compute obviousness scores for the standard MMPI validity and clinical scales, the Zero and X items,[5] and Wiener and Harmon's Obvious and Subtle items. A score of 3 indicated a neutral (neither subtle nor obvious) rating. The mean obviousness ratings for the validity and clinical scales, in order from most subtle to most obvious, were:

5 (Masculinity-Femininity)	2.21
K	2.28
L (Lie)	2.41
0 (Social Introversion)	2.64
3 (Hysteria)	2.81
9 (Hypomania)	2.82
2 (Depression)	2.94

1 (Hypochondriasis)	3.13
4 (Psychopathic Deviate)	3.13
7 (Psychasthenia)	3.47
6 (Paranoia)	3.52
8 (Schizophrenia)	3.64
F	3.70

The two surprising ratings are the somewhat subtle mean rating for the L scale, which is routinely described as an obvious scale that does not detect students instructed to underreport psychopathology (Dahlstrom et al., 1972), and the relatively neutral mean rating of Scale 1 (Hypochondriasis), which has been described as a marker variable for obviousness (cf. Wiener, 1948). It is possible that the students insightfully interpreted the L scale items as representing minor social foibles and the Hypochondriasis scale items as representing physical/medical problems rather than interpreting any of these items as representing psychological problems.

The mean ratings for the Zero and X items were 2.04 and 3.16, respectively, and the mean ratings for Wiener's (1948) obvious and subtle items were 2.44 and 3.45, respectively. Christian and associates (1978) noted that the mean ratings for both the X items and Wiener's obvious items fall in their neutral category of neither suble nor obvious. Researchers who are interested in using the Christian and colleagues' ratings of the obviousness of the MMPI items need to remember that their data are reported by Form R item numbers. A table for converting Form R item numbers to Group Booklet item numbers can be found in Dahlstrom and associates (1972).

Using Christian and associates' (1978) five categories of subtlety (very subtle, subtle, neutral, obvious, very obvious), Burkhart, Christian, and Gynther (1978) found that when instructed to overreport psychopathology, students endorsed more neutral, obvious, and very obvious items and fewer very subtle items. When instructed to underreport psychopathology, students endorsed fewer neutral, obvious, and very obvious items and more items in the two subtle categories.

These results suggest that obvious and subtle items can help detect overreporting as well as underreporting response sets, as was outlined above. The pattern of students endorsing more subtle items in the pathologic direction when instructed to underreport confirms previous findings by Vesprani and Seeman (1974). Although the cause of this paradox is unclear, Burkhart and colleagues (1978) conjectured that subtle items may be endorsed more frequently when students are instructed to underreport because such responses are socially desirable.

Using these same five categories of item subtlety (Christian et al., 1978), Gynther Burkhart, and Hovanitz (1979) examined the relationship between subtle, neutral, and obvious subscales of Scale 4 (Psychopathic Deviate) and scores on a nonconformity questionnaire. On the nonconformity scale the obvious and subtle subscales were directly related to the scale score for males; for females, only the obvious and neutral subscales were directly related to nonconformity. They concluded that the obvious subscale predicted nonconformity scores better than the subtle or neutral subscales and that the obvious subscale in conjunction with the subtle subscale was a better predictor than either subscale alone. In this situation the subtle subscale apparently enhanced the predictive power of the obvious subscale.

Gynther and colleagues have extended this same methodology to Scales 2 (Burkhart, Gynther, & Fromuth, 1980), 3 (Gynther & Burkhart, 1983; Wilson, 1980), and 9 (Hovanitz & Gynther, 1980). They found that subtle items supplied little additional information on Scales 2 and 3, and they probably could be omitted on these scales. Subtle items seemed to provide information that was not available from the obvious items on Scale 9. Weed, Ben-Porath, and Butcher (1990)

found that the Wiener and Harmon (Wiener, 1948) Subtle subscales attenuated validity to the same degree as the addition of a random variable.

Snyter and Graham (1984) using a different definition of item subtlety also found that subtle items may have some utility on Scale 9. Similar to Gynther and associates (1979), both Snyter and Graham (1984) and Worthington and Schlottmann (1986) found that the subtle items on Scale 4 did not contribute significantly to the prediction of other test scores.

Grossman and Wasyliw (1988; Wasyliw, Grossman, Haywood, & Cavanaugh, 1988) and Posey and Hess (1984, 1985) have investigated the use of the obvious and subtle subscales in forensic settings to assess malingering. Since Grossman and Wasyliw used the Wiener and Harmon (Wiener, 1948) Obvious and Subtle subscales, and Posey and Hess used the Christian and associates' (1978) ratings of obvious and subtle items, their results are not easily integrated. Their research did generally support the use of obvious and subtle subscales, to assess malingering and can provide direction for future work in this area.

Research on the obvious and subtle items again has raised the issue of the relative merits of empirical versus content strategies of developing personality tests. Are obvious items or subtle items more directly related to the criterion being assessed? And do obvious items or subtle items provide the most efficient means of measuring the criterion? Jackson (1971), Hathaway (1972), Holden and Jackson (1979), and Gynther and Burkhart (1983) have presented overviews of this issue.

ENDNOTES

1. A condensed version of this section can be found in Greene (1989).

2. Reproduced from the MMPI-2 by per-

mission. Copyright © 1943, (renewed 1970), 1989 by the University of Minnesota. Published by the University of Minnesota Press. All rights reserved.

    3. Ibid.

    4. Ibid.

    5. The Zero items used by Christian and colleagues (1978), which are based on the Zero items found in Dahlstrom and colleagues (1972), are not the same as the Zero items used by Seeman and colleagues (cf. Wales & Seeman, 1968).

CHAPTER 4

Clinical Scales

The clinician will need to become thoroughly familiar with the clinical scales reviewed in this chapter, for the information presented forms the basis for understanding combinations of scales to be described in Chapter 6. For each scale the following areas will be surveyed:

1. The content areas tapped by the scale
2. How the scale was developed and the criterion group
3. General psychometric and clinical information
4. Interpretation and behavioral correlates of high scores in psychiatric and normal populations
5. Interpretations of low scores, usually in a normal population
6. The effects on scale scores in adults of moderator variables such as gender, age, education, and social class (ethnic group membership will be discussed in Chapter 8)
7. A summary table of interpretations for the levels of elevation of the scale

Although a few comments have been made about the behavioral correlates of some low points in the MMPI profile, little systematic research has been done. The question of whether the specific elevation of the low point is critical has scarcely been examined. This neglect of investigation of low points on the MMPI in part reflects the tradition that low points represent adjustment, not psychopathology (Carson, 1969); there is some debate, however, regarding the interpretation of low points (Listiak & Stone, 1971).

While interpretation of high-point pairs or codetypes is the primary focus on the MMPI, low points on several scales deserve careful attention regardless of the codetype or overall elevation of the profile. Specifically, those MMPI scales for which low points need particular attention are Scales *3* (Hysteria), *4* (Psychopathic Deviate), *5* (Masculinity-Femininity), *6* (Paranoia), and *9* (Hypomania).

This chapter will discuss, therefore, low points on each of these scales, although it is not clear that these scales will be low points on the MMPI-2 because of the use of uniform T scores. All MMPI-2 scales have been truncated at a T score of 30, which also limits how low scores can go. Clinicians should remember that uniform T scores are used for all of the clinical scales except for Scales *5* and *0* (Social Introversion), which still use linear T scores.

Clinicians generally emphasize interpretation of the codetype (the one or two highest clinical scales elevated at or above a T score of 65) of the MMPI-2. Most of them, however, also rely on individual scales to modify and supplement their interpretations. Contrary to widespread assumptions, little actuarial research has been done on the behavioral correlates of individual MMPI scales. Some investigators (Boerger, Graham, & Lilly, 1974; Hedlund, 1977; Hovey & Lewis, 1967; Zelin, 1971) have begun to examine the correlates of individual MMPI scales, and their results will be reported throughout this chapter. Obviously, there has been little research on the behavioral correlates of individual MMPI-2 scales.

The reader should note that comments in the text to specific T scores reflecting high scores, moderate scores, and low scores on a specific scale refer to the MMPI-2. Rather than indicate parenthetically each time the comparable score on the MMPI, these scores will only be noted in the tables describing the interpretation of each scale below.

SCALE *1*: HYPOCHONDRIASIS (*Hs*)

A wide variety of vague and nonspecific complaints about bodily functioning are tapped by the 32 items (33 items on the MMPI) of Scale *1*. These complaints tend to focus on the abdomen and back, and they persist despite all reassurances and negative medical tests to the contrary. Scale *1* is designed to assess a neurotic concern over bodily functioning (i.e., psychotic concerns about bodily functioning are not found on this scale).

The criterion group used in developing the scale was a group of hypochondriacs with abnormal, psychoneurotic concern over bodily functioning (McKinley & Hathaway, 1940). (The development of Scale *1* was described in detail in Chapter 1; the reader should review that material if necessary. The reader also should note that the current DSM-III-R [American Psychiatric Association, 1987] definition of *hypochondriasis* emphasizes the fear or belief of the existence of a *serious* disease rather than abnormal concern over bodily functioning.)

Examples of Scale *1* items with the deviant answer indicated in parentheses are:

"I hardly ever feel pain in the back of my neck." (false)

"I have a great deal of stomach trouble." (true)

"The top of my head sometimes feels tender." (true)[1]

Most of the items on Scale *1* also are scored on the other clinical scales; only 8 items are unique to the scale. A majority of the items (20) overlap with Scale *3* (Hysteria) and are scored in the same direction. Only 5 of the items overlap with scales from the psychotic tetrad (the Paranoia, Psychasthenia, Schizophrenia, and Hypomania scales), 4 items with Scale *8* (Schizophrenia), and 1 item with Scale *6* (Paranoia).

The deviant response for two-thirds of the items on Scale *1* is "false"; hence, a tendency toward a "false" response set will elevate scores on this scale. The scale items appear to be obvious in content (Dahlstrom, Welsh, & Dahlstrom, 1972), although Christian, Burkhart, and Gynther (1978) found that students rated Scale *1* items as neutral (neither obvious nor subtle) when asked how clearly these items were indicative of a psychological problem.

Factor analyses of the items in several different populations have consistently identified one common factor, which has been labeled *poor physical health* (Comrey, 1957a; Eichman, 1962; O'Connor & Stefic, 1959; Stein, 1968) and a second factor, labeled *gastrointestinal difficulties* (Comrey, 1957a; O'Connor & Stefic, 1959).

The 33-item Tryon, Stein, and Chu (Stein, 1968) Bodily Symptoms scale (see Chapter 5), which was developed by a cluster analysis of all 550 items on the MMPI, contains 23 items from Scale *1*. Wiggins' (1966) content scales of Organic Symptoms and Poor Health from the MMPI, which were developed on a rational or intuitive basis (see Chapter 5), also overlap substantially with Scale *1*. The 36-item Organic Symptoms scale has 13 items in common with Scale *1* and the 28-item Poor Health scale also contains 13 Scale *1* items. Butcher, Graham, Williams, and Ben-Porath's (1989) content scale of Health Concerns from the MMPI-2 (see Chapter 5) has 23 items of its 36 items in common with Scale *1*.

Thus, it seems whether an empirical, rational, or statistical procedure is used, a general dimension of poor physical health and vague somatic complaints can be identified in the MMPI-2 item pool in a variety of populations, and Scale *1* adequately assesses this dimension.

A person who is actually physically ill will obtain only a moderate elevation (T score of 58 to 64) on Scale *1*. Such persons will endorse their legitimate physical complaints, but they will not endorse the entire gamut of vague physical complaints tapped by the scale. Scale *2* (Depression) is more likely to be elevated by actual physical illness than Scale *1*. If a client with actual physical illness obtains a T score of 65 or higher on Scale *1*, there are likely to be hypochondriacal features in addition to the physical condition, and the client is probably trying to manipulate or control significant others in the environment with the hypochondriacal complaints. Although the client may vehemently argue that the complaints reflect legitimate physical con-

cerns, the clinician should not ignore the elevation on Scale *1*. The hypochondriacal features in these individuals usually are evident despite their protests to the contrary.

Scale *1* is a crude index of psychological mindedness or sophistication, with high scorers lacking these attributes. It also is negatively correlated with intelligence (Brower, 1947). This would substantiate the lack of psychological mindedness in high scorers. Such persons are uninterested in exploring any psychological reasons for their bodily complaints. In fact, pity the clinician who directly suggests such a relationship; the client concludes that the clinician is poorly trained since he or she does not recognize the symptoms as genuine. With disparaging comments about their clinician's lack of training and skills to understand them, these clients trudge off to seek a more favorable second, third, and fourth opinion.

The robustness of these hypochondriacal features often amazes the neophyte clinician, who seemingly can readily recognize the client's motives. Despite, or perhaps because of, the transparency of the motives, any form of psychological intervention is almost surely doomed to fail. Thus, Scale *1* can be understood as a characterologic scale (i.e., it reflects a long-term personality style that is stable over time and resistant to change).

High scorers (T scores of 65 or higher) on Scale *1* in any population are characterized by their abnormal concern over bodily functions and vague hypochondriacal complaints, which attests to the construct validity of the scale. In addition, high scorers are described as pessimistic, sour on life, and evidencing long-standing personal inadequacy and ineffectualness. They seem to relish exaggerating the ills of the world and of their own situation. They rarely express hostility overtly; instead, they express their resentment covertly by using physical complaints to control and manipulate others. Finally, they are unlikely to be diagnosed psychotic, although an occasional psychotic individual with somatic delusions may simultaneously elevate Scales *1* and *8*.

Low scorers (T scores less than 45) on Scale *1* are a heterogeneous group since their common characteristic is the nonendorsement of hypochondriacal complaints. They are described as alert, spontaneous, and not unduly concerned about the adverse reactions of others. Good and Brantner (1961) commented that low scorers may be denying hypochondriacal complaints, but no research has documented this hypothesis. Persons who have worked or lived with hypochondriacs also tend to earn low scores on Scale *1*. Whether the difficulty in working with or relating to hypochondriacs results in a rejection of this personality style or some other factor is involved has not been investigated. Mental health professionals also score in this range.

Test-retest reliability coefficients for Scale *1* are among the largest for any of the MMPI clinical scales, with correlations ranging from .79 to .86 for up to a two-week interval and .38 to .65 for a one-year interval (Dahlstrom, Welsh, & Dahlstrom, 1975). Test-retest reliability coefficients for Scale *1* on the MMPI-2 for approximately a one-week interval are .85 for men and .85 for women (Butcher, Dahlstrom, Graham, Tellegen, & Kaemmer, 1989).

Women tend to endorse a few more Scale *1* items than men (Butcher et al., 1989; Colligan, Osborne, Swenson, & Offord, 1989; Dahlstrom et al., 1972). Scores on Scale *1* also tend to increase slightly with age in normal individuals; persons older than age 65 endorse on the average about two to three more items than their younger counterparts (Colligan et al., 1989; Dahlstrom et al., 1972). However, medical patients do *not* endorse more Scale *1* items with increasing age (Swenson, Pearson, & Osborne, 1973). Persons from lower socioeconomic classes also are more likely to endorse Scale *1* items.

A summary of the interpretations for four levels of elevation of Scale *1* is provided in Table 4–1.

SCALE *2:* DEPRESSION (*D*)

The 57 items (60 items on the MMPI) of Scale *2* measure symptomatic depression, which is a general attitude characterized by poor morale, lack of hope in the future, and general dissatisfaction with one's own status (Hathaway & McKinley, 1942). The major content areas deal with a lack of interest in activities expressed as general apathy, physical symptoms including sleep disturbances and gastrointestinal complaints, and excessive sensitivity and lack of sociability (Dahlstrom et al., 1972).

Scale *2* was derived empirically, using an approach identical to that used for Scale *1*. The criterion group used in developing Scale *2* consisted of 50 patients who represented relatively uncomplicated cases of the depressed phase of manic-depressive psychosis. Their responses were contrasted with a normal group to produce a preliminary depression scale.

As with Scale *1*, it was found that some nondepressed clients also scored high on this preliminary depression scale. Consequently, the responses of 50 such nondepressed patients who scored high on this preliminary scale of depression were compared with those of the criterion group, resulting in the identification of 11 correction items that distinguished these two groups of patients. These correction items were scored so that patients who were actually clinically depressed achieved higher scores on the scale. The addition of the 11 correction items resulted in the 60 items that currently appear on Scale *2* of the MMPI.

Each of these 60 items was required to meet the following criterion: The frequency of its endorsement had to increase progressively from the normal group through a normal group with depression (normals who

TABLE 4–1 Interpretation of Levels of Elevation on Scale *1:* Hypochondriasis (*Hs*)

MMPI-2 T Score	MMPI T Score	Interpretation
44 and below	40 and below	1. *Low.* These clients may be denying the presence of vague physical complaints. Scores in this range are typical for persons in helping professions and for children of a hypochondriacal parent.
45–57	41–59	2. *Normal.* These clients have a typical number of physical complaints.
58–64	60–69	3. *Moderate.* Scores in the lower end of this range are typical for physically handicapped persons and persons with actual physical illness. These clients have some concern about their bodily functioning and are likely to be seen as immature, stubborn, and lacking drive. Review of content and/or supplementary scales may facilitate interpretation in this range.
65 and above	70 and above	4. *Marked.* These clients are excessively concerned about vague physical complaints and use them to manipulate and control others. They are cynical, whiny, demanding of attention, and generally negative and pessimistic. The prognosis for either psychological or physical intervention is guarded. These clients focus on vague bodily complaints and resist any form of resolution. Conservative interventions reassuring these clients about their bodily complaints are indicated. Review of the content and/or supplementary scales may facilitate interpretation at the lower end of this range.

achieved high scores on the preliminary depression scale) to the criterion group. The depressed normal group was used to help establish the meaning of intermediate scale values between the normal and criterion groups, which would have been impossible if only the two extreme groups were contrasted.

Examples of Scale *2* items with the deviant response indicated in parentheses are:

"I am easily awakened by noise." (true)

"I usually feel that life is worthwhile." (false)

"I believe I am no more nervous than most others." (false)[2]

Scale *2* is thought to measure reactive or exogenous depression rather than "neurotic" or endogenous depression. Accordingly, scores are expected to fluctuate as the client's mood changes. Thus, Scale *2* is an index of how comfortable and secure clients feel about themselves and the environment, with higher scores indicating dissatisfaction. As clients' evaluations of themselves or of the situation changes, scores on Scale *2* should change concomitantly.

It may seem unusual that a psychotic criterion group was used to develop a scale that is part of the neurotic triad (Scales *1, 2,* and *3*) and is thought to measure reactive depression (Carson, 1969; Dahlstrom et al., 1972). This paradox may be partially explained by Hathaway and McKinley's interest in developing this scale to measure symptomatic depression, which can be a reaction to a variety of causes (such as economic crises, vocational difficulties, or personal problems) and which occurs in a multitude of psychopathologic conditions.

With Hathaway and McKinley's (1942) interest in assessing reactive depression, the specific diagnosis of the criterion group was not important as long as depression was a

central feature. Since reactive depression is
not a stable trait and will vary markedly over
time, using patients in the depressed phase of
manic-depressive psychosis as a criterion
group insured that the depressive features
were pronounced and central.

Most of the items on Scale 2 are scored
on the other clinical scales as well. Only 10
items are unique to Scale 2 on the MMPI-2,
and 3 of these are correction items; 13 items
are unique to Scale 2 on the MMPI, and 6 of
these are correction items. The overlapping
items are relatively evenly distributed among
the other clinical scales. The deviant response
for two-thirds of the items on Scale 2 is
"false" so that a tendency to endorse the
MMPI-2 items as "false" inflates the scores
on Scale 2. (A score on *TRIN* that is less than
9 would be expected in such cases; see Chapter 3.)

Wiener and Harmon (Wiener, 1948)
judged two-thirds of the items to be obvious
in content. Clients who are severely depressed
are more likely to endorse obvious items,
whereas mildly depressed persons tend to endorse
subtle items (Dahlstrom et al., 1972).
Thus, it seems that persons are unlikely to endorse
items with obvious depressive content
until they are significantly depressed (Nelson,
1987).

Comrey's (1957b) factor analysis of
MMPI items on Scale 2 revealed that 28 of
the items loaded on a factor that he labeled
neuroticism; 12 other items loaded on a factor
called *poor physical health*. Only 8 items
from Scale 2 are found on Wiggins' (1966)
content scale of Depression, and 10 items are
contained within the Tryon, Stein, and Chu
(Stein, 1968) cluster scale of Depression.
Butcher and associates' (1989) content scale
of Depression from the MMPI-2 (see Chapter
5) has only 9 of its 33 items in common with
Scale 2.

Apparently, all of these depression
scales vary dramatically depending on how
they were constructed. Moreover, due to the

ubiquitous nature of depression, the developers
of the various depression scales may have
used divergent samples in constructing their
measures. Research that investigates the relationships
among these different depression
scales and their relationship to depressive behaviors
is urgently needed.

Harris and Lingoes (1955) formed subscales
on Scale 2 of the MMPI by subjectively
grouping together the items that were either
similar in content or seemed to reflect a single
attitude or trait. Following this procedure,
they identified five groups of items within
Scale 2: Subjective Depression, Psychomotor
Retardation, Physical Malfunctioning, Mental
Dullness, and Brooding (see Table 4–2).
The Harris and Lingoes subscales have not
been changed on the MMPI-2.

The purpose of the Harris and Lingoes
(1955) subscales is to facilitate interpretation
of identical scores on Scale 2. A client can obtain
a specific raw score on the scale by endorsing
items from any one or various combinations
of the subscales. Knowing the
subscale scores should help the clinician understand
the exact nature of each client's depression,
especially when two or more clients
have identical raw scores.

Harris and Lingoes (1955) did not restrict
items to only one subscale; consequently,
there is extensive item overlap between
some of the subscales. For example, all
10 items on the Brooding subscale also appear
on the Subjective Depression subscale,
and 12 of the 15 items on the Mental Dullness
subscale are on the Subjective Depression
subscale. Other subscales, such as the Physical
Malfunctioning subscale, have few or no
items in common with the other subscales.

Miller and Streiner (1985) found that
judges who were asked to reproduce the
groups of items from the Harris and Lingoes
subscales agreed reliably only on 9 of the 28
subscales (Physical Malfunctioning [D_3]; Denial
of Social Anxiety [Hy_1]; Need for Affection
[Hy_2]; Somatic Complaints [Hy_4]; Family

TABLE 4–2 Description of High Scorers on the Harris and Lingoes Subscales for Scale *2* (Depression)

| Subscale | | | |
Name	Abbre-viation	Number of Items	Description of High Scorers
Subjective Depression	D_1	32	These clients lack joy in doing things, are pessimistic, and have poor morale and low self-esteem; they complain about psychological inertia and lack of energy for coping with problems.
Psychomotor Retardation	D_2	14	These clients are nonparticipative in social relations and are immobile.
Physical Malfunctioning	D_3	11	These clients complain about physical malfunctioning and are preoccupied with themselves.
Mental Dullness	D_4	15	These clients are unresponsive and distrustful of their own psychological functioning.
Brooding	D_5	10	These clients are ruminative and irritable.

Discord [Pd_1]; Naivete [Pa_3]; Lack of Ego Mastery, Cognitive [Sc_3]; Bizarre Sensory Experiences [Sc_6]; and Amorality [Ma_1]). For 10 of these subscales, the judges did not agree on a single item. It appears that this subset of 9 Harris and Lingoes subscales warrant clinical use and further research.

Little research has been conducted on the Harris and Lingoes subscales. The research that does exist consists primarily of reporting means and standard deviations for these subscales for various samples of individuals (cf. Gordon & Swart, 1973; Panton, 1959b).

Lingoes (1960) identified seven factors in his factor analysis of all 28 of the Harris and Lingoes subscales, which suggests that these subscales are capable of providing information beyond that contained within the standard clinical scales. However, Bernstein and Garbin (1985) concluded that none of the subscales (Comrey or Harris and Lingoes) could explain the item structure of Scale *2*

and they suggested that the entire Scale should be used rather than any set of subscales.

Unless some form of computer scoring of the MMPI-2 is used, it is extremely time-consuming to score all MMPI-2 supplementary scales and subscales, such as the Harris and Lingoes subscales. Given all the caveats noted above, the Harris and Lingoes subscales may provide helpful interpretive information when Scale *2* is between a T score of 60 and 80. When Scale *2* exceeds a T score of 80, all subscales usually are elevated above a T score of 70, and when there is a T score below 60, none of the subscales will likely be elevated above a T score of 70.

These subscales should not be interpreted unless they exceed a T score of 70 because of their restricted variance; on some subscales, endorsing one additional or one fewer item will change the client's score by 5 to 10 T score points. These general guidelines for interpreting the Harris and Lingoes subscales for Scale *2* also apply to the Harris and Lingoes subscales for Scales *3* (Hysteria), *4* (Psychopathic Deviate), *6* (Paranoia), *8* (Schizophrenia), and *9* (Hypomania). Harris and Lingoes (1955) did not develop subscales for the other clinical scales.

A description of high scorers on the Harris and Lingoes subscales for Scale *2* appears in Table 4–2.

Interpretation of Scale *2* varies markedly depending on which other clinical scales are elevated in conjunction with it; consequently, the scale is one of the most difficult clinical scales to interpret in isolation. An elevated score on Scale *2* reveals that the client is upset and feeling depressed about something; the precise source of the distress, however, cannot be deduced from the scale alone.

For example, a person in legal custody who is unhappy about being incarcerated and a client in psychotherapy who is concerned about self-worth may obtain similar raw scores on Scale *2*; their depressions, however, clearly emanate from different sources. These sources will be evident from the elevations on the other clinical scales: Scales *4* (Psychopathic Deviate) and *9* (Hypomania) are likely to be the two highest scales for the person in custody, whereas Scales *2* and *7* (Psychasthenia) will probably be the highest scales for the client in psychotherapy.

When Scale *2* is the only clinical scale elevated above a T score of 65, a careful evaluation of suicidal risk is indicated, particularly if there are no overt behavioral signs of depression (Carson, 1969; Graham, 1987). Suicide risk in such clients is generally considered to be greater than when depression is more demonstrable clinically. The MMPI-2 contains four items (150, 506, 520, and 524) that directly inquire about suicidal ideation and attempts. These four items should be reviewed routinely in all clients regardless of the consistency or accuracy of item endorsement.

Other than these three specific items, the MMPI-2 does not adequately assess suicide risk, and the clinician is well advised to use more appropriate assessment techniques, such as a directive clinical interview if suicide risk is an issue. Even using the MMPI-2 to identify groups of individuals who may be suicide risks is questionable because of the inordinate number of false positives and false negatives that may be generated by any MMPI-2 index used to predict suicide risk. The use of the MMPI-2 in assessing suicide risk will be examined more fully in Chapter 5.

High scorers (T scores of 65 or higher) on Scale *2* have been described in a variety of ways; this variety reflects the fact that depressive features are found as a concomitant to all types of behavior and psychopathology. General descriptions of high scorers indicate that they are depressed, anxious, moody, and inhibited. They display excessive sensitivity to their own depressed level of functioning and usually are withdrawn and isolated. To the extent that these negative attributes represent dissatisfaction with oneself, they will serve as an internal pressure to change and hence are a good prognostic sign.

High scorers also frequently have somatic symptoms and complaints, sleep difficulties, and a loss of appetite. Moreover, they are rather consistently described as not being hyperactive, excited, or belligerent toward others.

Persons with elevated scores on Scale *2* are acknowledging their personal discomfort and dissatisfaction with their current level of functioning. Their subjective distress may represent anxiety and its concomitants, or it may represent a genuine depressive condition. Thus, persons with elevations on Scale *2* will not always be diagnosed as being depressed, since their diagnosis will reflect their prominent symptoms and behaviors. Regardless of their diagnosis, these clients are acknowledging their dissatisfaction with their present circumstances.

Clinicians have been cautioned about

the interpretation of high Scale 2 scores in the aged because of the increase in scores that occurs in normal individuals (cf. Colligan, Osborne, Swenson, & Offord, 1983, 1989; Dahlstrom et al., 1975). It has been conjectured that the elderly may be reporting more physical symptoms, which elevates Scale 2.

However, Dye, Bohm, Anderten, and Won Cho (1983) reported that older psychiatric patients (age 60+) did not express concern over declining physical health as symptoms of their depression, although concern over physical well-being did become more important as reflected by the factor structure. They also noted that there were subtle qualitative changes in the expression of depression across their three age groups. The performance of the aged on the MMPI-2 is a topic that needs additional research (see Chapter 8).

Persons with moderate elevations (T scores from 58 to 64) on Scale 2 are generally described in similar but less extreme terms. Such persons are seen as shy, prone to worry and depression, and dissatisfied, either with themselves or their personal situation. Bieliauskas and Shekelle (1983) found that normal males with moderate elevations on Scale 2 of the MMPI frequently felt nervous or upset and they spent a lower percentage of time in bed sleeping. They also were more likely to be rated as appearing emotionally tense.

Low scorers (T scores below 45) should be evaluated carefully since some kind of depressive mood should be present in most, if not all, clients in psychiatric settings. Scores in this range suggest that the clients are not affected adversely by the behaviors that led to their referral for an evaluation. *The clinician should note well that scores in the normal range or below are not appropriate in psychiatric clients.* Low scorers are generally described as active, alert, socially outgoing, and effective in a variety of tasks. Some persons with low scores also are described as un-

dercontrolled; this can be manifested by ostentatiousness, sarcasm, or exhibitionism. For some, their activity, aggressiveness, and tendency to show off interferes with their interpersonal relationships.

It is unclear whether other scales in the profile will help to differentiate among these subtypes of persons with low scores. Very low scores (T scores of approximately 35) seem to represent an inability to tolerate anxiety and a tendency to act out, which could play a role in some of the negative behaviors described above. Although this inability to tolerate anxiety makes sense logically, it has not been tested empirically.

Reliability coefficients for Scale 2 on the MMPI are not as low as might be anticipated, given that the scale is a measure of reactive depression that should vary over time. Generally, reliability coefficients for this scale are comparable to those for the other clinical scales. Reliability coefficients of .80 to .90 for intervals up to a month and .40 to .50 for intervals up to a year or more are common (Dahlstrom et al., 1975). Test-retest reliability coefficients for Scale 2 on the MMPI-2 for approximately a one-week interval are .75 for men and .77 for women (Butcher et al., 1989).

Women tend to endorse more items on Scale 2 than men, and older, normal persons tend to endorse more items than younger, normal persons (Colligan et al., 1983, 1989; Dahlstrom et al., 1972; Leon, Gillum, Gillum, & Gouze, 1979). However, scores on Scale 2 do *not* increase with age in medical patients (Swenson et al., 1973) or psychiatric patients (Hedlund & Won Cho, 1979).

The interpretation of Scale 2 at four levels of elevation is summarized in Table 4–3.

SCALE 3: HYSTERIA (*Hy*)

The 60 items of Scale 3 consist of two general types: items reflecting specific somatic complaints and items that show that the client

TABLE 4–3   Interpretation of Levels of Elevation on Scale *2:* Depression (*D*)

MMPI-2 T Score	MMPI T Score	Interpretation
44 and below	40 and below	1. *Low.* These clients tend to be alert, gregarious, and active. Be sure that these behaviors are appropriate for the person's situation and setting (i.e., clients should rarely be scoring in this range).
45–57	41–59	2. *Normal.* These clients have a typical number of attitudes and behaviors that reflect symptomatic depression.
58–64	60–69	3. *Moderate.* These clients are dissatisfied with something or with themselves, but they may not recognize this state as depression. Their mild degree of dissatisfaction may appropriately represent the situation. Or they may not really be concerned about what is happening to them, or they may have learned to adjust to a chronic depressed existence. Review of the content and/or supplementary scales may facilitate interpretation in this range.
65 and above	70 and above	4. *Marked.* These clients exhibit a general sadness and depressed mood either about life or themselves. The clinician can determine the source of this depressed mood either by asking the client or by examining the clinical scales. As the scores increase, the pessimism, depression, and hopelessness begin to pervade the client's entire life. These clients tend to be depressed, withdrawn, guilty, and self-deprecating. Review of the content and/or supplementary scales may assist the clinician in interpretation at the lower end of this range.

considers himself or herself well socialized and adjusted. Although these two types of items are either unrelated or negatively correlated in normal individuals, they are closely associated in persons whose personality revolves around histrionic dynamics. Such persons generally maintain a facade of superior adjustment and only when they are under stress does their proneness to develop conversion-type symptoms as a means of resolving conflict and avoiding responsibility appear.

Scale *3* was developed on an empirical basis, using a criterion group composed of 50 patients with either a diagnosis of hysteria or identifiable histrionic personality components. The original Hysteria scale included numerous somatic complaint items that also appeared on Scale *1* (Hypochondriasis). In an effort to differentiate Scales *1* and *3*, McKinley and Hathaway (1944) eliminated the duplicate items from Scale *3*; this, however,

reduced the validity of Scale *3*. Therefore, these items were returned to Scale *3* and deleted from Scale *1* (see discussion of the construction of Scale *1* in Chapter 1). The result was the current 60 items on Scale *3*.

Examples of the items with the deviant answer indicated in parentheses are:

"Much of the time my head seems to hurt all over." (true)

"I often wonder what hidden reason another person may have for doing something nice for me." (false)

"It is safer to trust nobody." (false)[3]

Preliminary use of Scale *3* revealed that clients tended to score similarly on Scales *1* and *3*. Clinical experience, however, demonstrated valid clinical differences in prognosis and treatment for clients who scored relatively higher on Scale *1* or Scale *3*, so Mc-

Kinley and Hathaway (1944) decided to retain both scales.

Clients who scored higher on Scale *1* than Scale *3* tended to have diffuse, vague physical complaints, and the role of psychological factors in their disability was readily apparent. Clients who scored higher on Scale *3* than Scale *1* were less obviously neurotic; in fact, they appeared normal psychologically except when under stress. Their physical complaints tended to be specific and were likely to be psychosomatic in nature. Further differences between high scorers on these two scales will be detailed in Chapter 6.

Almost all items on Scale *3* are scored on other clinical scales; only 10 items are unique to Scale *3*. One-third of the Scale *3* items overlap with Scale *1* (even after the duplicate somatic complaints items were deleted from Scale *1*) and are scored in the same direction. Thus, it stands to reason that these two scales often are simultaneously elevated due to their shared variance.

The other overlapping Scale *3* items are distributed relatively evenly across the other clinical scales. There are 10 items on Scale *3* that overlap with the *K* scale, and they are scored in the same direction. Although Scale *3* is not *K*-corrected, the fact that they share 10 items functionally produces a result similar to a *K*-correction of .33. Consequently, when a non-*K*-corrected profile is constructed (see Chapter 2), the contribution of the *K* scale to Scale *3* cannot be removed directly.

As with the other scales in the neurotic triad (Scales *1*, *2*, and *3*), "false" is the deviant response for 47 (78 percent) of the items on Scale *3*. The profile for an "all false" response set in Chapter 3 illustrates the emphasis on "false" as the deviant response on the neurotic triad scales. Wiener and Harmon (Wiener, 1948) judged the items on Scale *3* to be almost evenly split between obvious and subtle items.

Studies of the associations among individual items on Scale *3* have yielded generally convergent results. Using factor analysis, Comrey (1957c) identified five factors: *poor physical health*, *shyness*, *cynicism*, *headaches*, and *neuroticism*. Through cluster analysis, Little and Fisher (1958) identified two relatively independent clusters of items: *admission of physiologic symptoms* and *denial*.

These two clusters were used to develop the Admission (*Ad*) and Denial (*Dn*) scales. The *Ad* scale correlates positively (.89–.90) with Scale *1*, which is logical since the two scales have 18 items in common. The *Dn* scale correlates positively (.78–.88) with the *K* scale, with which it has 9 items in common. Clients who score high on the *Ad* scale complain about their somatic functioning and have poor interpersonal relationships. High scorers on the *Dn* scale are described as lacking insight into their own behavior and morally virtuous. Little and Fisher (1958) believe that when both of these scales are elevated, the person should have conversion reaction dynamics.

Harris and Lingoes (1955) identified five subscales within Scale *3*: Denial of Social Anxiety, Need for Affection, Lassitude-Malaise, Somatic Complaints, and Inhibition of Aggression (see Table 4–4). Two of these subscales overlap substantially with the *Ad* scale: Lassitude-Malaise has 14 of its 15 items in common with the *Ad* scale, and Somatic Complaints has 16 of its 17 items in common with the *Ad* scale. The other three subscales—Denial of Social Anxiety, Need for Affection, and Inhibition of Aggression— overlap completely with the *Dn* scale, except that Inhibition of Aggression has one item that does not appear on *Dn*.

Because of this almost complete overlap between the *Ad* and *Dn* scales and the Harris and Lingoes subscales for Scale *3*, it is unnecessary to score both groups of scales. If the clinician chooses to score the Harris and Lingoes subscales, it is possible to obtain a close

TABLE 4-4 Description of High Scorers on the Harris and Lingoes Subscales for Scale *3* (Hysteria)

Subscale			
Name	Abbre-viation	Number of Items	Description of High Scorers
Denial of Social Anxiety	Hy_1	6	These clients are characterized by social extroversion.
Need for Affection	Hy_2	12	These clients obtusely deny that they have a critical or resentful attitude toward others. They consider themselves impunitive, and they overly protest their optimism and faith in other people.
Lassitude-Malaise	Hy_3	15	These clients complain about functioning below par physically and mentally. They effortfully keep up a good front, but they need attention and reassurance.
Somatic Complaints	Hy_4	17	These clients exhibit somatic complaints of a kind that suggest repression and conversion of affect.
Inhibition of Aggression	Hy_5	7	These clients express concurrence with others and disavow violence.

approximation of the *Ad* and *Dn* scale scores by combining the raw scores on the appropriate subscales and converting these to T scores using the means and standard deviations for *Ad* and *Dn* (see Appendix D).

Two of Wiggins' (1966) content scales share items with the subscales for Scale *3*: the Organic Symptoms scale has 11 items, and the Poor Health scale has 3 items in common with the Somatic Complaints subscale. Prokop (1986) has shown how the Harris and Lingoes subscales for Scale *3* can be useful in the treatment of low back pain patients, and Miller and Streiner (1985) found that the items on three of these five subscales could be replicated by judges. The subscales for Scale *3* seem to be assessing similar functions in a variety of populations, and they appear to warrant continued clinical use and experimental investigation.

The *Dn* scale (Little & Fisher, 1958) has been used in many studies of defensive styles and their effects on behavior (cf. Weinstein, Averill, Opton, & Lazarus, 1968). The *Dn* scale also shares 19 of its 26 items with Byrne, Barry, and Nelson's (1963) Repression-Sensitization scale, which has been extensively investigated as a measure of personality. The clinician who is interested in pursuing this line of research should consult Dahlstrom and associates (1975) for a review.

High scorers on Scale *3* (T scores of 65 or higher) are described as self-centered, immature, and infantile. They are demanding of attention and manipulative in interpersonal relationships. They tend to be uninhibited and outgoing in their social relationships, although they relate with others on a superficial and immature level. As their T score on Scale *0* (Social Introversion) approaches 30, the superficiality and lack of real intimacy in their interpersonal relationships becomes even more apparent.

Their insensitivity to others and lack of

empathy reflect their egocentric involvement. Their primary defenses are denial and repression, and they generally appear to be defensive and overcontrolled. They tend to be emotionally immature and labile. A profound fear of pain, both emotional and physical, may characterize high scorers. When under stress, high scorers are likely to display specific physical complaints such as headaches, chest pains, or tachycardia. At these times they also display transient depressive features and anxiety. High scorers on Scale 3 are rarely psychotic, although their symptomatology may be quite dramatic during periods of stress.

Because of their strong need to be liked and their desire to make a good initial impression on others, high scorers appear to be good candidates for psychological interventions since they probably will respond positively to the clinician. Their desire for attention and support further suggests that they will enjoy interacting with the clinician. They are, however, generally intolerant of analysis of their personality dynamics and frequently place inordinate demands on their clinician. Their histrionic style usually is so deeply ingrained that they are unaware of it. When the clinician points out the realities of their situation, they frequently cannot see their role in it and complain that the clinician does not understand them. Thus, despite the positive initial impression, any form of psychological intervention will be a trying task for the clinician.

Low scorers on Scale 3 (T scores less than 45) are described as socially isolated, conforming, and relatively unadventurous. They are likely to have limited interests. They tend to feel that life is tough and are sarcastic and caustic. They are seen as having few defenses to protect them from the external environment and consequently are vulnerable to a harsh and overwhelming environment.

Elevated scores on Scale 3 can be interpreted relatively successfully in isolation from the other clinical scales since the behavioral and clinical correlates of Scale 3 are usually stable regardless of scores on the other clinical scales. The clinician should be sure, however, that the client has endorsed both sets of items within Scale 3—specific somatic complaints and denial of psychological problems—before interpreting it in isolation; that is, all subscales should be elevated above a T score of 70.

However, McGrath and O'Malley (1986) found that Scales K, 1, and 3 needed to be elevated to insure that both denial of problems and specific somatic complaints were present. The statement is sometimes made (Duckworth & Anderson, 1986) that the client will see and acknowledge behaviors indicated by clinical scales whose elevations are higher than Scale 3 but deny and fail to see behaviors indicated by scales whose elevations are lower than Scale 3. Thus, if Scales 2 and 3 are at T scores of 80 and 70, respectively, the client is reputed to see and acknowledge the depressive features. If these T scores are reversed, however, the client purportedly will deny the depressive features. Since no research has investigated this hypothesized relationship, the clinician is cautioned against a noncritical use of such interpretations.

Test-retest reliability coefficients for Scale 3 on the MMPI range from .63 to .84 for intervals up to two weeks and from .36 to .72 for intervals up to one year (Dahlstrom et al., 1975). Test-retest reliability coefficients for Scale 3 on the MMPI-2 for approximately a one-week interval are .72 for men and .76 for women (Butcher et al., 1989).

Females endorse more Scale 3 items than males. Age appears to have little impact on Scale 3 in normal individuals (Colligan et al., 1983, 1989), medical patients (Swenson et al., 1973), or psychiatric patients (Hedlund & Won Cho, 1979). Scale 3 is likely to be a peak score in normal women and unlikely to be a low point in either normal men or women (Gulas, 1974). Scale 3 will reliably separate groups of clients with psychophysiological symptoms (Lair & Trapp, 1962) and conversion symptoms (Fricke, 1956) from other groups, but pronounced overlap usually exists among the individual scale scores in these groups of clients.

The interpretation of Scale *3* at four levels of elevation is summarized in Table 4–5.

Neurotic Triad Configurations

Four configurations encompass the most frequently encountered relationships among the three scales in the neurotic triad—Scales *1* (Hypochondriasis), *2* (Depression), and *3* (Hysteria). Since these configurations will be described in more detail in Chapter 6 under their respective codetypes, the review here will be brief.

The first configuration is a conversion "V" (see Figure 4–1). A client with this configuration is converting personally distressing troubles into more rational or socially acceptable problems; that is, the person is convert-

ing psychological problems into somatic complaints. The overall elevation of this configuration reflects the amount of psychological distress that the client is experiencing.

As Scales *1* and *3* both approach a T score of 90, the tenuousness of these defenses becomes readily apparent to everyone except the client. The relative elevation of Scale *2* compared to Scales *1* and *3* also reflects the adequacy of the "conversion defenses." The greater the relative elevation of Scales *1* and *3* compared to Scale *2*, the more severe, long-standing, and resistant to change are the client's defenses against facing the actual source of distress in his or her life.

The other important characteristic of this configuration is the relative elevation of Scales *1* and *3*. When Scale *3* is higher than Scale *1*, the client tends to be optimistic about physical complaints, which are specific and usually focused in the head and the extremities. In contrast, the client with Scale *1* higher than Scale *3* tends to be bitter and pessimistic about vague and general physical complaints.

TABLE 4–5   Interpretation of Levels of Elevation on Scale *3:* Hysteria (*Hy*)

MMPI-2 T Score	MMPI T Score	Interpretation
44 and below	40 and below	1. *Low.* These clients tend to be caustic, sarcastic, and socially isolated. They have few defenses. They are seen as having narrow interests and being socially conforming.
45–57	41–59	2. *Normal.* These clients have a typical number of attitudes and behaviors that relate to hysteric dynamics.
58–64	60–69	3. *Moderate.* These clients are likely to be exhibitionistic, extroverted, and superficial. They are naive, self-centered, and deny any problems. They prefer to look on the optimistic side of life and avoid unpleasant issues. Review of the content and/or supplementary scales may facilitate interpretation in this range.
65 and above	70 and above	4. *Marked.* These clients are naive, suggestible, lack insight into their own and others' behavior, and deny any psychological problems. Under stress, specific physical complaints will appear. Despite the initial positive impression they make on the clinician, any form of psychological intervention will be difficult. They look for simplistic, concrete solutions to their problems, solutions that do not require self-examination. Review of the content and/or supplementary scales may facilitate interpretation at the lower end of this range.

FIGURE 4-1 Neurotic Triad Configuration: Conversion "V"

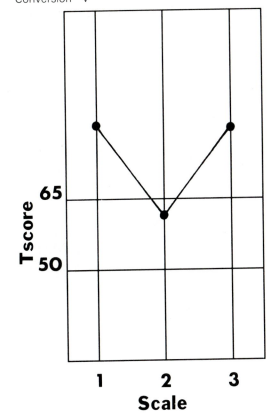

FIGURE 4-2 Neurotic Triad Configuration: Descending Slope

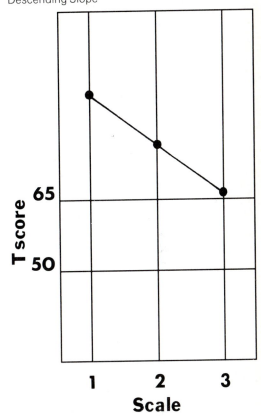

The emphasis on physical complaints along with the denial of any psychological basis for them makes all members of this group poor candidates for any form of psychological treatment. It is common for this neurotic triad configuration to be accompanied by a similar validity scale configuration (see page 120).

Another common neurotic triad configuration is the descending pattern (see Figure 4-2). The essential feature of this pattern is that all three scales are elevated above a T score of 65, with Scale *1* being the highest, followed by Scales *2* and *3* in descending order. Clients with this configuration have a long-standing somatic overconcern mani-

fested by hypersensitivity to even the most minor dysfunction, and they have constant physical complaints without adequate physical pathology.

Somatic symptoms often include nausea, dizziness, insomnia, and headaches. These clients typically have stable work records and marital relationships. As would be expected, they see little if any correlation between their physical complaints and any psychological problems. Prognosis is poor for any short-term psychological intervention. This configuration is frequently found in males over the age of 35 who feel "over the hill."

Figure 4-3 illustrates a third common

FIGURE 4–3   Neurotic Triad Configuration: Caret

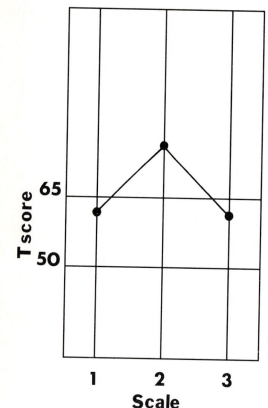

scribed as dependent and immature. Such persons often have learned to tolerate great unhappiness and a high level of discomfort; consequently, they may have poor motivation for treatment. They seem to operate at low levels of efficiency for extended periods of time.

The fourth common neurotic triad configuration is the ascending pattern (see Figure 4–4). In this configuration all three scales are greater than a T score of 65 and each succeeding scale is higher than the previous one. This pattern typically is found in females who present a history of gynecologic complaints. (Duckworth and Anderson [1986] call this the "hysterectomy" profile.) The women report

FIGURE 4–4   Neurotic Triad Configuration: Ascending Slope

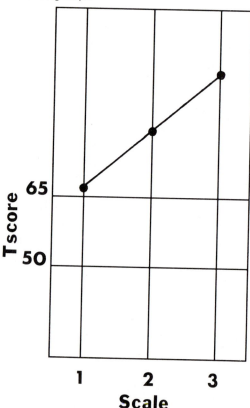

neurotic triad configuration. Its main feature is the elevation of Scale *2*; although all three scales are elevated, Scale *2* is higher than Scales *1* and *3*. These clients have a chronic neurotic condition with mixed symptomatology. Multiple somatic complaints, depression, and hysteroid features are typical, particularly as this configuration increases in overall elevation. When Scale *1* is below a T score of 65 and Scales *2* and *3* are above a T score of 70, the client frequently is overcontrolled emotionally and reports feeling "bottled up."

These clients usually are fatigued, anxious, and filled with self-doubts, which prevent them from doing anything. They are demany marital problems, including sexual complaints such as frigidity and a lifelong history of ill health. Males with this configuration are likely to be in chronic states of anxiety and exhibit physical effects of prolonged tension and worrying, such as gastric distress and ulcers.

In both men and women this configuration reflects a mixed neurotic pattern with depression and somatization predominating. A high level of anxiety with insomnia and anorexia usually accompanies the clinical picture. Lack of psychological insight and resistance to psychological interpretation of behavior are typical of clients with this configuration.

SCALE 4: PSYCHOPATHIC DEVIATE (*Pd*)

General social maladjustment and the absence of strongly pleasant experiences are assessed by the 50 items of Scale *4* (McKinley & Hathaway, 1944). The major content areas of the items are diverse and in some cases seem contradictory. Items tap complaints about family and authority figures in general, self- and social alienation, and boredom. Other items assess the denial of social shyness and the assertion of social poise and confidence. As with Scale *3*, the simultaneous endorsement of apparently contradictory groups of items was particularly characteristic of the criterion group used to construct Scale *4*.

Scale *4* was constructed empirically using a criterion group of young persons primarily between the ages of 17 and 22 diagnosed as psychopathic personality, asocial and amoral type, who were referred for testing by the courts because of their delinquent activities. None of the criterion cases was a major criminal type; most were characterized by a long history of minor delinquency. When they engaged in delinquent behavior, they generally did so without planning or

forethought and with little effort to avoid being caught.

All members of the criterion group, which included more females than males, were involved in legal proceedings, and many were incarcerated. Hence, their emotional responses of depression and boredom could have reflected their current circumstances rather than any real, inherent characteristics. The responses of this criterion group were contrasted with those of a sample of the married members of the original Minnesota normative group and a sample of college applicants. This procedure resulted in the 50 items currently on Scale *4*.

Examples of this scale's items with the deviant response in parentheses are:

"In school I was sometimes sent to the principal for bad behavior." (true)

"My way of doing things is apt to be misunderstood by others." (true)

"I have been quite independent and free from family rule." (false)[4]

McKinley and Hathaway (1944) also cross-validated Scale *4* by examining two other groups' total score on the scale. These two groups were a sample of psychiatric inpatients and a group of prison inmates, all diagnosed as psychopathic personality. A T score of 70 or above on Scale *4* was achieved by 59 percent of the prisoners and 45 percent of the inpatients. McKinley and Hathaway called this scale *psychopathic deviate* to indicate that it was not expected to differentiate all cases of psychopathic personality. Rather, Scale *4* could identify about one-half or more of those clients diagnosed as psychopathic personality.

Scale *4* has substantial overlap with most of the validity and clinical scales. It shares five to ten items with all clinical scales except Scales *1* (Hypochondriasis) and *5* (Masculinity-Femininity), and it shares five and seven items with scales *F* and *K*, respectively. Scale *4* has almost an equal number of "true" and "false" deviant responses, and it has slightly more obvious than subtle items (Wiener, 1948).

Factor analyses of the items have yielded similar results in a variety of populations. Generally five factors are identified: *shyness*, *hypersensitivity*, *delinquency*, *impulse control*, and *neuroticism* (Astin, 1959, 1961; Comrey, 1958a). Comrey (1958a) also identified a family dissension factor in his mixed sample of normals and psychiatric patients, but Astin (1959) did not in his sample of adult male narcotic addicts. Monroe, Miller, and Lyle (1964) extended Astin's factor-analytic scales to assist in screening adult addict patients.

Harris and Lingoes (1955) identified four subscales within Scale *4*: Familial Discord, Authority Conflict, Social Imperturbability, and Alienation (see Table 4-6). They further subdivided their Alienation scale into Social Alienation and Self-Alienation. In constructing these subscales, Harris and Lingoes added to each subscale two to six items not found on Scale *4*. They did not provide a rationale for adding these items, nor did they add items to the subscales for any of the other clinical scales.

Several of Harris and Lingoes' subscales overlap substantially with the factors identified by factor analysis that were described above: Social Alienation overlaps with hypersensitivity, Self-Alienation with neuroticism, and Social Imperturbability with shyness. Further, the Familial Discord subscale shares 8 of its 11 items with Wiggins' (1966) Family Problems scale, and the Authority Conflict subscale shares 3 of its 11 items with the Wiggins Authority Conflict scale. Thus, it appears that regardless of the method used to construct subscales within Scale *4*, four or five factors are frequently identified in most populations.

High scorers on Scale *4* usually are described in unfavorable terms: angry, impulsive, emotionally shallow, and unpredictable.

TABLE 4–6 Description of High Scorers on the Harris and Lingoes Subscales for Scale *4* (Psychopathic Deviate)

| Subscale | | | |
Name	Abbreviation	Number of Items	Description of High Scorers
Familial Discord	Pd_1	9	These clients struggle against familial control.
Authority Conflict	Pd_2	8	These clients resent societal demands and conventions and parental standards.
Social Imperturbability	Pd_3	6	These clients deny social anxiety, exhibit blandness, and deny dependency needs.
Social Alienation	Pd_4	13	These clients feel isolated from other people; they lack feelings of belongingness, externalize blame for their difficulties, and lack gratification in their social relations.
Self-Alienation	Pd_5	12	These clients lack self-integration; they avow guilt, exhibitionistically stated, and are despondent.

They are socially nonconforming, disregarding social rules and conventions in general and authority figures in particular. They harbor a brooding resentment and hostility toward authority figures, which may or may not be overtly displayed. In the absence of an antisocial history, this hostility may have been directed inward toward the self. Thus, a marked elevation on Scale *4* indicates the presence of antisocial behavior and attitudes, *but it does not necessarily mean that these behaviors will be expressed overtly.*

Other clinical scales, especially Scale *9* (Hypomania), usually are elevated if these antisocial behaviors are overtly expressed. High scorers have a perfectionistic and narcissistic conception of themselves, and they use these personal standards as a rationalization for ignoring social conventions. This perfectionistic self-concept is illustrated by the typical profile for a high scorer: Scale *4* is the only clinical scale elevated above a T score of 65 (a Spike *4* codetype). Rather than representing conscious avoidance of deviant responses, this codetype seems to reflect their perfectionistic conception of themselves.

High scorers (T scores of 65 or higher) are socially outgoing, energetic, and socially facile; thus, they make a good initial impression on others. Longer exposure to them soon reveals, however, their irresponsibility, unreliability, moodiness, and resentment. Novice clinicians frequently are awed by this initial impression and then dismayed when underlying qualities begin to emerge. The clinician should be aware of the favorable initial impression typical of high scorers and not be overly influenced by it.

Depression, when evident in a high scorer, usually consists of depressive thoughts and feelings but not actually psychomotor retardation nor the other vegetative signs of depression. The depression most often represents dissatisfaction about the current limits being placed on the high scorer's behavior rather than any actual concern or guilt about his behavior. Frequently, a high scorer will not elevate Scale *2* at all even when external constraints are being placed on his or her behavior. In these circumstances, a successful psychotherapeutic intervention is highly unlikely because the clients lack concern about their behavior. For most high scorers on Scale *4*, personal maturation rather than some other form of intervention is usually most effective in changing their behavior.

High scorers on Scale *4* are very likely to be diagnosed as having some form of personality disorder; they are unlikely to receive a psychotic diagnosis. They often have a long history of inadequate familial and social relationships, which seems to reflect a characterologic adjustment.

Elevations on Scale *4* are positively correlated with the frequency of delinquent and criminal behaviors and recidivism rates (Forgac, Cassel, & Michaels, 1984; Gearing, 1979; Holland & Levi, 1983). Hare's (1985) finding of little agreement between clinical judgments or behavioral measures and self-report measures for assessing psychopathy should be noted by clinicians who are interested in researching this area and trying to integrate the information.

Heilbrun (1979) found that an index of psychopathy based in part on the raw score on Scale *4* was directly related to the frequency of violent crimes in a sample of white prisoners, but only in those prisoners with IQs less than 95. Since violent crimes tend to be impulsive, Heilbrun speculated that the relationship between violent crime and lower levels of intelligence may reflect a limit on or lack of temporary cognitive restraints.

Gearing (1979) provides a comprehensive review of the use of the MMPI in prison settings. Walters (1985) reported that prisoners with behavioral diagnoses of Antisocial Personality Disorder scored higher on Scale *4* than prisoners without such behavioral diagnoses.

Normal persons who achieve high scores on Scale *4* (T scores of 65 or higher) are described in fairly similar and unflattering terms: rebellious, immature, exhibitionistic, unconventional, and nonconforming. Such persons may display a generalized deviancy from societal standards and conventions, although they are not displaying psychopathic behaviors per se.

Nearly 10 percent of college students obtain T scores greater than 70 on Scale *4* of the MMPI, and the possibility of developing separate norms for college populations has been discussed (Forsyth, 1967; Goodstein, 1954; Murray, Munley, & Gilbart, 1965). King and Kelley (1977a), however, found that college students requesting counseling who elevated Scale *4* above a T score of 70 had a history of legal, academic, and criminal difficulties. These students also were likely to be diagnosed as having a personality disorder. Thus, at least in this sample, elevation of Scale *4* seems to reflect significant pathology. Whether similar psychopathology accompanies elevations of Scale *4* among college students who are not seeking psychological services remains to be examined.

Butcher, Graham, and Bowman (1990) reported that normal college students had similar scores on Scale *4* and the other validity and clinical scales of the MMPI-2 as the MMPI-2 normative group. They concluded that the MMPI-2 norms were appropriate for college students so separate norms would not be needed.

Low scorers on Scale *4* (T scores less than 45) are generally described as conventional, conforming, and submissive. These persons are socially constricted, rigid, and have narrow interests. Males are frequently described as being uninterested in sexual activity, particularly when Scale *4* is the low point in the profile.

Scores on Scale *4* on the MMPI tend to be fairly stable with test-retest reliability coefficients of .59 to .84 for intervals up to one month and coefficients of .49 to .61 for intervals up to a year (Dahlstrom et al., 1975). Test-retest reliability coefficients for Scale *4* on the MMPI-2 for approximately a one-week interval are .81 for men and .79 for women (Butcher et al., 1989).

There are few gender differences in the distribution of raw scores on Scale *4*. In fact, the T score equivalents of each raw score are identical on the standard MMPI profile sheet, and they are generally within one or two T points on the MMPI-2. Scores on Scale *4* tend to decrease significantly (5 to 10 T points) with age in all populations (Colligan et al., 1983, 1989; Hedlund & Won Cho, 1979; Swenson et al., 1973); this pattern is thought to reflect the slow maturational changes that occur in persons with elevated scores. Several normal groups score in the high-normal and low-moderate range on Scale *4*: social activists, adolescents, and mental health professionals.

The interpretations of Scale *4* at four levels of elevation are summarized in Table 4–7.

SCALE *5*: MASCULINITY-FEMININITY (*Mf*)

The 56 items (60 items on the MMPI) comprising Scale *5* are very heterogeneous in content. Major content areas include interests in vocations and hobbies, aesthetic preferences, activity-passivity, and personal sensitivity.

Scale *5* was developed in a slightly different manner than the other clinical scales. Hathaway and McKinley (Hathaway, 1956) had intended to use a large sample of homosexual males and females in empirically developing a scale of masculinity-femininity, but they quickly discovered that homosexual samples were too heterogeneous to use as a single criterion group. They identified at least three subgroups of homosexuals within their samples, each with an apparently different source or cause of homosexuality.

TABLE 4-7   Interpretation of Levels of Elevation on Scale *4:* Psychopathic Deviate (*Pd*)

MMPI-2 T Score	MMPI T Score	Interpretation
44 and below	40 and below	1. *Low.* These clients tend to be rigid and conventional. They usually are able to tolerate much mediocrity and boredom. Males may lack interest in heterosexual activity, particularly if this scale is the low point.
45–57	45–59	2. *Normal.* These clients have a typical number of complaints about authority, alienation, and boredom.
58–64	60–69	3. *Moderate.* These clients may be genuinely concerned about social problems and issues; they may be responding to situational conflicts, or they may have adjusted to an habitual level of interpersonal and social conflict. If the conflict is situational, the score should return to the normal range as the conflict is resolved. Review of the content and/or supplementary scales may facilitate interpretation of scores in this range.
65 and above	70 and above	4. *Marked.* These clients are fighting against something, which is usually some form of conflict with authority figures. These conflicts may *not* necessarily be acted out overtly; the rebelliousness and hostility toward authority figures are readily apparent even in these cases. They are likely to be unreliable, egocentric, and irresponsible. They may be unable to learn from experience or to plan ahead. These clients have a good social facade and make a good initial impression, but the psychopathic features will surface in longer interactions or under stress. Psychological interventions are less effective than maturation in achieving change. Review of the content and/or supplementary scales may be helpful at the lower end of this range.

Because of their difficulty in obtaining a large number of cases within each subgroup, they decided to restrict their criterion sample to one subgroup—male homosexual inverts. Such persons were thought to engage in homoerotic behavior as a part of their feminine (i.e., inverted) personality characteristics; many such men, however, are too inhibited or conflicted to express their homosexuality overtly (Dahlstrom et al., 1972). The primary criterion group then consisted of 13 homosexual invert males who were selected for their freedom from any form of psychopathology.

Since most of the items used to identify sexual inversion were added to the item pool after the data had already been collected from the original Minnesota normative sample, separate groups of normals had to be gathered to contrast with the criterion group. These normal groups consisted of 54 male soldiers and 67 female airline employees. The initial item selection for Scale *5* resulted from contrasting the normal males with the criterion group (Dahlstrom et al., 1972). Items selected on this basis were then checked to insure that they separated the "normal" males from the "normal" females.

Finally, a group of feminine males was defined by the Attitude-Interest Analysis Test of Terman and Miles (1938), and the responses of these feminine males were contrasted with those of the normal males. The 60 items that contrasted the groups in all three comparisons became Scale *5* on the MMPI.

Hathaway and McKinley (Hathaway, 1956) were unsuccessful in their attempt to develop a separate scale (*Fm*) to identify female homosexual inversion. They found that their *Fm* scale correlated positively with Scale 5, so they abandoned it in favor of a single scale of Masculinity-Femininity.

Examples of Scale 5 items with the deviant response for men in parentheses are:

"I think I would like the work of a librarian." (true)

"I like collecting flowers or growing house plants." (true)

"I like mechanics magazines." (false)[5]

The items on Scale 5 have not been investigated as extensively as the other clinical scales. Part of this lack of research is because the scale was not routinely scored in the early years of the MMPI. In fact, some clinicians still refer to the clinical scales excluding Scales 5 and 0 (Social Introversion), which reflects the early tradition of MMPI usage.

Pepper and Strong (1958) rationally identified five subgroups of items within Scale 5: Personal and Emotional Sensitivity, Sexual Identification, Altruism, Feminine Occupational Identification, and Denial of Masculine Occupations. Serkownek (1975) developed six subscales within Scale 5 based on the factor analysis carried out by Graham, Schroeder, and Lilly (1971): Narcissism-Hypersensitivity; Stereotypic Feminine Interests; Denial of Stereotypic Masculine Interests; Heterosexual Discomfort-Passivity; Introspective-Critical; and Socially Retiring (see Table 4–8).

There is extensive item overlap between the Pepper and Strong (1958) item groupings and the Serkownek (1975) subscales. For example, 12 of the 14 items on Serkownek's

TABLE 4–8 Description of High Scorers on the Serkownek Subscales for Scale 5 (Masculinity-Femininity)

Subscale			
Name	Abbreviation	Number of Items	Description of High Scorers
Narcissism-Hypersensitivity	Mf_1	18	These clients are sensitive to reactions of others; they worry constantly and are easily hurt and upset.
Stereotypic Feminine Interests	Mf_2	12	These clients profess interests that are clearly feminine in character.
Denial of Stereotypic Masculine Interests	Mf_3	8	These clients deny interests that are clearly masculine in character.
Heterosexual Discomfort-Passivity	Mf_4	3	These clients admit homosexual impulses but feel uncomfortable talking about sexual matters.
Introspective-Critical	Mf_5	6	These clients neither enjoy nor feel comfortable in loud, active social gatherings.
Socially Retiring	Mf_6	9	These clients deny a liking for a number of social and cultural activities in which a dominant and conspicuous role is possible.

Stereotypic Feminine subscale overlap with Pepper and Strong's Feminine Occupational Identification. Consequently, both sets of items do not need to be routinely scored. Serkownek's subscales were selected for use in this manual because of their empirical derivation and because of the lack of construct validity for some of the Pepper and Strong groups of items (Martin & Greene, 1979).

Harris and Lingoes (1955) did not develop subscales for Scale 5, nor did Wiener and Harmon (Wiener, 1948) develop obvious and subtle subscales. Dahlstrom and colleagues (1972) state that most of the items are psychologically obvious, which supports the contention that homosexuals can conceal their sexual orientation without being detected by this scale (Bieliauskas, 1965). There are approximately the same number of "true" and "false" deviant responses to Scale 5 items, which means that either an "all true" or "all false" response set will not appreciably affect raw scores on this scale.

The same 56 items are used to assess masculinity-femininity for males and females. Responses to these items are scored as deviant when they reflect femininity in men and masculinity in women. Thus, high T scores result when a client endorses the items like a person of the opposite gender. For 4 of the items (121, 166, 209, 268), which deal with the admission of sexually deviant behaviors, the same response is considered deviant for both males and females. For the other 52 items, the scoring for a deviant response is reversed for the genders. For these latter 52 items, if "true" is the deviant response to a specific item for males reflecting femininity, "false" is the deviant response for females reflecting masculinity.

This procedure was intended to provide a basis of uniform interpretations of elevated scores since these scores would indicate that the person was endorsing the items like a person of the opposite sex. Immense differences exist, however, between the behavioral correlates of males and females at various elevations on Scale 5; thus, separate interpretations for males and females must be used.

Hathaway and McKinley (Hathaway, 1956) apparently assumed that masculinity-femininity was a bipolar dimension with masculinity at one end and femininity at the other. Numerous investigators (cf. Aaronson, 1959; Gonen & Lansky, 1968; Sines, 1977) have suggested that Scale 5 is not bipolar and that it is more likely to be multidimensional. Both factor-analytic (Graham et al., 1971) and rational (Pepper & Strong, 1958) subscales formed with Scale 5 items, which were described above, also support its multidimensional nature.

Constantinople (1973) provided an excellent review questioning whether masculinity-femininity is a bipolar dimension that can be adequately measured by a single score; Baucom (1976) empirically demonstrated that independent measures of masculinity and femininity can be developed from the California Psychological Inventory (Gough, 1957); and Peterson (1989) developed independent scales of masculinity and femininity for the MMPI-2 (see the Supplementary Scales for Gender Role—Masculine and Gender Role—Feminine in Chapter 5).

There also is a paucity of data on the behavioral correlates of Scale 5 in various populations, again reflecting the early history of the MMPI in which this scale was not routinely scored nor described in most research. What research has been done discusses males and females separately because of the very different correlates of specific T scores for the two genders.

High-scoring males (T scores of 65 or higher) in psychiatric populations are described as passive, socially sensitive and perceptive, having a wide range of aesthetic and social interests, and inner-directed. They also are seen as being dependent and insecure regarding their masculine role; often they tend to identify with a feminine role. Depression, anxiety, tension, and guilt frequently are reported (Ward & Dillon, 1990). If males are homosexual or have homosexual concerns and are willing to acknowledge openly these behaviors or concerns, they will achieve high scores on Scale 5 (Aaronson & Grumpelt, 1961; Dean & Richardson, 1964; Friberg, 1967; Manosevitz, 1971; Singer, 1970). If they cannot acknowledge these behaviors, they will not elevate the scale at all since item content on Scale 5 is psychologically obvious (Wong, 1984).

The fact that a variety of factors, such as education and vocational interests, tend to be associated with elevated scores on Scale 5 of the MMPI in males further reduces the usefulness of this scale in diagnosing homosexuality (Burton, 1947; Friberg, 1967), since the elevation on the scale may reflect these factors rather than homosexual behaviors or concerns. Raw scores on Scale 5 are positively correlated with level of education, particularly in the T score range of 55 to 65. Education per se, however, is insufficient to elevate scores much above a T score of 65 on the MMPI (Dean & Richardson, 1964; Manosevitz, 1971). Consequently, high scores in males cannot simply be dismissed as reflecting their humanistic and liberal arts-oriented college education.

The interpretation of Scale 5 on the MMPI-2 may be problematic because of the relatively high education level of the normative sample (see Chapter 1). It is apparent that scores on Scale 5 tend to be about 10 T points lower in men and 2 to 3 T points higher in women on the MMPI-2 than on the original MMPI. Research is clearly needed to determine whether the MMPI correlates of Scale 5 that are described below can be applied directly to the MMPI-2. Clinicians should recall that linear T scores are used on Scales 5 and 0 of the MMPI-2 rather than uniform T scores.

When only Scale 5 is elevated without accompanying elevations on other clinical scales, clients are likely to be seen as not having a psychiatric disorder even in a psychiatric setting (King & Kelley, 1977b; Rosen, 1974). High-scoring normal males are generally described in positive terms: curious, socially perceptive, peaceable, tolerant, and psychologically complex. They also are described as passive and prone to worry. They have wide philosophical and aesthetic interests.

Among females in psychiatric populations, high scorers (T scores of 65 or higher) are seen as being aggressive, unfriendly, dominating, and competitive. In an inpatient psychiatric setting high-scoring females have features of a psychotic thought disorder (Boerger et al., 1974). They have difficulty remembering, are slow moving and sluggish, and report hallucinations, thinking disturbances, and psychomotor withdrawal-retardation.

High-scoring normal females (T scores of 65 or higher) are seen as being adventurous. Somewhat surprisingly, no one has reported that they have masculine interests or that they do not have feminine interests. The lack of additional correlates of high scores in normal females reflects the infrequency with which such scores occur on the MMPI.

Low-scoring males (T scores less than 40) are easygoing, adventurous, and coarse. They may display an almost compulsive masculinity and will emphasize their masculine interests. They tend to lack individuality and originality.

Low-scoring females (T scores less than 40) are passive, submissive, yielding, and demure. They strongly identify with a traditional feminine role. Extremely low-scoring females (T scores below 35) are likely to be constricted, self-pitying, faultfinding, and self-deprecating. They frequently display almost a caricature of an extreme feminine role. They appear helpless and utterly dependent on significant others to take care of them. This behavior often is manipulative but can occasionally represent genuine help-lessness.

Test-retest reliability coefficients for Scale *5* of the MMPI range from .72 to .91 for intervals up to two weeks, with very similar coefficients for males and females. Reliability coefficients range from .34 to .63 for intervals up to one year, again with little difference between males and females (Dahlstrom et al., 1975). Test-retest reliability coefficients for Scale *5* on the MMPI-2 for approximately a one-week interval are .82 for men and .73 for women (Butcher et al., 1989).

Education has a predominant influence on raw scores on Scale *5* in males and somewhat less influence on raw scores in females. T scores for males can be expected to be in the range of 55 to 70 as a result of a college education and the vocational interests and training that are part of the education process. A male who has a liberal arts education can be expected to score at the upper end of this range, whereas a male who has an engineering or basic sciences oriented degree will score at the lower end of this range.

Males with education below the college level also can be expected to score at the lower end of this range or below. Consequently, either a low T score in a male liberal arts major or a high T score in a male high school graduate should be investigated by the clinician because of the unusualness of such scores. To the extent that social class will affect a male's vocational interests and his conceptions of what behaviors are appropriate within a masculine role, social class affects Scale *5* T scores, as does education.

Graham and Tisdale (1983) reported a number of differences between female graduate and undergraduate students with low scores on Scale *5*. The graduate students described themselves and were described as being more conscientious, insightful, reflective, unaffected, and unconventional than the undergraduates. The graduate students also described themselves and were described

as being less formal, mild, opportunistic, and silent than the undergraduates. It appears that women with low scores on Scale *5* may be described in a variety of different terms depending upon their level of education.

Summary tables of the interpretations of four levels of scores on Scale *5* are provided for men (see Table 4–9) and for women (see Table 4–10).

SCALE *6:* PARANOIA (*Pa*)

Interpersonal sensitivity, moral self-righteousness, and suspiciousness are revealed by the 40 items that make up Scale *6* (Paranoia). The content of some items is clearly psychotic, acknowledging the existence of delusions and paranoid thought processes. Hathaway and McKinley (Hathaway, 1956) never described the criterion group of paranoid patients used to develop Scale *6* empirically. They considered Scale *6* to be a weak preliminary scale although they were unable to develop a better scale.

In any case, the exact number and composition of patients in the paranoid criterion group are not known. These patients were judged to have paranoid symptoms, although few of them were classified as "only" paranoid. Most were diagnosed as having a paranoid state, paranoid condition, or paranoid schizophrenia. It can be assumed that Scale *6* was empirically derived by contrasting the item endorsements of this unspecified paranoid criterion group with the original Minnesota normative group.

Examples of scale items with the deviant response indicated in parentheses are:

"I have certainly had more than my share of things to worry about." (true)

"I have no enemies who really wish to harm me." (false)

"I believe I am being plotted against." (true)[6]

TABLE 4–9 Interpretation of Levels of Elevation for Men on Scale *5:* Masculinity-Femininity (*Mf*)

MMPI-2 T Score	MMPI T Score	Interpretation
44 and below	40 and below	1. *Low.* These men identify very strongly with the traditional masculine role, and they may be compulsive and inflexible about their masculinity.
45–57	41–59	2. *Normal.* These men are interested in traditional masculine interests and activities. This also is the typical range for college-educated males in the more masculine-oriented fields, such as engineering and agriculture.
58–64	60–69	3. *Moderate.* These men tend toward aesthetic interests such as art, music, and literature. They are rather passive and prefer to work through problems in a covert and indirect manner. This is the typical range for most college-educated males.
65 and above	70 and above	4. *Marked.* These men are passive, inner-directed, and have aesthetic interests and activities. They do not identify with the traditional masculine role. Self-proclaimed homosexuals and persons willing to admit overtly their homosexual concerns will score in this range. Homosexual behavior and/or concerns, however, can be easily concealed without elevating Scale *5* or the validity scales. Be very wary of diagnosing a client as homosexual solely on the basis of a score in this range.

There has been only limited study of the individual items on Scale *6*. Comrey's (1958b) factor analysis of the items revealed four factors of paranoia—*actual persecution, imagined persecution, delusion,* and *hopelessness, guilt-ridden*—as well as several other factors that are not clearly related to paranoia—neuroticism, cynicism, hysteria, and rigidity. Harris and Lingoes (1955) developed three subscales within Scale *6*: Persecutory Ideas, Poignancy, and Naivete (see Table 4–11). There is nearly complete overlap between Comrey's (1958b) paranoid, neuroticism, and cynicism factors and Harris and Lingoes' (1955) three subscales of Persecutory Ideas, Poignancy, and Naivete, respectively. Wiggins' (1966) Psychoticism scale overlaps with 19 of the 40 items on Scale *6* and shares numerous items with Comrey's four paranoid factors. The Tryon, Stein, and Chu (Stein, 1968) subscale of Suspicion and Mistrust shares only one item with Scale *6*. The

MMPI-2 content scale (Butcher et al., 1989) of Bizarre Mentation (see Chapter 5) overlaps with only 8 of the 40 items on Scale *6*.

Since Endicott, Jortner, and Abramoff (1969) reported only small positive correlations between clinical ratings of suspiciousness and Scale *6* scores, it may be that Scale *6* is an inadequate measure of the construct of suspiciousness, which is a central feature of paranoid behavior. Nevertheless, it appears that regardless of the method used to develop subscales within Scale *6*, three factors are identified, and these can be adequately assessed by the Harris and Lingoes' (1955) subscales.

Wiener and Harmon (Wiener, 1948) felt that more Scale *6* items were obvious (23) than subtle (17). Only 7 items are unique to the scale; 1 to 4 items are shared with most of the other clinical scales and even more substantial overlap occurs with Scales *F* (9 items), *4* (8 items), and *8* (13 items). There are

TABLE 4–10 Interpretation of Levels of Elevation for Women on Scale *5:*
Masculinity-Femininity (*Mf*)

MMPI-2 T Score	MMPI T Score	Interpretation
34 and below	34 and below	1. *Markedly Low.* These women tend to be coy, seductive, and appear helpless. They overidentify with the feminine role and at times are almost a caricature of it. This behavior may be subtly manipulative or they may conceive of themselves as actually helpless. These clients should elevate the supplementary scale of Gender Role-Feminine.
35–44	35–44	2. *Low.* These women are genuinely interested in traditional feminine interests and activities. They may be passive in their role.
45–64	45–59	3. *Normal and Moderate.* These women are less traditionally oriented toward a feminine role than women who score low, and they have an interest in masculine activities as well.
65 and above	60 and above	4. *Marked.* It is unusual for most women to score in this range. Check for scoring or profiling errors. The male template instead of the female template may have been used in scoring; male norms instead of female norms may have been used (i.e., the wrong table in an appendix was used); or the woman's profile was plotted on the male side of the profile sheet instead of the female side. These women may or may not have actual masculine interests, but they are definitely *not* interested in appearing or behaving according to a traditional feminine role. They may become anxious if they are expected to limit their behavior to what is prescribed by a traditional feminine role. Aggressive behavior is likely to be seen. Homosexual behavior is unlikely to be seen.

slightly more "true" (24) than "false" (16) deviant responses to Scale *6* items. As the "all true" profile (page 125) illustrates, Scale *6* and the succeeding scales have an increasingly larger proportion of "true" responses as deviant. Thus, "all true" response sets can be identified by the extreme elevations on the psychotic tetrad (Scales *6, 7, 8,* and *9*).

High scorers on Scale *6* are generally described as being suspicious, hostile, guarded, overly sensitive, argumentative, and prone to blame others. They often express their hostility overtly and rationalize it as a result of what others have done to them. In addition, an egocentric self-righteousness seems to permeate all of their behavior. Although they may not actually evidence a psychotic thought disorder, usually the paranoid character structure is evident.

Dahlstrom and associates (1972) observed that Scale *6* is quite sensitive to fluctuations in the degree and intensity of delusional material in psychiatric cases; the research support for this statement, however, is limited at best. Vestre and Watson (1972) could not identify a linear or a curvilinear relationship between Scale *6* scores and paranoid symptomatology, and Endicott and colleagues (1969) actually found an inverse relationship between Scale *6* scores and clinical ratings of suspiciousness.

It also is commonly reported that Scale *6* on the MMPI has few false positives (nonparanoid persons scoring above a T score of 70), presumably because of the rather obvious nature of the scale items (cf. Carson, 1969). Vestre and Watson (1972) found, however, that 9 of 22 patients with T scores

TABLE 4–11 Description of High Scorers on the Harris and Lingoes Subscales
for Scale *6* (Paranoia)

Subscale			
Name	Abbreviation	Number of Items	**Description of High Scorers**
Persecutory Ideas	Pa_1	17	These clients have ideas of external influence; they externalize blame for their problems, frustrations, and failures; in the extreme degree, they have persecutory ideas; they also project responsibility for their negative feelings.
Poignancy	Pa_2	9	These clients consider themselves something special and different from other people; they are high-strung and "thin-skinned"; they cherish sensitive feelings; they are overly subjective.
Naivete	Pa_3	9	These clients affirm moral virtue; they are excessively generous about the motives of others; they are righteous about ethical matters; they display an obtuse naivete; they deny distrust and hostility.

greater than 75 on Scale *6* had no rated paranoid symptomatology. Consequently, high scorers are likely to show a paranoid thought process if not a psychotic thought disorder, but there are more exceptions to this statement than was formerly thought. Because of the rigidity and suspiciousness of high scorers, interpersonal contact is difficult.

Numerous investigators have found that Scale *6* does not reliably separate groups of paranoid clients from other diagnostic groups (Harris, Wittner, Koppell, & Hilf, 1970; Scagnelli, 1975; Tarter & Perley, 1975). Scagnelli (1975) reported that the Dependency (*Dy*) scale (see Chapter 5) reliably separated female paranoid patients from other diagnostic groups, with the paranoid patients scoring lower on the *Dy* scale. Further research on

the *Dy* scale seems warranted to determine whether it can reliably separate paranoid groups from other diagnostic groups.

Normal individuals who score in the moderate range (T scores of 58 to 64) on Scale *6* are described very differently from high scorers in psychiatric populations; this appears to reflect the shift in behavioral correlates in moving from moderate to marked scores as well as the population differences. High scorers in psychiatric settings have been described. High-scoring normals are described as being interpersonally sensitive, emotional, rational, and clear thinking. To the extent that sensitivity to others and empathy reflects some of the same underlying dynamics as suspiciousness and projection, this shift in correlates from moderate to marked scores is logical.

Clients who score in the normal range on Scale 6 (T scores of 45 to 57) fall into two major categories: clients without any paranoid symptomatology, and clients whose paranoid symptomatology is well ingrained and who have sufficient reality testing to avoid endorsing the obvious items on Scale 6. The latter group would be expected to elevate the subtle subscale of Scale 6 (Wiener, 1948), but no research has addressed this issue. This group also provides ample evidence for the statement that scores in the normal range on a scale may not reflect normality.

It is sometimes stated that extremely paranoid patients will get scores in the low range (T scores less than 40) (Carson, 1969; Good & Brantner, 1961), but the available research indicates that their scores are more likely to fall above the low range (Endicott et al., 1969; Vestre & Watson, 1972).

Low-scoring individuals (T scores less than 45) in a psychiatric population are frequently described as stubborn, evasive, and overly cautious. As previously discussed, there seems to be little evidence that they are paranoid. Low-scoring normals are described in generally positive terms: socially competent, having narrow interests, trusting, balanced, and conventional. They sometimes are characterized as being overly trusting and unaware of or insensitive to the motives of others; they frequently appear gullible as a result. Anderson (1956) found that low-scoring college students generally were in academic difficulty due to underachievement and reported difficulties with their parents. He conjectured that repressed or denied hostility may interfere with academic success.

Scores on Scale 6 tend to be less stable over time than scores on the other clinical scales. Test-retest reliability coefficients for intervals up to two weeks range from .49 to .89, and for intervals of one year from .32 to .65 (Dahlstrom et al., 1975). Test-retest reliability coefficients for Scale 6 on the MMPI-2 for approximately a one-week interval are .67 for men and .58 for women (Butcher et al., 1989).

There are no reported gender differences on Scale 6 of the MMPI since the same T scores are used for men and women; T scores are very similar in men and women on the MMPI-2. Scores tend to decrease slightly (2 to 4 T points) with age in all populations (Colligan et al., 1983, 1989; Hedlund & Won Cho, 1979; Swenson et al., 1973).

A summary of the interpretations of four levels of elevation on Scale 6 is presented in Table 4–12.

Scale 4-5-6 Configurations

One configuration of Scales 4, 5, and 6 is seen frequently in women. Scales 4 and 6 are above a T score of 65, and Scale 5 is below a T score of 35 (see Figure 4–5). It is not necessary that Scales 4 and 6 be the high points in the profile, but it is mandatory that the T scores be in the indicated ranges since Scale 5 will be 10–20 T points lower than Scales 4 and 6 in most women. This configuration is sometimes called the "Scarlett O'Hara V."

These women are hostile and angry but unable to express these feelings directly. They resort to irritating other people into attacking them, and then seem to revel over how badly they are mistreated. They are excessively demanding, dependent, and have an almost inordinate need for affection. Unfortunately, their behaviors only serve to alienate significant others, and this decreases the likelihood that their needs will be met. As would be expected, marital difficulties, familial problems, and sexual dysfunctions are common. These women are very adept at getting clinicians to aggress against them, which makes therapeutic intervention very difficult.

When Scale 3 is elevated higher than this configuration, women will be superficially

TABLE 4–12   Interpretation of Levels of Elevation on Scale *6:* Paranoia (*Pa*)

MMPI-2 T Score	MMPI T Score	Interpretation
44 and below	40 and below	1. *Low.* These clients have narrow interests and tend to be insensitive to and unaware of the motives of other people. Students are frequently underachievers.
45–57	41–59	2. *Normal.* These clients may be very sensitive and suspicious, yet able to avoid endorsing the obvious items. The clinician should score the subtle and obvious scales. The client's suspiciousness should be relatively apparent in an interview. Otherwise, scores in this range are normal.
58–64	60–69	3. *Moderate.* These clients are interpersonally sensitive and think clearly and rationally. Mental health workers frequently score in this range. These clients may be overly sensitive to criticism and personalize the action of others toward themselves. Review of the content and/or supplementary scales may facilitate interpretation of scores in this range.
65 and above	70 and above	4. *Marked.* These clients are likely to be suspicious, hostile, and overly sensitive and usually overtly verbalize these qualities. A thought disorder may be readily apparent. At the lower end of this range review of the content and/or supplementary scales may aid in interpretation.

sociable and deny the existence of any hostile feelings toward others. These women are particularly adept at enraging others without any real understanding of their involvement in the process. Their demanding, manipulative, and hostile qualities are readily apparent to everyone but themselves. This pattern of behavior represents a chronic means of manipulating and controlling others, which is difficult to alter through psychological intervention.

SCALE *7:* PSYCHASTHENIA (*Pt*)

The 48 items of Scale *7* are designed to assess the neurotic syndrome of psychasthenia, which is characterized by the person's inability to resist specific actions or thoughts regardless of their maladaptive nature. This diagnostic label is no longer used, and such persons are now diagnosed as having obsessive-compulsive reactions.

In addition to obsessive-compulsive features, Scale *7* taps abnormal fears, self-criticism, difficulties in concentration, and guilt feelings. The item content does not reflect specific obsessions or compulsive rituals; instead a characterologic basis for a wide variety of psychasthenic symptoms is tapped (Dahlstrom et al., 1972). The anxiety assessed by this scale is of a long-term nature or trait anxiety, although the scale is somewhat responsive to situational stress as well.

McKinley and Hathaway (1942) developed Scale *7* empirically by contrasting a criterion group of 20 patients whose final diagnosis was psychasthenia with a subgroup of the original Minnesota normative sample and the college normative sample. At least one and possibly two of the criterion group patients were diagnosed incorrectly.

Since many patients with psychasthenia are not so disabled as to require hospitalization, McKinley and Hathaway (1942) were

FIGURE 4–5.   Scales *4-5-6* Configuration:
''Scarlett O'Hara V''

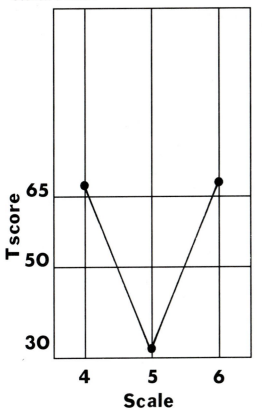

Examples of scale items with the deviant
response indicated in parentheses are:

> ''I feel anxiety about something or
> someone almost all the time.'' (true)

> ''I have a habit of counting things that
> are not important such as bulbs on elec-
> tric signs, and so forth.'' (true)

> ''Bad words, often terrible words, come
> into my mind and I cannot get rid of
> them.'' (true)[7]

There have been limited studies of the
items on Scale *7*. Comrey (1958c) identified
seven principal factors: *neuroticism, anxiety,
withdrawal, poor concentration, agitation,
psychotic tendencies,* and *poor physical
health.* None of these factors could be labeled
psychasthenia, although some of the features
of this syndrome can be seen in the factor
names.

There is limited overlap between the
items on Scale *7* and Wiggins' (1966) content
scales or the Tryon, Stein, and Chu (Stein,
1968) cluster scales. Scale *7* has 5 items in
common with Wiggins' Phobia scale, 6 items
with Wiggins' Poor Morale scale, and 9 items
with Wiggins' Depression scale. It has 11
items in common with Tryon, Stein, and
Chu's Tension, Worry, and Fear scale, 8
items with their Depression and Apathy
scale, and 7 items with their Autism and Disruptive Thought scale. Scale *7* has 9 items in
common with the MMPI-2 content scale of
Depression, 6 items with Anxiety, 5 items
with Obsessionality, and 4 items with Low
Self-esteem.

Harris and Lingoes (1955) found that the
Scale *7* items did not lend themselves to sub-
classification, and hence they were unable to
identify any subscales. Thus, it appears that
the use of an internal consistency approach in
selecting items for Scale *7* resulted in the selection of a wide variety of heterogeneous
items that tap general maladjustment and

limited in the number of criterion cases available. They were reluctant to use outpatient
cases because of the difficulty of studying
such patients in depth to confirm their diagnosis. Once items were selected by contrasting the criterion group with the two normative samples, additional items were chosen
that correlated with the total score on this
preliminary scale in a sample of 100 normal
persons. An analogous procedure was followed in a sample of 100 randomly selected
psychiatric patients, and a few more items
were added that correlated with the total
score on the preliminary scale. As a result of
all these procedures, 48 items were selected
for Scale *7.*

feeling bad; consequently, the items cannot be separated meaningfully into subscales.

Scale 7 has substantial item overlap with the other clinical scales: only 9 items are unique to it. It shares 17 items with Scale 8, 13 items with Scale 2, and from 2 to 8 items with the other clinical scales. Consequently, Scale 7 can be expected to covary directly with the other clinical scales because of the extensive item overlap. Scale 7 shares only 1 item with the F scale and none with the other validity scales. Wiener and Harmon (Wiener, 1948) were unable to develop subtle and obvious scales for Scale 7 since almost all of the items were obvious in nature. The deviant response to most of the Scale 7 items is "true" (39 of 48).

High scorers on Scale 7 (T scores of 65 or higher) are usually described as being anxious, tense, indecisive, and unable to concentrate. They frequently display obsessive thoughts and ruminations, self-doubt, and associated depressive features. Although specific phobias or compulsive behaviors may be seen in high scorers, they are not characteristically seen. In fact, many rigidly compulsive clients may not elevate Scale 7 at all, since their intellectual defenses are sufficient to control their anxieties, feelings of insecurity, and so on.

Basically, high scorers are clients whose characteristic defenses of intellectualization, rationalization, and undoing are no longer capable of controlling their anxiety and tension. High scorers display an extreme concern over their physical functioning; their complaints typically center around the cardiovascular system, although complaints about gastrointestinal and gastrourinary functioning are common. Their physical complaints generally reflect their high anxiety levels and the effects of anxiety on their physical functioning. Symptomatic treatment of their anxiety is frequently necessary before initiating any other form of therapeutic intervention.

High-scoring normals (T scores of 65 or higher) are generally described in positive terms although some of them, particularly women, display neurotic features to some degree. High-scoring males are described as being sentimental, responsible, conscientious, verbal, formal, unemotional, and idealistic. High-scoring females, however, are described as being prone to worry, emotional, high strung, and generally dissatisfied with themselves.

Griffith, Upshaw, and Fowler (1958) found that high scorers on Scale 7 were more doubtful than high scorers on Scale 9 (Hypomania) in their judgments in a psychophysiological weight discrimination task. Griffith and Fowler (1960) found that high scorers on Scale 7 were more compliant with an administrator's request to participate in an experiment than high scorers on Scale 4.

Low scorers on Scale 7 (T scores less than 45) are described in generally positive terms. They are seen as being responsible, easygoing, capable, and efficient. They also are seen as relaxed and not anxious or prone to worry.

Test-retest reliability coefficients for Scale 7 tend to be higher for intervals up to two weeks than for the other clinical scales, with correlations ranging from .74 to .93. For intervals up to one year, test-retest correlations are much lower, ranging from .37 to .58 (Dahlstrom et al., 1975). Test-retest reliability coefficients for Scale 7 on the MMPI-2 for approximately a one-week interval are .89 for men and .88 for women (Butcher et al., 1989).

There is little change in scores on Scale 7 with increasing age in normal samples (Colligan et al., 1983, 1989), however, scores in medical patients (Swenson et al., 1973) and psychiatric patients (Hedlund & Won Cho, 1979) tend to decrease slightly. Females endorse two to three more Scale 7 items than men.

A summary of the interpretations of four levels of elevations on Scale 7 is presented in Table 4–13.

TABLE 4–13 Interpretation of Levels of Elevation on Scale *7:* Psychasthenia (*Pt*)

MMPI-2 T Score	MMPI T Score	Interpretation
44 and below	40 and below	1. *Low.* These clients are secure and comfortable with themselves and are emotionally stable. They are success oriented, persistent, and capable. There is an absence of worries and a relaxed attitude toward responsibilities.
45–57	41–59	2. *Normal.* These clients can handle work and personal responsibilities without undue worry or anxiety.
58–64	60–69	3. *Moderate.* These clients are generally punctual in meeting their obligations and may worry if unable to do so. They do not see themselves as anxious nor do others see them as anxious. Review of the content and/or supplemental scales may facilitate interpretation in this range.
65 and above	70 and above	4. *Marked.* These clients are worried, tense, and indecisive. Agitation may develop and overt anxiety is usually apparent both to themselves and to others. At extreme scores ($T > 85$), there usually are agitated ruminations and obsessions that no longer control anxiety. Disabling guilt feelings may be present. Psychopharmacologic treatment of the anxiety may be necessary before other forms of therapeutic interventions are instituted.

SCALE *8:* SCHIZOPHRENIA (*Sc*)

In Scale *8* there are 78 items, which is 25 to 125 percent more items than in the other clinical scales. The items assess a wide variety of content areas, including bizarre thought processes and peculiar perceptions, social alienation, poor familial relationships, difficulties in concentration and impulse control, lack of deep interests, disturbing questions of self-worth and self-identity, and sexual difficulties.

Scale *8* was developed empirically by contrasting the item endorsements of the original Minnesota normative group with the responses of two partly overlapping groups of 50 patients who had been diagnosed as schizophrenic (Hathaway, 1956). The criterion group included assorted subtypes of schizophrenia and included slightly more females (60 percent) than males (40 percent).

Hathaway (1956) reported that four separate preliminary schizophrenia scales were derived in an attempt to improve the ratio of true to false positive cases identified. Each of the preliminary scales adequately separated schizophrenics from normals, but they also identified a number of other diagnostic groups as schizophrenic.

Hathaway and McKinley (Hathaway, 1956) also attempted to develop scales to identify each of the major subtypes of schizophrenia without success. They finally selected the fourth of the preliminary scales as being the best, despite its problem of identifying other diagnostic groups as schizophrenic. Using the *K*-correction procedure (see Chapters 1 and 3) reduced the number of false positives on this 78-item scale.

Examples of Scale *8* items with the deviant response in parentheses are

"I dislike having people around me." (true)

"I often feel as if things are not real." (true)

"I hear strange things when I am alone." (true)[8]

Investigations of the individual items on Scale *8* have not been extensive. Comrey's (Comrey & Marggraff, 1958) factor analysis of this scale included only 58 items because of limited computer capacity. (He omitted the 17 items that overlap with Scale *7* and 3 additional items.) Comrey identified seven major factors: *paranoia, poor concentration, poor physical health, psychotic tendencies, rejection, withdrawal,* and *sex concern.* It is surprising that in spite of the increased computer capacity now available, no one has factor analyzed all 78 items on Scale *8* in the two decades since Comrey reported his analysis.

Harris and Lingoes (1955) identified three subscales within the scale items and divided these first two subscales into two and three smaller subscales, respectively (see Table 4–14). Thus, the Object Loss subscale is divided into Social Alienation and Emotional Alienation subscales. The Lack of Ego Mastery, Intrapsychic Autonomy subscale is divided into Lack of Ego Mastery, Cognitive; Lack of Ego Mastery, Conative; and Lack of Ego Mastery, Defective Inhibition sub-

TABLE 4–14 Description of High Scorers on the Harris and Lingoes Subscales for Scale *8* (Schizophrenia)

| Subscale | | | |
Name	Abbre-viation	Number of Items	Description of High Scorers
Social Alienation	Sc_1	21	These clients feel a lack of rapport with other people; they withdraw from meaningful relationships with others.
Emotional Alienation	Sc_2	11	These clients feel a lack of rapport with themselves; they experience the self as strange and alien; they display flattened or distorted affect and apathy.
Lack of Ego Mastery, Cognitive	Sc_3	10	These clients admit autonomous thought processes; they have strange and puzzling ideas.
Lack of Ego Mastery, Conative	Sc_4	14	These clients have feelings of "psychological weakness"; they show abulia, inertia, massive inhibition, and regression.
Lack of Ego Mastery, Defective Inhibition	Sc_5	11	These clients have feelings of not being in control of their impulses; they experience their emotions as strange and alien; they are at the mercy of impulse and feeling and show dissociation of affect.
Bizarre Sensory Experiences	Sc_6	20	These clients have feelings of change in the perception of themselves and their body image; they experience feelings of depersonalization and estrangement.

scales. Since Comrey (Comrey & Marggraff, 1958) omitted 20 items in his factor analysis of Scale *8*, there is no meaningful way to compare his factors with the Harris and Lingoes (1955) subscales.

Scale *8* overlaps somewhat with Wiggins' (1966) content scales of Psychoticism (17/48), Organic Symptoms (13/36), and Depression (9/33). The rather substantial overlap with the Organic Symptoms scale and the small overlap with the Psychoticism scale illustrate both the heterogeneity of the Scale *8* items and the differences in the processes of rational and empirical item selection. Scale *8* overlaps minimally with the Tryon, Stein, and Chu (Stein, 1968) cluster scales, sharing some items with the Autism and Disruptive Thought (8/23), Depression (8/28), and Tension, Worry, and Fear (7/36) scales. Scale *8* also overlaps with the MMPI-2 (Butcher et al., 1989) content scales of Bizarre Mentation (9/23), Depression (7/33), Health Concerns (6/36), and Family Problems (6/16).

Again, it is apparent that the method of item selection produces different items to measure similar content areas. Further research is needed to establish the empirical correlates of these various groupings of items.

Scale *8* shares a substantial number of items with the other clinical scales, particularly Scales *6* (13), *7* (17), and *9* (11), and Scale *F* (15). It also shares from 3 to 10 items with the rest of the clinical scales. Only 16 items are unique to Scale *8*. Wiener and Harmon (Wiener, 1948) were unable to develop subtle and obvious scales within the scale since most of the items were obvious in content. The deviant response to almost three-fourths (59/78) of the items is "true."

Scale *8* is probably the single most difficult scale to interpret in isolation because of the variety of factors that can result in an elevated score. Since the total number of the *K* scale items endorsed in the deviant direction

is added to the raw score on Scale *8* to plot a *K*-corrected profile, approximately 20 Scale *8* items endorsed in the deviant direction are sufficient to produce a T score greater than 65 when the client has an average score on the *K* scale. Consequently, a client can endorse any combination of 20 or more of the 78 items on Scale *8* to obtain a T score greater than 65.

It also is important to know the specific combination of items from Scales *K* and *8* that the client is endorsing to produce a specific T score. For example, men can obtain a T score of 74 by endorsing any combination of 40 items from Scales *K* and *8*. A man who endorsed 30 *K* scale items and 10 Scale *8* items will be very different from a man who endorsed 5 *K* scale items and 35 Scale *8* items. The clinician is strongly encouraged to construct a non-*K*-corrected profile anytime the *K* scale exceeds a raw score of 18 (T score of 56) in order to have an appreciation of the relative contributions of the *K* scale and the item content of the *K*-corrected scales in the standard *K*-corrected profile.

Several attempts have been made to develop subscales using item analysis within Scale *8* to distinguish between actual cases of schizophrenia and other diagnostic groups (Benarick, Guthrie, & Snyder, 1951; Harding, Holz, & Kawakami, 1958). These studies, however, have not been successfully replicated (Quay & Rowell, 1955; Rubin, 1954). Virtually none of the items selected by Benarick and colleagues (1951) or Harding and colleagues (1958) overlap with either Wiggins' (1966) Psychoticism scale or the Tryon, Stein, and Chu (Stein, 1968) Autism and Disruptive Thought scale. This suggests that research is warranted with these latter two scales on differentiating schizophrenics from other diagnostic groups, although the scales are more likely to be sensitive to psychotic behaviors in general than to schizophrenia per se.

Newmark, Gentry, Simpson, and Jones

(1978) developed four criteria that were successful in identifying 72 percent of hospitalized patients with an admitting diagnosis of schizophrenia. Their MMPI criteria follow:

1. Scale *8* is in the T score of 80 to 100, inclusive.
2. The total raw score on Scale *8* with the K-correction includes 35 percent or fewer K items.[9]
3. Scale *F* is in the T score range of 75 to 95, inclusive.
4. Scale *8* is greater than or equal to Scale *7*.

Newmark and associates found that only 5.5 percent of patients in other diagnostic categories were labeled schizophrenic (false positives) using their criteria. They also reported that the Harris and Lingoes subscales for Scale *8* did not accurately identify the schizophrenic patients. The fact that Newmark and associates had to include both Scales *F* and *7* to identify correctly 72 percent of their sample further demonstrates the futility of trying to diagnose schizophrenia on the basis of Scale *8* alone.

This latter point is supported by Walters' (1984) finding that Scale *8* produced a 61 percent classification accuracy in distinguishing between schizophrenic and schizophrenia-spectrum and general psychiatric patients. However, Walters (1988) found that codetypes containing Scale *8* were more likely (64.4 percent) in schizophrenic patients than bipolar disorder, manic patients (35.5 percent).

High scorers on Scale *8* (T scores of 65 or higher) are described as cold, apathetic, alienated, misunderstood, and having difficulties in thinking and communication, which may reflect an actual psychotic thought disorder. These individuals feel that they are lacking something essential to be a real person. They tend to prefer daydreaming and fantasy to interpersonal relationships. They feel isolated, inferior, and self-dissatisfied.

As Scale *8* approaches and exceeds a T score of 75, particularly when these T scores are the result of a small *K*-correction, peculiarities in logic and thinking become more apparent or actual schizoid thought processes may even be evident. High scorers may appear confused and disoriented and may exercise poor judgment. They frequently display associated depressive features and psychomotor retardation. All of these behaviors may be the result of a schizophrenic process, a schizoid adjustment, or severe and prolonged stress.

Extremely high scorers (T scores greater than 100) usually are characterized by severe and prolonged stress, accompanied by an acute decompensation, if the items have been endorsed consistently and accurately (see Chapter 3). These persons typically are not schizophrenic; they are more likely to be undergoing acute psychotic reactions. For example, an adolescent going through an identity crisis will frequently score in this extreme range.

Normals who achieve high scores on Scale *8* (T scores of 65 or higher) are described in a variety of terms that seem to reflect the changing correlates of the scale as elevations increase. Normals who achieve T scores of 75 or higher, which are the result of small *K*-corrections, are generally described in a similar manner as high scorers in psychiatric populations (see above).

Anderson and Kunce (1984) found that their university counseling center clients, whose highest clinical scale was Scale *8* ($M = 91$), were more difficult than other clients and shared a number of characteristics such as feeling socially isolated, relationship difficulties, stressful home life, and so on. However, these clients did not display the severe symptoms that might be expected with such a high T score on Scale *8*.

Normals with less extreme elevations (T scores of 57 to 64) are described as self-dissatisfied, irritable, having wide interests, and immature. They are unlikely to be perceived as being deviant or withdrawn and may be seen as creative, individualistic, and imaginative. They like theoretical and abstract philosophical issues.

Low scorers (T scores less than 45) are seen as being compliant, submissive, and overly accepting of authority. They tend to have very practical interests with little concern about theoretical or philosophical issues. They also have difficulty understanding persons who approach issues in a theoretical or philosophical manner.

Test-retest reliability coefficients for Scale *8* for intervals up to two weeks range from .74 to .95, and for intervals up to one year from .37 to .64 (Dahlstrom et al., 1975). Test-retest reliability coefficients for Scale *8* on the MMPI-2 for approximately a one-week interval are .87 for men and .80 for women (Butcher et al., 1989).

There are small gender differences on Scale *8*, with females likely to endorse slightly more items than males. Scores tend to decrease 5 to 10 T points with age in psychiatric patients (Hedlund & Won Cho, 1979) and 2 to 5 T points in medical patients (Swenson et al., 1973) and normal individuals (Colligan et al., 1983, 1989). Scores also decline with chronicity so that older patients frequently score in the normal range (Davis, 1972; Wauck, 1950). Marital status has been reported to be unrelated to Scale *8* scores (Lacks, Rothenberg, & Unger, 1970).

A summary of the interpretations of five levels of elevation on Scale *8* is presented in Table 4–15.

Scale *6*-*7*-*8* Configurations

One configuration of Scales *6*, *7*, and *8* is seen frequently. It consists of Scales *6* and *8* being above a T score of 80, and Scale *7* being above a T score of 65 (see Figure 4–6). Scales *6* and *8* will be the high-point pair of this configuration. This configuration is sometimes called the paranoid valley or a psychotic "V."

Clients exhibiting this configuration are likely to be emotionally withdrawn, socially isolated, suspicious, hostile, and lacking insight into their own behavior. They also may have thought disorders, delusions, and hallucinations. They usually are labeled as being psychotic with the most frequent diagnosis being paranoid schizophrenia. (The clinician should examine the description of a *6*-*8*/*8*-*6* codetype in Chapter 6 for more information on this configuration.)

This configuration probably occurs most frequently in invalid profiles! It is characteristic of an "all true" response set (see page 125) and many random response sets (see page 127) so the clinician needs to examine measures of the consistency of item endorsement (see Chapter 3). It also occurs frequently when clients are overreporting psychopathology; the clinician should examine measures of the accuracy of item endorsement (see Chapter 3).

If the clinician has determined that this *6*-*7*-*8* configuration is valid (i.e., measures of the consistency and accuracy of item endorsement are in the appropriate ranges), Scales *2* (Depression) and *0* (Social Introversion) may be helpful in distinguishing between clients with a thought disorder and clients with a mood disorder with psychotic features (Post, Clopton, Keefer, Rosenberg, Blyth, & Stein, 1986). Walters and Greene (1988) found similar mean differences on Scales *2* and *0* between groups of inpatients with thought and mood disorders, but they could not identify any decision rule to discriminate the individ-

TABLE 4–15   Interpretation of Levels of Elevation on Scale *8:* Schizophrenia (*Sc*)

MMPI-2 T Score	MMPI T Score	Interpretation
44 and below	40 and below	1. *Low.* These clients are conventional, realistic, and uninterested in theoretical or philosophical issues. They are unimaginative and concrete and may have difficulty with persons who perceive the world differently.
45–57	45–59	2. *Normal.* Chronic schizophrenics who have adjusted to their psychotic process may score in this range. Otherwise, scores in this range are normal.
58–64	60–69	3. *Moderate.* These clients think differently from others, though this may reflect creativity, an avant-garde attitude, or actual schizoid-like processes. These clients tend to avoid reality through fantasy and daydreams. Review of the content and/or supplementary scales may help to differentiate among these alternatives; the clinician also should examine what other clinical scales are elevated.
65–90	70–99	4. *Marked.* These clients feel alienated and remote from their environment, which may reflect an actual schizophrenic process or situational or personal distress. Review of the content and/or supplementary scales may be helpful at the lower end of this range. Difficulties in logic and concentration and poor judgment become apparent as scores move higher in this range. As scores approach a T score of 80, the presence of a thought disorder is likely. Therapeutic interventions should be directive and supportive and frequently require psychotropic medications.
91 and above	100 and above	5. *Extreme.* These clients are under acute, severe situational stress. A client going through an identity crisis will score in this range. These clients typically are *not* schizophrenic.

ual patients accurately. Consequently, clinicians should consider this decision rule to be tentative.

Scales *2* and *0* usually are above a T score of 60 in clients with thought disorders and below a T score of 55 in clients with a manic mood disorder. Wiggins' (1966) Psychoticism scale and the MMPI-2 content scale (Butcher et al., 1989) of Bizarre Mentation will *not* distinguish between these two disorders since they are general measures of psychoticism. However, Wiggins' Hypomania scale will be higher in clients with a manic mood disorder.

SCALE *9:* HYPOMANIA (*Ma*)

The milder degrees of manic excitement, characterized by an elated but unstable mood, psychomotor excitement, and flight of ideas are covered by the 46 items comprising Scale *9* (McKinley & Hathaway, 1944). The items range over a wide variety of content areas including overactivity, both behaviorally and cognitively, grandiosity, egocentricity, and irritability.

The criterion group for Scale *9* consisted of 24 manic patients of moderate or mild severity since more severe cases would not cooperate with testing. The item endorsements of this criterion group were contrasted with those of the original Minnesota normative group to develop Scale *9* empirically, resulting in the 46 items currently on the scale. The clinician should remember that the label of hypomania refers to elevated scores, not T scores below 50 as the prefix ''hypo'' might suggest.

A normal activity level is indicated by T

FIGURE 4–6   Scales *6-7-8* Configuration: Psychotic "V"

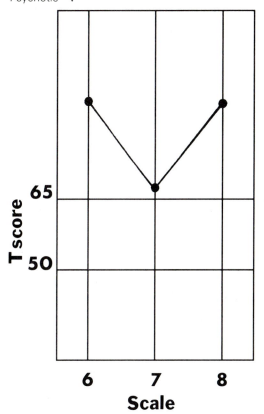

scores in the normal range (45 to 57), and more elevated scores indicate increasing levels of mania. Hence, elevated scores indicate hypomania, and increasingly higher scores reflect mania and ultimately hypermania. Since manic cases are usually readily identified behaviorally, it is the more moderate cases that need to be identified by Scale 9.

Examples of scale items with the deviant response in parentheses are:

"When I get bored I like to stir up some excitement." (true)

"I am an important person." (true)

"I don't blame people for trying to grab everything they can get in this world." (true)[10]

Comrey (1958d) found that Scale *9* had the most diversified factor content of any of the clinical scales and that most of the factor content was unique to this scale. He identified 11 major sources of variance: *shyness*, *bitterness*, *acceptance of taboos*, *poor reality contact*, *thrill seeking*, *social dependency*, *psychopathic personality*, *high water consumption*, *hypomania*, *agitation*, and *defensiveness*.

Harris and Lingoes (1955) identified four subscales within Scale *9*: Amorality, Psychomotor Acceleration, Imperturbability, and Ego Inflation (see Table 4–16). There is little overlap between Comrey's factors and the Harris and Lingoes subscales. The Psychomotor Acceleration subscale shares some items with thrill seeking and agitation, and Imperturbability shares a few items with shyness.

Scale *9* also shares few items with any of Wiggins' (1966) content scales; even with Wiggins' Hypomania scale the overlap is minimal (7/25). There is even less overlap with any of the Tryon, Stein, and Chu (Stein, 1968) cluster scales; Scale *9* has no more than 4 items in common with any of these scales. Finally, Scale *9* shares few items with the MMPI-2 content scales (Butcher et al., 1989). As with Scale *8*, it appears that different methods of item grouping produce quite different results, and the correlates of these groups need to be empirically investigated.

Scale *9* has substantial overlap with Scale *8* (11 items), but shares only from 1 to 6 items with the rest of the validity and clinical scales. There are 15 items unique to Scale *9*. Wiener and Harmon (Wiener, 1948) found that the scale had an equal number of obvious and subtle items. Again, the preponderance of deviant responses are "true" (35/46), as with the other scales in the psychotic tetrad.

Scale *9* also is difficult to interpret in isolation. It can be conceptualized as providing energy to activate the qualities identified by

TABLE 4–16 Description of High Scorers on the Harris and Lingoes Subscales for Scale *9* (Hypomania)

Subscale			
Name	Abbre-viation	Number of Items	Description of High Scorers
Amorality	Ma_1	6	These clients have a callousness about their own motives and ends and those of other people; they are disarmingly frank; they deny guilt.
Psychomotor Acceleration	Ma_2	11	These clients are hyperactive and labile; they show flight from "inner life" and anxiety, and pressure for action.
Imperturbability	Ma_3	8	These clients are confident in social situations; they deny sensitivity; they proclaim independence from the opinions of other persons.
Ego Inflation	Ma_4	9	These clients feel self-important to the point of unrealistic grandiosity.

other elevated clinical scales. Thus, a client who elevates Scale *4* along with Scale *9* will display very different behaviors than a client who simultaneously elevates Scales *8* and *9* (see the description of these two codetypes in Chapter 6).

Scale *9* is often described as being elevated in persons with brain damage (cf. Carson, 1969). Although some brain-damaged persons may display hyperactive and impulsive behaviors, virtually any type of emotional response may occur in brain-damaged persons, particularly depression. The MMPI-2 is an excellent instrument to assess the response of a person to brain damage, but there is not a typical score on Scale *9* or a typical clinical profile for brain-damaged persons. Some persons may respond to brain damage by becoming depressed; others may become apathetic, withdrawn, and display psychotic features; still others may be virtually unaffected. Farr and Martin (1988) have reviewed the performance of neuropsychological samples on a number of MMPI scales and indexes.

Post and colleagues (1986) found that bipolar disorder, manic patients had higher scores on Scale *9* than other psychotic psychiatric patients and general psychiatric patients. They found that discriminant analysis, with Scales *2*, *9*, and *0* as predictors, correctly classified 82.5 percent of the patients in their derivation sample and 74.2 percent in the cross-validation sample. However, Walters and Greene (1988) found that Scale *9* did not discriminate between bipolar disorder, manic patients and schizophrenic patients. Similar to Post and associates (1986), they found that Scale *0* did discriminate between these two groups of patients with schizophrenics earning higher scores.

High scorers on Scale *9* (T scores of 65 or higher) are described as being impulsive, competitive, talkative, narcissistic, amoral, extroverted, and superficial in social relationships. They typically have problems in controlling their behavior and display hostile, irritable qualities. They are not described as depressed. They may display actual manic features: flight of ideas, lability of mood, delusions of grandeur, impulsivity, and hyper-activity.

High-scoring normals (T scores of 65 or higher) are described in generally positive terms: friendly, sociable, energetic, talkative, and enthusiastic. Basically they have a pleasant, outgoing temperament. If scores become elevated over a T score of 75, some other features become apparent—hyperactivity, impulsivity, and irritability. There may even be acting out of conflicts in such persons.

Low scorers (T scores less than 45) also are described in positive terms. They are considered dependable, reliable, mature, and conscientious. They frequently participate very little in social activities.

Extremely low scores (T scores below 40 in most groups; see below) are described as apathetic, having little energy, and listless. Such persons usually are significantly depressed regardless of their score on Scale 2. The possibility of serious depression should be considered when Scale 9 is in this range even if the rest of the profile is within normal limits. In fact, low scores on Scale 9 are generally better indicators of the presence of significant depression than high scores on Scale 2. The clinician should evaluate suicide potential in these clients, particularly if the client seems to be getting more energized.

Test-retest reliability coefficients for Scale 9 for intervals up to two weeks range from .63 to .96; for intervals up to one year they range from .43 to .64 (Dahlstrom et al., 1975). Test-retest reliability coefficients for Scale 9 on the MMPI-2 for approximately a one-week interval are .83 for men and .68 for women (Butcher et al., 1989).

There are no gender differences on Scale 9; in fact, identical T score conversions are used for both males and females in the standard MMPI profile. Scores on Scale 9 change significantly with increasing age. Adolescents and college students usually score in the T score range of 55 to 65, whereas aged persons score in the range of 40 to 50. Thus, interpre-tations of high and low scores on Scale 9 must take into account these normal variations as a function of age. Clients whose scores on Scale 9 are 15 or more T points higher or lower than these expected ranges should be evaluated for the presence of a mood disorder.

A summary of the interpretations of four levels of elevation of Scale 9 is presented in Table 4–17.

SCALE 0: SOCIAL INTROVERSION (Si)

The 69 items (70 items on the MMPI) in Scale 0 were selected to assess the social introversion-extroversion dimension with high scores reflecting social introversion. The social introvert is uncomfortable in social interactions and typically withdraws from such interactions when possible. This individual may have limited social skills or simply prefer to be alone or with a small group of friends. The social extrovert is socially outgoing, gregarious, and seeks social interactions. Item content on Scale 0 reflects personal discomfort in social situations, isolation, general maladjustment, and self-deprecation.

Scale 0 was not based on a psychiatric syndrome; rather it was developed by using a psychological test—the Minnesota T-S-E Inventory (Evans & McConnell, 1941)—to form criterion groups. The Minnesota T-S-E Inventory assesses introversion-extroversion in three areas: thinking (T), social (S), and emotional (E).

Drake (1946) limited his investigation of introversion-extroversion to the social area as assessed by the Minnesota T-S-E Inventory. He selected items for Scale 0 by contrasting groups of students in the guidance program at the University of Wisconsin. Two groups were formed: 50 female students scoring above the 65th percentile on the social introversion-extroversion subscale of the Minnesota T-S-E Inventory, and 50 female students scoring below the 35th percentile. After those

TABLE 4–17   Interpretation of Levels of Elevation on Scale *9:* Hypomania (*Ma*)

MMPI-2 T Score	MMPI T Score	Interpretation
44 and below	40 and below	1. *Low.* These clients have a low energy and activity level that may reflect situational circumstances such as fatigue or actual depression. Extremely low scores (*T* < 35) indicate depression irrespective of the elevation of Scale *2.* Normal, aged persons score in the upper end of this range.
45–57	41–59	2. *Normal.* Normal college students and adolescents score in the upper end of this range. The client has a normal activity level.
58–64	60–69	3. *Moderate.* These clients are active, outgoing, and energetic. External restrictions on their activity level may result in agitation and overtly expressed dissatisfaction. Review of the content and/or supplementary scales may facilitate interpretation in this range.
65 and above	70 and above	4. *Marked.* These clients are overactive, emotionally labile, and may experience flight of ideas. Although the client's mood is typically euphoric, outbursts of temper may occur. These clients are impulsive and may have an inability to delay gratification. Manic features become increasingly pronounced with more elevated scores. The narcissistic and grandiose features also become more apparent. Review of the content and/or supplementary scales may facilitate interpretation at the lower end of this range.

items were eliminated that had a very high or very low frequency of endorsement in either or both groups, 70 items were selected that discriminated these two groups.

Drake (1946) later tested male students on Scale *0* and computed separate norms for males and females. The distributions of the total raw score for these two groups were so similar that Drake combined them into a single group to establish the norms on the MMPI.

Examples of Scale *0* items with the deviant response in parentheses are:

"At parties I am more likely to sit by myself or with just one other person than to join in with the crowd." (true)

"Whenever possible I avoid being in a crowd." (true)

"If given the chance I would make a good leader of people." (false)[11]

Comrey (1957a) did not factor analyze the items on Scale *0,* and Harris and Lingoes (1955) did not attempt to create subscales for this scale. Graham and associates (1971) identified six factors among Scale *0* items: Inferiority and Discomfort, Affiliation, Social Excitement, Sensitivity, Interpersonal Trust, and Physical-Somatic Concerns. Serkownek (1975) used the results of Graham and associates' factor analysis to create six subscales for Scale *0* (see Table 4–18). Williams (1983) found that Serkownek's subscales were in the acceptable ranges of reliability in college students and provided preliminary interpretive information for males and females. Clinicians can continue to use the Serkownek (1975) subscales on the MMPI-2 if desired since only one item was dropped from Scale *0.*

Ben-Porath, Hostetler, Butcher, and Graham (1989) developed new content-homogenous subscales for Scale *0* as an alternative to the Serkownek (1975) subscales. Ben-Porath and colleagues identified three subscales in college students: Shyness/Self-

TABLE 4–18 Description of High Scorers on the Serkownek Subscales for Scale *0* (Social Introversion)

Subscale			
Name	Abbre- viation	Number of Items	Description of High Scorers
Inferiority-Personal Discomfort	Si_1	27	These clients are unhappy and uncomfortable because of their perceived lack of interpersonal skills.
Discomfort with Others	Si_2	13	These clients do not enjoy being with other people and have problems being assertive.
Staid-Personal Rigidity	Si_3	16	These clients participate in few active social groups.
Hypersensitivity	Si_4	10	These clients are sensitive to the reactions of others; they are shy, easily embarrassed, and generally anxious; they are likely to avoid facing up to stressful situations.
Distrust	Si_5	12	These clients feel that others are dishonest, insincere, selfish, and generally anxious.
Physical-Somatic	Si_6	10	These clients admit somatic ailments and concern about their physical appearance.

Consciousness, Social Avoidance, and Self/Other Alienation (see Table 4–19). These three subscales accounted for nearly 90 percent of the variance in Scale *0* scores.

Scale *0* overlaps significantly with Wiggins' (1966) Social Maladjustment scale (21/27), which Wiggins characterized as corresponding roughly to an introversion-extroversion dimension. Scale *0* also has substantial item overlap with the Tryon, Stein, and Chu (Stein, 1968) Social Introversion scale (20/26). Regardless of the method of item grouping, a dimension of social introversion-extroversion appears to permeate the MMPI items.

Scale *0* shares fewer items proportionally with other validity and clinical scales than any other scale. There are 26 items unique to Scale *0*. Scales *2* and *7* share 7 and 8 items, respectively, with Scale *0*. Most scales share only 1 item with Scale *0*. Wiener and Harmon (Wiener, 1948) did not develop subtle and obvious scales for this scale. Christian and colleagues (1978) found that students rated Scale *0* items as being neutral, neither subtle nor obvious. There are almost exactly the same number of "true" (34) as "false" (35) deviant responses to Scale *0* items.

High scorers on Scale *0* (T scores of 65 or higher) in both psychiatric and normal populations are described similarly. They are seen as socially introverted, shy, and withdrawn. More extreme groups (T scores greater than 70 in most groups; see below) are described as socially inept, aloof, self-deprecating, and anxious in their interactions with others. Scale *0* scores tend to be unrelated to psychopathology since elevations may reflect a schizoid withdrawal from interpersonal relationships, neurotic withdrawal, and self-dep-

TABLE 4–19 Description of High Scorers on the Ben-Porath et al. Subscales for Scale *0* (Social Introversion)

| | Subscale | | |
Name	Abbre-viation	Number of Items	Description of High Scorers
Shyness/Self-Consciousness	Si_1	14	These clients are shy around others and easily embarrassed. They are uncomfortable in social and new situations, and avoid contact with people.
Social Avoidance	Si_2	8	These clients dislike and avoid group activities of all types, and act to keep people at a distance.
Self/Other Alienation	Si_3	17	These clients have low self-esteem and lack self-confidence. They question their own judgment. They are nervous, fearful, and indecisive. They lack interest in things.

recation as a function of personal distress, or merely an introverted orientation. In other words, the exact interpretation of Scale *0* will depend on the client's situation and which other clinical scales are elevated.

Low scorers (T scores less than 45) are essentially described as being extroverted. They are sociable, outgoing, and versatile in their interactions with others. They participate in many social activities. They may be unable to delay gratification and be undercontrolled emotionally. Extremely low scorers (T scores below 35) are described as being flighty, superficial in their relationships with others, and lacking any real intimacy. These characteristics are especially likely if the client simultaneously elevates Scale *3* or *4*.

Test-retest reliability coefficients for Scale *0* on the MMPI usually are higher than for the other clinical scales. Correlations for intervals up to two weeks range from .80 to .96 and for intervals up to one year from .54 to .76 (Dahlstrom et al., 1975). Test-retest re-

liability coefficients for Scale *0* on the MMPI-2 for approximately a one-week interval are .92 for men and .91 for women (Butcher et al., 1989).

Scores on Scale *0* increase with age. Adolescents and college students usually achieve T scores in the range of 40 to 50, while aged persons score from 50 to 60. Scale *0* appears to have an important role in marital relationships. Couples with T scores on Scale *0* that differ by 20 points or more will frequently report marital conflicts over their social relationships. One partner prefers to be alone or with small groups of friends while the other prefers larger social functions. This difference in social orientation may have appealed to them initially, but it can become a source of marital conflict.

Elevation of Scale *0* typically suppresses the acting out seen with elevations of Scales *4* and *9*, whereas it may accentuate the ruminating behaviors seen with elevations on Scales *2* or *7* and especially Scale *8*.

Linear T scores are used on Scale *0* for

TABLE 4–20   Interpretation of Levels of Elevation on Scale *0:* Social Introversion (*Si*)

MMPI-2 T Score	MMPI T Score	Interpretation
44 and below	40 and below	1. *Low.* These clients are socially extroverted, gregarious, and socially poised. A person with an extremely low score (*T* < 35) may have very superficial social relationships without any real depth. Adolescents and college students normally score at the upper end of this range. The clinician should be very cautious of labeling these clients as being schizophrenic.
45–57	41–59	2. *Normal.* These clients report a balance between socially extroverted and introverted attitudes and behaviors.
58–64	60–69	3. *Moderate.* These clients prefer to be alone or with a small group of friends. They have the ability to interact with others, but generally prefer not to. Review of the content and/or supplementary scales may facilitate interpretation in this range.
65 and above	70 and above	4. *Marked.* These clients are introverted, shy, and socially insecure. In addition, they withdraw from and avoid significant others, which serves to exacerbate their problems since others might be able to help them. The likelihood of acting out is decreased and ruminative behavior is increased. Intervention should specifically address the client's tendency to withdraw. Review of the content and/or supplementary scales may facilitate interpretation at the lower end of this range.

the MMPI-2 as was the case on the MMPI. T scores on Scale *0* of the MMPI seldom get very high or very low. It is one of the few MMPI scales on which T scores closely represent the frequency with which a score will be obtained (i.e., a T score of 65 or higher will occur two to three times in 100 cases). Consequently, clinicians can begin to interpret Scale *0* on the MMPI when T scores reach 65 or higher and 35 and lower.

A summary of the interpretations of four levels of elevation of Scale *0* is given in Table 4–20.

ENDNOTES

1. Reproduced from the MMPI-2 by permission. Copyright © 1943, (renewed 1970), 1989 by the University of Minnesota. Published by the University of Minnesota Press. All rights reserved.

2. Ibid.

3. Ibid.

4. Ibid.

5. Ibid.

6. Ibid.

7. Ibid.

8. Ibid.

9. This second criterion can be stated more simply as follows: The raw score on Scale *8 without* the *K*-correction should be twice the raw score on the *K* scale.

10. Reproduced from the MMPI-2 by permission. Copyright © 1943, (renewed 1970), 1989 by the University of Minnesota. Published by the University of Minnesota Press. All rights reserved.

11. Ibid.

CHAPTER 5

Supplementary Scales, Content Scales, Critical Items, and Short Forms

The popularity of the MMPI quickly led to the proliferation of additional means of garnering information from the item pool. The apparent ease with which investigators can identify a criterion group and contrast their responses to all 550 items on the MMPI with a normal group has resulted in more than 450 supplementary scales (Dahlstrom, Welsh, & Dahlstrom, 1975).

A large number of these MMPI scales are too limited or specialized for widespread use and few of them are cross-validated. Consequently, only some of the more widely used supplementary scales will be considered here. It is necessary to administer all 567 MMPI-2 items if all the supplementary and content scales and critical items are to be evaluated. The client can stop after answering the first 370 items of the MMPI-2 (see Chapter 2) and the clinician can still score the standard validity and clinical scales and plot the standard profile.

The clinician must realize, however, that most of the supplementary and content scales and critical item lists that will be discussed in this chapter also require scoring many of the last 200 items. Consequently, these addi-tional sources of information about the client must be sacrificed if only the first 370 items are administered.

Next, certain items within the MMPI have been identified as "critical" or "stop" items because by endorsing any one of these items, the client is acknowledging the existence of behavior or psychopathology that may demand immediate attention.

This chapter will review various lists of critical items and the problems of identifying what and how many items are actually "critical." Finally, this chapter will review the MMPI short forms (i.e., abbreviated versions of the MMPI that attempt to predict the scores on the validity and clinical scales from a limited number of items), and their use in clinical practice.

SUPPLEMENTARY SCALES

Before undertaking the development of a new supplementary scale on the MMPI-2, the clinician is strongly encouraged to review Clopton's (1974, 1978b, 1979a, 1982; Clopton & Neuringer, 1977a; Levitt, 1978) description of the methodology for the development of supplementary scales and Butcher and Tellegen's (1978) description of the common methodologic problems in MMPI research.

The associated issue of whether the supplementary scales generate redundant information already provided by the standard validity and clinical scales has not been investigated widely. Clopton and Klein (1978) found that three supplementary scales (Prejudice, Ego Strength, and MacAndrew Alcoholism) were highly related to the scores on the standard validity and clinical scales. They found, however, that a client's individual scores on these three scales could not be predicted accurately. This issue of the possible redundancy of the supplementary scales with the standard validity and clinical scales needs further investigation.

The interest in supplementary scales of the MMPI has increased in the last several years as evidenced by two recent texts (Caldwell, 1988; Levitt, 1989). Caldwell has provided interpretive information on 104 different supplementary scales and Levitt on 68. Both Caldwell and Levitt reviewed the Harris and Lingoes (1955) subscales, Wiggins' (1966) Content scales, and the Tryon, Stein, and Chu Cluster scales (Stein, 1968). The interpretive information in both books reflects the authors' clinical experience in using the various scales with little empirical data presented.

Levitt (1989) also included a list of supplementary scales that are not recommended for clinical use (pp. 113–114). The rationale for including a specific scale in this list was not made explicit other than a general statement about lack of experimental evaluation. No doubt some clinicians will be concerned that their favorite scale is on Levitt's "hit" list. Levitt also recommended the use of several scales in his text that would seem to reflect the same lack of experimental validation such as the Tryon, Stein, and Chu Cluster scales (Stein, 1968), Over-controlled Hostility (Megargee, Cook, & Mendelsohn, 1967),

and the Wiener and Harmon (Wiener, 1948) Depression-Subtle subscale. Colligan, Osborne, Swenson, and Offord (1989) have provided percentile ranks from their contemporary normative sample by gender for many of the scales reviewed in this chapter.

Templates for hand scoring many of the MMPI-2 and MMPI supplementary scales are available from National Computer Systems (P.O. Box 1416, Minneapolis MN 55440, 800–627–7271); Psychological Assessment Resources (P.O. Box 998, Odessa FL 33556, 800–331–8378) provides templates only for the MMPI.

TRADITIONAL SUPPLEMENTARY SCALES

Welsh Anxiety (*A*) and Repression (*R*) Scales

Factor-analytic studies of the MMPI clinical scales have consistently identified two factors that are variously labeled and interpreted. Welsh (1956) constructed his Anxiety (*A*) and Repression (*R*) scales to measure these two factors. The first factor has been interpreted in two different ways, and investigators debated for nearly ten years over which interpretation was more appropriate.

Welsh found that this factor has high positive loadings on Scales *7* (Psychasthenia) and *8* (Schizophrenia) and high negative loadings on the *K* scale. This factor has been identified as reflecting a personality factor labeled anxiety (Welsh, 1956), lack of ego resiliency (Block, 1965), and general maladjustment (Tyler, 1951). This factor also has been identified as reflecting a response bias factor labeled social desirability (Edwards & Diers, 1962) or the deviation hypothesis (Berg, 1955, 1957). In the deviation hypothesis, the actual item content and personality characteristics are deemed to be unimportant since a general response tendency is the primary determinant of whether or not the client endorses a specific item.

After a decade of debate, Block (1965) demonstrated that the factor structure of the MMPI was virtually unchanged when the potential of response bias, particularly social desirability and acquiescence, was controlled. Although Jackson (1967) questioned Block's research on several methodologic issues, Block's findings convinced most investigators that the first factor should be interpreted as a personality factor rather than a response bias factor. More recently, Shweder (1977a, 1977b) renewed the debate when he posited that the first factor reflects a conceptual linkage among test items that is not a personality factor.

The reader is encouraged to examine Shweder's (1977a) proposed interpretation, Block's (1977) and Edwards' (1977) response to Shweder, and Shweder's (1977b) reply to Block and Edwards for further information on this heated debate. Dahlstrom and colleagues (1975) provided an in-depth analysis of the major sources of variance in the MMPI, which is also pertinent to this debate. Most MMPI researchers concur with Block's position; however, the informed reader can decide for himself or herself which interpretation of the first factor of the MMPI seems most appropriate.

Unlike the first factor, the second factor of the MMPI has not involved controversy. Through factor analysis, Welsh (1956) found that the second factor has moderate positive loadings on Scales 2 (Depression), 3 (Hysteria), 5 (Masculinity-Femininity), and 6 (Paranoia), and a moderate negative loading on Scale 9 (Hypomania). He identified it as reflecting a personality factor, which he labeled repression.

To develop the A and R scales, Welsh selected male Veterans Administration (VA) patients who scored at or beyond the upper and lower 10 percent of a preliminary scale designed to assess each factor; he then contrasted the responses of these extreme groups on all 550 MMPI items. The A scale consists of 39 items that showed at least a 75 percent separation between high and low scores in two separate VA samples. The R scale consists of 37 items (40 items on the MMPI) that showed at least a 60 percent separation of high and low scorers in the same two samples. The items on the A and R scales are provided in Appendix A for the MMPI-2 and Appendix D for the MMPI.

The major content areas represented in the A scale are:

1. Problems in thinking and thought processes
2. Negative emotional tone and dysphoria
3. Lack of energy and pessimism
4. Personal sensitivity
5. Deviant thought processes

In the R scale the major content areas are the denial of or constriction of interests in:

1. Health and physical symptoms
2. Emotionality, violence, and activity
3. Enjoyable reactions to others in a social situation
4. Social dominance, feelings of personal adequacy, and interest in personal appearance
5. Interest in personal and vocational pursuits

High A scores (T scores of 65 or higher) are related to behaviors in which anxiety is prominent, whereas high R scores (T scores of 65 or higher) are characterized by repression and denial. The anxiety being assessed by the A scale has been found to reflect situational anxiety rather than long-term characterologic anxiety, which is assessed by Scale 7 (Psychasthenia). The deviant response is "true" for all but one of the *A* scale items and "false" for all of the *R* scale items, which means that either a "true" or "false" response set will substantially affect scores on both of these scales. *TRIN* (True Response Inconsistency scale) scores above 9 would be expected with high *A* scores and below 9 with high *R* scores (see Chapter 3, pages 74–76).

High scorers on the *A* scale (T scores of 65 or higher) are described as anxious, lacking confidence in their own abilities, inhibited, and overcontrolled. They are characterized as reacting to situational stress or personal distress with anxiety. These persons are often seen as being generally maladjusted, and the elevation of the *A* scale reflects their discomfort. Because of this discomfort, they are usually motivated to enter into psychological treatment.

Low scorers on the *A* scale (T scores less than 45) are usually described as well adjusted and not overtly anxious. They may be impulsive and display behavioral problems, although these behaviors are not upsetting to them. They also are described as verbally fluent and competent in social situations.

A summary of the interpretations of four levels of elevation of the *A* scale is provided in Table 5–1.

High scorers on the *R* scale (T scores of 65 or higher) are seen as being unwilling to discuss their problems, which may reflect conscious suppression and constriction of interests in events around them or actual repression and denial. In the latter situation they also will typically elevate the *K* scale and Scale *3* (Hysteria), which would substantiate their repressive nature. These persons appear constricted and overcontrolled and lack insight into their own behavior. They are unwilling to discuss any form of psychopathology even though it may be apparent to everyone but themselves.

Low scorers on the *R* scale (T scores less than 45) are described as being able to discuss what problems they may perceive themselves

TABLE 5–1   Interpretation of *A* Scale Elevations

MMPI-2 T Score	MMPI T Score	Interpretation
44 and below	40 and below	1. *Low.* These clients are not overtly anxious. They are extroverted, verbally fluent, and confident in their own abilities. They may be impulsive. Such low scores in clients in clinical settings would not be expected. Be sure that a score in this range is appropriate for the client.
45–57	41–59	2. *Normal.* These clients have a normal amount of anxiety.
58–64	60–69	3. *Moderate.* These clients are reporting a significant degree of anxiety and distress that should be readily apparent. They usually are motivated to seek treatment because of their level of distress.
65 and above	70 and above	4. *Marked.* These clients are reporting an ever increasing level of anxiety and distress that may be totally debilitating. They frequently are seen as maladjusted and emotionally upset, which may reflect a situational crisis or a more chronic problem. Extreme scores (T scores of 80 and higher) frequently are produced by the client overreporting psychopathology (see Chapter 3).

as having. They tend to be socially extroverted and outgoing in their relationships with others.

A summary of the interpretations of three levels of elevation of the R scale is given in Table 5-2.

Welsh (1965) provided a summary of interpretations of the A and R scales when both scales are employed conjointly. (This summary table also appears in Dahlstrom, Welsh, and Dahlstrom [1972], pp. 238–239.) Welsh cautioned clinicians against making cookbook interpretations of these descriptions; rather he suggested that the interpretations be considered as tentative hypotheses for further investigation. Duckworth and Anderson (1986) reported that Welsh's system was not accurate for college students except for the high A and high R description. They furnished a more limited summary of the joint elevations of the A and R scales, which they found useful in college students. The clinician who is interested in using the A and R scales in profile interpretation should consult both of these sources.

Age does not appear to affect performance on the A and R scales; however, women tend to endorse a few more items than men (Swenson, Pearson, & Osborne, 1973). Since T scores for the A and R scales are provided by gender (see Appendix B), these gender differences will not affect the interpretation of these scales.

The A scale has substantial item overlap with a number of the standard clinical scales: Scale 2 (Depression)—6 items; Scale 7 (Psychasthenia)—13 items; Scale 8 (Schizophrenia)—8 items; and Scale 0 (Social Introversion)—10 items (see Table 5-3). The A scale also has substantial item overlap with several of the other supplementary scales: Mt (College Maladjustment)—12 items; PK (Post Traumatic Stress Disorder—Keane)—9 items; and PS (Post Traumatic Stress Disorder—Schlenger)—14 items (see Table 5-4).

All of these scales that share items with the A scale can be conceptualized as "first factor" scales (i.e., general measures of maladjustment and emotional distress). Since these scales are redundant measures of the first factor, it is not clear what additional information is gained by scoring all of these supplementary scales beyond the A scale. Research that demonstrates the unique variance accounted for by each of these first factor scales is needed if all of these scales are to be

TABLE 5–2   Interpretations of R Scale Elevations

MMPI-2 T Score	MMPI T Score	Interpretation
44 and below	40 and below	1. *Low.* These clients either do not have problems or are willing to discuss the problems that they perceive themselves as having.
45–57	41–59	2. *Normal.* These clients show an appropriate level of willingness to discuss their behavior and problems.
58 and above	60 and above	3. *Moderate and Marked.* These clients are unwilling to discuss their behavior and any problems they may have. They may be merely suppressing this material or repressing and denying that any problems exist. Scales K and 3 (Hysteria) are typically elevated in this latter situation. These clients typically lack insight into their own behavior.

TABLE 5-3 Item Overlap between the MMPI-2 Supplementary Scales and the Standard Validity and Clinical Scales

	A S O	R S O	Es S O	MAC-R S O	F_B S O	OH S O	Do S O	Re S O	Mt S O	GM S O	GF S O	PK S O	PS S O
L	0 0	0 0	0 0	1 0	0 0	3 0	0 1	1 0	0 1	0 0	2 0	0 1	0 0
F	0 0	2 1	0 3	5 0	0 0	0 0	0 0	0 1	0 0	0 0	0 2	5 0	4 0
K	0 5	4 0	1 1	0 0	0 0	3 0	1 0	1 0	1 3	0 0	0 0	0 3	0 2
Hs	0 0	3 0	0 7	1 1	0 0	1 0	0 0	1 0	6 0	0 5	0 0	5 0	5 0
D	6 0	10 0	1 10	0 4	0 0	1 2	0 4	1 0	16 0	0 4	2 0	11 2	11 2
Hy	2 2	4 0	1 10	1 4	0 0	4 0	1 2	3 0	9 2	0 5	0 1	9 1	10 2
Pd	3 1	0 0	1 5	7 1	0 0	2 2	2 4	0 5	5 0	1 2	1 4	11 0	9 0
Mf	1 0	5 3	2 5	2 5	0 0	3 1	1 1	4 1	0 0	0 9	16 0	1 0	0 0
Pa	1 0	2 0	0 3	3 0	2 0	2 1	1 0	0 3	2 2	1 2	0 1	7 0	6 0
Pt	13 0	0 0	0 9	1 2	2 0	1 1	0 6	0 1	14 0	1 4	0 0	17 0	17 0
Sc	8 0	1 2	1 9	2 5	10 0	0 0	0 2	0 2	9 0	0 2	0 1	19 0	27 0
Ma	0 1	0 2	2 3	5 0	0 0	0 3	2 3	0 3	3 1	1 1	0 5	3 0	5 0
Si	10 1	8 0	2 5	0 5	0 0	1 2	0 5	3 1	6 0	0 8	2 1	7 2	4 2

Note: "S" indicates that the deviant response for the item is the same on both scales; "O" indicates that the deviant response is "true" on one scale and "false" on the other scale.

scored routinely. Nine *A* scale items also are scored on the *Es* (Ego Strength) scale, but with the opposite response as deviant.

The *R* scale shares fewer items with other scales than the *A* scale. The *R* scale has 10 items in common with Scale *2* (Depression), 5 items with Scale *5* (Masculinity-Femininity), and 8 items with Scale *0* (Social Introversion). The *R* scale has even less overlap with the other supplementary scales. It shares

6 items with the *MAC-R* (MacAndrew Alcoholism Scale—Revised), and all of these items are scored in the opposite direction on the two scales.

Ego Strength (*Es*) Scale

Barron (1953) developed the Ego Strength (*Es*) scale by correlating the MMPI item responses of 33 neurotic clients at two separate

TABLE 5-4 Item Overlap among the MMPI-2 Supplementary Scales

	A S O	R S O	Es S O	MAC-R S O	F_B S O	OH S O	Do S O	Re S O	Mt S O	GM S O	GF S O	PK S O
R	0 0											
Es	0 9	1 3										
MAC-R	1 2	0 6	0 4									
F_B	1 0	0 0	1 0	2 1								
OH	0 2	2 0	0 3	1 2	0 0							
Do	0 5	0 0	4 0	2 6	0 0	1 0						
Re	0 0	4 1	2 1	0 9	2 0	2 1	5 0					
Mt	12 0	1 1	0 6	1 3	0 0	0 1	0 4	0 0				
GM	0 3	0 2	7 1	3 0	0 1	0 2	2 0	3 1	1 4			
GF	0 0	3 4	0 3	4 5	0 0	2 1	2 1	6 1	1 0	0 0		
PK	9 0	0 2	0 10	3 1	2 0	1 0	0 3	0 1	10 0	0 1	0 0	
PS	14 0	1 2	0 10	1 3	4 0	2 2	1 2	0 2	13 0	0 3	0 0	26 0

Note: "S" indicates that the deviant response for the item is the same on both scales; "O" indicates that the deviant response is "true" on one scale and "false" on the other scale.

test administrations. Each client completed all 550 items on the MMPI before psychotherapy was initiated and then again after six months of psychotherapy. The clients were divided into two groups: 17 of them were judged to have clearly improved after six months of psychotherapy, and the other 16 were judged to be unimproved after the same interval.

Barron identified 68 items (only 52 items remain on the MMPI-2) that significantly correlated with rated improvement in these 33 clients. He concluded that these items (see Appendix A for the MMPI-2 items) measured a general factor of capacity for personality integration, or ego strength—hence the name of the scale. He believed that the Es scale assessed the latent ego strength of the person and that this would be an important determinant of response to psychotherapy.

Although all the clients were seeking psychotherapy for some sort of psychological difficulty, a high Es score, which indicates good ego strength, suggested that the person had resources that would emerge as therapy progressed. Since Es has a moderate negative correlation with all validity and clinical scales except one (it has a moderate positive correlation with the K scale), Barron hypothesized that clients with high Es scores were more likely to be facing situational stresses while clients with low Es scores were more likely to be experiencing chronic, characterologic problems.

Probably no other supplementary scale has generated as much research with contradictory results as the Es scale; various studies have reported positive, no, and inverse relationships between the Es scale and outcome in psychotherapy. Dahlstrom and associates (1975) provided a comprehensive review of these studies. They also pointed out the paradoxical relationship between psychotherapy outcome and Es scores as reported by Barron (1953).

Clients with high Es scores would be expected to have relatively normal profiles because of the inverse relationship between the Es scale and the clinical scales. Their normal profile would suggest that either they have no problems or they are extremely unwilling to admit any problems; yet they are requesting psychological treatment. Psychological intervention may be unnecessary in the former instance and very difficult in the latter because of their defensiveness and resistance. Clients with high Es scale scores and an elevated profile may be indicating that they have the appropriate resources for dealing with their problems, which probably are of recent origin. As a consequence of these different profiles that could be obtained with high Es scores, sampling differences could produce the variety of relationships to psychotherapy outcome described above.

The plethora of studies reporting no relationship between the Es scale and psychotherapy outcome indicates that the Es scale is of little usefulness in routinely predicting the response of a given client to psychotherapy. If further research on the Es scale is deemed necessary, it should try to identify those subgroups of clients in whom positive or negative psychotherapy outcome is expected.

The contradictory nature of the research on the Es scale makes it inappropriate to describe correlates of high and low scores on this scale.

The Es scale has substantial item overlap with a number of the standard clinical scales with the items being scored in the opposite direction on the Es scale: Scale 1 (Hypochondriasis)—7 items; Scale 2 (Depression)—10 items; Scale 3 (Hysteria)—10 items; Scale 7 (Psychasthenia)—9 items; and Scale 8 (Schizophrenia)—9 items (see Table 5-3).

The Es scale also has substantial item overlap with several of the other supplementary scales (see Table 5-4), and again the items are scored in the opposite direction: A (Anxiety)—9 items; Mt (College Maladjustment)—6 items; PK (Post Traumatic Stress

Disorder—Keane)—10 items; and *PS* (Post Traumatic Stress Disorder—Schlenger)—10 items.

Thus, the *Es* scale could be conceptualized as a negative marker for the first factor rather than as a measure of ego strength (i.e., high scorers on the *Es* scale are saying that they are not generally maladjusted or emotionally distressed, which would seem to make them poor candidates for psychotherapy).

MacAndrew Alcoholism (*MAC*) Scale

Several early investigators (Hampton, 1953; Holmes, 1953; Hoyt & Sedlacek, 1958) attempted to develop supplementary MMPI scales to detect alcoholism with limited success (cf. Clopton, 1978a; MacAndrew & Geertsma, 1964). MacAndrew (1965) was more successful in developing his Alcoholism (*MAC*) scale. He selected items that differentiated alcoholic outpatients from nonalcoholic, psychiatric outpatients. All patients were male, and most were white. MacAndrew identified 51 MMPI items that reliably separated these groups. Two of these 51 MMPI items (215 and 460) actually refer to alcohol use, and most investigators eliminate these two items, leaving a total of 49 items on the *MAC* scale.[1]

In the original sample, a raw score of 24 items or more to identify a patient as alcoholic correctly classified 81.8 percent of the patients. In a cross-validation sample this same cutting score correctly classified 81.5 percent of the patients, which is an unusually small loss of accuracy in classification. Through a factor analysis of the *MAC* scale, Schwartz and Graham (1979) found that the scale taps several discrete dimensions of personality and behavior, including impulsivity, high energy levels, interpersonal shallowness, and general psychological maladjustment, but not general antisociality.

Although MacAndrew (1965) developed the *MAC* scale on men and intended it to be used only with men, researchers quickly extended its use to women (cf. Rich & Davis, 1969; Schwartz & Graham, 1979). In fact, popular usage of the *MAC* scale does not recognize that the scale was developed originally for men; consequently the use of the *MAC* scale in men and women will be reviewed here.

Recently MacAndrew has developed substance abuse scales specifically for use with young men (Substance Abuse Proclivity scale [*SAP*]: MacAndrew, 1986) and women (MacAndrew, 1988). Research on these two scales has been limited since they were only recently developed. MacAndrew (1987) reported that the *SAP* scale was negatively correlated with age, which suggested that it was "tapping something more fundamental than the accumulated consequences of chronic substance abuse" (p. 145).

MacAndrew also found that the detection rates with the *SAP* and *MAC* scales were almost identical in these young adults. The very similar detection rates for the two scales are somewhat surprising since they share only nine items in common. If other studies reveal that the *SAP* and *MAC* produce similar results, it would appear unnecessary to score both scales.

Probably no single MMPI scale has generated more research than the *MAC* scale, and numerous reviews are available (cf. Apfeldorf, 1978; Gottesman & Prescott, 1989; Greene & Garvin, 1988; MacAndrew, 1981; Megargee, 1985). In the interests of brevity only a summary of the prolific research on the *MAC* scale will be provided here. This summary will draw heavily on the review by Greene and Garvin (1988). The interested reader should consult that review or any of the other reviews cited above for more specific information and references on the *MAC* scale. Table 5–5 provides a summary of

TABLE 5–5 Summary Table of the Performance on the MacAndrew Alcoholism Scale (*MAC*) as a Function of Age, Gender, and Ethnicity

Sample	*N*	Age	MAC (Raw Score) M	SD	False Positives	Hit Rate
Normal Individuals						
White						
Male adults	2975	34.5	23.1	4.3	26.5	76.2
Male adolescents	352	17.0	22.7	3.7	19.2	77.8
Female adults	1460	40.6	20.3	3.8	19.0	80.4
Female adolescents	213	15.8	20.9	4.0	7.4	86.6
Black						
Male adults	19	23.3	21.3	3.3	—	—
Psychiatric Patients						
White						
Male adults	2285	37.2	23.3	4.6	31.4	72.3
Male adolescents	749	16.7	19.8	7.8	42.3	68.0
Female adults	485	36.8	21.7	4.8	21.7	77.4
Female adolescents	444	16.4	20.4	6.9	37.0	74.0
Black						
Male adults	128	23.3	26.3	4.9	59.5	60.0
Medical Patients						
White						
Male adults	5353	49.0	—	—	37.3	—
Female adults	6737	48.8	—	—	20.3	—

Sample	*N*	Age	MAC (Raw Score) M	SD	False Negatives	Hit Rate
Alcoholics						
White						
Male adults	6512	40.8	28.4	5.5	20.4	73.1
Male adolescents	409	17.6	27.1	4.0	18.4	77.6
Female adults	1045	40.8	25.3	4.3	46.5	76.4
Female adolescents	163	15.8	26.2	4.6	11.5	87.9
Black						
Male adults	297	29.3	27.4	4.7	21.6	60.5
Polydrug Patients						
White						
Male adults	952	26.9	27.7	4.1	37.6	—
Female adults	127	41.5	—	—	72.5	—
Black						
Male adults	607	27.9	28.0	5.8	20.8	—

Note: From ''Substance abuse/dependence'' by R. L. Greene & R. D. Garvin in R. L. Greene (Ed.), *The MMPI: Use with specific populations,* 1988, p. 181. Philadelphia: Grune & Stratton. Reprinted by permission.

the performance on the *MAC* scale as a function of sample, age, gender, and ethnicity (Greene & Garvin, 1988).

The weighted (by sample size) mean score on the *MAC* scale in normal, white, adult male samples is 23.1 (*SD* = 4.3), which is only slightly below MacAndrew's traditional cutting score of 24. Gender differences in these normal, white, adult and adolescent samples are very consistent with men scoring approximately two raw-score points higher than women (*M* = 20.3; *SD* = 3.8). Normal, white adults and adolescents seem to have similar means and standard deviations; this finding is consistent with the report by Colligan and Offord (1987b) of no age differences on the *MAC* scale in their contemporary normative sample. Essentially no data exist on the *MAC* scale in normal samples of nonwhite ethnic groups. Hit rates in these normal samples ranged around 80 percent with approximately 20 percent false positives (normal individuals classified as alcoholic).

Both white, adult male (*M* = 23.3; *SD* = 4.6) and female (*M* = 21.7; *SD* = 4.8) psychiatric samples score slightly higher than their normal counterparts (male: *M* = 23.1; *SD* = 4.3) (female: *M* = 20.3; *SD* = 3.8). Again, men score approximately two raw-score points higher than women. Both male and female psychiatric patients are more variable in their performance on the *MAC* scale with slightly larger standard deviations.

In contrast to the adult samples, both male and female adolescent psychiatric samples have lower weighted mean scores on the *MAC* scale than their normal counterparts. The adolescent psychiatric samples also are extremely variable in their performance with standard deviations that are almost twice as large as those found in their normal counterparts. This increase in variability in both adult and adolescent psychiatric samples implies that hit rates and classification accuracy will decrease when alcoholics are contrasted with psychiatric patients rather than normal individuals.

Hit rates in these white psychiatric samples ranged around 75 percent, with approximately 35 percent false positives. (The reader should note that these percentages do not add to 100 since they are weighted means.) Both the hit rate and the false positive percentage decreased about 5 percentage points in the adult samples as compared with normal samples; however, the false positive percentage more than doubled in the adolescent samples.

Black, male adult psychiatric patients have a weighted mean score of 26.3 (*SD* = 4.9) on the *MAC* scale that is significantly higher than MacAndrew's (1965) recommended cutting score of 24. These black patients had a mean score that was five raw-score points higher than their normal colleagues. Both the hit rate and the false positive percentage were nearly 60 percent in these black patients. Although the sample size in these black patients was significantly smaller than any of the other samples, which may limit the generalizability of the results, clinicians should be very cautious in using the *MAC* scale in nonwhite ethnic groups.

This caution about the use of the *MAC* scale with blacks has been noted by several authors (cf. Graham & Mayo, 1985; Walters, Greene, Jeffrey, Kruzich, & Haskin, 1983). Again, there is almost a total lack of data on the *MAC* scale in nonwhite ethnic groups of psychiatric samples.

There has been only limited data on the *MAC* scale in medical patients, which is somewhat surprising since nearly 90 percent of the individuals who misuse alcohol are seen by their physician in a year (Kamerown, Pincus, & Macdonald, 1986). Davis, Colligan, Morse, and Offord (1987) reported that their white, male medical patients had an average of 37.3 percent false positives, and their female patients averaged 20.3 percent false positives. These false positive percentages in medical patients are comparable with those reported in psychiatric patients, so it would be expected that hit rates also would be comparable.

Colligan, Davis, Morse, and Offord (1988) found that none of seven alcoholism scales, one of which was the *MAC*, could be recommended for use in a medical setting because of the unsatisfactory classification rates. They did find that MMPI item #215 (MMPI-2 item #264), "I have used alcohol excessively," provided better classification rates for their medical patients than any of the alcoholism scales they reviewed. The need for additional research on how to detect substance abuse and dependence in medical patients, particularly in other ethnic groups, should be evident.

White, adult, male alcoholics had weighted mean scores significantly higher ($M = 28.4$; $SD = 5.5$) than their female counterparts ($M = 25.3$; $SD = 4.3$), and both samples were substantially above MacAndrew's (1965) suggested cutting score of 24. The pattern already noted in normal individuals and psychiatric patients for men to score about two raw-score points higher than women also was apparent, and even larger in alcoholic samples.

Male and female, white adolescent alcoholics had weighted mean scores that were somewhat comparable to those for adults. Hit rates and false negative (alcoholics classified as being nonalcoholic) percentages were very comparable for white, male adult and adolescent alcoholics. However, the false negative percentage was significantly higher in adult female alcoholics and significantly lower in adolescent female alcoholics. Black, male alcoholics had a weighted mean score of 27.4 ($SD = 4.7$) that is only one raw-score point higher than their psychiatric counterparts.

These small differences in mean scores

between black alcoholic and psychiatric patients make it nearly impossible for the *MAC* scale to discriminate between these two groups; hence the caution about using the *MAC* scale with nonwhite ethnic groups that was noted above. As expected because of the small mean differences between groups, hit rates in black, male alcoholics averaged only 60 percent. There are limited data on the use of the *MAC* scale in black, female alcoholics and essentially no data for other ethnic groups. Again, the need for research on the *MAC* scale in all nonwhite ethnic groups should be evident.

White, adult male polydrug abusers had a weighted mean score of 27.7 ($SD = 4.1$); black, adult male polydrug abusers had a weighted mean score of 28.0 ($SD = 5.8$). The false negative percentage in white polydrug abusers was nearly double (37.6 percent) that seen in their alcoholic counterparts (20.4 percent), whereas it was nearly identical in black polydrug abusers (20.8 percent) and alcoholics (21.6 percent). It is evident that the *MAC* scale is not simply an alcoholism scale; rather it is a more general measure of substance abuse which includes alcohol as well as other drugs. The only data reported on white, adult female polydrug abusers revealed 72.5 percent false negatives.

Higher scores on the *MAC* sometimes are interpreted as suggesting that the client is more likely to be a substance abuser or a worse substance abuser. Actually, higher scores on the *MAC* simply indicate that the client is more likely to remain above whatever cutting score is being used despite any psychometric error that may be associated with the scale. The interested reader is referred to Wiggins (1973) for an indepth review of this issue.

A number of general conclusions can be drawn after this rather lengthy summary on the use of the *MAC* scale in a variety of samples:

1. Men score about two raw-score points higher than women across most samples, which indicates that different cutting scores will be necessary by gender.

2. There is not a single, optimal cutting score with scores anywhere from 24 to 29 being used in different studies.

3. Cutting scores appear to be influenced by a number of factors; clinicians need to begin to determine empirically the best cutting score for their specific treatment facility to optimize the percentage of patients correctly classified as alcoholic and nonalcoholic.

4. Clinicians need to be very cautious in using the *MAC* scale in nonwhite ethnic groups.

5. Hit rates and classification accuracy decrease when clinicians are trying to discriminate between alcoholics and non-alcoholic, psychiatric patients, which is a frequent differential diagnosis.

6. Hit rates and classification accuracy may be unacceptably low in medical samples.

In addition to the general conclusions that were drawn about the use of the *MAC* scale above, there is one overriding issue that cannot be disregarded and that is the base rate of alcoholism for the setting in which the *MAC* scale is being used. For example, a hit rate of 75 percent and a false positive percentage of 20 percent with the *MAC* scale is very respectable in a setting where the base rate for alcoholism is 50 percent. The base rates for alcoholism are much lower than 50 percent, however, in most settings.

It has been estimated that the lifetime prevalence rates for alcoholism are approximately 8 percent and approximately 20 percent of medical patients have substance abuse or substance-related problems (Robins, Helzer, Weisman, Orvaschel, Gruenberg, Burke, & Regier, 1984). Consequently, the hit rates and classification accuracies for the *MAC* scale that have been reported above will be of limited usefulness in most real-life settings such as personnel selection or screening medical patients. Gottesman and Prescott (1989) have presented a cogent review of this issue that should be read by all clinicians.

One group of investigators (Hoffmann, Loper, & Kammeier, 1974; Kammeier, Hoffmann, & Loper, 1973; Loper, Kammeier, & Hoffmann, 1973) examined the MMPI scores of male college students who were later treated for alcoholism. Among these men, an average of 13 years elapsed between college admission and entrance into an alcoholism treatment program.

These investigators compared the alcoholics' *MAC* scale scores upon admission to college and at entrance into treatment with the scores of a control group of students who were admitted to college at the same time. The alcoholics had higher *MAC* scale scores both at college admission and at entrance into treatment than the control group of students. Using a cutting score of 26, the *MAC* scale correctly classified 72 percent of the alcoholic sample both at college admission and at entrance into treatment.

The consistency of classification by the *MAC* scale across such an extensive time interval suggests that the *MAC* scale is tapping a dimension of behavior that is resistant to change. This conclusion also is supported by the finding that the *MAC* scale scores in alcoholics remain elevated after treatment (Huber & Danahy, 1975; Gallucci, Kay, & Thornby, 1989; Rohan, Tatro, & Rotman, 1969).

High scorers on the *MAC* scale are described as being very likely to abuse alcohol and/or other drugs. They also are usually described as being antisocial with a tendency to act out, although Schwartz and Graham (1979) were unable to replicate this correlate in their sample. They have been found to be uninhibited, sociable individuals who appear to use repression and religion in an attempt to control their rebellious, delinquent impulses (Finney, Smith, Skeeters, & Auvenshine, 1971). They also are described as being impulsive, having a high energy level, having shallow interpersonal relationships, and being generally psychological maladjusted (Schwartz & Graham, 1979).

Personality and behavioral correlates of low scorers on the *MAC* scale have not been reported, although MacAndrew (1981) has suggested one possible interpretation of low scores. MacAndrew conjectured that the *MAC* scale taps a fundamental bipolar dimenison of personality with high scorers (raw scores of 24 or higher) being described as "moving (with 'boldness') into the world, albeit in a sometimes rancorous and ill-considered fashion, with little regard for future consequences" (p. 618), whereas low scores (raw scores of 23 or lower) "give every ap-

pearance of being 'neurotics-who-also-happen-to-drink-too-much'" (p. 620).

MacAndrew suggested that high scorers could be labeled primary alcoholics, and low scorers are reactive or secondary alcoholics. In this formulation of the *MAC* scale, substance abuse cannot be predicted since both high and low scorers can abuse substances. Rather the *MAC* scale is assessing a fundamental dimension of personality that will affect how the client will manifest his or her substance abuse. If this formulation by MacAndrew is accurate, clinicians would need to avoid using the *MAC* scale to predict whether a client will abuse substances, which has been the standard use of the *MAC* scale since it was first developed.

Greene (1990) reported the mean *MAC* scores by MMPI codetype, which would appear to support MacAndrew's conceptualiza-

TABLE 5–6   Mean *MAC* Scores as a Function of MMPI Codetype by Gender in Psychiatric Patients (Hedlund & Won Cho, 1979)

Codetype	MAC < 24	N	M	SD
Men				
All pts	15.9%	6593	27.2	4.8
2-8/8-2	31.5	336	24.5	4.8
2-7/7-2	28.4	310	24.7	4.4
1-3/3-1	22.0	177	26.1	4.6
2-4/4-2	15.6	748	26.8	4.5
7-8/8-7	15.3	308	27.4	4.7
4-6/6-4	8.3	278	28.3	4.3
6-8/8-6	9.8	389	28.5	4.4
6-9/9-6	3.3	121	29.6	3.9
4-9/9-4	2.3	686	30.2	3.9
Women				
All pts	43.7%	2726	23.2	4.6
2-7/7-2	80.0	95	19.7	3.8
2 8/8-2	65.0	120	20.8	4.2
7-8/8-7	59.0	105	22.0	4.2
1-3/3-1	51.3	113	22.3	3.7
2-4/4-2	48.0	179	22.5	4.3
4-6/6-4	33.8	195	24.2	4.0
6-8/8-6	27.6	225	25.1	4.5
6-9/9-6	12.8	86	26.6	4.3
4-9/9-4	12.1	214	26.8	3.9

tion of his scale as a measure of a dimension of personality (see Table 5–6) rather than as a measure of substance abuse per se. Some codetypes (*6-9/9-6, 4-9/9-4*) in men and women rarely have *MAC* scores less than 24 and it would seem inappropriate to assume that all of these psychiatric patients abused substances, whereas other codetypes (*2-7/7-2, 2-8/8-2*) rarely have scores above the cutting score of 24, particularly in women.

The correlates of these codetypes would suggest that high scorers on the *MAC* scale are impulsive, risk-taking, sensation-seeking individuals, who also may abuse substances, whereas low scorers are depressed, inhibited, overcontrolled individuals, who also may abuse substances, but in a different manner. Clinicians should see the apparent danger of identifying a client as a potential substance abuser or not based on the *MAC* scale without considering the codetype. For example, clients with *2-7/7-2* codetypes, who are likely to be "neurotic" and risk avoiders, would be unlikely to have elevated *MAC* scores regardless of whether they abuse substances, whereas clients with *6-9/9-6* codetypes, who are likely to act out, be impulsive, and to be risk takers, would be very likely to have elevated *MAC* scores again regardless of whether they abuse substances.

Four MMPI items (58, 378, 483, and 488) on the *MAC* scale were deleted in developing the MMPI-2. The rationale for dropping these items is apparent since they have either religious content or a sexist bias. Item 460, "I have used alcohol moderately (or not at all.),"[2] also was deleted, which along with item 215, is found on the 51-item version of the *MAC* scale. The deletion of item 460, since item 215 was retained is not clear because Colligan and colleagues (1988) found that this item, after item 215, provided better classification rates than any of the alcoholism scales in their medical patients. The deletion of item 460 may not be a problem, however, since items 215 and 460 are deleted frequently

from the *MAC* scale to create a 49-item, subtle scale of substance abuse.

Since interpretation of the *MAC* scale is based on raw scores instead of T scores, four items were added to the *MAC-R* scale on the MMPI-2 by contrasting the item responses of a group of male alcoholics with male psychiatric patients. Clinicians should note that item 387 on the MMPI-2, "I can express my true feelings only when I drink,"[3] is retained on the *MAC-R*, even though the item content directly relates to drinking.

There has been only one reported study of the comparability of the *MAC* and *MAC-R* scales (Greene, Arredondo, & Davis, 1990), and it appears that the two scales produce comparable scores (see Table 5–7). The only notable difference in the *MAC* and *MAC-R* scores for these groups of alcoholic and psychiatric inpatients was for male alcoholics to have slightly higher scores on the *MAC-R* scale than on the *MAC* scale. It appears that the *MAC-R* scale can be used in a similar manner to the *MAC* scale, although clinicians again are cautioned to note all the caveats described above.

The *MAC-R* has only limited item overlap with the other clinical and supplementary scales (see Tables 5–3 and 5–4). The *MAC-R* shares 5 items with the *F* scale, 7 items with Scale *4* (Psychopathic Deviate), and 5 items with Scale *9* (Hypomania). The *MAC-R* shares 6 items with *Do* (Dominance) and 9 items with *Re* (Social Responsibility), with the items being scored in the opposite direction on the *Do* and *Re* scales. It appears very logical that high scorers on the *MAC-R* scale are not socially responsible.

CONTENT SCALES

The content of individual items was basically ignored in the development of the MMPI scales because at that time methods of item selection that relied extensively on item con-

TABLE 5-7   Comparability between the MMPI *MAC* Scale and the MMPI-2 *MAC-R* Scale in Alcoholics and Psychiatric Inpatients

	Alcoholics				
	N	*M*	*SD*	Range	<24
MAC					
Men	279	26.8	4.7	10–39	24.0%
Women	147	24.6	4.2	15–36	41.5
MAC-R					
Men	66	28.1	4.3	19–38	16.8
Women	33	23.8	4.2	14–29	42.4

	Psychiatric Inpatients				
	N	*M*	*SD*	Range	>23
MAC					
Men	797	26.4	4.9	10–40	72.9%
Women	736	23.7	4.6	11–36	49.6
MAC-R					
Men	45	26.7	4.5	19–36	73.3
Women	54	23.0	4.9	14–34	42.6

Data are from Greene, Arredondo, and Davis (1990).

Note: Each sample consists of two separate groups of patients taking either the *MAC* or *MAC-R* scale in the same setting, *not* a single group of patients taking both scales.

tent had fallen into disfavor. Since these issues were reviewed in Chapter 1, they will not be reiterated here. Numerous investigators (cf. Jackson, 1971), however, believed that item content should not be ignored in test construction or interpretation.

Wiggins' (1966) Content scales represent a systematic attempt to develop a means of examining the client's responses to the content of individual MMPI items, and the Butcher, Graham, Williams, and Ben-Porath (1989) Content scales reflect a similar approach on the MMPI-2. Since Wiggins' Content scales were developed prior to the Butcher and colleagues content scales on the MMPI-2, Wiggins' scales will be reviewed first. Clinicians' interest in critical items, discussed in a later section, reflect a similar interest in item content.

Wiggins' MMPI Content Scales

Wiggins (1966) began by grouping the MMPI items into the 26-item content categories (see Table 1–2, page 5), originally proposed by Hathaway and McKinley (1940). He then applied both psychometric and intuitive procedures to produce 13 substantive dimensions of item content. He developed his Content scales on normal college students and validated them on additional normal populations and a psychiatric sample.

Wiggins selected the items for the Content scales so that they did not share common items with one another and so that scale homogeneity was maximized; each content scale was constructed to be a homogeneous measure of its substantive dimension that did not overlap with other scales. The name and abbreviation of each of these 13 scales appear in Table 5–8. The items found on each Content scale as well as the mean and standard deviation on each scale for males and females in the original Minnesota normative group are provided in Dahlstrom, Welsh, and Dahlstrom (1972, 1975).

Profile sheets to convert the raw scores directly to T scores are available from National Computer Systems (P.O. Box 1416, Minneapolis, Minnesota 55440, 800–627–7271) and Psychological Assessment Resources (P.O. Box 998, Odessa, Florida 33556, 800–331–8378). Fowler and Coyle (1969) also have provided normative data on college students that can be used to derive T scores for each content scale in college populations.

Wiggins (1966) construed the Content scales as reflecting the client's admission or self-report of symptomatology; the client's self-report is one way of communicating problems to the clinician. Since the Content scales are an obvious measure of symptomatology, it is possible for the client to present an inaccurate self-appraisal.

Lachar and Alexander (1978) suggested that the Content scales are indeed susceptible to a set to deny the presence of psychopathology. Therefore, low scores on the Content scales could represent the absence of the specific descriptors that are characteristic of high scorers or signify the client's refusal to acknowledge the presence of such symptomatology.

It also should be possible for clients to exaggerate the severity of their symptomatology and elevate their scores on the Content scales, although no research has addressed this issue. Thus, high scores on the Content scales may be the result of actual symptomatology or the client's overreporting of psychopathology. The procedures described in Chapter 3 for assessing the accuracy of item endorsement should be followed routinely and particularly when overreporting or un-

derreporting of psychopathology is suspected.

Research on the Wiggins Content scales has consistently supported their validity and generalizability to new populations. Wiggins, Goldberg, and Appelbaum (1971), Jarnecke and Chambers (1977), and Mezzich, Damarin, and Erickson (1974) found that the Content scales demonstrated the expected relationships to other test measures and behaviors. For example, clients who elevated the Wiggins Depression scale were more likely to exhibit depressive behaviors and to elevate other tests that measured depression than clients who did not elevate this scale.

Jarnecke and Chambers (1977), Lachar and Alexander (1978), and Mezzich and associates (1974) found that the Content scales were generalizable to psychiatric inpatients and Air Force personnel. Payne and Wiggins (1972) reported that hospitalized patients with the same profile type, as defined by the Gilberstadt and Duker (1965) profile classification system, tended to produce similar scores on the Content scales, and these scores were consistent with the established correlates of the codetype. Consequently, it seems that the Wiggins Content scales adequately assess their respective dimensions, and they can be generalized to new populations with little, if any, loss in predictive power.

The Wiggins Content scales can be understood through their relationship to the various clinical scales; these relationships are illustrated in Table 5–9. For example, Wiggins' Content scale of Poor Health (*HEA*) relates to Scale *1* (Hypochondriasis), Depression (*DEP*) relates to Scale *2* (Depression), and so on.

The Wiggins Content scales provide an additional source of information that the clinician can use in interpreting an MMPI profile. It is possible for two clients to have similar profiles on the standard clinical scales and very different patterns of scores on the Content scales. Thus, the Content scales can

TABLE 5–8   Description of Wiggins' MMPI Content Scales

Abbreviation	Name	Description
HEA	Poor Health	High *HEA* is concerned about his health and has admitted to a variety of gastrointestinal ailments centering around an upset stomach and difficulty in elimination.
DEP	Depression	High *DEP* experiences guilt, regret, worry, unhappiness, and a feeling that life has lost its zest. He experiences difficulty in concentrating and has little motivation to pursue things. His self-esteem is low, and he is anxious and apprehensive about the future. He is sensitive to slight, feels misunderstood, and is convinced that he is unworthy and deserves punishment. In short, he is classically depressed.
ORG	Organic Symptoms	High *ORG* admits to symptoms that are often indicative of organic involvement. These include headaches, nausea, dizziness, loss of motility and coordination, loss of consciousness, poor concentration and memory, speaking and reading difficulty, and problems with muscular control, skin sensations, hearing, and smell.
FAM	Family Problems	High *FAM* feels that he had an unpleasant home life characterized by a lack of love in the family and parents who were unnecessarily critical, nervous, quarrelsome, and quick tempered. Although some items are ambiguous, most are phrased with reference to the parental home rather than to the individual's current home.
AUT	Authority Conflict	High *AUT* sees life as a jungle and is convinced that others are unscrupulous, dishonest, hypocritical, and motivated only by personal profit. He distrusts others, has little respect for experts, is competitive, and believes that everyone should get away with whatever they can.
FEM	Feminine Interests	High *FEM* admits to liking feminine games, hobbies, and vocations. He denies liking masculine games, hobbies, and vocations. Here there is almost complete contamination of content and form that has been noted in other contexts by several writers. Individuals may score high on this scale by presenting themselves as liking many things since this item stem is present in almost all items. They may also score high by endorsing interests, which, although, possibly feminine, are also socially desirable, such as an interest in poetry, dramatics, news of the theater, and artistic pursuits. This has been noted in the case of Wiggins' *Sd* (Social Desirability) scale. Finally, of course, individuals with a genuine preference for activities that are conceived by our culture as "feminine" will achieve high scores on this scale.
REL	Religious Fundamentalism	High scorers on this scale see themselves as religious, church-going people who accept as true a number of fundamentalist religious convictions. They also tend to view their faith as the true one.

continued

TABLE 5-8 *continued*

Abbreviation	Name	Description
HOS	Manifest Hostility	High *HOS* admits to sadistic impulses and a tendency to be cross, grouchy, competitive, argumentative, uncooperative, and retaliatory in his interpersonal relationships. He is often competitive and socially aggressive.
MOR	Poor Morale	High *MOR* is lacking in self-confidence, feels that he has failed in life, and is given to despair and a tendency to give up hope. He is extremely sensitive to the feelings and reactions of others and feels misunderstood by them while at the same time being concerned about offending them. He feels useless and is socially suggestible. There is a substantive overlap here between the Depression and Social Maladjustment scales and the Poor Morale scale. The Social Maladjustment scale seems to emphasize a lack of social ascendance and poise, the Depression scale feelings of guilt and apprehension, while the present scale seems to emphasize a lack of self-confidence and hypersensitivity to the opinions of others.
PHO	Phobias	High *PHO* has admitted to a number of fears, many of them of the classically phobic variety such as heights, dark, closed spaces, etc.
PSY	Psychoticism	High *PSY* admits to a number of classic psychotic symptoms of a primarily paranoid nature. He admits to hallucinations, strange experiences, loss of control, and classic paranoid delusions of grandeur and persecution. He admits to feelings of unreality, daydreaming, and a sense that things are wrong, while feeling misunderstood by others.
HYP	Hypomania	High *HYP* is characterized by feelings of excitement, well-being, restlessness, and tension. He is enthusiastic, high strung, cheerful, full of energy, and apt to be hot-headed. He has broad interests, seeks change, and is apt to take on more than he can handle.
SOC	Social Maladjustment	High *SOC* is socially bashful, shy, embarrassed, reticent, self-conscious, and extremely reserved. Low *SOC* is gregarious, confident, assertive, and relates quickly and easily to others. He is fun loving, the life of a party, a joiner who experiences no difficulty in speaking before a group. This scale would correspond roughly with the popular concept of "introversion-extroversion."

Note: From "Substantive Dimensions of Self-report in the MMPI Item Pool" by J. S. Wiggins, 1966, *Psychological Monographs, 80* (22, Whole No. 630). Copyright © 1966 by the American Psychological Association. Reprinted by permission.

TABLE 5-9   Relationship between the Wiggins Content Scales and the MMPI Clinical Scales

Wiggins Content Scales		Related MMPI Clinical Scales
Abbreviation	Name	
HEA	Poor Health	Scale *1* (Hypochondriasis)
DEP	Depression	Scale *2* (Depression)
ORG	Organic Symptoms	Scale *3* (Hysteria)
FAM	Family Problems	Scale *4* (Psychopathic Deviate)
AUT	Authority Conflict	Scale *4* (Psychopathic Deviate)
FEM	Feminine Interests	Scale *5* (Masculinity-Femininity)
REL	Religious Fundamentalism	Scale *5* (Masculinity-Femininity)
HOS	Manifest Hostility	Scale *6* (Paranoia)
MOR	Poor Morale	Scale *7* (Psychasthenia)
PHO	Phobias	Scale *7* (Psychasthenia)
PSY	Psychoticism	Scale *8* (Schizophrenia)
HYP	Hypomania	Scale *9* (Hypomania)
SOC	Social Maladjustment	Scale *0* (Social Introversion)

be used to supplement and expand the interpretation of the standard MMPI profile. Clinicians are encouraged to score and interpret the Wiggins Content scales routinely because of the valuable information that can be obtained with little additional investment of time or effort.

Nichols (1987) has provided an excellent overview of the Wiggins Content scales and their relationship with their respective clinical scales as well as illustrative cases. Nichols' monograph should be consulted by every clinician who is interested in learning more about these scales.

Wiggins' descriptors of high scorers on the Content scales are presented in Table 5-8. Lachar and Alexander (1978) also presented preliminary interpretations of high scores on each content scale that were validated and replicated in an armed service setting (see Table 5-10). The clinician can use these interpretations of high scores in conjunction with Wiggins' descriptors (see Table 5-8) and Nichols' (1987) monograph as a basis for interpreting these scales.

Most of the items on the Wiggins Content scales have been retained on the MMPI-2

(see Table 5-11), so clinicians can continue to use these scales if desired. Only the Religious Fundamentalism scale has been totally dropped. Most of the Wiggins Content scales retain 90 percent or more of their items on the MMPI-2.

MMPI-2 Content Scales

Butcher and colleagues (1989) began to develop the MMPI-2 Content scales by sorting the 704 items of the AX booklet (the original 550 items from the MMPI plus 154 additional new items that were under consideration for inclusion in the MMPI-2) into possible categories based on their item content. These initial groupings of items were refined statistically to insure their psychometric homogeneity.

Finally, only those items whose content was homogeneous with the rest of the items were retained. This procedure resulted in 15 Content scales: their general clinical area, names, abbreviations, and description are provided in Table 5-12. An easy means of understanding each content scale is to review the actual items on each scale (see Appendix A for the item numbers or Butcher and asso-

TABLE 5–10 Proposed Interpretation of High Wiggins Content Scales

Abbreviation	Name	Description
HEA	Poor Health (T > 69)	A significant number of physical complaints are reflected by item endorsement centering mainly around the digestive system. Individuals who obtain high *HEA* elevations are often considerably worried about their health. Cardiac and pulmonary complaints are also occasionally reported.
DEP	Depression (T > 69)	This individual has admitted to symptoms associated with problematic depression, such as lack of interest in the environment, pessimism, self-criticism, and brooding. In client populations, social withdrawal, a negative self-concept, guilt feelings, and a reduced activity level may be suggested.
ORG	Organic Symptoms (T > 69)	This individual has admitted to a variety of sensory, motor, or general somatic concerns that may be related to psychological discomfort and general malaise as well as to reduced effectiveness in completing daily tasks. Clients who obtain high *ORG* elevations may complain of lack of stamina and strength, may present physical symptoms that often indicate emotional conflict, such as problematic headache or back pain.
FAM	Family Problems (T > 69)	Inventory responses include admission of pathology in and among family members. A history of poor relationships with parents is suggested, as well as the absence of positive supports in current family interactions, whether with parents, spouse, or extended family. Patient male: In adult male clients admission of family pathology may reflect not only marital conflict but may also suggest intolerant, overactive individuals and a negative self-concept. Drug abuse and other destructive behavior may be associated.
AUT	Authority Conflict (T > 59)	Endorsed item content reflects the belief that interpersonal relations are often exploitive in nature. Disregard for principles of ethical conduct and truthfulness is suggested, as well as a tendency to minimize the negative impact of antisocial behavior. In client populations these attitudes may be associated with problematic overassertive and manipulative social relations. Conflict with relatives may result.
FEM	Feminine Interests (T > 59)	Inventory responses suggest an interest in pursuits traditionally labeled as feminine and/or dislike of activities stereotyped as masculine. Patient male: In male clients this interest pattern may be associated with an indecisive, passive orientation that has proven to be problematic. Conflict may lead to confusion or self-blame. Evaluation for suicide ideation or previous attempts is suggested.
REL	Religious Fundamentalism (T > 59)	Endorsed item content reflects strong religious beliefs and religiously motivated behavior. In client populations this orientation suggests a reduced probability of sub-

continued

TABLE 5-10 *continued*

Abbreviation	Name	Description
		stance abuse, impulsive behaviors, and conflict with family members. Expression of strong religious beliefs may, at times, reflect a delusional system and associated thought disorder.
HOS	Mainfest Hostility ($T > 59$)	This individual admits to problems in adjustment related to unmodulated expressions of anger, resentment of perceived injustices, need for interpersonal dominance, and limited self-control. In client populations the combination of hostility, moodiness, and impulsivity may be associated with assaultive or other antisocial or violent behavior.
MOR	Poor Morale ($T > 69$)	Inventory responses reflect a pervasive lack of confidence in one's own abilities and a history of failure, which is related to these perceived limitations. Clients who obtain high *MOR* elevations may be insecure, despondent, withdrawn, intropunitive, and oversensitive, and may become easily upset by the actions of others.
PHO	Phobias ($T > 69$)	This individual admits to a variety of fears and appears to be significantly uncomfortable in many situations. Clients who obtain high *PHO* elevations are viewed as more anxious, tremulous, worrisome, and phobic than most patients. Depression and social withdrawal may also be indicated.
PSY	Psychoticism ($T > 69$)	Inventory responses include admission of unusual experiences and beliefs, many of which may include a clearly paranoid component. In client populations this response pattern often suggests an individual who finds comprehension of human motives and behavior difficult and is consequently suspicious of and worried about others. Symptoms associated with a psychotic adjustment, such as ideas of reference, hallucinations, and autistic or disorganized thought, may be present.
HYP	Hypomania ($T > 59$)	This individual's self-description suggests a fast personal tempo characterized by enthusiasm, cheerfulness, and perhaps irritability of emotional lability. Clients who obtain high *HYP* elevation are often described as immature, hyperactive, excitable, agitated, and restless. They are unlikely to respond intropunitively to conflict and may manipulate others to reach their goals.
SOC	Social Maladjustment ($T > 69$)	Endorsed item content reflects a lack of social skill and poise, discomfort in social interaction, and resultant inhibition and social isolation. In client populations this lack of social supports may be associated with a negative self-image, feelings of despair or fearfulness, thoughts of suicide, or a defensive orientation characterized by apathy and limited activity or compulsive attention to detail.

Note: From "Veridicality of self-report: Replicated correlates of the Wiggins MMPI content scales" by D. Lachar & R. S. Alexander, 1978, *Journal of Consulting and Clinical Psychology, 46,* 1355–1356. Copyright © 1978 by the American Psychological Association. Reprinted by permission. Also from "WPS TEST REPORT User's Manual for the MMPI" by D. Lachar, 1979, 9–10. Copyright © 1979 by Western Psychological Services. Reprinted by permission of the publisher, Western Psychological Services, 12031 Wilshire Blvd., Los Angeles, CA 90025.

TABLE 5–11 Wiggins' Content Scales Items on the MMPI-2

Wiggins Content Scale	Items on MMPI Scale	Number of Items Retained on MMPI-2
Poor Health	28	19 (67.9%)
Depression	33	33 (100.0%)
Organic Symptoms	36	32 (88.9%)
Family Problems	16	16 (100.0%)
Authority Conflict	20	20 (100.0%)
Feminine Interests	30	23 (76.7%)
Religious Fundamentalism	12	1 (8.3%)
Manifest Hostility	27	25 (92.6%)
Poor Morale	23	22 (95.6%)
Phobias	27	26 (96.3%)
Psychoticism	48	45 (93.8%)
Hypomania	25	23 (92.0%)
Social Maladjustment	27	26 (96.2%)

ciates [1989, pp. 192–199] for a listing of the actual items).

As can be seen in Table 5–13, most of the items on the MMPI-2 Content scales are from the original MMPI item pool except for the Low Self-Esteem, Work Interference, and Negative Treatment Indicators scales. That is, the MMPI-2 Content scales are *not* composed primarily of new items.

There is a substantial degree of item overlap within the MMPI-2 Content scales (see Table 5–14). Only three scales (Fears, Health Concerns, and Social Discomfort) have no items in common with the other Content scales. Four scales (Obsessiveness, Cynicism, Work Interference, and Negative Treatment Indicators) have almost one-half of their items in common with the other Content scales. There also is significant overlap among the standard validity and clinical scales and the MMPI-2 Content scales (see Table 5–15).

Some of the scales that share items make good intuitive sense: Health Concerns with Scales *1* (Hypochondriasis) and *3* (Hysteria); Bizarre Mentation with Scales *6* (Paranoia) and *8* (Schizophrenia); and Social Discomfort with Scale *0* (Social Introversion). How-

ever, other relationships among these scales would not be expected: Depression has only nine items in common with Scale *2* (Depression) and shares items with most of the other clinical scales; Antisocial Practices, Cynicism, and Anger have few items in common with Scale *4* (Psychopathic Deviate), and Cynicism and Anger share few items with any of the standard validity and clinical scales; and Anxiety shares items with 11 of the standard validity and clinical scales.

It also is informative to examine the item overlap between the Wiggins and the MMPI-2 Content scales that share the same or similar names (see Table 5–16). Only two Content scales (Fears and Phobias; Bizarre Mentation and Psychoticism) have substantial item overlap.

In most instances, MMPI-2 and Wiggins' Content scales with the same or similar names have a limited number of items in common. For example, the Wiggins Depression scale and the MMPI-2 Content scale of Depression have only 16 of their 33 items in common, and both of these scales have few items in common with Scale *2* (Depression). Whether these three "Depression" scales are measuring different facets of depressive phe-

TABLE 5–12   Description of the MMPI-2 Content Scales

Clinical Area		
Abbreviation	Name	**Description**

Internal Symptomatic Behaviors

ANX	Anxiety	These clients report general symptoms of anxiety, nervousness, worries, and sleep and concentration difficulties. They have difficulty making decisions. They fear losing their minds and are afraid that they are about to go to pieces. They find life a strain and work under a great deal of tension and stress.
FRS	Fears	These clients report a large number of specific fears: animals (snakes, mice, spiders); events in nature (dirt, earthquakes, fire, lightning, windstorms, water); dark, blood, money, high places, and so on.
OBS	Obsessiveness	These clients have great difficulty making decisions, ruminate excessively, worry excessively, and have intrusive thoughts. They dislike change. They count and save unimportant things.
DEP	Depression	These clients have a depressive mood and depressive thoughts. They feel blue and unhappy, and are likely to brood. They are uncertain about their future and find their lives empty and meaningless. They cry easily. They are self-critical, guilty, and lonely. They may report suicidal ideation or attempts.
HEA	Health Concerns	These clients report specific physical symptoms across several body systems as well as general physical ailments such as nausea, vomiting, and pain. They have pains in the chest, neck, and head. Their muscles may be paralyzed or twitch and jump. They have fainting and dizzy spells. They worry about their health and catching disease. They believe that they are sicker than most people.
BIZ	Bizarre Mentation	These clients report strange thoughts and experiences, paranoid ideation, and hallucinations; in short, they report psychotic thought processes.

External Aggressive Tendencies

ANG	Anger	These clients report being irritable, grouchy, impatient, hotheaded, annoyed, and stubborn. In addition, they may swear or lose control and smash objects, pick fights, and hurt someone in a fight.
CYN	Cynicism	These clients expect other people to lie, cheat, and steal, and if they do not engage in these behaviors, it is because they fear being caught. They trust nobody. People use each other and are friendly only for selfish reasons.
ASP	Antisocial Practices	These clients report stealing things, other problem behaviors, and antisocial practices during their school years. They have attitudes similar to individuals who break the

continued

TABLE 5–12   *continued*

Clinical Area		Description
Abbreviation	**Name**	
		law, even if not actually engaging in antisocial behavior. They expect other people to lie.
TPA	Type A	These clients are hard-driving, fast-moving, and work-oriented individuals, who frequently become impatient, grouchy, irritable, and annoyed. They do not like to wait, be interrupted, or believe that someone has gotten the best of them.
Negative Self-Views		
LSE	Low Self-Esteem	These clients have very low opinions of themselves, and they are uncomfortable if people say nice things about them. They believe that they are unattractive, awkward and clumsy, useless, and a burden to others, who do not like them. They lack self-confidence. They see themselves as not as good or capable as others, and they see themselves as not being able to do anything well.
General Problem Areas: Social, Familial, Work, and Treatment		
SOD	Social Discomfort	These clients are very uneasy around others and are happier by themselves. They see themselves as shy. They dislike parties and other group events, because they do not like meeting people and find it hard to talk.
FAM	Family Problems	These clients report considerable familial discord. Their families are lacking love, support, and companionship, and these clients wanted to leave home. Family members are described as being nervous and having quick tempers, and are to be avoided at best, or may even be hated.
WRK	Work Interference	These clients report that they are not as able to work as they once were and that they work under a great deal of tension. They are tired, lack energy, and sick of what they have to do. They dislike making decisions and lack self-confidence. They give up easily and shrink from facing a crisis or problem.
TRT	Negative Treatment Indicators	These clients dislike going to doctors and they believe that they should not discuss their personal problems with others. They prefer to take drugs or medicine, since talking about problems does not help them. They do not believe that anyone understands or cares about them. They give up quickly and do not care about what is happening to them, since nothing can be done about their problems. They have a hard time making decisions.

Note: Adapted from: Butcher, Dahlstrom, Graham, Tellegen, and Kaemmer (1989), *Manual for administration and scoring of the MMPI-2.* Minneapolis: University of Minnesota Press; and Butcher, Graham, Williams, and Ben-Porath (1989), *Development and use of the MMPI-2 content scales.* Minneapolis: University of Minnesota Press.

TABLE 5–13   Source of Items on MMPI-2 Content Scales

Content Scale	Abbre-viation	Number of Items	MMPI Items	New Items
Anxiety	*ANX*	23	20	3
Fears	*FRS*	23	22	1
Obsessiveness	*OBS*	16	10	6
Depression	*DEP*	33	25	8
Health Concerns	*HEA*	36	36	0
Bizarre Mentation	*BIZ*	23	19	4
Anger	*ANG*	16	10	6
Cynicism	*CYN*	23	21	2
Antisocial Practices	*ASP*	22	21	1
Type A	*TPA*	19	12	7
Low Self-Esteem	*LSE*	24	13	11
Social Discomfort	*SOD*	24	21	3
Family Problems	*FAM*	25	16	9
Work Interference	*WRK*	33	22	11
Negative Treatment Indicators	*TRT*	26	8	18

nomenology, or different types of depression remains to be determined.

Similarly, the Wiggins Family Problems scale and the MMPI-2 Content scale of Family Problems have only 10 items in common, and the Wiggins Manifest Hostil-ity scale and the MMPI-2 Content scale of Anger share only 8 items. Clinicians may find it beneficial to score both the MMPI-2 and the Wiggins Content scales to determine whether these scales with similar names and limited item overlap have dif-

TABLE 5–14   Item Overlap within the MMPI-2 Content Scales

Scale	Abbre-viation	Number of Items	Unique Items	Overlapping Content Scales and Number of Overlapping Items
Anxiety	*ANX*	23	18 (78.3%)	WRK-5 OBS-2
Fears	*FRS*	23	23 (100.0%)	
Obsessiveness	*OBS*	16	9 (56.3%)	WRK-4 TRT-3 ANX-2
Depression	*DEP*	33	23 (69.7%)	TRT-6 LSE-2 CYN-1 WRK-1
Health Concerns	*HEA*	36	36 (100.0%)	
Bizarre Mentation	*BIZ*	23	22 (95.7%)	FAM-1
Anger	*ANG*	16	14 (87.5%)	TPA-3 WRK-1
Cynicism	*CYN*	23	12 (52.2%)	ASP-7 DEP-1 TPA-1 WRK-1 TRT-1
Antisocial Practices	*ASP*	22	16 (72.7%)	CYN-7 TPA-1
Type A	*TPA*	19	14 (73.7%)	ANG-3 WRK-2 ASP-1 CYN-1
Low Self-Esteem	*LSE*	24	20 (83.3%)	DEP-2 TRT-2 WRK-1
Social Discomfort	*SOD*	24	24 (100.0%)	
Family Problems	*FAM*	25	24 (96.0%)	BIZ-1 WRK-1
Work Interference	*WRK*	33	18 (54.5%)	ANX-5 OBS-4 TRT-4 TPA-1 ANG-1 CYN-1 DEP-1 LSE-1 FAM-1
Negative Treatment Indicators	*TRT*	26	14 (53.8%)	DEP-6 WRK-4 OBS-3 LSE-2 CYN-1

TABLE 5–15 Item Overlap among the MMPI-2 Standard Validity and Clinical Scales and the MMPI-2 Content Scales

	L	F	K	Hs	D	Hy	Pd	Mf	Pa	Pt	Sc	Ma	Si	Total
HEA	0	3	0	23	8	16	0	1	1	3	6	0	2	63
DEP	0	3	0	1	9	4	6	0	4	9	7	0	2	45
FAM	0	2	0	0	0	1	5	2	1	0	6	4	0	21
ASP	0	3	0	0	0	0	3	0	1	0	1	4	3	15
CYN	0	0	0	0	0	0	1	0	0	0	0	1	4	6
ANG	0	0	0	0	0	0	0	0	0	1	0	0	1	2
ANX	0	1	0	2	5	3	1	1	1	6	4	1	1	26
FRS	0	1	0	0	0	1	0	1	1	2	2	0	0	8
OBS	0	0	0	0	0	0	0	1	0	5	0	2	1	9
BIZ	0	9	0	0	0	0	1	0	8	1	8	0	0	27
LSE	0	1	0	0	3	0	0	0	0	4	0	0	3	11
SOD	0	1	0	0	2	0	0	1	0	2	3	0	18	27
WRK	0	3	0	1	5	2	3	0	1	3	4	2	6	30
TRT	0	1	0	0	1	0	1	0	1	0	3	0	2	9
TPA	0	0	0	0	0	0	0	0	0	1	0	1	1	3
Totals	0	28	0	27	33	27	21	7	19	37	44	15	44	

Note: Since an individual item may overlap with several scales, the totals represent how many times items overlap on the various scales when stored in the same directory, not how many individual items on a given scale overlap with other scales.

ferent correlates. As noted earlier, most of the Wiggins Content scales can still be scored on the MMPI-2.

Several general comments need to be made about the MMPI-2 Content scales in concluding this section. First, since the MMPI-2 Content scales are obvious measures of symptomatology, it is possible for the client to present an inaccurate self-appraisal. The cautions noted earlier for the

TABLE 5–16 Item Overlap between the Wiggins Content Scales and Related MMPI-2 Content Scales

Wiggins	Items on Scale	Item Overlap[a]	MMPI-2	Items on Scale
Poor Health	28	13(36.1%)	Health Concerns	36
Depression	33	16(48.5%)	Depression	33
Organic Symptoms	36	20(55.6%)	Health Concerns	33
Family Problems	16	10(40.0%)	Family Problems	25
Authority Conflict	20	12(52.2%)	Cynicism	23
Authority Conflict	20	12(54.5%)	Antisocial Practices	22
Manifest Hostility	27	8(50.0%)	Anger	16
Poor Morale	23	6(25.0%)	Low Self-Esteem	24
Phobias	27	19(82.6%)	Fears	23
Psychoticism	48	19(82.6%)	Bizarre Mentation	23
Social Maladjustment	27	16(66.7%)	Social Discomfort	24

[a]The percentages indicate the percent of items on the related MMPI-2 Content Scale that are also on the Wiggins Content scale

Wiggins Content scales also need to be considered for the MMPI-2 Content scales.

Low scores on the MMPI-2 Content scales (T scores less than 45) could represent the absence of the specific descriptors characteristic of high scorers or the client's refusal to acknowledge the presence of such symptomatology. Similarly, high scores on the MMPI-2 Content scales may be the result of actual symptomatology or the client's over-reporting of psychopathology. The procedures described in Chapter 3 for assessing the accuracy of item endorsement should be followed routinely and particularly when over-reporting or underreporting of psychopathology is suspected.

Second, the deviant response for a majority of the items on the MMPI-2 Content scales is "true," so a *TRIN* (True Response Inconsistency scale) score of 12 or higher would be expected to produce elevations on most of these scales. Third, a number of the items on these scales are clustered in the last 100 items so any waning of the client's motivation toward the end of the test could adversely affect these scales. Finally, the MMPI-2 Content scales use uniform T scores.

ADDITIONAL MMPI-2 SUPPLEMENTARY SCALES

Overcontrolled-Hostility (*O-H*) Scale

Megargee and Mendelsohn (1962) attempted to cross-validate 12 MMPI indexes of hostility by contrasting groups of male criminals who were classified as extremely assaultive, moderately assaultive, and nonassaultive. None of these 12 scales correctly identified the extremely assaultive groups of criminals. In fact, Megargee and Mendelsohn found that the extremely assaultive criminals were more likely to score significantly lower on these scales (i.e., the extremely assaultive

criminals demonstrated lower hostility scores and better impulse control than the other groups). In a similar study of 21 MMPI scales and indexes of hostility Deiker (1974) also reported that his extremely assaultive group scored significantly lower than other assaultive groups on 13 of 17 scales that were significantly different.

In light of these paradoxical results, Megargee and associates (1967) developed a new scale to assist in the identification of assaultive individuals. They began by distinguishing between undercontrolled and overcontrolled assaultive individuals because they believed that different factors led to assaultive outbursts in these two groups. They believed that undercontrolled individuals have failed to learn to control their aggressive impulses, and their aggressive behaviors occur in response to some external form of provocation. Overcontrolled individuals, however, rigidly defend against any expression of aggressive impulses irrespective of the provocation until finally some provocation or other factor results in their acting out, frequently in an extremely destructive fashion.

Megargee and colleagues (1967) felt that the latter group was more important to identify since their assaultive behaviors occur unexpectedly and frequently very violently. They contrasted the item responses of four groups of men: 14 extremely assaultive prisoners, 25 moderately assaultive prisoners, 25 nonassaultive prisoners, and 46 normals. The 55 items that differentiated between the assaultive and nonassaultive prisoners were then cross-validated in new groups of extremely assaultive, moderately assaultive, and nonassaultive prisoners. They eliminated items that did not differentiate among these new groups of assaultive and nonassaultive prisoners, and the 31 (28 items on the MMPI-2) remaining items became the Overcontrolled-Hostility (*O-H*) Scale (see Appendix A).

Megargee and associates (1967) did not

suggest a specific cutting score to be used on this scale. Instead, they recommended that investigators determine the most appropriate cutting score in their own treatment setting based on which errors are more tolerable—false positives (identifying a person as over-controlled and hostile who is not) or false negatives (identifying a person as not being overcontrolled and hostile who actually is).

Prisoners whose crimes were judged to reflect overcontrolled hostility scored higher on the *O-H* scale than prisoners whose crimes were judged to reflect undercontrolled hostility (Megargee et al., 1967). Deiker (1974) found that the *O-H* scale was one of the few MMPI scales that could accurately identify male prisoners who were extremely assaultive. He questioned whether a negative response bias might account for the obtained results since two-thirds of the items on the *O-H* scale have "false" as the deviant response.

Megargee and Cook (1975) demonstrated, however, that *O-H* scales balanced for "naysaying" (equivalent numbers of "true" and "false" deviant responses) yielded similar if not better results than the original *O-H* scale, which indicated that a negative response bias cannot explain the results obtained with the *O-H* scale. Lane and Kling (1979) also found that the *O-H* scale reliably discriminated between overcontrolled assaultive forensic psychiatric patients and undercontrolled assaultive patients.

Quinsey, Maguire, and Varney (1983) reported that murderers who scored high on the *O-H* scale were less assertive than murderers who scored low on this scale. They suggested that assertiveness training may be beneficial with persons who have high scores on the *O-H* scale.

Several studies found that the *O-H* scale does not discriminate between violent and nonviolent criminals (Hoppe & Singer, 1976; Mallory & Walker, 1972; Truscott, 1990). The first two of these studies administered the *O-H* scale out of context of the entire MMPI, but it is not clear if this factor would be sufficient to invalidate the results.

Werner, Becker, and Yesavage (1983) found that the *O-H* scale was not correlated with assaultiveness in psychotic, male psychiatric inpatients. Most investigators, including Megargee and colleagues (1967) and Deiker (1974), found only small mean differences (two items) between assaultive and non-assaultive groups, so it is possible that even minor variations in procedure may be sufficient to obscure these differences. Investigators also have been inconsistent in whether or not they distinguish between overcontrolled and undercontrolled hostility in their assaultive groups; this inconsistency may further obscure the reported results.

Graham (1978) cited two unpublished studies that reported that blacks and females score higher on the *O-H* scale than white males on whom the scale was developed. Graham also noted an unpublished study that found that the *O-H* scale differentiated female assaultive prisoners from female non-assaultive prisoners. Both Leonard (1977) and Lester and Clopton (1979) reported that the *O-H* scale did not reliably distinguish between psychiatric patients who completed suicide and nonsuicidal psychiatric patients.

Additional research on the *O-H* scale is needed to validate its use in minority and female samples. The apparent finding that even minor procedural changes such as administering the *O-H* scale in isolation may alter the effectiveness of the *O-H* scale suggests that it should be used cautiously in identifying specific individuals as overcontrolled and hostile. Investigators also will need to determine the most efficient cutting score for the *O-H* scale in their treatment setting, as Megargee and colleagues (1967) recommended.

Finally, Gearing (1979) pointed out the similarity between the behaviors characteristic of persons with *4-3* codetypes (Davis & Sines, 1971; Persons & Marks, 1971) and the behaviors expected of a high scorer on the

O-H scale. Research is needed to determine whether similar behaviors are being assessed in these two instances.

High scorers on the *O-H* scale are described as displaying excessive control of their hostile impulses and as being socially alienated. They are reluctant to admit any form of psychological symptoms, even though they are sometimes diagnosed as being psychotic. They are seen as being rigid and not displaying anxiety overtly. They may candidates for assertiveness training.

There are no reported correlates of low scorers on the *O-H* scale.

The *O-H* scale shares few items with any of the standard validity and clinical scales or the supplementary scales (see Tables 5-3 and 5-4). It is one of the few supplementary scales that appears to be assessing something unique since it shares so few items with the other scales.

Dominance (*Do*) Scale

Gough, McClosky, and Meehl (1951) developed the Dominance (*Do*) scale by contrasting the item responses of both high school and college students who were judged by their peers to be most and least dominant. Their intent in the development of the *Do* scale was to identify strong, dominant, influential persons who were able to take initiative and exercise leadership.

Gough and associates (1951) identified 60 items that differentiated subgroups of male and female students who were most and least dominant. Only 28 of these items are found on the MMPI, and they comprise the MMPI *Do* scale. These 28 items (25 items remain on the MMPI-2) are keyed so that high scores indicate more dominant behaviors. The total 60 items identified by Gough and associates make up the Dominance scale on the California Psychological Inventory (Gough, 1957). Gough and colleagues noted that since their items were validated in nor-

mal student populations, additional research would be necessary to validate the use of the MMPI *Do* scale with adults and in psychopathologic groups.

Research on the MMPI *Do* scale has been exceedingly sparse. Olmsted and Monachesi's (1956) finding that firefighters achieved only slightly higher scores on the *Do* scale than students suggests that student norms could be generalized to adult samples. Olmsted and Monachesi also found that firefighters with the rank of captain did not have higher *Do* scores than regular firefighters; this finding led them to question the validity of the *Do* scale. On the other hand, Knapp (1960) found that military officers achieved higher *Do* scores than enlisted men, and Knapp questioned whether dominance played the same role in firefighters as in military personnel.

Age does not seem to affect *Do* scores in adults (Swenson et al., 1973). Duckworth and Anderson (1986) reported that college students have an average T score of 60 on the *Do* scale (i.e., current college students score somewhat higher on *Do* than the students on which Gough and associates [1951] developed the scale). The lack of further research on the *Do* scale makes conclusions difficult to draw. The Dominance scale on the California Psychological Inventory (Gough, 1957), which shares 28 of 60 items with the MMPI *Do* scale, is one of the better validated scales (Megargee, 1972). The MMPI *Do* scale also deserves serious attention. Research is needed on the MMPI *Do* scale to determine whether it is an adequate measure of interpersonal dominance and to document the generalization of student norms and test correlates to adult samples.

High scorers on the *Do* scale (T scores of 65 or higher) are described as being able to take charge of and responsibility for their lives. They are poised, self-assured, and confident of their own abilities. They address problems in a realistic, task-oriented fashion and feel adequate in their ability to overcome any obstacles that they may encounter. At higher elevations (T scores > 75) domineering qualities may be seen, but these qualities appear to be a function of which clinical scales are elevated. For example, elevations on Scales *4* (Psychopathic Deviate) and *9* (Hypomania) in conjunction with a high *Do* scale are more likely to indicate domineering behavior (Duckworth & Anderson, 1986).

Low scorers on the *Do* scale (T scores less than 45) have been less adequately investigated. These persons prefer to have others take responsibility for their lives. They frequently have high scores on the MMPI Dependency (*Dy*) scale, which further substantiates their reliance on others to meet their needs. Since the Dependency scale is not routinely scored on the MMPI-2 even though 48 of its 57 items have been retained, research is needed to determine the correlates of low scores on the *Do* scale.

The *Do* scale has limited item overlap with any of the standard validity and clinical scales. Those scales with which the *Do* scale does share the most items have the items scored in the opposite direction on the *Do* scale: Scale *2* (Depression)—4 items; Scale *4* (Psychopathic Deviate)—4 items; Scale *7* (Psychasthenia)—6 items; and Scale *0* (Social Introversion)—5 items (see Table 5–3). The *Do* scale also has limited item overlap with any of the other supplementary scales (see Table 5–4); again, the items are scored in the opposite direction on the *Do* scale: *A* (Anxiety)—5 items; and *MAC-R* (MacAndrew Alcoholism—Revised)—6 items.

Social Responsibility (*Re*) Scale

Gough and colleagues (1952) developed the Social Responsibility (*Re*) Scale by contrasting the item responses of both high-school and college students who were judged by their peers to be most and least responsible members, ignoring such considerations as friendliness, popularity, and so on. The responsible person was defined as "one who shows a ready willingness to accept the consequences of his own behavior, dependability, trustworthiness, and a sense of obligation to the group" (Gough et al., 1952, p. 74). Such a person would have a sense of commitment to the group and others, is dependable, and possesses integrity. They identified 56 items that reliably distinguished between students who were the most and least socially responsible. These 56 items comprise the Social Responsiblity Scale on the California Psychological Inventory (Gough, 1957). Only 32 of these items are found on the MMPI, and these 32 items comprise the MMPI *Re* scale, and 30 of these items are retained on the MMPI-2 *Re* scale.

Gough and colleagues (1952) described high scorers on the *Re* scale as showing greater concern for social and moral issues, disapproving of favoritism, emphasizing carrying one's own share of duties and burdens, having a sense of trust and confidence in the world, and being poised and self-assured. They did not describe low scorers on the *Re* scale. They noted that since their items were validated in normal student populations, additional research would be necessary to validate the use of the MMPI *Re* scale with adults and in clinical settings.

There has been virtually no research on the *Re* scale. Knapp (1960) reported that Marine Corps officers had higher scores than enlisted men, and Olmstead and Monachesi (1956) found that fire captains had higher scores than firemen, although these differences were not statistically reliable.

Duckworth and Anderson (1986) suggest that high scorers on the *Re* scale are accepting of a previously held value system, whereas low scorers are changing away from such a value system. They also provide suggested interpretations of ranges of scores on the *Re* scale. Such interpretations should be used cautiously until empirical research is available to validate them.

The *Re* scale shares few items with any of the standard validity and clinical scales (see Table 5–3) or the supplementary scales (see Table 5–4). The *Re* scale does share 9 items with the *MAC-R* (MacAndrew Alcoholism—Revised); these items are scored in the opposite direction on the two scales. The *Re* scale also shares 5 items with the *Do* (Dominance) scale.

College Maladjustment (*Mt*) Scale

Kleinmuntz (1960, 1961a) developed the College Maladjustment (*Mt*) scale by contrasting the item responses of 40 students who were referred to a university mental hygiene clinic for routine mental health screening required by their teacher's college with 40 students who were referred for treatment and who had remained in psychotherapy for at least three sessions. He excluded Scale *5* (Masculinity-Femininity) items since they were selected to differentiate between men and women. He identified 43 items that separated these two groups of students at the .01 level; 41 of these items are retained on the MMPI-2. The maladjusted student, who was defined by a score of 15 or higher, was an ineffectual, pessimistic, procrastinating, anxious, and worried person who tended to somatize and who found life to be a strain much of the time.

Kleinmuntz (1961b) found that his *Mt* scale did not accurately separate college students with potential maladjustment from those students who made a satisfactory adjustment during their first year of college. Subsequently, Kleinmuntz (1963) developed a computerized system based in part on the *Mt* scale to differentiate maladjusted and well-adjusted students. His use of the *Mt* scale and the MMPI in general quickly evolved into the issue of automated versus clinical judgment in the identification of maladjusted college students. The interested clinician should see Wiggins (1973) for an overview of this topic.

The *Mt* scale has substantial item overlap with a number of the standard clinical scales: Scale *1* (Hypochondriasis)—6 items; Scale *2* (Depression)—16 items; Scale *3* (Hysteria)—9 items; Scale *7* (Psychasthenia)—14 items; Scale *8* (Schizophrenia)—9 items; and Scale *0* (Social Introversion)—6 items (see Table 5–3).

The *Mt* scale also has substantial item overlap with several of the other supplementary scales: *A* (Anxiety)—12 items; *PK* (Post Traumatic Stress Disorder—Keane)—10 items; and *PS* (Post Traumatic Stress Disorder—Schlenger)—13 items (see Table 5–4). The *Mt* scale is another of the numerous MMPI-2 and MMPI scales that measure the first factor like the *A* scale. As noted above, there is little reason to score all of these first-factor scales since they tend to provide redundant information.

Gender Role Scales

Peterson (1989) developed separate gender role scales for men (Gender Role-Masculine [*GM*]) and women (Gender Role-Feminine [*GF*]) on the MMPI-2. She included an item on one of the gender scales if it was endorsed by a majority of one gender and by at least 10 percent fewer of the opposite gender. Nine items from *GM* and 15 items from *GF* overlap with Scale *5* (Masculinity-Femininity) so it is apparent that the *GM* and *GF* scales are not totally redundant to Scale *5* despite the substantial item overlap.

The availability of separate gender role scales for men and women avoids some of the pitfalls of the bipolar Scale *5* (see Chapter 4) and allows for the determination of the client's score separately on each scale. A quick perusal of the items on *GM* and *GF* (see Appendix A) will reveal that a very stereotypic characterization of each gender has been produced by this method of selecting the items for each scale. The items on each scale are so stereotypic for each gender that it does not seem likely that a person would score high on both scales and be classified as androgynous.

No research is available that reports the correlates of these two scales.

The *GM* and *GF* scales have little item overlap with any of the standard validity and clinical scales (see Table 5–3). The largest overlap is between the *GM* scale and Scale *0* (Social Introversion), sharing eight items. The *GM* and *GF* scales also have little item overlap with any of the supplementary scales (see Table 5–4). The *GM* scale shares 7 items with the *Es* (Ego Strength) scale, and the *GF* scale shares 6 items with the *Re* (Social Responsibility) scale.

Post Traumatic Stress Disorder Scales

Keane, Malloy, and Fairbank (1984) developed their Post Traumatic Stress Disorder *(PK)* scale by contrasting the item responses of 100 male veterans who had Post Traumatic Stress Disorder with 100 male veterans who had psychiatric diagnoses other than Post Traumatic Stress Disorder. They identified 49 items from the first 400 items of Form R of the MMPI that differentiated the two groups at the .001 level. They found that a cutting score of 30 was optimal for separating the two groups with a hit rate of 82 percent. The MMPI-2 retains 46 of these 49 items.

Hit rates in cross-validation studies of the *PK* scale have ranged from 38 percent (Gayton, Burchstead, & Matthews, 1986) to 80 percent (Schlenger & Kulka, 1987) and averaged in the 70 to 75 percent range (Penk, Keane, Robinowitz, Fowler, Bell, & Finkelstein, 1988). Denny, Robinowitz, and Penk (1987) and Penk and colleagues (1988) have provided recent reviews of the research on various PTSD scales.

Schlenger and Kulka (1987) developed their Post Traumatic Stress Disorder *(PS)* scale by contrasting the item responses of healthy Vietnam-era veterans with veterans with Post Traumatic Stress Disorder who did not have any other psychiatric diagnosis. Their scale consists of 60 items on the MMPI-2.

The *PK* and *PS* scales share 26 items (i.e., almost one-half of their items). The *PK* and *PS* scales have substantial item overlap with a number of the standard validity and clinical scales (see Table 5–3). The *PK* scale shares 11 items with Scale *2* (Depression); 9 items with Scale *3* (Hysteria); 11 items with Scale *4* (Psychopathic Deviate); 17 items with Scale *7* (Psychasthenia); and 19 items with Scale *8* (Schizophrenia).

The *PS* scale has an almost identical pattern of item overlap. The *PS* scale shares 11 items with Scale *2*; 10 items with Scale *3*; 9 items with Scale *4*; 17 items with Scale *7*; and 27 items with Scale *8*.

The *PK* and *PS* scales also have substantial item overlap with the other supplementary scales. The *PK* scale shares 9 items with Scale *A* (Anxiety) and 10 items with Scale *Mt* (College Maladjustment), whereas the *PS* scale shares 14 items with Scale *A* and 13 items with Scale *Mt*. Both the *PK* and *PS* scales share 10 items with the *Es* (Ego Strength) with the items scored in the opposite direction on the *Es* scale.

The *PK* and *PS* scales are saturated with first-factor variance as measures of general maladjustment and emotional distress rather than Post Traumatic Stress Disorder per se, as can be seen clearly in the extensive item overlap described above. Clinicians should be very cautious of diagnosing any client as having Post Traumatic Stress Disorder based on their scores on these two scales because of the significant amount of first-factor variance in both scales. Research is needed that outlines the relative advantages and disadvantages of the *PK* and *PS* scales. In the interim little is to be gained by scoring and using both of these scales since they are so redundant and saturated with first-factor variance.

ADDITIONAL MMPI SUPPLEMENTARY SCALES

Dependency (*Dy*) Scale

Navran (1954) developed the Dependency (*Dy*) scale by having 16 judges examine all MMPI items and select those items that they thought would be related to dependency. These judges identified 157 items, which were administered to two groups of 50 psychiatric patients. Through internal consistency procedures, Navran then identified those items that correlated most highly with one another in these two samples.

The 57 items (48 items on the MMPI-2) that resulted from this procedure comprise the *Dy* scale (See Appendix A for the MMPI-2). The items on the *Dy* scale are keyed so that high scores indicate more dependency. *Dy* has moderate positive correlations with Scales *2* (Depression), *6* (Paranoia), and *8* (Schizophrenia), and moderate negative correlations with the *K* scale. Navran's psychiatric patients scored higher on the *Dy* scale than the Minnesota normative group, who scored higher than a group of graduate students tested by Navran. Within the psychiatric sample nonparanoid schizophrenics scored higher than paranoid schizophrenics.

Little systematic research has been conducted on the *Dy* scale. High scores on the *Dy* scale has been found to be related to peer ratings and self-ratings of dependency (Zuckerman, Levitt, & Lubin, 1961); greater chronicity in welfare recipients (Pruitt & Van de Castle, 1962); and being female, having neurotic symptoms, being a psychiatric patient, being depressed, and attempting suicide (Birtchnell & Kennard, 1983). Birtchnell and Kennard suggest that these correlates of the *Dy* scale may largely reflect covariance with depression (i.e, the *Dy* scale is actually measuring some aspects of depression rather than dependency per se).

Age does not appear to affect performance on the *Dy* scores (Swenson et al., 1973), but women tend to score higher than men (Birtchnell & Kennard, 1983; Evans, 1984a). Duckworth and Anderson (1986) reported that college students have an average T score of 44 on the *Dy* scale.

At best, the present research provides modest support for the *Dy* scale. Since dependency is an important dimension of interpersonal behavior that could interact with and affect the success of treatment interventions, additional research on the *Dy* scale is needed to document its continued use. It appears particularly important to develop a dependency scale that measures the full range of dependent behaviors and that is *not* confounded with measures of depression.

High scorers on the *Dy* scale are described as being dependent, submissive, and passive. They also are frequently seen as being maladjusted. The dependency that they are manifesting may either be characterologic in nature or reflect their need for help in dealing with situational crises. Ambivalence about dependency may be present when they simultaneously elevate the Dominance (*Do*) scale or when they do not display dependent behaviors on other tests or in their interactions with others. In these circumstances they are likely to display passive-aggressive or passive-dependent behaviors.

Low scorers on the *Dy* scale are described as being independent and self-reliant.

Low-Back Pain (*Lb*) Scale

Hanvik (1949, 1951) developed the Low-Back Pain (*Lb*) scale by contrasting the item responses of 30 male inpatients with verifiable organic causes of their low-back pain and the responses of 30 male inpatients with no clear organic causes for their low-back pain. The two groups were matched on age, socioeconomic status, marital status, intelligence, and race.

Hanvik found 25 items that discriminated the two groups. He found that the optimal cutting score for identifying functional (nonorganic) low-back pain was a raw score of 11 or higher; this cutting score yielded an accuracy score of 80 percent on cross-validation. Hanvik (1951) reported that the mean profile for the clients with functional low-back pain had simultaneous elevations above a T score of 70 on Scales *1* (Hypochondriasis) and *3* (Hysteria), whereas Scale *2* (Depression) was about a T score of 60 (i.e., a conversion "V" profile [see Chapter 4 for a description of this profile]).

Hanvik (1951) also reported that experienced judges could reliably discriminate the profiles between these two groups, although some judges were more accurate at the task than others. Finally, Hanvik suggested that men with functional low-back pain demonstrated a slower return to normal functioning after surgery than those whose low-back pain had organic causes.

Dahlstrom (1954) found similar results in patients referred to neurosurgery for chronic low-back pain. Patients with no known physical cause for their complaints scored higher on the *Lb* scale and recovered more slowly after surgery than those with a known physical cause.

More recent research has obtained less consistent results. Most investigators have found small mean differences on the *Lb* scale between groups of patients with functional or mixed functional and organic low-back pain and patients with organic low-back pain, with the former groups scoring higher (Calsyn, Louks, & Freeman, 1976; Freeman, Calsyn, & Louks, 1976; Louks, Freeman, & Calsyn, 1978). None of these investigators, however, have found the *Lb* scale capable of reliably distinguishing between individual patients with functional or organic low-back pain (Haven & Cole, 1972; Pichot, Perse, Lebeaux, Dureau, Perez, & Rychewaert, 1972; Sternbach, Wolf, Murphy, & Akeson, 1973; Towne & Tsushima, 1978).

In France, Pichot and colleagues (1972) developed a 63-item scale that separated female patients with functional low-back pain from nonhospitalized persons without any pain complaints. Several studies have found that the *Lb* scale in conjunction with the Pichot and colleagues scale was somewhat successful in separating clients with functional low-back pain from clients with organic causes of their low-back pain. Until the Pichot and associates scale receives further validation in American samples, however, it should be used cautiously. It also seems that the *Lb* scale either by itself or in conjunction with the Pichot and colleagues scale may have limited usefulness in determining whether a specific client's pain is primarily functional in nature.

Several factors may have confounded the previous research on the *Lb* scale. First, investigators have used different cutting scores on the *Lb* scale; some have used a raw score of 11 (T score of 57) as suggested by Hanvik (1949), while others have used a T score of 70. Few investigators have identified and cross-validated the specific cutting score that classifies clients most accurately in their particular setting.

Second, investigators have paid little attention to the demographic factors that may influence how a client perceives and tolerates pain (cf. Weisenberg, 1977). The classification of clients into functional or organic subgroups on the basis of whether there are demonstrable organic reasons for their low-back pain appears to assume that all clients react to and tolerate pain in the same manner. Almost all investigators of clients with low-back pain have concluded that there is not a single profile type that is characteristic of these individuals. Profiles with conversion "V"'s are frequently seen in clients with functional low-back pain as well as in clients who have demonstrated organic causes for their low-back pain.

Finally, investigators have classified clients into categories of a functional, mixed, or organic basis for their low-back pain without consideration of either the reliability of these categories or their meaningfulness for treatment intervention. Future research on low-back pain and other forms of chronic pain may be more fruitful if investigators delineate subgroups among pain patients on the MMPI and then determine what forms of treatment interventions are most appropriate for each subgroup (Bradley, Prieto, Hopson, & Prokop, 1978; Bradley, Prokop, Margolis, & Gentry, 1978). Prokop (1988) and Snyder (1989) have provided a recent review of the literature on the use of the MMPI in patients with chronic pain that should be consulted by clinicians.

Personality Disorder Scales

Morey, Waugh, and Blashfield (1985) developed separate MMPI Personality Disorder Scales for each of the 11 DSM-III (American Psychiatric Association, 1980) personality disorders: Histrionic; Narcissistic; Borderline; Antisocial; Dependency; Compulsive; Passive-Aggressive; Paranoid; Schizotypal; Avoidant; and Schizoid.

Morey and associates developed their Personality Disorder Scales in a similar manner as Wiggins (1966) devised his Content scales, so their methodology will not be described here. The MMPI items found on each Personality Disorder Scale as well as the mean and standard deviation on each Scale for males and females in the original Minnesota normative group are provided in Dahlstrom, Welsh, and Dahlstrom (1972, 1975).

Since many items were common to more than one Scale, Morey and colleagues developed both a complete and a nonoverlapping version of these scales. They created the nonoverlapping version of each Scale by assigning overlapping items to the one scale with which these items had their highest correlation. "As a result, two sets of scales were developed: a complete set and a nonoverlapping set, which contained the same total number of items as the complete set but which eliminated item overlap" (p. 247). A comprehensive review of these Scales can be found in Morey and Smith (1988).

Only two validation studies of the Personality Disorder Scales have been published to date. Morey, Blashfield, Webb, and Jewell (1988) found that these Scales discriminated effectively between patients with a specific personality disorder diagnosis, normal individuals, and patients with other personality disorder diagnoses. Dubro, Wetzler, and Kahn (1988) found that the Personality Disorder Scales were only successful in identifying patients with avoidant personality disorder from four individual disorders (avoidant, borderline, dependent, and histrionic).

Overall, the Personality Disorder Scales had a sensitivity of 78 percent (patients with a personality disorder/all patients) and a specificity of 67 percent (patients without a personality disorder/all patients) for the presence of any personality disorder. It is difficult to draw any firm conclusions based on the limited research on the Morey and associates (1985) Personality Disorder Scales. Clinicians can use the scores from these Scales in conjunction with the other data from the MMPI in order to assess patients with personality disorders. Additional research will be necessary to determine the usefulness of these Scales.

The Morey and colleagues (1985) Personality Disorder scales are virtually intact on the MMPI-2. No scale has lost more than two items and eight of the nonoverlapping scales and six of the overlapping scales have lost no items.

Tryon, Stein, and Chu (TSC) Cluster Scales

Cluster scales on the MMPI based on an extensive cluster analysis of the entire MMPI item pool were developed by Tryon, Stein, and Chu (Stein, 1968). By analyzing responses to individual items rather than scale scores, they avoided the problem of items that are scored on more than one scale. For the 10 clinical scales the percentage of overlapping items ranges from 17 to 83 percent. This item overlap introduces a source of interrelatedness among the clinical scales, which is a problem in cluster analysis, factor analysis, or any other statistical procedure that assumes independent sources of variance.

For their analysis Tryon, Stein, and Chu used three samples totaling 310 males: 70 Veterans Administration (VA) hospital outpatient schizophrenics, 150 VA outpatient neurotics diagnosed as anxiety reaction, and 90 military officers. The officers and the VA patients were matched for age and education.

Items were selected for a cluster scale on both statistical and content bases. Through cluster analysis, Tryon, Stein, and Chu calculated communality estimates for each item within the three samples. They eliminated 317 items for reasons of trivial communality and an additional 57 items for being rationally ambiguous in relation to the general content meaning of items within a cluster scale. Seven cluster scales containing 192 items were derived following these procedures (see Table 5–17).

The items in each cluster scale are listed in Dahlstrom, Welsh, and Dahlstrom (1972, 1975).

High scores on each cluster scale indicate the presence of the behavior for which the scale is named, whereas low scores indicate the absence of this behavior. For example, a high score on the I (Social Introversion) cluster scale indicates that the client has endorsed the items like a person who is socially introverted, and a low score on this scale would indicate that the client has not endorsed the items like a socially introverted person.

Clusters I, B (Bodily Symptoms), and S (Suspicion) are the pivots or most independent clusters with modest intercorrelations (the highest correlation of .33 was between I and B). The other four clusters are highly correlated with all the clusters. The reliabilities of these clusters range from .85 to .94 with a median correlation of .92.

There has been virtually no reported research on the TSC scales. Graham (1987) provided some tentative interpretations of high scores on the TSC scales based on unpublished research by Boerger (1975). Boerger was unsuccessful in identifying correlates for low scores on these scales. Since low scores indicate the absence of the qualities

TABLE 5–17   Description of TSC Cluster Scales

Abbreviation	Number of Items	Description
I	26	Social Introversion versus Interpersonal Poise and Outgoingness
B	33	Bodily Symptoms versus Lack of Physical Complaints
S	25	Suspicion and Mistrust versus Absence of Suspicion
D	28	Depression and Apathy versus Positive and Optimistic Outlook
R	21	Resentment and Aggression versus Lack of Resentment and Aggression
A	23	Autism and Disruptive Thought versus Absence of Such Disturbance
T	36	Tension, Worry, Fear versus Absence of Such Complaints

Note: The descriptions are from Stein (1968).

manifested by high scores, it is not surprising that there are not consistent correlates of low scores. This situation may be similar to that on Scale *1* (Hypochondriasis), where high scorers are fairly homogeneous but low scorers are heterogeneous with the absence of somatic complaints as their only common characteristic.

The TSC scales need more empirical investigation in order to determine their function with various psychopathologic groups in a variety of settings.

Suicide Scales

Numerous attempts have been made to use the MMPI to predict the occurrence of suicide and/or suicide threats through supplementary scales such as the Suicide Threat scale (Farberow & Devries, 1967); profile analysis (cf. Clopton, Pallis, & Birtchnell, 1979; Leonard, 1977); and clinical judgment (Clopton & Baucom, 1979). Clopton (1979b) provided a comprehensive review of the use of the MMPI in predicting suicide, a review that the interested reader should consult.

The initial hurdle faced in predicting suicide with the MMPI or any other assessment device is the extremely low frequency with which suicide occurs in most populations. Even if a test were 75 percent accurate in predicting suicide, which would be unusually high for most tests, a more accurate prediction can be made by simply stating that all patients will be nonsuicidal since the frequency of suicide is less than 25 percent in any group. Consequently, any index of suicide will yield a large number of false positives (clients identified as suicidal who are nonsuicidal) because of this low frequency of occurrence.

Although it would seem that false positives are of less concern than false negatives (clients who are identified as nonsuicidal who commit suicide), the ethical and practical implications of falsely identifying a client as suicidal also must be considered (Rosen, 1954).

The clinical literature on the MMPI is replete with references to specific scales or codetypes that are frequently associated with suicide. For example, significant elevations (T scores $\geq$ 70) on Scales *2* (Depression) and/or *7* (Psychasthenia) are described as increasing the likelihood of suicide attempts (cf. Carson, 1969; Dahlstrom et al., 1972; Graham, 1987).

Dahlstrom and colleagues (1972) also noted that when the client has a Spike *2* profile (Scale *2* [Depression] is the only clinical scale elevated above a T score of 70) but denies depressive thoughts and feelings, the risk of suicide is increased. On the other hand, numerous studies have found no difference in Scale *2* scores of suicidal and nonsuicidal individuals (Clopton & Jones, 1975; Farberow, 1956; Simon & Gilberstadt, 1958). Suicidal and nonsuicidal persons also do not differ consistently on any of the other standard MMPI scales (Clopton, 1979b; Clopton, Post, & Larde, 1983; Spirito, Faust, Myers, & Bechtel, 1988; Watson, Klett, Walters, & Vassar, 1984).

Both Leonard (1977) and Clopton and associates (1979) found that multivariate statistical procedures, which simultaneously consider scores from a number of the clinical scales, could reliably distinguish female suicidal groups from control groups but not male suicidal groups from control groups. Leonard (1977) did not cross-validate her results; Clopton and associates (1979) found upon cross-validation that the percentage of female patients correctly classified decreased from 36 to 28 percent.

Clopton and colleagues (1979) reported the following relationship between Scales *1* (Hypochondriasis) and *2* (Depression) in their study, which deserves further investigation. Among clients with *7-8/8-7* codetypes, the relative elevation of Scales *1* and *2* was significantly associated with whether the client had attempted suicide. Scale *1* was greater than Scale *2* in 60 percent of the nonsuicidal clients, whereas Scale *2* was greater than Scale *1* in 64 percent of the suicidal clients.

Clopton and associates (1983) did find that discriminant analysis could reliably distinguish between patients who recently attempted suicide and nonsuicidal patients that held up on cross-validation. However, neither the original results (58.8 percent for females; 63.3 percent for males) nor the cross-validation results (53.9 percent for females; 58.6 percent for males) were particularly impressive.

Clopton and Baucom (1979) presented six psychologists who had extensive experience in MMPI interpretation with the profiles of male suicidal and nonsuicidal clients. None of the psychologists could reliably identify the clients in each group. The psychologists' ratings of eight variables thought to be related to suicide risk also did not differ for the suicidal and nonsuicidal clients.

Thus, any method using the MMPI or the MMPI-2—whether it involves single scales, profile analysis, supplementary scales, or item analysis—appears disappointing in the prediction of suicide. The few studies that reported statistical significance in identifying female suicidal groups appears to have limited clinical utility because of the small mean differences between groups on the individual scales.

As Clopton (1979b) pointed out, the research question of most interest is whether the MMPI can increase the accuracy of identifying suicidal clients, not whether the MMPI by itself is sufficient to predict suicide. Some investigators appear to assume that both suicide gestures or attempts and actual suicides result from a single cause without fully appreciating the multitude of factors that lead the client to attempt or commit suicide. Future research should discriminate among the various causes and types of suicide to determine whether specific scale patterns can assist in successfully

identifying some subgroups of suicidal clients.

Psychotic-Neurotic Indexes

Numerous MMPI indexes, those that involve combining various validity and/or clinical scales in a linear or a configural pattern, have been proposed as an additional means of determining how a client should be diagnosed. Peterson (1954) developed six diagnostic signs that he found were characteristic of psychotic (schizophrenic) MMPI patterns:

1. Four or more clinical scales are greater than a T score of 70.
2. The *F* scale is greater than a T score of 64.
3. Scales *6* (Paranoia), *8* (Schizophrenia), and *9* (Hypomania) are greater than Scales *1* (Hypochondriasis), *2* (Depression), and *3* (Hysteria).
4. Scale *2* is greater than Scales *1* and *3*.
5. Scale *8* is greater than Scale *7* (Psychasthenia).
6. Scales *6* or *9* is greater than a T score of 70.

The presence of three or more of these signs was characteristic of a psychotic profile pattern.

Taulbee and Sisson (1957) developed 16 signs, which involve comparison of one clinical scale with another clinical scale, as an index of whether the profile suggests a neurotic or a psychotic disorder (see Table 5–18). Each of these signs is scored as being present or absent. The presence of 13 or more of these signs suggests a neurotic pattern, whereas the presence of 6 or fewer signs suggests a schizophrenic pattern.

Meehl and Dahlstrom (1960) developed a set of complex configural rules (Meehl-Dahlstrom rules) to classify a MMPI profile

TABLE 5-18 Taulbee-Sisson Signs for Neurotic Patterns[a]

Sign	Sign
Scale *1* > Scale *3*	Scale *2* > Scale *6*
Scale *1* > Scale *4*	Scale *3* > Scale *4*
Scale *1* > Scale *5*	Scale *3* > Scale *5*
Scale *1* > Scale *6*	Scale *3* > Scale *6*
Scale *1* > Scale *7*	Scale *3* > Scale *9*
Scale *1* > Scale *8*	Scale *7* > Scale *5*
Scale *1* > Scale *9*	Scale *7* > Scale *6*
Scale *2* > Scale *4*	Scale *7* > Scale *8*

Note: The signs are from Taulbee and Sisson (1957).
[a]Each sign is scored as present or absent. Scores from 13 to 16 are indicative of a neurotic pattern; scores from 0 to 6 are indicative of a psychotic pattern.

as neurotic, psychotic, or indeterminate. (These rules are found in Dahlstrom et al. [1972].) Henrichs (1964, 1966) expanded the Meehl-Dahlstrom rules to include another category, character or behavior disorders.

Three studies are particularly relevant to the use of linear or configural indexes to make decisions about MMPI profile patterns. In a task examining linear and configural models of clinical judgment, Wiggins and Hoffman (1968) asked experienced clinicians to sort MMPI profiles on a distribution from neurotic through normal to psychotic. Slightly more than half of their clinicians (16/29) appeared to use configural cues in making their judgments, but a linear model could accurately estimate their judgments.

In two similar studies Goldberg (1965, 1969) found that a linear model accounted for most of the variance in clinicians' judgments of whether an MMPI profile should be classified as neurotic or psychotic, and a linear model was superior to all other models in estimating these judgments. Goldberg suggested a linear index [(Scale *L* + Scale *6* + Scale *8*) − (Scale *3* + Scale *7*)] as being one

of the most accurate in making this distinction between neurotic and psychotic profiles.[4]

Of course, these findings that a linear model can accurately estimate a clinician's judgments of whether an MMPI profile is neurotic or psychotic does not necessarily imply that the clinician makes decisions in this manner; they do suggest that the clinician should give greater considerations to such models in making judgments. Wiggins (1973) provided an extensive examination of the issues involved in clinical prediction, which the interested clinician is urged to read.

Little research has been conducted to validate these indexes to discriminate between neurotic and psychotic MMPI profiles. Meehl (1959) found that both the Meehl-Dahlstrom rules and the Taulbee-Sisson signs were better than individual clinicians in determining whether an MMPI profile should be classified as neurotic or psychotic. Winter and Stortroen (1963) reported that the Peterson signs were more accurate than the Meehl-Dahlstrom rules or the Taulbee-Sisson signs in discriminating among MMPI profiles from normals, patients with physical illness, and hospitalized schizophrenics.

Since neither the Meehl-Dahlstrom rules nor the Taulbee-Sisson signs were designed to identify normal profiles or profiles of patients with physical illness, it is unclear what meaning to assign to the superiority of the Peterson signs in their study.

Giannetti, Johnson, Klingler, and Williams (1978) found that the Goldberg index was superior to the Meehl-Dahlstrom rules, the Taulbee-Sisson signs, and the Peterson signs in discriminating neurotic from psychotic MMPI profiles. They also found that the Meehl-Dahlstrom rules and the Taulbee-Sisson signs achieved less than chance accuracy in making this discrimination.

The paucity of research in this area makes it difficult to draw definitive conclusions. It does appear that the Goldberg index may be superior to the other indexes in discriminating neurotic from psychotic MMPI profiles, although additional research is needed to investigate their utility thoroughly.

CRITICAL ITEMS

Despite the inherent difficulties in understanding responses to individual MMPI items (difficulties that provided the original impetus for the empirical selection of items on the MMPI), clinicians have been unwilling to ignore the information that might be contained in those responses. The original set of individual items, which were thought to require careful scrutiny if answered in the deviant direction, was rationally or intuitively selected by Grayson (1951). These 38 MMPI items were selected as being highly indicative of severe psychopathology and have accordingly been considered "stop" or "critical" items.

Caldwell (1969) developed on a rational basis a more comprehensive set of 68 MMPI items to identify severe, generally psychotic symptomatology. The content areas of his 66 MMPI-2 items are given in Table 5–19.

Koss and Butcher (1973) and Koss, Butcher, and Hoffmann (1976) examined the MMPI items endorsed by patients in crisis situations. They obtained MMPI responses from 723 male Veterans Administration hospital patients in six separate crisis situations: acute anxiety, depressed-suicidal ideation, threatened assault, situational stress due to alcoholism, mental confusion, and persecutory ideas.

The number of items that significantly discriminated each crisis group from a noncrisis control group ranged from 10 items in the threatened assault group to 89 items in the depressed-suicidal ideation group. If all of the items that discriminated a crisis group from the control group at a probability less than .001 and that are unique to only one cri-

TABLE 5–19 Content Areas for Caldwell MMPI-2 Critical Items

Number of Items	Content Areas
11	Distress and Depression
5	Suicidal Thoughts
10	Ideas of Reference, Persecution, and Delusions
9	Peculiar Experiences and Hallucinations
6	Sexual Difficulties
5	Authority Problems
3	Alcohol and Drugs
7	Family Discord
10	Somatic Concerns

Note: The content area names are from Caldwell (1969).

sis group are used, there are 67 items that are "critical" for these six crisis situations.

Examination of these 67 items reveals that the item content generally relates directly to the crisis situations. Thus, it appears that these patients were both willing and able to reveal accurate information about themselves.

All but three of the original Koss and Butcher (1973) critical items have been retained on the MMPI-2, although numerous items were added to the various item groups (see Appendix C). These item changes can be seen in Table 5–20.

The rationale for these changes has not been provided other than to state that empirical criteria were used to add items to the depressed suicidal ideation and situational stress due to alcoholism item groups (Butcher et al., 1989, p. 44). The latter point is particularly unclear since the original MMPI situational stress due to alcoholism item group had 15 items and this group has only 7 items on the MMPI-2.

Koss and Butcher (1973) also asked eight

TABLE 5–20   Changes in Items on the Koss and Butcher Critical Items

Crisis Area	Number of Items on the MMPI	Items Dropped on the MMPI-2	Number of Items on the MMPI-2
Acute Anxiety	9	2	17
Depressed-Suicidal Ideas	25	0	22
Threatened Assault	3	0	5
Situational Stress			
Due to Alcoholism	15	1	7
Mental Confusion	3	0	11
Persecutory Ideas	12	0	16
TOTAL	67	3	78

Note: Names and number of items are from Koss and Butcher (1973) and Butcher, Dahlstrom, Graham, Tellegen, & Kaemmer (1989).

clinical judges to select those MMPI items that would be relevant (face valid) to the six crisis groups. This procedure resulted in 96 items that four of the eight judges agreed would be relevant. When Koss and Butcher checked the responses of the patients to these items, they found that 67 items actually discriminated a crisis group from the control group. The fact that 24 percent (23/96) of these items did not significantly discriminate a crisis group from the control group illustrates the problem of generating critical item lists on a rational basis at least for these six crisis situations.

More importantly, Koss and Butcher could not find any apparent differences between face-valid items that were empirically related to a crisis situation and those face valid items that were not. Koss and colleagues (1976) indicated that the Grayson (1951) and Caldwell (1969) critical items are inadequate samples of behavior of potential interest to the clinician and that better critical items could be identified. Since most of these items are face valid for a specific crisis situation, the clinician could use these 67 items to identify significant problem areas that warrant further exploration.

A question that needs to be addressed, however, is the frequency with which these items are endorsed by normal clients. Even though a client in a crisis may endorse an item, it may still be true that normal clients endorse the items more often than not. For example, perhaps 75 percent of a crisis group endorsed a specific item, whereas 60 percent of a normal group endorsed the same item. This difference could be statistically significant; if an individual endorsed the item, however, that would not necessarily indicate that the individual is in a crisis since 60 percent of a normal sample also endorse that item. This question needs to be explored on the items identified by Koss and Butcher as well as sets of critical items identified by other investigators.

Lachar and Wrobel (1979) developed a set of critical items designed to be face-valid descriptors of psychological concerns. They first identified 14 categories of symptoms that summarized problems that motivate people to seek psychological treatment and that help the clinician make diagnostic decisions. Then 14 clinical psychologists read each MMPI item and nominated items that would be face-valid indicators of psychopathology in one of these 14 categories. Items nominated by at least 6 of the 14 clinicians, together with the Grayson (1951) and Caldwell (1969) critical items, were empirically validated by contrasting item response frequencies for normals and psychiatric samples matched for sex and race.

Lachar and Wrobel were able to validate 130 of the 177 items nominated. After eliminating 19 items that were highly duplicative of item content in other items on the list, they arrived at a final list of 111 critical items. The content areas for these items appear in Table 5–21. Lachar and Wrobel reported that 80 percent of the 111 items reliably differentiated normal from psychiatric samples for adult males, females, blacks, and whites. They concluded that responses to these critical items could serve as accurate representations of the client's psychological concerns.

All but four of the Lachar and Wrobel (1979) critical items have been retained on the MMPI-2 (see Appendix C). Two items were dropped from the Sexual Concern and Deviation group, and one item from Deviant Thinking and Experience and Substance Abuse (see Table 5–21).

Although critical item lists are widely employed in both automated and individual

TABLE 5–21   Content Areas for the Lachar and Wrobel MMPI-2 Critical Items

Number of Items	Content Areas
	Psychological Discomfort
11	Anxiety and Tension
16	Depression and Worry
6	Sleep Disturbance
	Bodily Distortions
15	Deviant Beliefs
10	Deviant Thinking and Experience
	Characterologic Adjustment
3	Substance Abuse
9	Antisocial Attitude
4	Family Conflict
4	Problematic Anger
6	Sexual Concern and Deviation
23	Somatic Symptoms

Note: The content area names are from Lachar and Wrobel (1979).

clinical interpretations of the MMPI and MMPI-2, there is little information on what meaning or clinical importance to assign to a deviant response to a specific critical item. Most clinicians seem to assume that any deviant response is worthy of further investigation, even without any information on the base rate (frequency) with which a given critical item is endorsed by normal or pathologic samples. In addition, until recently, the individual critical items had not been validated to determine whether deviant responses were empirically related to the actual behavior of the individual.

Regarding the Grayson (1951) critical items, Saunders and Gravitz (1974) found that normal females were more likely to endorse items reflecting internal conflict or stress, whereas normal males were more likely to endorse items reflecting acting-out behaviors. Newton (1968) reported that psychiatric samples endorsed on the average about 9 of the 38 Grayson critical items. Gravitz (1968) reported that normal adults infrequently endorse any of the items, although 5 of the 38 items were endorsed by more than 10 percent of his sample. The frequency of endorsement of these items ranged from .5 percent to 12.5 percent in males and from .9 percent to 29.3 percent in females. These results certainly question the appropriateness of considering these items critical.

Similarly, the university student sample described in Greene (1980), which can be assumed to be relatively normal, endorsed an average of six of the Grayson critical items. Only 36.4 percent of this student sample endorsed three or fewer items. Again, it seems that the high frequency of endorsement of the Grayson critical items by normal samples seriously questions how "critical" these items actually are. In addition, none of the above studies provides any empirical validation of the Grayson critical items.

In comparing the responses of their six crisis groups with the normal group, Koss and associates (1976) found substantial overlap between the distributions of the total number of their deviant responses to the Grayson critical items. Consequently, they could not identify any cutting score that accurately classified normal and crisis samples. Thus, there is little evidence that the Grayson critical items are useful either in identifying behaviors that need attention or in classifying clients as normal or pathologic.

No research has been published on the Caldwell (1969) critical items. Caldwell used procedures similar to Grayson's in constructing his critical items; therefore, it seems likely that the above reservations about the Grayson critical items also would apply to the Caldwell critical items.

Since critical items are face valid, clients can overreport or underreport the item content if they so desire (see Chapter 3). Hence, endorsement of the critical items will indicate the areas of psychological concern only if the items have been endorsed accurately.

There has been very little research with either the Koss and Butcher (1973) and Lachar and Wrobel (1979) critical items. Comparing items within similar content areas on these two lists reveals little item overlap, which suggests that a different meaning of the word *critical* is being used by these investigators. Koss and Butcher identified items that are critical for specific crisis groups; Lachar and Wrobel identified items that are face-valid descriptors of psychological concerns. Researchers should understand these differences in item selection and determine which critical item list is appropriate for their specific use.

Evans (1984b) found that his sample of normal adults endorsed more critical items than groups of psychiatric patients and alcoholics in the areas of Acute Anxiety and Situational Stress Due to Alcoholism of the Koss and Butcher (1973) critical items. His normal adults also endorsed more items than patients in the area of Problematic Anger of

the Lachar and Wrobel (1979) critical items. Finally, his normal adults endorsed an average of 16 of the Koss and Butcher critical items and 12 of the Lachar and Wrobel critical items.

Holmes, Sabalis, Chestnut, and Khoury (1984) reported that parents of children referred for outpatient psychiatric services significantly increased the number of critical items that they endorsed from the period of 1970–1974 to 1975–1979.

The frequency with which the Koss and Butcher (1973) MMPI critical items were endorsed by men and women for four samples are presented in Tables 5–22 and 5–23, respectively.

Several general comments can be made about the mean number of critical items endorsed by each sample. First, the university student sample endorsed more items in the Situational Stress Due to Alcoholism and Mental Confusion categories than any of the other three samples; thus, the items in these two categories may be influenced by some extraneous variables, such as the willingness to report problem behaviors. Second, females are more likely to endorse items within the Acute Anxiety and Depressed-Suicidal Ideas categories than males. Third, the Threatened Assault category does not distinguish any of the samples, probably because of the few items in it. Finally, even normal samples endorse a moderate percentage of critical items within any category, which suggests that exploring every critical item endorsed by a client may likely be a very time-consuming process.

The frequency of endorsement of the Lachar and Wrobel (1979) MMPI critical items in the same four samples for men and women is presented in Tables 5–24 and 5–25 respectively. Again, some general conclusions can be drawn.

First, females irrespective of the sample were more likely than males to endorse items in the Anxiety and Tension, Depression and Worry, and Sleep Disturbance areas. Second,

TABLE 5–22 Frequency of Endorsement of Koss and Butcher Critical Items by Sample for Men

Crisis Situation	Number of Items	Sample							
		Clinic Clients (N = 140)		Medical Patients (N = 86)		Prison Inmates (N = 200)		University Students (N = 96)	
		M	SD	M	SD	M	SD	M	SD
Acute Anxiety	9	3.58	1.49	4.86	1.53	2.78	1.41	3.10	1.28
Depressed-Suicidal Ideas	25	9.83	5.65	5.35	4.85	5.30	4.69	6.76	5.22
Threatened Assault	3	.91	.72	.79	.81	1.38	.65	.87	.76
Situational Stress Due to Alcoholism	15	7.84	2.14	8.85	2.16	9.65	1.82	8.95	1.95
Mental Confusion	3	1.08	.83	.95	.83	.82	.84	1.25	.97
Persecutory Ideas	12	2.41	1.84	1.13	1.14	2.39	1.99	1.86	1.34

males irrespective of the sample were more likely than females to endorse items in the Deviant Beliefs, Deviant Thinking, Antisocial Attitude, and Family Conflict areas. Third, the university students endorsed more items in the Deviant Thinking, Substance Abuse, and Problematic Anger areas than the other three samples, which would cause one

to question how critical the items are within these three areas.

Finally, even the university students, who are supposedly normal, endorsed about one-quarter of these critical items, and only 11 students (5.3 percent) endorsed 10 or fewer items. Consequently, if the clinician intends to pursue every critical item endorsed by the

TABLE 5–23 Frequency of Endorsement of Koss and Butcher Critical Items by Sample for Women

Crisis Situation	Number of Items	Sample					
		Clinic Clients (N = 275)		Medical Patients (N = 155)		University Students (N = 113)	
		M	SD	M	SD	M	SD
Acute Anxiety	9	4.03	1.49	5.44	1.40	3.54	1.31
Depressed-Suicidal Ideas	25	11.80	6.01	6.82	4.75	5.30	3.38
Threatened Assault	3	.70	.74	.60	.70	.50	.71
Situational Stress Due to Alcoholism	15	6.52	2.15	7.24	2.03	8.58	1.94
Mental Confusion	3	1.63	.76	1.22	.54	1.54	.84
Persecutory Ideas	12	2.11	1.50	1.55	2.22	1.73	.15

TABLE 5–24   Frequency of Endorsement of Lachar and Wrobel Critical Items by Sample for Men

Content Area	Number of Items	Sample							
		Clinic Clients (N = 140)		Medical Patients (N = 86)		Prison Inmates (N = 200)		University Students (N = 96)	
		M	SD	M	SD	M	SD	M	SD
Anxiety and Tension	11	4.43	2.41	3.17	2.29	2.14	1.94	3.21	2.32
Depression and Worry	16	5.78	3.49	3.38	2.99	2.85	1.31	4.13	3.19
Sleep Disturbance	6	2.05	1.53	1.47	1.43	1.59	1.42	1.75	1.56
Deviant Beliefs	15	2.83	2.76	1.08	1.74	2.07	2.83	2.12	1.95
Deviant Thinking and Experience	11	2.86	2.29	1.41	1.58	2.38	2.20	3.11	2.11
Substance Abuse	4	1.29	1.10	.71	.92	1.35	1.15	1.54	1.30
Antisocial Attitude	9	3.41	1.98	2.21	1.87	4.41	1.90	3.62	1.97
Family Conflict	4	1.98	1.19	.74	1.03	1.14	1.00	1.31	1.19
Problematic Anger	4	1.51	1.17	1.13	1.14	.97	1.16	1.74	1.27
Sexual Concern and Deviation	8	2.36	1.79	1.09	1.25	1.03	1.21	1.97	1.73
Somatic Symptoms	23	5.84	4.50	6.13	4.29	3.56	3.45	4.46	3.89

client, there appears to be a potential problem of expending a large amount of time because of the frequency of endorsement of these items even in a normal sample.

The sheer number of items (107 items on the MMPI-2; 111 items on the MMPI) in the Lachar and Wrobel (1979) critical items list, which includes 97 items scored on the standard validity and clinical scales, would make routine inspection of all the items a laborious process in a clinical sample. The Lachar and Wrobel critical items contain 39 percent of the 69 items that Clavelle and Butcher (1977) found most strongly to discriminate MMPI codetypes from one another. This suggests that psychopathologic samples will likely endorse a large number of these items.

The Koss and Butcher and Lachar and Wrobel critical items lists appear to warrant further research to determine how well these items identify critical areas of psychological concern in a variety of settings and populations. No criteria have been established to determine how many items within a given area can be answered before the clinician should investigate further; research is needed to establish such criteria although this violates the initial assumption that any item endorsed was deemed critical.

Additionally, items need to be identified that do not effectively discriminate among groups so that the number of items can be reduced to a manageable size. Some items within the Deviant Thinking, Substance Abuse, and Problematic Anger content areas seem to be likely candidates for deletion since the normal university students were more likely to endorse items within these areas than any of the other three samples studied.

Finally, the influence of a client's tendency to overreport or underreport psychopathology on the endorsement of these criti-

TABLE 5-25 Frequency of Endorsement of Lachar and Wrobel Critical Items by Sample for Women

Content Area	Number of Items	Clinic Clients (N = 275)		Medical Patients (N = 155)		University Students (N = 113)	
		M	SD	M	SD	M	SD
Anxiety and Tension	11	5.10	2.65	3.46	2.26	2.95	2.00
Depression and Worry	16	6.85	3.89	4.28	3.08	3.17	2.18
Sleep Disturbance	6	2.80	1.76	2.05	1.51	1.96	1.38
Deviant Beliefs	15	2.15	2.07	1.05	1.43	1.52	1.25
Deviant Thinking and Experience	11	2.67	1.96	1.64	1.42	2.68	1.68
Substance Abuse	4	1.02	1.16	.38	.66	.90	1.07
Antisocial Attitude	9	2.23	1.84	1.10	1.22	1.80	1.56
Family Conflict	4	2.10	1.25	.86	1.03	1.18	1.02
Problematic Anger	4	1.46	1.14	.86	.94	1.09	1.10
Sexual Concern and Deviation	8	2.65	1.60	1.55	1.22	1.82	1.15
Somatic Symptoms	23	7.55	5.06	7.64	4.36	3.98	2.77

cal items needs to be investigated, since the fact that a client endorses a specific critical item does not mean that he or she is providing an accurate self-report.

SHORT FORMS

The extensive number of items in the MMPI-2 (567) and MMPI (566) and the length of time required to complete the test (an hour for most clients and ranging upward to several hours for a few individuals) has led to numerous proposals to shorten or reduce the number of items on the test. Three of the more commonly used short forms of the MMPI will be reviewed here—Kincannon's (1968) Mini-Mult, Faschingbauer's Abbreviated MMPI (FAM: 1974), and Overall and Gomez-Mont's (1974) MMPI-168.

The clinician who desires more in-depth analysis of these short forms of the MMPI or other less frequently used short forms should consult Faschingbauer and Newmark (1978). Stevens and Reilley (1980) have provided an-

other review of the literature on short forms. The interested reader also should consult Greene's (1982) response to the review by Stevens and Reilley. Butcher and Hostetler (1990) have reviewed the research on the use of short forms on the MMPI with suggestions for how these issues might be addressed on the MMPI-2. Any clinician who is contemplating research on short forms on the MMPI-2 should consult this article before starting.

Kincannon's (1968) short form of the MMPI was developed based on Comrey's factor analyses of the validity and clinical scales (cf. Comrey, 1957a). Kincannon selected items to represent each cluster within each scale. He chose items that were scored on the greatest number of scales (i.e., items with the most overlap across scales), and most of his items are scored on three to five different scales.

Following this procedure, he identified 71 items, which he called the Mini-Mult. Kincannon also reworded these 71 items because he intended that they be used in an interrogative fashion in an interview format. The Mini-Mult yields an estimate of all the validity and clinical scales except Scales *5* (Masculinity-Femininity) and *0* (Social Introversion). Graham and Schroeder (1972) provided items that can be added to the Mini-Mult so that Scales *5* and *0* can be scored. The actual items on the Mini-Mult, the procedures for transforming raw scores on the shortened scales into estimates of the raw scores on the original scales, and the instructions for administration can be found in Kincannon's (1968) original article.

Faschingbauer's (1974) short form of the MMPI, the FAM, also was developed based on Comrey's factor analyses of the standard validity and clinical scales (cf. Comrey, 1957). In addition, Faschingbauer used Graham, Schroeder, and Lilly's (1971) factor analyses of Scales *5* and *0*, which were not factored by Comrey, and the results of research on deficiencies in Kincannon's (1968) Mini-Mult.

One-third of the items were selected on the basis of the greatest amount of overlap with other scales, one-third for the least amount of overlap, and one-third for the greatest number of intercorrelations > 0.29 with the other items. This procedure yielded preliminary short-form scales, which then were correlated with their corresponding original scales in a sample of 100 college males. For the FAM scales that did not correlate > 0.84 with their corresponding scale, items were added and deleted until this criterion was met. This final step yielded the 166 items in the FAM, which estimates all the standard validity and clinical scales.

Faschingbauer (1974) reported that when the FAM and MMPI were administered as two separate tests in a psychiatric sample, 60 percent of the profiles had an identical high-point scale and 28 percent had the same two high-point scales in any order. The FAM was more accurate in predicting high-point

scales in the standard profile and detecting invalid profiles than other short forms.

The MMPI-168 was developed by Overall and Gomez-Mont (1974) because of their need for a brief screening test in view of the disappointing results that they obtained from evaluation of the validity of the Mini-Mult in their psychiatric setting. They selected the first 168 items of the MMPI as a screening test largely because item 168 appears as the last item at the bottom of page 7 of the Form R test booklet, providing a convenient stopping point for the client. Of course, if the group booklet form is used, item 168 will have to be marked as the last item to be answered since it is in the middle of the fourth page.

One advantage of the MMPI-168 is that the regular scoring templates can be used, and Overall and Gomez-Mont (1974) provide regression equations for estimating the scores on all the validity and clinical scales from the obtained raw scores. They believe that most of the information in the standard profile is well represented in the first 168 items of the MMPI.

Research on the frequency with which short forms can predict the standard MMPI codetype has yielded mixed results. Hoffmann and Butcher (1975) found that the Mini-Mult, FAM, and MMPI-168 were comparable in their ability to predict specific codetypes, with hit rates ranging from .0 percent to 65 percent, 13.0 percent to 74.0 percent, and 6.8 percent to 74.0 percent, respectively. Hedlund, Won Cho, and Powell (1975) found that the Mini-Mult and MMPI-168 concurred with the standard MMPI high-point pair in 33 percent and 45 percent of their clients, respectively.

Evans (1984c) reported an average concordance rate of 35 percent for codetypes between the MMPI-168 and the standard MMPI in a sample of alcoholic patients. Concordance rates for specific codetypes ranged from 78 percent for a *2-4/4-2* codetype to 15 percent for a *7-8/8-7* codetype. In all of these studies the short forms were not independently administered; rather each short form was extracted from the standard MMPI, which would inflate the relationship between the short form and standard MMPI.

Hoffmann and Butcher (1975) concluded that there was insufficient evidence to advocate the clinical use of any of the short forms. They particularly cautioned against trying to use a short form with existing interpretive systems based on the standard MMPI because of the low frequency of concordance between the two tests in terms of high-point pairs. Graham (1987) voiced the same caution.

A virtual flood of studies have reported comparisons between a specific short form and the standard MMPI to document subject or setting characteristics. Almost all these studies have focused exclusively on how well the short form can predict the standard MMPI without considering the direct validity of the short form. Since the MMPI is an imperfect predictor of an external criterion, using a short form with questionable validity to predict the standard MMPI only seems to compound the potential for error. As Hoffmann and Butcher (1975) suggested, it would make more sense to use direct predictive approaches with short-form tests whereby a specific criterion is predicted.

Vincent (1984) has devised an actuarial system for use with the MMPI-168 (Overall & Gomez-Mont, 1974) that can be seen as one attempt to determine the specific correlates of a short form test. His actuarial system is very preliminary since it is based on a sample of 400 patients referred to a private psychiatric clinic. This approach is one that should be followed in using a short form test (i.e., it needs to be construed as a new test that must be validated directly). However, if the clinician is going to devote the time and effort to validate a short form as a new test, it would make more sense to begin with a new item pool and not be limited by any inherent short-

comings of the MMPI item pool and scales (Streiner & Miller, 1986).

Only a few studies have directly compared the utility of short forms and the standard MMPI in predicting an external criterion. Poythress and Blaney (1978) compared psychologists' *Q*-sort ratings of the FAM, Mini-Mult, and the standard MMPI in 36 patients with a wide variety of psychopathology. The standard MMPI yielded moderately higher but not statistically significant *Q*-sort ratings than the FAM, and the standard MMPI was significantly better than the Mini-Mult.

Using a similar procedure, Rand (1979) also found that *Q*-sorts produced by psychologists from the standard MMPI were significantly different from the Mini-Mult for 10 college students. Newmark, Ziff, Finch, and Kendall (1978) reported that the correlations of the FAM, MMPI-168, and standard MMPI with direct measures of psychopathology seemed comparable. Butcher, Kendall, and Hoffman (1980) pointed out that Newmark and associates' (1978) results appear to represent an atypical sample and they questioned whether these results can be generalized to other settings. Moreland (1984) found that neither the FAM nor the MMPI-168 could be substituted for the standard MMPI in predicting ratings of psychiatric patients.

Until further research has been conducted on the FAM, Mini-Mult, and MMPI-168, clinicians should be extremely cautious in using any short form routinely. Clinicians should be particularly wary of trying to use a short form to predict the standard MMPI profile and then follow existing interpretive systems based on the standard MMPI since concordance between codetypes is generally limited.

The research on the Mini-Mult (Kincannon, 1968) has yielded consistently negative results, which should cause the clinician to question its appropriateness in most situations. The fact that the MMPI-168 (Overall &

Gomez-Mont, 1974) seems to yield comparable results to the FAM is interesting because of the more elaborate statistical procedures that Faschingbauer (1974) used in developing the FAM. If future comparisons of the FAM and MMPI-168 with external validity criteria continue to produce similar results, the MMPI-168 would have some inherent advantages because the standard booklets and scoring templates can be retained.

There seems to be little justification for the use of short forms of the MMPI on a psychometric basis (McLaughlin, Helmes, & Howe, 1983; Streiner & Miller, 1986), from a clinical perspective (Edinger, 1981), based on their clinical utility (Helmes & McLaughlin, 1983), or based on their concordance with the standard MMPI (Evans, 1984c; Hedlund et al., 1975; Hoffmann & Butcher, 1975). Consequently, short forms of the MMPI should *not* be used as a predictor of or substitute for the standard MMPI, and clinicians who continue to use them will have to demonstrate their usefulness empirically for whatever purpose they have in mind. It also would seem that these same caveats should hold for the MMPI-2.

ENDNOTES

1. W. G. Dahlstrom (personal communication, November 13, 1979) noted that item 356 ("false") on the MAC was listed incorrectly as item 357 ("false") in Dahlstrom and associates (1975).

2. Reproduced from the MMPI by permission. Copyright © 1943, (renewed 1970), by the University of Minnesota. Published by the University of Minnesota Press. All rights reserved.

3. Ibid.

4. These scales are all *K*-corrected T scores. A score greater than 45 on the Goldberg index indicates a psychotic profile pattern, and a score of 44 or below indicates a neurotic profile pattern.

CHAPTER 6

Codetypes

The correlates of MMPI-2 and MMPI codetypes (specific combinations of the 10 clinical scales) will be considered in this chapter. These codetypes typically have been studied according to high-point pairs, that is, the two scales with the highest elevation above a T score of 65 (MMPI-2) or 70 (MMPI).

A codetype is referred to by writing the numbers of the two scales involved with the most elevated one first. For example, if a client's two highest scores on the MMPI-2 are on Scales *2* and *7*, and both are above a T score of 65 but Scale *7* is higher than Scale *2*, then the client's codetype would be *7-2*. If the two highest clinical scales have identical T scores, they are listed in numerical order. In this example, if both Scales *2* and *7* had identical T scores of 75, the client's codetype would be *2-7*. There are 90 possible codetypes on the MMPI-2 and MMPI following this procedure.

The order of the scales within the codetype will *not* be differentiated unless empirical data indicate that the correlates of the codetype do change depending on which scale is elevated higher. For example, *1-2/2-1* codetypes will not be distinguished from each other, whereas *1-3* and *3-1* codetypes will be. When scale order within a codetype does produce different correlates, these will be noted explicitly.

The amount of material presented on a codetype is a rough index of the frequency with which the codetype is encountered. Some codetypes occur frequently, such as *2-4/4-2*, *4-9/9-4*, and *6-8/8-6*; other codetypes are rarely encountered in any setting, such as *3-0/0-3*, *1-6/6-1*, and *1-5/5-1*. The actual frequency with which codetypes are encountered in psychiatric and medical settings will be provided below.

Generally, the relationships among any of the validity scales are not discussed because the validity scales serve primarily to establish whether a specific clinical scale profile can be safely interpreted. When an important relationship does exist between a validity scale and a codetype, this relationship will be mentioned.

The correlates of profiles in which only one clinical scale is elevated above a T score of 65 on the MMPI-2 or a T score of 70 on the MMPI (spike profiles) also will be discussed. Finally, the correlates of high-point triads

231

(three highest elevated clinical scales) will be examined when the addition of a third scale significantly modifies the interpretation of the codetype.

This chapter will provide only the general correlates of each codetype. The clinician is strongly encouraged to become familiar with the available references providing more detailed information on profile interpretations that have been developed within a specific population, and to know under what circumstances each source might be most useful.

MMPI COOKBOOK INTERPRETIVE SYSTEMS

Gilberstadt (Gilberstadt, 1970; Gilberstadt & Duker, 1965) and Marks and Seeman (Marks & Seeman, 1963; Marks, Seeman, & Haller, 1974) have developed the most widely known actuarial cookbooks for the MMPI. Gilberstadt developed his interpretive system on male inpatients at a Veterans Administration hospital. He used five criteria for including a client in his preliminary analysis: (1) MMPI administered within 21 days before or after admission; (2) age range from 20 to 60; (3) primary diagnosis not brain damage; (4) $L \leq 60$, $F \leq 85$, and $K \leq 70$; and (5) Shipley Institute of Living Scale IQ estimate ≥ 105. Gilberstadt cautioned the clinician about applying his cookbook when any of these criteria are not met. He identified 19 codetypes among these clients, for which he provided the following data:

1. The most probable diagnosis
2. The list of complaints, traits, and symptoms associated with the specific codetype
3. The cardinal features of the client as a summary description
4. Descriptive clinical information about the client

Gilberstadt also provided actuarial rules for identifying each codetype. For example, the rules for specifying a *1-2-3* codetype are:

Scales *1*, *2*, and *3* ≥ 70

Scale *1* > Scale *2* $\geq$ Scale *3*

No other clinical scale greater than 70

Scales $L \leq 65$, $F \leq 85$, and $K \leq 70$

Clopton (1975) has developed a computerized version of the Gilberstadt and Duker (1965) system.

Marks and Seeman (1963; Marks et al., 1974) developed their MMPI interpretive system on hospitalized psychiatric clients seen in a university medical center, two-thirds of whom were women. These clients were literate, over 18 years of age, and voluntarily seeking treatment for problems of personal adjustment.

Marks and Seeman (1963) identified 9 preliminary codetypes in an original sample; in new samples they revised and refined these 9 codetypes and identified 11 additional codetypes. Before including a codetype within their system, Marks and associates insisted on studying at least 20 clients with that codetype; Gilberstadt and Duker (1965), on the other hand, used as few as 6 clients in some of their codetypes. In their system Marks and Seeman determined the actual correlates of each codetype for women only. When they were able to examine differences between males and females within a codetype, they found no significant differences.

Marks and Seeman (1963) originally defined their codetypes by complex configural rules; later they modified their classification procedure (Marks et al., 1974) in view of Gynther, Altman, and Sletten's (1973) demonstration that codetypes were more useful than their original configural rules. For example, Marks and Seeman (1963) originally defined a *2-7* codetype by the following criteria:

Scales *2* and *7* ≥ 70

Scale *2* minus Scale *8* ≥ 15 points

Scale *7* > Scales *1* and *3*

Scale *7* minus Scale *4* ≥ 10 points

Scale *7* minus Scale *6* ≥ 10 points

Scale *7* minus Scale *8* ≥ 10 points

Scale *9* ≤ 60

Scales *L, F,* and *K* ≤ 70.

In their revised classification procedure (Marks et al., 1974), a *2-7* codetype is simply that: Scales *2* and *7* are the two highest clinical scales. Thus, 12 of their 16 current codetypes are defined simply by the two highest clinical scales. The other 4 codetypes are defined by the more complex configural rules as in their original system. They also developed 29 codetypes for adolescents, which will be discussed in Chapter 8.

Marks and Seeman did not report the percentage of profiles that could be classified in their revised system, although they did report that nearly 75 percent of their profiles could be classified in their original system. It would be expected that even more profiles should be classifiable in their revised system. Whether the simplified criteria for classifying profiles within codetypes significantly alters the applicability of the system will need to be determined empirically.

Although these two profile interpretation systems are specific and rather extensive, some interpretive problems remain. When either Gilberstadt's (Gilberstadt & Duker, 1965) or Marks and Seeman's (1963) original system is used, surprising variation occurs among the clinical scales obtained by clients with a specific codetype (cf. Sines, 1966).

Moreover, it is commonly reported that only 15 to 35 percent of codetypes from a given clinical setting will fit into any of the codetypes (Fowler & Coyle, 1968a; Meikle & Gerritse, 1970; Shultz, Gibeau, & Barry, 1968). Even when some of the configural rules for codetypes are relaxed, the number of profiles that can be interpreted with either system does not increase appreciably (Pauker, 1966).

Two additional MMPI profile interpretation systems have been developed, one by Gynther and colleagues (Gynther et al., 1973) and the other by Lachar (1974). Gynther and associates developed replicated correlates of 14 MMPI codetypes that occurred at least 30 or more times in a sample of 3,400 inpatients in public mental health facilities. They reported that 55 to 60 percent of MMPIs for white clients could be classified into one of these codetypes.

They also produced other interesting findings: no evidence could be found that the correlates of a high-point triad differed significantly from the codetype; absolute elevation of the codetype above a T score of 70 did not affect the obtained correlates; it seemed that gender may have affected the correlates within a given codetype; and similar codetypes obtained from blacks and whites seemed to require different interpretations.

The only rule required for classifying a profile within the Gynther system is that the raw score on the *F* scale be less than 26. Gynther and colleagues (1973) also provide a separate interpretation of profiles in which the raw score on the *F* scale equals or exceeds 26. As Gynther acknowledges, the interpretive narratives generated by this system are exceedingly brief compared to other systems.

For example, the complete narrative for a *1-3/3-1* codetype is: "This type of client may display an unusual amount of bodily concern, often in the form of multiple somatic complaints, that sometimes reach the proportions of hypochondriasis. However, it should be noted that sometimes real physical problems are the cause of the client's concerns" (Gynther et al., 1973, p. 273).

The very limited number of replicated correlates in the Gynther system for specific MMPI codetypes should be kept in mind when interpretation of profiles is discussed in Chapter 7 so that one can appreciate the amount of nonvalidated material that may be included.

Lachar (1974) developed an automated MMPI interpretive system in a manner very different from the three systems examined. His system was developed predominantly with a young, male, military sample, and each paragraph in this system was evaluated by having clinicians familiar with the client rate its accuracy. In the description of Lachar's (1974) system, the clinician can readily see what rules were used to select a specific statement and how frequently clinicians judged the paragraph to be accurate.

For example, if only Scale *9* on the MMPI exceeds a T score of 69 in the client's profile, the following paragraph will be used: "Similar individuals are often seen as talkative, distractible, and restless. A low frustration tolerance and an insufficient capacity for delay is often accompanied by irritability and maladaptive hyperactivity of thought and action [1/19]" (Lachar, 1974, p. 119). The numbers in brackets indicate that this paragraph was used in 19 of 1,472 clients and was judged inaccurate once.

Lachar's system has the unique advantage of providing some statement or paragraph for all MMPI profiles, and it provides correlates of 28 codetypes. It also attempts to provide at least rudimentary validation of the common interpretations made about individual scales and codetypes. Unfortunately, Lachar's instructions to his clinicians to judge the accuracy of each paragraph may have biased his system toward overgeneralized (high base rate) statements that are accurate but also not discriminating in describing clients. The reader interested in this area of research should consult Meehl (1956) or Greene (1977, 1978b).

King and Kelley (1977a, 1977b; Kelley & King, 1978, 1979a, 1979b, 1979c) reported the behavioral correlates of specific MMPI codetypes in a college student outpatient sample. The students were almost exclusively white, predominantly single, and mostly self-referred. King and Kelley required a minimum of five students within each codetype, and they analyzed for gender differences within a codetype if there were five or more males and females.

Since they have not summarized their research into a single source, it is necessary to consult each of the original articles for the behavioral correlates of that codetype. The codetypes for which behavioral correlates have been reported by King and Kelley, as well as the original article to be consulted, will be indicated following the descriptions of the respective codetypes.

So far, MMPI cookbooks have not been the panacea that was originally thought. Increasing the specificity of a particular codetype helps by enhancing the homogeneity of the group and increasing the probability of finding reliable empirical correlates; however, it also substantially reduces the number of profiles that could be classified within a codetype.

If the rules for defining codetypes are relaxed so that other profiles can be classified, the probability of finding reliable correlates decreases because of the heterogeneity of profiles within the codetype. Furthermore, when correlates of a codetype are being assessed, it is difficult to identify sufficient numbers of profiles while controlling for significant demographic variables. MMPI cookbooks, nevertheless, can assist clinicians who are working in certain settings and with certain sample characteristics.

It should be emphasized that the correlates of a specific codetype found in one population or setting may not be found in a new population or setting. Hence, the generalization of the correlates of a codetype to new groups or environmental settings needs to be made cautiously until the necessary research has been conducted. Confident application of these interpretive systems to other populations and settings requires empirical research, which is sorely needed.

In the interim the clinician needs to be familiar with MMPI codetypes in order to (1) understand and validate cookbooks when they are available for use, (2) modify and adapt the cookbook descriptions to fit the specific client in question, and (3) interpret meaningfully those profiles that do not fit into any interpretive system.

In a nutshell, if there is an empirically derived cookbook that is appropriate for a specific client and setting, the clinician should use it. In the absence of such information, the clinician will need to do the best job possible with whatever information is available. The clinician is currently in no real danger of being replaced by a cookbook or even a computer, but discussion of this topic will be reserved for the next chapter.

One critical issue for which there are no data at the present time is whether these cookbooks or correlates generated on the MMPI may be generalized to the MMPI-2. Clinical impressions suggest that well-defined MMPI codetypes are very similar on the MMPI-2. However, research that assesses whether or not the correlates of specific MMPI-2 codetypes are similar to their MMPI counterparts is needed. Until such empirical data are available, clinicians will need to use the correlates of MMPI codetypes carefully in the interpretation of the MMPI-2.

FREQUENCIES OF CODETYPES

The clinician needs to be aware of the relative frequency with which MMPI-2 and MMPI codetypes are encountered in specific settings. Each codetype does not occur equally often for several reasons. First, the specific forms of psychopathology that are associated with each clinical scale have different prevalence rates. Second, the specific setting in which the MMPI-2 or MMPI are administered affects which codetypes are likely to be seen. It should not come as a surprise that codetypes emphasizing Scales *1* (Hypochondriasis), *2* (Depression), and *3* (Hysteria) occur frequently in medical settings, while Scales *4* (Psychopathic Deviate), *8* (Schizophrenia), and *9* (Hypomania) occur frequently in psychiatric settings.

Finally, the linear T scores that were used with the original Minnesota normative group are not equivalent from scale to scale, as was discussed in Chapter 2; the transition to uniform T scores on the MMPI-2 also has changed the relationships among the clinical scales as will be seen below.

The information on the frequency of MMPI codetypes will be reported first, followed by similar information on the MMPI-2.

MMPI

Tables 6–1 and 6–2 provide the frequency with which each MMPI codetype occurred in a subset of a large sample ($N \cong 21,000$) of psychiatric inpatients and outpatients collected by Hedlund and Won Cho (1979) in the 1970s. Approximately 7,500 of these clients were administered the 399-item Form R and they were excluded from further analyses. Using criteria specified by Nichols, Greene, and Schmolck (1989) to assess consistency of item endorsement, an additional 1,874 clients were excluded because of inconsistent item endorsement and 1,014 clients were excluded because they omitted more than 30 items, which resulted in a final sample of 10,423 clients.

The careful reader might note that the sample sizes in Tables 6–1 and 6–2 are 6,152 and 2,575, respectively, or a total of 8,727 clients—and wonder what happened to the other 1,696 clients. These 1,696 (16.3 per-

TABLE 6-1   Frequency of MMPI Codetypes in *Male* Psychiatric Inpatients and Outpatients (Hedlund & Won Cho, 1979)

Highest Clinical Scale	Second Highest Clinical Scale										
	1	*2*	*3*	*4*	*5*	*6*	*7*	*8*	*9*	*0*	*Total*
1	1.1%	2.5%	1.7%	0.8%	0.1%	0.2%	0.2%	0.8%	0.4%	0.0%	7.6%
2	2.4	3.0	1.2	3.4	0.3	0.7	3.5	2.4	0.1	0.7	17.8
3	0.7	0.3	0.3	0.3	0.0	0.0	0.1	0.1	0.0	0.0	1.7
4	1.1	4.3	1.2	9.1	1.2	2.3	1.7	3.5	4.0	0.2	28.4
5	0.1	0.3	0.2	0.4	1.1	0.2	0.2	0.4	0.4	0.0	3.2
6	0.1	0.3	0.1	0.8	0.2	0.8	0.2	1.7	0.3	0.1	4.5
7	0.2	1.2	0.0	0.6	0.1	0.2	0.4	1.3	0.2	0.1	4.4
8	1.8	3.1	0.2	3.8	0.3	5.5	4.3	0.6	2.1	0.1	21.6
9	0.2	0.1	0.2	2.4	0.4	0.8	0.3	1.5	4.1	0.0	10.1
0	0.0	0.3	0.0	0.1	0.0	0.0	0.1	0.0	0.0	0.3	0.8
Total	7.7	15.4	4.9	21.7	3.7	10.6	10.9	12.1	11.6	1.4	100.0
											(*N* = 6,152)

Note: When the highest and second highest clinical scales are identical, the codetype is a Spike profile. For example, there are 1.1% Spike *1* profiles in these male psychiatric patients.

cent) clients had no MMPI clinical scale greater than a T score of 69 and consequently are not classifiable in a specific codetype. Thus, the most frequent codetype in these two tables is a Within-Normal-Limit (*WNL*) codetype. Duckworth and Barley (1988) have provided an extensive review of *WNL* codetypes that should be reviewed by clinicians.

Several conclusions can be drawn quickly even from a cursory review of Tables 6-1 and 6-2. First, it is apparent that all MMPI codetypes did not occur equally often. Some codetypes are very common (Spike *4*, *8-6*, Spike *9*, *4-9*, *8-7*, etc.), whereas other codetypes are very rare *(1-0*, *3-0*, *5-0*, *9-0*, *0-1*, *0-3*, etc.).

TABLE 6-2   Frequency of MMPI Codetypes in *Female* Psychiatric Inpatients and Outpatients (Hedlund & Won Cho, 1979)

Highest Clinical Scale	Second Highest Clinical Scale										
	1	*2*	*3*	*4*	*5*	*6*	*7*	*8*	*9*	*0*	*Total*
1	0.4%	0.7%	2.4%	0.2%	0.1%	0.2%	0.1%	0.4%	0.1%	0.0%	4.5%
2	1.2	1.7	2.2	2.5	0.0	0.9	2.9	2.4	0.0	1.5	15.2
3	1.4	0.9	1.0	0.9	0.0	0.4	0.3	0.5	0.2	0.1	5.5
4	0.9	2.8	2.3	7.4	0.4	3.7	0.7	4.4	3.3	0.5	26.3
5	0.0	0.1	0.0	0.2	1.7	0.0	0.0	0.1	0.2	0.0	2.3
6	0.2	0.3	0.3	2.8	0.0	2.1	0.1	4.0	1.3	0.3	11.3
7	0.0	0.9	0.2	0.2	0.0	0.2	0.4	1.1	0.1	0.2	3.3
8	0.7	2.4	0.6	4.4	0.1	5.6	3.1	0.7	1.5	0.5	19.7
9	0.2	0.2	0.2	1.7	0.2	1.1	0.1	2.0	3.6	0.0	9.3
0	0.1	0.7	0.1	0.2	0.1	0.1	0.1	0.1	0.0	1.4	2.8
Total	5.2	10.5	9.1	20.3	2.6	14.3	7.7	15.6	10.3	4.5	100.0
											(*N* = 2,575)

Note: When the highest and second highest clinical scales are identical, the codetype is a Spike profile. For example, there are 0.4% Spike *1* profiles in these female psychiatric patients.

Second, Scale *4* is the most frequent highest (males: 28.4 percent; females: 26.3 percent) and second highest clinical scale (males: 21.7 percent; females: 20.3 percent). If the Spike *4* codetypes are subtracted from these two numbers, since they are counted twice, 41.0 percent of the male (28.4 percent + 21.7 percent − 9.1 percent) and 39.2 percent of the female (26.3 percent + 20.3 percent − 7.4 percent) clients had Scale *4* as their highest or second highest clinical scale. It is no wonder that clinicians get the impression that Scale *4* is being interpreted in every profile. The frequent occurrence of codetypes that include Scale *4* indicates that such codetypes are an excellent place to begin to identify common subgroups who could have different treatment interventions and outcomes.

Third, Scale *0* is the least frequent highest (0.8 percent) and second highest (1.4 percent) clinical scale in men. Scale *0* also is infrequently the highest or second highest clinical scale in women, although Scale *5* is the highest or second highest clinical scale even less frequently. This relatively infrequent occurrence of Scale *0* as one of the two highest clinical scales no doubt reflects that T scores on Scale *0* tend to have a restricted range when compared to the other clinical scales.

Fourth, the frequency of the various codetypes tends to correspond to the amount of clinical literature that is available. For example, little interpretive information is available on *1-0/0-1*, *3-0/0-3*, and *6-0/0-6* codetypes, as can been seen below, which occurred infrequently in either male or female clients. Conversely, Spike *4* codetypes occur frequently in male and female clients and have a large body of interpretive information.

It would be instructive for every clinician to construct tables such as these in his or her own setting so that frequent codetypes can be identified. Such frequent codetypes could be examined more closely to determine whether specific subgroups are apparent that could enhance treatment interventions and outcomes. These subgroups within frequent codetypes will not be reported here because of limited space.

Finally, there are few gender differences in the frequency of codetypes, although some codetypes are more frequent in men (e.g., *1-2*, *2-1*, *4-2*) and some are more frequent in women (e.g., *2-3*, *6-4*, *6-8*).

The clinician also needs to be aware that the setting in which the MMPI is administered will affect the frequency with which specific codetypes are found. Tables 6–3 and 6–4 provide the frequency with which each MMPI codetype occurred in a large sample of male and female medical outpatients who were referred for a psychiatric evaluation at the Mayo Clinic (Colligan & Offord, 1986). It must be noted that these clients are a subset of general medical clients since their physician referred them for a psychiatric evaluation.

It is readily apparent that Scales *1*, *2*, and *3* are much more likely to be elevated in these clients than in psychiatric clients. Approximately 70 percent (men, 69.5; women, 72.7) of the profiles in these medical outpatients referred for psychiatric evaluations had their highest MMPI clinical scale among the neurotic triad (Scales *1*, *2*, and *3*), compared to approximately 25 percent (men, 27.1; women, 25.2) of the profiles of psychiatric clients.

The most frequent codetypes in these female medical outpatients were *1-3* (15.5 percent), *3-1* (12.8 percent), and Spike *3* (8.5 percent), whereas the most frequent codetypes in female psychiatric clients were Spike *4* (7.4 percent), *8-6* (5.6 percent), *4-8* (4.4 percent), and *8-4* (4.4 percent). The most frequent codetypes in male medical outpatients were *1-3* (12.8 percent), *2-1* (7.9 percent), *1-2* (6.8 percent), *3-1* (5.1 percent), and Spike *2* (4.7 percent), whereas the most frequent code-

TABLE 6–3 Frequency of MMPI Codetypes in *Male* Medical Outpatient Referrals for a Psychiatric Evaluation at the Mayo Clinic (Colligan & Offord, 1986)

Highest Clinical Scale	Second Highest Clinical Scale										Total
	1	2	3	4	5	6	7	8	9	0	
1	3.7%	6.8%	12.8%	0.6%	0.4%	0.2%	0.7%	1.1%	0.4%	0.3%	26.9%
2	7.9	4.7	4.1	2.0	1.3	0.8	7.4	2.8	0.2	1.2	32.4
3	5.1	1.1	2.1	0.6	0.5	0.0	0.3	0.3	0.1	0.0	10.2
4	0.4	1.4	0.8	2.6	0.6	0.4	0.5	0.7	0.7	0.0	8.1
5	0.3	0.6	0.3	0.4	2.6	0.3	0.2	0.3	0.3	0.0	5.2
6	0.1	0.2	0.1	0.1	0.1	0.6	0.1	0.4	0.1	0.0	1.6
7	0.3	1.9	0.1	0.3	0.2	0.1	0.6	0.9	0.1	0.1	4.5
8	0.6	1.5	0.2	0.8	0.1	0.9	1.4	0.4	0.7	0.0	6.6
9	0.3	0.1	0.1	0.6	0.2	0.1	0.1	0.6	2.0	0.0	4.2
0	0.0	0.1	0.0	0.0	0.0	0.0	0.0	0.1	0.0	0.3	0.4
Total	18.6	18.4	20.6	7.9	5.9	3.4	11.3	7.5	4.7	1.7	100.0
											(N = 3,614)

Note: When the highest and second highest clinical scales are identical, the codetype is a Spike profile. For example, there are 3.7% Spike *1* profiles in these male medical outpatients who were referred for a psychiatric evaluation.

types in male psychiatric clients were Spike *4* (9.1 percent), *8-6* (5.5 percent), *4-2* (4.3 percent), and Spike *9* (4.1 percent).

It is evident both that there is no overlap in the most frequent codetypes between these two settings and that gender has only minimal impact within a setting. These data should help the clinician realize the potential effect

of the setting in which the MMPI is administered on the frequency with which the various codetypes are encountered.

Clinicians also need to be aware of the frequency with which low points among the clinical scales are encountered in frequently occurring codetypes. Codetype interpretation of the MMPI-2 or the MMPI emphasizes the

TABLE 6–4 Frequency of MMPI Codetypes in *Female* Medical Outpatient Referrals for a Psychiatric Evaluation at the Mayo Clinic (Colligan & Offord, 1986)

Highest Clinical Scale	Second Highest Clinical Scale										Total
	1	2	3	4	5	6	7	8	9	0	
1	2.8%	2.6%	15.5%	0.3%	0.1%	0.2%	0.1%	0.5%	0.3%	0.3%	22.6%
2	3.5	3.3	5.2	1.8	0.1	1.0	4.1	1.5	0.1	2.1	22.6
3	12.8	3.2	8.5	1.1	0.0	0.5	0.3	0.4	0.5	0.0	27.5
4	0.4	1.6	1.2	2.3	0.0	1.1	0.4	1.0	0.8	0.2	8.9
5	0.0	0.0	0.0	0.0	0.4	0.0	0.0	0.0	0.1	0.0	0.6
6	0.1	0.5	0.3	0.4	0.0	0.9	0.2	0.5	0.2	0.1	3.1
7	0.1	1.0	0.3	0.1	0.0	0.1	0.3	0.6	0.0	0.1	2.7
8	0.5	1.3	0.4	0.9	0.0	0.8	1.0	0.2	0.3	0.0	5.4
9	0.4	0.0	0.3	0.4	0.1	0.3	0.0	0.5	2.0	0.0	4.0
0	0.1	0.7	0.0	0.1	0.0	0.1	0.2	0.0	0.0	1.4	2.7
Total	20.7	14.2	31.8	7.4	0.7	5.0	6.6	5.3	4.3	4.2	100.0
											(N = 4,792)

Note: When the highest and second highest clinical scales are identical, the codetype is a Spike profile. For example, there are 2.8% Spike *1* profiles in these female medical outpatients who were referred for a psychiatric evaluation.

high point(s) among the clinical scales and consequently less attention is paid to low-point scales. Since the low-point scale already is available in the standard profile, clinicians can make use of this information without any additional work.

For example, a low point on Scale 9 (Hypomania) in conjunction with a high point on Scale 2 (Depression) should alert the clinician to the presence of significant depressive symptoms. Hathaway and Meehl (1951, pp. xxvii–xxix) provided data on the frequency with which low points occur with each high-point scale, but they did not report low points for specific codetypes.

Table 6–5 provides the frequency of low points on the MMPI clinical scales for the 27 most frequent codetypes. Scale 9 is a common low point when Scale 2 is the highest

clinical scale in both male and female psychiatric clients. However, Scale 9 is much less often the low point when Scale 4 (Psychopathic Deviate) is the highest clinical scale; instead Scale 0 (Social Introversion) is a frequent low point.

As might be expected, Scale 5 is the most common low point in female psychiatric clients. Scale 0 is the most common low point in male psychiatric clients. It also is interesting to note that Scale 7 is rarely a low point with any codetype in either males or females. The clinician could consult Table 6–5 with every profile to determine whether a person's low-point scale is one that occurs commonly, and incorporate that information into the profile interpretation.

As the clinician amasses data in his or her specific setting, it is highly recommended

TABLE 6–5   Frequency of Low-Point Scales for 27 Frequent MMPI Codetypes by Gender

Codetype	Low-Point Scale									
	1	2	3	4	5	6	7	8	9	0
1-2										
Male	—	—	2.0%	2.0%	27.8%	9.3%	4.6%	6.6%	26.5%	21.2%
Female	—	—	0.0	5.3	52.6	10.5	5.3	0.0	26.3	0.0
1-3										
Male	—	1.0%	—	0.0	18.3	2.9	2.9	1.9	17.3	55.8
Female	—	1.6	—	4.9	42.6	6.6	1.6	0.0	31.2	11.5
Spike *2*										
Male	10.1%	—	2.7	3.2	14.4	14.9	1.6	17.6	28.7	6.9
Female	7.0	—	2.3	11.6	30.2	9.3	0.0	4.7	32.6	2.3
2-1										
Male	—	—	0.0	4.7	22.3	12.2	0.0	9.5	39.2	12.2
Female	—	—	0.0	0.0	38.7	6.5	3.2	0.0	51.6	0.0
2-3										
Male	0.0	—	—	0.0	12.0	8.0	1.3	1.3	40.0	37.3
Female	0.0	—	—	0.0	63.2	0.0	0.0	0.0	33.3	3.5
2-4										
Male	13.3	—	1.4	—	16.7	8.6	0.0	6.2	33.8	20.0
Female	1.6	—	0.0	—	71.4	4.8	1.6	0.0	20.6	0.0
2-7										
Male	6.4	—	4.1	2.3	19.7	8.3	0.0	1.4	52.3	5.5
Female	0.0	—	0.0	1.4	64.9	1.4	0.0	0.0	32.4	0.0
2-8										
Male	7.4	—	3.4	1.3	28.2	4.0	0.7	—	43.6	11.4
Female	6.6	—	3.3	1.6	63.9	1.6	0.0	—	21.3	1.6
Spike *4*										
Male	9.5	2.1	3.6	—	16.9	9.1	4.6	4.3	8.0	41.9
Female	10.9	6.3	3.7	—	34.0	6.8	6.8	3.1	6.8	21.5

continued

TABLE 6–5 *continued*

Codetype				Low-Point Scale						
	1	2	3	4	5	6	7	8	9	0
4-2										
Male	16.4%	—	2.7%	—	20.5%	4.9%	2.3%	5.7%	16.4%	31.2%
Female	9.9	—	0.0	—	60.6	0.0	0.0	0.0	18.3	11.3
4-3										
Male	0.0	0.0%	—	—	5.6	4.2	0.0	1.4	12.7	76.1
Female	1.7	1.7	—	—	51.7	1.7	1.7	0.0	6.9	34.5
4-6										
Male	26.2	3.6	3.6	—	16.3	—	4.3	1.4	2.1	42.6
Female	23.2	6.3	2.1	—	48.4	—	4.2	0.0	7.4	8.4
4-7										
Male	26.9	1.0	2.9	—	19.2	5.8	—	1.0	7.7	35.6
Female	17.7	0.0	0.0	—	47.1	0.0	—	0.0	23.5	11.8
4-8										
Male	18.7	0.5	6.5	—	20.6	3.3	2.8	—	7.0	40.7
Female	14.3	1.8	3.6	—	57.1	0.9	0.9	—	8.9	12.5
4-9										
Male	15.1	5.7	5.7	—	10.2	3.7	2.5	0.4	—	56.7
Female	11.6	7.0	2.3	—	36.1	0.0	3.5	0.0	—	39.5
Spike 6										
Male	31.2	4.2	12.5	0.0%	10.4	—	8.3	4.2	8.3	20.8
Female	16.7	0.0	18.5	3.7	33.3	—	3.7	1.9	11.1	11.1
6-4										
Male	17.7	5.9	9.8	—	13.7	—	5.9	2.0	7.8	37.3
Female	8.5	1.4	5.6	—	59.2	—	4.2	0.0	9.9	11.3
6-8										
Male	20.2	5.8	12.5	1.0	20.2	—	2.9	—	11.5	26.0
Female	10.8	5.9	13.7	1.0	59.8	—	1.0	—	1.0	6.9
8-1										
Male	—	0.0	0.0	0.9	41.4	4.5	0.9	—	9.9	42.3
Female	—	0.0	0.0	0.0	89.5	0.0	0.0	—	5.3	5.3
8-2										
Male	10.4	—	8.9	1.6	30.7	3.7	0.0	—	31.8	13.0
Female	4.9	—	3.3	0.0	70.5	1.6	0.0	—	19.7	0.0
8-4										
Male	17.2	1.7	10.8	—	23.3	1.7	0.0	—	8.2	37.1
Female	9.7	3.5	0.9	—	64.0	0.9	0.0	—	6.1	14.9
8-6										
Male	11.6	1.5	11.3	0.9	37.7	—	0.6	—	6.5	30.0
Female	4.2	4.2	9.8	5.6	68.5	—	0.7	—	2.1	4.9
8-7										
Male	11.5	3.4	9.5	1.9	32.4	2.3	—	—	13.4	25.6
Female	8.8	0.0	5.0	1.3	78.8	0.0	—	—	5.0	1.3
8-9										
Male	10.3	7.1	20.6	0.0	17.5	0.8	0.0	—	—	43.7
Female	2.6	15.8	21.1	5.3	42.1	0.0	0.0	—	—	13.2
Spike 9										
Male	13.3	13.7	13.3	1.6	9.8	6.3	2.4	2.8	—	36.9
Female	19.4	23.7	12.9	0.0	16.1	2.2	4.3	2.2	—	19.4
9-4										
Male	12.2	11.5	8.1	—	10.1	4.1	2.7	0.7	—	50.7
Female	0.0	20.5	6.8	—	25.0	2.3	0.0	0.0	—	45.5
9-8										
Male	7.5	20.4	14.0	0.0	10.8	5.4	1.1	—	—	40.9
Female	11.5	26.9	13.5	1.9	30.8	0.0	0.0	—	—	15.4
Total										
Male	11.6	3.0	6.3	0.8	20.6	5.2	1.9	2.7	15.4	32.5
Female	8.7	5.0	5.1	1.4	51.8	1.9	1.9	0.6	11.3	12.4

that codetype frequency and low-point frequency tables be constructed so that the effects of this specific setting can be ascertained. Sample sizes as small as several hundred clients are sufficient to start providing reasonable estimates of the relative frequencies of the codetypes.

MMPI-2

Tables 6–6 and 6–7 provide the frequency with which each MMPI-2 codetype occurred in the sample of psychiatric inpatients and outpatients collected by Hedlund and Won Cho (1979) that were described earlier. These data were developed by dropping the 13 MMPI items that were not retained on the MMPI-2, and rescoring the data on uniform T scores. This procedure allows for a comparison between the frequency of MMPI-2 and MMPI codetypes in the same sample of patients by contrasting Table 6–1 with Table 6–6 and Table 6–2 with Table 6–7.

There are a number of differences between the frequencies with which the various codetypes occurred on the MMPI and the MMPI-2 in this sample of psychiatric pa-

tients. Scales *4* (Psychopathic Deviate) and *8* (Schizophrenia) occurred less frequently and Scale *6* (Paranoia) more frequently as the highest clinical scale on the MMPI-2 in both the male (Tables 6–1 and 6–6) and female (Tables 6–2 and 6–7) patients, although these changes were slightly smaller in the female patients. There was little change in the frequency of the second highest clinical scale other than for Scale *4* to be slightly more common in both the male and female patients.

There also are a number of differences when specific codetypes are examined in these psychiatric patients. Some codetypes in the male patients (*2-0, 3-1, 3-2, 6-4, 6-8, 6-9,* and Spike *0*) occurred twice as often on the MMPI-2, whereas others (*2-4, 2-8, 4-7, 4-8, 8-2,* and *8-4*) occurred less than half as often (Tables 6–1 and 6–6). There were somewhat fewer changes in specific codetypes in the female patients. Several codetypes (*2-6, 3-1, 6-2*) were twice as frequent and a number of codetypes (Spike *4, 4-8, 8-4, 8-9*) were less than half as frequent in the female patients (Tables 6–2 and 6–7).

A simple rule that describes the changes

TABLE 6–6   Frequency of MMPI-2 Codetypes in *Male* Psychiatric Inpatients and Outpatients (Hedlund & Won Cho, 1979)

Highest Clinical Scale	Second Highest Clinical Scale										
	1	*2*	*3*	*4*	*5*	*6*	*7*	*8*	*9*	*0*	*Total*
1	1.7%	2.0%	3.0%	0.4%	0.0%	0.4%	0.4%	0.8%	0.4%	0.1%	9.2%
2	1.9	2.8	1.3	1.5	0.1	0.8	2.5	0.9	0.1	2.0	14.0
3	2.3	1.0	0.7	0.7	0.1	0.2	0.2	0.2	0.2	0.0	5.5
4	0.9	2.5	1.2	7.8	0.2	2.3	1.0	1.8	2.3	0.4	20.3
5	0.0	0.1	0.1	0.2	0.9	0.1	0.1	0.1	0.2	0.0	1.8
6	0.6	1.1	0.4	2.6	0.2	1.5	1.1	6.5	1.4	0.5	15.8
7	0.2	1.7	0.2	0.5	0.0	0.4	0.5	1.7	0.2	0.6	6.0
8	0.7	1.1	0.4	1.0	0.1	5.0	2.2	0.4	1.2	0.3	12.4
9	0.5	0.2	0.2	1.8	0.2	1.7	0.4	1.5	4.7	0.1	11.2
0	0.2	1.1	0.0	0.2	0.1	0.2	0.2	0.1	0.1	1.7	3.9
Total	8.9	13.7	7.4	16.5	1.8	12.7	8.7	13.9	10.7	5.6	100.0
											(*N* = 5,663)

Note: When the highest and second highest clinical scales are identical, the codetype is a Spike profile. For example, there are 1.7% Spike *1* profiles in these male psychiatric patients.

TABLE 6–7 Frequency of MMPI-2 Codetypes in *Female* Psychiatric Inpatients and Outpatients (Hedlund & Won Cho, 1979)

Highest Clinical Scale	Second Highest Clinical Scale										Total
	1	*2*	*3*	*4*	*5*	*6*	*7*	*8*	*9*	*0*	
1	0.8%	1.3%	2.8%	0.5%	0.3%	0.3%	0.1%	0.5%	0.3%	0.0%	6.9%
2	2.2	2.1	3.5	2.2	0.3	1.8	5.4	2.1	0.2	1.6	21.3
3	3.3	1.4	1.1	1.1	0.0	0.5	0.5	0.3	0.2	0.0	8.3
4	0.6	2.1	1.4	3.5	0.5	2.3	0.6	1.6	1.8	0.3	14.6
5	0.3	0.3	0.0	0.4	3.2	0.1	0.1	0.2	0.5	0.2	5.0
6	1.0	1.4	0.6	2.7	0.3	1.6	0.7	5.3	2.1	0.3	16.0
7	0.2	1.2	0.5	0.1	0.0	0.3	0.5	1.5	0.2	0.3	4.8
8	0.9	1.8	0.2	1.4	0.2	3.1	2.4	0.7	0.6	0.2	11.4
9	0.3	0.2	0.1	1.5	0.5	1.1	0.3	1.8	3.1	0.0	8.8
0	0.1	0.9	0.0	0.1	0.1	0.0	0.2	0.4	0.0	1.0	2.8
Total	9.6	12.6	10.3	13.3	5.4	11.1	10.7	14.3	8.9	3.9	100.0
											(N = 2,687)

Note: When the highest and second highest clinical scales are identical, the codetype is a Spike profile. For example, there are 0.8% Spike *1* profiles in these female psychiatric patients.

on the MMPI-2 in these patients is that codetypes involving Scales *3* (Hysteria) and *6* (Paranoia) have increased in frequency and codetypes involving Scales *4* (Psychopathic Deviate) and *8* (Schizophrenia) have decreased in frequency.

Tables 6–8 and 6–9 provides the frequency with which each MMPI-2 codetype occurred in the medical outpatients who were referred for a psychiatric evaluation at the Mayo Clinic (Colligan & Offord, 1986). Again, it should be noted that these MMPI data were rescored to simulate MMPI-2 data as described earlier.

The pattern of changes from the MMPI to the MMPI-2 was slightly different in these medical patients. Scales *2* (Depression), *4* (Psychopathic Deviate), and *8* (Schizophre-

TABLE 6–8 Frequency of MMPI-2 Codetypes in *Male* Medical Outpatient Referrals for a Psychiatric Evaluation at the Mayo Clinic (Colligan & Offord, 1986)

Highest Clinical Scale	Second Highest Clinical Scale										Total
	1	*2*	*3*	*4*	*5*	*6*	*7*	*8*	*9*	*0*	
1	5.0%	5.2%	13.6%	0.3%	0.2%	0.4%	0.4%	0.5%	0.4%	0.5%	26.4%
2	4.8	4.1	3.5	1.0	0.5	1.4	4.8	0.9	0.2	2.7	23.8
3	12.1	3.9	3.3	0.6	0.3	0.3	0.6	0.2	0.1	0.0	21.4
4	0.2	0.9	0.4	1.4	0.2	0.6	0.2	0.5	0.3	0.1	4.7
5	0.1	0.1	0.1	0.0	1.2	0.2	0.0	0.1	0.2	0.0	2.0
6	0.3	0.8	0.4	0.5	0.1	1.0	0.5	0.9	0.3	0.1	4.8
7	0.4	2.4	0.4	0.3	0.1	0.3	0.6	1.2	0.1	0.2	5.9
8	0.3	0.6	0.1	0.3	0.0	0.7	0.8	0.3	0.4	0.1	3.5
9	0.3	0.2	0.2	0.5	0.1	0.2	0.2	0.4	2.0	0.0	4.0
0	0.4	1.2	0.0	0.0	0.1	0.0	0.2	0.0	0.0	1.6	3.6
Total	23.7	19.2	22.0	4.9	2.7	5.1	8.4	4.9	3.8	5.3	100.0
											(N = 3,411)

Note: When the highest and second highest clinical scales are identical, the codetype is a Spike profile. For example, there are 5.0% Spike *1* profiles in these male medical outpatients who were referred for a psychiatric evaluation.

TABLE 6–9   Frequency of MMPI-2 Codetypes in *Female* Medical Outpatient Referrals for a Psychiatric Evaluation at the Mayo Clinic (Colligan & Offord, 1986)

Highest Clinical Scale	Second Highest Clinical Scale										
	1	*2*	*3*	*4*	*5*	*6*	*7*	*8*	*9*	*0*	*Total*
1	4.8%	3.8%	17.4%	0.2%	0.5%	0.3%	0.2%	0.4%	0.5%	0.3%	28.3%
2	5.0	3.2	5.4	1.1	0.2	1.2	5.6	1.3	0.1	1.8	25.0
3	17.8	4.2	3.8	0.5	0.1	0.4	0.7	0.2	0.2	0.0	27.9
4	0.2	0.9	0.3	0.8	0.1	0.3	0.2	0.2	0.3	0.1	3.3
5	0.2	0.2	0.0	0.0	1.2	0.1	0.1	0.0	0.1	0.1	1.9
6	0.4	0.7	0.3	0.5	0.0	0.5	0.2	0.7	0.1	0.0	3.3
7	0.3	1.3	0.2	0.2	0.0	0.2	0.5	0.4	0.0	0.1	3.2
8	0.2	0.3	0.2	0.2	0.0	0.6	0.5	0.2	0.1	0.0	2.3
9	0.5	0.1	0.3	0.3	0.1	0.2	0.1	0.3	1.1	0.0	3.1
0	0.1	0.6	0.0	0.0	0.0	0.1	0.1	0.0	0.0	0.9	1.9
Total	29.4	15.2	27.8	3.7	2.4	3.8	8.1	3.7	2.5	3.4	100.0
											(*N* = 5,331)

Note: When the highest and second highest clinical scales are identical, the codetype is a Spike profile. For example, there are 4.8% Spike *1* profiles in these female medical outpatients who were referred for a psychiatric evaluation.

nia) occurred less frequently and Scales *3* (Hysteria) and *6* (Paranoia) occurred more frequently as the highest clinical scale in the male patients. The only changes seen in the female patients were for Scales *4* and *8* to occur less frequently as the highest clinical scale; otherwise, the frequency with which the highest clinical scale occurred on the MMPI and MMPI-2 in these women was very similar.

There were similar changes in the second highest clinical scale in both the male and female patients: Scale *1* (Hypochondriasis) increased in frequency and Scale *4* decreased in frequency. Scale *0* (Social Introversion) also increased in frequency as the second highest clinical scale in the male patients.

The changes within specific codetypes in the male medical patients were very similar to what was seen in the male psychiatric patients. Several codetypes (*2-0*, *3-1*, *3-2*, *0-2*, and Spike *0*) occurred twice as often on the MMPI-2, whereas others (*1-8*, *2-4*, *2-8*, *8-2*, and Spike *5*) occurred less than half as often (Tables 6–3 and 6–8). However, these female medical patients only had Spike *5* codetypes occurring twice as frequently on

the MMPI-2, whereas a number of codetypes (Spike *3*, *3-4*, Spike *4*, *4-3*, *4-6*, *4-8*, *8-2*, *8- 7*) occurred less frequently (Tables 6–4 and 6– 9).

The same rule of thumb noted above describes the changes on the MMPI-2 in the male medical patients: codetypes involving Scale *3* (Hysteria) have increased in frequency and codetypes involving Scales *4* (Psychopathic Deviate) and *8* (Schizophrenia) have decreased in frequency. There does not appear to be a simple rule that describes in the changes in the frequency with which specific codetypes are seen in the female medical patients. This latter point suggests that changes from the MMPI to the MMPI-2 will be affected by the setting in which the test is administered.

Table 6–10 provides the frequency of low points on the MMPI-2 clinical scales for the 27 most frequent codetypes. There are three major differences between the frequency of low points on the MMPI and the MMPI-2: (1) Scale *5* (Masculinity-Femininity) is much less likely to be a low point on the MMPI-2 in women; (2) Scale *5* is almost as twice as likely to be a low point on the MMPI-2 in men; and (3) Scale *0* (Social In-

TABLE 6–10   Frequency of Low-Point Scales for 27 Frequent MMPI-2 Codetypes by Gender

Codetype	Low-Point Scale									
	1	2	3	4	5	6	7	8	9	0
Spike *1*										
Male	—	1.0%	0.0%	2.0%	45.9%	13.3%	10.2%	6.1%	9.1%	12.2%
Female	—	0.0	0.0	19.1	19.1	9.5	23.8	19.1	4.8	4.8
1-2										
Male	—	—	1.8	4.5	49.1	7.1	2.7	4.5	23.2	7.1
Female	—	—	0.0	11.4	34.3	14.3	2.9	5.7	28.6	2.9
1-3										
Male	—	1.2	—	3.6	46.1	6.0	3.6	1.8	19.8	18.0
Female	—	1.3	—	12.0	28.0	14.3	2.9	5.7	28.6	2.9
Spike *2*										
Male	3.7%	—	1.9	1.2	34.8	11.1	1.9	19.2	22.4	3.7
Female	5.3	—	8.8	15.8	12.3	10.5	0.0	10.5	35.1	1.8
2-1										
Male	—	—	0.9	0.9	39.6	13.2	0.9	6.6	36.8	0.9
Female	—	—	3.5	10.3	34.5	6.9	1.7	3.5	39.7	0.0
2-3										
Male	0.0	—	—	0.0	32.0	8.0	0.0	5.3	48.0	6.7
Female	0.0	—	—	2.2	49.5	4.3	1.1	1.1	37.6	4.3
2-4										
Male	2.3	—	2.4	—	33.3	7.1	0.0	9.5	40.4	4.8
Female	5.2	—	3.5	—	43.1	6.9	0.0	3.5	34.5	3.5
2-7										
Male	4.9	—	4.2	3.5	31.9	4.9	0.0	0.7	49.3	0.7
Female	2.1	—	2.1	1.4	52.1	6.9	0.0	0.0	33.6	2.1
2-8										
Male	2.0	—	2.0	2.0	39.2	7.8	0.0	—	43.1	3.9
Female	3.6	—	7.1	1.8	50.0	10.7	0.0	—	23.2	3.6
2-0										
Male	2.6	—	8.7	1.7	23.5	8.7	0.9	9.6	44.4	—
Female	2.3	—	6.8	4.6	36.4	6.8	0.0	0.0	43.2	—
3-1										
Male	—	0.0	—	0.0	40.6	3.9	1.6	6.3	19.5	28.1
Female	—	0.0	—	3.4	51.1	9.1	3.4	2.3	17.1	13.6
Spike *4*										
Male	7.6	1.2	5.5	—	37.2	9.7	5.3	5.8	6.4	21.4
Female	5.3	4.3	11.7	—	24.5	8.5	7.5	7.5	4.3	26.6
4-2										
Male	8.3	—	4.9	—	41.7	6.3	3.5	6.3	20.1	9.0
Female	8.8	—	1.8	—	47.4	7.0	3.5	1.8	19.3	10.5
4-6										
Male	16.7	1.5	8.3	—	34.1	—	6.1	1.5	10.6	21.2
Female	16.4	1.6	11.5	—	54.1	—	3.3	0.0	1.6	11.5
4-8										
Male	6.9	0.5	16.8	—	43.6	4.0	2.0	—	10.9	15.8
Female	9.1	2.3	13.6	—	54.6	2.3	0.0	—	4.6	13.6
4-9										
Male	12.3	3.1	10.8	—	30.0	7.7	1.5	0.0	—	34.6
Female	10.4	4.2	4.2	—	25.0	6.3	2.1	0.0	—	47.9
Spike *6*										
Male	15.5	3.6	23.8	1.2	21.4	—	6.0	8.3	7.1	13.1
Female	14.3	0.0	16.7	0.0	31.0	—	9.5	0.0	11.9	16.7
6-4										
Male	18.5	0.7	8.9	—	38.4	—	2.7	0.7	7.5	22.6
Female	15.3	2.8	12.5	—	37.5	—	2.8	0.0	11.1	18.1

continued

TABLE 6–10   *continued*

Codetype	Low-Point Scale									
	1	2	3	4	5	6	7	8	9	0
6-8										
Male	4.9%	1.9%	16.5%	1.6%	53.7%	—	0.8%	—	11.9%	8.7%
Female	5.0	2.1	19.2	5.7	51.8	—	1.4	—	2.8	12.1
8-2										
Male	0.0	—	13.9	9.2	44.6	6.2%	0.0	—	24.6	1.5
Female	0.0	—	4.3	0.0	72.3	2.1	0.0	—	19.2	2.1
8-4										
Male	6.9	1.7	17.2	—	39.7	1.7	0.0	—	15.5	17.2
Female	0.0	0.0	10.8	—	54.1	0.0	0.0	—	8.1	27.0
8-6										
Male	4.6	2.1	14.0	1.1	57.5	—	0.0	—	10.9	9.8
Female	2.4	3.6	19.3	3.6	54.2	—	0.0	—	6.0	10.8
8-7										
Male	3.2	1.6	12.0	3.2	48.8	0.8	—	—	26.4	4.0
Female	1.6	1.6	17.2	3.1	67.2	1.6	—	—	3.1	4.7
8-9										
Male	4.6	0.0	30.3	1.5	47.0	1.5	0.0	—	—	15.2
Female	0.0	11.8	11.8	17.7	35.3	0.0	0.0	—	—	23.5
Spike 9										
Male	8.6	11.2	20.5	0.8	23.5	5.6	5.2	1.1%	—	23.5
Female	13.4	11.0	18.3	0.0	18.3	6.1	4.9	2.4	—	25.6
9-4										
Male	6.9	7.8	10.8	—	31.4	8.8	3.9	0.7	—	30.4
Female	2.6	5.1	12.8	—	30.8	2.6	0.0	0.0	—	46.2
9-8										
Male	1.2	10.8	27.7	0.0	27.7	6.0	2.4	—	—	24.1
Female	2.1	16.7	33.3	4.2	22.9	4.2	0.0	—	—	16.7
Total										
Male	6.7	2.0	9.8	1.5	37.0	5.2	2.1	3.4	17.2	15.2
Female	4.6	2.2	10.6	3.7	39.4	5.6	3.2	1.9	15.7	13.1

troversion) is much less likely to be a low point on the MMPI-2 in men.

Low points on Scale 5 of the MMPI-2 now occur almost equally often in men and women, whereas low points on Scale 5 of the MMPI occurred over twice as often in women. Other than these three changes, it appears that the same low points on the MMPI-2 tend to be associated with specific codetypes as was found on the MMPI. Again, clinicians are encouraged to consult Table 6–10 for every profile to determine whether a person's low-point scale is one that occurs commonly, and incorporate that information into the profile interpretation.

CONCORDANCE BETWEEN MMPI-2 AND MMPI CODETYPES

One of the critical issues with the advent of the MMPI-2 is the concordance between the MMPI-2 and MMPI codetypes (i.e., how frequently the MMPI-2 and MMPI codetype would be similar or identical for a specific client). Two general comments need to be made about codetype concordance before examining the data on this issue. First, if the rationale for the revising the MMPI is valid in that the items and norms on the MMPI do not accurately reflect our contemporary society (see Chapter 1), then it makes little sense to expect the MMPI-2 and the MMPI to have perfect concordance. In fact, perfect concordance would suggest that there is little reason to revise the MMPI.

Second, it is not clear whether the MMPI or the MMPI-2 should serve as the "gold" standard against which the other test is evaluated (i.e., if the MMPI-2 and MMPI codetype do not agree for a specific client is the MMPI-2 or the MMPI inaccurate?). It is typically assumed that the MMPI should serve as the standard, but it is equally plausible that the MMPI-2 could be the standard.

There are two different methods for developing data that can be used for assessing concordance between the MMPI-2 and the MMPI. First, MMPI data can be quickly transformed to simulate the MMPI-2 by dropping the 13 items that were not retained on the MMPI-2 and converting the raw scores into the appropriate T scores. This procedure assumes that the changes made at the item level on the MMPI-2 will not have a systematic effect on the data. It is also possible to score both the MMPI-2 and the MMPI if Form AX, the form used to collect the restandardization data, was administered since it contains all of the items on the MMPI and the MMPI-2.

Second, the MMPI and the MMPI-2 can be administered to the same clients with some interval of time between the two test administrations (cf. Honaker, 1990). This latter method has been used infrequently, because it requires a significant amount of time and effort on the part of the clinician. It also tends to confound test-retest reliability changes with the differences between the MMPI and the MMPI-2.

Table 6–11 provides the concordance between specific MMPI-2 and MMPI codetypes in the sample of psychiatric inpatients and outpatients collected by Hedlund and Won Cho (1979). The left-hand column indicates the specific MMPI-2 codetype and the next columns report the concordance rates on the MMPI by gender and then for the entire sample. For instance, there were 92 men with Spike *1* codetypes on the MMPI-2 in this sample of psychiatric patients, and 64.1 percent of them also had a Spike *1* codetype on the MMPI.

The concordance rate within each gender is reported twice for each codetype: first with the requirement that the two highest clinical scales be in the same order, and second allowing the two highest clinical scales to be in either order. For example, there were 218 men with *1-2/2-1* codetypes on the MMPI-2. When it was required that these men have the same codetype on the MMPI-2 and the MMPI (i.e., if the man had a *1-2* codetype on the MMPI-2 then he had to have a *1-2* codetype on the MMPI), the concordance rate was 67.0 percent. When Scales *1* and *2* were allowed to be in either order as the two highest clinical scales, the concordance rate in these men was 81.7 percent.

The average concordance rate across all MMPI-2 codetypes was around 50 percent when the two highest clinical scales had to be in the same order, and around 65 percent when the two highest clinical scales could be in either order. Several codetypes (*2-4/4-2*, *2-8/8-2*, *4-8/8-4*, and *4-9/9-4*) had very high concordance rates in men, whereas a different set of codetypes (Spike *2*, Spike *3*, Spike *4*, *4-8/8-4*, *4-9/9-4*, Spike *7*, and Spike *0*) had very high concordance rates in women. There also were a number of codetypes that had very low concordance rates: *1-6/6-1* and *2-6/6-2* codetypes in men and women, and *2-0/0-2*, *4-0/0-4*, and *6-9/9-6* codetypes in men.

Butcher, Dahlstrom, Graham, and Tellegen (1989) provided information on the concordance between the MMPI-2 and the MMPI using Form AX in a sample of 423 psychiatric patients. They reported concordance rates for specific codetypes that were very similar to those seen in Table 6–11, which would suggest that the simulation of MMPI-2 data provided in Table 6–11 is rea-

TABLE 6–11   Concordance between MMPI-2 and MMPI Codetypes

		MMPI Codetype							
		Men			Women			Total	
		Two Highest Scales			Two Highest Scales			Two Highest Scales	
MMPI-2 Codetype	N	Same Order	Either Order	N	Same Order	Either Order		Same Order	Either Order
Spike *1*	92	64.1	—	20	60.0	—		63.4	—
1-2/2-1	218	67.0	81.7	93	50.6	50.6		62.1	72.4
1-3/3-1	295	34.2	47.8	163	48.5	57.7		39.3	51.3
1-4/4-1	71	49.3	64.8	28	21.4	53.6		41.4	61.6
1-6/6-1	60	20.0	26.7	37	21.6	21.6		20.6	24.8
1-8/8-1	83	50.6	84.3	36	38.9	50.0		47.1	73.9
Spike *2*	128	53.1	—	38	81.6	—		59.6	—
2-3/3-2	134	28.4	53.7	130	50.8	56.9		39.4	55.3
2-4/4-2	228	81.6	92.1	115	47.8	61.7		70.3	81.9
2-6/6-2	107	21.5	43.9	86	31.4	32.6		25.9	38.9
2-7/7-2	242	63.2	78.9	177	46.9	52.0		56.3	67.5
2-8/8-2	116	85.3	94.8	103	38.8	63.1		63.4	79.9
2-0/0-2	210	11.9	21.9	86	40.7	51.2		20.3	30.4
Spike *3*	37	48.7	—	29	82.8	—		63.7	—
3-4/4-3	107	34.6	56.1	67	35.8	67.2		35.1	60.4
Spike *4*	416	68.5	—	88	100.0	—		74.0	—
4-6/6-4	278	30.9	56.5	133	60.2	85.7		40.4	65.9
4-7/7-4	84	65.5	76.2	19	36.8	42.1		60.2	69.9
4-8/8-4	159	83.6	97.5	81	92.6	98.8		86.6	97.9
4-9/9-4	232	75.0	89.7	87	75.9	96.6		75.2	91.6
4-0/0-4	51	2.0	15.7	16	37.5	56.3		10.5	25.4
Spike *5*	47	53.2	—	75	73.3	—		65.6	—
Spike *6*	80	50.0	—	36	75.0	—		57.8	—
6-8/8-6	654	23.7	58.0	224	52.2	82.6		31.0	64.3
6-9/9-6	174	29.9	37.9	87	54.0	66.7		37.9	47.5
Spike *7*	11	45.8	—	12	100.0	—		74.1	—
7-8/8-7	221	58.8	81.4	105	54.3	74.3		57.4	79.1
Spike *8*	22	36.4	—	28	46.4	—		42.0	—
8-9/9-8	149	60.4	83.9	65	75.4	87.7		65.0	85.1
Spike *9*	256	63.7	—	70	70.7	—		65.2	—
Spike *0*	97	48.5	—	25	92.6	—		57.5	—
Mean		48.7	64.0		57.9	62.3		51.9	66.4
Weighted Mean		49.2	65.3		56.1	65.8		51.4	69.2
N		5059	3873		2359	1938		7418	5811

sonably accurate. Thus, clinicians could use the data in Table 6–11 as a good approximation of the concordance to be expected between the MMPI-2 and the MMPI in psychiatric samples until larger psychiatric samples are available on the MMPI-2.

Honaker (1990) reported codetype concordance of 32 percent between the MMPI-2 and the MMPI using a test-retest format in a sample of 55 psychiatric patients. This concordance rate was similar to the concordance if the MMPI had been readministered (40 percent) or the MMPI-2 had been readministered (35 percent). Basically, Honaker found low concordance rates when either the MMPI-2 or the MMPI was readministered regardless of which test was administered initially.

Table 6–12 provides similar information as Table 6–11 on the concordance between specific MMPI-2 and MMPI codetypes in the sample of psychiatric inpatients and outpatients collected by Hedlund and Won Cho (1979), except that now MMPI codetypes are reported in the left-hand column and the concordance rates are reported for the MMPI-2. A quick perusal of Tables 6–11 and 6–12 will reveal that concordance rates for specific codetypes can vary drastically, depending on whether the MMPI-2 or the MMPI is used as the criterion.

For example, *4-8/8-4* codetypes on the

TABLE 6–12   Concordance between MMPI and MMPI-2 Codetypes

		MMPI-2 Codetype							
		Men				Women		Total	
		Two Highest Scales				*Two Highest Scales*		*Two Highest Scales*	
MMPI Codetype	*N*	*Same Order*	*Either Order*	*N*	*Same Order*	*Either Order*	*Same Order*	*Either Order*
Spike *1*	66	89.4	—	23	52.2	—	79.8	—
1-2/2-1	299	48.8	59.5	50	78.0	82.0	53.0	62.7
1-3/3-1	144	70.1	97.9	97	81.4	96.9	74.6	97.5
1-4/4-1	112	31.3	41.1	28	21.4	53.6	29.3	43.6
1-6/6-1	16	75.0	100.0	10	80.0	80.0	76.9	92.3
1-8/8-1	160	26.3	43.8	28	50.0	64.3	29.8	46.9
Spike *2*	141	48.2	—	76	40.8	—	45.6	—
2-3/3-2	93	40.9	77.4	79	83.5	93.7	60.5	67.9
2-4/4-2	458	40.6	45.9	134	33.6	53.0	39.0	66.9
2-6/6-2	100	23.0	71.0	60	45.0	48.3	31.3	59.0
2-7/7-2	292	52.4	65.4	98	84.7	93.9	60.5	47.9
2-8/8-2	338	29.3	32.5	122	32.8	53.3	30.2	74.5
2-0/0-2	56	44.6	82.1	55	63.6	80.0	54.0	39.6
Spike *3*	37	48.7	—	29	82.8	—	63.7	—
3-4/4-3	88	42.0	65.9	80	30.0	56.3	36.3	61.9
Spike *4*	315	90.5	—	172	51.2	—	76.6	—
4-6/6-4	192	44.8	81.8	166	48.7	62.7	46.6	71.9
4-7/7-4	134	41.0	47.8	21	33.3	38.1	40.0	43.5
4-8/8-4	438	30.4	35.4	226	33.2	35.4	31.4	35.4
4-9/9-4	373	46.6	55.8	130	50.8	64.6	47.7	60.4
4-0/0-4	14	35.7	85.7	18	33.3	50.0	34.4	68.5
Spike *5*	30	83.3	—	72	76.4	—	78.4	—
Spike *6*	49	81.6	—	55	49.1	—	64.4	—
6-8/8-6	440	35.2	86.1	246	47.6	75.2	39.6	79.8
6-9/9-6	69	75.4	95.7	63	74.6	92.1	75.0	93.9
Spike *7*	18	61.1	—	19	63.2	—	62.2	—
7-8/8-7	341	38.1	53.1	109	52.3	71.6	41.5	63.8
Spike *8*	12	66.7	—	28	46.4	—	52.5	—
8-9/9-8	216	41.7	57.9	90	54.4	63.3	45.4	61.0
Spike *9*	177	92.1	—	99	70.7	—	84.4	—
Spike *0*	47	100.0	—	50	50.0	—	74.2	—
Mean		54.0	65.8		54.7	67.1	53.5	63.8
Weighted Mean		47.5	58.5		52.4	65.9	49.1	62.7
N		5265	4373		2533	1910	7798	6283

MMPI have a concordance rate of 35 percent on the MMPI-2 in men and women (Table 6-12), whereas *4-8/8-4* codetypes on the MMPI-2 have a concordance rate over 90 percent on the MMPI in men and women (Table 6-11). Thus, *4-8/8-4* codetypes on the MMPI-2 should be a very homogeneous subset of *4-8/8-4* codetypes on the MMPI, and it would be expected that *4-8/8-4* codetypes on the MMPI-2 should have more reliable correlates since the codetype is more homogeneous.

The opposite pattern for concordance rates between the MMPI-2 and the MMPI also can be found. For example, *1-3/3-1* codetypes on the MMPI have a concordance rate over 90 percent on the MMPI-2 in men and women (Table 6-12), whereas *1-3/3-1* codetypes on the MMPI-2 have a concordance rate around 50 percent on the MMPI in men and women (Table 6-11). Thus, *1-3/3-1* codetypes on the MMPI-2 are a more heterogeneous subset of *1-3/3-1* codetypes on the MMPI, and it would be expected that *1-3/3-1* codetypes on the MMPI-2 should have less reliable correlates since the codetype is more heterogeneous.

Despite these differences in concordance rates between specific codetypes depending on whether the MMPI-2 or the MMPI is used as the criterion, the average concordance rate is around 50 percent if the two highest clinical scales are required to be in the same order, and around 60 percent if the two highest clinical scales can be in either order.

Another way of examining the concordance between the MMPI-2 and the MMPI is to require that the specific codetype be "well-defined" (i.e., that there be at least a 5 to 10 T point difference between the scales in the codetype and the next highest clinical scale). Such a requirement is thought to produce a codetype that would be relatively stable over time if the client were to retake the MMPI-2 or the MMPI.

Table 6-13 provides the concordance rates for "well-defined" codetypes when the MMPI-2 is used as the criterion, and Table 6-14 provides similar information when the MMPI is used as the criterion. Two conclusions are apparent when Tables 6-13 and 6-14 are contrasted with Tables 6-11 and 6-12, respectively: (1) concordance rates have increased dramatically and now average around 80 percent in men and over 90 percent in women, and (2) almost three-fourths of the profiles do not meet this criterion of a well-defined codetype.

Graham (1990a) reported similar concordance rates for well-defined codetypes in the Butcher and associates' (1989) sample of psychiatric patients: 82 percent for male psychiatric patients and 97 percent for the female patients. Graham did not indicate how many profiles did not meet the criterion to be well-defined. Again, it seems that the simulation of MMPI-2 data based on the MMPIs collected by Hedlund and Won Cho (1979) in their psychiatric patients is reasonably accurate and can be used by clinicians until such information is available on large samples of psychiatric patients with the MMPI-2.

This discussion of concordance rates between the MMPI-2 and the MMPI leaves unanswered whether a specific codetype on the MMPI-2 will have the same correlates as has been found with that codetype on the MMPI. Harrell (1990) reported symptom correlates of MMPI-2 and MMPI clinical scales to be very similar in 55 psychiatric patients with most correlations in the .40 to .60 range.

Research is needed that reports the empirical correlates of specific MMPI-2 codetypes regardless of the concordance between the MMPI-2 and the MMPI. In fact, clinicians should be discouraged from reporting information on the concordance rates between the MMPI-2 and the MMPI since it could impede the investigation of the empirical correlates of specific MMPI-2 codetypes. Until such research is available, clinicians can use concordance rates as another piece of in-

TABLE 6–13 Concordance between MMPI-2 and MMPI Codetypes for ''Well-Defined'' Codetypes

MMPI-2 Codetype	N	MMPI Codetype							
		Men			Women			Total	
		Two Highest Scales			Two Highest Scales			Two Highest Scales	
		Same Order	Either Order	N	Same Order	Either Order		Same Order	Either Order
Spike *1*	20	80.0	—	1	100.0	—		81.0	—
1-2/2-1	24	100.0	100.0	8	75.0	75.0		93.8	93.8
1-3/3-1	24	83.3	91.7	17	94.1	94.1		87.8	92.7
Spike *2*	53	71.7	—	27	100.0	—		81.3	—
2-3/3-2	6	66.7	83.3	14	92.9	92.9		85.0	90.0
2-4/4-2	36	100.0	100.0	10	90.0	90.0		97.8	97.8
2-7/7-2	34	100.0	100.0	25	76.0	76.0		89.8	89.8
2-0/0-2	70	21.4	21.4	29	93.1	93.1		42.4	42.4
Spike *3*	5	100.0	—	10	100.0	—		100.0	—
3-4/4-3	5	80.0	100.0	5	60.0	80.0		70.0	90.0
Spike *4*	200	70.0	—	56	100.0	—		76.5	—
4-6/6-4	20	80.0	90.0	14	100.0	100.0		88.2	94.1
4-8/8-4	19	100.0	100.0	12	100.0	100.0		100.0	100.0
4-9/9-4	49	93.9	93.9	20	100.0	100.0		95.7	95.7
4-0/0-4	13	7.7	7.7	7	85.7	85.7		35.0	35.0
Spike *5*	20	70.0	—	36	100.0	—		89.3	—
Spike *6*	23	78.3	—	22	90.9	—		84.4	—
6-8/8-6	111	25.2	86.5	35	80.0	94.3		38.4	88.4
6-9/9-6	18	72.2	72.2	10	100.0	100.0		82.1	82.1
Spike *7*	5	80.0	—	5	100.0	—		90.0	—
7-8/8-7	26	100.0	100.0	14	92.7	92.7		97.5	97.5
8-9/9-8	21	95.2	100.0	12	100.0	100.0		97.0	100.0
Spike *9*	130	81.5	—	51	94.1	—		85.1	—
Mean		76.4	83.1		92.4	91.6		82.1	86.0
Weighted Mean		69.4	80.0		93.4	92.2		77.1	84.0
N		932	476		440	232		1372	708

formation in evaluating how to interpret an MMPI-2 codetype.

CODETYPE STABILITY

There is little empirical data that indicate how consistently clients will obtain the same codetype on two successive administrations of the MMPI or the MMPI-2. The research on the stability of the MMPI historically focused either upon the individual validity and clinical scales (these coefficients were reported in Chapters 3 and 4, respectively) or

group mean profiles (cf. Lichenstein & Bryan, 1966; Pauker, 1966; Warman & Hannum, 1965), which leaves unanswered whether individual clients' codetypes have remained unchanged. Clearly, there would be at least some cause for concern if a client obtained a *4-9/9-4* codetype on one occasion and upon a second administration of the MMPI a few months later in another setting obtained a *2-7/7-2* codetype.

Graham, Smith, and Schwartz (1986) have provided the only empirical data on the stability of MMPI codetypes for a large sam-

TABLE 6-14   Concordance between MMPI and MMPI-2 Codetypes for "Well-Defined" Codetypes

MMPI Codetype	N	MMPI-2 Codetype			N					
		Men				Women			Total	
		Two Highest Scales				Two Highest Scales			Two Highest Scales	
		Same Order	Either Order			Same Order	Either Order		Same Order	Either Order
Spike 1	19	84.2	—		3	33.3	—		77.3	—
1-2/2-1	28	85.7	85.7		5	100.0	100.0		87.9	87.9
1-3/3-1	22	90.9	100.0		16	100.0	100.0		94.7	100.0
Spike 2	64	59.4	—		30	90.0	—		69.1	—
2-3/3-2	6	66.7	66.7		13	100.0	100.0		89.5	89.5
2-4/4-2	63	30.2	30.2		9	100.0	100.0		38.9	38.9
2-7/7-2	53	64.2	64.2		19	100.0	100.0		73.6	73.6
2-8/8-2	29	24.1	24.1		3	33.3	33.3		25.0	25.0
2-0/0-2	15	100.0	100.0		34	79.4	79.4		85.7	85.7
Spike 3	5	100.0	—		11	90.9	—		93.8	—
3-4/4-3	6	66.7	66.7		4	75.0	75.0		70.0	70.0
Spike 4	145	96.6	—		63	88.9	—		94.2	—
4-6/6-4	20	80.0	90.0		16	87.5	87.5		83.3	88.9
4-8/8-4	38	50.0	50.0		13	92.3	92.3		60.8	60.8
4-9/9-4	92	50.0	50.0		23	87.0	87.0		57.4	57.4
Spike 5	15	93.3	—		38	94.7	—		94.3	—
Spike 6	21	85.7	—		24	83.3	—		84.4	—
6-8/8-6	105	26.7	91.4		34	82.4	97.1		40.3	92.8
6-9/9-6	13	100.0	100.0		10	100.0	100.0		100.0	100.0
Spike 7	4	100.0	—		6	83.3	—		90.0	—
7-8/8-7	31	83.9	83.9		13	100.0	100.0		88.6	88.6
Spike 8	1	100.0	—		3	66.7	—		75.0	—
8-9/9-8	27	63.0	77.8		12	100.0	100.0		74.4	84.6
Spike 9	107	99.1	—		49	98.0	—		98.7	—
Mean		75.0	72.1			86.1	90.1		77.0	76.0
Weighted Mean		68.3	67.2			90.2	92.4		75.4	74.2
N		929	548			451	224		1380	772

ple ($N = 405$) of psychiatric inpatients. They reported 42.7 percent, 44.0 percent, and 27.7 percent agreement across an average interval of approximately three months for high-point, low-point, and two-point codetypes, respectively. Only seven specific codetypes (2-3/3-2, 2-4/4-2, 4-8/8-4, 4-9/9-4, 6-8/8-6, 7-8/8-7, and 8-9/9-8) occurred frequently enough to assess their stability; the agreement for these seven codetypes ranged from 26.4 percent (6-8/8-6) to 41.4 percent (4-9/9-4). If the patients were classified into the categories of neurotic, psychotic, and characterologic, 58.1 percent remained in the same category when retested.

These data on codetype stability suggest several important conclusions. First, clinicians should be cautious about making long-term predictions from a single administration of the MMPI-2 or the MMPI. Second, it is not clear whether the shifts that do occur in codetypes across time reflect meaningful changes in the patients' behaviors, psychometric instability of the MMPI or MMPI-2, or some combination of both of these factors. Finally, research is needed to provide additional information on this issue.

RELATIONSHIP BETWEEN CODETYPES AND PSYCHIATRIC DIAGNOSES

Clinicians may be prone to believe that specific diagnoses are associated with certain codetypes. Unfortunately, there is more heterogeneity in psychiatric diagnoses within a given codetype than clinicians might expect. For example, Marks and colleagues (1974) reported that 68 percent of adult patients with a *6-8/8-6* codetype were diagnosed as being psychotic (schizophrenic or paranoid were the most frequent diagnoses), 18 percent as personality disordered (paranoid), and 14 percent as chronic organic brain syndrome.

Gilberstadt and Duker (1965) reported that the diagnosis for their *8-6* codetype was paranoid schizophrenia; since they reported prototypic codetypes, they did not provide information on the frequency with which *8-6* codetypes were diagnosed as being schizophrenic. Hathaway and Meehl (1951) found that 16 (46 percent) of their 35 patients with *6-8/8-6* codetypes had some form of schizophrenic diagnosis. Their patients also were twice as likely to be diagnosed as schizophrenic when they had an *8-6* codetype as compared with a *6-8* codetype. It appears that patients with a *6-8/8-6* codetype have a significant probability of receiving a schizophrenic diagnosis although a number of other diagnoses also can be encountered.

Similar data can be provided for *8-9/9-8* codetypes so that the clinician can see that heterogeneity in psychiatric diagnoses is characteristic of all codetypes. Marks and associates (1974) found that 70 percent of adult patients with an *8-9/9-8* codetype were diagnosed as being psychotic (schizophrenic or mixed were the most common diag-

noses), 17 percent as neurotic (depression), and 9 percent as acute organic brain syndrome.

Gilberstadt and Duker (1965) reported that the diagnosis for their prototypic *8-9* codetype was schizophrenic reaction, catatonic type with alternative diagnoses of "schizo-manic" psychosis and paranoid schizophrenia. Hathaway and Meehl found that 3 (37.5 percent) of their 8 patients with *9-8* codetypes were diagnosed as manic-depressive, manic type. Only 5 patients had *8-9* codetypes and none was diagnosed as manic-depressive, manic type. Thus, it appears that bipolar disorder, manic diagnoses may be common in *8-9/9-8* codetypes but such diagnoses occur less than one-half the time at the best and probably closer to one-quarter.

Greene (1988a) has summarized the frequency with which various codetypes were found in specific diagnostic groups, and he found the expected relationship between codetypes and diagnostic groups. For example, *2-7/7-2* codetypes occurred frequently in depressed patients, *6-8/8-6* codetypes in schizophrenic patients, *8-9/9-8* codetypes in manic patients, and so on. However, the most frequent codetypes in these groups occurred less than 20 percent of the time. It also appeared that as the sample sizes increased, the variability in performance within a specific diagnostic group increased rather than decreased.

The clinician should consult the individual chapters in Greene (1988b) to review MMPI performance within specific diagnostic groups, namely, chronic pain (Prokop, 1988), schizophrenia (Walters, 1988b), mood disorders (Nichols, 1988), personality disorders (Morey & Smith, 1988), substance abuse/dependence (Greene & Garvin, 1988), Post-Traumatic Stress Disorder (Penk, Keane, Robinowitz, Fowler, Bell, & Finkelstein, 1988), neuropsychological dysfunction (Farr & Martin, 1988), and child abuse and sexual abuse (Friedrich, 1988).

PROTOTYPIC SCORES FOR CODETYPES

Although the primary focus of this chapter will be on the correlates of each codetype, it is important for the clinician to realize that the relative elevation of the other clinical scales as well as the elevation of a number of the supplementary scales can drastically alter the potential interpretation.

Profiles 6–1 and 6–2 provide examples of two individuals both of whom have a *4-9/9-4* codetype. Even a quick perusal of the two profiles reveals that these individuals would behave very differently in a clinical interview and they would have different reasons for being referred for treatment. The first individual (Profile 6–1) is very likely to have been referred for behavioral difficulties and/or criminal activities, whereas the other individual (Profile 6–2) is more likely to have interpersonal difficulties, probably with a spouse or other family member.

Profiles 6–1 and 6–2 illustrate the importance of assessing how well the obtained profile matches the "prototypic" scores for that specific codetype. Appendix D contains tables with the prototypic scores for every codetype discussed in this chapter. Each table provides the prototypic scores for all of the MMPI-2 and MMPI standard validity and clinical scales as well as several of the supplementary scales that are scored commonly in *psychiatric* samples. Examples of these tables are provided in this Chapter for five frequently occurring codetypes: Spike *1*, *2-4/4-2*, *2-7-7-2*, *4-9/9-4*, and *6-8/8-6*. The use of prototypic scores also will be illustrated in Chapter 7 when specific MMPI-2 profiles are interpreted.

There are little data to address the issue of whether prototypic scores for specific MMPI-2 and MMPI codetypes would be similar in different psychiatric settings even if their frequency of occurrence is not the same. Profiles 6–3 and 6–4 indicate the similarities between *2-4/4-2* and *6-8/8-6* codetypes in

psychiatric patients (Hedlund & Won Cho, 1976) and medical outpatients referred for a psychiatric evaluation (Colligan & Offord, 1986).

Despite the different frequencies with which these two codetypes are encountered in these settings (see Tables 6–6 to 6–9), their scores on the MMPI-2 standard validity and clinical scales are very similar. In fact, the prototypic scores for the same codetype in these two settings are so similar that it would be redundant to report both sets of scores. Consequently, Appendix D contains the prototypic scores for each codetype based on psychiatric patients (Hedlund & Won Cho, 1979).

Persons who are being screened for personnel selection would be expected to have very different patterns of scores on the standard validity and clinical scales, and are generally unlikely to elevate most scales. Research is needed to determine whether prototypic scores for a specific codetype in a personnel setting are similar to those in a psychiatric setting despite the relative differences in elevation that would be expected.

Since persons in a personnel setting would be expected to minimize or underreport any type of psychological problem if they are trying to qualify for a position, they generally will not elevate any clinical scale on the MMPI-2 to a T score of 65 or higher. In those rare instances in which they do produce a standard codetype, it would be interesting to determine whether the pattern of scores on the standard validity and clinical scales are similar to those found in psychiatric settings.

Broughton (1984) and Horowitz, Wright, Lowenstein, and Parad (1981) have described the use of prototypes as a means of assessing personality or psychopathologic constructs. These references can provide a starting point for the clinician who is interested in a more conceptual understanding of this approach to the assessment of psychopathology.

PROFILE 6-1 Prototypic Scores for a *4-9/9-4* Codetype

MMPI-2

S.R. Hathaway and J.C. McKinley

Minnesota Multiphasic Personality Inventory-2

Profile for Basic Scales

Name _____

Address _____

Occupation _____ Date Tested __/__/__

Education _____ Age _____ Marital Status _____

Referred By _____

MMPI-2 Code _____

Scorer's Initials _____

MALE

Prototypic Scores for

4-9/9-4 Codetypes

Raw Score ___

? Raw Score ___

K to be Added ___

Raw Score with K ___

PROFILE 6-2   Nonprototypic Scores for a *4-9/9-4* Codetype

MMPI-2
S.R. Hathaway and J.C. McKinley
Minnesota Multiphasic Personality Inventory - 2

Name _____

Address _____

Occupation _____ Date Tested ___ / ___ / ___

Education _____ Age _____ Marital Status _____

Referred By _____

MMPI-2 Code _____

Scorer's Initials _____

Profile for Basic Scales

Minnesota Multiphasic Personality Inventory-2
Copyright © by THE REGENTS OF THE UNIVERSITY OF MINNESOTA
1942, 1943 (renewed 1970), 1989. This Profile Form 1989.
All rights reserved. Distributed exclusively by NATIONAL COMPUTER SYSTEMS, INC.
under license from The University of Minnesota.

"MMPI-2" and "Minnesota Multiphasic Personality Inventory-2" are trademarks owned by
The University of Minnesota. Printed in the United States of America.

FEMALE

Non-prototypic Scores for

4-9/9-4 Codetypes

Raw Score ___ ___ ___

? Raw Score ___

K to be Added ___

Raw Score with K ___

NATIONAL
COMPUTER
SYSTEMS

24001

PROFILE 6-3 Prototypic *2-4/4-2* Codetypes for Missouri Psychiatric Patients and Mayo Medical Outpatients Referred for a Psychiatric Evaluation

MMPI-2
S.R. Hathaway and J.C. McKinley
*Minnesota Multiphasic
Personality Inventory -2*

Profile for Basic Scales

Minnesota Multiphasic Personality Inventory-2
Copyright © by THE REGENTS OF THE UNIVERSITY OF MINNESOTA
1942, 1943 (renewed 1970), 1989. This Profile Form 1989.
All rights reserved. Distributed exclusively by NATIONAL COMPUTER SYSTEMS, INC.
under license from The University of Minnesota.

"MMPI-2" and "Minnesota Multiphasic Personality Inventory-2" are trademarks owned by
The University of Minnesota. Printed in the United States of America.

Name
Address
Occupation _____ Date Tested __/__/__
Education ____ Age ____ Marital Status ____
Referred By
MMPI-2 Code
Scorer's Initials

Prototypic Scores for 2-4/4-2 Codetypes

Medical Outpatient Referrals
(Colligan & Offord, 1986)
▲——▲

Psychiatric Patients
(Hedlund & Won Cho, 1979)
●——●

MALE

Raw Score
? Raw Score
K to be Added
Raw Score with K

24001

PROFILE 6–4 Prototypic *6-8/8-6* Codetypes for Missouri Psychiatric Patients and Mayo Medical Outpatients Referred for a Psychiatric Evaluation

Prototypic Scores for 6-8/8-6 Codetypes

Medical Outpatient Referrals
(Colligan & Offord, 1986)

Psychiatric Patients
(Hedlund & Won Cho, 1979)

Several general comments need to be made about these prototypic scores that are provided for each codetype:

1. The percentage of clients who produced inconsistent patterns of item endorsement will be reported for each codetype but prototypic scores were based only on those clients who endorsed the items consistently.

2. The percentage of clients within each codetype who scored below the 25th percentile or above the 75th percentile on the total T score difference on the Wiener and Harmon (Wiener, 1948) Obvious and Subtle subscales (see Table 3–45, p. 100, for the MMPI-2; Table 3–46, p. 101, for the MMPI) for all psychiatric clients is provided as an index of the accuracy of item endorsement; however, these clients were included in computing the prototypic scores.

3. All scores are reported as T scores with the appropriate clinical scales K-corrected unless indicated otherwise. Raw scores are provided for the following scales: Cannot Say (?), total T score difference on the Wiener and Harmon (Wiener, 1948) Obvious and Subtle subscales, total number of Lachar and Wrobel (1979) critical items endorsed, and MacAndrew alcoholism scale (MacAndrew, 1965).

As a clinical rule of thumb, any score that varies by more than one standard deviation (approximately 10 T points) from the prototypic score for that scale should be evaluated as to whether and how it might modify the standard interpretation of that codetype. For example, the prototypic T scores on Scales *2* and *0* for an MMPI-2 *4-9/9-4* codetype are 53.2 and 45.4 (see Table 6–18), respectively. If a client has T scores of 65 and 60 for these two scales, the client is less likely

to act out and is reporting more emotional distress as a consequence of his or her behavior.

An intriguing research question that has not even been addressed yet is whether clients who deviate significantly from the prototypic scores for a codetype are less likely to manifest its correlates. It also would be interesting to see if profiles that deviate from the prototype for the codetype are more similar to the pattern of scores for another codetype.

Greene and Brown have developed a computer interpretive program for the MMPI (1988) and the MMPI-2 (1990) that also provide information on how well a client's scores on the standard validity and clinical scales match his or her codetype and all other codetypes.

Finally, it would be very appropriate for clinicians to develop their own prototypic scores for codetypes that occur frequently in their setting. Once these prototypes have been identified within a specific setting, the clinician also could begin to see if subgroups of profiles were occurring within the codetype, and determine whether they were clinical correlates for these subgroups.

CODETYPES

Any correlate of a codetype discussed in this chapter or in any interpretive system is a probabilistic statement that may or may not apply to a specific client. Each statement should be understood as applying to most clients or typical of clients with such a codetype. Consequently, most of these qualifiers have been omitted in the following pages.

It also will be assumed that the clinician has assessed the consistency and accuracy of item endorsement (see Chapter 3), so disclaimers will not be presented with each codetype as appropriate. For example, the clinician might recall that 43.0 percent of *6-8/8-6* codetypes on the MMPI and 28.7 percent on the MMPI-2 are a result of inconsistent patterns of item endorsement (see Table 3–47, p. 103, or Tables 6–19 or G–44).

A number of the codetypes occur infrequently and consequently there is little information available for interpretation, as was noted above. In such situations it is frequently helpful to note the third highest clinical scale, particularly when Scales *5* (Masculinity-Femininity) and/or *0* (Social Introversion) are among the two highest scales. If a client has a *1-5/5-1* codetype and Scale *3* (Hysteria) is the third highest scale, it probably would be instructive to consider that the client has a *1-3* codetype with a high Scale *5*.

Anytime Scales *5* and/or *0* are among the two highest clinical scales, it probably would be a good idea to examine which clinical scale(s) are next highest and to consider how the interpretation of the codetype might be changed by considering these scales. Research is needed to determine when the third highest clinical scale can and should be substituted for one of the two highest scales to improve the accuracy of the clinical interpretation.

Within-Normal-Limit (*WNL*)

Clients who do not elevate any clinical scale above a T score of 65 on the MMPI-2 or a T score of 70 on the MMPI are quite common in psychiatric settings. In fact, a *WNL* codetype is the most frequently occurring codetype in most, if not all, psychiatric settings (cf. Hathaway & Meehl, 1951; Hedlund & Won Cho, 1979).

These clients describe themselves as being happy, healthy, and contented. They see their relationships as being satisfying. It is very important to determine whether this self-description is consistent with the reason(s) for which the clients are being evaluated. These clients are not reporting any type of emotional distress either as a result of the behaviors or symptoms that led them to be evaluated or of the process of being evaluated.

Their problems tend to be chronically ingrained and they have become adjusted to them. They frequently are psychotic or manifest a severe characterologic disorder. They have little motivation to consider change.

Duckworth and Barley (1988) and Kelley and King (1978) provide interpretive information on *WNL* codetypes.

Spike *1*

Clients who elevate only Scale *1* (Hypochondriasis) will present a long history of vague physical symptoms and ailments. Their exaggerated complaints will reflect primarily a somatization process even if they also have some objective physical conditions. Their complaints may be used to control and manipulate others. They do not report any type of emotional distress despite their physical symptoms.

They are not psychologically minded and they invest little effort in understanding psychological problems in themselves or others. They have difficulty seeing how their physical symptoms could be related to their psychological functioning.

This pattern represents a stable, chronic mode of adjustment that is difficult to modify.

Tables 6–15 and D–1 provide the prototypic scores for Spike *1* codetypes.

1-2/2-1

Clients with *1-2/2-1* codetypes present themselves as concerned about their physical functioning. General physical symptoms are seen with manifestations of a somatization or psychophysiologic reaction. Even when or if they have real physical symptoms, clients exaggerate their severity. These clients often complain of nausea, vomiting, weakness, insomnia, and fatigue rather than classical depressive features. Dizziness, chest and back pains, and tachycardia may be reported.

TABLE 6-15 Prototypic Scores for Spike *1* Codetypes in Psychiatric Settings

	MMPI			MMPI-2		
Demographics						
		M	*SD*		*M*	*SD*
N	76			119		
Age		46.5	14.1		45.4	14.3
Men	86.8%			82.4%		
Women	13.2			17.6		
Test-Taking Scales/Indexes						
		M	*SD*		*M*	*SD*
Inconsistent		0.0%			2.1%	
Total (Obvious-Subtle)[a]		12.9	54.1		24.6	53.3
Critical items[b]		24.4	8.9		23.5	8.2
Overreported[c]		1.3%			1.7%	
Underreported[c]		34.2%			33.6%	
Standard Validity and Clinical Scales (K-Corrected)						
		M	*SD*		*M*	*SD*
?[d]		4.3	5.9		4.2	5.6
L		55.4	9.3		59.1	12.2
F		56.3	6.1		51.8	7.7
K		54.7	8.8		50.4	9.8
1(Hs)		74.0	4.7		69.3	4.0
2(D)		61.0	6.7		57.3	6.3
3(Hy)		62.8	4.4		56.3	5.6
4(Pd)		60.5	6.5		53.4	7.6
5(Mf)		51.9	8.4		43.6	8.8
6(Pa)		55.1	6.6		49.0	7.8
7(Pt)		53.6	6.7		47.5	7.0
8(Sc)		55.8	7.3		49.4	6.8
9(Ma)		56.2	7.7		48.7	6.7
0(Si)		52.8	7.4		49.8	6.9
Supplementary Scales						
		M	*SD*		*M*	*SD*
A		48.2	8.3		49.6	8.5
R		64.8	12.3		54.3	10.1
MAC/MAC-R[d]						
men		27.4	4.5		27.0	4.5
women		23.6	2.6		22.8	3.6

Codetype Concordance

	Men	Women		Men	Women
MMPI-2 Spike *1*	88.1%	52.2%	MMPI Spike *1*	64.1%	60.0%
1-2/2-1		21.7	Spike *4*		30.0
1-3/3-1		13.0			

[a]See Chapter 3, Table 3-24, for explanation of how this index is computed.

[b]The total number of Lachar and Wrobel (1979) critical items endorsed.

[c]Percentage of patients within this codetype scoring above the 75th percentile or below the 25th percentile on the total T score difference on the Wiener and Harmon Obvious and Subtle subscales for all patients (see Tables 3-45 and 3-46 for the cutting scores for the MMPI-2 and MMPI, respectively).

[d]Raw score.

They lack insight into their somatic symptoms and behavior, often refusing to acknowledge that their symptoms are related to emotional conflict and are used as a means of avoiding their psychological problems. The somatic symptoms are focused around the alimentary system, particularly on abdominal pain and backaches. Their symptoms are vague, nonspecific, and difficult to isolate medically. These clients return to their physicians repeatedly with limited change in their physical condition.

They think in a very concrete manner and tend to focus extensively on their physical symptoms. They see their judgment as being poor, particularly when compared to how they used to function. Sustained attention and concentration are difficult for them.

They are unwilling to seek psychological counseling since they do not see their problems as psychological in nature. More frequently they seek another medical opinion when a physician suggests that their problems could reflect psychological factors. Any medical intervention should be as conservative as possible because of the somatization features. Gynther and colleagues (1973) reported that these clients were frequently alcoholics, but no other researcher has found this codetype to be characteristic of alcoholics (cf. Clopton, 1978; Greene & Garvin, 1988).

Gilberstadt and Duker (1965), Gynther and colleagues (1973), and Marks and colleagues (1974) provide interpretive information on *1-2/2-1* codetypes. Table D–2 provides the prototypic scores.

1-3

Clients with *1-3* codetypes are found frequently in both normal and psychiatric populations. (Information on *3-1* codetypes is provided in a later section of this chapter.) When Scales *1* and *3* are greater than a T score of 65 on the MMPI-2 or a T score of 70 on the MMPI and Scales *1* and *3* are greater

than Scale *2* by 10 T points, this profile is a classic conversion "V" (see Chapter 4). In general, the higher the elevation of the conversion "V," the more rigid are the client's defenses. A conversion "V" above a T score of 80 suggests that many of the client's efforts are ineffectively directed toward trying to ward off anxiety, particularly if the *F* scale also is significantly elevated.

The absolute elevation of the conversion "V" is not related to whether a psychological or an organic diagnosis is likely to be made (Schwartz & Krupp, 1971), although persons above age 40 are more likely to receive an organic diagnosis and younger females are more likely to receive a psychological diagnosis (Schwartz, Osborne, & Krupp, 1972). Hence, elevations on Scales *1* and *3* cannot be used reliably to distinguish functional disorders from actual physical disease. In either case the client is using somatic symptoms to avoid thinking or dealing with psychological problems.

These clients are converting their psychological problems into physical symptoms that localize the difficulty outside of themselves. They report a wide variety of physical symptoms such as gastrointestinal difficulties, chest and neck pains, hay fever and/or asthma, and balance and coordination difficulties. They describe themselves as being tired, inefficient, and lethargic. They see themselves as being treated unfairly by life. Depression and worry are not overtly expressed, no matter how concerned the clients are about poor physical functioning. Suicidal ideation is quite unusual. Narcissistic and dependent features are more likely to be seen.

These clients lack insight into their own behavior and are very resistant to interpretations that there could be psychological involvement in the physical complaints. Even when their complaints seem bizarre, they are unlikely to be psychotic. Others are likely to experience these clients' physical symptoms as being used in a manipulative or passive-aggressive manner.

They are very passive, conventional individuals who invest little energy in understanding themselves or others. They value being seen as logical and without psychological problems.

Clients with a *1-3* codetype are more likely to show more somatization features than the histrionic features characteristic of clients with a *3-1* codetype. Their physical complaints are usually more nonspecific and vague and likely to involve backaches, gastrointestinal complaints, and so on.

Clients with a *1-3-9* profile have been described as having a chronic brain syndrome with trauma and personality disorder (Gilberstadt & Duker, 1965). Neither Schwartz (1969) nor Golden, Sweet, and Osmon (1979) were able to replicate this codetype as being characteristic of brain-damaged persons.

Additional interpretive information on *1-3* codetypes is available in Gilberstadt and Duker (1965), Gynther and associates (1973), Marks and associates (1974), and Prokop (1988). Table D–3 provides the prototypic scores for *1-3* codetypes.

1-4/4-1

Clients with *1-4/4-1* codetypes are relatively rare. Their primary features appear to reflect a somatization process rather than psychopathy. The elevation on Scale *4* seems to emphasize the pessimistic, whiny, nagging qualities of Scale *1*. They report general pain and discomfort with few specific symptoms. They do not report any type of emotional distress such as depression or anxiety as a result of their physical symptoms.

Their interpersonal and familial relationships are characterized by turmoil and chronic complaining. They often exhibit poor social skills, particularly with the opposite gender. These clients' focus on somatic symptoms is essentially chronic in nature and consequently quite resistant to change or intervention.

Gynther and colleagues (1973) provide further interpretive information on this codetype, and Table D–4 provides the prototypic scores.

1-5/5-1

Scale *1* generally is not elevated with any clinical scale other than Scales *2* and *3*. Consequently, there is little information on this and the five subsequent codetypes.

When a *1-5/5-1* codetype does occur, it usually is seen in men. Lachar (1974) has commented that Scale *5* points out the passivity and the fussy, complaining attitude of these men. They report vague physical symptoms that are used to avoid personal responsibilities. They focus their dissatisfaction with life on their physical problems and complaints. In response to stress, these clients will exhibit an increase in the frequency and/or severity of their physical symptoms, and become irritable and easily annoyed. They generally are not depressed, anxious, tired, or fatigued.

Interpretive information on this codetype is found in Tanner (1990). Table D–5 provides the prototypic scores for *1-5/5-1* codetypes.

1-6/6-1

Clients with *1-6/6-1* codetypes also appear to manifest some form of somatization disorder and display the hostile qualities tapped by Scale *6*. They are unaware of these hostile qualities or will attribute them to the way others treat them. Their interpersonal relationships are quite conflicted because of their propensity to blame and accuse others of any problems that might arise. They may be delusional or obsessive concerning their physical symptoms, especially when Scale *8* is elevated, even though it is unusual for them to report actual psychotic behaviors.

Their personality structure is very resistant to intervention or change.

Table D-6 provides the prototypic scores for *1-6/6-1* codetypes.

1-7/7-1

Clients with *1-7/7-1* codetypes exhibit a wide variety of physical complaints that reflect constant tension and anxiety as well as general pain and discomfort. Their somatization features are resistant to intervention or change. Intellectualization is quite common. They often feel insecure, inhibited, inferior, and guilty. They are bothered by obsessive thoughts, and are concerned that they may be losing their mind. They also manifest depressive features and may report sleep difficulties.

They are shy, introverted, and retiring in interpersonal relationships. They worry about their interpersonal skills or lack thereof.

Table D-7 provides the prototypic scores for *1-7/7-1* codetypes.

1-8/8-1

Clients with *1-8/8-1* codetypes are likely to present somatic complaints of a bizarre nature. They actually may have somatic delusions. The somatic complaints also may represent defenses against the emergence of actual psychotic material. They are easily distracted and confused. They report concentration and memory difficulties.

They are socially inept and inadequate, particularly when Scale *0* also is elevated. They often have poor work histories and a nomadic lifestyle. They feel alienated, isolated, and different from other people. They distrust others. Other people see them as odd, strange, or bizarre.

Interpretive information on this codetype is found in Gilberstadt and Duker (1965). Table D-8 provides the prototypic scores for *1-8/8-1* codetypes.

1-9/9-1

Clients with *1-9/9-1* codetypes would be expected to have multiple somatic complaints that may be exhibited with a high energy level or agitation.

They describe themselves as happy, carefree, and self-reliant regardless of what others think. They are described as agitated, angry, and difficult to interact with.

Table D-9 provides the prototypic scores for *1-9/9-1* codetypes.

1-0/0-1

Clients with *1-0/0-1* codetypes are quite rare so there is little information available. It seems likely that they would also elevate Scale *8* and represent a variant of a *1-8/8-1* codetype. They report a very limited number of physical symptoms. They do not indicate any form of psychological discomfort or emotional distress.

They are shy, introverted, and socially withdrawn. They are very conventional, law-abiding individuals primarily out of fear of being caught.

Table D-10 provides the prototypic scores for *1-0/0-1* codetypes.

Spike 2

Clients who elevate only Scale *2* (Depression) are likely to be experiencing a mild reactive depression even if they deny depressive feelings. If Scale *9* is below a T score of 45, particularly in persons under the age of 30, the probability of significant depression is even higher. Suicidal ideation and plans should be routinely evaluated in these clients, although suicide cannot be predicted by the MMPI-2 alone (see Chapter 5). Although clinicians should routinely check the client's responses to items 150, 506, 520, and 524 on the MMPI-2 since their content refers directly to suicidal ideation and/or suicide attempts, these items are especially relevant to understanding clients who have this codetype.

These clients will have the general characteristics of depressed individuals: feelings of inadequacy, lack of self-confidence, self-deprecation, pessimism about the future, and strong guilt feelings. They are good psychotherapy candidates, and they will show significant improvement within a relatively short period of time.

They are socially reserved and introverted. They tend to withdraw and isolate themselves when in conflict or under stress, which serves to exacerbate their depressive symptomatology. They are very conventional people who are unlikely to get in trouble because of their behavior. They are rarely psychotic.

Kelley and King (1979a) provide interpretive information on Spike 2 codetypes and Table D–11 provides the prototypic scores.

2-3/3-2

Clients with 2-3/3-2 codetypes evidence significant depression as well as lowered activity levels, apathy, and helplessness. The presence of significant depressive symptomatology can be the result of their ineffective use of histrionic mechanisms and defenses. They are characteristically described as being overcontrolled and having difficulty in expressing their feelings, being immature, inadequate, and dependent.

They have grown accustomed to their chronic problems, and they continue to function at a lowered level of efficiency for prolonged periods of time. Physical complaints are likely, often with a histrionic quality. Women are likely to be sexually dysfunctional; this may represent their control of sexual feelings or an expression of their unhappiness with their spouse.

These clients usually lack insight into their own behavior and are reluctant to seek psychological counseling. These factors, in addition to the chronic nature of their adjustment, make response to any form of psychological intervention very poor unless motivation for long-term psychotherapy can be discovered.

Gynther and associates (1973) furnish additional information on the 2-3/3-2 codetype, and Table D–12 provides the prototypic scores.

2-4/4-2

Clients may achieve 2-4/4-2 codetypes for a myriad of reasons. One critical factor, which should be assessed through an interview with the client or knowledge of the client's reason for taking the MMPI-2, is whether Scale 2 is being elevated by internal (intrapsychic) and/or external (situational) causes. Examples of the latter are psychopathic individuals who have been caught in some illicit or illegal activity and who are being evaluated as a consequence of their behavior.

The depression in these persons represents the constraints being placed on their behavior; their depression, or possibly boredom at being externally constrained, will alleviate itself quickly once they manage to extricate themselves from their present situation. The presence of even this situational depression in these persons suggests a better prognosis than persons in similar circumstances who achieve a Spike 4 or a 4-9/9-4 codetype.

These psychopathic clients with a 2-4/4-2 codetype can be understood best by examining the correlates of a Spike 4 codetype. They will display excellent intellectual insight into their behavior, make a positive impression of their earnestness on the clinician, and vehemently protest that they will change their behavior. Despite their ''sincere'' intentions, recurrences of acting out are very likely, followed by the same protestations to do better when caught again.

Another subgroup of clients with 2-4/4-2 codetypes is more likely to be chronically depressed and unhappy without evidence of antisocial acting out. These clients are displaying hostility and resentment, which often result from marital conflict, familial difficulties, or similar situations that make them feel trapped and hopeless.

They are immature, dependent, and egocentric and often vacillate between pitying themselves and blaming others for their difficulties. These behaviors are chronic in nature and difficult to resolve through psychological interventions. Involvement of the other members of the family or the spouse in the therapeutic interaction is important if meaningful behavior change is to occur.

Clients with *2-4/4-2* codetypes are frequently identified as alcoholics (cf. Clopton, 1978a; Graham & Strenger, 1988; Greene & Garvin, 1988). Hodo and Fowler (1976) reported that 21 percent of 1,009 white male alcoholics had this codetype and that this was the most frequent codetype among these males. Greene and Garvin (1988), in their summary of MMPI research on substance abuse samples found that 15.3 percent of male and 14.8 percent of female alcoholics had a *2-4/4-2* codetype. Gynther and colleagues (1973) also found that alcoholism was a replicated correlate of this codetype in their psychiatric sample. These clients will evidence depressive features, familial conflict, and vocational problems characteristic of alcoholics.

In determining which of the above descriptions fits a specific client, useful information can be obtained by analyzing the content scales; a number of the supplementary scales such as Dominance, MacAndrew Alcoholism, and so on (see Chapter 5); the reasons why the client is taking the MMPI-2; and the other clinical scales.

Further interpretive information on this codetype may be found in Gynther and associates (1973) and Kelley and King (1979a). Tables 6–16 and D–13 provide the prototypic scores for *2-4/4-2* codetypes.

2-5/5-2

There are almost no published data on *2-5/5-2* codetypes. It would be anticipated that males with liberal arts college educations who are undergoing situational depression would produce this codetype. The depressive symptomatology tends to be very mild and chronic in nature. As the situational depression is resolved, Scale *2* should decrease in elevation and Scale *9* should increase. Their depression tends to be more serious when Scale *2* is more elevated than Scale *5*.

They are very passive, dependent, introverted, and shy although they have adequate social skills. They are unlikely to get into trouble because of their behavior. They have poor interpersonal and marital relationships.

King and Kelley (1977b) found that male college students who were psychiatric outpatients with this codetype were anxious, disoriented, and withdrawn. These students dated infrequently, had somatic complaints, and had a physical history for their complaints and difficulties.

King and Kelley (1977b) and Tanner (1990) present more interpretive information on *2-5/5-2* codetypes, and Table D–14 provides the prototypic scores.

2-6/6-2

Clients with *2-6/6-2* codetypes are angry, depressed individuals with so much anger that it is directed both against themselves and others. Unlike most depressed clients who are unable to express their anger, clients with this codetype usually are openly hostile and resentful toward others. As a result, these clients often have poor interpersonal relationships and may be rejected by significant others. They are very sensitive to criticism and prone to overinterpret the most innocuous comments.

This configuration represents a chronic pattern of adjustment which is difficult to alter. Their behavior generally invites others to reject and avoid them. If Scale *6* is mark-

TABLE 6–16 Prototypic Scores for *2-4/4-2* Codetypes in Psychiatric Settings

	MMPI			MMPI-2	
Demographics					
	M	SD		M	SD
N	606			343	
Age	38.1	12.5		36.9	12.4
Men	78.1%			66.5%	
Women	21.9			33.5	
Test-Taking Scales/Indexes					
	M	SD		M	SD
Inconsistent	6.3%			3.2%	
Total (Obvious-Subtle)[a]	38.6	59.9		68.3	62.3
Critical items[b]	32.9	12.1		34.4	11.9
Overreported[c]	5.9%			16.3%	
Underreported[c]	22.8%			13.7%	
Standard Validity and Clinical Scales (K-Corrected)					
	M	SD		M	SD
?[d]	4.2	5.5		3.4	4.7
L	50.9	8.0		52.5	10.5
F	62.2	9.0		64.9	13.9
K	51.5	8.8		45.3	9.3
1(Hs)	61.1	10.8		58.1	10.3
2(D)	81.8	9.1		76.1	8.4
3(Hy)	65.7	8.8		60.1	10.1
4(Pd)	83.1	8.3		77.6	7.9
5(Mf)	56.3	10.1		48.1	10.1
6(Pa)	63.5	9.6		59.3	11.0
7(Pt)	68.5	9.6		63.8	10.3
8(Sc)	65.8	11.6		60.6	11.7
9(Ma)	57.8	9.7		51.3	9.0
0(Si)	60.0	9.7		58.9	9.4
Supplementary Scales					
	M	SD		M	SD
A	60.1	10.8		62.7	10.8
R	68.1	13.1		57.4	11.5
MAC/MAC-R[d]					
men	26.9	4.7		26.8	4.9
women	22.4	4.5		22.7	4.4
Codetype Concordance					
	Men	Women		Men	Women
MMPI-2 2-4/4-2	45.9%	53.0%	MMPI 2-4/4-2	92.1%	61.7%
2-7/7-2		15.7	Spike 4		15.6
Spike 4	10.4		4-8/8-4		13.0

[a] See Chapter 3, Table 3–24, for explanation of how this index is computed.

[b] The total number of Lachar and Wrobel (1979) critical items endorsed.

[c] Percentage of patients within this codetype scoring above the 75th percentile or below the 25th percentile on the total T score difference on the Wiener and Harmon Obvious and Subtle subscales for all patients (see Tables 3–45 and 3–46 for the cutting scores for the MMPI-2 and MMPI, respectively).

[d] Raw score.

edly elevated and is higher than Scale 2, the possibility of a psychotic reaction of a paranoid type should be carefully evaluated.

Kelley and King (1979a) provide interpretive information on 2-6/6-2 codetypes, and Table D–15 provides the prototypic scores.

2-7/7-2

Clients with 2-7/7-2 codetypes are very common in most types of psychiatric settings. These clients are anxious, tense, depressed, and constant worriers; this is apparent both to themselves and to others. They are guilt-ridden, intrapunitive individuals who can become obsessively preoccupied with their personal deficiencies despite frequent evidence of their personal achievements. Any problem is likely to be attributed to their personal inadequacies.

Suicidal ideation and plans should be assessed carefully. Clinicians should routinely evaluate the client's responses to items 150, 506, 520, and 524 on the MMPI-2 in all clients, and particularly in this codetype, since the item content reflects suicidal ideation and/or suicide attempts.

Clients often will report cardiovascular symptoms that reflect their chronic state of tension and anxiety, insomnia, and decreased appetite. Because of their willingness to examine their own behavior, often in infinite detail, they are excellent candidates for psychotherapy. They have a natural introspective orientation as well as the motivation to change, which augurs well for any psychotherapeutic intervention.

If Scale 7 is extremely elevated (T score > 85) and particularly if Scale 7 also is higher than Scale 2, they may be so agitated and worried that these symptoms should be addressed through methods such as psychopharmacologic treatment or situational intervention before treatment is initiated.

Since 2-7/7-2 codetypes occur so frequently, it often is possible to examine the third highest clinical scale to augment the interpretation. Three scales (3, 4, and 8) often are elevated with Scales 2 and 7, thus producing three high-point triads—2-7-3/7-2-3, 2-7-4/7-2-4, and 2-7-8/7-2-8.

Clients with 2-7-3/7-2-3 codetypes, which is the least frequent of the three triads, are likely to be docile, passive individuals who are most comfortable in very dependent interpersonal relationships. They are adept at inspiring others to take care of them and to protect them from their cruel fate. They may even persuade the clinician to try to save them. That is, these clients are very successful at tapping any tendency a clinician may have toward rescuing or saving a client. Intervention into this chronic behavior pattern is fraught with problems even for the experienced clinician, who must provide appropriate support and empathy while inducing significant behavior change by confronting or interpreting the client's behavior.

Clients with 2-7-4/7-2-4 codetypes are characterized by chronic, deeply ingrained depressive features in conjunction with extensive feelings of inadequacy and guilt. They are self-deprecating and try to make others feel superior by focusing on their weaknesses and inadequacies. They refuse to recognize their extensive dependency on others. The clinical extreme of the behavior shown by these clients is a psychotic depressive reaction, although few clients with this codetype are diagnosed as such.

They report financial difficulties, marital problems, and problems with alcohol. Because of the chronic, deep-seated nature of their problems and their reluctance to expose themselves to anxiety, prognosis for significant behavior change is poor. Treatment aimed at alleviating the depressive features may be most beneficial for short-term goals.

Clients with 2-7-8/7-2-8 codetypes often appear in psychiatric settings. These clients have multiple neurotic symptoms that are of a chronic nature. Their major symptoms include depression, nervousness, and obsessions. They are ruminatively introspective and evidence excessive indecision, doubts, and worry. They complain of difficulties in concentration and thinking. There is a real question of whether these multiple neurotic symptoms actually mask a thought disorder. Hence, careful evaluation for a thought disorder is indicated.

They may have suicidal ruminations; these need to be evaluated carefully. Again, clinicians are reminded to review the client's responses to items 150, 506, 520, and 524 on the MMPI-2. Such clients are withdrawn and socially introverted, and these characteristics exacerbate their obsessive and ruminative behaviors. Psychopharmacologic intervention is indicated frequently. Psychotherapeutic interventions should initially be directed toward solving the client's immediate problems and should avoid any introspective type of self-analysis.

Additional interpretive information on 2-7/7-2 codetypes and their triads may be found in Gilberstadt and Duker (1965), Gynther and colleagues (1973), Kelley and King (1979c, 1980), and Marks and associates (1974). Tables 6–17 and D–16 provide the prototypic scores.

2-8/8-2

Since there are a number of differences in the observed correlates of 2-8 and 8-2 codetypes, each will be described separately. These different correlates are somewhat surprising since the prototypes for 2-8 and 8-2 codetypes are very similar and consequently only one prototype is provided for the 2-8/8-2 codetype.

Clients with 8-2 codetypes scored one-half standard deviation higher or more on the following scales in Table D–17 than clients with 2-8 codetypes: the total T score difference on the Wiener and Harmon (Wiener, 1948) Obvious and Subtle subscales; the total number of the Lachar and Wrobel (1979) critical items endorsed; Scales F, 6 (Paranoia), and 0 (Social Introversion); and the Wiggins (1966) Content scales of Depression, Organic Symptoms, and Psychoticism. Clients with 8-2 codetypes appear to be reporting more psychological distress and to have a slightly higher probability of being psychotic. This pattern of scores is consistent with the differences in correlates reported below for these two codetypes.

Clients with 2-8 codetypes are experiencing severe depression with associated anxiety and agitation. They frequently fear loss of control. Their depression and agitation are usually sufficient to produce confusion, forgetfulness, and difficulties in concentration and attention. They often display obsessive ruminations. Evaluation for a thought disorder may be appropriate. Somatic complaints are common, such as difficulty in sleeping or fatigue. These clients tend to withdraw and isolate themselves from interpersonal relationships and activities, which will exacerbate their symptomatology.

Suicidal ideation is a prominent feature and suicide attempts are quite frequent; suicide potential should be evaluated carefully as well as the client's responses to items 150, 506, 520, and 524 on the MMPI-2. This codetype represents a chronic level of adjustment of marginal quality, so prognosis for intervention and change is poor.

Clients with 8-2 codetypes are more likely to evidence actual schizophrenic features in addition to the behaviors just described. Auditory and/or visual hallucinations and systematized delusions may be present. A careful evaluation for a thought disorder should be made. Somatic symptoms of a bizarre nature may be seen.

These clients also are depressed, isolated, and withdrawn. Suicidal ruminations

TABLE 6–17   Prototypic Scores for *2-7/7-2* Codetypes in Psychiatric Settings

		MMPI			*MMPI-2*	
Demographics						
		M	*SD*		*M*	*SD*
N	391			418		
Age		40.3	12.7		38.8	12.8
Men	75.2%			58.2%		
Women	24.8			41.8		
Test-Taking Scales/Indexes						
		M	*SD*		*M*	*SD*
Inconsistent		10.1%			4.5%	
Total (Obvious-Subtle)[a]		82.1	50.6		111.1	55.2
Critical items[b]		38.3	10.5		40.3	10.9
Overreported[c]		21.4%			34.8%	
Underreported[c]		4.7%			0.7%	
Standard Validity and Clinical Scales (K-Corrected)						
		M	*SD*		*M*	*SD*
?[d]		4.6	6.1		4.3	5.9
L		49.8	7.3		51.8	10.1
F		62.9	8.4		66.8	14.3
K		48.9	7.2		42.7	7.8
1(Hs)		65.9	11.5		63.5	11.1
2(D)		89.8	11.3		84.3	9.7
3(Hy)		68.0	9.7		64.5	11.5
4(Pd)		70.5	9.8		63.8	10.2
5(Mf)		57.7	10.4		48.9	10.4
6(Pa)		66.1	9.4		63.0	11.1
7(Pt)		85.2	9.2		82.0	9.2
8(Sc)		74.4	11.2		69.6	11.0
9(Ma)		54.4	9.7		49.1	8.8
0(Si)		68.9	8.2		67.8	9.0
Supplementary Scales						
		M	*SD*		*M*	*SD*
A		69.9	8.1		72.8	8.1
R		71.7	13.0		60.6	11.3
MAC/MAC-R[d]						
men		24.5	4.6		24.5	4.8
women		19.6	3.5		20.0	3.7

Codetype Concordance

	Men	Women		Men	Women
MMPI-2 *2-7/7-2*	65.4%	93.9%	MMPI *2-7/7-2*	78.9%	52.0%
			2-8/8-2	12.0	10.7
			2-4/4-2		10.2

[a] See Chapter 3, Table 3–24, for explanation of how this index is computed.

[b] The total number of Lachar and Wrobel (1979) critical items endorsed.

[c] Percentage of patients within this codetype scoring above the 75th percentile or below the 25th percentile on the total T score difference on the Wiener and Harmon Obvious and Subtle subscales for all patients (see Tables 3–45 and 3–46 for the cutting scores for the MMPI-2 and MMPI, respectively).

[d] Raw score.

and suicide attempts are quite frequent; suicide potential should be evaluated carefully as well as the client's responses to items 150, 506, 520, and 524 on the MMPI-2. This is a chronic pattern of adjustment that usually results in psychiatric hospitalization.

Gilberstadt and Duker (1965), Gynther and colleagues (1973), Kelley and King (1979b, 1980), and Marks and colleagues (1974) provide additional interpretive information on *2-8/8-2* codetypes. Table D–17 provides the prototypic scores.

2-9/9-2

Clients with *2-9/9-2* codetypes demonstrate an interesting example of a clinical scale configuration that might not be anticipated: clients who simultaneously evidence significant depression and hypomanic tendencies. It is frequently stated that *2-9/9-2* codetypes are characteristic of brain-damaged individuals (cf. Lachar, 1974), but subsequent research has not been able to replicate these findings (see Farr & Martin [1988] for a review of this research).

Clients with a *2-9/9-2* codetype are likely to embody a hypomanic process that is no longer sufficient to obscure their depressive features, at least on the MMPI. They may evidence a severe, agitated depression, although the depressive features may be masked by their activity level. These clients are narcissistically absorbed in their ruminations and may evidence a psychotic process. If a bipolar disorder is identified, psychopharmacologic intervention is indicated. Otherwise, psychological intervention is probably best directed toward the depressive features.

Table D–18 provides the prototypic scores for *2-9/9-2* codetypes.

2-0/0-2

Clients with *2-0/0-2* codetypes often show mild but chronic levels of depression in conjunction with their socially introverted features. They usually display feelings of inadequacy, shyness, and isolation in social settings; these characteristics reflect their actual ineptitude in and lack of social skills. They generally are passive, conventional individuals who are unlikely to display either aggressive or delinquent behaviors.

Although they are unhappy and worried, their depression is chronically ingrained and they have little motivation to change. Essentially they have adjusted to their depressive state, and engaging them in psychotherapeutic endeavors may be difficult. Directly addressing their lack of social skills through assertiveness training, role playing, or similar approaches may be beneficial in helping them form meaningful interpersonal relationships.

Interpretive information on *2-0/0-2* codetypes is found in Kelley and King (1979a), and Table D–19 provides the prototypic scores.

Spike 3

Clients who elevate only Scale *3* (Hysteria) are characteristically socially conventional individuals who emphasize their harmony with other people and express an almost unassailable optimism. Even when faced with overwhelming failure in their life, they maintain that everything is going fine. They are unwilling to express any type of feelings of anger. They believe that they think clearly and logically, while others perceive them to be flighty and unfocused.

They are typically immature and egocentric, and display other histrionic features. When under stress, they develop physical complaints that have obvious secondary gain characteristics. They are extremely resistant to entertaining the idea that psychological factors could in any way be involved in their current problems. Prognosis for significant behavior change is unlikely unless they can be involved in long-term psychotherapy. Generally, they will terminate any professional contact once they have weathered their current crisis.

Table D–20 provides the prototypic scores for Spike *3* codetypes.

3-1

Clients with a *3-1* codetype characteristically develop physical symptoms when under stress. When the stress is alleviated, the physical complaints will disappear, only to reappear when the client again experiences stress. There is rather obvious secondary gain to their complaints. When physical symptoms do appear, they are relatively restricted and specific both in location and nature, frequently involving pain in the extremities or the head.

Some anxiety and nervousness usually occur and are not controlled by their somatic preoccupations. When emotional reactions occur, they are of short duration and expressed by crying and emotional lability. When the *L* and/or *K* scales also are elevated, these clients are likely to be extremely defensive, presenting themselves as exceedingly normal. Such clients are very threatened by any suggestion of psychological problems. They are very unlikely to be psychotic.

Additional interpretive information on *3-1* codetypes is available in Gilberstadt and Duker (1965), Gynther and associates (1973), Marks and associates (1974), and Prokop (1988). Table D–21 provides the prototypic scores.

3-4/4-3

Clients with *3-4* codetypes have been found to display different correlates than clients with *4-3* codetypes, so each of these will be described in turn. These different correlates are somewhat surprising since the prototypes for *3-4* and *4-3* codetypes are virtually identical and do not show even the few differences that were found with *2-8/8-2* codetypes. Consequently, only one prototype is provided for the *3-4/4-3* codetype.

These clients tend to be defensive, guarded, and unwilling to acknowledge psychological problems even when they are readily apparent to others. They report little psychological or emotional distress and describe themselves as less depressed and anxious than do most psychiatric patients. Behavioral problems are more likely to occur in this codetype than in any other codetype that includes Scale *3*.

The relationship between Scales *3* and *4* serves as an index of whether persons will control and inhibit their socially unacceptable impulses, particularly aggression and hostility. Clients with a *3-4* codetype are immature, egocentric individuals who discharge their hostile feelings indirectly. Overtly, they appear to be quiet and conforming. They may become involved with acting-out individuals and satisfy their own hostile tendencies in a vicarious fashion.

Males may express fears of being homosexual, if Scale *5* also is elevated, but they are unlikely to have overtly acted out their homosexual impulses. They report marital or family problems with little understanding of their role in them. These clients generally have chronic problems that are difficult to change.

Clients with a *4-3* codetype are characterized by poorly controlled anger and hostility that is expressed in a cyclic fashion. Often these clients are eventually incarcerated for their violent acts. The presence of violent, acting-out behavior in these persons has been replicated in several studies (Davis & Sines, 1971; Persons & Marks, 1971). Buck and Graham (1978) failed to replicate this finding; this is not surprising, however, since Buck and Graham used a different population than the other studies.

Clients with a *4-3* codetype are quiet, withdrawn individuals, and their sudden outbursts come as a surprise to others. They display poor judgment under stress, but their emotional or violent outbursts may be only minimally related to external stress or provocation. Their outbursts are not illogical or irrational unless Scale 8 also is elevated. The cyclic pattern of violent outbursts with intermittent periods of appropriate behavior represents a chronic and stable personality disorder that is extremely difficult to change. Davis and Sines (1971) could not find any lasting effects of any form of psychological intervention or incarceration.

Gilberstadt and Duker (1965) and Kelley and King (1979a) provide additional interpretive information on 3-4/4-3 codetypes, and Table D–22 provides the prototypic scores.

3-5/5-3

There is little information on 3-5/5-3 codetypes. College-educated males with histrionic features would be expected to achieve this codetype. They see themselves as being well adjusted, happy, calm, and self-confident. Others see them as manipulative, crafty, immature, and demanding. They do not report behavioral problems or getting into trouble because of their behavior. They have many physical problems, and they may be narcissistic. They are seldom self-referred.

Interpretive information on this codetype is found in Tanner (1990). Table D–23 provides the prototypic scores for 3-5/5-3 codetypes.

3-6/6-3

Clients with 3-6/6-3 codetypes are seen as angry, hostile individuals who attempt to deny or rationalize these feelings. They deny their hostility and suspiciousness, even though these attributes are apparent to everyone but themselves. Their anger and hostility are frequently directed toward family members, often in indirect, passive ways. They often deny and resent any kind of psychological interpretation of their problems. They perceive their relationships in positive terms

and have difficulty understanding why others react to them the way they do.

The hostility, egocentricity, and uncooperativeness become readily apparent in any relationship of more than a casual nature. Such individuals are unwilling to consider that psychological factors might be involved in their interpersonal problems. The possibility of paranoid or psychotic features should be evaluated, even though these features are relatively unusual. The prognosis for significant behavior change is poor.

Table D–24 provides the prototypic scores for 3-6/6-3 codetypes.

3-7/7-3

Clients with 3-7/7-3 codetypes are tense, anxious individuals who develop chronic physical ailments in the head or the extremities resulting from psychological stress and conflicts. They tend to highly ruminative and obsessive. Despite the overt behavioral evidence of tension and anxiety, they will deny the existence of psychological problems and be unconcerned about their physical ailments. They are fearful and frequently phobic. They feel depressed and have problems sleeping.

Their lack of insight into their histrionic mechanisms makes psychological intervention slow and arduous at best.

Table D–25 provides the prototypic scores for 3-7/7-3 codetypes.

3-8/8-3

Clients with 3-8/8-3 codetypes are seen as strange and peculiar individuals who complain of difficulties in thinking and concentration. They are likely to be experiencing significant psychological distress despite their attempts to deny and repress problems. Psychological stress is converted into physical symptoms, which may consist of headaches, insomnia, fatigue, or bizarre complaints.

They display histrionic features, such as immaturity, egocentricity, and dependency, as well as hostility, tension, and worry. They may actually be psychotic, and the possibility of a thought disorder should be evaluated carefully. When psychotic reactions are seen, there are infantile, narcissistic qualities accompanied by behavioral regression. They are often emotionally inappropriate, apathetic, and fearful.

Supportive procedures that bolster the histrionic defenses are frequently sufficient to weather the current crisis. Any form of insight-oriented psychotherapy should be considered carefully because of the possibility of an underlying psychotic process.

Marks and colleagues (1974) furnish additional interpretive information on this codetype, and Table D–26 provides the prototypic scores.

3-9/9-3

Clients with *3-9/9-3* codetypes are gregarious, dramatic, outgoing individuals who readily make their presence known in any social setting. This configuration becomes particularly pathognomic if Scale *0* (Social Introversion) approaches a T score of 30 (see Scale *0* in Chapter 4). These clients report acute attacks of physical symptoms, such as chest pains, cardiovascular problems, and headaches. The symptoms improve rapidly with medical intervention only to recur at a later date. These clients are hostile, irritable, and emotionally labile.

They are unwilling to examine psychological factors in their behavior and will forget treatment once their physical symptoms abate.

Kelley and King (1979a) provide additional interpretive information on *3-9/9-3* codetypes, and Table D–27 provides the prototypic scores.

3-0/0-3

There is little information on *3-0/0-3* codetypes. The underlying processes tapped by these two scales should be antithetical, and the infrequent occurrence of this codetype seems to support this contention. The rarity of occurrence is all the more remarkable since other scales that supposedly tap antithetical processes are not infrequently seen, such as *2-9/9-2* and *4-7/7-4*.

These clients describe themselves as being very conventional, law-abiding individuals who do not get in trouble because of their behavior. They are very shy, withdrawn, and socially reserved. They tend to isolate themselves and avoid interacting with others. They are not experiencing any degree of psychological or emotional distress.

Table D–28 provides the prototypic scores for *3-0/0-3* codetypes.

Spike 4

Clients who elevate only Scale *4* (Psychopathic Deviate) may show impulsive behavior, rebelliousness, and poor relationships with authority figures. They are likely to be seen as egocentric, lacking insight, and shallow in their feelings for others. They have a low tolerance for frustration, and this quality combined with poorly controlled anger and poor self-control often results in outbursts of physical aggression. They form quick, superficial relationships, but have difficulty in more intimate interpersonal relationships.

Scale *0* is typically low (see Table 6–5 [MMPI] or Table 6–10 [MMPI-2]), and these qualities become more pathognomic as Scale *0* approaches a T score of 30. Problems with substance abuse are quite frequent, and the MacAndrew Alcoholism scale (see Chapter 5) should be scored for these individuals if it not routinely scored.

These clients are rarely self-referred; rather a social agency usually refers them. As soon as the social agency no longer requires treatment, the client will discontinue therapy. The psychopathic qualities found in these clients make them poor candidates for psychotherapy. They conceive of themselves as being better than other people, externalize blame for their problems onto others, and have little insight into their own behavior.

These psychopathic qualities tend to be alleviated by age; maturation is often seen as a viable though long-term treatment alternative. If they do not change with age, some form of vocational counseling and career guidance that draws on the clients' "skills and talents" may be useful. A low Scale 2 (T score ≤ 50) in combination with a Spike 4 codetype of even moderate elevation indicates an especially low probability of behavior change.

Several investigators have reported that Spike 4 codetypes occur frequently in college students and have questioned whether new norms are needed (cf. Goodstein, 1954). King and Kelley (1977a) found in their college student sample that Spike 4 codetypes were indicative of significant psychopathology, and they concluded that new norms were not needed in their psychiatric outpatient clinic.

For interpretive information on Spike 4 codetypes, consult Gilberstadt and Duker (1965) and King and Kelley (1977a), and see Table D–29 for prototypic scores.

4-5/5-4

Clients with 4-5/5-4 codetypes are almost always men because of the infrequency with which women elevate Scale 5 on the MMPI above a T score of 70. The one major exception to this statement is the finding by Sutker, Allain, and Geyer (1978) that this MMPI codetype was the most frequent (23 percent) among women convicted of murder. It does not appear that women are much more likely to produce this codetype on the MMPI-2 (see Table 6–7).

These clients are very satisfied with themselves and their behavior. They also are very defensive and guarded about revealing themselves. As a consequence, they report lit-

tle emotional distress. They think clearly and rationally and report good insight into their behavior.

Males with 4-5/5-4 codetypes are passively unconventional, usually in both their appearance and their behavior. They are rebelling against social conventions and mores and delight in defying and challenging any form of rule or regulation. Both dominance and dependence are key issues for them, and the supplementary scales for measuring these traits should be scored (see Chapter 5).

Although they have strong needs for dependency, they fear domination by significant others. They may be concerned about homoerotic impulses, and a subset of persons with this codetype will be actively homosexual. These active homosexuals display this codetype only if they want to acknowledge openly their homosexual status. If they so desire, they can deny the presence of homosexual impulses or behaviors without being detected by any validity or clinical scale configuration. Hence, the detection of homosexual behavior in 4-5/5-4 codetypes is best accomplished when the clinician directly asks the client about such activity. Erickson, Luxenberg, Walbek, and Seely (1987) reported that 4-5/5-4 codetypes were among the most frequent in their sample of sex offenders.

Male college students with 4-5/5-4 codetypes are described as experiencing general interpersonal difficulties of a transient nature with only slight indications of a significant personality disorder (King & Kelley, 1977b). Although these students are passive and experiencing heterosexual adjustment problems, homosexuality is not characteristic of them.

The probability for significant behavior change is poor because of the chronic, ingrained nature of their personality features.

King and Kelley (1977b) and Tanner (1990) provide interpretive information about 4-5/5-4 codetypes, and Table D–30 provides the prototypic scores.

4-6/6-4

Clients with *4-6/6-4* codetypes are angry, resentful, argumentative individuals who are difficult to interact with personally or socially because of these characteristics. They usually are able to control the acting out of their hostility but do exhibit violent outbursts on occasion. They will externalize blame for their anger. They often express rather vague emotional and physical complaints and they report feeling depressed and anxious. They are suspicious of the motives of other people, and the likelihood of paranoid features should be examined closely.

These clients have a long history of severe social maladjustment with poor work histories. Poor interpersonal relationships as well as marital problems are quite common. They are difficult to interact with because of their hostile attitudes and behaviors. Consequently, they are poor candidates for any type of psychological intervention. In women with a *4-6/6-4* codetype it is important to know the elevation on Scale *5* to understand how these behaviors will be exhibited (see page 163).

When Scale *8* is also elevated in this *4-6/6-4* codetype, the process is even more malignant. In addition to the above characteristics, these clients are even more evasive and defensive about admitting any form of psychological problem, and difficulties in logic and judgment begin to appear. They seethe with anger, which in conjunction with their sensitivity to criticism and suspiciousness can lead to unpredictable and irrational violent outbursts. They are likely to be openly defiant and hostile. Their solution for behavior change is to have others change to meet their expectations.

Additional interpretive information is available in Marks and associates (1974), and Table D–31 provides the prototypic scores for *4-6/6-4* codetypes.

4-7/7-4

Clients with *4-7/7-4* codetypes are an example of the apparently paradoxic elevation of two antithetical scales. Since Scale *4* (Psychopathic Deviate) assesses persons' insensitivity to and disregard of the social consequences of their behavior, and Scale *7* (Psychasthenia) assesses persons' excessive concern about and analysis of their own behavior, it does not seem likely that simultaneous elevations on these two scales should occur. Nevertheless, they do.

The primary characteristic of these clients is cyclic behavior between these two extremes. It is as if Scale *4* characteristics become dominant for a period of time and the clients act out impulsively with little regard for social conventions and the needs and wishes of other people. Following these periods of acting out, the Scale *7* characteristics become dominant, and the clients will feel guilty, remorseful, and self-deprecating about having exhibited such behaviors. They appear to be overcontrolled during this phase, but these controls are not sufficient to prevent recurrences of acting out.

The clinician will encounter these clients during their guilty, remorseful phase, and the clinician is likely to believe that significant therapeutic progress is being made. All too often, however, these individuals will again act out impulsively and return feeling more guilty, and so on. Successfully intervening in this behavior cycle is extremely difficult without a long-term therapeutic relationship.

Kelley and King (1979a) provide interpretive information on *4-7/7-4* codetypes, and Table D–32 provides the prototypic scores.

4-8/8-4

Clients with *4-8/8-4* codetypes are typically characterized by a chronic marginal schizoid adjustment if they are not actually schizophrenic. They have difficulty with close, emotional relationships, distrust others, and are socially withdrawn. They are dissatisfied with their relationships with other people, but their angry, resentful qualities, which they have difficulty modulating or expressing, only serve to exacerbate their alienation from others. They see the world as dangerous and other people as rejecting and unreliable. They are moody and emotionally inappropriate. Suicide attempts are quite frequent and should be evaluated carefully. Clinicians should note the client's responses to items 150, 506, 520, and 524 on the MMPI-2.

Their behavior is typically unpredictable and nonconforming at best. They frequently get into social and legal difficulties because of their judgment and their problems in logic and thinking. A history of criminal activity with numerous arrests is common. Their crimes are often poorly planned and executed and may involve bizarre or violent behaviors. This is a frequent codetype among child molesters (Hall, Maiuro, Vitaliano, & Proctor, 1986; McCreary, 1975), rapists (Armentrout & Hauer, 1978), rapists and exposers (Rader, 1977), sex offenders (Erickson et al., 1987). These clients are chronically maladjusted, which indicates that any form of psychological intervention will be of limited benefit.

Additional interpretive information on 4-8/8-4 codetypes may be found in Gynther and colleagues (1973) and Marks and colleagues (1974), and Table D–33 provides the prototypic scores.

4-9/9-4

Clients with 4-9/9-4 codetypes are likely to display some form of acting-out behavior. The hypomania seemingly energizes or activates the behaviors assessed by Scale 4 (Psychopathic Deviate). These clients are overactive, impulsive, irresponsible, and untrustworthy. Their interpersonal relationships are shallow and superficial. They exhibit an enduring tendency to get into trouble, usually only in a way that damages their own or their family's reputation, although antisocial and criminal acts are not uncommon.

This codetype is common in clients with marital problems, illegitimate pregnancies, child abuse (Paulson, Afifi, Thomason, & Chaleff, 1974), alcohol or drug abuse (Greene & Garvin, 1988; Hodo & Fowler, 1976; Loper, Kammeier, & Hoffmann, 1973), delinquency, repeated crimes of indecent exposure (McCreary, 1975), and sex offenders (Erickson et al., 1987; Hall et al., 1986).

These clients have an inordinate need for excitement, and their acting out frequently serves these purposes. They temporarily create a favorable impression because they are socially facile and are free from anxiety, worry, and guilt. Their judgment, however, is notably poor, and they do not seem to learn from experience. They lack the ability to postpone gratification and have difficulty in any activity requiring sustained effort. Sheppard, Smith, and Rosenbaum (1988) found that 50 percent of their patients within a 4-9/9-4 cluster type did not complete a 30-day alcohol treatment program.

Acting out is the primary defense mechanism used by these individuals, although rationalization also plays an important role. When Scales 6 and 8 are also elevated and with higher elevations on Scale 9, there is an increased probability of acting-out episodes that may be quite intense and violent. These persons exhibit very stable personality patterns, and they have poor prognosis for behavior change or even participation in therapy.

Huesmann, Lefkowitz, and Eron (1978) reported that the sum of the T scores on Scales F, 4, and 9 was a valid predictor of aggression in older adolescents. Normal males ($M = 183.3$) and females ($M = 178.9$) scored significantly lower than delinquent males ($M = 217.4$) and females ($M = 237.7$) on this index. Huesmann and associates did not report standard deviations by group or gender; they stated that the composite standard deviation was about 25. Since there is substantial overlap in these distributions, it remains to be seen how useful this index will be for predicting aggression in individual clients.

Additional interpretive information on *4-9/9-4* codetypes is reported by Gilberstadt and Duker (1965), Gynther and colleagues (1973), King and Kelley (1977a), and Marks and colleagues (1974). Tables 6–18 and D–34 provide the prototypic scores.

4-0/0-4

Clients with *4-0/0-4* codetypes are statistically rare (see Tables 6–1 to 6–4). In fact, this codetype is so unusual that it is not listed in any of the major MMPI references. Theoretically, this infrequency of occurrence makes sense because psychopathic persons who typically elevate Scale *4* (Psychopathic Deviate) are unconcerned and lack anxiety about interpersonal relationships and consequently should score low on Scale *0* (Social Introversion). Hence, at a theoretical level, no specific classification of psychopathology would be expected to show this particular codetype.

These clients are experiencing little emotional distress and they are generally free from anxiety and guilt. They are in good physical health. They report problems interacting with their family members and persons in positions of authority.

They are shy, retiring individuals who avoid social interactions. They tend to be very conventional and do not get into trouble because of their behavior.

Table D–35 provides the prototypic scores for *4-0/0-4* codetypes.

Spike *5*

There is little information on the empirical correlates of elevations on Scale *5* (Masculin-

ity-Femininity). The paucity of data reflects the fact that Scale *5* was not among the original clinical scales, and thus it was not included in the early clinical research on the MMPI. Only King and Kelley (1977b) and Tanner (1990) have examined the behavioral correlates of codetypes in which Scale *5* is one of the high-point scales.

In addition, Scale *5* is a frequently occurring high-point only in normal college educated men with liberal arts majors and avowed homosexuals who are not trying to hide their homoerotic behavior. The former group is rarely of interest to most clinical researchers, and the latter group is only starting to be recognized and evaluated. The psychometric qualities of Scale *5* on the MMPI make it very difficult for women to have this scale as a high point (it is unusual for most women to score above a T score of 60).

Finally, it is the least well-developed and standardized scale of the individual scales on the MMPI, which also has contributed to its lack of attention. It remains to be see whether Scale *5* will fare any better on the MMPI-2.

These clients describe themselves as self-confident, easygoing, and assured. They relate easily to others and will make a good impression on them. They are in good physical health and experiencing few psychological problems.

King and Kelley (1977b) found that student outpatients at a university mental health center with Spike *5* codetypes were generally normal students with no significant psychopathology despite their seeking treatment.

More information on Spike *5* codetypes is available in King and Kelley (1977b), and Table D–36 provides the prototypic scores.

5-6/6-5

There is little information *5-6/6-5* codetypes. These clients are reluctant to expose themselves to others and they frequently are described as being guarded, resistant, aloof, impulsive, abrasive, irritable, and easily an-

TABLE 6–18 Prototypic Scores for *4-9/9-4* Codetypes in Psychiatric Settings

				MMPI-2		
Demographics						
		M	*SD*		*M*	*SD*
N	522			318		
Age		30.6	12.3		29.9	11.8
Men	75.1%			73.0%		
Women	24.9			27.0		
Test-Taking Scales/Indexes						
		M	*SD*		*M*	*SD*
Inconsistent		3.0%			2.9%	
Total (Obvious-Subtle)[a]		20.2	56.9		46.6	60.0
Critical items[b]		32.2	12.1		33.7	12.4
Overreported[c]		2.7%			9.4%	
Underreported[c]		28.3%			20.1%	
Standard Validity and Clinical Scales (K-Corrected)						
		M	*SD*		*M*	*SD*
?[d]		4.5	5.9		3.8	5.0
L		48.9	7.0		50.8	9.9
F		63.6	10.5		67.3	16.1
K		51.3	8.0		45.9	8.7
1(Hs)		54.5	9.5		52.6	10.0
2(D)		56.0	9.9		53.2	9.6
3(Hy)		58.0	8.6		52.2	10.0
4(Pd)		81.3	7.3		76.1	7.7
5(Mf)		55.3	9.6		47.2	9.6
6(Pa)		62.4	9.9		57.6	10.9
7(Pt)		59.8	8.7		55.5	9.5
8(Sc)		65.4	9.5		60.1	10.0
9(Ma)		79.3	7.2		75.7	8.0
0(Si)		47.7	7.1		45.4	7.7
Supplementary Scales						
		M	*SD*		*M*	*SD*
A		54.5	9.9		57.2	10.3
R		52.5	10.2		43.4	8.9
MAC/MAC-R[d]						
men		31.0	3.8		31.4	3.7
women		28.1	4.1		27.9	3.8

Codetype Concordance

	Men	Women		Men	Women
MMPI-2 *4-9/9-4*	55.8%	64.6%	MMPI *4-9/9-4*	89.7%	96.6%
Spike *9*	15.8				

[a] See Chapter 3, Table 3–24, for explanation of how this index is computed.

[b] The total number of Lachar and Wrobel (1979) critical items endorsed.

[c] Percentage of patients within this codetype scoring above the 75th percentile or below the 25th percentile on the total T score difference on the Wiener and Harmon Obvious and Subtle subscales for all patients (see Tables 3–45 and 3–46 for the cutting scores for the MMPI-2 and MMPI, respectively).

[d] Raw score.

gered. They have difficulties with social relationships, especially heterosexual relationships.

They have little insight into their own behavior since they describe themselves as being happy, self-confident, and as having good judgment. They have strong religious and political beliefs that they express directly. They see themselves as mixing easily and enjoying being in social situations.

Interpretive information on *5-6/6-5* codetypes is provided by Tanner (1990), and Table D-37 provides the prototypic scores for *5-6/6-5* codetypes.

5-7/7-5

Clients with *5-7/7-5* codetypes are more likely to be depressed than anxious. They have restricted affect and lack spontaneity. They are bothered by recurring thoughts and ideas and mild depressive symptoms. They are easily excited. They are in good physical health.

These clients are shy, bashful, and easily embarrassed. They are more sensitive than most people and their feelings are easily hurt. They have interpersonal and/or heterosexual difficulties.

See King and Kelley (1977b) and Tanner (1990) for more information. Table D-38 provides the prototypic scores for *5-7/7-5* codetypes.

5-8/8-5

Clients with *5-8/8-5* codetypes are likely to have a family history of alcohol abuse, mental illness, and physical abuse. They frequently have long psychiatric histories that began in childhood. They report reactive depression, paresthesia, and religious preoccupations but have intact thought processes. They can be described as odd, eccentric individuals who have difficulty making emotional contact with others. They report numerous conflicts over sexuality both in

themselves and in their relationships with others. They also have many family problems. They are shy, reserved individuals who avoid interpersonal contact.

More information is presented in King and Kelley (1977b) and Tanner (1990). Table D-39 provides the prototypic scores for *5-8/8-5* codetypes.

5-9/9-5

There is little information on *5-9/9-5* codetypes. These clients are very comfortable with themselves and their behavior. They do not report any form of psychological problems, emotional distress, or physical symptoms. They like to keep active and become bored easily; hyperactive thoughts and behaviors are possible. They describe themselves as self-confident, easygoing, and assured. They relate easily to others and make a good social impression, but they have extremely unstable heterosexual relationships. These clients prefer to be leaders rather than followers in any activity. They seldom are self-referred. They tend to use alcohol to reduce anxiety with a relatively high incidence of violence when drinking.

See Tanner (1990) for additional information. Table D-40 provides the prototypic scores for *5-9/9-5* codetypes.

5-0/0-5

There is little information for *5-0/0-5* codetypes. These clients see themselves as extremely well adjusted. They do not report any psychological problems, emotional distress, or physical symptoms; they do not appear to be defensive or guarded. They describe themselves as happy and contented with their lives. Clients are socially introverted and tend to withdraw from social contact. They are easily embarrassed in social situations. They rarely get into trouble because of their behavior.

Table D–41 provides the prototypic scores for *5-0/0-5* codetypes.

Spike *6*

Clients who elevate only Scale *6* (Paranoia) are relatively rare. Since the item content on Scale *6* is obvious, the paranoid symptomatology is usually evident in clients with Spike *6* profiles, particularly if the Dominance scale is higher than the Dependency scale on the MMPI (see Chapter 5). The possibility of a paranoid process should be evaluated. These clients are suspicious, distrustful, and project blame for their problems onto others.

Table D–42 provides the prototypic scores for Spike *6* codetypes.

6-7/7-6

Clients with *6-7/7-6* codetypes are anxious, worried, suspicious individuals. They are also rigid, hypersensitive, and stubborn. They brood and ruminate over both their own and others' behavior. They express hostile feelings indirectly. They are unlikely to be actually paranoid. Their problems tend to be chronic and characterologic in nature.

They tend to keep people at a distance and to have poor social judgment. Their hypersensitivity and tendency to misinterpret the statements and behaviors of others often leads to volatile and distant relationships.

Kelley and King (1979a) provide interpretive information on *6-7/7-6* codetypes, and Table D–43 provides the prototypic scores.

6-8/8-6

Clients with *6-8/8-6* codetypes are likely to evidence a thought disorder with paranoid features as in paranoid schizophrenia. Systematized delusions may be present. Such individuals express significant personal stress through their complaints of tension, worry, depression, and so on. They are socially isolated and withdrawn. Any social relationship that they do maintain will be tinged with resentment, suspiciousness, and hostility.

Their behavior is frequently unpredictable and socially inappropriate. They may be preoccupied about and ruminate over abstract, theoretical issues, religion, and sexual themes. General apathy may permeate all of their behavior. Behavioral regression, autistic thought processes, inappropriate affect, and bizarre associations may be seen. Difficulties in concentration and attention, memory deficits, and poor judgment are quite common.

These clients are severely and chronically maladjusted even if they are not actually psychotic. They are suspicious and distrustful of others and have poor social skills. They generally feel apathetic, socially isolated, and withdrawn.

Gilberstadt and Duker (1965), Gynther and colleagues (1973), and Marks and colleagues (1974) present further interpretive information on *6-8/8-6* codetypes. Tables 6–19 and D–44 provide the prototypic scores.

6-9/9-6

Clients with *6-9/9-6* codetypes are usually encountered only in inpatient settings. They are angry, hostile individuals who may exhibit grandiosity and egocentricity. They are also irritable, excited, and energetic. They may report difficulty thinking and concentrating, and exercise poor judgment.

The presence of a psychotic process that is more likely to reflect a mood disorder than a thought disorder should be considered. They describe themselves as happy, calm, easygoing, and in good physical health. Others see them as angry, hostile, and overresponsive to minor stresses and problems; less frequently they are seen as tense and anxious.

Further information is found in Gynther and associates (1973) and Marks and associates (1974). Table D–45 provides the prototypic scores for *6-9/9-6* codetypes.

TABLE 6–19 Prototypic Scores for *6-8/8-6* Codetypes in Psychiatric Settings

	MMPI			*MMPI-2*	
Demographics					
	M	SD		M	SD
N	678		863		
Age		30.4	12.2	29.8	12.0
Men	67.9%		74.3%		
Women	36.1		25.7		
Test-Taking Scales/Indexes					
	M	SD		M	SD
Inconsistent	43.0%			28.7%	
Total (Obvious-Subtle)[a]	159.6	68.3		202.5	70.8
Critical items[b]	64.0	17.2		66.2	16.5
Overreported[c]	41.1%			84.5%	
Underreported[c]	1.1%			0.5%	
Standard Validity and Clinical Scales (K-Corrected)					
	M	SD		M	SD
?[d]	5.1	6.3		4.8	5.9
L	49.4	7.9		50.5	10.5
F	92.5	14.9		105.0	17.3
K	42.8	7.2		36.3	7.3
1(Hs)	70.3	15.1		69.4	14.3
2(D)	75.8	14.9		73.2	13.2
3(Hy)	67.1	12.1		64.6	15.3
4(Pd)	79.4	12.2		73.7	12.9
5(Mf)	60.3	11.3		54.0	10.5
6(Pa)	95.3	11.4		97.4	13.5
7(Pt)	80.7	13.4		78.0	13.7
8(Sc)	100.5	15.1		96.0	14.5
9(Ma)	75.2	10.9		69.6	12.3
0(Si)	65.5	9.4		65.7	10.2
Supplementary Scales					
	M	SD		M	SD
A	72.0	9.5		76.1	9.6
R	59.2	14.0		49.9	12.2
MAC/MAC-R[d]					
men	28.6	4.4		28.0	4.4
women	25.5	4.4		25.8	4.2

Codetype Concordance

	Men	Women			Men	Women
MMPI-2 *6-8/8-6*	86.1%	75.2%	MMPI	*6-8/8-6*	58.0%	82.6%
				7-8/8-7	12.2	
				4-8/8-4	11.6	
				2-8/8-2	10.9	

[a] See Chapter 3, Table 3–24, for explanation of how this index is computed.

[b] The total number of Lachar and Wrobel (1979) critical items endorsed.

[c] Percentage of patients within this codetype scoring above the 75th percentile or below the 25th percentile on the total T score difference on the Wiener and Harmon Obvious and Subtle subscales for all patients (see Tables 3–45 and 3–46 for the cutting scores for the MMPI-2 and MMPI, respectively).

[d] Raw score.

6-0/0-6

There is little information on *6-0/0-6* codetypes. These clients see themselves as calm, happy, well adjusted, and in good physical health. They believe that they think clearly and have good judgment and memory. They are not experiencing any form of psychological or emotional distress.

They are very shy, bashful, and easily embarrassed in social situations. Their feelings are easily hurt and they are unlikely to be assertive or confrontive with others. They have pleasant relationships with others.

Table D–46 provides the prototypic scores for *6-0/0-6* codetypes.

Spike 7

Clients who elevate only Scale 7 (Psychasthenia) are relatively uncommon because of the extensive item overlap between Scale 7 and the other clinical scales, especially Scales *2* and *8*. Clients with Spike *7* codetypes are seen as mildly tense and anxious. They usually exhibit obsessive-compulsive defenses that are no longer able to handle their problems completely. Phobias, compulsions, and obsessions may be seen. They are easily frightened.

They are very shy, reserved individuals who become embarrassed easily. Their social isolation and fear of social interaction keeps them out of behavioral problems.

These clients have a very stable personality structure, which requires long-term psychological treatment to produce significant behavior change. They are unlikely to require hospitalization, although their symptoms may seriously interfere with their jobs and general interpersonal relationships.

Table D–47 provides the prototypic scores for Spike *7* codetypes.

7-8/8-7

Clients with *7-8/8-7* codetypes share numerous clinical features in common, but scale order is important in understanding their behavior. When Scale *7* is higher than Scale *8*, they are still resisting the establishment of serious thought and behavior disorders. That is, the thoughts and behaviors that they are experiencing are still upsetting and distressing to them, which is a positive clinical sign. When Scale *8* is higher than Scale *7*, they may be adapting to the presence of serious psychopathology, which makes intervention more difficult.

Clients with *7-8/8-7* codetypes are chronically worried, tense, and agitated. They are socially uncomfortable and have poor social skills and judgment. They have difficulty forming close interpersonal relationships and usually are withdrawn, isolated, and introverted. These characteristics exacerbate their obsessive ruminations. They often engage in sexual fantasies and their sexual adjustment is poor. Hall and colleagues (1986) found this codetype to occur frequently in men who sexually assaulted children. They should be evaluated carefully for the presence of a thought disorder; a diagnosis of schizophrenia is very common.

Psychopharmacologic interventions are difficult because of the ingrained nature of their psychological conflicts and because of their difficulty in forming interpersonal relationships.

See Gilberstadt and Duker (1965), Gynther and colleagues (1973), and Kelley and King (1980) for further interpretive information on *7-8/8-7* codetypes. Table D–48 provides the prototypic scores.

7-9/9-7

Clients with *7-9/9-7* codetypes are chronically worried, tense, agitated, and depressed. Their high energy level seems only to enhance their obsessive ruminations. They talk excessively about unconnected ideas, which may be difficult to follow. They may alternate between periods of impulsive acting out and periods of guilt and self-deprecation. The possibility of manic or hypomanic features should be investigated. They find it difficult to relax and interrupt their obsessive ruminations about their fears and problems.

Their interpersonal relationships are often awkward since their inconsiderate and impulsive behavior makes it difficult to establish contact at more than a superficial level. They are immature and self-centered.

Psychopharmacologic intervention may be necessary because of their excessive level of anxiety.

Kelley and King (1979a) provide interpretive information on *7-9/9-7* codetypes, and Table D–49 provides the prototypic scores.

7-0/0-7

Clients with *7-0/0-7* codetypes are uncommon. They report a mild, general dissatisfaction with their lives. Their symptoms tend to be vague and nonspecific. They are unlikely to be psychotic.

They are very shy, reserved individuals who become embarrassed easily. They lack self-confidence and are easily threatened or intimidated by others. Their social isolation and fear of social interaction keeps them out of behavioral problems.

Table D–50 provides the prototypic scores for *7-0/0-7* codetypes.

Spike *8*

Clients who elevate only Scale *8* (Schizophrenia) relate poorly to other people and tend to escape from their own unacceptable impulses into need-fulfillment fantasies. Some original, unusual, or eccentric qualities may be present in their thinking. At best, these clients have abstract theoretical or philosophical interests and a tendency not to conform, although occasionally an intelligent and creative person will produce a Spike *8* codetype. They are confident in social situations and are not self-conscious. They tend to be aloof from others. They believe that their memory, concentration, and judgment are good.

A subset of clients with Spike *8* codetypes manifest serious psychopathology; review of the supplementary scales (see Chapter 5) will assist in their identification. Sexual preoccupation is frequent along with sexual confusion and bizarre sexual fantasies. These clients also are mentally disorganized, have vague goals, are indecisive and unhappy, worry a great deal, and suffer from insomnia. A careful evaluation to rule out the presence of a thought disorder is indicated in all cases.

These clients may be psychotic, with feelings of unreality, memory difficulties, and confused or bizarre thoughts or beliefs. Hallucinations, psychomotor retardation, and withdrawal are possible. A history of psychiatric hospitalizations is common in these clients. The chronic and characterologic nature of the problems represented in a Spike *8* codetype also does not augur well for therapeutic change.

Table D–51 provides the prototypic scores for Spike *8* codetypes.

8-9/9-8

Clients with *8-9/9-8* codetypes evidence serious psychopathology, even when these scales are only slightly elevated above a T score of 65 on the MMPI-2 or a T score of 70 on the MMPI. They have a rapid onset of excitement, confusion, disorientation, and hyperactivity. They may have difficulty thinking and concentrating. They excessively engage in daydreaming and fantasy, and their reality testing may be marginal. They are depressed, anxious, hostile, and irritable. They are unpredictable and prone to act out unexpectedly. Most of these clients have a psychotic process either of a bipolar manic or schizophrenic type. Autistic thinking, hallucinations, and delusions are frequent.

They are fearful of relating to others and focusing on a specific topic or idea, which interferes with their interpersonal relationships both at home and on the job. Their relationships are marked by distrust, suspicion, and anger. They are boastful, emotionally labile, and egocentric.

They are difficult to work with therapeutically because of their social withdrawal and fear of relating to others. They also flit so rapidly from topic to topic that addressing a specific issue in a therapeutic relationship is very difficult.

Gilberstadt and Duker (1965), Gynther and associates (1973), and Marks and colleagues (1974) have additional interpretive information on *8-9/9-8* codetypes. Table D–52 provides the prototypic scores.

8-0/0-8

Clients with *8-0/0-8* codetypes are relatively infrequent despite the common theme of problems with interpersonal relationships that is characteristic of both scales. They describe themselves as being mildly depressed and anxious and getting little pleasure from life. Their family life is conflictual and unsatisfying. They have trouble making decisions and they worry what others may think about the decisions they have made. They are easily frightened and frequently phobic.

These clients are extremely introverted, shy, and bashful. They are withdrawn, socially isolated, and avoid interpersonal relationships. They are very uncomfortable in any type of social setting or interaction. They give up easily and avoid conflict whenever possible.

They are generally nonverbal, which makes a psychotherapeutic relationship difficult. The presence of schizoid features should be considered.

Table D–53 provides the prototypic scores for *8-0/0-8* codetypes.

Spike 9

Clients who elevate only Scale *9* (Hypomania) are impulsive, acting-out individuals with a history of criminal and interpersonal problems. They are extroverted, outgoing, and sociable in their interpersonal relationships, but these relationships have no real depth or intimacy. They are rebellious and hostile, and they have difficulty controlling their impulses. They are grandiose, hyperactive, talkative, and not depressed. They also believe that they have good memory, judgment, and concentration.

These clients are in good physical health and do not tire easily. They may evidence manic features, which should be carefully investigated. Their thought processes may become bizarre during acute hypomanic phases, and they may become extremely belligerent if their grandiose plans are interrupted. If manic features are evident, a psychopharmacologic intervention is indicated.

Further interpretive information is available in Gilberstadt and Duker (1965) on Spike *9* codetypes. Table D–54 provides the prototypic scores.

9-0/0-9

Clients with *9-0/0-9* codetypes are very uncommon. They describe themselves as being happy and well adjusted. They are in good physical health and experience few pains or physical discomforts. They are elated, frequently excited individuals who definitely are not depressed.

These clients tend to be socially shy and withdrawn, although they have adequate social skills. They are egocentric, self-confident, and occasionally grandiose.

Table D–55 provides the prototypic scores for *9-0/0-9* codetypes.

Spike 0

Clients who elevate only Scale *0* (Social Introversion) are relatively unusual. They are experiencing only minor psychological and emotional distress that tends to be chronic in nature. They are easily frightened and frequently phobic. They are in good physical health. They do not get into trouble because of their behavior.

Clients are very shy, bashful, introverted individuals who are easily embarrassed in social situations. They lack self-confidence and are easily overwhelmed by others. They are uncomfortable in any type of interpersonal relationship. Whether this interpersonal dis-comfort represents a schizoid adjustment, a neurotic reaction, or simply a lifestyle preference will have to be determined by understanding the client's history and his or her reason for taking the MMPI-2.

Further interpretive information is available in King and Kelley (1977a) on Spike *0* codetypes. Table D–56 provides the prototypic scores.

CHAPTER 7

Interpreting the MMPI-2 Profile

The preceding chapters have reviewed the common interpretive statements made about specific elevations on the individual validity and clinical scales and have explored the various interscale relationships. Both of these sources of information provide the database used in profile interpretation of the MMPI-2. Consequently, the reader should be thoroughly familiar with the preceding chapters and refer back to specific sections when appropriate and necessary in interpreting individual profiles.

The task of this chapter will be to analyze the interpretive process for MMPI-2 profiles. In addition to a discussion of issues in profile interpretation, two profiles are presented to serve as examples of the interpretive process. Each profile will be interpreted by an individual clinician. This interpretation will then be compared and contrasted with interpretations produced by three computer-based interpretive systems.

PRELIMINARY ISSUES IN PROFILE INTERPRETATION

Several issues should be discussed prior to undertaking an analysis of the process of MMPI-2 interpretation. First, the interpretive process in this chapter will be "blind," that is, done without any additional sources of data about the client. This is not to suggest that the clinician in actual practice should follow such a procedure, but it is necessary here in order to limit the interpretation to a finite, known database. Such a procedure ensures that readers will know what data are used in making the interpretation and that they will become aware of what information can and cannot be obtained from the MMPI-2. There are obviously questions that the clinician cannot answer from the MMPI-2 alone, and this blind analysis should sensitize the clinician to the additional data that are needed to answer these particular questions.

Second, MMPI-2 data, like most clinical data, are amenable to more than one interpretation. Thus, the clinician's task, and the task in the examples provided, is not to find one and only one "correct" interpretation. It is, rather, to find an interpretation of the profile that is internally and theoretically consistent as well as empirically testable.

The focus of this chapter, then, is to explore how interpretations are made rather than to decide which alternative interpretation is "better." The reader should keep this in mind when it appears that only one "correct" interpretation is being made of each profile in this chapter. It is possible that each profile may have an alternative interpretation, and once the reader understands the procedure explained in this chapter, he or she may discover a "better" interpretation. This process of becoming an informed skeptic when interpreting MMPI-2 profiles is strongly encouraged.

Finally, even though the description of the process of analysis is being limited to the MMPI-2, the same general skills and procedures are involved in the interpretation of any clinical material, including the Rorschach, an interview, or dreams. Hopefully, the empirical nature of the MMPI-2 will make understanding of this basic process of interpretation easier. (The interested reader should consult Levy's [1963] text, *Psychological Interpretation*, for a more abstract discussion of this issue.)

THE INTERPRETIVE PROCESS

Even in a blind analysis, basic demographic data on the client whose profile is being interpreted are needed in order to help the clinician determine which reference group to use. At a minimum, the clinician needs to know the client's age, gender, education level, social class, and ethnic group; any of these variables can drastically alter the interpretation of particular scales or entire profiles. For example, a T score of 60 on Scale 9 (Hypomania) may be typical for an adolescent and extremely unusual for a 60-year-old. Thus, only after one knows the basic demographic data is one ready to start interpreting the profile.

The first step in profile interpretation is to insure that the client has endorsed the items in a consistent and accurate manner using the scales and indexes that were described in Chapter 3. Once it has been ascertained that the client has endorsed the items consistently and accurately, the clinician should examine the client's scores on each of the individual validity and clinical scales. For each scale, the clinician needs to decide whether this score is in the normal or deviant range for this particular client. (This procedure will be illustrated for the two sample profile interpretations later in this chapter.)

At this point the clinician should note what a score in this range for each scale means by referring back to the earlier sections of this text. It is important to remember that a score in the normal range on any scale may be as deviant as a score in the deviant range. For example, if the client has recently committed some heinous or bizarre crime and yet the MMPI-2 does not indicate the presence of any guilt, remorse, or depression, these "normal" scores should provide valuable information about the client's personality and potential for significant behavior change.

Each scale should be analyzed sequentially with the notes made on what each score means and any hypotheses recorded that occur to the clinician while proceeding through this process. Once familiar with all of the individual validity and clinical scales, the clinician should make predictions about ensuing scales on the basis of the score on a particular scale.

A frequently occurring example is significant elevations on scales/indexes measuring underreporting of psychopathology (see Chapter 3). When this happens, the clinician should suspect that all of the clinical scales will be somewhat less elevated, since the defensiveness tapped by these scales should serve to conceal the pathology measured by the clinical scales. In such a case the clinician should be more aware of any scales that are elevated significantly since they are atypical.

At this stage of the interpretive process the clinician should be willing to entertain virtually any hypothesis that fits the data. No hypothesis should be summarily dismissed unless there are absolutely no data to support it. This does not mean that great inferential leaps can be made from the data, but it is wise to acknowledge even tenuous hypotheses at this stage.

The neophyte clinician tends to alternate between the two extremes: refusing to make any inferences whatsoever from the data or making such great inferential leaps that virtually no one would give credence to his or her hypothesis. Hopefully, by being aware of these extremes, the clinician can learn to follow a more moderate course and cautiously assert hypotheses about the meaning of scores on particular scales.

A cautionary note concerning base rates (the frequency with which a specific behavior occurs) of reference groups also is in order. If 75 percent of the clients in a specific setting are psychotic, the clinician should realize that any hypothesis stating that the client is not psychotic is going against the base rates.

One also must be wary of making "Barnum"-type statements (Meehl, 1956), which are accurate for virtually everyone in the reference group and hence are meaningless in describing a specific client. Thus, to hypothesize that an acutely psychotic patient is having heterosexual difficulties is neither particularly brilliant nor insightful. On the other hand, the accuracy of such statements should not be ignored, and they should be tailored to make them more specific for the individual.

All too often, once clinicians are familiar with base rates and Barnum-type statements, they avoid any statement that could be even vaguely labeled as such. Unfortunately, such a reaction is much like throwing the baby out with the bath water. The clinician is afraid to make any base rate statement even when it may provide the most accurate appraisal of the situation. For example, if an elevated score on Scale *3* (Hysteria) virtually excludes the possibility of the person's being diagnosed as psychotic, the clinician should

not ignore the data simply because of the base rate.

Thus, the clinician is advised to use Barnum-type statements that have virtually 0 percent or 100 percent applicability only when they provide the most accurate appraisal of the client, and they should be individualized insofar as possible.

The next step in the process of interpreting an MMPI-2 profile is to examine the data gathered from the individual validity and clinical scales for consistent and inconsistent information. Inferences or hypotheses that are suggested by several scales are important to note since they may represent central features of the client. It is a rare profile, however, that does not also contain inconsistent information; the contradictory inferences that result are important since they will somehow need to be resolved in interpreting the profile. Occurrences of such inconsistent inferences are commonplace, and both sample profiles interpreted in this chapter contain at least one example. Any information from the validity or clinical scales that is inconsistent with the client's demographic data also should be noted.

The next level of analysis in profile interpretation involves subgroups of scales or interscale relationships. In many respects this is the most common type of interpretation, since at its least complex level it involves the relationship of only two scales. If the two scales examined are the highest or most deviant clinical scales, a codetype (high-point pair) analysis, the core of any MMPI-2 interpretive system, is being utilized.

In fact, many interpretive systems look no farther than the codetype for any profile. For this analysis it is only necessary that two clinical scales or a single clinical scale (a spike profile) be elevated at or above a T score of 65 on the MMPI-2 or a T score of 70 on the MMPI. Once the codetype for the profile has been determined, interpretation begins by selecting the appropriate statements from the description of this particular codetype for the reference group from which this person comes (see Chapter 6).

In selecting the appropriate statements from the description of the codetype, there are several issues to consider. The first is whether the order of the two scales in the codetype makes a difference in interpretation and whether the reference source being used discriminates order within this codetype. (Codetypes in which scale order is important have been noted explicitly in Chapter 6.)

Although order of scales within codetypes seems basic to any interpretive system, a little simple arithmetic will show how difficult it is to implement such a system. A codetype system based on all 10 clinical scales in any combination involves 45 ($[10 \times 9]/2 = 45$) possible codetypes. Controlling for gender (male, female), age (adolescent, adult, aged), and social class (upper, middle, lower), with a minimum of 10 persons per group, requires a sample of more than 8,000 ($2 \times 3 \times 3 \times 10 \times 45 = 8,100$) persons. Controlling for the order of the scales would double the number of persons required. Obviously, if finer discriminations in any of these groups are of interest, or if other variables such as ethnic group or reason for referral are of interest, the number of persons required for an interpretive system quickly becomes astronomical.

Consequently, the clinician should be aware of how each interpretive system was developed and must work within the limitations of the data each provides. A prime example of the importance of scale order is *1-3* and *3-1* codetypes. It is important to know which scale is higher in this codetype for accurate interpretation, since they represent two very different groups of individuals; interpretive systems that do not discriminate between these two codetypes will usually contain a single description filled with seemingly contradictory data.

A second issue in interpreting codetypes involves the criterion group on which the interpretive system is based. Possible criterion groups on which interpretive systems have been developed include male veterans (Gilberstadt, 1970; Gilberstadt & Duker, 1965), adolescents (Marks, Seeman, & Haller, 1974), psychiatric inpatients (Gynther, Altman, & Sletten, 1973; Lachar, 1974; Marks et al., 1974), a wide variety of diagnostic and pathological groups (Lanyon, 1968), and college students (Drake & Oetting, 1959; Kelley & King, 1978, 1979a, 1979b, 1979c, 1980; King & Kelley, 1977a, 1977b).

Several references in addition to this text also provide general interpretive data on codetypes: Archer (1987), Dahlstrom, Welsh, and Dahlstrom (1972), Duckworth and Anderson (1986), Friedman, Webb, and Lewak (1989), Good and Brantner (1961, 1974), Graham (1987, 1990b), and Lachar (1974).

When the client whose profile is being interpreted matches one of the above criterion groups, the clinician should consult the appropriate source. An even greater improvement, however, is when such information is available from the clinician's own institution or setting. It is unlikely that this goal will ever be reached for many discrete settings, but a serious student of the MMPI-2 should collect as much information as possible on local clientele. Since most clinicians will never have access to a sufficient number of clients to evolve a local interpretive system, the best that can be hoped for is the appropriate modifications of the most applicable system.

A third issue in interpreting codetypes involves elevation. Although there are some notable exceptions (e.g., Gilberstadt & Duker, 1965), most interpretive systems do not discriminate among scale elevations above a T score of 70 on the MMPI, the usual cutoff for inclusion as a codetype. This is not to say that the developers of such systems believe that distinguishing among scale elevations above a T score of 70 on the MMPI is unimportant. Rather, the problem is again one of how many variables it is feasible to incorporate into a system and still have it remain of manageable proportions.

The clinician, then, is faced with the need to take into consideration the degree of elevation of the codetype and has little empirical direction on how to do so. For some codetypes (e.g., *4-9/9-4*) a difference of 10 to 20 T score points seemingly has little clinical import, whereas for other pairs (e.g., *7-8/8-7*) such a difference cannot be ignored. To a certain extent, the higher the elevation of the codetype, the more distress the client is experiencing or reporting and the more ego alien or ego dystonic is the psychopathology. For personality disorders, the higher elevations indicate that the pathology is more ingrained and resistant to change.

Beyond these simple statements it seems that the importance of the degree of elevation of a codetype is a question that still needs to be researched. The degree of elevation of the entire profile has been researched more extensively, probably because it is easier to investigate. (This issue will be taken up when interpretation of the entire profile is discussed.) Finally, it is being assumed that a T score of 65 on the MMPI-2 is equivalent to a T score of 70 on the MMPI. This assumption is probably fairly safe since elevation does not appear to have any systematic effects on profile interpretation of the MMPI, but at a minimum clinicians need to be aware that this assumption is being made with the MMPI-2.

Once the appropriate statements have been selected from the description of the codetype, the clinician can again start generating hypotheses about the type of client who would produce such a description. The statements drawn from the description of the codetype should be compared with each of the individual scale interpretations for consistencies and inconsistencies. Redundant interpretations serve to highlight the important characteristics of the client, whereas inconsistent features represent areas that need to be examined more carefully.

It is extremely important, at any level of profile interpretation, for the clinician to be wary of focusing exclusively on any one feature and consequently ignoring, biasing, or misinterpreting the rest of the data. The clinician has always to be willing to entertain alternate hypotheses or inferences from the test data. All too often a novice clinician selects one characteristic or feature as being important and then cannot get away from this perceptual set in interpreting the test data. Instead, the clinician should acknowledge inconsistencies with the inference being made and consider other inferences that might be better able to fit the data. But even after the clinician feels that the best inferences have been selected from those available and all alternative inferences have been carefully rejected, he or she should come back to the data at a later time with an open mind.

Special mention should be made of the necessity to note the low-point clinical scales, which are essentially the converse of the high-point scales. Frequently, clinicians who are learning to interpret the MMPI-2 focus solely on the analysis of the codetype or some other feature of the profile and miss other significant data, usually the low points in the profile. This is unfortunate since there are several scales for which low points are particularly significant (see Chapter 4). Some interpreters of the MMPI even argue that focusing on low points is a means of determining the kinds of behavior the client is defending against and does not want to reveal (cf. Duckworth & Anderson, 1986). There is no known research to support the tenability of this inference.

On several clinical scales, moreover, low points do not represent the opposite end of the dimension measured by high points. At any rate, the clinician should note low points in the profile, keeping in mind that low-point interpretation is generally based on absolute rather than relative elevation of the low-point scale. For example, a low point on Scale *3* (Hysteria) at a T score of 47 does not indicate the same potential problem areas for the client as a low point at a T score of 31 on this scale. The latter score is much more unusual and hence clinically more important. The reader also should recall that Tables 6–5 (MMPI) and 6–10 (MMPI-2) provided the frequency with which low points are found in commonly occurring codetypes.

There is a tendency for clinicians using the MMPI-2 to discuss high-point triads in addition to codetypes (cf. Duckworth & Anderson, 1986; Friedman et al., 1989). This approach recognizes the amount of information not being used by a codetype system and the increased specificity offered by discriminating among subgroups within any particular codetype. The increase in specificity, however, is offset by the difficulty of obtaining a large enough sample of profiles to make such a system feasible. This approach to the analysis of high-point triads is not an analysis of scale configuration; rather, it simply follows the rationale for a high-point pair system with an additional scale.

Therefore, all of the above discussion of the procedures and problems of high-point pair analysis is equally applicable to high-point triads. Some investigators (cf. Gynther et al., 1973) also have been unable to find replicable correlates of high-point triads that differ from those of the respective codetype. For example, Gynther and associates found that the correlates of a *2-1-3* high-point triad did not differ from those for a *2-1* codetype.

The next level of analysis of the MMPI-2 profile involves configuration analysis of subsets of the validity and clinical scales. At this level of analysis, groups of scales, typically triads, are examined at the same time. The best example of such configuration analysis involves Scales *L*, *F*, and *K*, or Scales *1* (Hypochondriasis), *2* (Depression),

and *3* (Hysteria) (see pages 116–121 and 148–151.

For this type of analysis the complexity increases appreciably because the degree of relative elevation of each scale within the triad must be considered as well as the overall elevation of the entire triad. The initial step in this analysis is a close examination of the behavioral and clinical correlates of the specific elevation for each scale within the configuration. This information must then be combined and integrated with that for the configuration as a whole. In carrying out this second step, it is necessary to match the configuration as closely as possible to the various examples provided. Obviously, the closer the configuration being analyzed fits one of the examples, the better or more accurately the empirical and clinical correlates should describe the client in question.

Again, the inferences garnered from the configurations should be examined for consistencies and inconsistencies with all the previous information. At this point redundant inferences, all representing cardinal features of the client, should be appearing. Also, any glaring discrepancies with these inferences should be carefully noted, since they will need to be dealt with when all the material is finally integrated into one report.

The final level of analysis of the MMPI-2 involves configurational analysis of the entire profile. This level of analysis is typically limited to the clinical scales, since the validity scales lend themselves more readily to a triad configurational analysis as described above. It is clearly the most complex level and frequently it is given only passing consideration in interpreting the MMPI-2. The primary reason for its neglect is the difficulty involved in attempting to match an entire profile for configuration. Even though there is not an entire interpretive system at this level of analysis, there are characteristic profiles for specific diagnostic groups and subgroups.

Lanyon's (1968) text on group profiles

provides the most readily available data, but he does not furnish any information other than simply a mean profile for various diagnostic groups. That is, he does not give any empirical or clinical correlates for each profile. If the clinician can determine how closely the profile being interpreted matches one of Lanyon's diagnostic groups, this source may be of some help in interpretation. Even so, the primary features in interpreting the configuration of the profile are its elevation, slope, and phasicity. Each of these will be examined in turn.

The overall elevation of the clinical scales gives a fairly accurate representation of how much distress the client is experiencing and how ego alien or ego dystonic is the symptomatology that the client is acknowledging. The higher the elevation of the clinical scales, the more the client is saying that he or she is hurting. Sometimes, in their "cry for help," clients will even overemphasize their symptomatology in order to insure that they will receive assistance sooner. (A careful examination of the scales to assess overreporting of psychopathology that were discussed in Chapter 3 will be helpful in these circumstances.) In general, however, the higher the overall elevation of the clinical scales, the more distress the client is experiencing and the more likely the client is to resemble those individuals on whom the scales were constructed.

If sequential MMPI-2s are examined for the same client and that client is either neurotic or psychotic, there is a characteristic pattern in the overall elevation of the clinical scales. In psychotic disorders there is a gradual or sudden increase in the elevation of the entire profile that corresponds to the onset of the symptomatology. If the condition becomes chronic, there will be a gradual decrease, first in the neurotic triad (Scales *1, 2,* and *3*), while the psychotic tetrad (Scales *6, 7, 8,* and *9*) remains elevated. Finally, as the psychotic symptomatology becomes integrated into the client's personality, the psy-

chotic tetrad also decreases in elevation and none of the clinical scales is elevated.

Thus, without additional information it is difficult to discriminate the profile of a client with a chronic psychotic condition from the profile of a normal person. Confirmation of this point can be easily obtained by using the Meehl-Dahlstrom (1960) rules for profile classification, which were intended for use with hospitalized patients, on a normal person's MMPI. These rules will classify a normal profile as psychotic most of the time. (This fact should also be a reminder to use the appropriate criterion group for interpreting any MMPI-2 or MMPI profile.) The interested reader also could compare the mean MMPI profiles for chronic schizophrenics and normals in Lanyon's (1968) text; there are virtually no differences between the two profiles.

In neurotic disorders there is an elevation in the neurotic triad corresponding to the onset of the symptomatology. As the neurosis becomes more disturbing and upsetting to the client, there will be a concomitant increase in the elevation of the psychotic tetrad, although these scales rarely get much over a T score of 75. As the neurotic symptomatology subsides, there will be a gradual reversal of this sequence until a within-normal-limits (*WNL*) profile is achieved.

The interpretation of the slope of the MMPI-2 profile is based largely upon the relationship between the neurotic triad and the psychotic tetrad. Positive slope reflects the fact that the psychotic tetrad is elevated higher than the neurotic triad, and negative slope indicates the reverse relationship between these two groups of scales. Positive slope is generally related to psychological disorders in which the client is experiencing limited impulse control, poor contact with reality, or even disorientation and confusion. In short, positive slope is generally related to psychotic disorders, particularly when elevation is considered in conjunction with slope.

Negative slope is more characteristic of acute psychological upsets involving anxiety, depression, poor morale, and physical symptoms without psychotic distortions. The height of the general elevation in the profile with a negative or positive slope corresponds to the magnitude of the discomfort and distress the client is experiencing. At lower elevations, profiles with zero slope (flat profiles) typically are found in normal individuals, clients with a chronic psychotic condition, or clients with severe, ingrained behavior or personality disorders. At higher elevations, profiles with zero slope are characteristic of clients with psychological reactions that have recently come to be called borderline states. In these clients many psychotic symptoms can be detected, although actual psychotic disorders are not readily discerned.

Phasicity, which is a measure of the number of peaks in the profile, is the least commonly used index in profile interpretation. Primarily, this disinterest reflects the fact that this index is so confounded with elevation and slope of codetypes that there is little to be gained by considering it. Since most interpretive systems are based on codetypes, it seems that most profiles are best classified as being biphasic. There are only two additional comments that need to be made about phasicity.

First, the flatter the profile, the more likely the person is to be well adjusted, particularly at lower elevations, or the person has the characteristics discussed above for profiles with zero slope. Second, a "sawtoothed" profile in which Scales *2* (Depression), *4* (Psychopathic Deviate), *6* (Paranoia), and *8* (Schizophrenia) are significantly elevated above the other clinical scales is a particularly malignant profile. Clients with this saw-toothed profile are likely to be experiencing a very serious psychotic disorder. The clinician should note that the flat and the saw-toothed profiles represent the extremes of phasicity; most profiles, which are biphasic, fall between these two extremes.

Before turning to the two examples of MMPI-2 profile interpretation, a comment about automated interpretation of the MMPI-2 is necessary. The intent in the upcoming examples is to compare and contrast the process of MMPI-2 profile interpretation by an individual clinician with those provided by automated interpretive systems. Thus, three automated systems were selected to illustrate that method of profile interpretation, but this is not to suggest that these three systems are better or worse than other automated systems.

For the interested reader, a general description and review of all automated interpretive systems for the MMPI can be found in *The Eighth Mental Measurements Yearbook* (Buros, 1978, pp. 938–962). Dahlstrom and colleagues (1972) and Graham (1977) have examples of automated interpretation of a single MMPI profile by most of these systems.

EXAMPLES OF PROFILE INTERPRETATION

The procedure for interpreting the MMPI-2 profile, which was described above, will be illustrated for two clients. Each of these profiles was interpreted by an individual clinician and also by three computerized interpretive services. For each client background information and the MMPI-2 profiles are presented below. Then the clinician's interpretation of response consistency and accuracy and of the validity and clinical scales, subscales, and configurations is given. This sequence reflects the steps the clinician followed in gathering information to interpret the profile.

This information is followed by the clinician's integration of all these sources of information into a profile interpretation. Next, the three computer interpretations are provided. Finally, some general comments are made about the four interpretations of each profile. In addition to the MMPI-2 profile, the clinician was provided only the basic demographic data on each client, so the clinician and the computer interpretive systems had similar information on which to make the profile interpretation.

The two examples for profile interpretation were selected so that one example matched the prototype for the codetype as closely as possible; the second example had a number of the clinical and supplementary scales different from the prototype for the codetype. Readers can see these differences for themselves by comparing Profile 7–1 for the first example with Profile 7–4 for the second, which also have the prototypic scores plotted for the standard validity and clinical scales. It would be expected that the computer interpretations would be much more accurate when the profile matches the codetype then when it does not. The clinician may or may not be able to realize that the second profile varies in significant ways from the prototype and incorporate that information into the interpretation.

Interpreting the MMPI-2: Example 1

The client is a 41-year-old, separated, white male who was admitted for the second time to the state hospital. His previous hospitalization occurred two years ago following a separation from his wife, and resulted from his increasing agitation over trying to maintain his relationship with his wife. He had been telephoning her as many as 75 times a day, driving by her residence repeatedly, and physically abused her once. At that point the wife obtained a restraining order because the patient was "obsessed with keeping the family together."

He believes that he is in the state hospital because the judge and police are fabricating evidence against him. His wife reported continued harassment and he recently chased his son home from school. He states that it is God's will for him and his family to be reunited, and he insists that they were never actually separated. He believes that his family wants him to return home but he cannot because of constant interference from the police and judge.

There is no history of alcohol or drug use.

The client believes that there is no reason for him being in the state hospital and he has filed suit to be released immediately. The MMPI-2 (see Profiles 7–1, 7–2, and 7–3) was administered approximately one week after he entered the hospital. The prototypic scores for *6-9/9-6* codetypes can be found in Table 7–1.

Clinician's Interpretation

Item Omissions

(See Chapter 3) He endorsed all of the items
$? = 3$ except three. None of these three items is omitted by most clients. Item omissions are not a problem for profile interpretation. The content of these items is 88: "I believe women ought to have as much sexual freedom as men"; 258: "I can sleep during the day but not at night"; and 259: "I am sure I am being talked about."[1]

Consistency of Item Endorsement

(See Chapter 3) The score on *VRIN* and the
$VRIN = 9$ absolute difference be-
$F = 12$ tween F and F_B are at the
$F_B = 5$ lower end of the marginal range. By the next two rules for assessing consistency of item endorsement (see Table 3–45, p. 100),

PROFILE 7–1.   MMPI-2 Standard Validity and Clinical Scales for Example 1

Profile for Basic Scales

Minnesota Multiphasic Personality Inventory-2
Copyright © by THE REGENTS OF THE UNIVERSITY OF MINNESOTA
1942, 1943 (renewed 1970), 1989. This Profile Form 1989.
All rights reserved. Distributed exclusively by NATIONAL COMPUTER SYSTEMS, INC.
under license from The University of Minnesota.

"MMPI-2" and "Minnesota Multiphasic Personality Inventory-2" are trademarks owned by
The University of Minnesota. Printed in the United States of America.

Name **Example 1**

Address **2709 Elmwood**

Occupation **Auto Mechanic**   Date Tested **12/12/89**

Education **12th**   Age **41**   Marital Status **Divorced**

Referred by **Dr. Harry Davis**

MMPI-2 Code **6'948-0/25317**   **F'L-/K**

Scorer's Initials **HG**

Client ●——●

Prototype ▲——▲

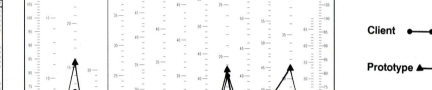

	L	F	K	Hs+5K 1	D 2	Hy 3	Pd+4K 4	Mf 5	Pa 6	Pt+1K 7	Sc+1K 8	Ma+2K 9	Si 0
Raw Score	6	12	13	3	17	18	24	24	18	9	19	24	31
K to be Added				7			5			13	13	3	
Raw Score with K				10		29				22	32	27	

? Raw Score **3**

PROFILE 7-2.   MMPI-2 Content Scales for Example 1

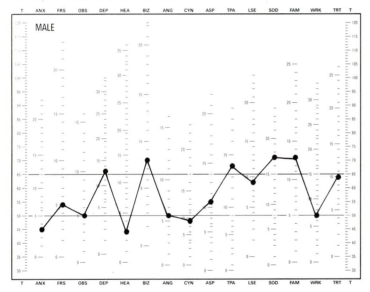

Name **Example 1**

Address **2709 Elmwood**

Occupation **Auto Mechanic**   Date Tested **12/12/89**

Education **12th**   Age **41**   Marital Status **Divorced**

Referred by **Dr. Harry Davis**

Scorer's Initials **HG**

	ANX	FRS	OBS	DEP	HEA	BIZ	ANG	CYN	ASP	TPA	LSE	SOD	FAM	WRK	TRT
Raw Score	3	5	5	13	3	8	6	9	11	14	9	17	13	7	10

PROFILE 7–3.   MMPI-3 Supplementary Scales for Example 1

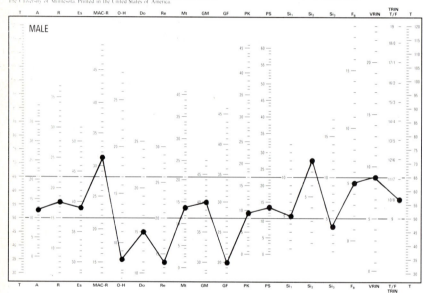

MMPI-2 S.R. Hathaway and J.C. McKinley
Minnesota Multiphasic
Personality Inventory -2

Profile for Supplementary Scales

Name **Example 1**

Address **2709 Elmwood**

Occupation **Auto Mechanic**   Date Tested **12/12/89**

Education **12th**   Age **41**   Marital Status **Divorced**

Referred by **Dr. Harry Davis**

Scorer's Initials **HG**

Raw Score: **12 18 39 31 8 15 14 14 40 20 9 14 5 8 4 5 9 10**

TABLE 7–1   Prototypic Scores for *6-9/9-6* Codetypes in Psychiatric Settings

		MMPI			MMPI-2	
Demographics						
		M	*SD*		*M*	*SD*
N	131			260		
Age		33.9	13.0		31.2	12.4
Men	51.9%			66.5%		
Women	48.1			33.5		
Test-Taking Scales/Indexes						
		M	*SD*		*M*	*SD*
Inconsistent		13.9%			15.0%	
Total (Obvious-Subtle)[a]		74.6	54.0		114.9	62.6
Critical items[b]		42.5	12.3		46.3	14.3
Overreported[c]		12.7%			41.8%	
Underreported[c]		12.0%			3.5%	
Standard Validity and Clinical Scales (K-Corrected)						
		M	*SD*		*M*	*SD*
?[d]		4.0	5.5		4.4	6.0
L		49.5	7.4		50.1	9.9
F		73.2	12.3		82.6	19.4
K		43.4	7.1		37.2	7.2
1(Hs)		53.0	11.0		52.7	12.5
2(D)		52.0	8.7		51.7	9.6
3(Hy)		52.6	9.7		48.3	11.7
4(Pd)		66.7	8.5		62.8	10.2
5(Mf)		57.0	9.1		51.4	9.4
6(Pa)		80.6	8.6		81.2	11.3
7(Pt)		59.6	8.0		58.2	10.6
8(Sc)		70.8	9.4		67.9	11.5
9(Ma)		82.5	8.6		80.5	10.3
0(Si)		51.8	8.1		49.5	8.2
Supplementary Scales						
		M	*SD*		*M*	*SD*
A		61.2	9.1		65.9	9.9
R		48.6	11.4		38.9	10.2
MAC/MAC-R[d]						
men		30.4	4.2		32.0	4.1
women		27.6	4.0		27.9	4.2

Codetype Concordance

	Men	Women		Men	Women
MMPI-2 *6-9/9-6*	84.2%	88.2%	MMPI *6-9/9-6*	38.5%	71.9%
Spike *6*	15.8		*6-8/8-6*	23.1%	12.3%
1-6/6-1		11.8			

[a] See Chapter 3, Table 3–24, for explanation of how this index is computed.

[b] The total number of Lachar and Wrobel (1979) critical items endorsed.

[c] Percentage of patients within this codetype scoring above the 75th percentile or below the 25th percentile on the total T score difference on the Wiener and Harmon Obvious and Subtle subscales for all patients (see Tables 3–45 and 3–46 for the cutting scores for the MMPI-2 and MMPI, respectively).

[d] Raw score.

the client endorsed the items consistently. Profile interpretation may proceed since the client has endorsed the items consistently.

Accuracy of Item Endorsement

(See Chapter 3)
Total (Ob-Sub) = 34
Crit items   = 28

Both scales/indexes are within the acceptable range. When his scores are compared to the prototype for a *6-9/9-6* codetype (see Table 7–1), he is almost two standard deviations lower on both scales/indexes. Although the client has endorsed the items accurately, he is reporting less distress than most clients with this codetype. Profile interpretation may proceed since the client has endorsed the items accurately.

Validity Scales

(See Chapter 3)
$L = 61$

He may have a tendency to resort to denial mechanisms.

$F = 73$

He is acknowledging the unusual experiences represented in this scale more than the typical individual.

$K = 45$

He describes himself as having adequate personal resources. He has a proper balance between self-disclosure and self-protection.

Validity Scale Configuration

(See Figure 3–3, dashed line)

This client is admitting to personal and emotional difficulties, and simultaneously trying to defend himself against these problems in an unsophisticated manner. This pattern of ineffective defenses with the simultaneous admission of fairly severe problems is typical of chronically maladjusted clients. He is not an optimal client for any type of psychological intervention.

Codetype

(See Chapter 6)

Clients with a *6-9/9-6* codetype are usually encountered only in inpatient settings. They are angry, hostile individuals who may exhibit grandiosity and egocentricity. They are also irritable, excited, and energetic. They may report difficulty thinking and concentrating, and exercise poor judgment.
The presence of a psychotic process that is more likely to reflect a mood disorder than a thought disorder should be considered. They describe themselves as happy, calm, easygoing, and in good physical health. Others see them as angry, hostile, and overresponsive to minor stresses and problems;

less frequently they are seen as tense and anxious.

Prototypic Scores

(See Table 7–1)   The client was more than one standard deviation above the mean on Scale *L*. He was more than one standard deviation below the mean on Scales *F*, *1*, *7*, and *9*. It will be important to insure that these atypical scores for the prototype are accounted for in the interpretation.

Clinical Scales

(See Chapter 4)

$1(Hs)$ = 42   He may be denying the presence of vague physical complaints. Clearly, he is not reporting any health-related problems.

$2(D)$ = 47   He reported a typical number of attitudes and behaviors that reflect symptomatic depression. Neither his presence in the state hospital (even though he believes that he is being confined unjustly) nor his problems with the judge and police that led him to be sent to the hospital are seen as being upsetting or distressful. His normal score is *not* normal!

$3(Hy)$ = 43   He tends to be caustic, sarcastic, and socially isolated. He has few defenses. He has narrow interests and is socially conforming.

$4(Pd)$ = 64   He has adjusted to an habitual level of interpersonal and social conflict.

Pd_1 = 65   He may struggle against familial control.

Pd_2 = 68   He may resent societal demands and conventions and parental standards.

$5(Mf)$ = 46   He has traditional masculine interests and activities.

$6(Pa)$ = 79   He is likely to be suspicious, hostile, and overly sensitive and overtly verbalizes these qualities. A thought disorder may be readily apparent.

Pa_1 = 82   He has ideas of external influence. He externalizes blame for his problems, frustrations, and failures. He may have persecutory ideas. He projects responsibility for his negative feelings.

Pa_2 = 62   He may consider himself as special and different from other people.

$7(Pt)$ = 41   He is secure and comfortable with himself and is emotionally stable. He is success oriented, persistent, and capable. There is an absence of worries and a relaxed attitude toward responsibilities. Again, like with Scale *2*, he is not reporting any type of anxiety or distress.

$8(Sc)$ = 60   He thinks differently than others. He tends to avoid reality through fantasy and daydreams.

$9(Ma)$ = 69   He is overactive, emotionally labile, and may experience flight of ideas. Although his mood is typically euphoric, outbursts of temper may occur. He is impulsive and may have an inability to delay gratification. Manic, narcissistic, and grandiose features may be seen.

$0(Si)$ = 56 He reported a balance between socially extroverted and introverted attitudes and behaviors.

Supplementary Scales

(See Chapter 5)

A = 53 He has a normal amount of anxiety. Again, he is not reporting any distress. Note the low scores on other first-factor scales (Mt = 54; PK = 52; and PS = 54).

R = 56 He shows an appropriate willingness to discuss his behavior and problems.

MAC = 31 (raw score) He has a significant probability of abusing alcohol or drugs. He is likely to be impulsive, have a high energy level, have shallow interpersonal relationships, and be psychologically maladjusted.

Content Scales

(See Chapter 5)

ANX = 45 He does not report general symptoms of anxiety as has been noted several times above.

FRS = 54 He has a typical number of specific fears.

OBS = 50 He does not report obsessional thoughts.

DEP = 66 He has depressive mood and thoughts. He feels blue, unhappy, and is likely to brood. He is prone to blame others for his problems. He did not endorse any of the items related to suicidal ideation or attempts.

HEA = 44 He does not report any concerns about his health.

BIZ = 70 He reported strange thoughts and experiences, paranoid ideation, and hallucinations.

ANG = 50 He does not see himself as being angry, moody, or irritable. He did not endorse any of the items directly related to anger.

CYN = 48 He is not cynical.

ASP = 55 He did not engage in problematic behaviors while in school.

TPA = 68 He is hard-driving, fast-moving, and work-oriented, who frequently becomes impatient, grouchy, irritable, and annoyed. He does not like to wait, be interrupted, or believe that someone has gotten the best of him.

LSE = 62 He has somewhat of a low opinion of himself. He lacks self-confidence and sees himself as not as good or capable as others.

SOD = 71 He is very uneasy around others and is happier by himself. He sees himself as shy. He dislikes parties and other group events.

FAM = 71 He reports considerable familial discord. His family was lacking love, support, and companionship. Family members are nervous and have quick tempers. They are to be avoided.

WRK = 50 He is as able to work as he ever was, and his current problems are not interfering with his ability to work.

TRT = 64 He dislikes going to doctors and he believes that he should not discuss his personal problems with others. He does not believe that anyone understands or cares about him.

Profile Interpretation[2]

Test-Taking Behaviors

The client endorsed the items consistently (*VRIN, F, F_B*) and accurately (Total T score difference; Total critical items), although he is reporting less distress than most clients with this codetype on the MMPI-2. He is admitting to personal and emotional difficulties, and simultaneously trying to defend himself against these problems in an unsophisticated manner (validity scale configuration). This pattern of ineffective defenses with the simultaneous admission of fairly severe problems is typical of chronically maladjusted clients (validity scale configuration).

Cognitive Processes

He has difficulty thinking and concentrating, and may exercise poor judgment (*6-9/9-6* codetype). He thinks differently than other people (Scale *8*), and he reported strange thoughts and experiences (*BIZ*). There is a strong likelihood of a potentially psychotic process that needs to be evaluated carefully (*6-9/9-6* codetype; *BIZ*). A review of his background and reasons for coming to the state hospital may be sufficient to document the presence of a psychotic process.

Mood

The client did not describe himself as being depressed (Scale *2*), anxious (Scale *7*), or emotionally distressed (*A, Mt, PK, PS, ANX*) despite his presence in the state hospital. Neither his being hospitalized nor the behaviors that led him to being hospitalized are creating any emotional distress. He does not see himself as being angry (*ANG*) or cynical *(CYN)*. Others are likely to see him as angry and hostile (*6-9/9-6* codetype; *TPA*) and blaming them for his problems (*Pa$_1$, DEP*). Outbursts of temper (Scale *9; TPA*) or physical acting-out

may occur (Scale *6*). He did not report suicidal ideation or any history of suicide attempts.

Interpersonal Relationships

The client reported a balance between socially extroverted and introverted attitudes and behaviors (Scale *0*). He has traditional masculine interests and activities (Scale *5*). He is very uneasy around others and is happier by himself (*SOD*). The client sees himself as shy and he avoids others when given the opportunity (*SOD*). He has shallow interpersonal relationships (*MAC-R*) and considerable familial discord (*FAM*).

Treatment

The client is a poor candidate for most forms of psychological interventions for a variety of reasons. He is experiencing little internalized distress (Scales *2, 7, A, Mt, PK, PS, ANX*), and he is prone to blame others for his problems (Scale *6, Pa$_1$*) and to expect them to change to meet his needs. His problems are chronic in nature (validity scale configuration), and he sees little hope of changing (*TRT*). He dislikes going to doctors and he believes that he should not discuss his personal problems with anyone (*TRT*). He also may be prone to abuse alcohol or other drugs (*MAC-R*), which will only exacerbate all of the problems described above.

Therapy will proceed slowly at best and should focus on his relationships with members of his family (*FAM*). It will be important for the therapist not to place any unusual demands on the client until some trust in the relationship is developed (Scale *6*). Despite all of his problems, he does not see his work as being affected by his problems (WRK). If his statement about his work is accurate, it could be used as a point of strength from which to work on other issues.

Diagnostic Impression

Axis I   296.44   Rule out Bipolar Disorder, Manic Type, with Mood-Congruent Psychotic Features

         301.13   Rule out Cyclothymia

Axis II   301.00   Rule out Paranoid Personality Disorder

Computer Interpretation — The Minnesota Report[TM3]

Profile Validity

This is a valid MMPI-2 profile. The client's responses to the MMPI-2 validity items suggest that he cooperated with the evaluation enough to provide useful interpretive information. The resulting clinical profile is an adequate indication of his present personality functioning.

Symptomatic Pattern

Individuals with this MMPI-2 profile are experiencing severe psychological adjustment problems. Extremely sensitive to criticism, the client tends to overreact to minor problems with anger or hostility. He trusts no one and is constantly on guard to prevent others from doing him harm or injustice. When he feels threatened, he may react with aloofness and self-righteous indignation, or take a rigidly moralistic stance. He blames others for his problems and rationalizes to avoid personal responsibility. Some individuals with this profile type harbor delusional beliefs or feel that they have a special mission in life of which others are unaware.

In addition, the following description is suggested by the content of this client's responses. He views the world as a threatening place, sees himself as having been unjustly blamed for others' problems, and feels that he is getting a raw deal out of life. He endorsed a number of extreme and bizarre thoughts suggesting the presence of delusions and/or hallucinations. He apparently believes that he has

special mystical powers or a special "mission" in life which others do not understand or accept. He considers himself in good health and does not complain of somatic difficulties.

Interpersonal Relations

He is overly sensitive and rigid in interpersonal relations. His hypersensitivity, lack of trust, and inability to compromise are likely to disrupt or strain relationships. He broods a great deal and becomes hostile when he feels threatened. He also tends to hold grudges and seeks to "get even" with others for perceived wrongs. His lack of trust may prevent him from developing warm, close relationships. He tends to feel insecure in personal relationships, is hypersensitive to rejection, and may become jealous at times. He tends to need a great deal of reassurance.

The content of this client's MMPI-2 responses suggests the following additional information concerning his interpersonal relations. He views his home situation as unpleasant and lacking in love and understanding. He feels like leaving home to escape a quarrelsome, critical situation, and to be free of family domination. His social relationships are likely to be viewed by others as problematic. He may visibly by uneasy around others, sits alone in group situations, and dislikes engaging in group activities.

Behavioral Stability

His suspicious and mistrusting behavior is long-standing. He is not likely to change significantly, although he may become less intensely angry or "clam up" to reduce attention. His interpersonal style is not likely to change significantly if retested at a later date.

Diagnostic Considerations

This profile strongly suggests a diagnosis of Paranoid Personality or Paranoid Disorder. His unusual thinking and bizarre ideas need to be considered in any diagnostic formulation.

His extremely high score on the Mac-

Andrew Alcoholism Scale—Revised suggests great proneness to the development of an addictive disorder. Further evaluation of substance use or abuse problems is strongly recommended. However, he seems to deny the possibility of a substance use or abuse disorder and would probably be reluctant to discuss the possibility freely.

Treatment Considerations

Individuals with this profile tend not to seek psychological help; instead, they are usually brought to treatment at the insistence of others. Because they are likely to be quite guarded, suspicious of the therapist, and oppositional or detached in treatment, their therapy sessions will probably be stormy. Treatment is likely to be terminated prematurely.

If psychological treatment is being considered it may be profitable for the therapist to explore the client's treatment motivation early in therapy. The item content he endorsed includes some feelings and attitudes that could be unproductive in psychological treatment and in implementing self-change. Examination of item content reveals a considerable number of problems with his home life. He feels extremely unhappy and alienated from his family. He related that he feels that his home life is unpleasant and feels pessimistic that the situation will improve. Any psychological intervention with him will need to focus upon his negative family feelings if treatment progress is to be made.

Computer Interpretation — MMPI-2 Adult Interpretive System[4]

Profile matches and scores for the client are provided in Table 7–2.

Configural Validity Scale Interpretation

There is no information available for this configuration of scores for scales L, F, and K. Interpretation for each of the individual validity scales is presented below.

Validity Scales

$?$ (raw) $= 3$

Scores in this range reflect a relatively small number of unanswered items, which in and of itself should not have an impact on the validity of the profile.

$L \quad T = 61$

L scores in this range are suggestive of individuals who may be defensive, lack insight, and be slightly more conforming and moralistic than usual. They may have a tendency to repress or deny problems and unfavorable traits.

$F \quad T = 73$

F scores in this range, if they are valid, suggest the increasing probability of serious psychological and emotional problems which are often characteristic of severe neurosis, psychosis, or behavioral problems. Scores in this range also may occur because individuals have had some difficulty reading or understanding the test items (evaluate measures of consistency of item endorsement), or because they have some motivation to overreport psychopathology (evaluate measures of accuracy of item endorsement).

$K \quad T = 45$

Scores in this range are typically obtained by individuals who exhibit an appropriate balance between self-disclosure and self-protection. These individuals usually are psychologically well adjusted and capable of dealing with problems in their daily lives. Scores in this range are also indicative of good ego strength, sufficient personal resources to deal with problems, a positive self-image, adaptability, and a wide range of interests. Prognosis for psychological intervention is generally good.

TABLE 7–2   MMPI-2 Adult Interpretive System: Profile Matches and Scores for Example 1

	Scale	Client Profile	Highest Scale Codetype	Best Fit Codetype
Codetype match:			6-9/9-6	6-9/9-6 (4)
Coefficient of Fit:			.91	.94
Scores:	? (raw)	3		
	L	61	50	50
	F	73	83	69
	K	45	37	41
	Hs (1)	42	53	47
	D (2)	47	52	49
	Hy (3)	43	48	46
	Pd (4)	64	63	65
	Mf (5)	46	51	48
	Pa (6)	79	81	73
	Pt (7)	41	58	52
	Sc (8)	60	68	58
	Ma (9)	69	81	75
	Si (0)	56	50	46
Mean Clinical Elevation:		55	59	58
Ave age-males:			30	30
Ave age-females:			34	36
% of male codetypes:			3.1%	1.4%
% of female codetypes:			3.2%	1.0%
% of males within codetype:			66.7%	74.5%
% of females within codetype:			33.3%	25.5%

Configural clinical scale interpretation is provided in the report for the following codetype(s):
6-9/9-6
6-9/9-6 (4)

Note: Reproduced by special permission of Psychological Assessment Resources, Inc., from MMPI-2 Adult Interpretive System by Greene, Brown, & PAR. Copyright 1990. Further reproduction is prohibited without permission from PAR, Inc.

Configural Clinical Scale Interpretation

6-9/9-6 Codetype (High Match)

Clinical Presentation

These individuals are very active and energetic. Sometimes they become so agitated and excited that they may report difficulty in thinking and concentration. At these times they may exhibit indications of a psychotic process that is more likely to reflect a mood disorder than a thought disorder.

They are distrustful of others and vulnerable to perceived threat. They often project their feelings and problems onto others. They have difficulty expressing their feelings appropriately. They may vacillate between overcontrolling and undercontrolling their emotions. These individuals are sometimes described as being tense, anxious, and irritable. They often exercise poor judgment, although they think that their judgment is very good.

The self-concept of these individuals is often grandiose and egocentric. They are cynical of the abilities of others.

The exaggerated need for affection exhibited by these individuals, coupled with their suspiciousness, hypersensitivity and fear of emotional involvement, often results in unsatisfying and volatile interpersonal relationships. They tend to be unconcerned about others' evaluations of them.

Treatment

The prognosis is generally poor with individuals who obtain this codetype.

Possible Diagnoses

Axis I   Rule Out Mood Disorders
           Manic Episode
           Hypomanic Episode
           Cyclothymia
Axis II   Rule Out Paranoid Personality
           Disorder
           Rule Out Schizoid Personality
           Disorder
           Rule Out Schizotypal Personality
           Disorder

6-9/9-6 (4) Codetype (Best Fit)

Clinical Presentation

These individuals are very active and energetic. Sometimes they become so agitated and excited that they may report difficulty in thinking and concentration. At these times they may exhibit indications of a psychotic process that is more likely to reflect a mood disorder than a thought disorder.

They are distrustful of others and vulnerable to perceived threat. They often project their feelings and problems onto others. They have difficulty expressing their feelings appropriately. They may vacillate between overcontrolling and undercontrolling their

emotions. They often exercise poor judgment, although they think that their judgment is very good. They believe that they are as able to work as they ever were. They are in good physical health. These individuals are sometimes described as being tense, anxious, and irritable.

The self-concept of these individuals is often grandiose and egocentric. They are cynical of the abilities of others.

The exaggerated need for affection exhibited by these individuals, coupled with their suspiciousness, hypersensitivity and fear of emotional involvement, often results in unsatisfying and volatile interpersonal relationships. They tend to be unconcerned about others' evaluations of them. They found their home life to be unpleasant and frequently wanted to leave home, if they did not do so.

Treatment

The prognosis is generally poor with individuals who obtain this codetype.

Possible Diagnoses

Axis I   Rule Out Mood Disorders
           Manic Episode
           Hypomanic Episode
           Cyclothymia
Axis II   Rule Out Paranoid Personality
           Disorder
           Rule Out Schizoid Personality
           Disorder
           Rule Out Schizotypal Personality
           Disorder

Computer Interpretation— Caldwell Report[5]

Test-Taking Attitude

He made a few atypical responses to the MMPI-2. Otherwise, he was straightforward and not unduly defensive. The basic validity scales were within acceptable limits.

The supplemental validity scales indicate extensive efforts to "look good" on the MMPI-2. He showed a moderately high level of conscious defensiveness, responding "too positively" to many of the MMPI-2 items. Despite this he showed little elevation on scale K, suggesting a rather limited to low level of verbal sophistication. His below-average score on the scale measuring his level of currently attained, recently experienced, or wished for socioeconomic status (Ss) is consistent with his having obtained an unsophisticated low K despite this degree of faking-good. His profile appears marginally valid or, at the least, several of his scales are apt to be significantly underelevated. (As with scale L, we cannot tell from the Mp and Sd scales which of his scales are most underelevated.)

There were no indications on the Ds of any attempt to malinger or exaggerate his level of disturbance. The scattered atypical and rarely given responses shown in his elevation on scale F appear, in the absence of any Ds elevation, to reflect the valid reporting of some unusual experiences and attitudes on the MMPI-2. The elevation on F also suggests an internally driven person who may be described by such terms as dissatisfied, restless, changeable, or complex. Despite the mildly elevated F score, his clinical scale scores are not likely to be overelevated; the F score does not appear to reflect any consciously self-critical distortion or biasing of his responses.

These scores suggest a person who is defensive in some areas but willing to report somewhat atypical reactions in other areas. The extent of distress that he did report indeed does appear genuine.

Symptoms and Personality Characteristics

His profile has typically been associated with episodes of intense hostility and resentment for which he lacks adaptive and constructive means of expression. He is apt to misinterpret the intentions of others and to overreact to anything he perceives or suspects to be a threat to his security. He would be quick to feel poorly treated and unfairly dealt with. When he feels "wronged" he would be quite slow to forgive and forget. Such projections, evasiveness when challenged, a circumstantial stream of thought, and breakdowns of his reality testing would reflect pervasive paranoid characteristics.

These distortions could prove to be delusional. Difficulties with alcohol would readily aggravate these problems. Nevertheless, his ego strength tests as well above average which predicts organized functioning and immediate practical self-sufficiency in many areas.

His profile indicates a general pattern of hypomanic excitability and overactivity. His plans and expectations could be seen by others as unrealistically optimistic. He is likely to take on multiple activities or commitments as if needing to distract himself as well as to prove his self-worth. He could be particularly conflicted around the importance of taking advantage of all the opportunities that he does get lest he "lose out" on an important experience. He may also be seen as stubborn about doing things "my own way," as if demanding validation that his way is "the right way."

Talkative and expansive when things are going well for him, he is apt to become abruptly emotional when under pressure. He tests as irritable and demanding when crossed, and personal setbacks could easily break down his controls over his aggressive impulses. Confused and high strung, he appears capable of sharp temper outbursts if not physical assaultiveness. These outbursts could be the adult equivalent of temper tantrums in his childhood. The profile would not rule out a potential for dangerous violence.

He tests as notably impulsive and as lacking in tolerance for frustrations. His chronic anger may be expressed through repeated resentments and defiance of authority figures. Needs for attention and approval are likely to conflict with his fears of being hurt and his underlying ambivalence about emotional closeness and vulnerability. This could focus specifically on sexual behavior and approach-avoidance conflicts about involvement with women. That is, his positive needs for sexual gratification could particularly conflict with his difficulties around emotional closeness.

Wanting of female company, he is vulnerable to problems around his sexual impulsiveness. The ego gratifications around his sexual activities could have become overemphasized, and thus they could distort the giving and receiving of love. However, he would be quickly resentful of external controls and especially of what he would see as "meddling" by friends or family members. His overall balance of masculine and feminine interests is within the normal range for his age and education.

His underlying moral code appears inflexible both toward himself and others. In some cases this was tied to religious beliefs, political convictions, or other principles and moral standards with an excessive rigidity. Phases of active involvement in church groups or other organizations would not be unusual. Employment, community involvement, church work, and other responsibilities may provide positive compensations for the deficient emotional gratifications in his interpersonal or family relationships.

He would have strong needs to be seen as normal, or at least "as normal as everyone else." His defenses against being seen as "not normal" would include rationalizations and such reaction formations as, "It is not my anger; I want to be kind and at peace."

In many cases this pattern has been associated with a "mistreated sibling" life role. During the childhoods of these patients, siblings and other family members had been openly favored because of physical or various

other handicaps. Unreleased resentments accumulated around the child's efforts to deal with feelings of not being appreciated along with increasingly fixed projections that served to explain why "they never treated me right."

In many cases one of the parents had been away from the home or had been an otherwise unavailable figure with whom to identify. Frequently the patient as a child had been particularly demanding of the mother's attention with a lack of substantial emotional gratifications. This led to a conflict between wanting affection and hating domination. Chronic patterns of blame and targets of resentment and unforgiving anger accumulated in these family interactions. As adults these feelings of being unappreciated and of seeing others as unfairly favored over them repeatedly led to resentments and projections as well as a defensive pride. Often these feelings had erupted in their marriages as acute mother-in-law conflicts along with overreactions to other outside interventions in their marriages.

Despite these interpersonal problems, past periods of good work adjustment are likely, although he could have repeatedly overreacted to threats to his career and especially to any clear or imminent job failures.

Diagnostic Impression

The typical diagnoses are of paranoid and schizo-affective schizophrenia and bipolar manic-depressive illness, manic type. Secondary personality disorder diagnoses such as narcissistic personality and passive-aggressive personality, aggressive type, are fairly common in these cases. Secondary diagnoses reflecting chronic dependence on alcohol, drugs, or other chemical agents were frequent in these cases. It should be reemphasized, however, that his general understatement of his problems and his mildly idealized self-presentation make his profile more ambiguous than most.

Treatment Considerations

The pattern indicates a major risk of a "paranoid explosion" if he felt trapped or cornered. Similar patients have often benefitted from anti-manic agents. In some cases lithium was combined with an initial use of a nonsedating phenothiazine, and the latter was gradually tapered off and discontinued over a period of weeks.

While the calming effects usually were desirable if not urgent, some of these patients reacted against such medications in part because of their secret fears of being poisoned. Others resisted such medications because of their fears of becoming depressed and their dislike of being "drugged." He tests as severely addiction prone. His makeup is often associated with histories of alcoholism or related forms of chronic chemical abuse and dependence. His responses suggest asking if he has been in trouble with the law. If currently involved, the stress of this could have precipitated or aggravated his symptoms or otherwise have led him to make professional contact.

His responses also suggest a careful review of his sexual history as to any repetitive pattern involving (1) increasing sexual tension, (2) hasty or ill-judged sexual encounters, and (3) subsequent struggles over his self-justification that block out his negative self-judgments.

If not already expressed in the interview, the therapist may wish to follow up the patient's "true" responses to the following items:

"There are persons who are trying to steal my thoughts and ideas."

"Someone has control over my mind."

Longstanding paranoid features and any fixed and defended projections of his anger would predict a relatively gradual recovery from the current episode. Previous breakdowns or emotional upheavals would be prognostically unfavorable, even if of a different nature from his current adjustment. The family histories of similar patients usually suggested genetic contributions, especially where these involved histories of major mood swings in family members.

The pattern suggests a great reluctance to open up in psychotherapy, to expose himself psychologically, and to risk his precarious pride. Projecting anger onto the therapist, he would be vigilantly sensitive to what he would perceive to be "hostile interpretations" by the therapist, and he could even try to provoke such interpretations as a way of testing the therapist. His strong needs to keep control over himself could help him to regain his previous level of practical functioning. However, these controls could also put a "tight lid" on exploring his emotional feelings.

The low level of expressed anxiety and depression would also tend to limit his involvement in treatment. Furthermore, his emphasis on action could conflict with introspection and with "talking about feelings." Contacts with family members and other informants could add considerable perspective to the situational variations of his behavior and the related current stresses.

The treatment of many similar cases has begun with reality confrontations around current frustrations, including what the patient is doing and what he is running around or away from facing. He would benefit from supportive reality testing when life becomes threatening and acutely disturbing to him. Accepting and then managing his many resentments of family members and of his ex-wife could be central, even if he were slow and roundabout in letting go of his denial.

Interviews are likely to focus on helping him to recognize and verbalize the immediate hurt-anger sequences in these interactions. This could involve a careful balance between enabling him to express his intensely angry feelings while also cultivating social ease and more mutually satisfying interpersonal roles. He may be slow to accept his own anger as a normal and sometimes desirable reaction lest he be "consumed" by rage.

The channeling and directing of his intense energies and needs for excitement and stimulation can be beneficial; vigorous physical activities were reported as a positive compensation for many patients with similar profiles. Ways in which he felt superior to his peers as child or now feels emotionally unique and different could lead to an exploration of his interpersonal ambivalences.

A related assertion of personal beliefs, of elaborated explanations of ongoing events, and of unchallengeable values may overprotect against painful criticism and threats to his self-esteem. A very gradual acceptance of the intensity and directions of his own angry feelings could help him to express them more appropriately and lead to an eventual relaxing and freeing up of his controls.

General Comments

All four interpretations for this first example are in general agreement about the profile's primary features: the client blames others for his problems, which are chronic in nature; he is angry, hostile, and may become physically assaultive; he has strange and unusual experiences that may reflect a psychotic process; he has significant familial problems; he is not motivated for treatment and will be difficult to treat; he has difficulties with substance abuse; and he has a paranoid disorder or bipolar disorder, manic type.

All four interpretations were incorrect as to the presence of substance abuse according to all available information since the client did not use alcohol or other substances and he had no history of such use. As noted in Chapter 5, *MAC* scores are typically elevated in *6-9/9-6* codetypes regardless of substance

use, which would indicate that the *MAC-R* was a false positive in this client.

The client was released from the hospital after a stay of approximately two weeks because of the threatened litigation. He was referred for outpatient treatment at his local mental health clinic. Once he was released from the hospital, he filed suit against all of the people and agencies that he believed were involved in his hospitalization. He did not keep any of his appointments at the mental health clinic.

The reader has probably already noticed the different types of interpretations provided by the three computer-based interpretive systems. Both The Minnesota Report™ and Caldwell Report are like the evaluations that the individual clinician would write, whereas the MMPI-2 Adult Interpretive System provides a briefer narrative that the clinician would have to integrate with other material.

All three computer-based interpretive systems appear to use a configural approach to profile interpretation, and the MMPI-2 Adult Interpretive System provides a quantitative estimate of how well the client's profile matches prototypic codetypes. The Caldwell Report provides the most detailed and dynamic interpretation of the client's profile and it suggests a number of issues that might be explored in treatment. The interested reader also can take each statement in these interpretations and try to deduce the scales and/or indexes that were used as the basis for making the statement.

Interpreting the MMPI-2: Example 2

The client is a 32-year-old married, white female, who was admitted to the hospital as a result of an overdose of medication and her verbalized statements of further suicidal attempts. She reported four previous suicidal gestures by overdose; the most recent attempt was due to her depression over her husband's physical disabilities. She also is addicted to heroin and needed to be withdrawn from it while she was hospitalized.

The client has been married for five years to an alcoholic, who is physically disabled. It was the second marriage for both of them. She had a five-year relationship prior to her present marriage that was very chaotic. That man committed suicide several years after the termination of their relationship.

She feels trapped in her dysfunctional marital relationship, but her dependency needs are so great that she cannot bring herself to terminate the relationship even though she has good skills for employment and some insight into the unhealthiness of their relationship. She was not seriously depressed, but rather chronically dysthymic and fearful of making changes in her life.

The MMPI-2 (see Profiles 7-4 to 7-6) was administered approximately one week after she entered the hospital. The prototypic scores for *2-4/4-2* codetypes can be found in Table 7-3.

Clinician's Interpretation

Item Omissions

(See Chapter 3)   She endorsed all of the
? = 0   items. Item omissions are not a problem for interpretation.

Consistency of Item Endorsement

(See Chapter 3)   Both indexes are well
VRIN = 4   within the acceptable
F = 10   range, which indicates
F_B = 6   that she endorsed the items consistently. Profile interpretation may proceed since she endorsed the items consistently.

Accuracy of Item Endorsement

(See Chapter 3)   Both scales/indexes are within
Total (Ob-Sub) = 103   the acceptable
Crit Items = 43   range. When her scores are compared to the prototype for a *2-4/4-2* codetype (see Table 7-3), she is about one standard deviation above the mean on both scales/indexes. She has endorsed the items accurately, and she is experiencing slightly more emotional distress than most clients with this codetype. Profile interpretation may proceed since she endorsed the items accurately.

Validity Scales

(See Chapter 3)   She may be trying to create
L = 38   an extremely pathologic picture of herself.
F = 72   She is willing to acknowledge more than the typical number of unusual experiences. She is experiencing a mild to moderate degree of emotional distress.
K = 41   She has a proper balance between self-disclosure and self-protection. She has sufficient personal resources to desire and tolerate a psychological intervention.

PROFILE 7–4.   MMPI-2 Standard Validity and Clinical Scales for Example 2

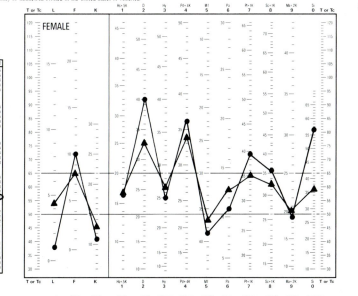

MMPI-2
S.R. Hathaway and J.C. McKinley
Minnesota Multiphasic
Personality Inventory -2™

Profile for Basic Scales

Minnesota Multiphasic Personality Inventory-2
Copyright © by THE REGENTS OF THE UNIVERSITY OF MINNESOTA
1942, 1943 (renewed 1970), 1989. This Profile Form 1989.
All rights reserved. Distributed exclusively by NATIONAL COMPUTER SYSTEMS, INC.
under license from The University of Minnesota.

"MMPI-2" and "Minnesota Multiphasic Personality Inventory-2" are trademarks owned by
The University of Minnesota. Printed in the United States of America.

Name **Example 2**

Address **3612 New Jersey**

Occupation **Medical Technician**   Date Tested **11/20/89**

Education **10th** Age **32** Marital Status **Married**

Referred by **Dr. Harry Davis**

MMPI-2 Code **2*40"7'8-136/95**   **F'-K:L**

Scorer's Initials **HG**

Client

Prototype

	L	F	K	Hs+5K 1	D 2	Hy 3	Pd+4K 4	Mf 5	Pa 6	Pt+1K 7	Sc+1K 8	Ma+2K 9	Si 0
Raw Score	1	10	11	10	40	25	32	39	11	28	25	17	56
? Raw Score 0			K to be Added	6			4			11	11	2	
			Raw Score with K	16			36			39	36	19	

NATIONAL
COMPUTER   NCS
SYSTEMS

24001

PROFILE 7–5. MMPI-2 Content Scales for Example 2

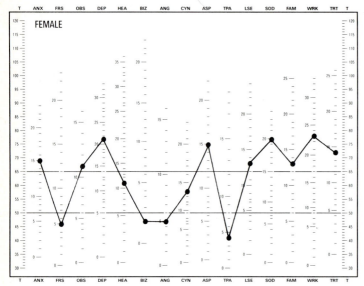

Name Example 2

Address 3612 New Jersey

Occupation Medical Technician   **Date Tested** 11/20/89

Education 10th   **Age** 32   **Marital Status** Married

Referred by Dr. Harry Davis

Scorer's Initials HG

	ANX	FRS	OBS	DEP	HEA	BIZ	ANG	CYN	ASP	TPA	LSE	SOD	FAM	WRK	TRT
Raw Score	15	5	11	21	11	1	5	14	15	4	13	20	13	23	14

PROFILE 7–6. MMPI-2 Supplementary Scales for Example 2

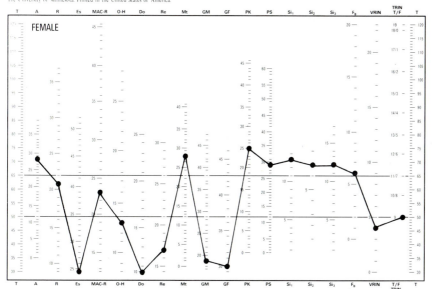

Name **Example 2**

Address **3612 New Jersey**

Occupation **Medical Technician**   Date Tested **11/20/89**

Education **10th** Age **32** Marital Status **Married**

Referred by **Dr. Harry Davis**

Scorer's Initials **HG**

FEMALE

Raw Score	A	R	Es	MAC-R	O-H	Do	Re	Mt	GM	GF	PK	PS	Si₁	Si₂	Si₃	F_B	VRIN	T/F
	28	21	24	23	13	9	17	28	19	30	25	29	13	7	12	6	4	9

TABLE 7-3 Prototypic Scores for *2-4/4-2* Codetypes in Psychiatric Settings

	MMPI			MMPI-2	
Demographics					
	M	SD		M	SD
N	606			343	
Age	38.1	12.5		36.9	12.4
Men	78.1%			66.5%	
Women	21.9			33.5	
Test-Taking Scales/Indexes					
	M	SD		M	SD
Inconsistent	6.3%			3.2%	
Total (Obvious-Subtle)[a]	38.6	59.9		68.3	62.3
Critical items[b]	32.9	12.1		34.4	11.9
Overreported[c]	5.9%			16.3%	
Underreported[c]	22.8%			13.7%	
Standard Validity and Clinical Scales (K-Corrected)					
	M	SD		M	SD
?[d]	4.2	5.5		3.4	4.7
L	50.9	8.0		52.5	10.5
F	62.2	9.0		64.9	13.9
K	51.5	8.8		45.3	9.3
1(Hs)	61.1	10.8		58.1	10.3
2(D)	81.8	9.1		76.1	8.4
3(Hy)	65.7	8.8		60.1	10.1
4(Pd)	83.1	8.3		77.6	7.9
5(Mf)	56.3	10.1		48.1	10.1
6(Pa)	63.5	9.6		59.3	11.0
7(Pt)	68.5	9.6		63.8	10.3
8(Sc)	65.8	11.6		60.6	11.7
9(Ma)	57.8	9.7		51.3	9.0
0(Si)	60.0	9.7		58.9	9.4
Supplementary Scales					
	M	SD		M	SD
A	60.1	10.8		62.7	10.8
R	68.1	13.1		57.4	11.5
MAC/MAC-R[d]					
men	26.9	4.7		26.8	4.9
women	22.4	4.5		22.7	4.4

Codetype Concordance

	Men	Women		Men	Women
MMPI-2 2-4/4-2	45.9%	53.0%	MMPI 2-4/4-2	92.1%	61.7%
2-7/7-2		15.7	Spike 4		15.6
Spike 4	10.4		4-8/8-4		13.0

[a] See Chapter 3, Table 3-24, for explanation of how this index is computed.

[b] The total number of Lachar and Wrobel (1979) critical items endorsed.

[c] Percentage of patients within this codetype scoring above the 75th percentile or below the 25th percentile on the total T score difference on the Wiener and Harmon Obvious and Subtle subscales for all patients (see Tables 3-45 and 3-46 for the cutting scores for the MMPI-2 and MMPI, respectively).

[d] Raw score.

Validity Scale Configuration

(See Figure 3–3, solid line)

This client is admitting to personal and emotional problems, is requesting assistance with these problems, and is unsure of her own capabilities for dealing with these problems.

Codetype

(See Chapter 6)

Clients may achieve *2-4/4-2* codetypes for a myriad of reasons. One critical factor, which should be assessed through an interview with the client or knowledge of the client's reason for taking the MMPI-2, is whether Scale *2* is being elevated by internal (intra-psychic) and/or external (situational) causes.

Examples of the latter are psychopathic individuals who have been caught in some illicit or illegal activity and who are being evaluated as a consequence of their behavior. The depression in these persons represents the constraints being placed on their behavior, and their depression, or possibly boredom at being externally constrained, will alleviate itself quickly once they manage to extricate themselves from their present situation. The presence of even this situational depression in these persons forebodes a better progno-

sis than persons in similar circumstances who achieve a Spike *4* or a *4-9/9-4* codetype.

These psychopathic clients with a *2-4/4-2* codetype can be understood best by examining the correlates of a Spike *4* codetype. They will display excellent intellectual insight into their behavior, make a positive impression of their earnestness on the clinician, and vehemently protest that they will change their behavior. Despite their "sincere" intentions, recurrences of acting out are very likely, followed by the same protestations to do better when caught again.

Another subgroup of clients with *2-4/4-2* codetypes is more likely to be chronically depressed and unhappy without evidence of antisocial acting out. These clients are displaying hostility and resentment, which often result from marital conflict, familial difficulties, or similar situations that make them feel trapped and hopeless.

They are immature, dependent, and egocentric and often vacillate between pitying themselves and blaming others for their difficulties. These behaviors are chronic in nature and difficult to resolve through psychological interventions. Involvement of the other members of the family or the spouse in the therapeutic interaction is important if meaningful behavior change is to occur.

Clients with *2-4/4-2* codetypes are frequently identified as alcoholics. These clients will evidence depressive features, familial conflict, and vocational problems characteristic of alcoholics.

The prototypic scores for a *2-4/4-2* codetype can be seen in Table 7–3.

Prototypic Scores

(See Table 7–3) The client was more than one standard deviation above the mean on Scales *2* and *0*. She was more than one standard deviation below the mean on Scale *L*. She is significantly more depressed and socially introverted than most clients with this codetype.

Clinical Scales

(See Chapter 4)
$1(Hs) = 57$
$2(D) = 92$

She has a typical number of physical ailments.
She exhibits a general sadness and depressed mood either about life or herself. Pessimism, depression, and hopelessness are prevading her life. She is depressed, withdrawn, guilty, and self-deprecating.

$3(Hy) = 56$ The client has a typical number of attitudes and behaviors that relate to histrionic dynamics.

$4(Pd) = 84$ She is fighting against something, which is usually some form of conflict with authority figures. These conflicts may not necessarily be acted out overtly; the rebelliousness and hostility toward authority figures are readily apparent even in these cases. She is likely to be unreliable, egocentric, and irresponsible. She may be unable to learn from experience or to plan ahead. She has a good social facade and makes a good initial impression, but the psychopathic features will surface in longer interactions or under stress. Psychological interventions are less effective than maturation in achieving change.

$Pd_1 = 80$ She is struggling against familial control.

$Pd_2 = 62$ She does not resent societal demands and conventions and parental standards. Her problems may involve more of the familial aspects of Scale *4* rather than the authority conflict seen in sociopathic individuals.

$5(Mf) = 43$ The client is genuinely interested in traditional feminine interests and activities. She may be passive in this role.

6(*Pa*) = 52   She may be very sensitive and suspicious, yet able to avoid endorsing the obvious items on this Scale. She has the normal degree of interpersonal sensitivity.

7(*Pt*) = 72   She is worried, tense, and indecisive. Agitation may develop and overt anxiety is usually apparent both to her and to others. Disabling guilt feelings may be present.

8(*Sc*) = 66   She feels alienated and remote from her environment. Therapeutic interventions should be directive and supportive.

9 (*Ma*) = 49   The client has a normal activity level.

0 (*Si*) = 81   She is introverted, shy, and socially insecure. In addition, she withdraws from and avoids significant others, which serves to exacerbate her problems since others might be able to help her. The likelihood of acting out is decreased and ruminative behavior is increased.

Supplementary Scales

(See Chapter 5)

A   = 71   She has a mild to moderate level of anxiety and distress. She is maladjusted and emotionally upset which may reflect a situational crisis or a more chronic problem. Note that other first factor scales (*Mt* = 72, *PK* = 75, *PS* = 69) are in the same range as *A*.

R   = 62   She is reluctant to discuss her behavior and any problems she may have. She may be merely suppressing this material or repressing and denying that any problems exist. She may lack insight into her own behavior.

MAC-R = 23   She has an average score
(raw score)   for her codetype. She reported that she used alcohol excessively and other drugs.

Content Scales

(See Chapter 5)

ANX = 69   She reported general symptoms of anxiety, nervousness, worries, and sleep and concentration difficulties. She has difficulty making decisions. She finds life a strain and works under a great deal of tension and stress.

FRS = 46   She has a typical number of specific fears.

OBS = 67   She has great difficulty making decisions, ruminates excessively, worries excessively, and has intrusive thoughts. She dislikes change. She counts and saves unimportant things.

DEP = 77   She has depressive mood and thoughts. She feels blue and unhappy, and is likely to brood. She is uncertain about her future and finds her life empty and meaningless. She cries easily. She is self-critical, guilty, and lonely. She reported suicidal ideation.

HEA = 61   She has an usual number of concerns about her health.

BIZ = 47   She does not report strange thoughts or experiences.

ANG = 47   She is not moody, irritable, or angry. She did not endorse items indicating that she is angry or has problems in controlling her anger.

CYN = 58   She is not cynical.

ASP = 75   She reported stealing things, other problem behaviors, and antisocial practices during her school years. She has attitudes similar individuals who break the law, even if she is not engaging in antisocial behavior.

TPA = 41   She is not a hard-driving, fast-moving, work-oriented person.

LSE = 68   She has a very low opinion of herself, and is uncomfortable if people say nice things about her. She believes that she is unattractive, awkward and clumsy, useless, and a burden to others, who do not like her. She sees herself as not as good or capable as others, and she cannot do anything well.

SOD = 77   She is very uneasy around others and is happier by herself. She sees herself as shy. She dislikes parties and other group events.

FAM = 68   She reports considerable familial discord. Her family lacks love, support, and companionship, and she wanted to leave home. Family members are nervous and have quick tempers. They are to be avoided and may be hated.

WRK = 78   She is not as able to work as she once was and she works under a great deal of tension. She is tired, lacks energy, and is sick of what she has to do. She dislikes making decisions and lacks self-confidence. She gives up easily and shrinks from facing a crisis or problem.

TRT = 72   She dislikes going to doctors and she believes that she should not discuss her personal problems with others. She prefers to take drugs or medicine, since talking about problems does not help. She does not believe that anyone understands or cares about her. She gives up quickly and does not care about what is happening to her, since nothing can be done about her problems.

Profile Interpretation[6]

Test-Taking Behaviors

The client endorsed the items consistently (*VRIN*, *F*, F_B) and accurately (Total T score difference; Total critical items). She is experiencing a mild to moderate degree of emotional distress (*F* scale). She is admitting to personal and emotional problems, is requesting assistance with these problems, and is unsure of her own capabilities for dealing with these problems (validity scale configuration).

Cognitive Processes

She has great difficulty making decisions, ruminates excessively, and has intrusive thoughts (*OBS*). She vacillates between pitying herself and blaming others for her difficulties (*2-4/4-2* codetype). She did not report any strange thoughts or unusual experiences (*BIZ*). She has concentration and memory difficulties because of her extensive depressive symptomatology, and does not trust her judgment (Scale *2*).

Mood

She is depressed, guilty, withdrawn, and self-deprecating (Scale *2*). Pessimism, depression, and hopelessness are prevading her life (Scale *2*). She is uncertain about her future and finds her life empty and meaningless (*DEP*). She reported suicidal ideation that should be evaluated carefully (*DEP*). She has a very low opinion of herself, and believes that she is unattractive, awkward and clumsy, useless, and a burden to others who do not like her (*LSE*). She is tired, lacks energy, and is sick of what she has to do (*WRK*). She does not believe that anyone understands or cares about her (*TRT*).

She also is worried, tense, and indecisive (Scales *7*, *A*, *ANX*). Her agitation and anxiety are readily apparent to her and to others (Scale *7*).

She does not describe herself as being angry or having problems in controlling her anger (*ANG*).

Interpersonal Relationships

She is significantly more introverted than her peers (Scale *0*). She is shy and socially insecure (*SOD*). She withdraws from and avoids significant others, which serves to exacerbate her problems since others might be able to help her (Scale *0*). She is very uncomfortable around others and is happier by herself (*SOD*).

She has traditional feminine interests and activities (Scale *5*).

She has considerable familial discord (*Pd₁*, FAM). Her family lacks love, support, and companionship. Her family members are nervous and have quick tempers.

Treatment

Her significant depressive symptomatology and general hopelessness about her life must be directly addressed (Scale *2*, *DEP*). Her suicidal ideation needs to be evaluated carefully and monitored on an ongoing basis, particularly as her mood begins to improve (*DEP*). Depending on the severity of her depression and the sources of distress in her current situation, antidepressant medication may be appropriate (Scale *2*).

Her family is a significant part of her current distress and should be an initial focus in therapy (*Pd₁*, *FAM*). Involvement of her spouse and/or other members of the family is important if meaningful behavior change is to occur (*2-4/4-2* codetype).

Therapeutic interventions should be directive and supportive (Scale *8*). Group therapy would be very beneficial since it would directly counteract her tendency to isolate herself and avoid other people (Scale *0*), and it would help her realize that other people have similar problems. Neither individual nor group therapy should be confrontive until a good therapeutic relationship has been established (*LSE*).

She reported a history of antisocial behaviors that needs to be reviewed to determine whether such behaviors are still being expressed (*ASP*). These antisocial behaviors may reflect issues around her family or more general antisocial behavior.

Diagnostic Impression

Axis I	300.40	Rule out Dysthymia
Axis II	301.82	Rule out Avoidant Personality Disorder
	301.60	Rule out Dependent Personality Disorder

Computer Interpretation— The Minnesota Report™⁷

Profile Validity

This is a valid MMPI-2 profile. The client has cooperated in the evaluation, admitting to a number of psychological problems in a frank and open manner. Individuals with this profile tend to be blunt and may openly complain to others about their psychological problems. The client tends to be quite self-critical and may appear to have low self-esteem and inadequate psychological defense mechanisms. She may be seeking psychological help at this time since she feels that things are out of control and unmanageable.

Symptomatic Pattern

Individuals with this MMPI-2 profile tend to show a pattern of chronic psychological maladjustment. The client appears to be quite anxious and depressed at this time. She may be feeling some tension and somatic distress along with her psychological problems and may want relief from situational pressures.

Apparently quite immature and hedonistic, she may show a recent history of impulsive acting-out behavior and substance abuse which resulted in considerable situational stress. She shows a pattern of superficial guilt or remorse over her behavior, but does not accept much responsibility for her actions. She may avoid confrontation and deny problems. She reports no significant sex-role conflicts.

In addition, the following description is suggested by the content of this client's responses. She is preoccupied with feeling guilty and unworthy. She feels that she deserves to be punished for wrongs that she has committed. She feels regretful and unhappy about her life, and seems plagued by anxiety and worry about the future. She feels hopeless at times and feels that she is a condemned person. She has difficulty managing routine affairs, and the item content she endorsed suggests a poor memory, concentration problems, and an inability to make decisions.

She appears to be immobilized and withdrawn and has no energy for life. She views her physical health as failing and reports numerous somatic concerns. She feels that life is no longer worthwhile and that she is losing control of her thought processes. According to her self-report, there is a strong possibility that she has seriously contemplated suicide. She has a self-acknowledged history of suicidal ideation. It is important to perform a suicide assessment and, if need be, take appropriate precautions. She has acknowledged having suicidal thoughts recently. Although she denies suicidal attempts in the past, given her current mood an assessment of suicidal potential appears indicated.

The client's recent thinking is likely to be characterized by obsessiveness and indecision. She feels somewhat self-alienated and expresses some personal misgivings or a vague sense of remorse about past acts. She feels that life is unrewarding and dull, and finds it hard to settle down. She reports holding some antisocial beliefs and attitudes, admits to rule violations, and acknowledges a history of antisocial behavior in the past.

Interpersonal Relations

She is probably experiencing disturbed interpersonal relationships, possibly owing to her acting-out behavior. Her acting-out behavior is likely to put great strain on her marriage. She may be experiencing marital discord at this time.

The content of this client's MMPI-2 responses suggests the following additional information concerning her interpersonal relations. She feels a moderate degree of family conflict at this time, and reported some troublesome family issues. She feels that her family life is not as pleasant as that of other people she knows. She feels like leaving home to escape a quarrelsome, critical situation, and to be free of family domination. Her social relationships are likely to be viewed by others as problematic. She may visibly by uneasy around others, sits alone in group situations, and dislikes engaging in group activities.

Behavioral Stability

Individuals with this profile tend to have long-standing personality problems and are presently experiencing situational distress. Although they might express a desire to change and feel remorse over past behavior, they tend to change only temporarily, eventually drifting back into the old pattern. Social introversion tends to be very stable personality characteristic. Her generally reclusive interpersonal behavior, introverted life style, and tendency toward interpersonal avoidance would likely be evident in any future test results.

Diagnostic Considerations

Individuals with this profile are often diagnosed as having a Personality Disorder (Dependent or Passive-Aggressive type) with a Substance Use Disorder. The content of her responses underscores the antisocial features in her history. These factors should be taken into consideration in arriving at a clinical diagnosis.

Treatment Considerations

Individuals with this profile may seek psychological therapy as an effort to reduce the current situational distress they are experiencing. The sincerity of their motivation to change their behavior should be carefully evaluated. They may verbalize a great need for help and show early gains, but as frustration mounts, they may terminate early. Acting-out behavior is a possibility once her anxiety and depression over her current problems diminish. She is probably experiencing multiple problems that make it difficult to focus treatment. Long-term behavioral change may be difficult to obtain in her case.

Individuals with this profile are often predisposed to Substance Use or Abuse Disorders. Any treatment program involving medication should be carefully monitored. Some individuals with this profile attempt to manipulate others through suicidal gestures. Thus, the possibility she might use prescription medication for that purpose should also be taken into consideration.

The client endorsed item content, which seems to indicate low potential for change. She may feel that her problems are not addressable through therapy and that she is not likely to benefit much from psychological treatment at this time. Her apparently negative treatment attitudes may need to be explored early in therapy if treatment is to be initiated successfully. Her item content suggests some family conflicts which are giving her considerable concern at this time. She feels unhappy about her life and resents having an unpleasant home life. Psychological intervention with her could profitably focus, in part, upon clarifying her feelings about her family.

In any intervention or psychological evaluation program involving occupational adjustment, her negative work attitudes could become an important problem to overcome. She holds a number of attitudes and feelings that could interfere with work adjustment.

Computer Interpretation—MMPI-2 Adult Interpretive System[8]

Profile matches and scores for the client are provided in Table 7–4.

Configural Validity Scale Interpretation

This validity scale configuration is usually obtained by individuals who are admitting personal and emotional problems, requesting help with these problems, and are unsure of their own resources for dealing with them. As the elevation of the F scale increases, these individuals are acknowledging that they are experiencing more problems and feeling worse or are overreporting their problems, perhaps to get help sooner.

This configural interpretation should be

TABLE 7–4 MMPI-2 Adult Interpretive System: Profile Matches and Scores for Example 2

Scale		Client Profile	Highest Scale Codetype	Best Fit Codetype
Codetype match:			2-4/4-2	2-4/4-2 (7)
Coefficient of Fit:			.95	.96
Scores:	? (raw)	0		
	L	38	53	51
	F	72	65	60
	K	41	45	47
	Hs (1)	57	58	53
	D (2)	92	76	71
	Hy (3)	56	60	55
	Pd (4)	84	78	73
	Mf (5)	43	48	46
	Pa (6)	52	59	54
	Pt (7)	72	64	65
	Sc (8)	66	61	57
	Ma (9)	49	51	50
	Si (0)	81	59	56
Mean Clinical Elevation:		66	56	60
Ave age-males:			38	36
Ave age-females:			34	33
% of male codetypes:			4.0%	1.8%
% of female codetypes:			4.3%	1.2%
% of males within codetype:			66.5%	75.6%
% of females within codetype:			33.5%	24.4%

Configural clinical scale interpretation is provided in the report for the following codetype(s):

2-4/4-2

2-4/4-2 (7)

Note: Reproduced by special permission of Psychological Assessment Resources, Inc., from MMPI-2 Adult Interpretive System by Greene, Brown, & PAR. Copyright 1990. Further reproduction is prohibited without permission from PAR, Inc.

the primary source of interpretive hypotheses for the *L, F,* and *K* validity scales. Individual validity scale hypotheses, however, are also presented in the following section.

Validity Scales

? (raw) = 0

Scores in this range reflect a relatively small number of unanswered items, which in and of itself should not have an impact on the validity of the profile.

L   T = 38

L scores in this range are usually obtained by individuals who generally respond frankly and openly to the test items and are willing to admit to minor faults.

F   T = 72

F scores in this range, if they are valid, suggest the increasing probability of serious psychological and emotional problems which are often characteristic of severe neurosis, psychosis, or behavioral problems. Scores in this range also may occur because individuals have had some difficulty reading or understanding the test items (evaluate measures of consistency of item endorsement), or because they have some motivation to overreport psychopathology (evaluate measures of accuracy of item endorsement).

K   T = 41

Scores in this range indicate limited personal resources and open acknowledgment of significant psychological distress. These individuals are likely to have a relatively poor self-concept, to be strongly dissatisfied with themselves but lacking the skills necessary to change their situation, to be self-critical, and/or to be extremely open and revealing. Scores in this range may also reflect low ego strength, a lack of insight into one's self-motivation and behavior, and ineffectiveness in dealing with the problems of daily life. Prognosis for psychological intervention is usually guarded.

Configural Clinical Scale Interpretation

2-4/4-2 Codetype (High Match)

Clinical Presentation

This codetype is very frequent and much more common in men than women. It also is one of the more difficult codetypes to interpret because of the multitude of factors that can produce it. It is imperative that the clinician note the other clinical scales that are elevated and the relative elevations of the supplementary and content scales. For example, a patient with this codetype who also elevates Pd_2 (Authority Problems), *ANG* (Anger), *CYN* (Cynicism), and *ASP* (Antisocial Practices), is very different from a patient who does not elevate these same scales and elevates *ANX* (Anxiety), *DEP* (Depression), *LSE* (Low Self-esteem) and Scale *0*.

A number of features are common to all individuals with this codetype regardless of the reasons for its occurrence: substance abuse, conflictual interpersonal and familial relationships, and depression.

These individuals often exhibit depression and agitation in response to vocational or family problems, financial problems, legal difficulties and/or substance abuse problems. They perceive themselves as playing a significant role in these problems and are distressed by them.

These individuals are usually very dissatisfied with themselves and very dependent upon others. They tend to be somewhat introverted and shy, although they have adequate social skills. They often are manipulative and passive-dependent in their relationships with others.

Treatment

The prognosis is generally poor with respect to traditional methods of individual psychotherapy. Marital or family therapy may be somewhat effective in instances other than characterologic or extremely severe pathology.

Possible Diagnoses

Axis I   Rule out Adjustment Disorder
          Rule out Mood Disorders
                  Dysthymia
                  Major Depression
          Rule out Psychoactive Substance-
          Abuse Disorders
Axis II   Rule out Antisocial Personality
                  Disorder
          Rule out Passive Aggressive Personality Disorder
          Rule out Borderline Personality
          Disorder

2-4/4-2 (7) Codetype (Best Fit)

Clinical Presentation

This codetype is very frequent and much more common in men than women. It also is one of the more difficult codetypes to interpret because of the multitude of factors that can produce it. It is imperative that the clinician note the other clinical scales that are elevated and the relative elevations of the supplementary and content scales. For example, a patient with this codetype who also elevates Pd_2 (Authority Problems), *ANG* (Anger), *CYN* (Cynicism), and *ASP* (Antisocial Practices), is very different from a patient who does not elevate these same scales and elevates *ANX* (Anxiety), *DEP* (Depression), *LSE* (Low Self-esteem) and Scale *0*.

These individuals often exhibit depression and agitation in response to vocational or family problems, financial problems, legal difficulties and/or substance abuse problems. They perceive themselves as playing a significant role in these problems and are distressed by them.

These individuals are usually very dissatisfied with themselves and very dependent upon others. They tend to be somewhat introverted and shy, although they have adequate social skills. They often are manipulative and passive-dependent in their relationships with others.

Treatment

The prognosis is fair with traditional methods of individual psychotherapy.

Possible Diagnoses

Axis I   Rule out Adjustment Disorder
           Rule out Mood Disorders
              Dysthymia
              Major Depression
           Rule out Psychoactive Substance-Abuse Disorders
Axis II   Rule out Avoidant Personality Disorder
           Rule out Passive Aggressive Personality Disorder
           Rule out Borderline Personality Disorder

Computer Interpretation — Caldwell Report[9]

Test-Taking Attitude

The client was open and mildly self-critical in taking the MMPI-2. The basic validity scales were well within the acceptable limits.

The supplemental validity scales show a mild to moderate elevation on the "fake-bad" scale (Ds). This suggests an open willingness to report distressing symptoms if not some overemphasis on or exaggeration of them. It should be noted, however, that a serious disorder, especially if it involved any mental confusion or even marginally psychotic elements, could also contribute to such a willingness to self-disclose. Thus, most of her mild elevation on scale F may be attributable to her self-criticalness, although some of it may be secondarily due to psychopathology.

The score on the scale measuring currently attained, recently experienced, or wished for socioeconomic status (Ss) is below average, which is consistent with her K score. This overall pattern of scores suggests a person of less than average sophistication and socioeconomic status identification who is openly reporting her distresses if not mildly exaggerating them. Unless the following interpretation is unequivocally a poor clinical fit, however, it would not be justified to reject the test results as malingered.

Symptoms and Personality Characteristics

The profile shows a severe level of anxiety and depression. The patterns suggests extreme low moods and complaints of nervousness, worry, fears, self-doubts, feelings of inferiority, and loss of initiative. She appears prone to overreact with excessive anxiety and poorly regulated emotions to minor matters or even fancied threats. She is apt to become quite tense and ruminative and to have chronic difficulties in getting to sleep.

The current level of her day-to-day coping and immediate practical self-sufficiency tests as partially disorganized in a variety of areas.

The profile indicates a severe passive-aggressive or related personality disorder. She is likely to get many secondary gains from her symptoms, even though her undercontrol of her impulses and lapses of judgment are self-defeating in the long run. Her ability to conform socially tests as poor. Repeated difficulties and conflicts over limits on her behavior are suggested. She appears quite immature and insecure with indications of repeated misunderstandings and longstanding resentments in her close personal relationships. She tests as vulnerable to increasing difficulties with alcohol.

Persisting problems in regulating her expressions of anger are indicated along with chronic, underlying resentments over dependency frustrations. Fears of confirming her self-dislike would lead to a self-protective interpersonal distancing. These fears would, however, repeatedly block self-assertive expressions of anger. She would be acutely sensitive to criticism.

She tests as severely introverted and socially shy. She appears mildly to moderately withdrawn. Her balance of masculine and feminine interests is within the normal range for women.

Her profile is related to the dependency manipulative ''Daddy's girl'' life-style pattern. She would play a daughter-to-father role toward her husband, relating in dependent and immature ways to him as well as to other males in her life. She is likely to be seen as clutching onto men in masochistic or even self-destructive relationships and as becoming symptomatic when she was threatened with losing such quasi-paternal supports. The husbands of patients with this pattern have a notably high frequency of psychological breakdowns. This pattern is typically associated with histories of almost no premarital dating.

Diagnostic Impression

The diagnoses most commonly associated with this profile are of depressive and anxiety neuroses. A secondary personality disorder diagnosis such as dependent or passive-aggressive personality would also be typical. A few of these patients showed secondary schizoid trends. A secondary diagnosis reflecting chronic dependence on alcohol may also be indicated.

Treatment Considerations

The profile suggests a mild to moderate suicide risk. In some similar cases the use of alcohol effectively became a slow form of suicide. Antidepressants and energizers have been of limited benefit with patients who obtained similar profiles. On the one hand, her pattern is often associated with episodes of serious if not uncontrolled chemical abuse; on the other hand, her score on the MacAndrew Alcoholism Scale was just below the chronic alcoholic and chemical dependence range. Her responses suggest asking if she has been in trouble with the law. If currently involved, the stress of this could have precipitated or aggravated her symptoms or otherwise have led her to make professional contact.

The profile emphasizes the importance of contacts with her relatives or other informants. The clarification of all the precipitating circumstances would be particularly indicated, including possible adjustments to them that she may fail to mention. The family can be of specific benefit in minimizing secondary gains.

Treatment motivation is apt to decline as soon as her situation begins to improve and external stresses are reduced. Many patients with this pattern have terminated treatment before the therapist felt it to be complete, some against therapeutic advice. She tests as very prone to manipulate treatment, and the character problems strongly warn against involvement in her manipulations. She is apt to outwardly obliging because of her needs for attention and affection, which would obscure her underlying resentments and passive-aggressive tendencies. The treatment relationship may develop slowly because of her fears of being hurt and her emotional distortions. In general her emotional constrictions and her tendency to declare certain topics "off limits" could necessitate careful handling and patience in therapy.

The expected response to short-term treatment is fair. She tests as prone to focus in interviews on her fears, worries, and shortcomings. She could benefit from a greater awareness of the ways in which she sacrifices long-term goals for immediate gratifications and relief of anxiety. She could also benefit from an increased awareness of the manipulations and countermanipulations of guilt around her victim role. New activities in which she needs to exert initiative with a risk of failure are apt to require repeated encouragement and reassurances. These could include projects to develop new activities and interests as well as initiative in dealing with current personal dilemmas.

General Comments

All four interpretations are in general agreement about the primary features of this client's profile: mild to moderate depression and anxiety with associated guilt; difficulties with interpersonal relationships, particularly with members of her family; significant social introversion and avoidance of social interaction; history of antisocial behavior; presence of suicidal ideation; and obsessive and ruminative thoughts.

The four interpretations did not concur whether the client was angry and hostile; antidepressant medications would be appropriate; acting-out will occur; substance use or abuse is a problem; and the client should have a personality disorder diagnosis. It is apparent that the computer-based test interpreta-

tions were having a hard time deciding whether the 2-4/4-2 codetype reflected a personality disorder, some form of depressive disorder, and/or a substance use disorder. This confusion is real since all three diagnoses were appropriate for the client given her history. Her discharge diagnoses from the hospital were Heroin Dependence; Alcohol Dependence, in Remission; Dysthymia; and Dependent Personality Disorder.

It is interesting to note that all four interpretations only discussed suicidal ideation since the client did not report any suicide attempts despite her history and reasons for being hospitalized. In this specific instance, all four interpretations were incorrect because the client did not provide accurate information. All four interpretations did stress the importance of evaluating her suicidal ideation carefully.

The client made satisfactory progress while hospitalized and was discharged with a significant improvement in her mood. Although she verbalized insight into her familial problems and the changes that she needed to make in her life, she chose to return to live with her disabled spouse. Subsequent followup interviews as an outpatient did not reveal any significant changes in her life circumstances.

ENDNOTES

1. Reproduced from the MMPI-2 by permission. Copyright © 1943, (renewed 1970), 1989 by the University of Minnesota. Published by the University of Minnesota Press. All rights reserved.

2. The parenthetical references to specific scales or indexes are provided so clinicians can see the source(s) for the statements in the interpretation. These parenthetical references would be deleted in an actual report.

3. The permission of the University of Minnesota Press to reproduce this report is gratefully acknowledged.

4. Reproduced by special permission of Psychological Assessment Resources, Inc., from MMPI-2 Adult Interpretive System by Greene, Brown, & PAR, Copyright 1990. Further repro-

duction is prohibited without permission from PAR, Inc.

5. The permission of Dr. Alex B. Caldwell, Caldwell Report, Los Angeles, California, to reproduce this report is gratefully acknowledged.

6. The parenthetical references to specific scales or indexes are provided so clinicians can see the source(s) for the statements in the interpretation. These parenthetical references would be deleted in an actual report.

7. The permission of the University of Min-

nesota Press to reproduce this report is gratefully acknowledged.

8. Reproduced by special permission of Psychological Assessment Resources, Inc., from MMPI-2 Adult Interpretive System by Greene, Brown, & PAR, Copyright 1990. Further reproduction is prohibited without permission from PAR, Inc.

9. The permission of Dr. Alex B. Caldwell, Caldwell Report, Los Angeles, California, to reproduce this report is gratefully acknowledged.

CHAPTER 8

Specific Groups: Adolescents, the Aged, Blacks, and Other Ethnic Groups

The original standardization sample of the MMPI consisted of white Minnesota adults, primarily between the ages of 16 and 55 (Hathaway & McKinley, 1940). Investigators suggest that the validity of the MMPI with persons who differ in age or ethnicity from the original standardization sample may be improved by modifying either the norms or the scales themselves. The MMPI-2, which has a more nationally representative normative sample, will begin to provide some current data on the issues that are raised in this chapter.

This chapter will review the use of the MMPI with adolescents, the aged, and several ethnic groups. The MMPI-2 as currently published is not intended for use with adolescents (i.e., anyone under 18 years of age) (Butcher, Dahlstrom, Graham, Tellegen, & Kaemmer, 1989, p. 15). An adolescent revision of the MMPI is planned for publication in August 1991. Until that revision is published, the original MMPI is intended to be used with adolescents.

ADOLESCENTS

Hathaway and Monachesi (1963), in an extensive study of the MMPI performance of adolescents, administered the MMPI to 3,971 ninth-graders (mean age about 15) in the Minneapolis public school system during the 1947–1948 school year. They also microfilmed each student's school record at the time of testing. Two and four years later, they determined how many of these students had records with the local juvenile division of the police department or probation office.

During the spring of 1954 these researchers tested 11,329 additional ninth-graders who represented a sample of the entire state of Minnesota. They again microfilmed each student's school record, had each student complete a personal data sheet, and obtained the teacher's prediction of which students were likely to have legal or emotional difficulties. Three years later they determined how many of these students had records by examining the student's local community police and court files.

In 1957, when most of this second set of ninth-graders were now twelfth-graders (mean age about 18), Hathaway and Monachesi readministered the MMPI to 3,976 students. Hathaway and Monachesi obviously have a wealth of data, only part of which is relevant to the issue of how adolescents differ from adults in terms of their MMPI performance. (The reader who is interested in the use of the MMPI to predict delinquency in adolescents, which was the main thrust of Hathaway and Monachesi's research project, should consult their book.)

Relevant to the current topic of MMPI norms, Hathaway and Monachesi found that ninth-graders had mean scores with *K*-corrections on Scales *4* (Psychopathic Deviate), *8* (Schizophrenia), and *9* (Hypomania), which were approximately 10 T score points higher than the original Minnesota normative sample of adults. On the rest of the validity and clinical scales, the ninth-graders scored very similarly to the adult sample. Thus, these adolescents were more likely to have sociopathic (Scale *4* elevations) or psychotic (elevations on Scales *8* and *9*) profile patterns if adult MMPI norms were used. They also were less likely to have profiles in which all clinical scales were below a T score of 70 than were the normal adults.

The issue that Hathaway and Monachesi did not directly address is whether these MMPI scale elevations in normal adolescents reflect some form of psychological distress and maladjustment that is characteristic of the turmoil of adolescence or whether these elevations reflect mere differences in the frequency of item endorsement that may not have psychopathologic implications.

Hathaway and Monachesi seem to favor the former interpretation since they did not advocate the use of special adolescent norms with the MMPI. Instead, they suggested that both the standard adult profile and an adolescent-normed profile should be plotted so that the clinician can understand the contrast between adolescents and adults. The clinician, however, when provided with the potentially divergent and contradictory information from two profiles on the same adolescent, needs to know which source of information is more accurate, and

Hathaway and Monachesi (1963) did not answer this question.

The students who were retested with the MMPI in the twelfth grade provided some interesting information on profile stability. Test-retest reliability coefficients were highest for the *K* scale—.52 for males and .56 for females—and Scale *0* (Social Introversion)—.54 for males and .61 for females. By contrast, Scales *4* (Psychopathic Deviate)—.36 for males and .38 for females—and *6* (Paranoia)—.32 for males and .36 for females—had the lowest reliability coefficients.

As might be expected, profile stability as defined by the single high-point scale was highest when that scale was greater than a T score of 69. For example, more than half of the adolescents, both male and female, with Scale *4* greater than a T score of 69 on initial testing, had Scale *4* as one of the two highest scales when retested. This relationship, however, did not hold for all scales. Scale *5* (Masculinity-Femininity), for example, was likely to shift from a high-point scale to one of the three lowest clinical scales across this three-year interval.

Hathaway and Monachesi wondered whether there may be an active differentiation of gender roles during this time span that results in Scale *5* scores changing so dramatically. Whatever the reason, Scale *5* scores did change drastically in some adolescents during this time interval.

Following the lead of Hathaway and Monachesi, Ball (1962) also examined the relationship of personality to social deviancy among Kentucky adolescents. Only the data on the nondelinquent adolescents will be reviewed here since it is germane to the issue of how normal adolescents differ from the original Minnesota normative sample on the MMPI. Both male and female adolescents achieved mean T scores near 60 on Scales *F*, *4* (Psychopathic Deviate), *7* (Psychasthenia), *8* (Schizophrenia), and *9* (Hypomania), with the other clinical scales averaging near a mean T score of 50. This pattern of scores is very similar to what Hathaway and Monachesi (1963) reported for their Minnesota adolescents who were tested nearly 10 years earlier.

In a comprehensive study of black-white differences on a variety of intellectual, academic, and personality factors, Baughman and Dahlstrom (1968) reported the MMPI performance of eighth-graders. Only discussion of the data on white adolescents will be reviewed in this section; the data examining black-white differences in MMPI performance will be reviewed in a later section of this chapter. Again, a similar pattern of MMPI scale scores was found in the white eighth-graders. Scales *F, 4* (Psychopathic Deviate), *7* (Psychasthenia), *8* (Schizophrenia), and *9* (Hypomania) were elevated to a mean T score of nearly 60 in both girls and boys, with Scales *8* and *9* elevated almost to a mean T score of 70 in boys.

It appears that normal adolescents display significant elevation on a number of the standard MMPI validity and clinical scales when the adult norms from the original Minnesota normative sample are used. If the clinician is interested in knowing how an adolescent client compares with normal adolescents rather than with the original, adult normative group on the MMPI, an adolescent-normed profile, described in the next section, should be constructed.

Marks, Seeman, and Haller (1974) have done the most extensive MMPI research on emotional disturbance in adolescents. They also have described how the adolescent norms for the MMPI were derived, primarily crediting Peter F. Briggs. Briggs selected 100 boys and 100 girls aged 14, 15, and 16 years, and 80 boys and 40 girls aged 17 years from the students studied by Hathaway and Monachesi (1963).

In order to obtain a larger and more nationally representative sample, 1,046 additional MMPI profiles were collected in 1964 and 1965 from both rural and urban, public and private school students residing in Alabama, California, Kansas, Missouri, North Carolina, and Ohio. All of these students were presumed to be white and at the time of testing were neither institutionalized nor being treated for emotional disturbance (Marks et al., 1974).

By combining these two groups of students, the adolescent norms for the standard validity and clinical scales for boys and girls in four age groups (14 and below, 15, 16, and 17 and 18) were constructed. Only if adolescents were still living with their parents were 18-year-olds included in the oldest group. If an 18-year-old was not living with his or her parents, it was deemed more appropriate to use adult norms, although there has not been any research to demonstrate which set of norms is better.

Although Marks and colleagues (1974) advocate that emotional disturbance in adolescents needs to be established against adolescent norms, they do concur with Hathaway and Monachesi (1963) that adolescent scores on the MMPI also should be compared to adult norms. Thus, Marks and colleagues recommend that both an adult- and an adolescent-normed profile should be constructed for adolescents.

The clinician who desires to construct a profile from adolescent norms must locate the correct table for the age and gender of the adolescent and determine the T score equivalent of the raw score on each scale; these tables are *not K*-corrected. These T scores are then directly plotted on the standard profile sheet. The clinician should indicate on the profile sheet that the profile was plotted using adolescent norms; this procedure will prevent another clinician who uses the profile from assuming that the profile has been misplotted, since the adolescent and adult T scores for each raw score will not be the same. Adolescent profile sheets are available from Psychological Assessment Resources

(P.O. Box 998, Odessa, FL 33566, 800–331–8378) so that clinicians can plot the T score equivalents of the raw scores directly without consulting other data.

In addition to describing the development of adolescent norms, Marks and associates (1974) assessed the empirical correlates of MMPI codetypes in a sample of 834 white boys and girls between the ages of 12 and 18 who were not mentally retarded but who had adjustment problems causing them to seek or be referred for professional services. Each of these teenagers completed a personal data sheet, and for each teenager a therapist completed a case data schedule, an adjective checklist, and a *Q*-sort after a minimum of 10 hours of therapy. All of the therapist's ratings were made independent of the MMPI.

Each of the descriptors from the information provided by the teenager and the therapist was evaluated for gender differences and deleted if significant. Marks and colleagues also eliminated descriptors with exceedingly high ($\geq$ 90 percent) or low ($\leq$ 10 percent) frequencies of occurrence. This procedure resulted in a pool of 1,265 descriptors, which were then related to the codetypes on the MMPI based on adolescent norms.

When ties occurred among the high-point scales, the profile was classified into a codetype on the basis of the scale with the lowest number. For example, if Scales *1*, *2*, and *3* were the three highest scales and had equivalent T scores, the profile was classified as a *1-2/2-1* codetype. Similarly, if Scale *2* was the highest and Scales *3*, *4*, and *7* were tied for the second highest scale, the profile was classified as a *2-3/3-2* codetype.

Marks and colleagues were able to identify 29 codetypes, irrespective of scale order, with a minimum of at least 10 cases per high-point pair. They then developed an actuarial description based on the descriptors that were significantly associated with each of these 29 codetypes. The narrative description for each of these codetypes is approximately two

pages long, and the clinician will need to consult Marks and associates' (1974) book to use their interpretive system.

For profiles that do not fit into one of these 29 codetypes, Marks and colleagues recommend that the second highest scale should be disregarded and that the profile should be reclassified using the first and third highest scales. If the profile is still not classifiable using the first and third highest scales, the profile is considered to be unclassifiable, and their interpretive system cannot be used.

Only one study (Williams & Butcher, 1989b) has attempted to validate the correlates of any of the codetypes developed by Marks and colleagues in another sample of adolescents; this study will be reviewed below.

Marks and associates (1974) dealt with the problem of testing adolescents with the MMPI by using adolescent norms, which sometimes lead to codetypes different from those that would be derived if the adult norms were used. In addition, they used an adolescent population to develop a set of behavioral correlates, or narrative descriptions, for these codetypes. Marks and associates' narrative descriptions have not been cross-validated in another adolescent population, and the research in this area has yielded mixed results.

Ehrenworth and Archer (1985) found that interpretations based on the descriptions by Marks and colleagues were rated as being less accurate than other interpretations in a sample of adolescent inpatients, whereas Archer, Gordon, Giannetti, and Singles (1988) reported that the clinical correlates of single clinical scales in adolescent inpatients were similar to those of Marks and colleagues. Consequently, clinicians should use the Marks and associates' descriptions cautiously.

There has been an almost geometric increase in research on the use of the MMPI with adolescents in the last few years. This increase in research has been spearheaded by the work of Archer (cf. Archer, 1984, 1987, 1988) and Williams (cf. Williams, 1986; Williams & Butcher, 1989a, 1989b). Their contributions should be reviewed by any clinician who is using the MMPI with adolescents. Archer (1987) provides a single, comprehensive overview of this entire area.

Several issues arise when the MMPI is used with adolescents. The first issue is whether adult norms, adolescent norms, or both sets of norms should be used with adolescents. As noted above, Hathaway and Monachesi (1963) and Marks and associates (1974) recommend that adult- and adolescent-normed profiles should be constructed for adolescents. However, Archer (1984, 1987) advocates that adolescent norms should be used exclusively with adolescents, and he presents a cogent rationale for their use that should be read by clinicians. Williams (1986) also indicated that adolescent norms are the most appropriate for adolescents, but she suggests that both profiles should be plotted for adolescents.

Once it has been decided that adolescent norms will be used, the next issue is whether T scores of 70 and above should continue to be the criterion for defining a significant elevation on the scales. Since adolescent norms produce a general lowering of the entire profile, Archer (1984, 1987; Ehrenworth & Archer, 1985) has recommended that T scores of 65 and above be used to define significant clinical elevations similar to the procedure now being used on the MMPI-2.

Additional empirical research that assesses whether a T score of 65 or 70 facilitates the interpretation of adolescent MMPIs is needed. In the interim, clinicians would seem to be well advised to follow Archer's (1984, 1987) suggestion and use adolescent norms for adolescents and interpret their profiles at T scores of 65 and above.

A final issue is whether the adolescent or the adult correlates provide a more accurate interpretation once adolescent norms serve as the base to derive a codetype. Using adolescent and adult norms, Lachar, Klinge, and Grisell (1976) obtained valid profiles on 100 adolescents, most of whom were hospitalized. Interpretations of the two profiles for each adolescent were generated using Lachar's (1974) automated interpretive system for adults. Clinicians were then asked to rate these interpretations for accuracy.

The interpretations of profiles generated from adolescent norms, in comparison to interpretations of profiles generated from adult norms, were rated more accurate 61 times, as accurate 13 times, and less accurate 26 times. Only 10 percent of the adolescent norm interpretations were judged to be inaccurate, and 20 percent of the adult norm interpretations were judged to be inaccurate. Wimbish (1984) reported similar findings in a sample of inpatient adolescent substance abusers.

Hence, it appears that even when an interpretive system (Lachar's) based on adults is used, profiles based on adolescent norms provide a more accurate description of adolescents than do profiles based on adult norms. It remains to be seen, however, whether other adult interpretive systems and individual clinicians will demonstrate the same improvement in accuracy with the use of adolescent norms.

Once the decision has been made to use adolescent norms, the clinician now has three different sets of norms from which to choose: (1) Marks and colleagues (1974), which have been described above and which have served as the standard for adolescent MMPIs since they were originally published; (2) Gottesman, Hanson, Kroeker, and Briggs (1987); and (3) Colligan and Offord (1989).

Gottesman and associates developed their norms by using the MMPI responses of 12,953 15-year-olds and 3,492 18-year-olds, who composed the entire sample of adolescents studied by Hathaway and Monachesi (1963). Instead of using linear T scores as traditionally had been done with the MMPI, Gottesman and colleagues used a normalizing procedure based on power transformations of the raw scores to produce T scores that had equivalent percentile ranks across the scales.

Colligan and Offord (1989) developed their norms by collecting a sample of adolescents in the Mayo Clinic catchment area in a similar manner as they had collected their adult data (see Chapter 1). Colligan and Offord also used normalized T scores in their adolescent sample as they had in their adult sample (see Chapter 2). Since the same issues of codetype concordance can be raised among these various sets of adolescent norms as were discussed in Chapter 6 about codetype concordance between the MMPI and the MMPI-2, they will not be reiterated here.

Archer, Pancoast, and Klinefelter (1989) reported the codetype concordance among these three sets of adolescent norms to range from 22 to 31 percent for an adolescent sample of 100 inpatients, 100 outpatients, and 100 normals. They did not find the two newer sets of norms to have higher hit rates in classifying adolescents as normal or psychologically distressed, but they did substantiate higher sensitivity rates using a T score of 65 rather than a T score of 70 to classify an adolescent as psychologically distressed. They cautioned clinicians about using these newer sets of adolescent norms to produce a codetype that would be interpreted based on the existing MMPI research because of the limited concordance rates.

Williams and Butcher reported the empirical correlates of the MMPI standard validity and clinical scales (1989a) and codetypes (1989b) in a large, inpatient, adolescent sample. These adolescents had similar descriptors associated to the individual MMPI scales that had been found in adults. Williams and Butcher (1989a) concluded that their results supported the use of adult descriptors for adolescent MMPI interpreta-

tions as suggested previously by Archer (1987) and Williams (1986).

Although, Williams and Butcher (1989b) found that the relative frequency of the various codetypes in their sample was very comparable to those reported by Marks and colleagues (1974), they were unable to replicate the correlates of specific codetypes found in Marks and colleagues or the adult codetype literature. This latter finding suggests that the validity of traditional MMPI codetypes in adolescents may be limited.

Since the development of an adolescent interpretive system for the MMPI is still in its infancy, one solution may be to use adolescent norms and empirical correlates of individual validity and clinical scales based on adolescents when testing this population. An alternative procedure, which can be followed while an adolescent interpretive system such as Marks and associates (1974) is being cross-validated, is to use adolescent norms to generate the profile and then to use an adult interpretive system.

This procedure, as Lachar and associates (1976) and Wimbish (1984) demonstrated, provides some improvement over utilizing both adult norms and adult correlates of a codetype to interpret an adolescent's MMPI. However, it must be noted that Williams and Butcher (1989b) were unable to replicate the correlates of specific adolescent codetypes, which suggests that clinicians should be cautious in using this procedure.

THE AGED

There have been only limited investigations of the performance of the normal aged on the MMPI. Brozek (1955) reported MMPI data on 233 business and professional men between the ages of 45 and 55 who were participating in a program examining the effects of aging on the cardiovascular system. All of these men had normal blood pressure and were in good physical health.

Brozek compared the performance of these older men with a group of 157 male college students. He reported T scores for only three validity scales (*?*, *L*, and *K*) and Scales *1* (Hypochondriasis) and *0* (Social Introversion). The mean T score on all five of these scales was nearly 50 in both groups of men; that is, no scale was noticeably different from the mean T score of the original Minnesota normative sample.

Brozek found that the older men endorsed four to nine more items on Scales *1* (Hypochondriasis), *2* (Depression), *3* (Hysteria), *5* (Masculinity-Femininity), *6* (Paranoia), and *0* (Social Introversion) and endorsed six to seven fewer items on Scales *7* (Psychasthenia), *8* (Schizophrenia), and *9* (Hypomania) than the younger men. He concluded that within the age ranges (20 to 55) of his study, the T scores derived from the original Minnesota normative sample were valid. Brozek also provided a detailed analysis of items that separated the older and younger age groups. The reader who is interested in this information should consult Brozek's (1955) article.

Leon, Gillum, Gillum, and Gouze (1979) have reported 30-year followup data on the MMPI performance of the healthy professional men described by Brozek. These researchers were able to obtain MMPI data on 71 of these men who had completed the MMPI at four different times (1947, 1953, 1960, and 1977). The mean age of the 71 men in 1977 was 77 years.

When the scale scores from 1947 were contrasted with those in 1977, these men achieved significantly higher scores on all validity and clinical scales except the *L* scale, although all scale scores were still below a mean T score of 62. When scale scores from 1960 were compared with those in 1977, these men achieved significantly higher scores on Scales *L*, *2*, *7*, *8*, and *0*. The largest difference in scale score between 1960 and 1977, however, was only 5 T points on Scale *2*. There was

striking stability of scores over this 30-year interval for Scales *5*, *9*, and *0*, and 23.9 percent of these men had the same codetype.

Leon and associates (1979) suggest that the elevations on Scales *2* and *3* in an aging sample may reflect realistic somatic concerns rather than the usual depressive and histrionics correlates found in younger adults.

The most comprehensive examination of MMPI performance in the aged was conducted by Swenson (1961). He asked 210 persons aged 60 years or more who had completed a brief attitude questionnaire to take the MMPI. Only 95 (45.1 percent) of these persons completed the MMPI: 31 men and 64 women with a median age of 71.4 years. None had a known mental disorder sufficient to warrant a psychiatric diagnosis. (It is possible that the large percentage of older individuals who did not complete the MMPI may somehow bias the representativeness of this sample, but the nature of these biases is unknown.)

The scores of these 95 persons served as the basis for constructing the T score norms for the aged. They scored from 6 to 9 T score points higher on Scales *1*, *2*, *3*, and *5* and 3 T score points lower on Scale *9* then the original Minnesota normative sample. Scales *1*, *2*, *3*, and *0* were the most frequently occurring high-point scales in both genders. The median profiles for this aged sample were commonly of a neurotic pattern (elevations on Scales *1*, *2*, and *3*) and only rarely gave evidence of a psychotic or a behavior disorder pattern.

Swenson, Pearson, and Osborne (1973) provided MMPI data on 1,733 male and 1,471 female medical outpatients 70 years of age and older who were seen at the Mayo Clinic between 1962 and 1965. They excluded any patient referred primarily for psychiatric evaluation and treatment. Both male and female patients scored about a T score of 60 on Scales *1*, *2*, and *3*, a T score of 55 on Scale *0*, and a T score of 48 on Scale *9*. This pattern of scores is very similar to what Swenson (1961) reported. Swenson and colleagues (1973), however, report similar elevations on Scales *1*, *2*, and *3* in medical patients aged 16 to 69. Thus, it is not possible to conclude whether the elevations on Scales *1*, *2*, and *3* in patients 70 years of age and older reflect age per se or some other factor.

Fillenbaum and Pfeiffer (1976) collected the Mini-Mult (Kincannon, 1968) as a portion of a broad questionnaire administered to a 10 percent random sample of noninstitutionalized persons 65 years and older living in a southern community. The Mini-Mult was read to the person by a trained interviewer, and responses were obtained to all 71 items on the Mini-Mult from 249 men (171 white, 78 black) and 391 women (250 white, 141 black). An additional 298 persons answered some of the items, and 59 answered none of the items; their responses were not analyzed.

Fillenbaum and Pfeiffer found only one item (25) that was endorsed differently as a function of gender or race. The mean T scores in both genders and races for the eight clinical scales measured by the Mini-Mult (which excludes Scales *5* and *0*) were approximately 60, except for Scale *9*, which was approximately 50. Despite there being only one item that was significantly different for blacks and whites, blacks had significantly higher T scores (2 to 5 points) on Scales *F*, *4*, *8*, and *9*.

If this sample can be considered to be relatively normal, it appears that the Mini-Mult overestimates the amount of psychopathology in an aged sample and hence will have limited usefulness. Clinicians should review the discussion of short forms of the MMPI in Chapter 5 before using them with any clients.

The limited amount of research on MMPI performance in normal-aged samples allows for only a few general conclusions. It appears that aged persons may elevate Scales *1*, *2*, and *3* about 10 T score points, elevate Scale *0* about 5 T score points, and lower Scale *9* about 3 T score points compared to the original Minnesota normative sample. Using aged norms in constructing a profile for a person 70 years or older will allow the clinician to compare the person's scores to others of similar age. There is no published research, however, on how to interpret an MMPI profile constructed on aged norms.

Again, research is needed to determine whether correlates of profiles constructed on the original Minnesota normative sample will apply in a similar fashion to an aged sample. Since the representativeness of the sample used in constructing the aged-norm tables is unclear because of the limited sample size and the large number of persons who did not complete the MMPI, the clinician should use the aged norms very cautiously.

It might be best for the clinician to plot two profiles for an aged client: the standard profile and an aged-norm profile. By examining the latter profile, the clinician could determine how the client compares on the various scales with persons in his or her age range. The clinician, however, probably should interpret the standard profile and use the aged norm profile only to supplement the interpretation.

ETHNIC GROUPS[1]

Most research on the MMPI in minority groups has focused on blacks, although recently there has been some research with Hispanics,[2] Asian-Americans, and American Indians. The first issue, of course, is whether minority group status does influence MMPI results when other potential confounding factors such as socioeconomic status and educational level are controlled. If minority group status does affect MMPI scale scores when these factors are controlled, the critical issue becomes whether MMPI interpretations based on white or minority group norms are more valid. Each of these issues will be examined in turn.

The MMPI also has been translated into a number of different languages for use around the world (cf. Butcher, 1985; Butcher & Clark, 1979; Butcher & Pancheri, 1976), which allows for the investigation of the effects of cultural factors on MMPI performance from an international perspective. The reader who is interested in this perspective should contact these resources for additional information.

Dahlstrom, Lachar, and Dahlstrom (1986) have provided a thorough, in-depth analysis of the influence of ethnic group membership on MMPI performance, and Dana (1990) has provided a general overview of multiethnic assessment. Also, there have been a number of other recent reviews of the research in this area that should be consulted for a variety of perspectives on this topic (Costello, Tiffany, & Gier, 1972; Gynther, 1972, 1979, 1989; Gynther & Green, 1980; Pritchard & Rosenblatt, 1980a, 1980b).

The prototypic investigation of the effect of ethnic group membership on MMPI performance consists of obtaining a sample of individuals from some specific ethnic group and then plotting the obtained profile against the original normative group or another ethnic group. If differences occur between the two groups on any scale, the typical conclusion is that the MMPI as a whole or some subset of scales is affected by membership in that ethnic group.

Rarely do such prototypic studies determine whether these obtained differences are of sufficient magnitude to affect clinical interpretation and, more importantly, they virtually never determine whether these different scores actually affect the empirical correlates of the scale. A number of issues must be considered before the conclusion is justified that the observed results reflect differences as a function of ethnic group membership. Greene (1987) has summarized a number of methodologic issues that need to

be considered that can potentially affect the interpretation of any ethnic differences that are found.

Researchers tend to be very casual about reporting the criteria used to specify membership within the ethnic group whose MMPI performance is being evaluated. Most often, the persons are described as black, Hispanic, Asian-American, and so on, with little consideration of whether they have any actual identification with their ethnic group.

Sometimes Hispanic subjects, and even less frequently, Asian-American subjects, will be classified on the basis of their surname, which at least assures that at some point in their family heritage they had membership in the ethnic group. However, a surname does not determine whether persons actually are members of the ethnic group, or more important, whether they have any identification with that group.

Recently, in an attempt to address this problem, some researchers have used the Acculturation scale for Mexican-Americans (Cuellar, Harris, & Jasso, 1980) as a moderator variable in examining MMPI performance in Hispanic individuals (e.g., Montgomery & Orozco, 1985). In a similar vein, Costello (1977) proposed a scale that can be used to assess "functional" identification with black culture, although it has not yet been used in any reported study.

Clearly, researchers need to become more sophisticated in assessing membership in and identification with a specific ethnic group when they are interested in examining MMPI performance, because the cultural factors that are so important in determining how psychopathology will be manifested in a person may be only loosely related to ethnic group membership.

Black-White Comparisons

The early research of black-white differences on the MMPI compared scores on the standard validity and clinical scales. The general procedure for these studies was to administer the MMPI to a group of blacks and whites and then to compare their mean scores on the validity and clinical scales.

Ball (1960) contrasted the MMPI performance of 31 black ninth-graders with 167 white students in the same classes. The black male students earned higher scores on Scale *1* (Hypochondriasis) than the white male students. The black female students earned higher scores on Scales *F*, *8* (Schizophrenia), and *0* (Social Introversion) and lower scores on Scales *K* and *3* (Hysteria) than the white female students. Ball noted that, in addition to ethnicity, his two groups differed in school grades, level of intelligence, and social class.

McDonald and Gynther (1962) conducted a similar study using black students from segregated high schools. The black male students achieved higher scores than white male students on Scales *L*, *F*, *K*, *1* (Hypochondriasis), *2* (Depression), and *9* (Hypomania), whereas the black female students achieved significantly different scores from white female students on all scales except *K* and *8*. McDonald and Gynther (1962) noted that their black students were primarily lower class, and the white students were middle and upper class. Since socioeconomic status could have been a factor in producing the black-white differences, McDonald and Gynther (1963) examined another group of black and white students from segregated high schools who were matched on the basis of their parents' occupation.

They reported that social class as measured by parents' occupation was not related to scores on any MMPI scale. Both male and female black students achieved higher scores on Scales *L*, *F*, *2*, *8*, and *9* and lower scores on Scale *3* than their white counterparts. McDonald and Gynther concluded that these black-white differences on the MMPI were culturally determined and did not reflect a bias in social class.

Table 8–1 summarizes the extant literature that has examined black-white differences on the standard validity and clinical scales of the MMPI. Since MMPI performance varies as a function of the setting, this table has been separated into normal, prison, substance abuse, medical/welfare, and psychiatric samples. Even a cursory review of Table 8–1 should suggest that there is no consistent pattern to black-white differences on the MMPI.

Clearly, a statement that blacks or whites routinely score higher on any specific validity or clinical scale is *not* warranted across this entire range of studies. Even within specific populations, there are few generalizations that can be made in a reliable manner.

For example, in normal populations it has been stated that blacks frequently score higher on the *F* scale and Scales *8* (Schizophrenia) and *9* (Hypomania) than whites. However, a majority of the 27 comparisons within normal samples found no reliable differences on these three scales, although when differences do occur, blacks score higher than whites. In fact, there is no scale on which a majority of the studies was consistently higher either in blacks or whites in any sample. Consequently, it appears inappropriate to conclude that blacks routinely score higher than whites on any of the standard validity or clinical scales in any sample.

It is possible that the black samples in these studies may have differed in their identification with a black culture, which would tend to obscure any real black-white differences. Harrison and Kass (1968), for example, found that northern blacks scored between southern blacks and whites on Scales *?*, *F*, *9*, and *0*, which led them to conjecture that northern blacks may be acquiring white culture. Moreover, Erdberg (1975) found that black-white differences were less in urban than in rural settings.

The three studies (Erdberg, 1975; Mc-

TABLE 8–1   Black-White Differences on MMPI Standard Validity and Clinical Scales

Study	Validity Scales			Clinical Scales									
	L	F	K	1	2	3	4	5	6	7	8	9	0
Normal Samples													
Ball (1960)													
Female		B	W		W						B		B
Male				B									
Butcher, Ball, & Ray (1964)													
Female	B							B	W				
Male	B		B				W	W	W			B	W
Erdberg (1975)													
Rural female	W	B	W			W	B	W	B		B	B	
Rural male	W	B	W	B			B		B	B	B	B	
Urban female	W		W	W	W	W					B		W
Urban male													
Gynther, Fowler, & Erdberg (1971)													
Female		B	W				B	B	B	B	B	B	B
Male		B	W	B			B	B	B	B	B	B	B
Harrison & Kass (1967), female													
King, Carroll, & Fuller (1977), male												B	
Kirk & Zucker (1979),[a] male													
McDonald & Gynther (1962)													
Female					B								
Male	B				B								
McDonald & Gynther (1963)[b]													
Female, social class 1–2	B							B					
Female, social class 3													
Female, social class 4													
Male, social class 1–2	B											B	
Male, social class 3	B		B										
Male, social class 4	B		B								B	B	
Moore & Handal (1980)													
Female									B				
Male		B							B	B	B	B	
Muller & Bruno (1988), male													
Sutker & Kilpatrick (1973)													
Female						B							
Male													
Walters, Greene, & Jeffrey (1984), male													
Prison Samples													
Caldwell (1953), male							B					B	
Cooke, Pogany, & Johnston (1974), male						W		B					

continued

TABLE 8-1 *continued*

Study	Validity Scales			Clinical Scales									
	L	F	K	1	2	3	4	5	6	7	8	9	0
Prison Samples													
Costello, Fine, & Blau (1973), male													
Elion & Megargee (1975),[c] male							B						
Flanagan & Lewis (1969), male												B	
Fry (1949), male												B	
Holcomb & Adams (1982), male												B	
Holcomb, Adams, & Ponder (1984), male		B											W
Ingram, Marchioni, Hill, Caraveo-Ramos, & McNeil (1985), male													
Recidivist		B											
Nonrecedivist	B												
McCreary & Padilla (1977), male		B				W						B	
Murphree, Karbelas, & Bryan (1962),[d] male													
Panton (1959a), male		B				W					B		
Rosenblatt & Pritchard (1978), male				B		W					B	B	
Stanton (1956), male													
Walters (1986), male													
Control									W				
Index		B					W	B					
Substance Abuse Samples													
Hill, Haertzen, & Glaser (1960), male					W							B	
Patalano (1978)													
Female					W			B	W				W
Male		B						W					W
Patterson, Charles, Woodward, Roberts, & Penk (1981), male													
Penk et al. (1982), male													
Penk, Robinowitz, Roberts, Dolan, & Atkins (1981), male													
Penk, Woodward, Robinowitz, & Hess (1978), male	W												W
Sutker, Archer, & Allain (1978), female & male	W				W			W	W				

TABLE 8–1 *continued*

Study	Validity Scales			Clinical Scales									
	L	F	K	1	2	3	4	5	6	7	8	9	0
Substance Abuse Samples													
Sutker, Archer, & Allain (1980)[e]													
Female (NARA)		W		W	W	W	W	B		W	W	W	
Male (NARA)													
Female (Fetter)		W		W	W	W	W	B	W	W	W		W
Male (Fetter)				W	W							B	W
Walters, Greene, & Jeffrey (1984), male													
Weiss & Russakoff (1977), female & male					W					W			
Medical/Welfare Samples													
Hokanson & Calden (1960), male							W	B			B	B	
McGill (1980), female													
Psychiatric Samples													
Bertelson, Marks, & May (1982), female & male	B							B				B	
Butcher, Braswell, & Raney (1983)													
Female	B											B	
Male													
Costello et al. (1973)													
Female	B	W					B		B		B	B	
Male	B												
Davis (1975), male													
Schizophrenic													
Nonschizophrenic													
Davis, Beck, & Ryan (1973), male													
High education		B	B	W				W	W	W			
Low education	W				W	W			W	W	W		
Davis & Jones (1974), male													
High education schizophrenic												W	
High education nonschizophrenic									W				
Low education schizophrenic								B	B		B	B	
Low education nonschizophrenic		B					W	W			B	B	
Genthner & Graham (1976), female & male	B										B		

continued

TABLE 8-1 *continued*

Study	Validity Scales			Clinical Scales									
	L	F	K	1	2	3	4	5	6	7	8	9	0
				Psychiatric Samples									
Kirk & Zucker (1979), male					B								
Klinge & Strauss (1976), female & male													
Liske & McCormick (1976), male													
Miller, Knapp, & Daniels (1968), male					B			W				B	
Miller, Wertz, & Counts (1961), male					B			W					
Peteroy & Pirrello (1982),[f] female & male													
Smith & Graham (1981),[g] female & male													

Adapted from "Ethnicity and MMPI Performance: A Review" by Roger L. Greene, 1987, *Journal of Consulting and Clinical Psychology, 55,* pp. 500–502. Copyright 1987 by the American Psychological Association. Reprinted by permission.

Note: B = Blacks scored higher than whites; W = Whites scored higher than blacks. Differences less than 5 T points between two groups were not charted, regardless of statistical significance. When a study reported multiple comparisons between two groups, only the results of the most rigorous comparisons were charted.

[a]Compared only Scale *2.*

[b]Social classes 1 and 2 = independent or dependent occupations involving skill and the supervision of others; Social class 3 = dependent occupations involving skill but little supervision of others; Social class 4 = dependent occupations involving little skill and little supervision of others.

[c]Compared only Scale *4.*

[d]Compared only Scales *K* and *4.*

[e]NARA = Narcotic Addict Rehabilitation Act Program, Tulane University School of Medicine; Fetter = Franklin C. Fetter Drug Abuse Program, Charleston, SC.

[f]Compared only Scale *F, 8,* and *9.*

[g]Compared only Scale *F.*

Donald & Gynther, 1962, 1963) that reported the preponderance of significant black-white differences on the MMPI in normal individuals were conducted in the South, which lends some credence to Harrison and Kass's (1968) hypothesis. Ball (1960) and Baughman and Dahlstrom (1968), however, also conducted their research in the South, and these investigators found few black-white differences.

Thus, some factor(s) other than ethnicity—perhaps identification with a black culture independent of geographic location—may be contributing to whether black-white differences are found. Costello (1977) has developed an index to help control for this factor in studying black-white differences on the MMPI.

In response to the finding that blacks usually score higher on the standard MMPI *F* scale, Gynther, Lachar, and Dahlstrom (1978) developed a new *F* scale for blacks. They identified 33 items that were endorsed by less than 10 percent of a combined normal male and female black sample. Only 22 of these 33 items (66.7 percent) are on the standard F scale.

Blacks and whites, however, responded quite similarly to the 33 items on the new F scale for blacks; 28 of these 33 items also were endorsed by less than 10 percent of a white sample. Gynther and colleagues (1978) suggest that raw scores of 3, 7, and 11 on the new F scale for blacks should be considered equivalent to T scores of 50, 60, and 70, respectively. This new F scale for blacks can be used as a measure of the black client's endorsement of items that are infrequently endorsed by black normals, in a fashion similar to the standard F scale. It remains to be seen, however, whether black clients who elevate the new F scale for blacks will demonstrate the same behavioral correlates as are found in white clients who elevate the standard F scale.

The specific population that is being examined also appears to play an important influence on the nature of the black-white differences that will be found. Thus, in substance abuse samples, whites rather frequently score higher than blacks on those scales for which reliable differences have been found, whereas in psychiatric samples there does not appear to be any reliable pattern to the black-white comparisons.

It has been conjectured (cf. Penk, Robinowitz, Roberts, Dolan, & Atkins, 1981) that whites who become substance abusers are more disturbed than blacks, which would account for the higher elevations in the former group. Since groups of substance abusers have not been matched for type or severity of psychopathology and then examined for black-white differences, there are no data to address this issue directly. However, when psychiatric patients were matched on education and for type of psychopathology (Davis, Beck, & Ryan, 1973), no black-white differences were found.

Again, it seems that any simple explanation of the pattern of black-white differences within and between populations is not readily apparent without giving adequate consideration to the multitude of moderator variables which may affect performance.

One final comment about black-white differences on the standard validity and clinical scales seems warranted. The more rigorously that moderator variables and profile validity issues are controlled by an investigator, the less likely it becomes that black-white differences will be found. For example, Costello and colleagues (1972) reported that no black-white differences were found if invalid profiles were excluded. Similarly, Penk and colleagues (Penk, Robinowitz, Dolan, Atkins, & Woodward, 1982; Penk et al., 1981) have found no black-white differences in substance abuse patients when age, education, socioeconomic status, and intelligence were controlled statistically.

Thus, it appears that moderator variables, such as socioeconomic status, education, and intelligence, as well as profile validity issues, are important factors to be controlled in any MMPI research and particularly when the potential effect of ethnic status is being examined. Rather than discussing the fact that normals from an ethnic minority tend to have more elevated scores on the standard validity and clinical scales than whites, it seems much more important to consider the role of the moderator variables listed above such as socioeconomic status, education, and intelligence.

As stated by Pritchard and Rosenblatt (1980a), it seems premature to conclude that new norms for blacks are needed. However, it does appear necessary for clinicians and researchers to become more aware of the multitude of potential factors which can affect MMPI performance.

The paucity of studies that have examined directly whether there are distinct empirical correlates of the obtained black-white differences is amazing, particularly when it is realized that this issue has been investigated for nearly 40 years. Investigators seem content to report small black-white differences in performance on a specific scale without considering whether these differences have any clinical correlates or relevance.

Gynther, Fowler, and Erdberg (1971) administered the MMPI to 88 rural, isolated blacks and found that almost half (41/88) of these persons had raw scores greater than 16 (T score of 80) on the *F* scale. Scale *8* (Schizophrenia) was the most frequent high-point scale, followed by Scale *9* (Hypomania) in men and Scale *6* (Paranoia) in women. The mean profile for this group of blacks would have been classified as psychotic by most MMPI interpretive systems. Clearly, this black sample was being overpathologized using standard MMPI interpretive criteria.

In a related study Gynther, Altman, and Warbin (1973b) were unable to replicate any of the correlates of raw scores greater than 25 (T score of 98) on the standard *F* scale in black psychiatric patients; they were, however, successful in replicating these correlates in white patients. Gynther and associates' findings suggest that the meaning of high *F* scale scores in blacks remains unclear.

In one of the few additional validity studies, Elion and Megargee (1975) tested the validity of Scale *4* (Psychopathic Deviate) in blacks and concluded that there was no need to derive a new Scale *4* to assess antisocial behavior patterns among blacks. They did suggest that 5 T points should be subtracted from Scale *4* after *K*-correction in black clients to offset the tendency that they found for blacks to score slightly higher than whites on this scale. Finally, Marks and associates (1974) found few black-white differences in the correlates of their adolescent codetypes, although they only had a small sample of 61 black adolescents.

Only three studies (Elion & Megargee, 1975; Genthner & Graham, 1976; Smith & Graham, 1981) have examined the empirical

correlates of the black-white differences that were found, and two of the three studies (Elion & Megargee, 1975; Genthner & Graham, 1976) concluded that there were no differences in the external correlates of the MMPI.

Four studies have examined the correlates of specific codetypes and scale elevations (Clark & Miller, 1971; Gynther, Altman, & Warbin, 1973a, 1973b; Strauss, Gynther, & Wallhermfechtel, 1974). In none of these four studies were the black correlates identical to the white correlates, although Clark & Miller (1971) reported that the cardinal features of their *8-6* profiles were remarkably similar. Shore (1976) reviewed the statistical analysis of the data reported by Strauss and colleagues (1974) and concluded that there was no clear evidence for greater misdiagnosis among blacks than whites.

Thus, at least three of these seven studies have found different correlates for blacks and whites on the MMPI. The interested reader should consult Pritchard and Rosenblatt's (1980a, 1980b) criticisms of these studies, however, before assuming that these correlates are reliable. Clearly, additional research is needed to investigate the clinical correlates of black-white differences in MMPI performance when the potential influence of moderator variables have been controlled adequately.

Only a few studies have investigated whether there are differences in the discriminability of blacks and whites within and between diagnostic groups using the MMPI. Both Cowan, Watkins, and Davis (1975) and Davis (1975) examined black-white differences in matched groups of schizophrenics and nonschizophrenics and found no significant differences for ethnicity. Cowan and associates did find that blacks with less than 12 years of education were more likely to be misclassified than blacks with 12 years or more of education or whites. Their results appear to be compatible with Rosenblatt and Pritchard (1978), who found race differences only in patients with IQs below 94.

Strauss and colleagues (1974) examined black-white differences between groups of patients diagnosed as exhibiting behavior disorders and psychoses. Using a discriminant function analysis, they reported that black patients with behavior disorders were misclassified more than any of the other groups of patients. But Shore (1976) indicated that this result reflected a computational error and concluded that there were no significant black-white differences in the Strauss and colleagues' (1974) study.

Because of the limited amount of research, it is difficult to conclude whether there are black-white differences between various diagnostic groups as assessed by the MMPI. There does appear to be a tendency for blacks with limited education and IQs below average to score differently than whites on the MMPI, and the clinician should consider this when interpreting a black client's MMPI.

There has been very little research on black-white differences for the numerous MMPI supplementary scales (see Table 8–2). The limited research appears to show that few reliable black-white differences are found with fewer significant results than on the standard validity and clinical scales. Even given the fact that moderator variables generally were not controlled in most of these studies, few reliable differences are found. It is interesting to note that black and white substance abusers seem to score in the same range on the MacAndrew Alcoholism scale (MacAndrew, 1965), yet normal blacks score higher than whites. Since the MacAndrew Alcoholism scale is used so widely, more research on potential ethnic differences, particularly in interaction with the type of setting, is needed.

A number of investigators have reported black-white differences at the item level on the MMPI (Costello, 1973, 1977; Gynther &

Witt, 1976; Harrison & Kass, 1967, 1968; Jones, 1978; Miller, Knapp, & Daniels, 1968; Witt & Gynther, 1975). Although from 58 to 213 items have been found to differentiate blacks from whites in a given study, there has been limited overlap among these items across the various studies. In reviewing six studies of item-level differences among blacks and whites, Costello (1977) reported that "three items differentiated [blacks and whites] six of six times, seven items discriminated five of six times, and 22 items discriminated four of six times" (p. 515).

Again, the need to control for the potential effect of moderator variables must be underscored in these studies. Consequently, there does not appear to be any real conclusion that can be drawn from these findings other than that item-level endorsement frequencies may vary in different samples with a small number of items consistently differentiating blacks and whites.

Harrison and Kass (1967) examined the individual validity and clinical scales to determine which ethnic group was more likely to endorse the items, and concluded that in many cases ethnic differences may cancel out because there are approximately the same number of items favoring each ethnic group on many of the scales. They discovered more items that whites were likely to endorse only on Scale *3* and found more items that blacks were likely to endorse on Scales *F, 1, 6, 8,* and *9*. These findings are somewhat consistent with the results presented in Table 8–1, which reveals a tendency for blacks to score higher on Scales *F, 1, 8,* and *9*; whites, however, tend to score higher on Scale *6* as well as on Scale *3*.

Harrison and Kass (1967) conducted a factor analysis of the 150 items that most reliably distinguished blacks from whites and identified 20 factors, 16 of which could be conceptually labeled. The first 8 of these factors are estrangement, intellectual and cultural interests, denial of major symptoms,

TABLE 8–2 Black-White Differences on MMPI Supplementary Scales

Study	Gender	Population	Result
Dependency scale (Navran, 1954)			
Ingram, Marchioni, Hill, Caraveo-Ramos, & McNeil (1985)	M	Prison	
King, Carroll, & Fuller (1977)	M	Normal	
Patalano (1978)	M & F	Substance abuse	
Dominance scale (Gough, McClosky, & Meehl, 1951)			
Ingram et al. (1985)			
Nonrecidivist	M	Prison	W
Redicivist	M	Prison	
King et al. (1977)	M	Normal	W
Patalano (1978)	M & F	Substance abuse	
MacAndrew Alcoholism scale (MacAndrew, 1965)			
McCreary & Padilla (1977)	M	Prison	
Snyder, Kline, & Podany (1985)	M	Substance abuse	
Snyder et al. (1985)	F	Substance abuse	
Walters, Greene, Jeffrey, Kruzich, & Haskin (1983)	M	Normal	B
Walters et al. (1983)	M	Substance abuse	
Zager & Megargee (1981)	M	Prison/substance abuse	
Overcontrolled Hostility scale (Megargee, Cook, & Mendelsohn, 1967)			
McCreary & Padilla (1977)	M	Prison	
Welsh Anxiety Scale (Welsh, 1965)			
Butcher, Ball, & Ray (1964)	F	Normal	
Butcher et al. (1964)	M	Normal	W
Hokanson & Calden (1960)	M	Medical	
King et al. (1977)	M	Normal	
Miller, Knapp, & Daniels (1968)	M	Psychiatric	
Miller, Wertz, & Counts (1961)	M	Psychiatric	
Sutker, Archer, & Allain (1978)	M	Substance abuse	
Sutker, Archer, & Allain (1980)	M & F	Substance abuse	
Welsh Repression scale (Welsh, 1965)			
Butcher et al. (1964)	F	Normal	
Butcher et al. (1964)	M	Normal	
King et al. (1977)	M	Normal	
Miller et al. (1961)	M	Psychiatric	
Miller et al. (1968)	M	Psychiatric	
Sutker et al. (1978)	M	Substance abuse	
Sutker et al. (1980)[a]			
Fetter	F	Substance abuse	B
Fetter	M	Substance abuse	
NARA	F	Substance abuse	B
NARA	M	Substance abuse	
Wiggins Content scales (Wiggins, 1966)[b]			
Dolan, Roberts, Penk, Robinowitz, & Atkins (1983)	M	Substance abuse	W(*FAM*) B(*FEM*)
Penk, Woodward, Robinowitz, & Hess (1978)	M	Substance abuse	W(*FAM*) B(*FEM*) B(*PHO*) W(*SOC*)

Adapted from "Ethnicity and MMPI Performance: A Review" by Roger L. Greene, 1987, *Journal of Consulting and Clinical Psychology, 55,* pp. 504–505. Copyright 1987 by the American Psychological Association. Reprinted by permission.

Note: B = Blacks scored higher than whites; W = Whites scored higher than blacks. Differences less than 5 T points between two groups were not charted, regardless of statistical significance. When a study reported multiple comparisons between two groups, only the results of the most rigorous comparison were charted.

[a]Fetter = Franklin C. Fetter Drug Abuse Program, Charleston, SC; NARA = Narcotic Addict Rehabilitation Act Program, Tulane University School of Medicine.

[b]*FAM* = Family Problems; *FEM* = Femininity; *PHO* = Phobias; *SOC* = Social Maladjustment.

cynicism, admission of minor faults, romantic interests, somatic tension, and impulse-ridden fantasy. Blacks achieved significantly higher scores on all 8 of these factors except denial of major symptoms, on which whites achieved significantly higher scores.

Baughman and Dahlstrom (1968) examined the performance of their sample of black and white eighth-graders on the first 5 of these factors. The black eighth-graders achieved significantly higher scores than white eighth-graders on 3 of the 5 factors: estrangement, intellectual and cultural interests, and cynicism. The white male eighth-graders achieved higher scores on denial of major symptoms than did white female or black eighth-graders. The similarity of the results between Baughman and Dahlstrom (1968) and Harrison and Kass (1967) on these factors is remarkable considering the differences in sample composition and geographic location.

Gynther (1972) suggested that the common theme in both of these studies is the marked distrust of society exhibited by blacks rather than any indication of psychopathology. Jones (1978) has contended that this conceptualization of blacks' performance on the MMPI may reflect the types of items found in the MMPI rather than blacks' marked distrust of society.

In support of this contention, Jones examined black-white differences in college students on 361 items, which included items from the California Psychological Inventory (Gough, 1957) that are less pathologic in content than many MMPI items. He found that 288 (80 percent) of these items significantly differentiated blacks and whites. Instead of the alienated and distrustful conceptualization of blacks' performance on the MMPI as proposed by Gynther (1972), Jones found his item differences to suggest that young blacks were assertive, poised, outspoken, tough-minded, and so on.

Further research is obviously necessary to determine which interpretation of black-white differences at the item level is more appropriate. In the interim, clinicians should be cautious of interpreting blacks' performances on Harrison and Kass' (1967) factors as reflecting either psychopathology or distrust of society. Jones' (1978) investigation suggests that other factors, such as the type of items found in the MMPI, may be contributing to these results.

Hispanic-White Comparisons

Table 8–3 summarizes the literature that has examined Hispanic-white differences on the standard validity and clinical scales of the MMPI. It should be apparent that there has been very little research in this area, and consequently, conclusions are even more difficult to make than in black samples. There does not appear to be any pattern to these comparisons and there are few data to support the contention that Hispanics frequently score higher on the *L* scale and lower on Scale 5 (Masculinity-Femininity; cf. Greene, 1980), although when differences are found they tend to be in that direction. There does appear to be a tendency for fewer Hispanic-white differences to be found than when black-white comparisons are made (see Table 8–1).

Velasquez and colleagues (Velasquez, 1984; Velasquez & Callahan, 1990a, 1990b; Velasquez, Callahan, & Carrillo, 1989; Velasquez & Gimenez, 1987) have provided the most systematic research on the use of the MMPI in Hispanics. There is not a simple generalization that summarizes their research, although their results tend to be similar to what has been reported by others. Velasquez and Gimenez (1987) did not find any relationship between DSM-III diagnosis and the standard validity and clinical scales on the MMPI in Hispanic inpatients; this failure to find a specific relationship between the MMPI and DSM-III diagnoses has been reported frequently (cf. Greene, 1988).

TABLE 8–3 Hispanic-White Differences on MMPI Standard Validity and Clinical Scales

Study	Validity Scales			Clinical Scales									
	L	F	K	1	2	3	4	5	6	7	8	9	0
Normal Samples													
Montgomery & Orozco (1985), female & male		H									H		
Padilla, Olmedo, & Loya (1982), female & male[a]													
N-L factor	H			H				W					
SES factor	W		W				H						
Reilley & Knight (1970), female & male													
Psychiatric Samples													
Hibbs, Kobos, & Gonzalez (1979)													
Female				H					H				
Male							W						
Lawson, Kahn, & Heiman (1982), female & male	H												
Plemons (1977), female & male	H	H					W	W		W		W	
Velasquez & Callahan (1990b)	H		H	H					H	H	H	H	
Prison Samples													
Holland (1979), male							W						
McCreary & Padilla (1977), male			H										
Substance Abuse Samples													
Page & Bozlee (1982), male				H									
Penk, Robinowitz, Roberts, Dolan, & Atkins (1981), male								W					
Velasquez & Callahan (1990a)				W		W	W	W	W	W			W
Welfare Sample													
McGill (1980), female							H					W	

Adapted from "Ethnicity and MMPI Performance: A Review" by Roger L. Greene, 1987, *Journal of Consulting and Clinical Psychology, 55,* p. 506. Copyright 1987 by the American Psychological Association. Reprinted by permission.

Note: H = Hispanics scored higher than whites; W = Whites scored higher than Hispanics. Differences less than 5 T points between two groups were not charted, regardless of statistical significance. When a study reported multiple comparisons between two groups, only the results of the most rigorous comparison were charted.

[a]N-L factor = Normality-Language factor; SES factor = socioeconomic status.

Velasquez and Callahan (1990a) found that Hispanic alcoholics had lower scores on the MMPI than white alcoholics similar to the relationship found in black-white comparisons in alcoholics (see Table 8–1). This latter finding that Hispanic alcoholics, like black alcoholics, have lower scores on the MMPI when differences are found requires that any study of ethnic differences on the MMPI include the setting in which the test is administered as a potential confounding factor. Finally, it must be noted that Velasquez, like many other investigators in this area of research, does not report how ethnicity is defined in any of his studies.

There have been only three studies (Dolan, Roberts, Penk, Robinowitz, & Atkins, 1983; McCreary & Padilla, 1977; Page & Bozlee, 1982) that have reported Hispanic-white differences on any supplementary scales, with almost no overlap in the scales reported. McCreary and Padilla (1977) found no differences between Hispanic and white prisoners, and Page and Bozlee (1982) found no differences between Hispanic and white substance abusers on the MacAndrew Alcoholism scale (MacAndrew, 1965). McCreary and Padilla reported that Hispanics scored higher on the Overcontrolled-Hostility scale (Megargee, Cook, & Mendelsohn, 1967), and Dolan and associates (1983) found no differences larger than 5 T points on any of the Wiggins (1966) Content scales.

There have been no studies of Hispanic-white differences at the item level.

Black-Hispanic Comparisons

Only five studies have investigated black-Hispanic differences on the standard validity and clinical scales (Holland, 1979; McCreary & Padilla, 1977; McGill, 1980; Penk et al., 1981; Velasquez & Callahan, 1990b).

Holland's (1979) sample of Hispanic prisoners scored lower on Scales *5* (Masculinity-Femininity) and *8* (Schizophrenia) than blacks, whereas McCreary and Padilla's (1977) Hispanic prisoners scored higher on Scales *K, 1* (Hypochondriasis), *2* (Depression), and *3* (Hysteria). McGill (1980) found that Hispanic women welfare recipients scored higher on Scales *L* and *K* and lower on Scale *9* (Hypomania) than blacks. Penk and colleagues (1981) reported that Hispanic male substance abusers scored higher on Scale *2* and lower on Scale *5* than blacks. Finally, Velasquez and Callahan (1990b) did not find any differences between black and Hispanic schizophrenics. It should be evident that there is no clear pattern to be found in these black-Hispanic comparisons.

McCreary and Padilla (1977) are the only investigators to report black-Hispanic comparisons on any MMPI supplementary scales. They found that Hispanic prisoners scored lower on the MacAndrew Alcoholism scale (MacAndrew, 1965) than blacks.

Indian-White Comparisons

Table 8–4 summarizes the literature that has examined Indian-white differences on the standard validity and clinical scales of the MMPI. For the first time in the comparison of the MMPI performance of two ethnic groups, there appears to be a clear pattern for normal Indians to score higher on most of the clinical scales than their white counterparts even though there are no differences on the validity scales. This conclusion must be tempered by the fact that only two studies have been conducted, especially since similar trends are not evident in psychiatric and substance abuse samples. In these latter two samples, much as in black-white and Hispanic-white comparisons, there is no consistent pattern at all.

Only one study (Uecker, Boutilier, & Richardson, 1980) has investigated the performance of Indian samples on any of the MMPI supplementary scales. Uecker and colleagues found no differences between In-

TABLE 8–4 Indian-White Differences on MMPI Standard Validity and Clinical Scales

| Study | Validity Scales | | | Clinical Scales | | | | | | | | | |
	L	F	K	1	2	3	4	5	6	7	8	9	0
Normal Samples													
Arthur (1944)[a]													
Female				I		I	I						
Male				I									
Herreid & Herreid (1966)													
Female native				I	I		I		I	I	I		
Male native				I					I	I			
Female nonnative											I		
Male nonnative									I				
Psychiatric Samples													
Butcher, Braswell, & Raney (1983)													
Female	W									W			
Male									W	W			
Pollack & Shore (1980), female & male[b]	I			I	I	I	I		I	I	I	I	I
Substance Abuse Samples													
Kline, Rozynko, Flint, & Roberts (1973), male										I			
Page & Bozlee (1982), male													
Uecker, Boutilier, & Richardson (1980), male					W	W							

Adapted from "Ethnicity and MMPI Performance: A Review" by Roger L. Greene, 1987, *Journal of Consulting and Clinical Psychology, 55*, p. 508. Copyright 1987 by the American Psychological Association. Reprinted by permission.

Note: I = Indian scored higher than whites; W = Whites scored higher than Indians. Differences less than 5 T points between two groups were not charted, regardless of statistical significance. When a study reported multiple comparisons between two groups, only the results of the most rigorous comparison were charted.

[a]Reported data only for Scales *1–4*.

[b]Compared their Indian psychiatric patients with the original Minnesota normative sample, which produced the larger number of significant results.

dian and white substance abusers on the Mac-Andrew Alcoholism scale (MacAndrew, 1965). Uecker and colleagues did not report data from an Indian sample who were not substance abusers, so it is not known whether they also would elevate the MacAndrew Alcoholism scale as seen in normal blacks as mentioned earlier.

There have been no studies of Indian-white differences at the item level, although Arthur (1944) discussed the various interpretations that her Indian students gave to some of the items. For example, one Indian student answered "true" to the items, "I worry about my wife," and "My children worry

me," because he worried about them even though he was not married and had no children.

Asian-American-White Comparisons

Table 8–5 summarizes the literature that has examined Asian-American-white differences on the standard validity and clinical scales. As can be readily seen in Table 8–5, there have been almost no studies of the performance of Asian-Americans on the MMPI. Since Sue and Sue (1974) found a number of differences between their samples, it appears clear that more research is need in this ethnic

TABLE 8–5 Asian-American-White Differences on MMPI Standard Validity and Clinical Scales

Study	Validity Scales			Clinical Scales									
	L	F	K	1	2	3	4	5	6	7	8	9	0
Normal Samples													
Marsella, Sanborn, Kameoka, Shizuru, & Brennan (1975)[a]													
Chinese female					A								
Chinese male													
Japanese female													
Japanese male					A								
Psychiatric Samples													
Sue & Sue (1974)													
Female	A	A											A
Male	A	A		A	A		A		A	A	A		A
Tsushima & Onorato (1982)													
Female													
Male							W						

Adapted from "Ethnicity and MMPI Performance: A Review" by Roger L. Greene, 1987, *Journal of Consulting and Clinical Psychology, 55,* p. 509. Copyright 1987 by the American Psychological Association.

Note: A = Asian-Americans scored higher than whites; W = Whites scored higher than Asian-Americans. Differences less than 5 T points between two groups were not charted, regardless of statistical significance. When a study reported multiple comparisons between two groups, only the results of the most rigorous comparison were charted.

[a]Compared only Scale *2.*

group. It is particularly important for the study by Sue and Sue to be replicated, since in the other ethnic groups that were reviewed above, there was a tendency toward fewer differences between groups in psychiatric samples than in normal samples.

There have been no studies which have examined Asian-American-white performance on any of the MMPI supplementary scales. There also have been no studies of the differences in the pattern of item endorsements between Asian-Americans and whites.

Summary

After reviewing the MMPI performance of various ethnic groups, there appear to be a number of comments that can be made about the research being conducted in this area. First, the failure to find any consistent pattern of scale differences between any two ethnic groups in any population would suggest that it is very premature to begin to develop new norms for various ethnic groups. It appears that moderator variables, such as socioeconomic status, education, and intelligence, as well as profile validity, are more important determinants of MMPI performance than ethnic status. Definitely, research is needed that examines the role of identified cultural factors on MMPI performance when appropriate controls are instituted for the multitude of factors which can affect the results.

Second, the frequent failure to assess in any manner the persons' identification with their ethnic group is quite notable. It seems very questionable to be making statements about the effects of ethnic status on MMPI performance without some means of insuring that the persons actually identify with and belong to the ethnic group. Thus, investigations

of the effect of ethnic status on MMPI performance need to give more serious consideration to the role of cultural factors and stop assuming that identity with the minority culture is defined by the person's race or surname. Some reliable and valid means of assessing persons' degree of identification with their culture would greatly enhance research on this topic.

Third, researchers need to stop reporting small mean differences between two groups, which are frequently poorly defined, and begin to assess the empirical correlates of any differences that are found. The fact that fewer than 10 studies actually have examined the empirical correlates of ethnic status and MMPI performance should indicate the direction for future research.

Finally, there is a real dearth of studies on the multitude of MMPI supplementary scales in any ethnic group. Since a number of these supplementary scales are scored routinely, research is needed to examine the effect of ethnic status on performance on these scales. It should go without saying that the above stated guidelines for research on the standard validity and clinical scales also apply to research on these supplementary scales.

ENDNOTES

1. This section has drawn substantially on Greene's (1987) review of ethnicity and MMPI performance.

2. A multitude of terms have been used to describe persons within a specific ethnic group such as *Chicano, Hispanic, Mexican, Mexican-American*, and so on. In order to provide consistency throughout this chapter, the terms *Asian-American, Hispanic*, and *Indian* will be used.

Appendixes

APPENDIX A

MMPI-2: Item Composition of Validity, Clinical, and Supplementary Scales

TABLE A-1 Basic Scales

L — Lie (15 items)

True

False

| 16 | 29 | 41 | 51 | 77 | 93 | 102 | 107 | 123 | 139 | 153 | 183 | 203 | 232 | 260 |

Males: Mean 3.53; S.D. 2.28.   Females: Mean 3.56; S.D. 2.08.

F – Infrequency (60 items)

True

18	24	30	36	42	48	54	60	66	72	84	96	114	138
144	150	156	162	168	180	198	216	228	234	240	246	252	258
264	270	282	288	294	300	306	312	324	336	349	355	361	

False

| 6 | 12 | 78 | 90 | 102 | 108 | 120 | 126 | 132 | 174 | 186 | 192 | 204 | 210 |
| 222 | 276 | 318 | 330 | 343 | | | | | | | | | |

Males: Mean 4.53; S.D. 3.24.   Females: Mean 3.66; S.D. 2.91.

continued

Source: From the *Minnesota Multiphasic Personality Inventory-2 Manual* by J. N. Butcher, W. G. Dahlstrom, J. R. Graham, A. Tellegen, & B. Kaemmer, Appendix B, pp. 65–84. Copyright © the University of Minnesota 1942, 1943, 1951, 1967 (renewal 1970), 1989. This *Manual*, 1989. Reproduced by permission.

TABLE A-1   *continued*

K – Correction (30 items)

True

83

False

29	37	58	76	110	116	122	127	130	136	148	157	158	167
171	196	213	243	267	284	290	330	338	339	341	346	348	356
365													

Males: Mean 15.30; S.D. 4.76.   Females: Mean 15.03; S.D. 4.58.

---

1 Hs – Hypochondriasis (32 items)

True

| 18 | 28 | 39 | 53 | 59 | 97 | 101 | 111 | 149 | 175 | 247 |

False

| 2 | 3 | 8 | 10 | 20 | 45 | 47 | 57 | 91 | 117 | 141 | 143 | 152 | 164 |
| 173 | 176 | 179 | 208 | 224 | 249 | 255 | | | | | | | |

Raw scores without K:
Males: Mean 4.92; S.D. 3.87.   Females: Mean 5.93; S.D. 4.51.
Raw scores with K:
Males: Mean 12.78; S.D. 3.86.   Females: Mean 13.69; S.D. 4.05.

---

2 D – Depression (57 items)

True

| 5 | 15 | 18 | 31 | 38 | 39 | 46 | 56 | 73 | 92 | 117 | 127 | 130 | 146 |
| 147 | 170 | 175 | 181 | 215 | 233 | | | | | | | | |

False

2	9	10	20	29	33	37	43	45	49	55	68	75	76
95	109	118	134	140	141	142	143	148	165	178	188	189	212
221	223	226	238	245	248	260	267	330					

Males: Mean 18.32; S.D. 4.59.   Females: Mean 20.14; S.D. 4.97.

TABLE A–1 *continued*

---

3 Hy – Conversion Hysteria (60 items)

True

11	18	31	39	40	44	65	101	166	172	175	218	230

False

2	3	7	8	9	10	14	26	29	45	47	58	76	81
91	95	98	110	115	116	124	125	129	135	141	148	151	152
157	159	161	164	167	173	176	179	185	193	208	213	224	241
243	249	253	263	265									

Males: Mean 20.87; S.D. 4.73.   Females: Mean 22.08; S.D. 4.72.

---

4 Pd – Psychopathic Deviate (50 items)

True

17	21	22	31	32	35	42	52	54	56	71	82	89	94
99	105	113	195	202	219	225	259	264	288				

False

9	12	34	70	79	83	95	122	125	129	143	157	158
160	167	171	185	209	214	217	226	243	261	263	266	267

Raw scores without K:
Males: Mean 16.57; S.D. 4.60.   Females: Mean 16.21; S.D. 4.65.
Raw scores with K:
Males: Mean 22.65; S.D. 4.67.   Females: Mean 22.21; S.D. 4.53.

---

5 Mf-m – Masculinity-Femininity (Masculine) (56 items)

True

4	25	62	64	67	74	80	112	119	122	128	137	166	177
187	191	196	205	209	219	236	251	256	268	271			

False

1	19	26	27	63	68	69	76	86	103	104	107	120	121
132	133	163	184	193	194	197	199	201	207	231	235	237	239
254	257	272											

Males: Mean 26.01; S.D. 5.08.

---

continued

TABLE A–1 *continued*

---

5 Mf-f – Masculinity-Femininity (Feminine) (56 items)

True

4	25	62	64	67	74	80	112	119	121	122	128	137	177
187	191	196	205	219	236	251	256	271					

False

1	19	26	27	63	68	69	76	86	103	104	107	120	132
133	163	166	184	193	194	197	199	201	207	209	231	235	237
239	254	257	268	272									

Females: Mean 35.94; S.D. 4.08.

---

6 Pa – Paranoia (40 items)

True

16	17	22	23	24	42	99	113	138	144	145	146	162	234
259	271	277	285	305	307	333	334	336	355	361			

False

81	95	98	100	104	110	244	255	266	283	284	286	297	314
315													

Males: Mean 10.10; S.D. 2.87.   Females: Mean 10.23; S.D. 2.97.

---

7 Pt – Psychasthenia (48 items)

True

11	16	23	31	38	56	65	73	82	89	94	130	147	170
175	196	218	242	273	275	277	285	289	301	302	304	308	309
310	313	316	317	320	325	326	327	328	329	331			

False

3	9	33	109	140	165	174	293	321

Raw scores without K:
Males: Mean 11.24; S.D. 6.61.   Females: Mean 12.69; S.D. 7.19.
Raw scores with K:
Males: Mean 26.43; S.D. 5.00.   Females: Mean 27.70; S.D. 5.10.

TABLE A–1 *continued*

8 Sc – Schizophrenia (78 items)

True

16	17	21	22	23	31	32	35	38	42	44	46	48	65
85	92	138	145	147	166	168	170	180	182	190	218	221	229
233	234	242	247	252	256	268	273	274	277	279	281	287	291
292	296	298	299	303	307	311	316	319	320	322	323	325	329
332	333	355											

False

6	9	12	34	90	91	106	165	177	179	192	210	255	276
278	280	290	295	343									

Raw scores without K:
Males: Mean 11.20; S.D. 7.12.   Females: Mean 11.24; S.D. 7.57.

Raw scores with K:
Males: Mean 26.40; S.D. 5.92.   Females: Mean 26.25; S.D. 5.97.

9 Ma – Hypomania (46 items)

True

13	15	21	23	50	55	61	85	87	98	113	122	131	145
155	168	169	182	190	200	205	206	211	212	218	220	227	229
238	242	244	248	250	253	269							

False

88	93	100	106	107	136	154	158	167	243	263

Raw scores without K:
Males: Mean 16.88; S.D. 4.51.   Females: Mean 16.07; S.D. 4.50.

Raw scores with K:
Males: Mean 19.93; S.D. 4.29.   Females: Mean 19.09; S.D. 4.26.

0 Si – Social Introversion (69 items)

True

31	56	70	100	104	110	127	135	158	161	167	185	215	243
251	265	275	284	289	296	302	308	326	337	338	347	348	351
352	357	364	367	368	369								

False

25	32	49	79	86	106	112	131	181	189	207	209	231	237
255	262	267	280	321	328	335	340	342	344	345	350	353	354
358	359	360	362	363	366	370							

Males: Mean 25.86; S.D. 8.57.   Females: Mean 27.98; S.D. 9.18.

TABLE A–2   Harris-Lingoes Subscales

D_1 – Subjective Depression (32 items)

True

31	38	39	46	56	73	92	127	130	146	147	170	175	215

233

False

2	9	43	49	75	95	109	118	140	148	178	188	189	223

260   267   330

Males: Mean 6.86; S.D. 3.79.   Females: Mean 7.65; S.D. 4.21.

D_2 – Psychomotor Retardation (14 items)

True

38   46   170   233

False

9   29   37   49   55   76   134   188   189   212

Males: Mean 5.34; S.D. 1.82.   Females: Mean 5.74; S.D. 1.83.

D_3 – Physical Malfunctioning (11 items)

True

18   117   175   181

False

2   20   45   141   142   143   148

Males: Mean 2.89; S.D. 1.23.   Females: Mean 3.22; S.D. 1.36.

D_4 – Mental Dullness (15 items)

True

15   31   38   73   92   147   170   233

False

9   10   43   75   109   165   188

Males: Mean 2.42; S.D. 2.09.   Females: Mean 2.55; S.D. 2.21.

TABLE A–2 *continued*

D_5 – Brooding (10 items)

True

| 38 | 56 | 92 | 127 | 130 | 146 | 170 | 215 |

False

| 75 | 95 |

Males: Mean 1.83; S.D. 1.77.   Females: Mean 2.50; S.D. 1.95.

Hy_1 – Denial of Social Anxiety (6 items)

True

False

| 129 | 161 | 167 | 185 | 243 | 265 |

Males: Mean 3.89; S.D. 1.86.   Females: Mean 3.85; S.D. 1.87.

Hy_2 – Need for Affection (12 items)

True

230

False

| 26 | 58 | 76 | 81 | 98 | 110 | 124 | 151 | 213 | 241 | 263 |

Males: Mean 6.69; S.D. 2.58.   Females: Mean 6.88; S.D. 2.44.

Hy_3 – Lassitude-Malaise (15 items)

True

| 31 | 39 | 65 | 175 | 218 |

False

| 2 | 3 | 9 | 10 | 45 | 95 | 125 | 141 | 148 | 152 |

Males: Mean 2.55; S.D. 2.20.   Females: Mean 2.73; S.D. 2.48.

---

continued

TABLE A-2 *continued*

Hy$_4$ – Somatic Complaints (17 items)

True

11	18	40	44	101	172

False

8	47	91	159	164	173	176	179	208	224	249

Males: Mean 2.50; S.D. 2.06.   Females: Mean 3.22; S.D. 2.53.

Hy$_5$ – Inhibition of Aggression (7 items)

True
none

False

7	14	29	115	116	135	157

Males: Mean 3.29; S.D. 1.32.   Females: Mean 3.46; S.D. 1.29.

Pd$_1$ – Familial Discord (9 items)

True

21	54	195	202	288

False

83	125	214	217

Males: Mean 1.78; S.D. 1.52.   Females: Mean 2.05; S.D. 1.65.

Pd$_2$ – Authority Problems (8 items)

True

35	105

False

34	70	129	160	263	266

Males: Mean 3.29; S.D. 1.52.   Females: Mean 2.35; S.D. 1.34.

TABLE A-2   *continued*

Pd$_3$ – Social Imperturbability (6 items)

True

False

70   129   158   167   185   243

Males: Mean 3.64; S.D. 1.71.   Females: Mean 3.37; S.D. 1.73.

Pd$_4$ – Social Alienation (13 items)

True

17   22   42   56   82   99   113   219   225   259

False

12   129   157

Males: Mean 3.74; S.D. 1.89.   Females: Mean 3.98; S.D. 1.93.

Pd$_5$ – Self-Alienation (12 items)

True

31   32   52   56   71   82   89   94   113   264

False

9   95

Males: Mean 3.39; S.D. 2.08.   Females: Mean 3.35; S.D. 2.07.

Pa$_1$ – Persecutory Ideas (17 items)

True

17   22   42   99   113   138   144   145   162   234   259   305   333   336
355   361

False

314

Males: Mean 1.74; S.D. 1.66.   Females: Mean 1.79; S.D. 1.67.

---

continued

TABLE A–2 *continued*

Pa$_2$ – Poignancy (9 items)

True

| 22 | 146 | 271 | 277 | 285 | 307 | 334 |

False

100   244

Males: Mean 2.36; S.D. 1.43.   Females: Mean 2.57; S.D. 1.58.

Pa$_3$ – Naïveté (9 items)

True

16

False

| 81 | 98 | 104 | 110 | 283 | 284 | 286 | 315 |

Males: Mean 4.84; S.D. 2.09.   Females: Mean 4.95; S.D. 2.09.

Sc$_1$ – Social Alienation (21 items)

True

| 17 | 21 | 22 | 42 | 46 | 138 | 145 | 190 | 221 | 256 | 277 | 281 | 291 | 292 |
| 320 | 333 |

False

| 90 | 276 | 278 | 280 | 343 |

Males: Mean 2.72; S.D. 2.42.   Females: Mean 3.11; S.D. 2.59.

Sc$_2$ – Emotional Alienation (11 items)

True

| 65 | 92 | 234 | 273 | 303 | 323 | 329 | 332 |

False

| 9 | 210 | 290 |

Males: Mean 1.05; S.D. 1.04.   Females: Mean 1.12; S.D. 1.09.

TABLE A–2 *continued*

Sc_3 – Lack of Ego Mastery, Cognitive (10 items)

True

31	32	147	170	180	299	311	316	325

False

165

Males: Mean 1.31; S.D. 1.66.   Females: Mean 1.18; S.D. 1.62.

Sc_4 – Lack of Ego Mastery, Conative (14 items)

True

31	38	48	65	92	233	234	273	299	303	325

False

9	210	290

Males: Mean 2.13; S.D. 1.85.   Females: Mean 2.17; S.D. 1.95.

Sc_5 – Lack of Ego Mastery, Defective Inhibition (11 items)

True

23	85	168	182	218	242	274	320	322	329	355

False

Males: Mean 1.42; S.D. 1.43.   Females: Mean 1.57; S.D. 1.57.

Sc_6 – Bizarre Sensory Experiences (20 items)

True

23	32	44	168	182	229	247	252	296	298	307	311	319	355

False

91	106	177	179	255	295

Males: Mean 1.90; S.D. 2.04.   Females: Mean 2.07; S.D. 2.20.

---

continued

TABLE A–2 *continued*

Ma$_1$ – Amorality (6 items)

True

131   227   248   250   269

False

263

Males: Mean 1.97; S.D. 1.29.   Females: Mean 1.56; S.D. 1.20.

Ma$_2$ – Psychomotor Acceleration (11 items)

True

15   85   87   122   169   206   218   242   244

False

100   106

Males: Mean 5.29; S.D. 2.07.   Females: Mean 5.07; S.D. 1.99.

Ma$_3$ – Imperturbability (8 items)

True

155   200   220

False

93   136   158   167   243

Males: Mean 3.51; S.D. 1.66.   Females: Mean 3.06; S.D. 1.56.

Ma$_4$ – Ego Inflation (9 items)

True

13   50   55   61   98   145   190   211   212

False

Males: Mean 3.04; S.D. 1.53.   Females: Mean 3.09; S.D. 1.64.

TABLE A–3 Wiener-Harmon Subtle-Obvious Subscales

D-O – Depression, Obvious (39 items)

True

15	18	31	38	39	46	56	73	92	127	130	146	147	170
175	215	233											

False

2	9	10	20	33	43	45	49	75	95	109	118	140	141
142	165	188	223	245	248	260	330						

Males: Mean 7.72; S.D. 4.29.   Females: Mean 8.75; S.D. 4.88.

D-S – Depression, Subtle (18 items)

True

5	117	181

False

29	37	55	68	76	134	143	148	178	189	212	221	226	238
267													

Males: Mean 10.60; S.D. 2.61.   Females: Mean 11.39; S.D. 2.44.

Hy-O – Hysteria, Obvious (32 items)

True

11	18	31	39	40	44	65	101	166	172	175	218

False

2	3	8	9	10	45	47	91	95	115	125	141	152	159
164	173	179	208	224	249								

Males: Mean 4.78; S.D. 3.61.   Females: Mean 5.67; S.D. 4.21.

Hy-S – Hysteria, Subtle (28 items)

True
230

False

7	14	26	29	58	76	81	98	110	116	124	129	135	148
151	157	161	167	176	185	193	213	241	243	253	263	265	

Males: Mean 16.09; S.D. 4.31.   Females: Mean 16.41; S.D. 4.09.

---

continued

TABLE A–3 *continued*

Pd-O – Psychopathic Deviate, Obvious (28 items)

True

17	22	31	32	35	42	52	54	56	71	82	94	99	105
195	202	225	259	264	288								

False

9	12	34	79	95	125	261	266

Males: Mean 6.16; S.D. 3.74.   Females: Mean 5.40; S.D. 3.72.

Pd-S – Psychopathic Deviate, Subtle (22 items)

True

21	89	113	219

False

70	83	122	129	143	157	158	160	167	171	185	209	214	217
226	243	263	267										

Males: Mean 10.41; S.D. 2.58.   Females: Mean 10.80; S.D. 2.48.

Pa-O – Paranoia, Obvious (23 items)

True

17	22	23	24	42	99	138	144	146	162	234	259	277	285
305	307	333	336	355	361								

False

255	266	314

Males: Mean 2.55; S.D. 2.19.   Females: Mean 2.76; S.D. 2.33.

TABLE A–3 *continued*

Pa-S – Paranoia, Subtle (17 items)

True

16	113	145	271	334

False

81	95	98	100	104	110	244	283	284	286	297	315

Males: Mean 7.55; S.D. 2.36.   Females: Mean 7.47; S.D. 2.34.

Ma-O – Hypomania, Obvious (23 items)

True

15	23	50	61	85	87	145	155	168	182	190	205	218	227
229	238	242	250	253	269								

False

100	106	107

Males: Mean 6.84; S.D. 2.95.   Females: Mean 6.38; S.D. 2.97.

Ma-S – Hypomania, Subtle (23 items)

True

13	21	55	98	113	122	131	169	200	206	211	212	220	244
248													

False

88	93	136	154	158	167	243	263

Males: Mean 10.04; S.D. 2.68.   Females: Mean 9.69; S.D. 2.60.

TABLE A–4   Si Subscales

Si_1 – Shyness/Self-Consciousness (14 items)

True

158   161   167   185   243   265   275   289

False

49   262   280   321   342   360

Males: Mean 4.80; S.D. 3.44.   Females: Mean 5.31; S.D. 3.69.

Si_2 – Social Avoidance (8 items)

True

337   367

False

86   340   353   359   363   370

Males: Mean 3.12; S.D. 2.33.   Females: Mean 2.75; S.D. 2.19.

Si_3 – Alienation—Self and Others (17 items)

True

31   56   104   110   135   284   302   308   326   328   338   347   348   358
364   368   369

False

Males: Mean 4.99; S.D. 3.35.   Females: Mean 5.23; S.D. 3.59.

TABLE A–5 Supplementary Scales

| A – Anxiety (39 items) |

True

31	38	56	65	82	127	135	215	233	243	251	273	277	289
301	309	310	311	325	328	338	339	341	347	390	391	394	400
408	411	415	421	428	442	448	451	464	469				

False

388

Males: Mean 10.02; S.D. 7.10.   Females: Mean 11.64; S.D. 7.90.

| R – Repression (37 items) |

True

False

1	7	10	14	37	45	69	112	118	120	128	134	142	168
178	189	197	199	248	255	256	297	330	346	350	353	354	359
363	365	422	423	430	432	449	456	465					

Males: Mean 15.18; S.D. 4.53.   Females: Mean 16.34; S.D. 3.81.

| Es – Ego Strength (52 items) |

True

2	33	45	98	141	159	169	177	179	189	199	209	213	230
245	323	385	406	413	425								

False

23	31	32	36	39	53	60	70	82	87	119	128	175	196
215	221	225	229	236	246	307	310	316	328	391	394	441	447
458	464	469	471										

Males: Mean 37.34; S.D. 4.46.   Females: Mean 34.37; S.D. 4.90.

continued

TABLE A–5 *continued*

MAC-R – MacAndrew Alcoholism-Revised (49 items)

True

7	24	36	49	52	69	72	82	84	103	105	113	115	128
168	172	202	214	224	229	238	257	280	342	344	387	407	412
414	422	434	439	445	456	473	502	506	549				

False

73	107	117	137	160	166	251	266	287	299	325

Males: Mean 21.72; S.D. 4.32.   Females: Mean 19.78; S.D. 3.65.

F_B – Back F (40 items)

True

281	291	303	311	317	319	322	323	329	332	333	334	387	395
407	431	450	454	463	468	476	478	484	489	506	516	517	520
524	525	526	528	530	539	540	544	555					

False

383	404	501

Males: Mean 1.86; S.D. 2.44.   Females: Mean 1.94; S.D. 2.58.

TABLE A–5 *continued*

VRIN – Variable Response Inconsistency (67 item-response pairs)
For each of the following response pairs add one point.

3 T – 39 T	125 T – 195 T	349 T – 515 F
6 T – 90 F	125 F – 195 F	349 F – 515 T
6 F – 90 T	135 F – 482 T	350 F – 521 T
9 F – 56 F	136 T – 507 F	353 T – 370 F
28 T – 59 F	136 F – 507 T	353 F – 370 T
31 T – 299 F	152 F – 464 F	364 F – 554 T
32 F – 316 T	161 T – 185 F	369 F – 421 T
40 T – 176 T	161 F – 185 T	372 T – 405 F
46 T – 265 F	165 F – 565 F	372 F – 405 T
48 T – 184 T	166 T – 268 F	380 T – 562 F
49 T – 280 F	166 F – 268 T	395 T – 435 F
73 T – 377 F	167 T – 243 F	395 F – 435 T
81 T – 284 F	167 F – 243 T	396 T – 403 F
81 F – 284 T	196 F – 415 T	396 F – 403 T
83 T – 288 T	199 T – 467 F	411 T – 485 F
84 T – 105 F	199 F – 467 T	411 F – 485 T
86 T – 359 F	226 T – 267 F	472 T – 533 F
95 F – 388 T	259 F – 333 T	472 F – 533 T
99 F – 138 T	262 F – 275 F	491 T – 509 F
103 T – 344 F	290 T – 556 F	506 T – 520 F
110 T – 374 F	290 F – 556 T	506 F – 520 T
110 F – 374 T	339 F – 394 T	513 T – 542 F
116 T – 430 F		

Males: Mean 4.52; S.D. 2.39.   Females: Mean 4.47; S.D. 2.28.

TRIN – True Response Inconsistency (23 item-response pairs)

1) For each of the following response pairs *add* one point:

3 T – 39 T	65 T – 95 T	209 T – 351 T
12 T – 166 T	73 T – 239 T	359 T – 367 T
40 T – 176 T	83 T – 288 T	377 T – 534 T
48 T – 184 T	99 T – 314 T	556 T – 560 T
63 T – 127 T	125 T – 195 T	

2) For each of the following response pairs *subtract* one point:

9 F – 56 F	140 F – 196 F	262 F – 275 F
65 F – 95 F	152 F – 464 F	265 F – 360 F
125 F – 195 F	165 F – 565 F	359 F – 367 F

3) Then add 9 points to the total raw score.

Males: Mean 8.95; S.D. 1.41.   Females: Mean 9.00; S.D. 1.32.

continued

TABLE A–5 *continued*

O-H – Overcontrolled Hostility (28 items)

True

67	79	207	286	305	398	471

False

1	15	29	69	77	89	98	116	117	129	153	169	171	293	344
390	400	420	433	440	460									

Males: Mean 12.51; S.D. 2.94.   Females: Mean 13.53; S.D. 2.74.

Do – Dominance (25 items)

True

55	207	232	245	386	416

False

31	52	70	73	82	172	201	202	220	227	243	244	275	309	325
399	412	470	473											

Males: Mean 16.62; S.D. 2.95.   Females: Mean 16.27; S.D. 2.89.

Re – Social Responsibility (30 items)

True

100	160	199	266	440	467

False

7	27	29	32	84	103	105	145	164	169	201	202	235	275	358
412	417	418	430	431	432	456	468	470						

Males: Mean 20.09; S.D. 3.89.   Females: Mean 21.02; S.D. 3.36.

Mt – College Maladjustment (41 items)

True

15	16	28	31	38	71	73	81	82	110	130	215	218	233	269
273	299	302	325	331	339	357	408	411	449	464	469	472		

False

2	3	9	10	20	43	95	131	140	148	152	223	405

Males: Mean 11.30; S.D. 6.44.   Females: Mean 12.31; S.D. 6.99.

TABLE A–5 *continued*

GM – Gender Role-Masculine (47 items)

True

8	20	143	152	159	163	176	199	214	237	321	331	350	385	388
401	440	462	467	474										

False

4	23	44	64	70	73	74	80	100	137	146	187	289	351	364
392	395	435	438	441	469	471	498	509	519	532	536			

Males: Mean 37.49; S.D. 4.56.   Females: Mean 28.81; S.D. 6.16.

GF – Gender Role-Feminine (46 items)

True

62	67	119	121	128	203	263	266	353	384	426	449	456	473	552

False

1	27	63	68	79	84	105	123	133	155	197	201	220	231	238
239	250	257	264	272	287	406	417	465	477	487	510	511	537	548
550														

Males: Mean 27.32; S.D. 4.70.   Females: Mean 36.86; S.D. 3.85.

PK – Post Traumatic Stress Disorder-Keane (46 items)

True

16	17	22	23	30	31	32	37	39	48	52	56	59	65	82
85	92	94	101	135	150	168	170	196	221	274	277	302	303	305
316	319	327	328	339	347	349	367							

False

2	3	9	49	75	95	125	140

Males: Mean 8.01; S.D. 5.99.   Females: Mean 8.52; S.D. 6.56.

continued

TABLE A-5 *continued*

PS – Post Traumatic Stress Disorder-Schlenger (60 items)

True

17	21	22	31	32	37	38	44	48	56	59	65	85	94	116
135	145	150	168	170	180	218	221	273	274	277	299	301	304	305
311	316	319	325	328	377	386	400	463	464	469	471	475	479	515
516	565													

False

3	9	45	75	95	141	165	208	223	280	372	405	564

Males: Mean 10.49; S.D. 7.98.   Females: Mean 11.82; S.D. 8.96.

TABLE A-6 Content Scales

ANX – Anxiety (23 items)

True

15	30	31	39	170	196	273	290	299	301	305	339	408	415	463
469	509	556											

False

140	208	223	405	496

Males: Mean 5.53; S.D. 4.17.   Females: Mean 6.53; S.D. 4.51.

FRS – Fears (23 items)

True

154	317	322	329	334	392	395	397	435	438	441	447	458	468	471
555													

False

115	163	186	385	401	453	462

Males: Mean 3.80; S.D. 2.96.   Females: Mean 6.59; S.D. 3.60.

TABLE A–6 *continued*

OBS – Obsessiveness (16 items)

True

55	87	135	196	309	313	327	328	394	442	482	491	497	509	547
553														

False

Males: Mean 4.93; S.D. 3.06.   Females: Mean 5.50; S.D. 3.32.

DEP – Depression (33 items)

True

38	52	56	65	71	82	92	130	146	215	234	246	277	303	306
331	377	399	400	411	454	506	512	516	520	539	546	554		

False

3	9	75	95	388

Males: Mean 4.79; S.D. 4.62.   Females: Mean 5.86; S.D. 5.02.

HEA – Health Concerns (36 items)

True

11	18	28	36	40	44	53	59	97	101	111	149	175	247

False

20	33	45	47	57	91	117	118	141	142	159	164	176	179	181
194	204	224	249	255	295	404								

Males: Mean 5.29; S.D. 3.91.   Females: Mean 6.16; S.D. 4.47.

BIZ – Bizarre Mentation (23 items)

True

24	32	60	96	138	162	198	228	259	298	311	316	319	333	336
355	361	466	490	508	543	551								

False

427

Males: Mean 2.30; S.D. 2.50.   Females: Mean 2.21; S.D. 2.49.

---

continued

TABLE A–6   *continued*

ANG – Anger (16 items)

True

| 29 | 37 | 116 | 134 | 302 | 389 | 410 | 414 | 430 | 461 | 486 | 513 | 540 | 542 | 548 |

False

564

Males: Mean 5.63; S.D. 3.31.   Females: Mean 5.68; S.D. 3.08.

CYN – Cynicism (23 items)

True

| 50 | 58 | 76 | 81 | 104 | 110 | 124 | 225 | 241 | 254 | 283 | 284 | 286 | 315 | 346 |
| 352 | 358 | 374 | 399 | 403 | 445 | 470 | 538 | | | | | | | |

False

Males: Mean 9.50; S.D. 5.35.   Females: Mean 8.73; S.D. 5.16.

ASP – Antisocial Practices (22 items)

True

| 26 | 35 | 66 | 81 | 84 | 104 | 105 | 110 | 123 | 227 | 240 | 248 | 250 | 254 | 269 |
| 283 | 284 | 374 | 412 | 418 | 419 | | | | | | | | | |

False

266

Males: Mean 7.91; S.D. 4.19.   Females: Mean 6.17; S.D. 3.70.

TPA – Type A (19 items)

True

| 27 | 136 | 151 | 212 | 302 | 358 | 414 | 419 | 420 | 423 | 430 | 437 | 507 | 510 | 523 |
| 531 | 535 | 541 | 545 | | | | | | | | | | | |

False

Males: Mean 8.08; S.D. 3.68.   Females: Mean 7.41; S.D. 3.34.

TABLE A-6 *continued*

LSE – Low Self-Esteem (24 items)

True

70	73	130	235	326	369	376	380	411	421	450	457	475	476	483
485	503	504	519	526	562									

False

61   78   109

Males: Mean 4.25; S.D. 3.69.   Females: Mean 5.16; S.D. 4.24.

SOD – Social Discomfort (24 items)

True

46	158	167	185	265	275	281	337	349	367	479	480	515

False

49	86	262	280	321	340	353	359	360	363	370

Males: Mean 7.65; S.D. 4.77.   Females: Mean 7.53; S.D. 4.80.

FAM – Family Problems (25 items)

True

21	54	145	190	195	205	256	292	300	323	378	379	382	413	449
478	543	550	563	567										

False

83   125   217   383   455

Males: Mean 5.32; S.D. 3.52.   Females: Mean 6.14; S.D. 3.77.

WRK – Work Interference (33 items)

True

15	17	31	54	73	98	135	233	243	299	302	339	364	368	394
409	428	445	464	491	505	509	517	525	545	554	559	566		

False

10   108   318   521   561

Males: Mean 7.30; S.D. 4.98.   Females: Mean 8.51; S.D. 5.45.

TABLE A–6 *continued*

TRT – Negative Treatment Indicators (26 items)

True

22	92	274	306	364	368	373	375	376	377	391	399	482	488	491
495	497	499	500	504	528	539	554							

False

493	494	501

Males: Mean 4.70; S.D. 3.71.   Females: Mean 5.02; S.D. 3.98.

MMPI-2: T Score Conversion Tables

Source: From the *Minnesota Multiphasic Personality Inventory-2 Manual* by J. N. Butcher, W. G. Dahlstrom, J. R. Graham, A. Tellegen, & B. Kaemmer, Appendix A, pp. 53–64. Copyright © the University of Minnesota 1942, 1943, 1951, 1967 (renewal 1970), 1989. This *Manual*, 1989. Reproduced by permission.

TABLE B-1 Uniform and Linear T Score Conversions for Basic Scales with K-Corrections

Males

RAW SCORE	L*	F*	K*	Hs +.5K	D	Hy	Pd +.4K	Mf*	Pa	Pt +1K	Sc +1K	Ma +.2K	Si*
73													
72													
71													
70													
69													100
68													99
67													98
66											120		97
65											118		96
64											117		94
63											115		93
62											113		92
61											111		91
60										120	110		90
59										119	108		89
58										117	106		87
57										115	105		86
56					120			109		113	103		85
55					119			107		111	101		84
54					117			105		109	98		83
53					115	120		103		106	96		82
52					114	119		101		104	94		80
51					112	116	120	99		102	93		79
50					110	114	117	97		100	91		78
49					108	111	115	95		98	89		77
48					106	109	112	93		96	87		76
47					104	106	110	91		94	84		75
46					102	104	107	89		91	82		73
45					100	102	105	87		89	81		72
44				120	98	100	102	85		87	79	120	71
43				119	97	98	100	83		85	77	117	70
42				116	95	97	97	81		83	75	114	69
41				114	93	95	95	79		81	74	110	68
40				112	91	93	92	78		79	72	107	66
39				110	89	91	90	76		77	70	104	65
38				108	87	89	87	74		74	69	101	64
37				105	85	87	84	72		72	67	98	63
36				103	83	86	82	70		70	65	94	62
35				101		84	79	68		68			61

Females

RAW SCORE	L*	F*	K*	Hs +.5K	D	Hy	Pd +.4K	Mf*	Pa	Pt +1K	Sc +1K	Ma +.2K	Si*
73													
72													
71													
70											120		
69											119		95
68											118		94
67											116		93
66										120	115		91
65										119	113		90
64										117	112		89
63										115	111		88
62										114	109		87
61										112	108		86
60										110	106		85
59										108	105		84
58										106	103		83
57										105	102		82
56					120					103	100		81
55					118					101	99		79
54					116					99	97		78
53					114	120				97	96		77
52					112	118				95	94		76
51					109	115				94	93		75
50					107	113	120			92	91		74
49					105	111	118			90	90		73
48					103	108	115			88	88		72
47					101	106	113			86	87		71
46				120	99	104	110			84	84		70
45				118	96	101	107			83	81		69
44				116	94	99	105	30		81	78	120	67
43				113	92	96	102	33		79	76	118	66
42				111	90	94	100	35		77	75	115	65
41				109	88	92	97	38		75	73	112	64
40				107	86	90	94	40		73	72	109	63
39				105	83	89	92	43		72	70	106	62
38				103	81	87	89	45		70	69	103	61
37				101		84	87	47		68	67	100	60
36				99		82	84	50		66	66	97	59
35				97		80	81	52		64	65	94	58

Males

Raw	L*	F*	K*	Hs +.5K	D	Hy	Pd +.4K	Mf*	Pa	Pt +1K	Sc +1K	Ma +.2K	Si*
34		120		99	81	81	77	66	120	66	63	91	59
33		119		97	80	79	74	64	119	64	62	88	58
32		116		94	78	78	72	62	116	62	60	85	57
31		113		92	76	76	69	60	113	59	58	81	56
30		110	81	90	74	74	67	58	112	57	56	78	55
29		107	77	88	72	71	64	56	108	55	55	75	54
28		104	75	86	70	69	62	54	105	53	53	72	52
27		101	72	84	68	66	59	52	101	51	51	69	51
26		98	70	81	66	64	57	50	97	49	49	65	50
25		95	68	79	64	61	54	48	94	47	47	62	49
24		92	66	77	62	59	52	46	90	44	45	59	48
23		89	64	75	61	57	50	44	86	43	44	56	47
22		85	62	73	59	54	48	42	83	41	42	53	45
21		82	60	70	57	52	46	40	79	39	40	51	44
20		79	58	68	54	50	44	38	75	37	39	49	43
19		76	56	66	52	47	42	36	72	36	37	47	42
18		73	54	64	50	45	40	34	68	34	36	45	41
17		70	51	62	47	43	39	32	64	33	35	43	40
16		67	49	59	45	42	37	30	61	32	34	41	38
15	100	64	47	57	42	40	35		57	31	33	39	37
14	96	61	45	54	40	38	34		53	30	32	38	36
13	91	58	43	51	38	37	33		49		31	36	35
12	87	55	41	48	36	35	31		46		30	35	34
11	83	51	39	45	34	34	30		42			33	33
10	78	48	37	42	32	33			39			31	31
9	74	45	35	39	30	32			37			30	30
8	70	42	33	37		31			34				
7	65	39	30	35		30			32				
6	61	36		33					31				
5	56			32					30				
4	52			31									
3	48			30									
2	43												
1	39												
0	35												
K-FRACTION				+.5K			+.4K			+1K	+1K	+.2K	

Females

Raw	L*	F*	K*	Hs +.5K	D	Hy	Pd +.4K	Mf*	Pa	Pt +1K	Sc +1K	Ma +.2K	Si*
34		120		95	79	77	79	55	120	62	63	91	57
33		116		92	77	75	76	57	118	61	62	88	55
32		113		90	75	73	73	60	114	59	60	85	54
31		109		88	72	70	71	62	111	57	59	82	53
30		106	83	86	70	68	68	65	107	55	57	79	52
29		103	81	84	68	65	66	67	103	53	55	76	51
28		99	78	82	66	63	63	69	100	51	53	74	50
27		96	76	80	64	61	60	72	96	49	52	71	49
26		92	74	78	62	58	58	74	92	47	50	68	48
25		89	72	76	59	56	55	77	89	44	48	65	47
24		85	70	74	57	54	53	79	85	42	46	62	46
23		82	67	71	55	51	51	82	81	40	44	59	45
22		79	65	69	53	49	49	84	78	39	42	56	43
21		75	63	67	51	47	47	87	74	37	41	53	42
20		72	61	65	49	45	45	89	70	35	39	51	41
19		68	59	63	47	43	43	92	67	34	37	49	40
18		65	56	61	46	41	41	94	63	32	36	47	39
17		61	54	59	44	39	39	96	59	31	34	45	38
16		58	52	57	42	38	37	99	56	30	33	43	37
15	105	55	50	54	40	36	36	101	52		32	41	36
14	100	51	48	51	38	35	34	104	49		31	39	35
13	95	48	46	49	36	34	32	106	45		30	37	34
12	90	44	43	46	34	32	30	109	42			35	33
11	86	41	41	43	32	31		111	39			33	32
10	81	37	39	41	30	30		114	37			31	30
9	76		37	40				116	34			30	
8	71		35	38				118	32				
7	66		32	35				120	31				
6	62		30	33					30				
5	57			30									
4	52												
3	47												
2	43												
1	38												
0	33												
K-FRACTION				+.5K			+.4K			+1K	+1K	+.2K	

*Linear T Scores

TABLE B-2 Uniform and Linear T Score Conversions for Basic Scales without K-Corrections

RAW SCORE					Males													Females								RAW SCORE
	L*	F*	K*	Hs	D	Hy	Pd	Mf*	Pa	Pt	Sc	Ma	Si*	L*	F*	K*	Hs	D	Hy	Pd	Mf*	Pa	Pt	Sc	Ma	Si*	
72													100											120			72
71													99											118			71
70													98											117			70
69											120		97											116		95	69
68											119		96											115		94	68
67											117		94											114		93	67
66											116		93											113		91	66
65											115		92											112		90	65
64											114		91											111		89	64
63											113		90											109		88	63
62											111		89											108		87	62
61											110		87											107		86	61
60											109		86											106		85	60
59											108		85											105		84	59
58											107		84											104		83	58
57											105		83											103		82	57
56								109			104		82											102		81	56
55					120			107			103		80											100		79	55
54					119			105			102		79											99		78	54
53					117			103			100		78					120						98		77	53
52					115			101			99		77					118	120					97		76	52
51					114			99			98		76					116	118					96		75	51
50					112	120		97			97		75					114	115					95		74	50
49					110	119		95			96		73					112	113					94		73	49
48					108	116	120	93		104	94		72					109	111				98	93		72	48
47					106	114	117	91		103	93		71					107	108	120			97	92		71	47
46					104	111	115	89		101	92		70					105	106	118			95	90		70	46
45					102	109	113	87		100	91		69					103	104	116			94	89		69	45
44					100	106	111	85		98	90		68					101	101	113	30		93	88		67	44
43					98	104	109	83		97	88		66					99	99	111	33		91	87	120	66	43
42					97	101	106	81		95	87	120	65					96	96	109	35		90	86	119	65	42
41					95	99	104	79		94	86	118	64					94	94	106	38		89	85	116	64	41
40					93	96	102	78		92	85	115	63					92	92	104	40		87	84	114	63	40
39					91	94	100	76		91	84	112	62					90	89	102	43		86	83	111	62	39
38					89	91	97	74		89	82	109						88	87	99	45		84	81	108	61	38
37					87	89	95	72		88	81	106						86	84	97	47		83	80	105	60	37
36					85	86	93	70		86		103						83	82	95	50		82	79	102	59	36

Females

RAW SCORE	L*	F*	K*	Hs	D	Hy	Pd	Mf*	Pa	Pt	Sc	Ma	Si*
35					81	80	92	52		80	78	100	58
34					79	77	90	55	120	79	77	97	57
33				100	77	75	88	57	118	78	76	94	55
32				98	75	73	85	60	114	76	75	91	54
31				97	72	70	83	62	111	75	74	89	53
30		120	83	95	70	68	81	65	107	73	72	86	52
29		116	81	93	68	65	78	67	103	72	71	83	51
28		113	78	91	66	63	76	69	100	71	70	80	50
27		109	76	89	64	61	74	72	96	69	69	77	49
26		106	74	87	62	58	72	74	92	68	68	75	48
25		103	72	85	59	56	69	77	89	67	67	72	47
24		99	70	83	57	54	67	79	85	65	65	69	46
23		96	67	81	55	51	65	82	81	64	63	66	45
22		92	65	80	53	49	62	84	78	62	62	64	43
21		89	63	78	51	47	60	87	74	61	61	61	42
20		85	61	76	49	45	58	89	70	60	60	58	41
19		82	59	74	47	43	55	92	67	58	59	55	40
18		79	56	72	46	41	53	94	63	57	58	53	39
17		75	54	70	44	39	51	96	59	56	57	51	38
16		72	52	69	42	38	49	99	56	55	55	49	37
15	105	68	50	67	40	36	47	101	52	53	53	47	36
14	100	65	48	65	38	35	45	104	49	52	52	45	35
13	95	61	46	63	36	33	43	106	45	51	51	43	34
12	90	58	43	61	34	32	39	109	42	50	50	41	33
11	86	55	41	59	32	31	37	111	39	48	48	40	32
10	81	51	39	57	30	30	35	114	37	47	47	38	30
9	76	48	37	56			33	116	34	46	45	36	
8	71	44	35	54			31	118	32	44	43	34	
7	66	41	32	52			30	120	31	43	42	32	
6	62	37	30	49					30	41	39	30	
5	57			47						39	37		
4	52			44						37	35		
3	47			41						35	32		
2	43			37						33	30		
1	38			33						30			
0	33												

Males

RAW SCORE	L*	F*	K*	Hs	D	Hy	Pd	Mf*	Pa	Pt	Sc	Ma	Si*
35					83	84	91	68	120	85	80	100	61
34					81	81	89	66	119	83	79	97	59
33				107	80	79	86	64	116	82	78	94	58
32				105	78	76	84	62	112	80	76	91	57
31				103	76	74	82	60	108	79	75	88	56
30		120	81	101	74	71	80	58	105	78	74	85	55
29		119	79	99	72	69	77	56	101	76	73	82	54
28		116	77	97	70	66	75	54	97	75	72	78	52
27		113	75	95	68	64	73	52	94	73	70	76	51
26		110	72	93	66	61	71	50	90	72	69	73	50
25		107	70	91	64	59	68	48	86	70	68	70	49
24		104	68	89	62	57	66	46	83	69	67	67	48
23		101	66	87	61	54	64	44	79	67	66	64	47
22		98	64	85	59	52	62	42	75	66	64	61	45
21		95	62	83	57	50	60	40	72	64	63	58	44
20		92	60	81	54	47	57	38	68	63	62	56	43
19		89	58	79	52	45	55	36	64	61	61	53	42
18		85	56	77	50	43	53	34	61	60	60	51	41
17		82	54	75	47	42	51	32	57	58	58	49	40
16		79	51	73	45	40	49	30	53	57	57	47	38
15	100	76	49	71	42	38	46		49	56	56	45	37
14	96	73	47	69	40	37	44		46	54	55	43	36
13	91	70	45	67	38	35	42		42	53	54	42	35
12	87	67	43	65	36	34	40		39	52	52	40	34
11	83	64	41	63	34	33	38		37	50	51	38	33
10	78	61	39	61	32	31	36		34	49	49	37	31
9	74	58	37	59	30	30	34		32	47	48	35	30
8	70	55	35	57			33		31	46	46	33	
7	65	51	33	54			31		30	44	45	31	
6	61	48	30	52			30			42	43	30	
5	56	45		49						41	41		
4	52	42		46						39	39		
3	48	39		42						37	37		
2	43	36		38						34	35		
1	39			34						32	32		
0	35									30	30		

*Linear T Scores

TABLE B-3 Linear T Score Conversions for Harris-Lingoes Subscales for Males

RAW SCORE	D_1	D_2	D_3	D_4	D_5	Hy_1	Hy_2	Hy_3	Hy_4	Hy_5	Pd_1	Pd_2	Pd_3	Pd_4	Pd_5	Pa_1	Pa_2	Pa_3	Sc_1	Sc_2	Sc_3	Sc_4	Sc_5	Sc_6	Ma_1	Ma_2	Ma_3	Ma_4	RAW SCORE
32	116																												32
31	114																												31
30	111																												30
29	108																												29
28	106																												28
27	103																												27
26	100																												26
25	98																												25
24	95																												24
23	93																												23
22	90																												22
21	87																												21
20	85																		120										20
19	82																		117										19
18	79																		113										18
17	77								120							120			109					120					17
16	74								115							118			105					119					16
15	71			110				106	111							112			101			114		114					15
14	69			105				102	106							106			97			109		109					14
13	66	98		101				97	101					99		100			92			103		104					13
12	64	92		96				93	96						91	94			88			103		99					12
11	61	87	116	91			71	88	91					88	87	88			84			98	117	95					11
10	58	81	108	86	96		67	84	86					83	82	82			80		103	92	110	90		78			10
9	56	76	100	82	91		63	79	82		98			78	77	76	96	70	76	120	96	87	103	85		73		89	9
8	53	70	91	77	85		59	75	77		91	81		73	72	70	89	65	72	117	90	82	96	80		68	77	82	8
7	50	65	83	72	79		55	70	72	78	84	74		67	67	64	82	60	68	107	84	76	89	75		63	71	76	7
6	48	59	75	67	74	61	51	67	67	71	78	68	64	62	63	58	76	56	64	98	78	71	82	70	81	58	65	69	6
5	45	54	67	62	68	56	47	61	62	63	71	61	58	57	58	52	69	51	59	88	72	65	75	65	74	53	59	63	5
4	42	48	59	58	62	51	43	57	57	55	65	55	52	51	53	46	62	46	55	78	66	60	68	60	66	49	53	56	4
3	40	43	51	53	57	45	40	52	52	48	58	48	46	46	48	40	55	41	51	69	60	55	61	55	58	44	47	50	3
2	37	37	43	48	51	40	36	48	48	40	51	42	40	41	43		48	36	47	59	54	49	54	51	50	39	41	43	2
1	35	32	35	43	45	34	32	43	43	33	45	35	35	36	38		41	32	43	50	48	44	47	46	42	34	35	37	1
0	32	30	30	38	40	30	30	38	38	30	38	30	30	30	34		34	30	39	40	42	39	40	41	35	30	30	30	0

388

TABLE B–4 Linear T Score Conversions for Harris-Lingoes Subscales for Females

RAW SCORE	D_1	D_2	D_3	D_4	D_5	Hy_1	Hy_2	Hy_3	Hy_4	Hy_5	Pd_1	Pd_2	Pd_3	Pd_4	Pd_5	Pa_1	Pa_2	Pa_3	Sc_1	Sc_2	Sc_3	Sc_4	Sc_5	Sc_6	Ma_1	Ma_2	Ma_3	Ma_4	RAW SCORE
32	108																												32
31	105																												31
30	103																												30
29	101																												29
28	98																												28
27	96																												27
26	94																												26
25	91																												25
24	89																												24
23	86																												23
22	84																												22
21	82																		119										21
20	79																		115										20
19	77																		111										19
18	75								105										108					120					18
17	72								101										104					118					17
16	70																		100					113					16
15	67			106				99	97										96					109					15
14	65	95		102				95	93							120			92			111		104					14
13	63	90		97			71	91	89					97		117			88			106		100					13
12	60	84	107	93			67	87	85					92	92	111			84			100	110	95					12
11	58	79	100	88			63	83	81					86	87	105			81			95	104	91					11
10	56	73	93	84	89		59	79	77					81	82	99			77		104	90	97	86		80			10
9	53	68	85	79	83		55	75	73		92			76	77	93	91	69	73	120	98	85	91	81		75		86	9
8	51	62	78	75	78		50	71	69		86	92		71	72	87	84	65	69	113	92	80	85	77		70	82	80	8
7	48	57	70	70	73		46	67	65	77	80	85		66	68	81	78	60	65	104	86	75	78	72		65	75	74	7
6	46	51	63	66	68	61	42	63	61	70	74	77	65	60	63	75	72	55	61	95	80	70	72	68	87	60	69	68	6
5	44	46	56	61	63	56	38	59	57	62	68	70	59	55	58	69	65	50	57	86	74	65	65	63	79	55	62	62	5
4	41	41	48	57	58	51	34	55	53	54	62	62	54	50	53	63	59	45	53	76	67	59	65	59	70	50	56	56	4
3	39	35	41	52	53	45	30	51	49	46	56	55	48	45	48	57	53	41	50	67	61	54	59	54	62	45	50	49	3
2	37	30	34	48	47	40		47	45	39	50	47	42	40	43	51	46	36	46	58	55	49	53	50	54	40	43	43	2
1	34		30	43	42	35		43	41	31	44	40	36	35	39	45	40	31	42	49	49	44	46	45	45	35	37	37	1
0	32			38	37	30		39	37	30	38	32	31	30	34	39	34	30	38	40	43	39	40	41	37	30	30	31	0

TABLE B–5 Linear T Score Conversions for Wiener-Harmon Subtle-Obvious Subscales for Males and Females

RAW SCORE	Males										Females									
	D-O	D-S	Hy-O	Hy-S	Pd-O	Pd-S	Pa-O	Pa-S	Ma-O	Ma-S	D-O	D-S	Hy-O	Hy-S	Pd-O	Pd-S	Pa-O	Pa-S	Ma-O	Ma-S
39	120										112									
38	118										110									
37	116										108									
36	114										106									
35	111										104									
34	109										102									
33	107										100									
32	104										98									
31	104										96									
30	102		120								94		112							
29	100		117								92		110							
28	97		114		108						89		108		111					
27	95		111		106						87		105		108					
26	93		109		103						85		103		105					
25	90		106		100						83		101		103					
24	88		103		98						81		98		100					
23	86		100		95						79		96		97					
22	83		98		92				105		77		93		95				106	
21	81		95		90				101		75		91		92				103	
20	79		92	78	87				98		73		89		89				99	
19	76		89	75	84				95		71		86	78	87		120		96	
18	74		87	73	82				91	98	69		84	76	84		115		92	101
17	72		84	71	79		116		88	95	67		82	73	81		111		89	97
16	69		81	68	76	95	112		84	91	65		79	71	79	95	107		86	93
15	67		78	66	74	91	107		81	87	63		77	69	76	91	103		82	90
14	65		76	64	71	87	102	90	78	83	61		75	66	73	87	98	91	79	86
13	62		73	61	68	83	98	86	74	80	59		72	64	70	83	94	87	76	82
12	60	78	70	59	66	79	93	82	71	76	57		70	61	68	79	90	82	72	78
11	58	75	67	57	63	76	89	77	67	72	55	77	67	59	65	75	85	78	69	74
10	55	71	64	54	60	72	84	73	64	69	53	73	65	56	62	71	81	74	66	70
9	53	67	62	52	58	68	80	69	61	65	51	69	63	54	60	67	77	69	62	67
8	51	63	59	50	55	64	75	65	57	61	48	65	60	51	57	63	72	65	59	63
7	48	59	56	47	52	60	70	60	54	57	46	61	58	49	54	59	68	61	55	59
6	46	55	53	45	50	56	66	56	51	54	44	57	56	47	52	55	64	57	52	55
5	44	52	51	43	47	52	61	52	47	50	42	53	53	44	49	51	60	52	49	51
4	41	48	48	41	44	48	57	48	44	46	40	48	51	42	46	47	55	48	45	47
3	39	44	45	38	42	45	52	43	40	42	38	44	48	39	44	43	51	44	42	44
2	37	40	42	36	39	41	47	39	37	39	36	40	44	37	41	39	47	39	39	40
1	34	36	40	34	36	37	43	35	34	35	34	36	41	34	38	35	42	35	35	36
0	32	32	37	31	34	33	38	31	30	31	32	32	37	32	35	31	38	31	32	32

TABLE B–6 Linear T Score Conversions for Si Subscales

RAW SCORE	Males				Females		
	Si_1	Si_2	Si_3		Si_1	Si_2	Si_3
17			86				83
16			83				80
15			80				77
14	77		77		73		74
13	74		74		71		72
12	71		71		68		69
11	68		68		65		66
10	65		65		63		63
9	62		62		60		60
8	59	71	59		57	74	58
7	56	67	56		55	69	55
6	53	62	53		52	65	52
5	51	58	50		49	60	49
4	48	54	47		46	56	47
3	45	49	44		44	51	44
2	42	45	41		41	47	41
1	39	41	38		38	42	38
0	36	37			36	37	

TABLE B–7 Linear T Score Conversions for Supplementary Scales for Males and Females

RAW SCORE	Males															Females															RAW PS SCORE
	A	R	Es	MAC-R	F_B	TRIN	VRIN	O-H	Do	Re	Mt	GM	GF	PK	PS	A	R	Es	MAC-R	F_B	TRIN	VRIN	O-H	Do	Re	Mt	GM	GF	PK	PS	
60															112															104	60
59															111															103	59
58															110															102	58
57															108															100	57
56															107															99	56
55															106															98	55
54															104															97	54
53															103															96	53
52			83												102			86												95	52
51			81												101			84												94	51
50			78												99			82												93	50
49			76	113											98			80												92	49
48			74	111											97			78												90	48
47			72	109								71			96			76									80			89	47
46			69	106								69	90	113	94			74	120								78	74	107	88	46
45			67	104								66	88	112	93			72	119								76	71	106	87	45
44			65	102								64	85	110	92			70	116								75	69	104	86	44
43			63	99								62	83	108	91			68	114								73	66	103	85	43
42			60	97								60	81	107	89			66	111								71	63	101	84	42
41			58	95							96	58	79	105	88			64	108							91	70	61	100	83	41
40			56	92							95	56	77	103	87			61	105							90	68	58	98	81	40
39	91		54	90							93	53	75	102	86	85		59	103							88	67	56	96	80	39
38	89	98	51	88							91	51	73	100	84	83		57	100							87	65	53	95	79	38
37	88	96	49	85							90	49	71	98	83	82	104	55	97							85	63	50	93	78	37
36	87	94	47	83							88	47	68	97	82	81	102	53	94							84	62	48	92	77	36
35	85	92	45	81							87	45	66	95	81	80	99	51	92							82	60	45	90	76	35
34	84	92	42	78							85	42	64	93	79	78	96	49	89							81	58	43	89	75	34
33	82	89	40	76							84	40	62	92	78	77	94	47	86							80	57	40	87	74	33
32	81	87	38	74							82	38	60	90	77	76	91	45	84							78	55	37	86	73	32
31	80	85	36	72							81	36	58	88	76	75	88	43	81							77	54	35	84	71	31
30	78	83	34	69						76	79	34	56	87	74	73	86	41	78						77	75	52	32	83	70	30

Females

RAW SCORE	A	R	Es	MAC-R	F_B	TRIN	VRIN	O-H	Do	Re	Mt	GM	GF	PK	PS	RAW PS SCORE
29	72	83	39	75	116	120T	120	103	80	74	74	50	30	81	69	29
28	71	81	37	73	112	118T	118	99	77	71	72	49		80	68	28
27	69	78	35	70	108	111T	114	96	73	68	71	47		78	67	27
26	68	75	33	67	105	103T	110	92	70	65	70	45		77	66	26
25	67	73	31	64	101	95T	106	88	66	62	68	44		75	64	25
24	66	70	30	62	97	88T	102	85	63	59	67	42		74	63	24
23	64	67		59	93	80T	98	81	59	56	65	41		72	62	23
22	63	65		56	89	73T	94	77	56	53	64	39		71	61	22
21	62	62		53	85	65T	90	74	53	50	62	37		69	60	21
20	61	60		51	81	58T	86	70	49	47	61	36		68	59	20
19	59	57		48	77	50	82	66	46	44	60	34		66	58	19
18	58	54		45	74	58F	78	63	42	41	58	32		64	57	18
17	57	52		42	70	65F	74	59	39	38	57	31		63	56	17
16	56	49		40	66	73F	70	55	35	35	55			61	55	16
15	54	46		37	62	80F	66	52	30	32	54			60	54	15
14	53	44		34	58	88F	62	48		30	52			58	52	14
13	52	41		31	54	95F	58	44			51			57	51	13
12	50	39		30	50	103F	54	41			50			55	50	12
11	49	36			46	111F	50	37			48			54	49	11
10	48	33			42	118F	46	33			47			52	48	10
9	47	31					42	30			45			51	47	9
8	45	30									44			49	46	8
7	44										42			48	45	7
6	43										41			46	43	6
5	42										40			45	42	5
4	40										38			43	41	4
3	39										37			42	40	3
2	38										35			40	39	2
1	37										34			39	38	1
0	35										32			37	37	0

Males

RAW SCORE	A	R	Es	MAC-R	F_B	TRIN	VRIN	O-H	Do	Re	Mt	GM	GF	PK	PS
29	77	81	31	67	120	120T	103	78	73		77	31	54	85	73
28	75	78	30	65	116	114T	99	75	70		76	30	51	83	72
27	74	76		62	112	107T	96	72	68		74		49	82	71
26	73	74		60	108	100T	93	68	65		73		47	80	69
25	71	72		58	104	93T	89	65	63		71		45	78	68
24	70	69		55	100	86T	86	61	60		70		43	77	67
23	68	67		53	96	79T	82	58	57		68		41	75	66
22	67	65		51	92	72T	79	55	55		67		39	73	64
21	65	63		48	87	65T	76	51	52		65		37	72	63
20	64	61		46	83	57T	72	48	50		64		34	70	62
19	63	58		44	79	50	69	45	47		62		32	68	61
18	61	56		41	75	57F	65	41	45		60		30	67	59
17	60	54		39	71	64F	61	38	42		59			65	58
16	58	52		37	67	71F	57	34	39		57			63	57
15	57	50		34	63	78F	54	31	37		56			62	56
14	56	47		32	59	85F	50	30	34		54			60	54
13	54	45		30	55	92F			32		53			58	53
12	53	43			51	99F			30		51			57	52
11	51	41			46	107F					50			55	51
10	50	39			42	114F					48			53	49
9	49	36									46			52	48
8	47	34									45			50	47
7	46	32									43			48	46
6	44	30									42			47	44
5	43										40			45	43
4	42										39			43	42
3	40										37			42	41
2	39										36			40	39
1	37										34			38	38
0	36										32			37	37

TABLE B-8 Uniform T Score Conversions for Content Scales

Males

RAW SCORE	ANX	FRS	OBS	DEP	HEA	BIZ	ANG	CYN	ASP	TPA	LSE	SOD	FAM	WRK	TRT
36					112										
35					110										
34					108										
33				100	106									98	
32				99	105									96	
31				97	103									94	
30				95	101									92	
29				94	99									90	
28				92	97									89	
27				90	95									87	
26				88	93									85	104
25				87	91								105	83	101
24				85	89						101	89	102	81	99
23	92	113		83	87	120		83			98	86	99	79	96
22	90	110		82	85	119		80	94		96	84	97	78	94
21	87	107		80	83	115		77	90		93	81	94	76	91
20	85	103		78	81	112		74	87		91	78	91	74	89
19	82	100		77	80	108		71	83	89	88	76	88	72	86
18	80	97		75	78	105		68	79	85	85	73	85	70	84
17	77	93		73	76	101		65	76	81	83	71	82	68	81
16	75	90	87	71	74	98	86	62	72	77	80	68	80	67	79
15	72	87	84	70	72	94	82	59	69	72	77	65	77	65	76
14	70	84	80	68	70	91	78	56	65	68	75	63	74	63	74
13	67	80	77	66	68	88	74	54	62	64	72	60	71	61	71
12	65	77	73	65	66	84	70	52	58	60	70	58	68	59	69
11	62	74	70	63	64	81	67	51	55	56	67	55	66	57	66
10	60	70	66	61	62	77	63	49	53	53	64	52	63	56	64
9	57	67	63	59	60	74	59	48	51	50	62	50	60	54	61
8	55	64	59	58	58	70	56	47	49	48	59	47	57	52	59
7	53	60	56	56	56	67	53	46	46	46	57	45	55	50	56
6	52	57	53	55	53	63	50	44	44	44	55	43	52	48	54
5	50	54	50	53	51	60	48	43	42	43	53	41	50	46	52
4	47	51	47	51	48	57	46	41	40	41	51	39	47	44	49
3	45	48	44	48	44	54	43	40	37	38	48	35	44	41	47
2	42	45	41	44	41	51	40	38	34	36	45	32	41	39	43
1	39	41	37	41	37	46	36	35	30	32	41		37	36	39
0	35	35	33	36	33	39	32	32		30	35		33	33	35

Females

RAW SCORE	ANX	FRS	OBS	DEP	HEA	BIZ	ANG	CYN	ASP	TPA	LSE	SOD	FAM	WRK	TRT
36					107										
35					105										
34					103										
33				97	101									99	
32				95	100									97	
31				93	98									95	
30				92	96									92	
29				90	94									90	
28				88	92									88	
27				87	90									86	
26				85	89									84	102
25				83	87								99	82	100
24				82	85						97	87	96	80	97
23	89	101		80	83	113		83			94	84	94	78	95
22	86	98		78	81	110		80	98		92	82	91	76	92
21	84	94		77	79	108		77	94		89	80	89	73	89
20	81	91		75	77	105		75	91		86	77	86	71	87
19	79	88		73	76	102		72	88	94	84	75	83	69	84
18	76	85		72	74	99		69	85	90	81	72	81	67	82
17	74	81		70	72	96		67	82	86	78	70	78	65	79
16	71	78	87	68	70	93	88	64	79	81	76	68	75	63	77
15	69	75	83	67	68	90	84	61	75	77	73	65	73	61	74
14	66	72	79	65	66	87	80	58	72	73	70	63	70	59	72
13	64	68	75	63	64	84	76	56	69	69	68	60	68	57	69
12	61	65	71	62	63	81	72	54	66	64	65	58	65	55	67
11	59	62	67	60	61	79	68	53	63	60	62	56	62	53	64
10	56	59	63	59	59	76	64	51	59	56	60	54	60	51	61
9	55	56	59	57	57	73	60	50	56	53	57	52	57	50	59
8	53	53	56	55	55	70	56	48	54	50	55	51	55	48	57
7	51	51	53	53	53	67	53	47	51	48	54	49	52	46	55
6	49	48	50	52	51	64	50	46	49	45	52	46	50	45	53
5	47	46	48	51	49	61	47	44	47	43	51	44	47	43	51
4	45	43	46	49	46	58	45	42	45	41	49	41	45	40	49
3	43	41	44	46	43	56	42	40	42	38	47	39	42	37	46
2	40	38	41	43	40	52	39	38	39	36	44	35	39	34	43
1	37	35	37	40	36	47	36	35	36	33	40	32	36	31	39
0	34	31	32	34	32	39	31	32	33	30	35		32		35

MMPI-2: Critical Items

TABLE C–1 Koss-Butcher Critical Items Sets, Revised

Acute Anxiety State			
2F	28T	208F	463T
3F	39T	218T	469T
5T	59T	223F	
10F	140F	301T	
15T	172T	444T	

Depressed Suicidal Ideation				
9F	92T	233T	411T	520T
38T	95F	273T	454T	524T
65T	130T	303T	485T	
71T	146T	306T	506T	
75F	215T	388F	518T	

Threatened Assault
37T
85T
134T
213T
389T

Situational Stress Due to Alcoholism	
125F	511T
264T	518T
487T	
489T	
502T	

Mental Confusion		
24T	180T	325T
31T	198T	
32T	299T	
72T	311T	
96T	316T	

Persecutory Ideas			
17T	144T	241T	361T
42T	145T	251T	
99T	162T	259T	
124T	216T	314F	
138T	228T	333T	

Source: From the *Minnesota Multiphasic Personality Inventory-2 Manual* by J. N. Butcher, W. G. Dahlstrom, J. R. Graham, A. Tellegen, & B. Kaemmer, Appendix C, pp. 85–86. Copyright © the University of Minnesota 1942, 1943, 1951, 1967 (renewal 1970), 1989. This *Manual*, 1989. Reproduced by permission.

TABLE C–2 Lachar-Wrobel Critical Item Sets

Anxiety and Tension		
15T	261F	463T
17T	299T	
172T	301T	
218T	320T	
223F	405F	

Depression and Worry			
2F	75F	273T	454T
3F	130T	303T	
10F	150T	339T	
65T	165F	411T	
73T	180T	415T	

Sleep Disturbance	
5T	471T
30T	
39T	
140F	
328T	

Deviant Beliefs		
42T	162T	333T
99T	216T	336T
106F	228T	355T
138T	259T	361T
144T	314F	466T

Deviant Thinking and Experience	
32T	298T
60T	307T
96T	316T
122T	319T
198T	427F

Substance Abuse
168T
264T
429F

Antisocial Attitude	
27T	240T
35T	254T
84T	266F
105T	324T
227T	

Family Conflict
21T
83F
125F
288T

TABLE C–2 *continued*

Problematic Anger
85T
134T
213T
389T

Sexual Concern and Deviation	
12F	268T
34F	
62T/F	
121F	
166T	

Somatic Symptoms				
18T	47F	111T	176F	255F
28T	53T	142F	182T	295F
33F	57F	159F	224F	464T
40T	59T	164F	229T	
44T	101T	175T	247T	

Prototypic Scores for Specific Codetypes in Psychiatric Settings

TABLE D-1 Prototypic Scores for Spike *1* Codetypes in Psychiatric Settings

	MMPI			MMPI-2	
Demographics					
	M	SD		M	SD
N	76		119		
Age		46.5	14.1		45.4	14.3
Men	86.8%		82.4%		
Women	13.2		17.6		
Test-Taking Scales/Indexes					
	M	SD		M	SD
Inconsistent	0.0%			2.1%	
Total (Obvious-Subtle)[a]	12.9	54.1		24.6	53.3
Critical items[b]	24.4	8.9		23.5	8.2
Overreported[c]	1.3%			1.7%	
Underreported[c]	34.2%			33.6%	
Standard Validity and Clinical Scales (K-Corrected)					
	M	SD		M	SD
?[d]	4.3	5.9		4.2	5.6
L	55.4	9.3		59.1	12.2
F	56.3	6.1		51.8	7.7
K	54.7	8.8		50.4	9.8
1(Hs)	74.0	4.7		69.3	4.0
2(D)	61.0	6.7		57.3	6.3
3(Hy)	62.8	4.4		56.3	5.6
4(Pd)	60.5	6.5		53.4	7.6
5(Mf)	51.9	8.4		43.6	8.8
6(Pa)	55.1	6.6		49.0	7.8
7(Pt)	53.6	6.7		47.5	7.0
8(Sc)	55.8	7.3		49.4	6.8
9(Ma)	56.2	7.7		48.7	6.7
0(Si)	52.8	7.4		49.8	6.9
Supplementary Scales					
	M	SD		M	SD
A	48.2	8.3		49.6	8.5
R	64.8	12.3		54.3	10.1
MAC/MAC-R[d]					
men	27.4	4.5		27.0	4.5
women	23.6	2.6		22.8	3.6

Codetype Concordance

	Men	Women		Men	Women
MMPI-2 Spike *1*	88.1%	52.2%	MMPI Spike *1*	64.1%	60.0%
1-2/2-1		21.7	Spike *4*		30.0
1-3/3-1		13.0			

[a] See Chapter 3, Table 3–24, for explanation of how this index is computed.

[b] The total number of Lachar and Wrobel (1979) critical items endorsed.

[c] Percentage of patients within this codetype scoring above the 75th percentile or below the 25th percentile on the total T score difference on the Wiener and Harmon Obvious and Subtle subscales for all patients (see Tables 3–45 and 3–46 for the cutting scores for the MMPI-2 and MMPI, respectively).

[d] Raw score.

TABLE D–2 Prototypic Scores for *1-2/2-1* Codetypes in Psychiatric Settings

	MMPI			*MMPI-2*	
Demographics					
	M	*SD*		*M*	*SD*
N	347			309	
Age	46.8	11.7		46.5	12.3
Men	85.9%			70.2%	
Women	14.1			29.8	
Test-Taking Scales/Indexes					
	M	*SD*		*M*	*SD*
Inconsistent	12.2%			5.3%	
Total (Obvious-Subtle)[a]	78.6	59.6		98.2	64.9
Critical items[b]	40.0	12.7		38.6	13.2
Overreported[c]	17.7%			33.1%	
Underreported[c]	8.5%			7.1%	
Standard Validity and Clinical Scales (K-Corrected)					
	M	*SD*		*M*	*SD*
?[d]	4.7	6.2		4.6	6.0
L	52.5	8.7		55.7	11.9
F	62.1	9.2		62.4	13.7
K	49.6	8.2		43.4	9.8
1(Hs)	86.9	10.6		78.8	9.1
2(D)	88.3	11.0		80.0	9.8
3(Hy)	75.6	9.4		68.2	10.6
4(Pd)	69.3	10.4		59.5	10.6
5(Mf)	56.4	9.0		47.2	9.6
6(Pa)	62.5	10.3		56.6	11.9
7(Pt)	71.5	12.1		64.3	12.0
8(Sc)	68.3	13.5		59.7	12.4
9(Ma)	56.4	10.1		49.4	9.5
0(Si)	63.3	9.4		62.1	9.6
Supplementary Scales					
	M	*SD*		*M*	*SD*
A	62.0	10.5		64.0	11.1
R	71.4	12.7		60.7	11.2
MAC/MAC-R[d]					
men	26.9	4.8		26.8	4.9
women	21.4	4.1		21.3	4.5
Codetype Concordance					
	Men	Women		Men	Women
MMPI-2 *1-2/2-1*	81.7%	44.1%	MMPI *1-2/2-1*	59.5%	82.0%
Spike *2*		14.0	*1-3/3-1*	24.1	
2-4/4-2		11.8			

[a] See Chapter 3, Table 3–24, for explanation of how this index is computed.

[b] The total number of Lachar and Wrobel (1979) critical items endorsed.

[c] Percentage of patients within this codetype scoring above the 75th percentile or below the 25th percentile on the total T score difference on the Wiener and Harmon Obvious and Subtle subscales for all patients (see Tables 3–45 and 3–46 for the cutting scores for the MMPI-2 and MMPI, respectively).

[d] Raw score.

TABLE D–3 Prototypic Scores for *1-3* Codetypes in Psychiatric Settings

	MMPI			MMPI-2	
Demographics					
	M	*SD*		*M*	*SD*
N	164		241		
Age	46.6	13.1		45.8	12.4
Men	62.8%		68.9%		
Women	37.2		31.1		
Test-Taking Scales/Indexes					
	M	*SD*		*M*	*SD*
Inconsistent	6.5%			5.7%	
Total (Obvious-Subtle)[a]	25.3	61.0		61.2	71.0
Critical items[b]	35.1	12.7		35.9	13.6
Overreported[c]	3.9%			15.3%	
Underreported[c]	35.0%			22.5%	
Standard Validity and Clinical Scales (K-Corrected)					
	M	*SD*		*M*	*SD*
?[d]	5.1	5.8		5.0	6.0
L	56.1	9.6		60.0	13.5
F	59.6	8.4		60.4	13.3
K	56.2	10.0		50.3	11.7
1(Hs)	88.4	9.5		84.2	8.7
2(D)	70.8	9.4		68.4	9.6
3(Hy)	81.6	7.0		78.8	8.3
4(Pd)	68.1	9.3		60.6	10.5
5(Mf)	55.3	9.9		48.0	10.0
6(Pa)	62.4	9.3		57.5	11.9
7(Pt)	64.8	9.1		60.5	10.8
8(Sc)	67.7	9.8		61.5	10.8
9(Ma)	59.1	10.0		52.0	9.6
0(Si)	55.1	9.0		54.3	9.1
Supplementary Scales					
	M	*SD*		*M*	*SD*
A	52.6	10.7		55.4	11.8
R	72.0	14.4		60.3	12.8
MAC/MAC-R[d]					
men	26.3	5.1		26.5	4.9
women	22.1	3.7		22.8	3.7

Codetype Concordance

	Men	Women			Men	Women
MMPI-2 *1-3*	61.5%	78.7%	MMPI *1-3*		38.3%	64.0%
3-1	36.5	16.4	*1-2*		28.1	
			1-4		12.0	

[a] See Chapter 3, Table 3–24, for explanation of how this index is computed.

[b] The total number of Lachar and Wrobel (1979) critical items endorsed.

[c] Percentage of patients within this codetype scoring above the 75th percentile or below the 25th percentile on the total T score difference on the Wiener and Harmon Obvious and Subtle subscales for all patients (see Tables 3–45 and 3–46 for the cutting scores for the MMPI-2 and MMPI, respectively).

[d] Raw score.

TABLE D–4   Prototypic Scores for *1-4/4-1* Code Types in Psychiatric Settings

		MMPI			MMPI-2	
Demographics						
		M	SD		M	SD
N	140			99		
Age		41.3	13.5		39.9	13.1
Men	80.0%			71.8%		
Women	20.0			28.2		
Test-Taking Scales/Indexes						
		M	SD		M	SD
Inconsistent		10.0%			10.7%	
Total (Obvious-Subtle)[a]		14.8	60.3		40.4	67.9
Critical items[b]		31.4	12.5		32.4	13.5
Overreported[c]		2.6%			8.1%	
Underreported[c]		30.1%			27.3%	
Standard Validity and Clinical Scales (K-Corrected)						
		M	SD		M	SD
?[d]		5.5	6.9		5.0	6.7
L		54.1	9.9		57.6	13.2
F		59.9	8.8		61.6	13.7
K		57.3	10.0		52.0	11.2
1(Hs)		79.9	8.2		73.3	7.1
2(D)		67.5	9.3		63.1	8.2
3(Hy)		71.5	7.7		65.1	7.9
4(Pd)		81.1	6.5		74.4	6.8
5(Mf)		54.0	8.7		46.7	8.9
6(Pa)		60.7	8.5		56.3	10.6
7(Pt)		62.3	8.3		57.1	9.2
8(Sc)		65.4	8.5		59.6	9.2
9(Ma)		60.5	10.3		55.6	10.4
0(Si)		52.8	7.7		51.1	8.8
Supplementary Scales						
		M	SD		M	SD
A		49.9	10.3		53.1	11.1
R		69.2	13.3		56.2	11.5
MAC/MAC-R[d]						
men		28.3	5.2		29.2	4.5
women		24.1	4.4		24.0	3.5
Codetype Concordance						
		Men	Women		Men	Women
MMPI-2 *1-4/4-1*		41.1%	53.6%	MMPI *1-4/4-1*	64.8%	53.6%
1-3/3-1		28.6	25.0	Spike *4*		17.9
Spike *1*		14.3		*4-8/8-4*	12.7	

[a] See Chapter 3, Table 3–24, for explanation of how this index is computed.

[b] The total number of Lachar and Wrobel (1979) critical items endorsed.

[c] Percentage of patients within this codetype scoring above the 75th percentile or below the 25th percentile on the total T score difference on the Wiener and Harmon Obvious and Subtle subscales for all patients (see Tables 3–45 and 3–46 for the cutting scores for the MMPI-2 and MMPI, respectively).

[d] Raw score.

TABLE D–5 Prototypic Scores for *1-5/5-1* Codetypes in Psychiatric Settings

		MMPI			MMPI-2	
Demographics						
		M	SD		M	SD
N	13			18		
Age		37.1	11.4		40.9	13.4
Men	76.9%			22.2%		
Women	23.1			77.8		
Test-Taking Scales/Indexes						
		M	SD		M	SD
Inconsistent		0.0%			14.3%	
Total (Obvious-Subtle)[a]		41.0	59.4		58.3	60.7
Critical items[b]		33.8	9.9		29.9	10.9
Overreported[c]		0.0%			5.6%	
Underreported[c]		12.5%			16.7%	
Standard Validity and Clinical Scales (K-Corrected)						
		M	SD		M	SD
?[d]		2.5	2.4		7.2	9.0
L		49.8	9.4		56.9	10.4
F		60.5	9.5		56.9	11.5
K		51.4	9.5		47.4	11.7
1(Hs)		76.8	5.0		71.1	5.4
2(D)		62.7	8.4		58.5	5.5
3(Hy)		67.5	6.1		58.7	7.5
4(Pd)		63.0	10.4		53.7	9.2
5(Mf)		76.7	3.5		73.1	6.4
6(Pa)		60.9	5.8		51.4	8.7
7(Pt)		60.9	9.1		53.9	6.9
8(Sc)		63.3	6.7		55.3	5.1
9(Ma)		60.3	6.6		51.2	6.5
O(Si)		55.0	9.2		51.7	7.4
Supplementary Scales						
		M	SD		M	SD
A		55.8	9.4		55.7	10.1
R		58.9	8.6		56.8	12.0
MAC/MAC-R[d]						
men		25.2	5.8		26.0	3.5
women		29.7	3.2		24.7	3.7

Codetype Concordance

	Men	Women			Men	Women
MMPI-2 *1-3/3-1*	30.0%		MMPI *1-5/5-1*		75.0%	14.3%
1-5/5-1	30.0	100.0%	Spike 4			21.4
			Spike 2			14.3
			Spike 5			14.3

[a] See Chapter 3, Table 3–24, for explanation of how this index is computed.

[b] The total number of Lachar and Wrobel (1979) critical items endorsed.

[c] Percentage of patients within this codetype scoring above the 75th percentile or below the 25th percentile on the total T score difference on the Wiener and Harmon Obvious and Subtle subscales for all patients (see Tables 3–45 and 3–46 for the cutting scores for the MMPI-2 and MMPI, respectively).

[d] Raw score.

TABLE D–6 Prototypic Scores for *1-6/6-1* Codetypes in Psychiatric Settings

	MMPI			MMPI-2	
Demographics					
	M	*SD*		*M*	*SD*
N	26		96		
Age	44.4	13.2		42.6	12.1
Men	61.5%			61.5%	
Women	38.5			38.5	
Test-Taking Scales/Indexes					
	M	*SD*		*M*	*SD*
Inconsistent	14.6%			15.7%	
Total (Obvious-Subtle)[a]	101.9	61.6		128.6	68.3
Critical items[b]	46.5	13.6		47.6	14.9
Overreported[c]	22.0%			49.5%	
Underreported[c]	4.9%			3.1%	
Standard Validity and Clinical Scales (K-Corrected)					
	M	*SD*		*M*	*SD*
?[d]	5.9	6.9		5.6	6.4
L	51.3	6.9		53.7	10.6
F	70.8	11.0		77.4	16.8
K	47.8	6.5		41.6	9.3
1(Hs)	84.9	10.5		79.3	9.8
2(D)	69.2	11.0		67.1	10.3
3(Hy)	71.3	9.2		66.8	12.5
4(Pd)	68.8	8.3		62.9	10.3
5(Mf)	53.7	11.3		47.4	9.7
6(Pa)	85.1	10.9		83.4	11.4
7(Pt)	67.0	12.6		63.8	12.8
8(Sc)	73.5	12.9		68.6	12.7
9(Ma)	61.8	10.7		58.9	11.1
0(Si)	61.0	7.3		56.6	8.8
Supplementary Scales					
	M	*SD*		*M*	*SD*
A	62.7	10.1		64.4	11.0
R	64.8	12.9		52.0	10.9
MAC/MAC-R[d]					
men	27.6	5.3		28.2	5.0
women	24.0	4.5		24.9	3.6

Codetype Concordance

	Men	Women			Men	Women
MMPI-2 *1-6/6-1*	100.0%	80.0%	MMPI	*1-6/6-1*	26.7%	21.6%
				1-8/8-1	21.7	
				1-2/2-1	20.0	
				4-6/6-4		27.0
				6-8/8-6		21.6
				6-9/9-6		10.8

[a] See Chapter 3, Table 3–24, for explanation of how this index is computed.

[b] The total number of Lachar and Wrobel (1979) critical items endorsed.

[c] Percentage of patients within this codetype scoring above the 75th percentile or below the 25th percentile on the total T score difference on the Wiener and Harmon Obvious and Subtle subscales for all patients (see Tables 3–45 and 3–46 for the cutting scores for the MMPI-2 and MMPI, respectively).

TABLE D–7   Prototypic Scores for *1-7/7-1* Codetypes in Psychiatric Settings

	MMPI			MMPI-2	
Demographics					
	M	SD		M	SD
N	29		41		
Age	40.9	13.5		40.2	12.7
Men	89.7%		80.5%		
Women	10.3		19.5		
Test-Taking Scales/Indexes					
	M	SD		M	SD
Inconsistent	17.1%			5.5%	
Total (Obvious-Subtle)[a]	91.7	64.7		126.3	63.2
Critical items[b]	45.3	13.5		46.0	13.3
Overreported[c]	26.8%			50.0%	
Underreported[c]	7.3%			0.0%	
Standard Validity and Clinical Scales (K-Corrected)					
	M	SD		M	SD
?[d]	5.6	6.5		5.5	6.8
L	48.2	7.0		54.6	11.8
F	64.9	10.6		71.1	14.2
K	50.2	8.4		44.3	8.6
1(Hs)	86.0	9.6		80.8	10.5
2(D)	77.5	9.9		71.7	11.5
3(Hy)	75.5	9.5		70.3	12.3
4(Pd)	70.5	11.3		63.2	10.0
5(Mf)	61.1	12.6		48.8	12.1
6(Pa)	66.8	12.0		62.4	12.4
7(Pt)	85.1	8.9		79.8	9.8
8(Sc)	75.8	11.2		70.8	11.4
9(Ma)	62.3	10.7		55.5	9.1
0(Si)	62.6	9.2		60.2	10.2
Supplementary Scales					
	M	SD		M	SD
A	66.2	10.7		69.2	9.9
R	65.0	15.0		53.9	12.9
MAC/MAC-R[d]					
men	27.1	5.0		27.3	4.5
women	25.0	5.0		24.5	5.2

Codetype Concordance					
	Men	Women		Men	Women
MMPI-2 *1-7/7-1*	55.6%	100.0%	MMPI *1-7/7-1*	47.1%	37.5%
1-6/6-1	14.8		*1-8/8-1*	23.5	
3-7/7-3	14.8		*4-7/7-4*		25.0

[a] See Chapter 3, Table 3–24, for explanation of how this index is computed.

[b] The total number of Lachar and Wrobel (1979) critical items endorsed.

[c] Percentage of patients within this codetype scoring above the 75th percentile or below the 25th percentile on the total T score difference on the Wiener and Harmon Obvious and Subtle subscales for all patients (see Tables 3–45 and 3–46 for the cutting scores for the MMPI-2 and MMPI, respectively).

[d] Raw score.

TABLE D–8 Prototypic Scores for *1-8/8-1* Codetypes in Psychiatric Settings

	MMPI				MMPI-2	
Demographics						
	M	SD			M	SD
N	186			117		
Age		38.5	14.1		37.5	15.0
Men	84.9%			70.1%		
Women	15.1			29.9		
Test-Taking Scales/Indexes						
		M	SD		M	SD
Inconsistent		36.8%			30.7%	
Total (Obvious-Subtle)[a]		134.8	72.5		155.0	73.8
Critical items[b]		58.6	16.0		55.4	15.6
Overreported[c]		41.3%			65.6%	
Underreported[c]		5.2%			1.7%	
Standard Validity and Clinical Scales (K-Corrected)						
		M	SD		M	SD
?[d]		6.3	7.0		5.2	6.7
L		51.3	9.1		54.7	12.1
F		80.4	14.4		85.2	19.2
K		47.0	9.5		40.8	10.0
1(Hs)		92.4	10.7		82.9	10.6
2(D)		80.7	12.7		71.8	11.0
3(Hy)		78.1	10.1		71.1	12.9
4(Pd)		76.9	11.0		66.0	11.8
5(Mf)		59.4	10.8		50.0	9.0
6(Pa)		76.0	12.8		68.7	13.5
7(Pt)		79.9	12.2		71.4	13.3
8(Sc)		95.6	13.8		83.5	13.1
9(Ma)		70.6	10.6		61.9	11.2
0(Si)		63.0	9.2		61.9	9.1
Supplementary Scales						
		M	SD		M	SD
A		68.3	10.6		68.7	9.9
R		65.0	13.3		55.4	11.2
MAC/MAC-R[d]						
men		27.7	4.8		28.0	4.9
women		23.8	4.7		24.7	3.7
Codetype Concordance						
		Men	Women		Men	Women
MMPI-2 *1-8/8-1*		84.3%	50.0%	MMPI *1-8/8-1*	43.8%	64.3%
4-8/8-4			19.4	*1-3/3-1*	13.1	14.3

[a] See Chapter 3, Table 3–24, for explanation of how this index is computed.

[b] The total number of Lachar and Wrobel (1979) critical items endorsed.

[c] Percentage of patients within this codetype scoring above the 75th percentile or below the 25th percentile on the total T score difference on the Wiener and Harmon Obvious and Subtle subscales for all patients (see Tables 3–45 and 3–46 for the cutting scores for the MMPI-2 and MMPI, respectively).

[d] Raw score.

TABLE D–9   Prototypic Scores for *1-9/9-1* Codetypes in Psychiatric Settings

	MMPI				MMPI-2	
Demographics						
		M	SD		M	SD
N	46			68		
Age		40.3	12.1		40.6	12.2
Men	82.6%			75.0%		
Women	17.4			25.0		
Test-Taking Scales/Indexes						
		M	SD		M	SD
Inconsistent		4.2%			4.9%	
Total (Obvious-Subtle)[a]		61.0	62.7		88.3	61.4
Critical items[b]		42.7	12.3		42.6	12.5
Overreported[c]		12.6%			26.1%	
Underreported[c]		12.6%			5.8%	
Standard Validity and Clinical Scales (K-Corrected)						
		M	SD		M	SD
?[d]		4.7	6.0		4.3	5.2
L		48.4	6.0		50.8	10.0
F		65.0	10.8		67.6	15.4
K		47.5	8.7		41.4	9.3
1(Hs)		80.6	8.1		74.9	6.7
2(D)		62.1	11.2		57.4	9.5
3(Hy)		68.5	7.2		61.5	9.0
4(Pd)		67.9	7.9		60.2	9.1
5(Mf)		55.9	8.8		45.8	9.2
6(Pa)		62.0	7.9		56.6	9.4
7(Pt)		61.2	7.7		56.4	8.3
8(Sc)		67.7	8.8		62.0	8.1
9(Ma)		80.8	6.9		77.4	8.2
0(Si)		49.1	7.7		49.1	8.6
Supplementary Scales						
		M	SD		M	SD
A		59.2	10.0		60.8	9.9
R		53.2	10.2		45.8	9.3
MAC/MAC-R[d]						
men		31.9	4.1		32.2	4.2
women		25.4	3.9		27.7	4.0
Codetype Concordance						
		Men	Women		Men	Women
MMPI-2 *1-9/9-1*		81.6%	87.5%	MMPI *1-9/9-1*	60.8%	38.9%
				8-9/9-8	17.6	16.7
				4-9/9-4	11.8	22.2
				Spike *9*		16.7

[a] See Chapter 3, Table 3–24, for explanation of how this index is computed.

[b] The total number of Lachar and Wrobel (1979) critical items endorsed.

[c] Percentage of patients within this codetype scoring above the 75th percentile or below the 25th percentile on the total T score difference on the Wiener and Harmon Obvious and Subtle subscales for all patients (see Tables 3–45 and 3–46 for the cutting scores for the MMPI-2 and MMPI, respectively).

[d] Raw score.

TABLE D–10 Prototypic Scores for *1-0/0-1* Codetypes in Psychiatric Settings

	MMPI				MMPI-2	
Demographics						
	M	*SD*			*M*	*SD*
N	5			19		
Age		53.6	16.0		42.1	13.8
Men	60.0%			84.2%		
Women	40.0			15.8		
Test-Taking Scales/Indexes						
	M	*SD*			*M*	*SD*
Inconsistent	0.0%				0.0%	
Total (Obvious-Subtle)[a]	39.0	18.9			85.7	41.9
Critical items[b]	27.6	2.2			33.1	6.6
Overreported[c]	5.3%				21.1%	
Underreported[c]	10.5%				0.0%	
Standard Validity and Clinical Scales (K-Corrected)						
	M	*SD*			*M*	*SD*
?[d]	3.2	4.7			4.9	6.5
L	53.0	7.7			52.9	11.6
F	58.2	3.9			58.8	6.8
K	49.8	7.0			40.4	7.5
1(Hs)	73.4	6.5			71.3	5.8
2(D)	64.8	9.1			62.9	6.6
3(Hy)	61.6	6.7			57.6	7.8
4(Pd)	54.4	10.2			51.0	7.3
5(Mf)	54.6	12.3			46.1	8.9
6(Pa)	53.4	10.6			50.9	10.1
7(Pt)	56.8	7.8			54.4	11.0
8(Sc)	59.4	4.8			51.2	8.0
9(Ma)	55.2	7.1			46.5	6.7
0(Si)	74.6	3.3			71.5	3.8
Supplementary Scales						
	M	*SD*			*M*	*SD*
A	51.4	2.5			60.4	9.1
R	78.8	8.5			59.5	9.4
MAC/MAC-R[d]						
men	22.7	1.5			26.9	5.1
women	22.0	2.8			22.0	6.2
Codetype Concordance						
	Men	Women			Men	Women
MMPI-2 *1-0/0-1*	100.0%	50.0%	MMPI Spike *1*		31.8%	
1-2/2-1		50.0	*1-2/2-1*		27.3	
			1-0/0-1		13.6	
			Spike *0*			50.0%

[a] See Chapter 3, Table 3–24, for explanation of how this index is computed.

[b] The total number of Lachar and Wrobel (1979) critical items endorsed.

[c] Percentage of patients within this codetype scoring above the 75th percentile or below the 25th percentile on the total T score difference on the Wiener and Harmon Obvious and Subtle subscales for all patients (see Tables 3–45 and 3–46 for the cutting scores for the MMPI-2 and MMPI, respectively).

[d] Raw score.

TABLE D-11   Prototypic Scores for Spike *2* Codetypes in Psychiatric Settings

	MMPI			MMPI-2	
Demographics					
	M	SD		M	SD
N	228			217	
Age	44.5	13.2		42.3	12.9
Men	81.6%			74.2%	
Women	18.4			25.8	
Test-Taking Scales/Indexes					
	M	SD		M	SD
Inconsistent	0.0%			3.0%	
Total (Obvious-Subtle)[a]	23.0	47.5		36.4	50.8
Critical items[b]	23.3	8.3		23.7	8.0
Overreported[c]	1.8%			4.1%	
Underreported[c]	26.8%			20.6%	
Standard Validity and Clinical Scales (K-Corrected)					
	M	SD		M	SD
?[d]	5.7	6.4		4.8	5.7
L	52.3	8.0		56.2	11.2
F	55.0	5.8		52.4	8.2
K	50.1	7.9		44.6	8.9
1(Hs)	56.0	8.0		52.9	8.4
2(D)	74.1	4.2		69.1	3.5
3(Hy)	58.3	6.4		51.5	7.7
4(Pd)	60.2	7.6		53.7	7.6
5(Mf)	53.4	7.4		45.1	7.9
6(Pa)	54.6	7.1		49.4	8.2
7(Pt)	58.8	6.2		53.3	6.9
8(Sc)	53.8	8.1		47.4	7.6
9(Ma)	51.3	8.9		45.5	7.4
0(Si)	59.5	6.8		56.1	6.4
Supplementary Scales					
	M	SD		M	SD
A	55.3	9.4		57.4	9.7
R	67.8	12.0		56.6	10.5
MAC/MAC-R[d]					
men	25.3	4.5		25.8	4.8
women	20.7	4.0		21.4	4.1
Codetype Concordance					
	Men	Women		Men	Women
MMPI-2 Spike *2*	53.1%	81.6%	MMPI Spike *2*	48.2%	40.8%
2-4/4-2	35.9		*2-0/0-2*	44.7	23.7
			1-2/2-1		17.1

[a] See Chapter 3, Table 3-24, for explanation of how this index is computed.

[b] The total number of Lachar and Wrobel (1979) critical items endorsed.

[c] Percentage of patients within this codetype scoring above the 75th percentile or below the 25th percentile on the total T score difference on the Wiener and Harmon Obvious and Subtle subscales for all patients (see Tables 3-45 and 3-46 for the cutting scores for the MMPI-2 and MMPI, respectively).

[d] Raw score.

TABLE D–12   Prototypic Scores for *2-3/3-2* Codetypes in Psychiatric Settings

	MMPI			MMPI-2	
Demographics					
	M	*SD*		*M*	*SD*
N	172			264	
Age		45.0	12.9		42.9	13.0
Men	54.1%			50.8%	
Women	45.9			49.2	
Test-Taking Scales/Indexes					
	M	*SD*		*M*	*SD*
Inconsistent	7.3%			5.0%	
Total (Obvious-Subtle)[a]	22.5	62.1		68.4	67.9
Critical items[b]	30.9	11.6		35.5	13.0
Overreported[c]	5.8%			20.2%	
Underreported[c]	35.6%			11.9%	
Standard Validity and Clinical Scales (K-Corrected)					
	M	*SD*		*M*	*SD*
?[d]	4.8	6.2		4.7	6.3
L	55.4	8.9		59.3	12.5
F	58.7	7.2		61.7	12.3
K	55.4	9.3		47.7	10.7
1(Hs)	72.2	8.3		71.9	8.9
2(D)	84.9	8.9		83.0	9.7
3(Hy)	80.2	6.9		80.8	9.2
4(Pd)	69.4	8.5		63.2	9.3
5(Mf)	53.2	10.3		47.0	9.5
6(Pa)	63.6	8.6		59.6	10.8
7(Pt)	70.3	8.9		68.6	10.5
8(Sc)	65.2	9.9		62.4	11.8
9(Ma)	52.4	10.7		48.3	9.6
0(Si)	59.5	9.6		59.6	9.8
Supplementary Scales					
	M	*SD*		*M*	*SD*
A	56.3	10.1		61.9	10.9
R	79.1	13.8		65.3	12.7
MAC/MAC-R[d]					
men	24.0	4.8		24.0	4.9
women	19.8	4.4		20.1	4.2
Codetype Concordance					
	Men	Women		Men	Women
MMPI-2 *2-3/3-2*	53.7%	53.8%	MMPI *2-3/3-2*	77.4%	93.7%
2-4/4-2	15.7	10.0			
1-2/2-1	12.7				

[a] See Chapter 3, Table 3–24, for explanation of how this index is computed.

[b] The total number of Lachar and Wrobel (1979) critical items endorsed.

[c] Percentage of patients within this codetype scoring above the 75th percentile or below the 25th percentile on the total T score difference on the Wiener and Harmon Obvious and Subtle subscales for all patients (see Tables 3–45 and 3–46 for the cutting scores for the MMPI-2 and MMPI, respectively).

[d] Raw score.

TABLE D-13 Prototypic Scores for *2-4/4-2* Codetypes in Psychiatric Settings

	MMPI			*MMPI-2*	
Demographics					
	M	SD		M	SD
N	606			343	
Age	38.1	12.5		36.9	12.4
Men	78.1%			66.5%	
Women	21.9			33.5	
Test-Taking Scales/Indexes					
	M	SD		M	SD
Inconsistent	6.3%			3.2%	
Total (Obvious-Subtle)[a]	38.6	59.9		68.3	62.3
Critical items[b]	32.9	12.1		34.4	11.9
Overreported[c]	5.9%			16.3%	
Underreported[c]	22.8%			13.7%	
Standard Validity and Clinical Scales (K-Corrected)					
	M	SD		M	SD
?[d]	4.2	5.5		3.4	4.7
L	50.9	8.0		52.5	10.5
F	62.2	9.0		64.9	13.9
K	51.5	8.8		45.3	9.3
1(Hs)	61.1	10.8		58.1	10.3
2(D)	81.8	9.1		76.1	8.4
3(Hy)	65.7	8.8		60.1	10.1
4(Pd)	83.1	8.3		77.6	7.9
5(Mf)	56.3	10.1		48.1	10.1
6(Pa)	63.5	9.6		59.3	11.0
7(Pt)	68.5	9.6		63.8	10.3
8(Sc)	65.8	11.6		60.6	11.7
9(Ma)	57.8	9.7		51.3	9.0
0(Si)	60.0	9.7		58.9	9.4
Supplementary Scales					
	M	SD		M	SD
A	60.1	10.8		62.7	10.8
R	68.1	13.1		57.4	11.5
MAC/MAC-R[d]					
men	26.9	4.7		26.8	4.9
women	22.4	4.5		22.7	4.4

Codetype Concordance

		Men	Women		Men	Women
MMPI-2	2-4/4-2	45.9%	53.0%	MMPI 2-4/4-2	92.1%	61.7%
	2-7/7-2		15.7	Spike 4		15.6
	Spike 4	10.4		4-8/8-4		13.0

[a] See Chapter 3, Table 3–24, for explanation of how this index is computed.

[b] The total number of Lachar and Wrobel (1979) critical items endorsed.

[c] Percentage of patients within this codetype scoring above the 75th percentile or below the 25th percentile on the total T score difference on the Wiener and Harmon Obvious and Subtle subscales for all patients (see Tables 3–45 and 3–46 for the cutting scores for the MMPI-2 and MMPI, respectively).

[d] Raw score.

TABLE D–14 Prototypic Scores for *2-5/5-2* Codetypes in Psychiatric Settings

		MMPI			MMPI-2	
Demographics						
		M	SD		M	SD
N	43			26		
Age		37.6	14.7		42.0	15.1
Men	93.0%			34.6%		
Women	7.0			65.4		
Test-Taking Scales/Indexes						
		M	SD		M	SD
Inconsistent		1.1%			3.7%	
Total (Obvious-Subtle)[a]		47.8	60.8		71.3	55.2
Critical items[b]		32.3	12.2		30.1	11.2
Overreported[c]		7.4%			19.2%	
Underreported[c]		25.5%			3.9%	
Standard Validity and Clinical Scales (K-Corrected)						
		M	SD		M	SD
?[d]		3.2	3.9		3.7	4.0
L		48.6	6.0		57.0	13.0
F		58.9	7.1		60.0	8.8
K		47.3	8.2		44.8	7.3
1(Hs)		58.9	12.2		56.2	9.8
2(D)		79.8	9.5		73.9	7.6
3(Hy)		62.4	8.8		56.0	10.4
4(Pd)		64.0	8.8		53.4	8.8
5(Mf)		79.0	7.6		73.8	6.8
6(Pa)		60.7	9.1		54.4	11.3
7(Pt)		67.4	9.7		60.7	11.8
8(Sc)		62.3	12.3		60.2	9.7
9(Ma)		53.7	10.0		45.8	7.4
0(Si)		61.8	9.3		60.5	8.4
Supplementary Scales						
		M	SD		M	SD
A		63.3	10.3		62.2	11.4
R		64.0	11.3		61.5	9.9
MAC/MAC-R[d]						
men		22.2	5.1		19.1	4.0
women		24.7	2.3		21.6	3.4

Codetype Concordance

	Men	Women		Men	Women
MMPI-2 *2-5/5-2*	22.2%	100.0%	MMPI *2-5/5-2*	88.9%	17.6%
2-0/0-2	22.2		Spike *2*		29.4
Spike *2*	11.1		Spike *5*		17.6
2-6/6-2	11.1				

[a] See Chapter 3, Table 3–24, for explanation of how this index is computed.

[b] The total number of Lachar and Wrobel (1979) critical items endorsed.

[c] Percentage of patients within this codetype scoring above the 75th percentile or below the 25th percentile on the total T score difference on the Wiener and Harmon Obvious and Subtle subscales for all patients (see Tables 3–45 and 3–46 for the cutting scores for the MMPI-2 and MMPI, respectively).

[d] Raw score.

TABLE D–15 Prototypic Scores for *2-6/6-2* Codetypes in Psychiatric Settings

	MMPI				MMPI-2	
Demographics						
	M	SD			M	SD
N	86			192		
Age	40.0	12.8			39.4	12.7
Men	66.3%			55.2%		
Women	33.7			44.8		
Test-Taking Scales/Indexes						
	M	SD			M	SD
Inconsistent	10.5%				10.4%	
Total (Obvious-Subtle)[a]	89.4	65.4			119.8	63.4
Critical items[b]	41.8	13.7			43.3	13.3
Overreported[c]	19.3%				42.5%	
Underreported[c]	15.8%				1.0%	
Standard Validity and Clinical Scales (K-Corrected)						
	M	SD			M	SD
?[d]	6.1	7.2			4.7	5.9
L	50.4	6.9			53.9	10.6
F	68.4	12.2			74.4	19.5
K	45.7	6.9			39.8	8.0
1(Hs)	63.1	13.7			61.8	13.3
2(D)	84.1	10.0			80.5	10.8
3(Hy)	64.9	10.5			61.8	13.2
4(Pd)	72.1	9.4			65.9	10.6
5(Mf)	56.0	10.2			47.7	9.3
6(Pa)	82.1	10.2			81.9	11.7
7(Pt)	71.9	10.3			69.1	11.0
8(Sc)	70.9	14.0			66.9	14.1
9(Ma)	58.2	9.5			51.3	8.9
0(Si)	66.0	9.0			64.7	8.7
Supplementary Scales						
	M	SD			M	SD
A	66.7	8.6			69.6	8.7
R	70.8	14.3			58.5	12.3
MAC/MAC-R[d]						
men	25.8	5.2			25.8	5.1
women	20.7	4.9			21.3	4.3

Codetype Concordance

	Men	Women		Men	Women
MMPI-2 *2-6/6-2*	34.6%	32.6%	MMPI *2-6/6-2*	81.0%	96.6%
2-4/4-2	21.5	10.5			
2-8/8-2	15.0	14.0			
6-8/8-6		18.6			

[a] See Chapter 3, Table 3–24, for explanation of how this index is computed.

[b] The total number of Lachar and Wrobel (1979) critical items endorsed.

[c] Percentage of patients within this codetype scoring above the 75th percentile or below the 25th percentile on the total T score difference on the Wiener and Harmon Obvious and Subtle subscales for all patients (see Tables 3–45 and 3–46 for the cutting scores for the MMPI-2 and MMPI, respectively).

[d] Raw score.

TABLE D–16 Prototypic Scores for *2-7/7-2* Codetypes in Psychiatric Settings

	MMPI			MMPI-2	
Demographics					
	M	SD		M	SD
N	391			418	
Age		40.3	12.7		38.8	12.8
Men	75.2%			58.2%	
Women	24.8			41.8	
Test-Taking Scales/Indexes					
	M	SD		M	SD
Inconsistent	10.1%			4.5%	
Total (Obvious-Subtle)[a]	82.1	50.6		111.1	55.2
Critical items[b]	38.3	10.5		40.3	10.9
Overreported[c]	21.4%			34.8%	
Underreported[c]	4.7%			0.7%	
Standard Validity and Clinical Scales (K-Corrected)					
	M	SD		M	SD
?[d]	4.6	6.1		4.3	5.9
L	49.8	7.3		51.8	10.1
F	62.9	8.4		66.8	14.3
K	48.9	7.2		42.7	7.8
1(Hs)	65.9	11.5		63.5	11.1
2(D)	89.8	11.3		84.3	9.7
3(Hy)	68.0	9.7		64.5	11.5
4(Pd)	70.5	9.8		63.8	10.2
5(Mf)	57.7	10.4		48.9	10.4
6(Pa)	66.1	9.4		63.0	11.1
7(Pt)	85.2	9.2		82.0	9.2
8(Sc)	74.4	11.2		69.6	11.0
9(Ma)	54.4	9.7		49.1	8.8
0(Si)	68.9	8.2		67.8	9.0
Supplementary Scales					
	M	SD		M	SD
A	69.9	8.1		72.8	8.1
R	71.7	13.0		60.6	11.3
MAC/MAC-R[d]					
men	24.5	4.6		24.5	4.8
women	19.6	3.5		20.0	3.7

Codetype Concordance						
	Men	Women			Men	Women
MMPI-2 *2-7/7-2*	65.4%	93.9%	MMPI *2-7/7-2*		78.9%	52.0%
				2-8/8-2	12.0	10.7
				2-4/4-2		10.2

[a] See Chapter 3, Table 3–24, for explanation of how this index is computed.

[b] The total number of Lachar and Wrobel (1979) critical items endorsed.

[c] Percentage of patients within this codetype scoring above the 75th percentile or below the 25th percentile on the total T score difference on the Wiener and Harmon Obvious and Subtle subscales for all patients (see Tables 3–45 and 3–46 for the cutting scores for the MMPI-2 and MMPI, respectively).

[d] Raw score.

TABLE D–17 Prototypic Scores for *2-8/8-2* Codetypes in Psychiatric Settings

	MMPI				MMPI-2	
Demographics						
		M	SD			M	SD
N	461				219		
Age		35.8	12.8			35.7	12.7
Men	73.8%				53.0%		
Women	26.2				47.0		
Test-Taking Scales/Indexes						
		M	SD			M	SD
Inconsistent		22.2%				11.1%	
Total (Obvious-Subtle)[a]		137.2	68.0			155.0	73.0
Critical items[b]		54.7	16.1			52.5	16.4
Overreported[c]		45.2%				56.1%	
Underreported[c]		3.3%				1.9%	
Standard Validity and Clinical Scales (K-Corrected)						
		M	SD			M	SD
?[d]		5.5	6.7			5.2	6.1
L		49.1	7.7			51.7	10.6
F		79.9	14.6			88.4	20.7
K		45.7	8.0			39.5	8.4
1(Hs)		75.1	14.8			69.7	13.4
2(D)		95.4	12.1			86.3	11.5
3(Hy)		72.4	11.1			66.4	14.3
4(Pd)		79.2	11.4			69.2	12.4
5(Mf)		60.8	11.9			52.0	10.2
6(Pa)		76.6	13.5			70.7	14.9
7(Pt)		84.9	11.9			77.2	12.3
8(Sc)		97.2	14.2			86.8	13.4
9(Ma)		63.2	10.5			56.6	9.6
0(Si)		71.8	8.3			69.2	9.5
Supplementary Scales						
		M	SD			M	SD
A		72.3	9.3			73.0	9.5
R		72.2	13.3			59.6	11.6
MAC/MAC-R[d]						
men		24.6	4.9			24.4	4.7
women		21.0	4.4			21.7	4.3
Codetype Concordance						
		Men	Women			Men	Women
MMPI-2 *2-8/8-2*		32.5%	53.3%	MMPI *2-8/8-2*	94.8%	63.1%
6-8/8-6		21.0			*4-8/8-4*		22.3
2-7/7-2			20.5				

[a] See Chapter 3, Table 3–24, for explanation of how this index is computed.

[b] The total number of Lachar and Wrobel (1979) critical items endorsed.

[c] Percentage of patients within this codetype scoring above the 75th percentile or below the 25th percentile on the total T score difference on the Wiener and Harmon Obvious and Subtle subscales for all patients (see Tables 3–45 and 3–46 for the cutting scores for the MMPI-2 and MMPI, respectively).

[d] Raw score.

TABLE D–18 Prototypic Scores for *2-9/9-2* Codetypes in Psychiatric Settings

	MMPI			MMPI-2	
Demographics					
	M	SD		M	SD
N	18			25	
Age	39.3	11.0		39.5	12.2
Men	72.2%			64.0%	
Women	27.8			36.0	
Test-Taking Scales/Indexes					
	M	SD		M	SD
Inconsistent	8.8%			3.6%	
Total (Obvious-Subtle)[a]	73.1	33.8		86.1	49.7
Critical items[b]	38.9	9.6		40.1	10.0
Overreported[c]	2.2%			12.0%	
Underreported[c]	24.2%			8.0%	
Standard Validity and Clinical Scales (K-Corrected)					
	M	SD		M	SD
?[d]	4.9	6.6		4.4	5.8
L	49.0	5.7		51.6	8.2
F	64.4	9.4		66.6	11.1
K	44.4	7.6		38.8	8.6
1(Hs)	58.2	9.3		56.1	10.2
2(D)	77.1	5.3		73.0	5.3
3(Hy)	62.5	9.7		57.9	10.7
4(Pd)	69.1	9.0		62.4	8.6
5(Mf)	56.1	9.2		50.0	9.7
6(Pa)	61.5	9.8		57.1	11.1
7(Pt)	66.6	8.4		62.6	7.6
8(Sc)	65.5	8.3		59.5	8.7
9(Ma)	79.5	6.8		74.9	7.1
0(Si)	54.5	8.3		53.2	8.7
Supplementary Scales					
	M	SD		M	SD
A	63.4	7.7		66.5	9.5
R	58.9	10.2		48.2	10.7
MAC/MAC-R[d]					
men	29.5	2.3		28.6	2.9
women	25.8	4.0		25.6	4.1

Codetype Concordance

	Men	Women			Men	Women
MMPI-2 *2-9/9-2*	83.3%	100.0%	MMPI	*2-9/9-2*	62.5%	55.6%
				2-4/4-2	25.0	
				8-9/9-8		22.2

[a] See Chapter 3, Table 3–24, for explanation of how this index is computed.

[b] The total number of Lachar and Wrobel (1979) critical items endorsed.

[c] Percentage of patients within this codetype scoring above the 75th percentile or below the 25th percentile on the total T score difference on the Wiener and Harmon Obvious and Subtle subscales for all patients (see Tables 3–45 and 3–46 for the cutting scores for the MMPI-2 and MMPI, respectively).

[d] Raw score.

TABLE D–19 Prototypic Scores for *2-0/0-2* Codetypes in Psychiatric Settings

	MMPI		MMPI-2	
Demographics				
	M	SD	M	SD
N	111		243	
Age	40.7	13.0	41.5	13.0
Men	50.5%		72.4%	
Women	49.5		27.6	
Test-Taking Scales/Indexes				
	M	SD	M	SD
Inconsistent	1.4%		2.6%	
Total (Obvious-Subtle)[a]	69.2	39.0	93.0	46.1
Critical items[b]	31.5	8.4	31.5	9.7
Overreported[c]	5.1%		20.5%	
Underreported[c]	8.3%		1.6%	
Standard Validity and Clinical Scales (K-Corrected)				
	M	SD	M	SD
?[d]	4.7	6.4	4.0	5.4
L	49.9	6.1	51.4	8.9
F	59.7	7.4	59.4	11.6
K	44.5	5.8	38.9	6.8
1(Hs)	56.7	9.3	55.3	10.3
2(D)	79.4	6.9	75.3	7.3
3(Hy)	58.6	7.4	52.4	9.4
4(Pd)	63.1	8.3	56.2	9.1
5(Mf)	52.5	10.4	47.3	9.1
6(Pa)	59.7	9.2	53.6	9.7
7(Pt)	65.7	6.9	61.6	8.9
8(Sc)	61.0	9.4	55.0	11.0
9(Ma)	48.5	8.7	43.5	7.4
0(Si)	76.0	3.9	73.2	5.3
Supplementary Scales				
	M	SD	M	SD
A	64.9	6.9	67.1	8.6
R	74.0	10.3	60.6	9.8
MAC/MAC-R[d]				
men	23.7	4.4	24.2	4.4
women	19.1	3.8	19.2	3.9

Codetype Concordance

	Men	Women		Men	Women
MMPI-2 *2-0/0-2*	82.1%	80.0%	MMPI *2-0/0-2*	21.9%	51.2%
Spike *0*	10.7		Spike *2*	30.0	20.9
			Spike *0*		17.4
			2-4/4-2	16.2	
			2-7/7-2	11.4	

[a] See Chapter 3, Table 3–24, for explanation of how this index is computed.

[b] The total number of Lachar and Wrobel (1979) critical items endorsed.

[c] Percentage of patients within this codetype scoring above the 75th percentile or below the 25th percentile on the total T score difference on the Wiener and Harmon Obvious and Subtle subscales for all patients (see Tables 3–45 and 3–46 for the cutting scores for the MMPI-2 and MMPI, respectively).

[d] Raw score.

TABLE D–20 Prototypic Scores for Spike *3* Codetypes in Psychiatric Settings

	MMPI				MMPI-2	
Demographics						
		M	*SD*		*M*	*SD*
N	44			66		
Age		41.1	12.0		42.5	12.1
Men	40.9%			56.1%		
Women	59.1			43.9		
Test-Taking Scales/Indexes						
		M	*SD*		*M*	*SD*
Inconsistent		0.0%			0.0%	
Total (Obvious-Subtle)[a]		−39.4	41.4		−18.3	51.4
Critical items[b]		19.6	8.3		18.3	8.2
Overreported[c]		0.0%			0.0%	
Underreported[c]		70.5%			60.6%	
Standard Validity and Clinical Scales (K-Corrected)						
		M	*SD*		*M*	*SD*
?[d]		6.7	7.0		5.0	5.7
L		54.0	8.9		59.1	12.1
F		51.8	4.5		49.5	8.2
K		57.6	8.1		54.4	10.4
1(Hs)		63.1	4.4		60.5	3.7
2(D)		59.1	6.9		56.4	6.5
3(Hy)		72.6	2.8		67.6	2.7
4(Pd)		60.7	6.9		53.8	7.2
5(Mf)		52.0	8.4		45.9	8.4
6(Pa)		56.0	7.4		49.7	7.7
7(Pt)		54.1	7.1		49.5	7.3
8(Sc)		54.7	7.2		48.8	7.5
9(Ma)		53.7	7.6		47.2	6.4
0(Si)		50.6	7.0		47.7	7.0
Supplementary Scales						
		M	*SD*		*M*	*SD*
A		45.8	7.9		47.0	8.1
R		67.7	11.0		57.2	11.2
MAC/MAC-R[d]						
men		24.5	3.9		24.4	4.7
women		22.4	3.3		22.8	4.4

Codetype Concordance

	Men	Women		Men	Women
MMPI-2 Spike *3*	100%	57.1%	MMPI Spike *3*	48.7%	82.8%
1-3/3-1		28.5	*3-4/4-3*	29.7	
			2-3/3-2	13.5	
			Spike *4*		13.8

[a] See Chapter 3, Table 3–24, for explanation of how this index is computed.

[b] The total number of Lachar and Wrobel (1979) critical items endorsed.

[c] Percentage of patients within this codetype scoring above the 75th percentile or below the 25th percentile on the total T score difference on the Wiener and Harmon Obvious and Subtle subscales for all patients (see Tables 3–45 and 3–46 for the cutting scores for the MMPI-2 and MMPI, respectively).

[d] Raw score.

TABLE D–21 Prototypic Scores for Spike *3-1* Codetypes in Psychiatric Settings

	MMPI			MMPI-2	
Demographics					
	M	SD		M	SD
N	76		215		
Age		44.6	11.7	43.3	12.8
Men	52.6%		59.1%		
Women	47.4		40.9		
Test-Taking Scales/Indexes					
	M	SD		M	SD
Inconsistent	6.5%			5.7%	
Total (Obvious-Subtle)[a]	1.8	56.7		48.7	70.9
Critical items[b]	30.4	11.9		35.7	14.9
Overreported[c]	0.0%			15.3%	
Underreported[c]	56.6%			22.5%	
Standard Validity and Clinical Scales (K-Corrected)					
	M	SD		M	SD
?[d]	3.9	5.2		4.1	5.5
L	55.1	9.6		57.5	12.3
F	56.8	7.0		58.9	12.3
K	56.1	9.5		49.7	11.2
1(Hs)	77.0	6.2		79.0	9.1
2(D)	69.1	7.6		69.1	10.6
3(Hy)	82.0	6.8		85.1	9.9
4(Pd)	66.7	8.4		63.4	10.2
5(Mf)	51.9	10.0		47.6	10.1
6(Pa)	61.0	7.6		59.5	11.8
7(Pt)	62.7	8.3		62.6	11.8
8(Sc)	62.5	9.6		61.3	12.7
9(Ma)	57.3	9.6		52.2	9.7
0(Si)	52.3	7.3		52.4	9.6
Supplementary Scales					
	M	SD		M	SD
A	51.8	10.5		57.6	12.1
R	71.6	12.3		59.5	11.4
MAC/MAC-R[d]					
men	26.5	3.8		26.5	5.2
women	22.5	3.8		22.7	4.1
Codetype Concordance					
	Men	Women		Men	Women
MMPI-2 Spike 1	88.1%	52.2%	MMPI Spike 1	64.1%	60.0%
1-2/2-1		21.7	Spike 4		30.0
1-3/3-1		13.0			

[a] See Chapter 3, Table 3–24, for explanation of how this index is computed.

[b] The total number of Lachar and Wrobel (1979) critical items endorsed.

[c] Percentage of patients within this codetype scoring above the 75th percentile or below the 25th percentile on the total T score difference on the Wiener and Harmon Obvious and Subtle subscales for all patients (see Tables 3–45 and 3–46 for the cutting scores for the MMPI-2 and MMPI, respectively).

[d] Raw score.

TABLE D–22   Prototypic Scores for *3-4/4-3* Codetypes in Psychiatric Settings

		MMPI			MMPI-2	

Demographics

		M	SD		M	SD
N	168			174		
Age		39.1	13.1		36.4	12.6
Men	52.4%			61.5%		
Women	47.6			38.5		

Test-Taking Scales/Indexes

	M	SD		M	SD
Inconsistent	2.7%			0.5%	
Total (Obvious-Subtle)[a]	−21.8	58.8		18.7	66.0
Critical items[b]	27.6	12.9		31.1	14.0
Overreported[c]	0.6%			7.5%	
Underreported[c]	50.2%			36.2%	

Standard Validity and Clinical Scales (K-Corrected)

	M	SD		M	SD
?[d]	4.4	5.7		4.0	5.3
L	53.9	8.9		55.9	11.7
F	57.4	7.1		59.5	13.0
K	59.4	10.0		53.1	10.8
1(Hs)	67.1	7.9		66.3	8.5
2(D)	66.2	7.9		65.3	9.2
3(Hy)	77.2	6.2		76.8	9.0
4(Pd)	82.2	7.4		78.7	8.1
5(Mf)	53.3	10.1		48.8	10.0
6(Pa)	62.5	8.2		59.0	11.3
7(Pt)	63.6	7.8		61.5	9.9
8(Sc)	64.4	8.8		60.8	10.7
9(Ma)	59.2	9.1		54.4	10.3
0(Si)	49.8	7.6		48.2	7.8

Supplementary Scales

	M	SD		M	SD
A	49.6	9.9		54.5	11.3
R	68.9	13.4		56.0	10.9
MAC/MAC-R[d]					
men	26.8	4.7		26.9	4.1
women	23.2	3.6		24.3	4.1

Codetype Concordance

	Men	Women			Men	Women
MMPI-2 *3-4/4-3*	65.9%	56.3%	MMPI *3-4/4-3*		54.2%	67.2%
Spike *3*	12.5		*2-4/4-2*		15.0	
1-3/3-1	10.2	22.5	Spike *4*			11.9
			4-8/8-4			10.4

[a] See Chapter 3, Table 3–24, for explanation of how this index is computed.

[b] The total number of Lachar and Wrobel (1979) critical items endorsed.

[c] Percentage of patients within this codetype scoring above the 75th percentile or below the 25th percentile on the total T score difference on the Wiener and Harmon Obvious and Subtle subscales for all patients (see Tables 3–45 and 3–46 for the cutting scores for the MMPI-2 and MMPI, respectively).

[d] Raw score.

TABLE D–23 Prototypic Scores for *3-5/5-3* Codetypes in Psychiatric Settings

		MMPI			MMPI-2	
Demographics						
		M	SD		M	SD
N	12			9		
Age		35.8	14.4		33.4	15.0
Men	91.7%			77.8%		
Women	8.3			22.2		
Test-Taking Scales/Indexes						
		M	SD		M	SD
Inconsistent		1.4%			0.0%	
Total (Obvious-Subtle)[a]		−14.3	50.3		−7.6	49.9
Critical items[b]		26.7	9.3		24.6	8.7
Overreported[c]		0.0%			0.0%	
Underreported[c]		64.8%			55.6%	
Standard Validity and Clinical Scales (K-Corrected)						
		M	SD		M	SD
?[d]		2.0	2.9		1.7	2.7
L		51.3	5.9		55.2	12.4
F		54.7	8.1		53.1	10.0
K		54.2	7.0		51.0	8.5
1(Hs)		66.4	4.8		63.0	5.2
2(D)		64.6	7.3		62.6	5.7
3(Hy)		73.3	4.5		70.4	6.4
4(Pd)		67.8	7.3		61.8	6.8
5(Mf)		78.4	5.8		70.6	4.1
6(Pa)		60.6	6.9		53.9	9.1
7(Pt)		59.7	6.4		53.0	6.7
8(Sc)		59.0	8.9		49.1	9.0
9(Ma)		60.8	8.0		48.0	6.4
0(Si)		49.4	9.4		45.3	6.8
Supplementary Scales						
		M	SD		M	SD
A		51.6	7.5		51.6	7.3
R		63.4	9.9		54.2	12.1
MAC/MAC-R[d]						
men		24.8	3.9		24.4	4.4
women		25.0	—		27.5	3.5

Codetype Concordance

	Men	Women		Men	Women
MMPI-2 *3-5/5-3*	54.5%	100.0%	MMPI *3-5/5-3*	85.7%	
			Spike *3*		50.0%
			Spike *4*		50.0%

[a] See Chapter 3, Table 3–24, for explanation of how this index is computed.
[b] The total number of Lachar and Wrobel (1979) critical items endorsed.
[c] Percentage of patients within this codetype scoring above the 75th percentile or below the 25th percentile on the total T score difference on the Wiener and Harmon Obvious and Subtle subscales for all patients (see Tables 3–45 and 3–46 for the cutting scores for the MMPI-2 and MMPI, respectively).
[d] Raw score.

TABLE D-24 Prototypic Scores for *3-6/6-3* Codetypes in Psychiatric Settings

		MMPI			MMPI-2	
Demographics						
		M	SD		M	SD
N	22			64		
Age		40.1	14.5		36.9	12.7
Men	31.8%			53.1%		
Women	68.2			46.9		
Test-Taking Scales/Indexes						
		M	SD		M	SD
Inconsistent		6.3%			12.2%	
Total (Obvious-Subtle)[a]		37.5	60.7		85.9	74.2
Critical items[b]		36.5	11.3		43.6	16.7
Overreported[c]		6.3%			28.1%	
Underreported[c]		41.3%			12.5%	
Standard Validity and Clinical Scales (K-Corrected)						
		M	SD		M	SD
?[d]		5.3	7.4		5.3	6.9
L		52.9	6.7		55.3	11.2
F		59.1	8.5		72.0	20.0
K		49.4	8.9		44.5	9.5
1(Hs)		66.0	6.8		71.5	10.8
2(D)		65.9	6.6		67.7	12.2
3(Hy)		75.7	4.6		80.7	10.6
4(Pd)		68.6	7.7		68.1	10.3
5(Mf)		51.7	12.6		51.4	12.6
6(Pa)		78.9	5.9		83.6	9.8
7(Pt)		61.8	7.0		64.3	13.2
8(Sc)		62.0	8.8		68.5	14.7
9(Ma)		58.6	6.9		56.5	10.3
0(Si)		57.0	8.0		53.1	8.6
Supplementary Scales						
		M	SD		M	SD
A		58.4	9.6		62.5	11.5
R		66.1	10.0		55.3	10.3
MAC/MAC-R[d]						
men		27.7	5.2		26.3	5.7
women		22.5	5.6		23.7	4.9

Codetype Concordance

	Men	Women			Men	Women
MMPI-2 *3-6/6-3*	100.0%	80.0%	MMPI *3-6/6-3*		20.6%	40.0%
1-3/3-1		20.0	*2-3/3-2*		11.8	
			4-6/6-4			26.7
			6-8/8-6			20.0

[a] See Chapter 3, Table 3-24, for explanation of how this index is computed.

[b] The total number of Lachar and Wrobel (1979) critical items endorsed.

[c] Percentage of patients within this codetype scoring above the 75th percentile or below the 25th percentile on the total T score difference on the Wiener and Harmon Obvious and Subtle subscales for all patients (see Tables 3-45 and 3-46 for the cutting scores for the MMPI-2 and MMPI, respectively).

[d] Raw score.

TABLE D–25   Prototypic Scores for *3-7/7-3* Codetypes in Psychiatric Settings

	MMPI			MMPI-2	
Demographics					
	M	SD		M	SD
N	16		51		
Age		37.4	12.8		36.3	13.0
Men	25.0%		49.0%		
Women	75.0		51.0		
Test-Taking Scales/Indexes					
	M	SD		M	SD
Inconsistent	3.8%			1.6%	
Total (Obvious-Subtle)[a]	43.5	50.0		85.1	57.8
Critical items[b]	40.8	9.8		42.0	11.9
Overreported[c]	0.0%			27.5%	
Underreported[c]	34.6%			9.8%	
Standard Validity and Clinical Scales (K-Corrected)					
	M	SD		M	SD
?[d]	4.8	6.1		5.8	6.1
L	50.3	8.8		51.2	10.3
F	60.4	6.3		62.7	11.4
K	53.0	6.4		47.1	8.4
1(Hs)	74.6	8.9		72.6	10.4
2(D)	74.0	10.7		74.3	9.9
3(Hy)	83.8	7.6		83.2	10.1
4(Pd)	70.7	9.4		68.3	10.3
5(Mf)	49.1	12.0		47.9	10.6
6(Pa)	67.6	10.4		66.1	12.0
7(Pt)	82.9	7.5		82.9	9.8
8(Sc)	75.3	8.5		73.0	10.3
9(Ma)	58.2	9.5		54.3	10.2
0(Si)	63.1	11.4		58.9	11.0
Supplementary Scales					
	M	SD		M	SD
A	65.3	7.2		69.4	9.0
R	73.8	13.2		58.0	10.3
MAC/MAC-R[d]					
men	26.3	4.5		27.1	5.7
women	20.4	4.1		21.2	3.6

Codetype Concordance					
	Men	Women		Men	Women
MMPI-2 3-7/7-3	75.0%	66.7%	MMPI 2-7/7-2	24.0%	
2-4/4-2		25.0	4-7/7-4	20.0	26.9%
			1-7/7-1	16.0	
			7-8/8-7	16.0	
			3-7/7-3	12.0	30.8
			3-8/8-3		19.2

[a] See Chapter 3, Table 3–24, for explanation of how this index is computed.

[b] The total number of Lachar and Wrobel (1979) critical items endorsed.

[c] Percentage of patients within this codetype scoring above the 75th percentile or below the 25th percentile on the total T score difference on the Wiener and Harmon Obvious and Subtle subscales for all patients (see Tables 3–45 and 3–46 for the cutting scores for the MMPI-2 and MMPI, respectively).

[d] Raw score.

TABLE D–26 Prototypic Scores for *3-8/8-3* Codetypes in Psychiatric Settings

	MMPI			MMPI-2	
Demographics					
	M	*SD*		*M*	*SD*
N	41			46	
Age	34.2	12.6		32.7	11.7
Men	31.7%			69.6%	
Women	68.3			30.4	
Test-Taking Scales/Indexes					
	M	*SD*		*M*	*SD*
Inconsistent	15.7%			26.9%	
Total (Obvious-Subtle)[a]	53.7	56.5		122.5	87.5
Critical items[b]	46.0	13.4		53.9	17.6
Overreported[c]	10.0%			51.1%	
Underreported[c]	24.3%			8.5%	
Standard Validity and Clinical Scales (K-Corrected)					
	M	*SD*		*M*	*SD*
?[d]	5.1	6.6		5.9	7.4
L	53.1	9.6		57.9	14.5
F	67.7	8.4		85.9	20.5
K	50.8	7.8		45.6	10.9
1(Hs)	74.9	9.1		80.1	12.2
2(D)	73.8	9.0		74.6	11.8
3(Hy)	82.6	7.1		87.8	11.5
4(Pd)	72.1	9.6		71.5	13.2
5(Mf)	53.1	13.0		54.2	12.5
6(Pa)	71.2	9.1		74.4	13.0
7(Pt)	74.2	8.4		76.6	12.6
8(Sc)	85.1	8.1		89.5	14.2
9(Ma)	65.7	7.6		65.1	11.0
0(Si)	57.9	7.6		58.0	10.2
Supplementary Scales					
	M	*SD*		*M*	*SD*
A	61.7	9.9		66.5	12.7
R	67.4	12.2		57.0	11.4
MAC/MAC-R[d]					
men	25.8	7.4		26.1	3.9
women	23.1	3.3		23.3	3.0

Codetype Concordance

		Men	Women			Men	Women
MMPI-2	*3-8/8-3*	46.2%	39.3%	MMPI	*1-8/8-1*	36.4%	
	3-6/6-3	23.1			*2-8/8-2*	18.2	
	1-3/3-1		32.1		*3-8/8-3*	18.2	73.3%
	3-7/7-3		17.9		*4-8/8-4*		13.3

[a] See Chapter 3, Table 3–24, for explanation of how this index is computed.

[b] The total number of Lachar and Wrobel (1979) critical items endorsed.

[c] Percentage of patients within this codetype scoring above the 75th percentile or below the 25th percentile on the total T score difference on the Wiener and Harmon Obvious and Subtle subscales for all patients (see Tables 3–45 and 3–46 for the cutting scores for the MMPI-2 and MMPI, respectively).

[d] Raw score.

TABLE D-27 Prototypic Scores for *3-9/9-3* Codetypes in Psychiatric Settings

		MMPI			MMPI-2	
Demographics						
		M	SD		M	SD
N	20			27		
Age		35.0	10.3		37.9	12.7
Men	55.0%			70.4%		
Women	45.0			29.6		
Test-Taking Scales/Indexes						
		M	SD		M	SD
Inconsistent		0.0%			8.8%	
Total (Obvious-Subtle)[a]		14.5	48.7		42.7	46.0
Critical items[b]		35.1	10.3		35.5	10.4
Overreported[c]		0.0%			3.7%	
Underreported[c]		62.0%			22.2%	
Standard Validity and Clinical Scales (K-Corrected)						
		M	SD		M	SD
?[d]		5.3	5.7		5.8	7.1
L		51.8	6.1		54.0	8.8
F		59.2	6.0		59.8	9.4
K		50.0	5.9		44.8	6.7
1(Hs)		66.9	6.7		64.4	6.3
2(D)		61.3	8.3		58.6	9.2
3(Hy)		75.6	4.8		74.1	7.0
4(Pd)		67.8	5.1		63.1	7.0
5(Mf)		55.8	9.6		51.4	9.7
6(Pa)		58.9	7.5		55.8	9.2
7(Pt)		58.9	7.4		55.0	8.5
8(Sc)		64.1	7.9		59.1	7.6
9(Ma)		79.4	6.0		75.0	6.2
0(Si)		47.2	8.1		45.4	7.5
Supplementary Scales						
		M	SD		M	SD
A		53.8	7.3		57.0	7.4
R		58.4	8.6		48.6	6.9
MAC/MAC-R[d]						
men		30.4	2.7		29.3	3.9
women		25.0	5.7		25.1	6.2

Codetype Concordance

	Men	Women			Men	Women
MMPI-2 *3-9/9-3*	90.9%	44.4%	MMPI *3-9/9-3*		52.6%	50.0%
1-3/3-1		33.3	*3-4/4-3*		10.5	
			4-9/9-4		10.5	37.5

[a] See Chapter 3, Table 3-24, for explanation of how this index is computed.

[b] The total number of Lachar and Wrobel (1979) critical items endorsed.

[c] Percentage of patients within this codetype scoring above the 75th percentile or below the 25th percentile on the total T score difference on the Wiener and Harmon Obvious and Subtle subscales for all patients (see Tables 3-45 and 3-46 for the cutting scores for the MMPI-2 and MMPI, respectively).

[d] Raw score.

TABLE D–28 Prototypic Scores for *3-0/0-3* Codetypes in Psychiatric Settings

	MMPI			*MMPI-2*
Demographics				
	M	*SD*		*M*
N	4		2	
Age	39.0	12.6		36.5
Men	0.0%		50.0%	
Women	100.0		50.0	
Test-Taking Scales/Indexes				
	M	*SD*		*M*
Inconsistent	0.0%			0.0%
Total (Obvious-Subtle)[a]	60.5	56.9		49.5
Critical items[b]	32.3	10.8		29.0
Overreported[c]	0.0%			0.0%
Underreported[c]	45.5%			50.0%
Standard Validity and Clinical Scales (K-Corrected)				
	M	*SD*		*M*
?[d]	8.8	7.4		9.5
L	52.3	11.0		61.5
F	62.5	5.3		63.0
K	48.8	6.2		46.5
1(Hs)	65.5	3.0		65.5
2(D)	69.8	4.3		67.0
3(Hy)	73.0	2.9		69.5
4(Pd)	57.3	5.3		55.0
5(Mf)	48.8	12.2		53.0
6(Pa)	59.8	3.8		60.0
7(Pt)	64.3	3.5		65.0
8(Sc)	63.8	7.9		59.0
9(Ma)	44.0	11.6		42.5
0(Si)	75.0	2.2		73.5
Supplementary Scales				
	M	*SD*		*M*
A	60.0	6.1		63.0
R	82.3	3.5		69.0
MAC/MAC-R[d]				
men	—	—		16.0
women	19.3	5.3		17.0

Codetype Concordance

		Men	Women			Men	Women
MMPI-2	*1-3/3-1*	none	25.0%	MMPI	*2-0/0-2*	100.0%	
	2-3/3-2		25.0		*3-0/0-3*		100.0%
	2-0/0-2		25.0				
	3-0/0-3		25.0				

[a] See Chapter 3, Table 3–24, for explanation of how this index is computed.

[b] The total number of Lachar and Wrobel (1979) critical items endorsed.

[c] Percentage of patients within this codetype scoring above the 75th percentile or below the 25th percentile on the total T score difference on the Wiener and Harmon Obvious and Subtle subscales for all patients (see Tables 3–45 and 3–46 for the cutting scores for the MMPI-2 and MMPI, respectively).

[d] Raw score.

TABLE D–29 Prototypic Scores for Spike 4 Codetypes in Psychiatric Settings

	MMPI			MMPI-2	
Demographics					
	M	SD		M	SD
N	752			529	
Age	34.0	12.6		32.7	11.8
Men	74.6%			82.2%	
Women	25.4			17.8	
Test-Taking Scales/Indexes					
	M	SD		M	SD
Inconsistent	0.0%			2.0%	
Total (Obvious-Subtle)[a]	−36.0	52.2		−15.0	54.4
Critical items[b]	18.4	8.2		19.4	8.2
Overreported[c]	0.1%			0.6%	
Underreported[c]	71.4%			59.6%	
Standard Validity and Clinical Scales (K-Corrected)					
	M	SD		M	SD
?[d]	4.6	6.0		3.9	5.2
L	53.0	8.0		56.0	10.5
F	55.1	6.2		53.4	8.9
K	58.5	9.2		53.7	10.5
1(Hs)	53.1	7.0		50.2	7.8
2(D)	57.3	7.0		54.5	6.5
3(Hy)	58.0	6.6		51.0	7.3
4(Pd)	76.6	5.2		71.3	5.2
5(Mf)	52.3	8.2		44.3	8.7
6(Pa)	55.5	7.1		50.4	8.2
7(Pt)	55.2	6.6		50.0	6.7
8(Sc)	56.7	6.8		51.0	6.9
9(Ma)	57.6	7.3		51.2	6.8
0(Si)	49.3	7.5		47.2	7.4
Supplementary Scales					
	M	SD		M	SD
A	46.0	8.3		48.4	8.7
R	62.8	11.2		52.1	9.4
MAC/MAC-R[d]					
men	27.6	4.1		27.7	4.1
women	23.9	3.7		24.1	3.7

Codetype Concordance

	Men	Women		Men	Women
MMPI-2 2-7/7-2	65.4%	93.9%	MMPI 2-7/7-2	78.9%	52.0%
			2-8/8-2	12.0	10.7
			2-4/4-2		10.2

[a] See Chapter 3, Table 3–24, for explanation of how this index is computed.

[b] The total number of Lachar and Wrobel (1979) critical items endorsed.

[c] Percentage of patients within this codetype scoring above the 75th percentile or below the 25th percentile on the total T score difference on the Wiener and Harmon Obvious and Subtle subscales for all patients (see Tables 3–45 and 3–46 for the cutting scores for the MMPI-2 and MMPI, respectively).

[d] Raw score.

TABLE D–30 Prototypic Scores for *4-5/5-4* Codetypes in Psychiatric Settings

		MMPI			*MMPI-2*	
Demographics						
		M	*SD*		*M*	*SD*
N	113			45		
Age		32.9	11.7		28.4	10.2
Men	87.6%			51.1%		
Women	12.4			48.9		
Test-Taking Scales/Indexes						
		M	*SD*		*M*	*SD*
Inconsistent		1.3%			3.8%	
Total (Obvious-Subtle)[a]		−14.7	56.6		−2.0	53.8
Critical items[b]		24.7	10.2		23.3	9.7
Overreported[c]		0.7%			2.2%	
Underreported[c]		48.5%			55.6%	
Standard Validity and Clinical Scales (K-Corrected)						
		M	*SD*		*M*	*SD*
?[d]		4.8	6.6		3.8	6.2
L		50.1	8.0		53.7	11.5
F		58.9	7.1		56.6	11.1
K		55.8	9.4		52.1	9.6
1(Hs)		54.7	8.2		49.6	7.9
2(D)		60.1	8.7		53.2	8.7
3(Hy)		61.3	6.5		52.3	7.3
4(Pd)		79.8	6.1		73.2	5.9
5(Mf)		76.7	5.1		73.0	6.0
6(Pa)		60.2	8.2		51.8	10.0
7(Pt)		60.7	7.2		52.9	8.2
8(Sc)		62.2	7.9		54.3	7.2
9(Ma)		61.6	9.0		55.0	9.0
0(Si)		49.5	8.1		45.5	7.3
Supplementary Scales						
		M	*SD*		*M*	*SD*
A		50.9	10.2		51.0	9.3
R		59.6	12.3		48.7	11.1
MAC/MAC-R[d]						
men		25.9	4.2		27.3	4.4
women		26.8	4.1		25.8	4.9

Codetype Concordance		Men	Women		Men	Women
MMPI-2 *4-5/5-4*		26.1%	85.7%	MMPI *4-5/5-4*	100.0%	54.5%
Spike *4*		25.0		Spike *4*		27.3
4-6/6-4		12.5				
Spike *5*		10.2				

[a] See Chapter 3, Table 3–24, for explanation of how this index is computed.

[b] The total number of Lachar and Wrobel (1979) critical items endorsed.

[c] Percentage of patients within this codetype scoring above the 75th percentile or below the 25th percentile on the total T score difference on the Wiener and Harmon Obvious and Subtle subscales for all patients (see Tables 3–45 and 3–46 for the cutting scores for the MMPI-2 and MMPI, respectively).

[d] Raw score.

TABLE D-31 Prototypic Scores for *4-6/6-4* Codetypes in Psychiatric Settings

	MMPI			MMPI-2	
Demographics					
	M	SD		M	SD
N	358			410	
Age	34.1	13.2		32.1	12.6
Men	53.6%			67.6%	
Women	46.4			32.4	
Test-Taking Scales/Indexes					
	M	SD		M	SD
Inconsistent	8.8%			7.4%	
Total (Obvious-Subtle)[a]	47.1	62.8		82.6	68.8
Critical items[b]	37.5	13.0		39.5	13.6
Overreported[c]	8.5%			23.6%	
Underreported[c]	21.2%			13.4%	
Standard Validity and Clinical Scales (K-Corrected)					
	M	SD		M	SD
?[d]	4.9	6.0		4.5	6.0
L	51.5	7.8		52.6	10.7
F	68.6	11.6		73.8	18.1
K	49.9	8.2		43.4	9.4
1(Hs)	56.4	10.4		54.0	11.1
2(D)	64.2	10.2		62.8	10.1
3(Hy)	61.2	8.6		55.5	10.9
4(Pd)	83.7	8.3		79.0	9.1
5(Mf)	54.9	10.8		49.3	10.1
6(Pa)	81.0	8.6		80.6	10.8
7(Pt)	63.4	9.6		61.1	10.8
8(Sc)	70.1	10.2		65.4	11.2
9(Ma)	64.9	9.0		59.1	10.2
0(Si)	55.8	9.2		54.1	9.4
Supplementary Scales					
	M	SD		M	SD
A	58.6	10.2		62.8	10.7
R	60.9	13.2		49.8	10.5
MAC/MAC-R[d]					
men	28.7	4.4		28.7	4.3
women	24.5	4.0		24.9	4.5

Codetype Concordance

	Men	Women		Men	Women
MMPI-2 *4-6/6-4*	81.8%	68.7%	MMPI *4-6/6-4*	52.4%	85.7%
			4-8/8-4	18.2	12.0

[a] See Chapter 3, Table 3-24, for explanation of how this index is computed.

[b] The total number of Lachar and Wrobel (1979) critical items endorsed.

[c] Percentage of patients within this codetype scoring above the 75th percentile or below the 25th percentile on the total T score difference on the Wiener and Harmon Obvious and Subtle subscales for all patients (see Tables 3-45 and 3-46 for the cutting scores for the MMPI-2 and MMPI, respectively).

[d] Raw score.

TABLE D–32 Prototypic Scores for *4-7/7-4* Codetypes in Psychiatric Settings

		MMPI			*MMPI-2*	
Demographics						
		M	*SD*		*M*	*SD*
N	161			102		
Age		32.3	12.0		30.1	10.6
Men	87.0%			81.4%		
Women	13.0			18.6		
Test-Taking Scales/Indexes						
		M	*SD*		*M*	*SD*
Inconsistent		7.4%			4.2%	
Total (Obvious-Subtle)[a]		49.8	53.7		76.6	60.7
Critical items[b]		34.9	11.2		36.9	11.8
Overreported[c]		6.3%			21.4%	
Underreported[c]		16.3%			8.7%	
Standard Validity and Clinical Scales (K-Corrected)						
		M	*SD*		*M*	*SD*
?[d]		5.8	7.1		4.6	6.3
L		46.9	6.5		47.5	8.0
F		61.8	7.8		65.0	12.8
K		51.4	8.5		46.0	8.8
1(Hs)		59.0	11.6		55.1	10.5
2(D)		70.3	7.7		67.0	8.1
3(Hy)		63.5	9.5		57.6	10.0
4(Pd)		83.1	7.9		79.9	8.5
5(Mf)		56.7	9.6		49.2	8.8
6(Pa)		64.7	9.2		61.4	11.2
7(Pt)		79.7	7.1		76.4	8.1
8(Sc)		70.4	9.5		65.7	10.1
9(Ma)		62.4	10.5		57.0	10.0
0(Si)		58.9	9.9		57.3	9.8
Supplementary Scales						
		M	*SD*		*M*	*SD*
A		63.7	10.2		67.1	10.8
R		61.0	13.3		51.2	11.5
MAC/MAC-R[d]						
men		28.7	4.1		28.3	3.8
women		22.2	4.0		24.3	3.5

Codetype Concordance

	Men	Women		Men	Women
MMPI-2 *4-7/7-4*	47.8%	38.1%	MMPI *4-7/7-4*	76.2%	42.1%
3-7/7-3		33.3	*4-8/8-4*		31.6
			Spike *4*		15.8

[a] See Chapter 3, Table 3–24, for explanation of how this index is computed.

[b] The total number of Lachar and Wrobel (1979) critical items endorsed.

[c] Percentage of patients within this codetype scoring above the 75th percentile or below the 25th percentile on the total T score difference on the Wiener and Harmon Obvious and Subtle subscales for all patients (see Tables 3–45 and 3–46 for the cutting scores for the MMPI-2 and MMPI, respectively).

[d] Raw score.

TABLE D–33   Prototypic Scores for *4-8/8-4* Codetypes in Psychiatric Settings

	MMPI				MMPI-2	
Demographics						
		M	*SD*		*M*	*SD*
N	664			238		
Age		29.1	11.3		27.8	10.5
Men	66.3%			66.0%		
Women	33.7			34.0		
Test-Taking Scales/Indexes						
		M	*SD*		*M*	*SD*
Inconsistent		19.3%			15.5%	
Total (Obvious-Subtle)[a]		84.6	77.7		104.7	77.9
Critical items[b]		47.1	17.6		45.9	17.5
Overreported[c]		25.9%			40.8%	
Underreported[c]		14.1%			8.3%	
Standard Validity and Clinical Scales (K-Corrected)						
		M	*SD*		*M*	*SD*
?[d]		5.1	6.3		4.4	5.9
L		49.2	8.2		51.3	11.2
F		77.8	14.3		85.1	19.8
K		49.6	10.0		44.7	11.2
1(Hs)		64.0	12.5		61.2	11.9
2(D)		72.8	12.1		68.3	10.2
3(Hy)		65.9	10.2		60.0	12.4
4(Pd)		88.7	9.4		83.0	9.6
5(Mf)		58.1	10.6		51.2	10.7
6(Pa)		74.1	12.0		69.2	13.2
7(Pt)		74.4	11.5		69.5	12.1
8(Sc)		89.6	13.7		82.1	12.9
9(Ma)		69.7	10.8		63.2	11.6
0(Si)		61.1	10.7		59.1	10.7
Supplementary Scales						
		M	*SD*		*M*	*SD*
A		64.2	12.4		65.6	12.8
R		62.7	13.0		52.1	11.3
MAC/MAC-R[d]						
men		27.5	4.4		27.4	4.6
women		24.0	4.5		24.0	4.5
Codetype Concordance						
		Men	Women		Men	Women
MMPI-2 *4-8/8-4*		35.4%	35.3%	MMPI *4-8/8-4*	97.5%	98.8%
6-8/8-6		16.0				
4-6/6-4		12.3				
7-8/8-7			12.4			
2-8/8-2			10.2			

[a] See Chapter 3, Table 3–24, for explanation of how this index is computed.

[b] The total number of Lachar and Wrobel (1979) critical items endorsed.

[c] Percentage of patients within this codetype scoring above the 75th percentile or below the 25th percentile on the total T score difference on the Wiener and Harmon Obvious and Subtle subscales for all patients (see Tables 3–45 and 3–46 for the cutting scores for the MMPI-2 and MMPI, respectively).

[d] Raw score.

TABLE D–34 Prototypic Scores for *4-9/9-4* Codetypes in Psychiatric Settings

		MMPI			MMPI-2	
Demographics						
		M	*SD*		*M*	*SD*
N	522			318		
Age		30.6	12.3		29.9	11.8
Men	75.1%			73.0%		
Women	24.9			27.0		
Test-Taking Scales/Indexes						
		M	*SD*		*M*	*SD*
Inconsistent		3.0%			2.9%	
Total (Obvious-Subtle)[a]		20.2	56.9		46.6	60.0
Critical items[b]		32.2	12.1		33.7	12.4
Overreported[c]		2.7%			9.4%	
Underreported[c]		28.3%			20.1%	
Standard Validity and Clinical Scales (K-Corrected)						
		M	*SD*		*M*	*SD*
?[d]		4.5	5.9		3.8	5.0
L		48.9	7.0		50.8	9.9
F		63.6	10.5		67.3	16.1
K		51.3	8.0		45.9	8.7
1(Hs)		54.5	9.5		52.6	10.0
2(D)		56.0	9.9		53.2	9.6
3(Hy)		58.0	8.6		52.2	10.0
4(Pd)		81.3	7.3		76.1	7.7
5(Mf)		55.3	9.6		47.2	9.6
6(Pa)		62.4	9.9		57.6	10.9
7(Pt)		59.8	8.7		55.5	9.5
8(Sc)		65.4	9.5		60.1	10.0
9(Ma)		79.3	7.2		75.7	8.0
0(Si)		47.7	7.1		45.4	7.7
Supplementary Scales						
		M	*SD*		*M*	*SD*
A		54.5	9.9		57.2	10.3
R		52.5	10.2		43.4	8.9
MAC/MAC-R[d]						
men		31.0	3.8		31.4	3.7
women		28.1	4.1		27.9	3.8
Codetype Concordance						
		Men	Women		Men	Women
MMPI-2 *4-9/9-4*		55.8%	64.6%	MMPI *4-9/9-4*	89.7%	96.6%
Spike *9*		15.8				

[a] See Chapter 3, Table 3–24, for explanation of how this index is computed.

[b] The total number of Lachar and Wrobel (1979) critical items endorsed.

[c] Percentage of patients within this codetype scoring above the 75th percentile or below the 25th percentile on the total T score difference on the Wiener and Harmon Obvious and Subtle subscales for all patients (see Tables 3–45 and 3–46 for the cutting scores for the MMPI-2 and MMPI, respectively).

[d] Raw score.

TABLE D–35 Prototypic Scores for *4-0/0-4* Codetypes in Psychiatric Settings

		MMPI			MMPI-2	
Demographics						
		M	SD		M	SD
N	31			42		
Age		29.4	9.7		30.6	10.1
Men	45.2%			76.2%		
Women	54.8			23.8		
Test-Taking Scales/Indexes						
		M	SD		M	SD
Inconsistent		0.8%			2.2%	
Total (Obvious-Subtle)[a]		56.7	45.7		77.8	46.5
Critical items[b]		31.5	9.1		31.5	9.4
Overreported[c]		1.6%			11.9%	
Underreported[c]		16.5%			7.1%	
Standard Validity and Clinical Scales (K-Corrected)						
		M	SD		M	SD
?[d]		4.2	5.4		3.4	3.8
L		48.6	6.6		50.0	9.2
F		62.4	9.1		64.7	11.8
K		45.8	7.5		40.2	8.0
1(Hs)		51.8	9.7		46.7	9.7
2(D)		63.9	7.0		62.5	6.2
3(Hy)		54.9	7.7		46.4	8.3
4(Pd)		77.3	5.4		72.4	5.4
5(Mf)		48.0	10.0		46.1	8.2
6(Pa)		59.9	8.0		56.1	10.5
7(Pt)		62.4	6.6		57.7	8.4
8(Sc)		59.7	8.3		54.4	9.1
9(Ma)		56.0	6.7		49.3	7.6
0(Si)		73.2	2.3		70.9	3.7
Supplementary Scales						
		M	SD		M	SD
A		62.1	9.5		64.8	9.9
R		65.9	11.6		54.4	9.5
MAC/MAC-R[d]						
men		27.4	3.4		27.0	4.3
women		21.1	4.2		20.0	3.3
Codetype Concordance						
		Men	Women		Men	Women
MMPI-2 4-0/0-4		75.0%	50.0%	MMPI Spike 4	39.2%	43.8%
Spike 0		12.5		2-4/4-2	17.6	
2-4/4-2			11.1	4-0/0-4	15.7	56.3
8-0/0-8			11.1			

[a] See Chapter 3, Table 3–24, for explanation of how this index is computed.

[b] The total number of Lachar and Wrobel (1979) critical items endorsed.

[c] Percentage of patients within this codetype scoring above the 75th percentile or below the 25th percentile on the total T score difference on the Wiener and Harmon Obvious and Subtle subscales for all patients (see Tables 3–45 and 3–46 for the cutting scores for the MMPI-2 and MMPI, respectively).

[d] Raw score.

TABLE D–36 Prototypic Scores for Spike 5 Codetypes in Psychiatric Settings

	MMPI			MMPI-2	
Demographics					
	M	SD		M	SD
N	113			135	
Age		34.8	14.1		35.2	13.6
Men	61.9%			37.0%	
Women	38.1			63.0	
Test-Taking Scales/Indexes					
	M	SD		M	SD
Inconsistent	0.0%			3.6%	
Total (Obvious-Subtle)[a]	−23.9	53.6		.8	54.3
Critical items[b]	18.1	8.8		17.8	8.4
Overreported[c]	0.0%			0.7%	
Underreported[c]	65.5%			45.9%	
Standard Validity and Clinical Scales (K-Corrected)					
	M	SD		M	SD
?[d]	4.4	5.7		3.9	6.2
L	53.0	7.5		58.5	11.9
F	55.5	7.2		54.9	11.0
K	54.8	8.4		49.9	10.0
1(Hs)	51.2	7.4		48.4	8.0
2(D)	55.3	7.4		50.4	7.2
3(Hy)	55.9	7.4		46.9	8.3
4(Pd)	60.6	6.0		51.8	7.3
5(Mf)	75.2	4.8		70.9	5.5
6(Pa)	54.8	7.7		47.0	8.7
7(Pt)	53.3	7.1		46.7	8.0
8(Sc)	54.1	7.1		47.7	7.8
9(Ma)	57.9	7.3		51.1	6.5
0(Si)	49.8	8.5		48.1	8.0
Supplementary Scales					
	M	SD		M	SD
A	47.3	8.9		48.9	9.1
R	60.9	10.7		50.2	10.0
MAC/MAC-R[d]					
men	24.2	4.7		24.0	4.2
women	23.5	3.8		24.3	3.6

Codetype Concordance						
	Men	Women			Men	Women
MMPI-2 Spike-5	83.3%	76.4%	MMPI Spike 5		53.2%	73.3%
5-0/0-5	16.7	13.9	4-5/5-4		19.2	
			Spike 4			18.7

[a]See Chapter 3, Table 3–24, for explanation of how this index is computed.

[b]The total number of Lachar and Wrobel (1979) critical items endorsed.

[c]Percentage of patients within this codetype scoring above the 75th percentile or below the 25th percentile on the total T score difference on the Wiener and Harmon Obvious and Subtle subscales for all patients (see Tables 3–45 and 3–46 for the cutting scores for the MMPI-2 and MMPI, respectively).

[d]Raw score.

TABLE D–37　Prototypic Scores for *5-6/6-5* Codetypes in Psychiatric Settings

	MMPI			MMPI-2	
Demographics					
	M	SD		M	SD
N	21		26		
Age	36.5	14.7		36.2	14.2
Men	90.5%		57.7%		
Women	9.5		42.3		
Test-Taking Scales/Indexes					
	M	SD		M	SD
Inconsistent	8.2%			26.1%	
Total (Obvious-Subtle)[a]	18.8	58.1		70.5	70.9
Critical items[b]	32.2	11.2		35.4	13.5
Overreported[c]	3.3%			23.1%	
Underreported[c]	31.1%			19.2%	
Standard Validity and Clinical Scales (K-Corrected)					
	M	SD		M	SD
?[d]	4.0	5.0		3.5	4.4
L	51.9	7.5		54.3	12.3
F	63.6	8.7		72.4	17.3
K	51.0	8.8		42.7	10.9
1(Hs)	57.8	9.7		52.3	13.4
2(D)	58.0	10.7		55.2	10.7
3(Hy)	61.0	11.5		50.0	15.7
4(Pd)	66.4	10.0		57.7	9.5
5(Mf)	79.0	8.8		73.8	7.9
6(Pa)	78.3	6.3		78.2	10.1
7(Pt)	62.5	7.8		56.3	11.0
8(Sc)	66.1	9.6		64.2	9.0
9(Ma)	62.9	8.1		58.3	9.4
0(Si)	53.3	8.9		53.2	8.6
Supplementary Scales					
	M	SD		M	SD
A	56.2	10.3		60.0	11.7
R	60.5	10.7		48.8	12.6
MAC/MAC-R[d]					
men	25.3	5.2		24.4	3.5
women	25.0	2.8		26.1	5.1

Codetype Concordance

	Men	Women		Men	Women
MMPI-2 *5-6/6-5*	47.4%	100.0%	MMPI *5-6/6-5*	60.0%	18.2%
Spike *6*	31.6		*4-5/5-4*	20.0	
			Spike *6*		45.5
			6-8/8-6		27.3

[a] See Chapter 3, Table 3–24, for explanation of how this index is computed.

[b] The total number of Lachar and Wrobel (1979) critical items endorsed.

[c] Percentage of patients within this codetype scoring above the 75th percentile or below the 25th percentile on the total T score difference on the Wiener and Harmon Obvious and Subtle subscales for all patients (see Tables 3–45 and 3–46 for the cutting scores for the MMPI-2 and MMPI, respectively).

[d] Raw score.

TABLE D–38 Prototypic Scores for *5-7/7-5* Codetypes in Psychiatric Settings

	MMPI			MMPI-2		
Demographics						
		M	SD		M	SD
N	16			10		
Age		35.7	13.5		33.2	12.2
Men	93.7%			70.0%		
Women	6.3			30.0		
Test-Taking Scales/Indexes						
		M	SD		M	SD
Inconsistent		0.0%			10.0%	
Total (Obvious-Subtle)[a]		41.4	48.8		83.1	59.4
Critical items[b]		31.2	9.7		36.5	11.3
Overreported[c]		4.0%			10.0%	
Underreported[c]		16.0%			10.0%	
Standard Validity and Clinical Scales (K-Corrected)						
		M	SD		M	SD
?[d]		4.1	4.1		4.4	5.1
L		48.1	5.5		51.7	14.2
F		59.4	5.1		63.9	8.0
K		50.1	6.8		42.7	8.8
1(Hs)		58.3	11.1		56.0	9.5
2(D)		63.5	10.3		59.9	8.6
3(Hy)		58.8	9.9		52.8	9.0
4(Pd)		63.8	8.5		57.8	9.9
5(Mf)		80.8	7.2		76.4	8.8
6(Pa)		63.3	5.5		59.5	10.7
7(Pt)		77.1	5.6		72.6	5.5
8(Sc)		68.3	7.4		64.5	7.1
9(Ma)		62.0	9.1		59.2	8.0
0(Si)		60.4	9.2		58.1	7.8
Supplementary Scales						
		M	SD		M	SD
A		64.6	6.8		67.4	9.1
R		64.5	8.4		50.6	6.5
MAC/MAC-R[d]						
men		25.4	5.2		24.3	6.0
women		30.0	—		28.7	1.5

Codetype Concordance

	Men	Women		Men	Women
MMPI-2 *5-7/7-5*	35.7%	100.0%	MMPI *5-7/7-5*	71.4%	33.3%
Spike *5*	21.4		*5-8/8-5*	28.6	
			Spike *4*		33.3
			Spike *5*		33.3

[a] See Chapter 3, Table 3–24, for explanation of how this index is computed.

[b] The total number of Lachar and Wrobel (1979) critical items endorsed.

[c] Percentage of patients within this codetype scoring above the 75th percentile or below the 25th percentile on the total T score difference on the Wiener and Harmon Obvious and Subtle subscales for all patients (see Tables 3–45 and 3–46 for the cutting scores for the MMPI-2 and MMPI, respectively).

[d] Raw score.

TABLE D-39   Prototypic Scores for *5-8/8-5* Codetypes in Psychiatric Settings

		MMPI			MMPI-2	
Demographics						
		M	SD		M	SD
N	39			21		
Age		31.1	11.4		29.4	7.7
Men	92.3%			61.9%		
Women	7.7			38.1		
Test-Taking Scales/Indexes						
		M	SD		M	SD
Inconsistent		16.2%			41.3%	
Total (Obvious-Subtle)[a]		67.1	52.5		82.8	45.2
Critical items[b]		40.6	12.4		41.6	9.9
Overreported[c]		13.2%			18.2%	
Underreported[c]		7.4%			0.0%	
Standard Validity and Clinical Scales (K-Corrected)						
		M	SD		M	SD
?[d]		4.9	6.3		3.4	5.5
L		48.6	8.7		54.1	12.1
F		70.3	12.1		75.7	17.6
K		47.6	7.8		43.0	8.7
1(Hs)		57.3	12.7		57.1	12.3
2(D)		65.3	11.9		58.2	10.5
3(Hy)		60.3	10.7		54.2	11.9
4(Pd)		68.7	7.4		60.1	7.8
5(Mf)		82.6	7.6		74.9	7.2
6(Pa)		68.9	8.2		63.9	8.7
7(Pt)		69.4	9.5		61.2	8.8
8(Sc)		83.9	11.2		75.6	10.7
9(Ma)		69.0	8.2		61.2	9.6
0(Si)		59.6	9.1		55.7	9.6
Supplementary Scales						
		M	SD		M	SD
A		65.3	10.1		65.3	11.2
R		58.5	10.7		49.3	9.5
MAC/MAC-R[d]						
men		25.3	3.4		25.7	4.0
women		23.7	7.8		24.9	3.9

Codetype Concordance						
	Men	Women		Men	Women
MMPI-2 *5-8-/8-5*	35.1%	50.0%	MMPI *5-8/8-5*	100.0%	22.2%
Spike *5*	10.8		*4-8/8-4*		22.2
			Spike *8*		22.2

[a] See Chapter 3, Table 3-24, for explanation of how this index is computed.

[b] The total number of Lachar and Wrobel (1979) critical items endorsed.

[c] Percentage of patients within this codetype scoring above the 75th percentile or below the 25th percentile on the total T score difference on the Wiener and Harmon Obvious and Subtle subscales for all patients (see Tables 3-45 and 3-46 for the cutting scores for the MMPI-2 and MMPI, respectively).

[d] Raw score.

TABLE D–40   Prototypic Scores for *5-9/9-5* Codetypes in Psychiatric Settings

		MMPI			**MMPI-2**	
Demographics						
		M	*SD*		*M*	*SD*
N	57			45		
Age		31.7	11.0		30.2	11.3
Men	86.0%			44.4%		
Women	14.0			55.6		
Test-Taking Scales/Indexes						
		M	*SD*		*M*	*SD*
Inconsistent		1.7%			7.7%	
Total (Obvious-Subtle)[a]		−0.5	55.0		27.6	56.7
Critical items[b]		26.9	11.0		27.1	10.7
Overreported[c]		0.6%			6.5%	
Underreported[c]		35.3%			30.4%	
Standard Validity and Clinical Scales (K-Corrected)						
		M	*SD*		*M*	*SD*
?[d]		4.1	5.3		5.1	6.3
L		50.1	7.3		54.2	11.3
F		59.8	7.9		61.2	15.7
K		51.2	8.5		46.2	9.2
1(Hs)		50.4	9.4		47.1	10.8
2(D)		49.4	8.9		45.8	8.6
3(Hy)		56.4	8.9		47.4	10.5
4(Pd)		63.0	9.2		56.0	7.6
5(Mf)		76.5	5.9		72.1	5.6
6(Pa)		59.6	8.1		52.5	10.8
7(Pt)		56.6	7.7		49.6	6.9
8(Sc)		62.4	8.5		56.8	8.1
9(Ma)		76.8	5.4		73.0	6.3
0(Si)		44.5	7.8		43.1	8.0
Supplementary Scales						
		M	*SD*		*M*	*SD*
A		52.7	10.9		53.7	10.3
R		49.1	10.1		40.0	9.2
MAC/MAC-R[d]						
men		28.0	4.6		28.1	5.4
women		27.4	5.0		27.7	4.3

Codetype Concordance					
	Men	Women		Men	Women
MMPI-2 *5-9/9-5*	44.2%	100.0%	MMPI *5-9/9-5*	95.0%	30.8%
Spike *9*	34.9		Spike *9*		42.3

[a] See Chapter 3, Table 3–24, for explanation of how this index is computed.

[b] The total number of Lachar and Wrobel (1979) critical items endorsed.

[c] Percentage of patients within this codetype scoring above the 75th percentile or below the 25th percentile on the total T score difference on the Wiener and Harmon Obvious and Subtle subscales for all patients (see Tables 3–45 and 3–46 for the cutting scores for the MMPI-2 and MMPI, respectively).

[d] Raw score.

TABLE D–41 Prototypic Scores for *5-0/0-5* Codetypes in Psychiatric Settings

		MMPI				MMPI-2	
Demographics							
		M	SD			M	SD
N	4				10		
Age		37.5	9.5			34.4	13.2
Men	50.0%				40.0%		
Women	50.0				60.0		
Test-Taking Scales/Indexes							
		M	SD			M	SD
Inconsistent		0.0%				0.0%	
Total (Obvious-Subtle)[a]		70.5	44.1			47.1	40.0
Critical items[b]		24.8	6.9			22.1	9.1
Overreported[c]		2.3%				0.0%	
Underreported[c]		27.9%				20.0%	
Standard Validity and Clinical Scales (K-Corrected)							
		M	SD			M	SD
?[d]		14.5	11.3			4.8	5.0
L		44.0	4.9			49.5	7.7
F		52.0	2.4			53.6	7.2
K		40.8	7.1			42.0	10.3
1(Hs)		43.0	9.1			43.3	11.3
2(D)		61.3	9.6			58.2	7.6
3(Hy)		44.0	6.5			40.4	6.8
4(Pd)		58.5	7.2			50.2	6.1
5(Mf)		71.5	1.3			69.3	3.3
6(Pa)		50.8	5.7			47.0	8.3
7(Pt)		54.8	7.5			56.2	5.3
8(Sc)		53.0	5.6			50.6	8.4
9(Ma)		58.0	4.1			46.3	5.9
0(Si)		74.0	2.8			68.9	3.8
Supplementary Scales							
		M	SD			M	SD
A		60.3	12.0			57.8	10.9
R		60.0	20.5			59.5	10.2
MAC/MAC-R[d]							
men		25.0	2.8			19.8	4.6
women		23.0	4.2			21.0	3.5
Codetype Concordance							
		Men	Women			Men	Women
MMPI-2 Spike *0*		100.0%			MMPI Spike *5*	71.4%	62.5%
5-0/0-5			100.0%		Spike *0*		25.0
					5-0/0-5		12.5

[a] See Chapter 3, Table 3–24, for explanation of how this index is computed.

[b] The total number of Lachar and Wrobel (1979) critical items endorsed.

[c] Percentage of patients within this codetype scoring above the 75th percentile or below the 25th percentile on the total T score difference on the Wiener and Harmon Obvious and Subtle subscales for all patients (see Tables 3–45 and 3–46 for the cutting scores for the MMPI-2 and MMPI, respectively).

[d] Raw score.

TABLE D–42   Prototypic Scores for Spike 6 Codetypes in Psychiatric Settings

	MMPI			MMPI-2		
Demographics						
		M	SD		M	SD
N	102			126		
Age		39.5	13.4		36.9	13.6
Men	47.1%			66.7%		
Women	52.9			33.3		
Test-Taking Scales/Indexes						
		M	SD		M	SD
Inconsistent		0.0%			5.2%	
Total (Obvious-Subtle)[a]		12.8	52.7		34.7	55.4
Critical items[b]		25.5	8.4		25.9	8.9
Overreported[c]		2.0%			2.4%	
Underreported[c]		38.2%			26.2%	
Standard Validity and Clinical Scales (K-Corrected)						
		M	SD		M	SD
?[d]		6.8	7.7		5.9	6.7
L		53.2	9.1		56.2	11.8
F		59.6	7.8		59.9	11.9
K		50.5	8.4		44.9	9.2
1(Hs)		50.2	8.2		47.8	8.7
2(D)		57.2	7.1		52.9	6.9
3(Hy)		53.7	7.7		46.7	7.6
4(Pd)		61.5	5.7		54.5	5.9
5(Mf)		53.0	9.3		47.3	8.5
6(Pa)		74.0	5.3		73.1	6.5
7(Pt)		55.6	7.6		50.5	8.2
8(Sc)		57.3	7.3		52.1	7.9
9(Ma)		57.4	7.6		51.8	6.5
0(Si)		55.2	8.6		50.7	7.4
Supplementary Scales						
		M	SD		M	SD
A		53.1	9.2		55.5	9.6
R		61.2	10.6		48.4	9.2
MAC/MAC-R[d]						
men		26.8	4.4		27.1	4.4
women		22.7	3.6		23.8	3.5

Codetype Concordance

	Men	Women		Men	Women
MMPI-2 Spike 6	81.6%	49.1	MMPI Spike 6	50.0%	75.0%
6-0/0-6	16.3	14.6	6-8/8-6	15.0	
			4-6/6-4		25.0

[a] See Chapter 3, Table 3–24, for explanation of how this index is computed.

[b] The total number of Lachar and Wrobel (1979) critical items endorsed.

[c] Percentage of patients within this codetype scoring above the 75th percentile or below the 25th percentile on the total T score difference on the Wiener and Harmon Obvious and Subtle subscales for all patients (see Tables 3–45 and 3–46 for the cutting scores for the MMPI-2 and MMPI, respectively).

[d] Raw score.

TABLE D–43 Prototypic Scores for *6-7/7-6* Codetypes in Psychiatric Settings

	MMPI			MMPI-2	
Demographics					
	M	SD		M	SD
N	35			109	
Age		34.9	11.0		34.3	11.8
Men	74.3%			75.2%	
Women	25.7			24.8	
Test-Taking Scales/Indexes					
	M	SD		M	SD
Inconsistent	12.5%			8.5%	
Total (Obvious-Subtle)[a]	83.8	56.9		139.1	62.0
Critical items[b]	42.2	12.4		48.0	13.0
Overreported[c]	23.2%			57.3%	
Underreported[c]	8.9%			0.9%	
Standard Validity and Clinical Scales (K-Corrected)					
	M	SD		M	SD
?[d]	7.4	7.1		5.8	7.2
L	47.5	7.3		48.7	8.5
F	66.8	12.6		75.6	17.9
K	47.2	7.0		39.4	6.6
1(Hs)	62.6	13.3		62.2	12.7
2(D)	71.5	12.0		70.4	10.9
3(Hy)	63.7	11.4		61.3	13.5
4(Pd)	71.2	9.7		66.6	10.6
5(Mf)	54.9	10.3		51.0	10.3
6(Pa)	81.9	9.3		85.6	12.5
7(Pt)	82.9	8.4		81.8	10.3
8(Sc)	74.7	11.3		74.4	12.4
9(Ma)	65.1	9.3		57.8	9.2
0(Si)	63.4	8.6		64.3	9.6
Supplementary Scales					
	M	SD		M	SD
A	69.9	7.7		74.7	8.3
R	62.8	14.5		53.3	11.7
MAC/MAC-R[d]					
men	29.7	5.9		27.8	5.3
women	21.1	2.6		23.4	4.1

Codetype Concordance					
	Men	Women		Men	Women
MMPI-2 *6-7/7-6*	77.8%	88.9%	MMPI *7-8/8-7*	36.1%	
6-0/0-6	11.1		*6-7/7-6*	25.3	29.6%
			6-8/8-6		44.4
			4-6/6-4		11.1

[a] See Chapter 3, Table 3–24, for explanation of how this index is computed.

[b] The total number of Lachar and Wrobel (1979) critical items endorsed.

[c] Percentage of patients within this codetype scoring above the 75th percentile or below the 25th percentile on the total T score difference on the Wiener and Harmon Obvious and Subtle subscales for all patients (see Tables 3–45 and 3–46 for the cutting scores for the MMPI-2 and MMPI, respectively).

[d] Raw score.

TABLE D–44   Prototypic Scores for *6-8/8-6* Codetypes in Psychiatric Settings

		MMPI			MMPI-2	
Demographics						
		M	SD		M	SD
N	678			863		
Age		30.4	12.2		29.8	12.0
Men	67.9%			74.3%		
Women	36.1			25.7		
Test-Taking Scales/Indexes						
		M	SD		M	SD
Inconsistent		43.0%			28.7%	
Total (Obvious-Subtle)[a]		159.6	68.3		202.5	70.8
Critical items[b]		64.0	17.2		66.2	16.5
Overreported[c]		41.1%			84.5%	
Underreported[c]		1.1%			0.5%	
Standard Validity and Clinical Scales (K-Corrected)						
		M	SD		M	SD
?[d]		5.1	6.3		4.8	5.9
L		49.4	7.9		50.5	10.5
F		92.5	14.9		105.0	17.3
K		42.8	7.2		36.3	7.3
1(Hs)		70.3	15.1		69.4	14.3
2(D)		75.8	14.9		73.2	13.2
3(Hy)		67.1	12.1		64.6	15.3
4(Pd)		79.4	12.2		73.7	12.9
5(Mf)		60.3	11.3		54.0	10.5
6(Pa)		95.3	11.4		97.4	13.5
7(Pt)		80.7	13.4		78.0	13.7
8(Sc)		100.5	15.1		96.0	14.5
9(Ma)		75.2	10.9		69.6	12.3
0(Si)		65.5	9.4		65.7	10.2
Supplementary Scales						
		M	SD		M	SD
A		72.0	9.5		76.1	9.6
R		59.2	14.0		49.9	12.2
MAC/MAC-R[d]						
men		28.6	4.4		28.0	4.4
women		25.5	4.4		25.8	4.2

Codetype Concordance

	Men	Women			Men	Women
MMPI-2 *6-8/8-6*	86.1%	75.2%	MMPI *6-8/8-6*		58.0%	82.6%
			7-8/8-7		12.2	
			4-8/8-4		11.6	
			2-8/8-2		10.9	

[a] See Chapter 3, Table 3–24, for explanation of how this index is computed.
[b] The total number of Lachar and Wrobel (1979) critical items endorsed.
[c] Percentage of patients within this codetype scoring above the 75th percentile or below the 25th percentile on the total T score difference on the Wiener and Harmon Obvious and Subtle subscales for all patients (see Tables 3–45 and 3–46 for the cutting scores for the MMPI-2 and MMPI, respectively).
[d] Raw score.

TABLE D–45 Prototypic Scores for *6-9/9-6* Codetypes in Psychiatric Settings

	MMPI			MMPI-2	
Demographics					
	M	SD		M	SD
N	131			260	
Age		33.9	13.0		31.2	12.4
Men	51.9%			66.5%	
Women	48.1			33.5	
Test-Taking Scales/Indexes					
	M	SD		M	SD
Inconsistent	13.9%			15.0%	
Total (Obvious-Subtle)[a]	74.6	54.0		114.9	62.6
Critical items[b]	42.5	12.3		46.3	14.3
Overreported[c]	12.7%			41.8%	
Underreported[c]	12.0%			3.5%	
Standard Validity and Clinical Scales (K-Corrected)					
	M	SD		M	SD
?[d]	4.0	5.5		4.4	6.0
L	49.5	7.4		50.1	9.9
F	73.2	12.3		82.6	19.4
K	43.4	7.1		37.2	7.2
1(Hs)	53.0	11.0		52.7	12.5
2(D)	52.0	8.7		51.7	9.6
3(Hy)	52.6	9.7		48.3	11.7
4(Pd)	66.7	8.5		62.8	10.2
5(Mf)	57.0	9.1		51.4	9.4
6(Pa)	80.6	8.6		81.2	11.3
7(Pt)	59.6	8.0		58.2	10.6
8(Sc)	70.8	9.4		67.9	11.5
9(Ma)	82.5	8.6		80.5	10.3
0(Si)	51.8	8.1		49.5	8.2
Supplementary Scales					
	M	SD		M	SD
A	61.2	9.1		65.9	9.9
R	48.6	11.4		38.9	10.2
MAC/MAC-R[d]					
men	30.4	4.2		32.0	4.1
women	27.6	4.0		27.9	4.2

Codetype Concordance

	Men	Women		Men	Women
MMPI-2 *6-9/9-6*	84.2%	88.2%	MMPI *6-9/9-6*	38.5%	71.9%
Spike *6*	15.8		*6-8/8-6*	23.1%	12.3%
1-6/6-1		11.8			

[a] See Chapter 3, Table 3–24, for explanation of how this index is computed.

[b] The total number of Lachar and Wrobel (1979) critical items endorsed.

[c] Percentage of patients within this codetype scoring above the 75th percentile or below the 25th percentile on the total T score difference on the Wiener and Harmon Obvious and Subtle subscales for all patients (see Tables 3–45 and 3–46 for the cutting scores for the MMPI-2 and MMPI, respectively).

[d] Raw score.

TABLE D–46   Prototypic Scores for *6-0/0-6* Codetypes in Psychiatric Settings

		MMPI			MMPI-2	
Demographics						
		M	SD		M	SD
N	13			50		
Age		39.8	15.1		36.5	13.5
Men	23.1%			82.0%		
Women	76.9			18.0		
Test-Taking Scales/Indexes						
		M	SD		M	SD
Inconsistent		1.8%			8.6%	
Total (Obvious-Subtle)[a]		60.2	39.6		124.3	49.4
Critical items[b]		32.2	8.0		37.0	11.1
Overreported[c]		1.8%			44.0%	
Underreported[c]		17.5%			0.0%	
Standard Validity and Clinical Scales (K-Corrected)						
		M	SD		M	SD
?[d]		4.4	4.6		4.4	5.9
L		54.2	7.0		50.5	10.0
F		65.4	9.0		71.2	13.4
K		47.2	7.5		36.4	6.8
1(Hs)		57.8	9.3		49.4	11.2
2(D)		65.3	4.6		63.3	7.7
3(Hy)		57.5	7.0		46.2	8.8
4(Pd)		59.8	7.9		57.5	9.0
5(Mf)		46.4	5.8		47.3	8.4
6(Pa)		75.3	5.8		75.9	7.1
7(Pt)		59.7	7.4		59.5	9.8
8(Sc)		63.9	5.5		61.1	10.3
9(Ma)		54.4	8.8		51.4	9.3
0(Si)		73.2	3.2		72.0	5.5
Supplementary Scales						
		M	SD		M	SD
A		59.0	7.4		69.7	10.6
R		77.3	12.7		57.1	9.8
MAC/MAC-R[d]						
men		25.7	5.9		25.5	5.3
women		22.1	4.6		19.9	1.8

Codetype Concordance

	Men	Women			Men	Women
MMPI-2 *6-0/0-6*	100.0%	50.0%	MMPI *6-8/8-6*		17.8%	
1-6/6-1		20.0	Spike *6*		17.8	53.3%
			6-0/0-6			33.3

[a] See Chapter 3, Table 3–24, for explanation of how this index is computed.

[b] The total number of Lachar and Wrobel (1979) critical items endorsed.

[c] Percentage of patients within this codetype scoring above the 75th percentile or below the 25th percentile on the total T score difference on the Wiener and Harmon Obvious and Subtle subscales for all patients (see Tables 3–45 and 3–46 for the cutting scores for the MMPI-2 and MMPI, respectively).

[d] Raw score.

TABLE D–47 Prototypic Scores for Spike 7 Codetypes in Psychiatric Settings

		MMPI			MMPI-2	
Demographics						
		M	SD		M	SD
N	33			43		
Age		32.5	14.0		31.4	12.2
Men	72.7%			69.8%		
Women	27.3			30.2		
Test-Taking Scales/Indexes						
		M	SD		M	SD
Inconsistent		0.0%			6.0%	
Total (Obvious-Subtle)[a]		28.5	52.7		50.2	57.2
Critical items[b]		27.4	8.9		28.1	9.4
Overreported[c]		6.1%			7.0%	
Underreported[c]		36.4%			27.9%	
Standard Validity and Clinical Scales (K-Corrected)						
		M	SD		M	SD
?[d]		4.9	5.7		3.2	3.8
L		49.8	7.6		53.0	11.4
F		57.9	7.1		57.9	9.9
K		51.4	8.6		46.1	10.8
1(Hs)		53.3	8.2		51.1	8.0
2(D)		61.4	5.2		58.3	5.2
3(Hy)		56.6	7.6		49.3	8.3
4(Pd)		61.1	7.8		53.9	7.3
5(Mf)		54.2	8.8		46.4	6.9
6(Pa)		59.2	5.8		52.4	6.7
7(Pt)		74.3	3.7		69.1	3.7
8(Sc)		62.5	5.9		56.4	5.8
9(Ma)		57.2	7.9		50.3	7.4
0(Si)		57.5	6.6		55.2	6.8
Supplementary Scales						
		M	SD		M	SD
A		61.4	8.9		62.4	9.5
R		60.2	11.3		49.3	7.6
MAC/MAC-R[d]						
men		26.6	4.0		26.8	3.8
women		18.4	3.4		22.0	4.3
Codetype Concordance						
		Men	Women		Men	Women
MMPI-2 Spike 7		61.1%	63.2%	MMPI Spike 7	45.8%	100.0%
7-0/0-7		38.3		4-7/7-4	33.3	
2-7/7-2			10.5			

[a] See Chapter 3, Table 3–24, for explanation of how this index is computed.

[b] The total number of Lachar and Wrobel (1979) critical items endorsed.

[c] Percentage of patients within this codetype scoring above the 75th percentile or below the 25th percentile on the total T score difference on the Wiener and Harmon Obvious and Subtle subscales for all patients (see Tables 3–45 and 3–46 for the cutting scores for the MMPI-2 and MMPI, respectively).

[d] Raw score.

TABLE D–48 Prototypic Scores for *7-8/8-7* Codetypes in Psychiatric Settings

		MMPI			MMPI-2	
Demographics						
		M	SD		M	SD
N	443			323		
Age		32.1	12.3		32.9	12.6
Men	75.8%			67.5%		
Women	24.2			32.5		
Test-Taking Scales/Indexes						
		M	SD		M	SD
Inconsistent		27.5%			20.2%	
Total (Obvious-Subtle)[a]		137.6	62.0		164.8	63.0
Critical items[b]		56.1	15.2		55.0	14.0
Overreported[c]		44.5%			70.3%	
Underreported[c]		1.9%			1.2%	
Standard Validity and Clinical Scales (K-Corrected)						
		M	SD		M	SD
?[d]		5.0	6.1		5.1	6.0
L		47.1	7.0		48.0	9.4
F		80.2	15.2		85.9	18.3
K		45.0	6.7		39.1	7.4
1(Hs)		70.5	14.4		67.7	12.5
2(D)		79.3	12.1		74.8	10.6
3(Hy)		68.8	11.0		64.7	13.0
4(Pd)		77.2	11.2		69.4	11.8
5(Mf)		60.5	11.6		52.2	10.5
6(Pa)		76.6	12.3		71.8	11.8
7(Pt)		90.8	10.5		86.7	10.4
8(Sc)		97.9	14.2		88.8	12.6
9(Ma)		70.6	10.5		63.0	11.4
0(Si)		67.6	8.8		67.5	9.7
Supplementary Scales						
		M	SD		M	SD
A		74.7	7.4		77.3	7.8
R		61.0	13.2		51.8	11.7
MAC/MAC-R[d]						
men		27.4	4.7		26.8	4.5
women		22.3	4.2		22.9	4.5
Codetype Concordance						
		Men	Women		Men	Women
MMPI-2 7-8/8-7		52.1%	71.6%	MMPI 7-8/8-7	81.9%	74.3%
6-8/8-6		23.8		2-8/8-2	10.4	
2-7/7-2			15.6	4-8/8-4		13.3

[a] See Chapter 3, Table 3–24, for explanation of how this index is computed.

[b] The total number of Lachar and Wrobel (1979) critical items endorsed.

[c] Percentage of patients within this codetype scoring above the 75th percentile or below the 25th percentile on the total T score difference on the Wiener and Harmon Obvious and Subtle subscales for all patients (see Tables 3–45 and 3–46 for the cutting scores for the MMPI-2 and MMPI, respectively).

[d] Raw score.

TABLE D–49   Prototypic Scores for *7-9/9-7* Codetypes in Psychiatric Settings

	MMPI			*MMPI-2*	
Demographics					
	M	SD		M	SD
N	36			46	
Age		36.8	12.3		34.9	14.9
Men	88.9%			73.9%	
Women	11.1			26.1	
Test-Taking Scales/Indexes					
	M	SD		M	SD
Inconsistent	8.8%			3.6%	
Total (Obvious-Subtle)[a]	67.9	53.1		94.6	54.4
Critical items[b]	38.5	11.8		40.0	11.4
Overreported[c]	6.3%			23.9%	
Underreported[c]	7.5%			4.4%	
Standard Validity and Clinical Scales (K-Corrected)					
	M	SD		M	SD
?[d]	4.5	5.5		4.4	5.7
L	45.5	6.3		46.6	8.4
F	62.3	9.0		65.3	13.6
K	45.4	6.8		39.0	6.7
1(Hs)	54.1	11.4		52.0	11.2
2(D)	64.0	10.2		59.1	9.0
3(Hy)	57.3	7.5		49.5	8.8
4(Pd)	69.3	6.4		61.0	8.0
5(Mf)	59.3	10.2		49.6	8.8
6(Pa)	62.7	7.5		57.7	9.2
7(Pt)	76.8	4.7		72.8	5.5
8(Sc)	67.4	8.5		63.9	9.3
9(Ma)	80.5	7.0		76.1	7.4
O(Si)	55.7	10.1		54.8	9.6
Supplementary Scales					
	M	SD		M	SD
A	67.4	8.6		69.5	7.9
R	49.8	9.8		43.0	7.2
MAC/MAC-R[d]					
men	29.4	3.7		29.4	3.5
women	25.3	7.2		24.7	3.9

Codetype Concordance						
		Men	Women		Men	Women
MMPI-2 *7-9/9-7*		66.7%	50.0%	MMPI *7-9/9-7*	64.7%	16.7%
Spike *9*		12.1		*7-8/8-7*	11.8	
				8-9/9-8		33.0
				Spike *9*		25.0

[a] See Chapter 3, Table 3–24, for explanation of how this index is computed.

[b] The total number of Lachar and Wrobel (1979) critical items endorsed.

[c] Percentage of patients within this codetype scoring above the 75th percentile or below the 25th percentile on the total T score difference on the Wiener and Harmon Obvious and Subtle subscales for all patients (see Tables 3–45 and 3–46 for the cutting scores for the MMPI-2 and MMPI, respectively).

[d] Raw score.

TABLE D–50   Prototypic Scores for *7-0/0-7* Codetypes in Psychiatric Settings

	MMPI				*MMPI-2*		
Demographics							
		M	*SD*			*M*	*SD*
N	17				57		
Age		34.3	12.0			36.1	14.1
Men	64.7%				77.2%		
Women	35.3				22.8		
Test-Taking Scales/Indexes							
		M	*SD*			*M*	*SD*
Inconsistent		0.0%				0.0%	
Total (Obvious-Subtle)[a]		75.8	48.9			106.3	49.6
Critical items[b]		34.1	8.8			34.8	10.2
Overreported[c]		13.2%				26.3%	
Underreported[c]		10.5%				1.8%	
Standard Validity and Clinical Scales (K-Corrected)							
		M	*SD*			*M*	*SD*
?[d]		2.1	3.1			3.6	4.9
L		48.9	7.0			49.0	7.9
F		62.1	6.6			61.8	11.8
K		47.5	8.5			40.2	8.6
1(Hs)		57.8	10.2			54.1	10.2
2(D)		70.4	6.8			67.0	7.1
3(Hy)		57.2	7.9			50.1	10.8
4(Pd)		66.0	6.6			60.0	7.7
5(Mf)		56.4	8.6			47.6	9.9
6(Pa)		60.6	7.0			55.7	8.9
7(Pt)		77.4	5.7			74.6	6.2
8(Sc)		69.5	6.1			61.7	7.6
9(Ma)		55.1	8.1			48.5	9.3
0(Si)		77.2	4.9			73.5	5.8
Supplementary Scales							
		M	*SD*			*M*	*SD*
A		67.6	8.8			72.8	9.1
R		71.8	13.0			57.9	11.0
MAC/MAC-R[d]							
men		25.0	4.6			26.3	4.7
women		19.7	2.0			19.6	2.7
Codetype Concordance							
		Men	Women			Men	Women
MMPI-2 *7-0/0-7*		54.5%	100.0%	MMPI *2-7/7-2*		26.0%	
Spike *0*		18.2		*4-7/7-4*		26.0	
				7-8/8-7		16.0	
				Spike *7*		12.0	
				7-0/0-7			42.9%
				8-0/0-8			14.3
				Spike *0*			14.3

[a] See Chapter 3, Table 3–24, for explanation of how this index is computed.

[b] The total number of Lachar and Wrobel (1979) critical items endorsed.

[c] Percentage of patients within this codetype scoring above the 75th percentile or below the 25th percentile on the total T score difference on the Wiener and Harmon Obvious and Subtle subscales for all patients (see Tables 3–45 and 3–46 for the cutting scores for the MMPI-2 and MMPI, respectively).

[d] Raw score.

TABLE D–51 Prototypic Scores for Spike *8* Codetypes in Psychiatric Settings

	MMPI				MMPI-2	
Demographics						
		M	*SD*			*M*	*SD*
N	54			41		
Age		35.6	15.4		35.3	15.7
Men	64.8%			53.7%		
Women	35.2			46.3		
Test-Taking Scales/Indexes						
		M	*SD*		*M*	*SD*
Inconsistent		0.0%			4.9%	
Total (Obvious-Subtle)[a]		15.9	62.1		33.4	62.2
Critical items[b]		27.4	11.5		26.5	10.5
Overreported[c]		5.6%			7.3%	
Underreported[c]		33.3%			26.8%	
Standard Validity and Clinical Scales (K-Corrected)						
		M	*SD*		*M*	*SD*
?[d]		4.9	6.1		4.5	5.9
L		54.0	9.6		58.4	12.1
F		62.1	8.2		66.3	14.9
K		53.5	10.7		49.3	11.4
1(Hs)		56.6	6.7		51.8	6.6
2(D)		58.1	5.7		54.7	5.9
3(Hy)		56.0	7.2		49.3	8.6
4(Pd)		61.5	7.6		55.3	7.0
5(Mf)		55.6	8.1		48.9	8.2
6(Pa)		59.7	6.0		55.5	7.2
7(Pt)		59.9	5.8		55.8	6.2
8(Sc)		73.7	4.3		67.7	4.0
9(Ma)		61.3	6.1		54.7	5.9
0(Si)		55.6	8.2		52.2	6.2
Supplementary Scales						
		M	*SD*		*M*	*SD*
A		54.4	10.0		55.3	8.9
R		61.5	10.9		51.3	11.8
MAC/MAC-R[d]						
men		25.0	5.5		26.5	4.6
women		20.8	2.7		21.9	3.9

Codetype Concordance

	Men	Women		Men	Women
MMPI-2 Spike *8*	66.7%	46.4%	MMPI Spike *8*	36.4	46.4
Spike *0*	16.7		*4-8/8-4*	36.4	
1-8/8-1		14.3	*8-9/9-8*	13.6	
8-0/0-8		10.7	*8-0/0-8*		10.7

[a] See Chapter 3, Table 3–24, for explanation of how this index is computed.

[b] The total number of Lachar and Wrobel (1979) critical items endorsed.

[c] Percentage of patients within this codetype scoring above the 75th percentile or below the 25th percentile on the total T score difference on the Wiener and Harmon Obvious and Subtle subscales for all patients (see Tables 3–45 and 3–46 for the cutting scores for the MMPI-2 and MMPI, respectively).

[d] Raw score.

TABLE D–52 Prototypic Scores for *8-9/9-8* Codetypes in Psychiatric Settings

		MMPI			MMPI-2	
Demographics						
		M	*SD*		*M*	*SD*
N	305			210		
Age		31.3	12.7		30.5	11.8
Men	71.1%			69.5%		
Women	28.9			30.5		
Test-Taking Scales/Indexes						
		M	*SD*		*M*	*SD*
Inconsistent		32.8%			22.9%	
Total (Obvious-Subtle)[a]		92.1	63.5		121.5	63.5
Critical items[b]		49.2	14.8		49.8	13.8
Overreported[c]		18.7%			45.8%	
Underreported[c]		6.3%			2.8%	
Standard Validity and Clinical Scales (K-Corrected)						
		M	*SD*		*M*	*SD*
?[d]		4.7	5.8		4.6	5.9
L		47.7	8.2		48.2	11.2
F		78.6	14.4		86.6	18.8
K		45.1	8.4		39.5	8.4
1(Hs)		61.4	12.3		59.8	11.9
2(D)		58.6	11.6		55.9	11.3
3(Hy)		58.3	10.6		52.8	12.7
4(Pd)		71.0	10.1		64.0	11.1
5(Mf)		59.3	9.8		51.7	10.4
6(Pa)		71.1	10.7		67.1	12.6
7(Pt)		69.7	10.0		65.9	10.1
8(Sc)		87.4	12.0		80.7	10.8
9(Ma)		86.9	8.5		84.4	10.9
0(Si)		54.6	9.0		52.9	9.0
Supplementary Scales						
		M	*SD*		*M*	*SD*
A		64.7	10.3		67.4	10.3
R		48.4	12.9		40.3	10.9
MAC/MAC-R[d]						
men		31.0	4.5		30.6	4.2
women		27.4	4.9		27.7	4.6
Codetype Concordance						
		Men	Women		Men	Women
MMPI-2 *8-9/9-8*		57.9%	63.3%	MMPI *8-9/9-8*	83.9%	87.7%
6-9/9-6		17.6	11.1			

[a] See Chapter 3, Table 3–24, for explanation of how this index is computed.

[b] The total number of Lachar and Wrobel (1979) critical items endorsed.

[c] Percentage of patients within this codetype scoring above the 75th percentile or below the 25th percentile on the total T score difference on the Wiener and Harmon Obvious and Subtle subscales for all patients (see Tables 3–45 and 3–46 for the cutting scores for the MMPI-2 and MMPI, respectively).

[d] Raw score.

TABLE D–53 Prototypic Scores for *8-0/0-8* Codetypes in Psychiatric Settings

	MMPI			MMPI-2	
Demographics					
	M	*SD*		*M*	*SD*
N	24		36		
Age		30.9	12.5		33.6	11.2
Men	29.2%			58.3%	
Women	70.8			41.7	
Test-Taking Scales/Indexes					
	M	*SD*		*M*	*SD*
Inconsistent	6.3%			4.9%	
Total (Obvious-Subtle)[a]	110.6	41.4		142.4	45.7
Critical items[b]	43.2	10.1		44.5	10.9
Overreported[c]	25.0%			64.9%	
Underreported[c]	8.3%			0.0%	
Standard Validity and Clinical Scales (K-Corrected)					
	M	*SD*		*M*	*SD*
?[d]	5.9	7.1		5.3	5.7
L	47.9	6.0		49.0	10.3
F	71.5	11.8		78.5	16.7
K	42.1	5.1		36.1	6.2
1(Hs)	56.9	10.1		54.7	10.2
2(D)	67.5	8.5		64.8	11.4
3(Hy)	55.9	8.6		49.5	10.1
4(Pd)	66.8	9.2		60.5	10.2
5(Mf)	52.6	8.4		50.7	9.5
6(Pa)	65.5	7.9		60.9	11.5
7(Pt)	70.0	8.9		66.5	10.5
8(Sc)	82.2	9.0		77.9	10.4
9(Ma)	59.7	7.9		54.6	8.9
0(Si)	78.2	5.2		75.9	7.2
Supplementary Scales					
	M	*SD*		*M*	*SD*
A	70.6	7.8		73.6	9.2
R	68.6	9.5		55.0	9.5
MAC/MAC-R[d]					
men	22.1	4.2		24.3	4.3
women	20.5	3.3		21.1	3.4
Codetype Concordance					
	Men	Women		Men	Women
MMPI-2 *8-0/0-8*	71.4%	64.7%	MMPI *2-8/8-2*	28.6%	
Spike *0*	28.6		*8-0/0-8*	23.8	61.1%
			4-8/8-4	19.0	
			Spike *8*		16.7

[a] See Chapter 3, Table 3–24, for explanation of how this index is computed.

[b] The total number of Lachar and Wrobel (1979) critical items endorsed.

[c] Percentage of patients within this codetype scoring above the 75th percentile or below the 25th percentile on the total T score difference on the Wiener and Harmon Obvious and Subtle subscales for all patients (see Tables 3–45 and 3–46 for the cutting scores for the MMPI-2 and MMPI, respectively).

[d] Raw score.

TABLE D–54 Prototypic Scores for Spike *9* Codetypes in Psychiatric Settings

		MMPI			MMPI-2	
Demographics						
		M	SD		M	SD
N	347			348		
Age		34.3	13.8		33.3	13.4
Men	73.2%			76.4%		
Women	26.8			23.6		
Test-Taking Scales/Indexes						
		M	SD		M	SD
Inconsistent		0.0%			1.8%	
Total (Obvious-Subtle)[a]		12.6	48.2		34.7	50.0
Critical items[b]		25.7	8.6		26.6	8.4
Overreported[c]		0.9%			2.9%	
Underreported[c]		38.9%			23.1%	
Standard Validity and Clinical Scales (K-Corrected)						
		M	SD		M	SD
?[d]		4.2	5.2		3.4	4.9
L		49.4	7.3		51.3	9.9
F		58.4	7.5		57.6	10.6
K		48.9	7.4		43.2	8.0
1(Hs)		49.3	7.6		46.0	8.5
2(D)		49.7	8.4		46.0	8.2
3(Hy)		51.1	7.3		43.6	7.6
4(Pd)		61.0	6.3		53.9	7.1
5(Mf)		53.6	8.7		45.8	9.0
6(Pa)		55.3	7.5		49.9	8.5
7(Pt)		53.6	7.1		47.9	7.5
8(Sc)		56.6	7.1		50.9	7.3
9(Ma)		75.5	5.8		72.1	6.6
0(Si)		47.3	7.6		44.4	8.0
Supplementary Scales						
		M	SD		M	SD
A		52.6	9.0		54.9	9.5
R		50.2	10.3		40.6	8.6
MAC/MAC-R[d]						
men		30.0	3.8		30.2	3.8
women		26.4	3.4		26.6	3.6
Codetype Concordance						
		Men	Women		Men	Women
MMPI-2 Spike *9*		92.1%	70.7%	MMPI Spike *9*	63.7%	70.7%
				3-9/9-3	21.5	

[a] See Chapter 3, Table 3–24, for explanation of how this index is computed.

[b] The total number of Lachar and Wrobel (1979) critical items endorsed.

[c] Percentage of patients within this codetype scoring above the 75th percentile or below the 25th percentile on the total T score difference on the Wiener and Harmon Obvious and Subtle subscales for all patients (see Tables 3–45 and 3–46 for the cutting scores for the MMPI-2 and MMPI, respectively).

[d] Raw score.

TABLE D-55 Prototypic Scores for *9-0/0-9* Codetypes in Psychiatric Settings

	MMPI				MMPI-2	
Demographics						
	M	*SD*			*M*	*SD*
N	3			7		
Age	43.0	16.5			38.1	13.5
Men	66.7%			100.0%		
Women	33.3			0.0		
Test-Taking Scales/Indexes						
	M	*SD*			*M*	*SD*
Inconsistent	5.3%				10.0%	
Total (Obvious-Subtle)[a]	71.3	29.7			104.7	48.3
Critical items[b]	32.8	8.4			35.7	5.4
Overreported[c]	0.0%				14.3%	
Underreported[c]	15.8%				0.0%	
Standard Validity and Clinical Scales (K-Corrected)						
	M	*SD*			*M*	*SD*
?[d]	1.0	1.7			2.6	3.6
L	43.3	3.1			46.4	4.9
F	62.0	10.1			73.4	6.3
K	41.0	8.7			35.3	5.7
1(Hs)	46.3	8.7			48.0	9.8
2(D)	58.3	12.7			58.3	9.2
3(Hy)	47.3	10.6			43.6	7.3
4(Pd)	60.0	7.0			56.7	9.5
5(Mf)	52.3	11.0			48.9	10.8
6(Pa)	59.0	6.0			58.6	6.2
7(Pt)	60.3	8.5			53.4	7.2
8(Sc)	61.3	7.2			57.1	8.7
9(Ma)	72.7	2.5			68.6	3.9
0(Si)	71.3	1.2			68.9	2.5
Supplementary Scales						
	M	*SD*			*M*	*SD*
A	66.3	8.6			68.3	8.0
R	62.3	5.1			51.1	5.8
MAC/MAC-R[d]						
men	26.5	.7			28.0	3.2
women	28.0	-			-.-	-.-

Codetype Concordance

	Men	Women		Men	Women
MMPI-2 *9-0/0-9*	50.0%	100.0%	MMPI Spike *9*	68.4%	100.0%
Spike *0*	50.0				

[a] See Chapter 3, Table 3–24, for explanation of how this index is computed.

[b] The total number of Lachar and Wrobel (1979) critical items endorsed.

[c] Percentage of patients within this codetype scoring above the 75th percentile or below the 25th percentile on the total T score difference on the Wiener and Harmon Obvious and Subtle subscales for all patients (see Tables 3–45 and 3–46 for the cutting scores for the MMPI-2 and MMPI, respectively).

[d] Raw score.

TABLE D–56   Prototypic Scores for Spike *0* Codetypes in Psychiatric Settings

		MMPI			MMPI-2	
Demographics						
		M	*SD*		*M*	*SD*
N	54			123		
Age		40.5	14.0		39.6	14.3
Men	33.3%			78.0%		
Women	66.7			22.0		
Test-Taking Scales/Indexes						
		M	*SD*		*M*	*SD*
Inconsistent		0.0%			4.4%	
Total (Obvious-Subtle)[a]		30.3	43.1		62.4	44.0
Critical items[b]		23.9	7.6		23.9	7.8
Overreported[c]		1.9%			4.0%	
Underreported[c]		20.4%			5.7%	
Standard Validity and Clinical Scales (K-Corrected)						
		M	*SD*		*M*	*SD*
?[d]		5.2	4.8		4.6	5.3
L		51.8	7.3		53.6	9.3
F		56.5	7.2		55.0	9.7
K		46.9	6.9		39.5	7.4
1(Hs)		49.5	8.2		46.2	8.6
2(D)		61.7	7.2		57.7	5.9
3(Hy)		52.1	8.0		42.3	6.4
4(Pd)		58.6	7.6		51.5	7.6
5(Mf)		51.0	8.1		45.0	7.3
6(Pa)		56.5	6.9		50.0	8.4
7(Pt)		57.8	6.0		50.3	7.2
8(Sc)		53.4	8.9		46.1	8.4
9(Ma)		50.6	10.0		45.4	7.2
0(Si)		72.5	2.5		68.7	3.5
Supplementary Scales						
		M	*SD*		*M*	*SD*
A		57.7	7.8		60.6	8.9
R		71.4	11.5		55.4	8.8
MAC/MAC-R[d]						
men		24.7	5.6		25.4	4.7
women		19.7	3.6		21.3	3.3

Codetype Concordance

	Men	Women		Men	Women
MMPI-2 Spike *0*	100.0%	50.0%	MMPI Spike *0*	48.5%	92.6%
2-0/0-2		22.0	Spike *2*	10.3	
			Spike *4*	10.3	

[a] See Chapter 3, Table 3–24, for explanation of how this index is computed.

[b] The total number of Lachar and Wrobel (1979) critical items endorsed.

[c] Percentage of patients within this codetype scoring above the 75th percentile or below the 25th percentile on the total T score difference on the Wiener and Harmon Obvious and Subtle subscales for all patients (see Tables 3–45 and 3–46 for the cutting scores for the MMPI-2 and MMPI, respectively).

[d] Raw score.

MMPI-2: Item Overlap among MMPI-2 Scales

Item	True	False
1		Mfm Mff R OH GF
2	Es	Hs D Hy Mt PK
3	VRIN TRIN	Hs Hy Pt Mt PK PS DEP
4	Mfm Mff	GM
5	D	
6	VRIN	F Sc VRIN
7	MAC-R	Hy R Re
8	GM	Hs Hy VRIN
9		D Hy Pd Pt Sc Mt PK PS DEP TRIN
10		Hs D Hy R Mt WRK
11	Hy Pt HEA	
12	TRIN	F Pd Sc
13	Ma	
14		Hy R
15	D Ma Mt ANX WRK	OH
16	Pa Pt Sc Mt PK	L
17	Pd Pa Sc PK PS WRK	
18	F Hs D Hy HEA	
19		Mfm Mff
20	GM	Hs D Mt HEA
21	Pd Sc Ma PS FAM	
22	Pd Pa Sc PK PS TRT	
23	Pa Pt Sc Ma PK	Es GM
24	F Pa MAC-R BIZ	
25	Mfm Mff	Si
26	ASP	Hy Mfm Mff
27	TPA	Mfm Mff Re GF
28	Hs Mt HEA VRIN	
29	ANG	L K D Hy OH Re
30	F PK ANX	
31	D Hy Pd Pt Sc Si A Mt PK PS ANX WRK VRIN	Es Do
32	Pd Sc PK PS BIZ VRIN	Si Es Re
33	Es	D Pt HEA
34		Pd Sc
35	Pd Sc ASP	
36	F MAC-R HEA	Es
37	PK PS ANG	K D R
38	D Pt Sc A Mt PS DEP	
39	Hs D Hy PK ANX VRIN TRIN	Es
40	Hy HEA VRIN TRIN	
41		L
42	F Pd Pa Sc	
43		D Mt
44	Hy Sc PS HEA	GM
45	Es	Hs D Hy R PS HEA
46	D Sc SOD VRIN	
47		Hs Hy HEA
48	F Sc PK PS VRIN TRIN	
49	MAC-R VRIN	D Si PK SOD
50	Ma CYN	
51		L
52	Pd MAC-R PK DEP	Do

Item	True	False
53	Hs HEA	Es
54	F Pd FAM WRK	
55	Ma Do OBS	D
56	D Pd Pt Si A PK PS DEP	VRIN TRIN
57		Hs HEA
58	CYN	K Hy
59	Hs PK PS HEA	VRIN
60	F BIZ	Es
61	Ma	LSE
62	Mfm Mff GF	
63	TRIN	Mfm Mff GF
64	Mfm Mff	GM
65	Hy Pt Sc A PK PS DEP TRIN	TRIN
66	F ASP	
67	Mfm Mff OH GF	
68		D Mfm Mff GF
69	MAC-R	Mfm Mff R OH
70	Si LSE	Pd Do Es GM
71	Pd Mt DEP	
72	F MAC-R	
73	D Pt Mt LSE WRK VRIN TRIN	MAC-R Do GM
74	Mfm Mff	GM
75		D PK PS DEP
76	CYN	K D Hy Mfm Mff
77		L OH
78		F LSE
79	OH	Pd Si GF
80	Mfm Mff	GM
81	Mt CYN ASP VRIN	Hy Pa VRIN
82	Pd Pt A MAC-R Mt PK DEP	Es Do
83	K VRIN TRIN	Pd FAM
84	F MAC-R ASP VRIN	Re GF
85	Sc Ma PK PS	
86	VRIN	Mfm Mff Si SOD
87	Ma OBS	Es
88		Ma
89	Pd Pt	OH
90	VRIN	F Sc VRIN
91		Hs Hy Sc HEA
92	D Sc PK DEP TRT	
93		L Ma
94	Pd Pt PK PS	
95	TRIN	D Hy Pd Pa Mt PK PS DEP VRIN TRIN
96	F BIZ	
97	Hs HEA	
98	Ma Es WRK	Hy Pa OH
99	Pd Pa TRIN	VRIN
100	Si Re	Pa Ma GM
101	Hs Hy PK HEA	
102		L F
103	MAC-R VRIN	Mfm Mff Re
104	Si CYN ASP	Mfm Mff Pa

Item	True	False
105	Pd MAC-R ASP	Re GF VRIN
106		Sc Ma Si
107		L Mfm Mff Ma MAC-R
108		F WRK
109		D Pt LSE
110	Si Mt CYN ASP VRIN	K Hy Pa VRIN
111	Hs HEA	
112	Mfm Mff	Si R
113	Pd Pa Ma MAC-R	
114	F	
115	MAC-R	Hy FRS
116	PS ANG VRIN	K Hy OH
117	D	Hs MAC-R OH HEA
118		D R HEA
119	Mfm Mff GF	Es
120		F Mfm Mff R
121	Mff GF	Mfm
122	Mfm Mff Ma	K Pd
123	ASP	L GF
124	CYN	Hy
125	VRIN TRIN	Hy Pd PK FAM VRIN TRIN
126		F
127	D Si A TRIN	K
128	Mfm Mff MAC-R GF	R Es
129		Hy Pd OH
130	D Pt Mt DEP LSE	K
131	Ma	Si Mt
132		F Mfm Mff
133		Mfm Mff GF
134	ANG	D R
135	Si A PK PS OBS WRK	Hy VRIN
136	TPA VRIN	K Ma VRIN
137	Mfm Mff	MAC-R GM
138	F Pa Sc BIZ VRIN	
139		L
140		D Pt Mt PK ANX TRIN
141	Es	Hs D Hy PS HEA
142		D R HEA
143	GM	Hs D Pd
144	F Pa	
145	Pa Sc Ma PS FAM	Re
146	D Pa DEP	GM
147	D Pt Sc	
148		K D Hy Mt
149	Hs HEA	
150	F PK PS	
151	TPA	Hy
152	GM	Hs Hy Mt VRIN TRIN
153		L OH
154	FRS	Ma
155	Ma	GF
156	F	

Item	True	False
157		K Hy Pd
158	Si SOD	K Pd Ma
159	Es GM	Hy HEA
160	Re	Pd MAC-R
161	Si VRIN	Hy VRIN
162	F Pa BIZ	
163	GM	Mfm Mff FRS
164		Hs Hy Re HEA
165		D Pt Sc PS VRIN TRIN
166	Hy Mfm Sc VRIN TRIN	Mff MAC-R VRIN
167	Si SOD VRIN	K Hy Pd Ma VRIN
168	F Sc Ma MAC-R PK PS	R
169	Ma Es	OH Re
170	D Pt Sc PK PS ANX	
171		K Pd OH
172	Hy MAC-R	Do
173		Hs Hy
174		F Pt
175	Hs D Hy Pt HEA	Es
176	GM VRIN TRIN	Hs Hy HEA
177	Mfm Mff Es	Sc
178		D R
179	Es	Hs Hy Sc HEA
180	F Sc PS	
181	D	Si HEA
182	Sc Ma	
183		L
184	VRIN TRIN	Mfm Mff
185	Si SOD VRIN	Hy Pd VRIN
186		F FRS
187	Mfm Mff	GM
188		D
189	Es	D Si R
190	Sc Ma FAM	
191	Mfm Mff	
192		F Sc
193		Hy Mfm Mff
194		Mfm Mff HEA
195	Pd FAM VRIN TRIN	VRIN TRIN
196	Mfm Mff Pt PK ANX OBS	K Es VRIN TRIN
197		Mfm Mff R GF
198	F BIZ	
199	Es Re GM VRIN	Mfm Mff R VRIN
200	Ma	
201		Mfm Mff Do Re GF
202	Pd MAC-R	Do Re
203		L GF
204		F HEA
205	Mfm Mff Ma FAM	
206	Ma	
207	OH Do	Mfm Mff Si
208		Hs Hy PS ANX

Item	True	False
209	Mfm Es TRIN	Pd Mff Si
210		F Sc
211	Ma	
212	Ma TPA	D
213	Es	K Hy
214	MAC-R GM	Pd
215	D Si A Mt DEP	Es
216	F	
217		Pd FAM
218	Hy Pt Sc Ma Mt PS	
219	Pd Mfm Mff	
220	Ma	Do GF
221	Sc PK PS	D Es
222		F
223		D Mt PS ANX
224	MAC-R	Hs Hy HEA
225	Pd CYN	Es
226	VRIN	D Pd
227	Ma ASP	Do
228	F BIZ	
229	Sc Ma MAC-R	Es
230	Hy Es	
231		Mfm Mff Si GF
232	Do	L
233	D Sc A Mt WRK	
234	F Pa Sc DEP	
235	LSE	Mfm Mff Re
236	Mfm Mff	Es
237	GM	Mfm Mff Si
238	Ma MAC-R	D GF
239	TRIN	Mfm Mff GF
240	F ASP	
241	CYN	Hy
242	Pt Sc Ma	
243	Si A WRK	K Hy Pd Ma Do
244	Ma	Pa Do
245	Do Es	D
246	F DEP	Es
247	Hs Sc HEA	
248	Ma ASP	D R
249		Hs Hy HEA
250	Ma ASP	GF
251	Mfm Mff Si A	MAC-R
252	F Sc	
253	Ma	Hy
254	CYN ASP	Mfm Mff
255		Hs Pa Sc Si R HEA
256	Mfm Mff Sc FAM	R
257	MAC-R	Mfm Mff GF
258	F	
259	Pd Pa BIZ	VRIN
260		L D

Item	True	False
261		Pd
262		Si SOD VRIN TRIN
263	GF	Hy Pd Ma
264	F Pd	GF
265	Si SOD	Hy VRIN TRIN
266	Re GF	Pd Pa MAC-R ASP
267		K D Pd Si VRIN
268	Mfm Sc VRIN	Mff VRIN
269	Ma Mt ASP	
270	F	
271	Mfm Mff Pa	
272		Mfm Mff GF
273	Pt Sc A Mt PS ANX	
274	Sc PK PS TRT	
275	Pt Si SOD	Do Re VRIN TRIN
276		F Sc
277	Pa Pt Sc A PK PS DEP	
278		Sc
279	Sc	
280	MAC-R	Sc Si PS SOD VRIN
281	Sc Fb SOD	
282	F	
283	CYN ASP	Pa
284	Si CYN ASP VRIN	K Pa VRIN
285	Pa Pt	
286	OH CYN	Pa
287	Sc	MAC-R GF
288	F Pd VRIN TRIN	
289	Pt Si A	GM
290	ANX VRIN	K Sc VRIN
291	Sc Fb	
292	Sc FAM	
293		Pt OH
294	F	
295		Sc HEA
296	Sc Si	
297		Pa R
298	Sc BIZ	
299	Sc Mt PS ANX WRK	MAC-R VRIN
300	F FAM	
301	Pt A PS ANX	
302	Pt Si Mt PK ANG TPA WRK	
303	Sc Fb PK DEP	
304	Pt PS	
305	Pa OH PK PS ANX	
306	F DEP TRT	
307	Pa Sc	Es
308	Pt Si	
309	Pt A OBS	Do
310	Pt A	Es
311	Sc A Fb PS BIZ	
312	F	

Item	True	False
313	Pt OBS	
314	TRIN	Pa
315	CYN	Pa
316	Pt Sc PK PS BIZ VRIN	Es
317	Pt Fb FRS	
318		F WRK
319	Sc Fb PK PS BIZ	
320	Pt Sc	
321	GM	Pt Si SOD
322	Sc Fb FRS	
323	Sc Es Fb FAM	
324	F	
325	Pt Sc A Mt PS	MAC-R Do
326	Pt Si LSE	
327	Pt PK OBS	
328	Pt A PK PS OBS	Si Es
329	Pt Sc Fb FRS	
330		F K D R
331	Pt Mt GM DEP	
332	Sc Fb	
333	Pa Sc Fb BIZ VRIN	
334	Pa Fb FRS	
335		Si
336	F Pa BIZ	
337	Si SOD	
338	Si A	K
339	A Mt PK ANX WRK	K VRIN
340		Si SOD
341	A	K
342	MAC-R	Si
343		F Sc
344	MAC-R	Si OH VRIN
345		Si
346	CYN	K R
347	Si A PK	
348	Si	K
349	F PK SOD VRIN	VRIN
350	GM	Si R VRIN
351	Si TRIN	GM
352	Si CYN	
353	GF VRIN	Si R SOD VRIN
354		Si R
355	F Pa Sc BIZ	
356		K
357	Si Mt	
358	CYN TPA	Si Re
359	TRIN	Si R SOD VRIN TRIN
360		Si SOD TRIN
361	F Pa BIZ	
362		Si
363		Si R SOD
364	Si WRK TRT	GM VRIN

Item	True	False
365		K R
366		Si
367	Si PK SOD TRIN	TRIN
368	Si WRK TRT	
369	Si LSE	VRIN
370	VRIN	Si SOD VRIN
371		
372	VRIN	PS VRIN
373	TRT	
374	CYN ASP VRIN	VRIN
375	TRT	
376	LSE TRT	
377	PS DEP TRT TRIN	VRIN
378	FAM	
379	FAM	
380	LSE VRIN	
381		
382	FAM	
383		Fb FAM
384	GF	
385	Es GM	FRS
386	Do PS	
387	Fb	MAC-R
388	GM VRIN	A DEP
389	ANG	
390	A	OH
391	A TRT	Es
392	FRS	GM
393		
394	A OBS WRK VRIN	Es
395	Fb FRS VRIN	GM VRIN
396	VRIN	VRIN
397	FRS	
398	OH	
399	DEP CYN TRT	Do
400	A PS DEP	OH
401	GM	FRS
402		
403	CYN VRIN	VRIN
404		Fb HEA
405	VRIN	Mt PS ANX VRIN
406	Es	GF
407	MAC-R Fb	
408	A Mt ANX	
409	WRK	
410	ANG	
411	A Mt DEP LSE VRIN	VRIN
412	MAC-R ASP	Do Re
413	Es FAM	
414	MAC-R ANG TPA	
415	A ANX VRIN	
416	Do	

Item	True	False
417		Re GF
418	ASP	Re
419	ASP TPA	
420	TPA	OH
421	A LSE VRIN	
422	MAC-R	R
423	TPA	R
424		
425	Es	
426	GF	
427		BIZ
428	A WRK	
429		
430	ANG TPA	R Re VRIN
431	Fb	Re
432		R Re
433		OH
434	MAC-R	
435	FRS VRIN	GM VRIN
436		
437	TPA	
438	FRS	GM
439	MAC-R	
440	Re GM	OH
441	FRS	Es GM
442	A OBS	
443		
444		
445	MAC-R CYN WRK	
446		
447	FRS	Es
448	A	
449	Mt GF FAM	R
450	Fb LSE	
451	A	
452		
453		FRS
454	Fb DEP	
455		FAM
456	MAC-R GF	R Re
457	LSE	
458	FRS	Es
459		
460		OH
461	ANG	
462	GM	FRS
463	Fb PS ANX	
464	A Mt PS WRK	Es VRIN TRIN
465		R GF
466	BIZ	
467	Re GM VRIN	VRIN
468	Fb FRS	Re

Item	True	False
469	A Mt PS ANX	Es GM
470	CYN	Do Re
471	OH PS FRS	Es GM
472	Mt VRIN	VRIN
473	MAC-R GF	Do
474	GM	
475	PS LSE	
476	Fb LSE	
477		GF
478	Fb FAM	
479	PS SOD	
480	SOD	
481		
482	OBS TRT VRIN	
483	LSE	
484	Fb	
485	LSE VRIN	VRIN
486	ANG	
487		GF
488	TRT	
489	Fb	
490	BIZ	
491	OBS WRK TRT VRIN	
492		
493		TRT
494		TRT
495	TRT	
496		ANX
497	OBS TRT	
498		GM
499	TRT	
500	TRT	
501		Fb TRT
502	MAC-R	
503	LSE	
504	LSE TRT	
505	WRK	
506	MAC-R Fb DEP VRIN	VRIN
507	TPA VRIN	VRIN
508	BIZ	
509	ANX OBS WRK	GM VRIN
510	TPA	GF
511		GF
512	DEP	
513	ANG VRIN	
514		
515	PS SOD VRIN	VRIN
516	Fb PS DEP	
517	Fb WRK	
518		
519	LSE	GM
520	Fb DEP VRIN	VRIN

Item	True	False
521	VRIN	WRK
522		
523	TPA	
524	Fb	
525	Fb WRK	
526	Fb LSE	
527		
528	Fb TRT	
529		
530	Fb	
531	TPA	
532		GM
533	VRIN	VRIN
534	TRIN	
535	TPA	
536		GM
537		GF
538	CYN	
539	Fb DEP TRT	
540	Fb ANG	
541	TPA	
542	ANG	VRIN
543	BIZ FAM	
544	Fb	
545	TPA WRK	
546	DEP	
547	OBS	
548	ANG	GF
549	MAC-R	
550	FAM	GF
551	BIZ	
552	GF	
553	OBS	
554	DEP WRK TRT VRIN	
555	Fb FRS	
556	ANX VRIN TRIN	VRIN
557		
558		
559	WRK	
560	TRIN	
561		WRK
562	LSE	VRIN
563	FAM	
564		PS ANG
565	PS	VRIN TRIN
566	WRK	
567	FAM	

MMPI-2 to MMPI Conversion Tables

TABLE F–1 Conversion from MMPI Group Form to MMPI-2*

1-1	51-45	101-88	151-162	201-185	251-229	301-273
2-2	52-46	102-89	152-140	202-234	252-306	302-34
3-3	53-	103-91	153-141	203-187	253-230	303-274
4-4	54-78	104-92	154-142	204-191	254-231	304-275
5-5	55-47	105-93	155-143	205-240	255-232	305-277
6-7	56-84	106-94	156-168	206-	256-312	306-278
7-8	57-49	107-95	157-145	207-188	257-318	307-279
8-9	58-	108-97	158-146	208-189	258-	308-21
9-10	59-50	109-98	159-147	209-246	259-233	309-280
10-11	60-51	110-99	160-148	210-252	260-235	310-12
11-13	61-52	111-100	161-149	211-258	261-236	311-35
12-14	62-53	112-120	162-151	212-190	262-237	312-281
13-15	63-	113-126	163-152	213-193	263-238	313-283
14-	64-55	114-101	164-174	214-194	264-239	314-16
15-16	65-90	115-132	165-153	215-264	265-241	315-17
16-17	66-96	116-103	166-154	216-195	266-242	316-284
17-6	67-56	117-104	167-155	217-196	267-243	317-285
18-20	68-57	118-105	168-180	218-270	268-244	318-9
19-19	69-	119-106	169-186	219-197	269-324	319-286
20-12	70-	120-107	170-157	220-276	270-245	320-287
21-21	71-58	121-138	171-158	221-199	271-248	321-289
22-23	72-59	122-109	172-161	222-200	272-330	322-290
23-18	73-61	123-144	173-160	223-201	273-247	323-32
24-22	74-62	124-110	174-159	224-202	274-249	324-291
25-25	75-102	125-111	175-164	225-203	275-336	325-292
26-26	76-65	126-112	176-163	226-205	276-343	326-23
27-24	77-64	127-113	177-192	227-282	277-250	327-297
28-27	78-67	128-115	178-165	228-206	278-251	328-31
29-28	79-63	129-116	179-166	229-207	279-253	329-293
30-29	80-68	130-117	180-167	230-208	280-254	330-295
31-30	81-69	131-118	181-169	231-209	281-255	331-42
32-31	82-70	132-119	182-170	232-211	282-256	332-296
33-32	83-108	133-121	183-171	233-212	283-257	333-22
34-36	84-71	134-122	184-198	234-213	284-259	334-298
35-42	85-114	135-123	185-204	235-214	285-260	335-299
36-33	86-73	136-124	186-172	236-215	286-349	336-302
37-34	87-74	137-125	187-177	237-217	287-261	337-301
38-35	88-75	138-127	188-173	238-218	288-18	338-305
39-37	89-76	139-150	189-175	239-219	289-263	339-303
40-48	90-77	140-128	190-176	240-220	290-15	340-304
41-38	91-79	141-129	191-178	241-221	291-355	341-307
42-54	92-80	142-130	192-179	242-223	292-265	342-308
43-39	93-81	143-131	193-181	243-224	293-361	343-309
44-40	94-82	144-133	194-182	244-225	294-266	344-310
45-41	95-	145-134	195-183	245-288	295-	345-311
46-43	96-83	146-156	196-210	246-294	296-267	346-313
47-44	97-85	147-135	197-216	247-300	297-268	347-314
48-60	98-	148-136	198-184	248-226	298-269	348-315
49-66	99-86	149-137	199-222	249-	299-271	349-316
50-72	100-87	150-139	200-228	250-227	300-272	350-319

TABLE F–1   *continued*

351-317	382-390	413-407	444-	475-433	506-444	537-
352-320	383-338	414-408	445-422	476-	507-445	538-
353-321	384-391	415-350	446-344	477-434	508-	539-462
354-322	385-392	416-409	447-423	478-	509-446	540-
355-323	386-393	417-410	448-424	479-360	510-447	541-
356-325	387-	418-411	449-353	480-435	511-448	542-
357-326	388-395	419-412	450-359	481-362	512-	543-463
358-327	389-394	420-	451-363	482-342	513-	544-464
359-328	390-396	421-413	452-	483-	514-	545-
360-329	391-340	422-	453-	484-	515-	546-
361-331	392-397	423-	454-	485-436	516-449	547-370
362-285	393-	424-	455-357	486-	517-450	548-
363-332	394-398	425-	456-	487-364	518-451	549-368
364-333	395-399	426-414	457-	488-	519-	550-465
365-334	396-400	427-351	458-425	489-	520-452	551-466
366-277	397-339	428-	459-	490-	521-262	552-467
367-385	398-348	429-	460-	491-	522-453	553-468
368-386	399-372	430-	461-356	492-438	523-	554-
369-	400-345	431-415	462-	493-	524-	555-469
370-	401-401	432-416	463-426	494-441	525-458	556-
371-335	402-402	433-	464-427	495-437	526-454	557-
372-	403-	434-417	465-428	496-	527-455	558-470
373-	404-403	435-	466-429	497-	528-	559-471
374-341	405-404	436-352	467-	498-	529-456	560-472
375-	406-346	437-418	468-430	499-442	530-	561-
376-	407-405	438-419	469-358	500-439	531-457	562-473
377-337	408-	439-420	470-	501-440	532-459	563-474
378-	409-	440-354	471-431	502-365	533-	564-369
379-388	410-406	441-	472-432	503-	534-460	565-
380-	411-347	442-	473-367	504-443	535-	566-
381-389	412-	443-421	474-	505-366	536-461	

*Missing numbers represent items from the original MMPI not included in the MMPI-2 booklet. The 16 items duplicated in the original MMPI are not duplicated in MMPI-2; hence they occur in only one location in MMPI-2 (e.g., items 8 and 318 are now equivalent to item 9).

TABLE F–2 Conversion from MMPI-2 to MMPI Group Form*

1-1	65-76	129-141	193-213	257-283	321-353	385-367
2-2	66-49	130-142	194-214	258-211	322-354	386-368
3-3	67-78	131-143	195-216	259-284	323-355	387-
4-4	68-80	132-115	196-217	260-285	324-269	388-379
5-5	69-81	133-144	197-219	261-287	325-356	389-381
6-17	70-82	134-145	198-184	262-521	326-357	390-382
7-6	71-84	135-147	199-221	263-289	327-358	391-384
8-7	72-50	136-148	200-222	264-215	328-359	392-385
9-8,318	73-86	137-149	201-223	265-292	329-360	393-386
10-9	74-87	138-121	202-224	266-294	330-272	394-389
11-10	75-88	139-150	203-225	267-296	331-361	395-388
12-20,310	76-89	140-152	204-185	268-297	332-363	396-390
13-11	77-90	141-153	205-226	269-298	333-364	397-392
14-12	78-54	142-154	206-228	270-218	334-365	398-394
15-13,290	79-91	143-155	207-229	271-299	335-371	399-395
16-15,314	80-92	144-123	208-230	272-300	336-275	400-396
17-16,315	81-93	145-157	209-231	273-301	337-377	401-401
18-23,288	82-94	146-158	210-196	274-303	338-383	402-402
19-19	83-96	147-159	211-232	275-304	339-397	403-404
20-18	84-56	148-160	212-233	276-220	340-391	404-405
21-21,308	85-97	149-161	213-234	277-305,366	341-374	405-407
22-24,333	86-99	150-139	214-235	278-306	342-482	406-410
23-22,326	87-100	151-162	215-236	279-307	343-276	407-413
24-27	88-101	152-163	216-197	280-309	344-446	408-414
25-25	89-102	153-165	217-237	281-312	345-400	409-416
26-26	90-65	154-166	218-238	282-227	346-406	410-417
27-28	91-103	155-167	219-239	283-313	347-411	411-418
28-29	92-104	156-146	220-240	284-316	348-398	412-419
29-30	93-105	157-170	221-241	285-317,362	349-286	413-421
30-31	94-106	158-171	222-199	286-319	350-415	414-426
31-32,328	95-107	159-174	223-242	287-320	351-427	415-431
32-33,323	96-66	160-173	224-243	288-245	352-436	416-432
33-36	97-108	161-172	225-244	289-321	353-449	417-434
34-37,302	98-109	162-151	226-248	290-322	354-440	418-437
35-38,311	99-110	163-176	227-250	291-324	355-291	419-438
36-34	100-111	164-175	228-200	292-325	356-461	420-439
37-39	101-114	165-178	229-251	293-329	357-455	421-443
38-41	102-75	166-179	230-253	294-246	358-469	422-445
39-43	103-116	167-180	231-254	295-330	359-450	423-447
40-44	104-117	168-156	232-255	296-332	360-479	424-448
41-45	105-118	169-181	233-259	297-327	361-293	425-458
42-35,331	106-119	170-182	234-202	298-334	362-481	426-463
43-46	107-120	171-183	235-260	299-335	363-451	427-464
44-47	108-83	172-186	236-261	300-247	364-487	428-465
45-51	109-122	173-188	237-262	301-337	365-502	429-466
46-52	110-124	174-164	238-263	302-336	366-505	430-468
47-55	111-125	175-189	239-264	303-339	367-473	431-471
48-40	112-126	176-190	240-205	304-340	368-549	432-472
49-57	113-127	177-187	241-265	305-338	369-564	433-475
50-59	114-85	178-191	242-266	306-252	370-547	434-477
51-60	115-128	179-192	243-267	307-341	371-	435-480
52-61	116-129	180-168	244-268	308-342	372-399	436-485
53-62	117-130	181-193	245-270	309-343	373-	437-495
54-42	118-131	182-194	246-209	310-344	374-	438-492
55-64	119-132	183-195	247-273	311-345	375-	439-500
56-67	120-112	184-198	248-271	312-256	376-	440-501
57-68	121-133	185-201	249-274	313-346	377-	441-494
58-71	122-134	186-169	250-277	314-347	378-	442-499
59-72	123-135	187-203	251-278	315-348	379-	443-504
60-48	124-136	188-207	252-210	316-349	380-	444-506
61-73	125-137	189-208	253-279	317-351	381-	445-507
62-74	126-113	190-212	254-280	318-257	382-	446-509
63-79	127-138	191-204	255-281	319-350	383-	447-510
64-77	128-140	192-177	256-282	320-352	384-	448-511

TABLE F-2 *continued*

449-516	466-551	483-	500-	517-	534-	551-
450-517	467-552	484-	501-	518-	535-	552-
451-518	468-553	485-	502-	519-	536-	553-
452-520	469-555	486-	503-	520-	537-	554-
453-522	470-558	487-	504-	521-	538-	555-
454-526	471-559	488-	505-	522-	539-	556-
455-527	472-560	489-	506-	523-	540-	557-
456-529	473-562	490-	507-	524-	541-	558-
457-531	474-563	491-	508-	525-	542-	559-
458-525	475-	492-	509-	526-	543-	560-
459-532	476-	493-	510-	527-	544-	561-
460-534	477-	494-	511-	528-	545-	562-
461-536	478-	495-	512-	529-	546-	563-
462-539	479-	496-	513-	530-	547-	564-
463-543	480-	497-	514-	531-	548-	565-
464-544	481-	498-	515-	532-	549-	566-
465-550	482-	499-	516-	533-	550-	567-

*Missing numbers represent items that did not appear in the original MMPI. Pairs of numbers refer to the two locations in which duplicate items appeared in the original MMPI.

References

Aaronson, B. S. (1958). Age and sex influences on MMPI profile peak distributions in an abnormal population. *Journal of Consulting Psychology, 22,* 203–206.

Aaronson, B. S. (1959). A comparison of two MMPI measures of masculinity-femininity. *Journal of Clinical Psychology, 15,* 48–50.

Aaronson, B. S., & Grumpelt, H. R. (1961). Homosexuality and some MMPI measures of masculinity-femininity. *Journal of Clinical Psychology, 17,* 245–247.

American Psychiatric Association (1980). *Diagnostic and statistical manual of mental disorders* (3rd ed.). Washington: Author.

American Psychiatric Association (1987). *Diagnostic and statistical manual of mental disorders* (3rd ed. revised). Washington: Author.

Anastasi, A. (1968). *Psychological testing* (3rd ed.). New York: Macmillan.

Anderson, W. (1956). The MMPI: Low *Pa* scores. *Journal of Counseling Psychology, 3,* 226–228.

Anderson, W. P., & Kunce, J. T. (1984). Diagnostic implications of markedly elevated MMPI *Sc* scores for nonhospitalized clients. *Journal of Clinical Psychology, 40,* 925–930.

Anthony, N. (1971). Comparison of clients' standard, exaggerated, and matching MMPI profiles. *Journal of Consulting and Clinical Psychology, 36,* 100–103.

Anthony, N. (1976). Malingering as role taking. *Journal of Clinical Psychology, 32,* 32–41.

Apfeldorf, M. (1978). Alcoholism scales and the MMPI: Contributions and future directions. *International Journal of the Addictions, 13,* 17–55.

Archer, R. P. (1984). Use of the MMPI with adolescents: A review of salient issues. *Clinical Psychology Review, 4,* 241–251.

Archer, R. P. (1987). *Using the MMPI with adolescents.* Hillsdale, NJ: Erlbaum.

Archer, R. P. (1988). Using the MMPI with adolescents. In C. D. Spielberger & J. N. Butcher (Eds.), *Advances in personality assessment* (Vol. 7, pp. 103–126). Hillsdale, NJ: Erlbaum.

Archer, R. P., Gordon, R. A., Giannetti, R., & Singles, J. (1988). MMPI scale clinical correlates for adolescent inpatients. *Journal of Personality Assessment, 52,* 707–721.

Archer, R. P., Gordon, R. A., & Kirchner, F. H. (1987). MMPI response-set characteristics among adolescents. *Journal of Personality Assessment, 51,* 506–516.

Archer, R. P., Pancoast, D. L., & Klinefelter, D. (1989). A comparison of MMPI code types produced by traditional and recent adolescent norms. *Psychological Assessment: A Journal of Consulting and Clinical Psychology, 1,* 23–29.

Armentrout, J. A., & Hauer, A. L. (1978). MMPIs of rapists of adults, rapists of children, and non-rapist sex offenders. *Journal of Clinical Psychology, 34,* 330–332.

Arthur, G. (1944). An experience in examining an Indian twelfth-grade group with the MMPI. *Mental Hygiene, 28,* 243–250.

Astin, A. W. (1959). A factor study of the MMPI Psychopathic Deviate scale. *Journal of Consulting Psychology, 23,* 550–554.

Astin, A. W. (1961). A note on the MMPI Psychopathic Deviate scale. *Educational and Psychological Measurement, 21,* 895–897.

Ball, J. C. (1960). Comparison of MMPI profile differences among Negro-white adolescents. *Journal of Clinical Psychology, 16,* 304–307.

Ball, J. C. (1962). *Social deviancy and adolescent personality.* Lexington: University of Kentucky Press.

Ball, J. C., & Carroll, D. (1960). Analysis of MMPI Cannot Say scores in an adolescent population. *Journal of Clinical Psychology, 16,* 30–31.

Barley, W. D., Sabo, T. W. , & Greene, R. L.

(1986). MMPI normal K^+ and other unelevated profiles. *Journal of Consulting and Clinical Psychology, 54*, 502–506.

Barron, F. (1953). An ego-strength scale which predicts response to psychotherapy. *Journal of Consulting Psychology, 17*, 327–333.

Baucom, D. H. (1976). Independent masculinity and femininity scales on the California Psychological Inventory. *Journal of Consulting and Clinical Psychology, 44*, 876.

Baughman, E. E., & Dahlstrom, W. G. (1968). *Negro and white children: A psychological study in the rural South*. New York: Academic Press.

Ben-Porath, Y. S., & Butcher, J. N. (1989). Psychometric stability of rewritten MMPI items. *Journal of Personality Assessment, 53*, 645–653.

Ben-Porath, Y. S., Hostetler, K., Butcher, J. N., & Graham, J. R. (1989). New subscales for the MMPI-2 Social Introversion (*Si*) scale. *Psychological Assessment, 1*, 169–174.

Benarick, S. J., Guthrie, G. M., & Snyder, W. U. (1951). An interpretive aid for the *Sc* scale of the MMPI. *Journal of Consulting Psychology, 15*, 142–144.

Berg, I. A. (1955). Response bias and personality: The deviation hypothesis. *Journal of Psychology, 40*, 61–72.

Berg, I. A. (1957). Deviant responses and deviant people: The formulation of the deviation hypothesis. *Journal of Counseling Psychology, 4*, 154–161.

Bernreuter, R. G. (1933). The theory and construction of the personality inventory. *Journal of Social Psychology, 4*, 387–405.

Bernstein, I. H., & Garbin, C. P. (1985). A comparison of alternative proposed subscale structures for MMPI Scale *2*. *Multivariate Behavioral Research, 20*, 223–235.

Bertelson, A. D., Marks, P. A., & May, G. D. (1982). MMPI and race: A controlled study. *Journal of Consulting and Clinical Psychology, 50*, 316–318.

Bieliauskas, L. A., & Shekelle, R. B. (1983). Stable behaviors associated with high-point D MMPI profiles in a nonpsychiatric population. *Journal of Clinical Psychology, 39*, 422–426.

Bieliauskas, V. J. (1965). Recent advances in psychology of masculinity and femininity. *Journal of Psychology, 60*, 255–263.

Birtchnell, J., & Kennard, J. (1983). What does the MMPI Dependency scale really measure? *Journal of Clinical Psychology, 39*, 532–543.

Blanchard, J. S. (1981). Readability of the MMPI. *Perceptual & Motor Skills, 52*, 985–986.

Block, J. (1965). *The challenge of response sets: Unconfounding meaning, acquiescence, and social desirability in the MMPI*. New York: Appleton-Century-Crofts.

Block, J. (1977). An illusory interpretation of the first factor of the MMPI: A reply to Shweder. *Journal of Consulting and Clinical Psychology, 45*, 930–935.

Blumberg, S. (1967). MMPI *F* scale as an indicator of severity of psychopathology. *Journal of Clinical Psychology, 23*, 96–99.

Boerger, A. R. (1975). *The utility of some alternative approaches to MMPI scale construction*. Unpublished doctoral dissertation, Kent State University, Kent, OH.

Boerger, A. R., Graham, J. R., & Lilly, R. S. (1974). Behavioral correlates of single-scale MMPI code types. *Journal of Consulting and Clinical Psychology, 42*, 398–402.

Bond, J. A. (1986). Inconsistent responding to repeated MMPI items: Is its major cause really carelessness? *Journal of Personality Assessment, 50*, 50–64.

Bradley, L. A., Prieto, E. J., Hopson, L., & Prokop, C. K. (1978). Comment on "Personality organization as an aspect of back pain in a medical setting." *Journal of Personality Assessment, 42*, 573–578.

Bradley, L. A., Prokop, C. K., Margolis, R., & Gentry, W. D. (1978). Multivariate analyses of the MMPI profiles of low-back pain patients. *Journal of Behavioral Medicine, 1*, 253–272.

Broughton, R. (1984). A prototype strategy for construction of personality scales. *Journal of Personality and Social Psychology, 47*, 1334–1346.

Brower, D. (1947). The relation between intelligence and MMPI scores. *Journal of Social Psychology, 25*, 243–245.

Brown, M. N. (1950). Evaluating and scoring the MMPI "Cannot Say" items. *Journal of Clinical Psychology, 6*, 180–184.

Brozek, J. (1955). Personality changes with age: An item analysis of the MMPI. *Journal of Gerontology, 10*, 194–206.

Buck, J, A., & Graham, J. R. (1978). The *4-3* MMPI profile type: A failure to replicate. *Journal of Consulting and Clinical Psychology, 46*, 344.

Buechley, R., & Ball, H. (1952). A new test of "validity" for the group MMPI. *Journal of Consulting Psychology, 16*, 299–301.

Burish, T. G., & Houston, B. K. (1976). Construct validity of the Lie scale as a measure of defensiveness. *Journal of Clinical Psychology*, *32*, 310–314.

Burkhart, B. R., Christian, W. L., & Gynther, M. D. (1978). Item subtlety and faking on the MMPI: A paradoxical relationship. *Journal of Personality Assessment*, *42*, 76–80.

Burkhart, B. R., Gynther, M. D., & Fromuth, M. E. (1980). The relative predictive validity of subtle versus obvious items on the MMPI depression scale. *Journal of Clinical Psychology*, *36*, 748–751.

Buros, O. K. (Ed.). (1978). *The eighth mental measurements yearbook*. Highland Park, NJ: Gryphon Press.

Burton, A. (1947). The use of the Masculinity-Femininity scale of the MMPI as an aid in the diagnosis of sexual inversion. *Journal of Psychology*, *24*, 161–164.

Butcher, J. N. (1985). Current developments in MMPI use: An international perspective. In C. D. Spielberger & J. N. Butcher (Eds.), *Advances in personality assessment* (Vol. 4, pp. 83–94). Hillsdale, NJ: Erlbaum.

Butcher, J. N. (1990). Education level and MMPI-2 measured psychopathology: A case of negligible influence. *MMPI-2 News and Profiles*, *1*, 3.

Butcher, J. N. (Ed.) (1972). *Objective personality assessment*. New York: Academic Press.

Butcher, J. N. (Ed.) (1987). *Computerized psychological assessment: A practitioner's guide*. New York: Basic.

Butcher, J. N., Ball, B., & Ray, E. (1964). Effects of socio-economic level on MMPI differences in Negro-white college students. *Journal of Counseling Psychology*, *11*, 83–87.

Butcher, J. N., Braswell, L., & Raney, D. (1983). A cross-cultural comparison of American Indian, black, and white inpatients on the MMPI and presenting symptoms. *Journal of Consulting and Clinical Psychology*, *51*, 587–594.

Butcher, J. N., & Clark, L. A. (1979). Recent trends in cross-cultural MMPI research and application. In J. N. Butcher (Ed.), *New developments in the use of the MMPI* (pp. 69–111). Minneapolis: University of Minnesota Press.

Butcher, J. N., Dahlstrom, W. G., Graham, J. R., Tellegen, A. M., & Kaemmer, B. (1989). *MMPI-2: Manual for administration and scoring*. Minneapolis: University of Minnesota Press.

Butcher, J. N., Graham, J. R., Dahlstrom, W. G. & Bowman, E. (1990). The MMPI-2 with college students. *Journal of Personality Assessment*, *54*, 1–15.

Butcher, J. N., Graham, J. R., Williams, C. L., & Ben-Porath, Y. (1989). *Development and use of the MMPI-2 content scales*. Minneapolis: University of Minnesota Press.

Butcher, J. N., & Hostetler, K. (1990). Abbreviating MMPI item administration: What can be learned from the MMPI for the MMPI-2? *Psychological Assessment: Journal of Consulting and Clinical Psychology*, *2*, 12–21.

Butcher, J. N., Kendall, P. C., & Hoffman, N. (1980). MMPI short forms: Caution. *Journal of Consulting and Clinical Psychology*, *48*, 275–278.

Butcher, J. N., & Pancheri, P. (1976). *A handbook of cross-cultural MMPI research*. Minneapolis: University of Minnesota Press.

Butcher, J. N., & Tellegen, A. (1966). Objections to MMPI items. *Journal of Consulting Psychology*, *30*, 527–534.

Butcher, J. N., & Tellegen, A. (1978). Common methodological problems in MMPI research. *Journal of Consulting and Clinical Psychology*, *46*, 620–628.

Byrne, D., Barry, J., & Nelson, D. (1963). Relation of the revised repression-sensitization scale to measures of self-description. *Psychological Reports*, *13*, 323–334.

Caldwell, A. B. (1969). *MMPI critical items*. Unpublished mimeograph. (Available from Caldwell Report, 1545 Sawtelle Boulevard, Los Angeles, CA 90025.)

Caldwell, A. B. (1988). *MMPI supplemental scale manual*. Los Angeles: Caldwell Report.

Caldwell, A. B. (1990, August). *MMPI, MMPI-2, and the measurement of the human condition*. Paper presented at the annual meeting of the American Psychological Association, Boston.

Caldwell, M. G. (1953). The youthful male offender in Alabama: A study in delinquency causation. *Sociology and Social Research*, *37*, 236–243.

Calsyn, D. A., Louks, J., & Freeman, C. W. (1976). The use of the MMPI with chronic low back pain patients with a mixed diagnosis. *Journal of Clinical Psychology*, *32*, 532–536.

Carson, R. C. (1969). Interpretative manual to the MMPI. In J. N. Butcher (Ed.), *MMPI.: Research development and clinical applications* (pp. 279–296). New York: McGraw.

Christian, W. L., Burkhart, B. R., & Gynther, M. D. (1978). Subtle-obvious ratings of MMPI items: New interest in an old concept. *Journal of Consulting and Clinical Psychology*, *46*, 1178–1186.

Clark, C. G., & Miller, H. L. (1971). Validation of Gilberstadt and Duker's *8-6* profile type on a black sample. *Psychological Reports*, *29*, 259–264.

Clavelle, P. R., & Butcher, J. N. (1977). An adaptive typological approach to psychiatric screening. *Journal of Consulting and Clinical Psychology*, *45*, 851–859.

Clopton, J. R. (1974). A computer program for MMPI scale development with contrasted groups. *Educational and Psychological Measurement*, *34*, 161–163.

Clopton, J. R. (1975). Automated MMPI interpretation based on a modification of Gilberstadt's codebook. *Journal of Clinical Psychology*, *31*, 648–651.

Clopton, J. R. (1978a). Alcoholism and the MMPI: A review. *Journal of Studies on Alcohol*, *39*, 1540–1558.

Clopton, J. R. (1978b). MMPI scale development methodology. *Journal of Personality Assessment*, *42*, 148–151.

Clopton, J. R. (1979a). Development of special MMPI scales. In C. S. Newmark (Ed.), *MMPI: Clinical and research trends* (pp. 354–372). New York: Praeger.

Clopton, J. R. (1979b). The MMPI and suicide. In C. S. Newmark (Ed.), *MMPI: Clinical and research trends* (pp. 149–166). New York: Praeger.

Clopton, J. R. (1982). MMPI scale development methodology reconsidered. *Journal of Personality Assessemnt*, *46*, 143–146.

Clopton, J. R., & Baucom, D. H. (1979). MMPI ratings of suicide risk. *Journal of Personality Assessment*, *43*, 293–296.

Clopton, J. R., & Jones, W. C. (1975). Use of the MMPI in the prediction of suicide. *Journal of Clinical Psychology*, *31*, 52–54.

Clopton, J. R., & Klein, G. L. (1978). An initial look at the redundancy of specialized MMPI scales. *Journal of Consulting and Clinical Psychology*, *46*, 1436–1438.

Clopton, J. R., & Neuringer, C. (1977a). FORTRAN computer programs for the development of new MMPI scales. *Educational and Psychological Measurement*, *37*, 783–786.

Clopton, J. R., & Neuringer, C. (1977b). MMPI Cannot Say scores: Normative data and degree of profile distortion. *Journal of Personality Assessment*, *41*, 511–513.

Clopton, J. R., Pallis, D. J., & Birtchnell, J. (1979). MMPI profile patterns of suicide attempters. *Journal of Consulting and Clinical Psychology*, *47*, 135–139.

Clopton, J. R., Post, R. D., & Larde, J. (1983). Identification of suicide attempters by means of MMPI profiles. *Journal of Clinical Psychology*, *39*, 868–871.

Coché, E., & Steer, R. A. (1974). The MMPI response consistencies of normal, neurotic and psychotic women. *Journal of Clinical Psychology*, *30*, 194–195.

Cofer, C. N., Chance, J., & Judson, A. J. (1949). A study of malingering on the MMPI. *Journal of Psychology*, *27*, 491–499.

Colligan, R. C., Davis, Jr., L. J., Morse, R. M., & Offord, K. P. (1988). Screening medical patients for alcoholism with the MMPI: A comparison of seven scales. *Journal of Clinical Psychology*, *44*, 582–592.

Colligan, R. C., & Offord, K. P. (1986). [MMPI data research tape for Mayo Clinic medical outpatients referred for psychiatric evaluations.] Unpublished raw data.

Colligan, R. C., & Offord, K. P. (1987a). Resiliency reconsidered: Contemporary MMPI normative data for Barron's Ego Strength Scale. *Journal of Clinical Psychology*, *43*, 467–471.

Colligan, R. C., & Offord, K. P. (1987b). The MacAndrew alcoholism scale applied to a contemporary normative sample. *Journal of Clinical Psychology*, *43*, 291–293.

Colligan, R. C., & Offord, K. P. (1988a). Changes in MMPI factor scores: Norms for the Welsh A and R dimensions from a contemporary normal sample. *Journal of Clinical Psychology*, *44*, 142–148.

Colligan, R. C., & Offord, K. P. (1988b). Contemporary norms for the Wiggins content scales: A 45-year update. *Journal of Clinical Psychology*, *44*, 23–32.

Colligan, R. C., & Offord, K. P. (1989). The aging MMPI: Contemporary norms for contemporary adolescents. *Mayo Clinic Proceedings*, *64*, 3–27.

Colligan, R. C., Osborne, D., & Offord, K. P. (1980). Linear transformation and the interpretation of MMPI *T* scores. *Journal of Clinical Psychology*, *36*, 162–165.

Colligan, R. C., Osborne, D., & Offord, K. P. (1984). Normalized transformations and the interpretation of MMPI *T* scores: A reply to Hsu. *Journal of Consulting and Clinical Psychology*, *52*, 824–826.

Colligan, R. C., Osborne, D., Swenson, W. M., & Offord, K. P. (1983). *The MMPI: A contemporary normative study*. New York: Praeger.

Colligan, R. C., Osborne, D., Swenson, W. M., & Offord, K. P. (1984). The MMPI: Development of contemporary norms. *Journal of Clinical Psychology*, *40*, 100–107.

Colligan, R. C., Osborne, D., Swenson, W. M., & Offord, K. P. (1985). Using the 1983 norms for the MMPI: Code type frequencies in four clinical samples. *Journal of Clinical Psychology*, *41*, 629–633.

Colligan, R. C., Osborne, D., Swenson, W. M., & Offord, K. P. (1989). *The MMPI: A contemporary normative study of adults* (2nd ed.). Odessa, FL: Psychological Assessment Resources.

Comrey, A. L. (1957a). A factor analysis of items on the MMPI Hypochondriasis scale. *Educational and Psychological Measurement*, 17, 568–577.

Comrey, A. L. (1957b). A factor analysis of items on the MMPI Depression scale. *Educational and Psychological Measurement*, *17*, 578–585.

Comrey, A. L. (1957c). A factor analysis of items on the MMPI Hysteria scale. *Educational and Psychological Measurement*, *17*, 586–592.

Comrey, A. L. (1958a). A factor analysis of items on the MMPI Psychopathic Deviate scale. *Educational and Psychological Measurement*, *18*, 91–98.

Comrey, A. L. (1958b). A factor analysis of items on the MMPI Paranoia scale. *Educational and Psychological Measurement*, *18*, 99–107.

Comrey, A, L. (1958c). A factor analysis of items on the MMPI Psychasthenia scale. *Educational and Psychological Measurement*, *18*, 293–300.

Comrey, A. L. (1958d). A factor analysis of items on the MMPI Hypomania scale. *Educational and Psychological Measurement*, *18*, 312–323.

Comrey, A. L., & Marggraff, W. M. (1958). A factor analysis of items on the MMPI Schizophrenia scale. *Educational and Psychological Measurement*, *18*, 301–311.

Constantinople, A. (1973). Masculinity-femininity: An exception to a famous dictum? *Psychological Bulletin*, *80*, 389–407.

Cooke, G., Pogany, E., & Johnston, N. G. (1974). A comparison of blacks and whites committed for evaluation of competency to stand trial on criminal charges. *Journal of Psychiatry and Law*, *2*, 319–337.

Costello, R. M. (1973). Item level racial differences on the MMPI. *Journal of Social Psychology*, *91*, 161–162.

Costello, R. M. (1977). Construction and cross-validation of an MMPI black-white scale. *Journal of Personality Assessment*, *41*, 514–519.

Costello, R. M., Fine, H. J., & Blau, B. I. (1973). Racial comparisons on the MMPI. *Journal of Clinical Psychology*, *29*, 63–65.

Costello, R. M., Tiffany, D. W., & Gier, R. H. (1972). Methodological issues and racial (black-white) comparisons on the MMPI. *Journal of Consulting and Clinical Psychology*, *38*, 161–168.

Cowan, M. A., Watkins, B. A., & Davis, W. E. (1975). Level of education, diagnosis and race-related differences in MMPI performance. *Journal of Clinical Psychology*, *31*, 442–444.

Coyle, Jr., F. A., & Heap, R. F. (1965). Interpreting the MMPI *L* scale. *Psychological Reports*, *17*, 722.

Craig, R. J. (1984). A comparison of MMPI profiles of heroin addicts based on multiple methods of classification. *Journal of Personality Assessment*, 48, 115–120.

Cuellar, I., Harris, L. C., & Jasso, R. (1980). An acculturation scale for Mexican-American normal and clinical populations. *Hispanic Journal of Behavioral Science*, *2*, 199–217.

Dahlstrom, W. G. (1954). Prediction of adjustment after neurosurgery. *American Psychologist*, *9*, 353–354.

Dahlstrom, W. G., Lachar, D., & Dahlstrom, L. E. (1986). *MMPI patterns of American minorities*. Minneapolis: University of Minnesota Press.

Dahlstrom, W. G., Welsh, G. S., & Dahlstrom, L. E. (1972). *An MMPI handbook: Vol. I. Clinical interpretation* (rev. ed.). Minneapolis: University of Minnesota Press.

Dahlstrom, W. G., Welsh, G. S., & Dahlstrom, L. E. (1975). *An MMPI handbook: Vol. II. Research applications* (rev. ed.). Minneapolis: University of Minnesota Press.

Dana, R. H. (1990). Cross-cultural and multi-ethnic assessment. In J. N. Butcher & C. D. Spielberger (Eds.), *Advances in personality assessment* (Vol. 8, pp. 1–26). Hillsdale, NJ: Erlbaum.

Davies, J., Nichols, D. S., & Greene, R. L. (1985, March). *A new schizophrenia scale for the MMPI.* Paper presented at the 20th Annual Symposium on Recent Advances in the Use of the MMPI, Honolulu.

Davis, K. R., & Sines, J. O. (1971). An antisocial behavior pattern associated with a specific MMPI profile. *Journal of Consulting and Clinical Psychology, 36,* 229–234.

Davis, L. J., Colligan, R. C., Morse, R. M., & Offord, K. P. (1987). Validity of the Mac-Andrew scale in a general medical population. *Journal of Studies on Alcohol, 48,* 202–206.

Davis, W. E. (1972). Age and the discriminative "power" of the MMPI with schizophrenic and nonschizophrenic patients. *Journal of Consulting and Clinical Psychology, 38,* 151.

Davis, W. E. (1975). Race and the differential "power" of the MMPI. *Journal of Personality Assessment, 39,* 138–140.

Davis, W. E., Beck, S. J., & Ryan, T. A. (1973). Race-related and educationally-related MMPI profile differences among hospitalized schizophrenics. *Journal of Clinical Psychology, 29,* 478–479.

Davis, W. E., & Jones, M. H. (1974). Negro versus Caucasian psychological test performance revisited. *Journal of Consulting and Clinical Psychology, 42,* 675–679.

Dean, R. B., & Richardson, H. (1964). Analysis of MMPI profiles of forty college-educated overt male homosexuals. *Journal of Consulting Psychology, 28,* 483–486.

Deiker, T. E. (1974). A cross-validation of MMPI scales of aggression on male criminal criterion groups. *Journal of Consulting and Clinical Psychology, 42,* 196–202.

Denny, N., Robinowitz, R., & Penk, W. E. (1987). Conducting applied research on Vietnam combat-related Post-traumatic Stress Disorder. *Journal of Clinical Psychology, 43,* 56–66.

Dolan, M. P., Roberts, W. R., Penk, W. E., Robinowitz, R., & Atkins, H. G. (1983). Personality differences among black, white, and Hispanic-American male heroin addicts on MMPI content scales. *Journal of Clinical Psychology, 39,* 807–813.

Drake, L. E. (1946). A social I-E scale for the MMPI. *Journal of Applied Psychology, 30,* 51–54.

Drake, L. E., & Oetting, E. R. (1959). *An MMPI*

codebook for counselors. Minneapolis: University of Minnesota Press.

Dubinsky, S., Gamble, D. J., & Rogers, M. L. (1985). A literature review of subtle-obvious items on the MMPI. *Journal of Personality Assessment, 49,* 62–68.

Dubro, A. F., Wetzler, S., & Kahn, M. W. (1988). A comparison of three self-report questionnaires for the diagnosis of DSM-III personality disorders. *Journal of Personality Disorders, 2,* 256–266.

Duckworth, J. C., & Anderson, W. (1986). *MMPI interpretation manual for counselors and clinicians* (3rd ed.). Muncie, IN: Accelerated Development.

Duckworth, J. C., & Barley, W. D. (1988). Within-Normal-Limit profiles. In R. L. Greene (Ed.), *The MMPI: Use in specific populations* (pp. 278–315). San Antonio: Grune & Stratton.

Dye, C. J., Bohm, K., Anderten, P., and Won Cho, D. (1983). Age group differences in depression on MMPI *D* Scale. *Journal of Clinical Psychology, 39,* 227–234.

Eaddy, M. L. (1962). An investigation of the Cannot Say scale of the group MMPI. *Dissertation Abstracts, 23,* 1070.

Edinger, J. D. (1981). MMPI short forms: A clinical perspective. *Psychological Reports, 48,* 627–631.

Edwards, A. L. (1959). *Edwards Personal Preference Schedule manual.* New York: Psychological Corporation.

Edwards, A. L. (1977). Comments on Shweder's "Illusory correlation and the MMPI controversy." *Journal of Consulting and Clinical Psychology, 45,* 925–929.

Edwards, A. L., & Diers, C. J. (1962). Social desirability and the factorial interpretation of the MMPI. *Educational and Psychological Measurement, 22,* 501–509.

Ehrenworth, N. V., & Archer, R. P. (1985). A comparison of clinical accuracy ratings of interpretive approaches for adolescent MMPI responses. *Journal of Personality Assessment, 49,* 413–421.

Eichman, W. J. (1962). Factored scales for the MMPI: A clinical and statistical manual. *Journal of Clinical Psychology, 18,* 363–395.

Elion, V. H., & Megargee, E. I. (1975). Validity of the MMPI *Pd* scale among black males. *Journal of Consulting and Clinical Psychology, 43,* 166–172.

Endicott, N. A., Jortner, S., & Abramoff, E.

(1969). Objective measures of suspiciousness. *Journal of Abnormal Psychology, 74,* 26–32.

Erdberg, S. P. (1975). MMPI differences associated with sex, race, and residence in a southern sample. In W. G. Dahlstrom, G. S. Welsh, & L. E. Dahlstrom (Eds.), *An MMPI handbook: Vol. II. Research applications* (pp. 155–157). Minneapolis: University of Minnesota Press.

Erickson, W. D., Luxenberg, M. G., Walbek, N. H., & Seely, R. K. (1987). Frequency of MMPI two-point code types among sex offenders. *Journal of Consulting and Clinical Psychology, 55,* 566–570.

Evans, C., & McConnell, T. R. (1941). A new measure of introversion-extroversion. *Journal of Psychology, 12,* 111–124.

Evans, R. G. (1984a). MMPI Dependency scale norms for alcoholics and psychiatric patients. *Journal of Clinical Psychology, 40,* 345–346.

Evans, R. G. (1984b). Normative data for two MMPI critical item sets. *Journal of Clinical Psychology, 40,* 512–515.

Evans, R. G. (1984c). Utility of the MMPI-168 with men inpatient alcoholics. *Journal of Studies on Alcohol, 45,* 371–373.

Evans, R. G., & Dinning, W. D. (1983). Response consistency among high F scale scorers on the MMPI. *Journal of Clinical Psychology, 39,* 246–248.

Exner, Jr., J. E., McDowell, E., Pabst, J., Stackman, W. & Kirk, L. (1963). On the detection of willful falsifications in the MMPI. *Journal of Consulting Psychology, 27,* 91–94.

Farberow, N. L. (1956). Personality patterns of suicidal mental hospital patients. In G. S. Welsh & W. G. Dahlstrom (Eds.), *Basic readings on the MMPI in psychology and medicine* (pp. 427–432). Minneapolis: University of Minnesota Press.

Farberow, N. L., & Devries, A. G. (1967). An item differentiation analysis of MMPIs of suicidal neuropsychiatric hospital patients. *Psychological Reports, 20,* 607–617.

Farr, S. P. & Martin, P. (1988). Neuropsychological dysfunction. In R. L. Greene (Ed.), *The MMPI: Use with specific populations* (pp. 214–245). San Antonio: Grune & Stratton.

Faschingbauer, T. R. (1974). A 166-item written short form of the group MMPI: The FAM. *Journal of Consulting and Clinical Psychology, 42,* 645–655.

Faschingbauer, T. R. (1979). The future of the MMPI. In C. S. Newmark (Ed.), *MMPI: Clinical and research trends* (pp. 373–398). New York: Praeger.

Faschingbauer, T. R., & Newmark, C. S. (1978). *Short forms of the MMPI.* Lexington, MA: Heath.

Fekken, G. C., & Holden, R. R. (1987). Assessing the person reliability of an individual MMPI protocol. *Journal of Personality Assessment, 51,* 123–132.

Ferguson, G. A. (1971). *Statistical analysis in psychology and education* (3rd ed.). New York: McGraw Hill.

Fillenbaum, G. G., & Pfeiffer, E. (1976). The Mini-Mult: A cautionary note. *Journal of Consulting and Clinical Psychology, 44,* 698–703.

Finney, J. C., Smith, D. F., Skeeters, D. E., & Auvenshine, C. D. (1971). MMPI alcoholism scales: Factor structure and content analysis. *Quarterly Journal of Studies on Alcohol, 32,* 1055–1060.

Fjordbak, T. (1985). Clinical correlates of high *Lie* scale elevations among forensic patients. *Journal of Personality Assessment, 49,* 252–255.

Flanagan, J., & Lewis, G. (1969). Comparison of Negro and white lower class men on the general aptitude test battery and the MMPI. *Journal of Social Psychology, 78,* 289–291.

Forgac, G. E., Cassel, C. A., & Michaels, E. J. (1984). Chronicity of criminal behavior and psychopathology in male exhibitionists. *Journal of Clinical Psychology, 40,* 827–832.

Forsyth, D. R. (1967). MMPI and college populations. *Journal of College Student Personnel, 8,* 90–96.

Fowler, R. D., & Coyle, F. A. (1968a). A comparison of two MMPI actuarial systems used in classifying an alcoholic out-patient population. *Journal of Clinical Psychology, 24,* 434–435.

Fowler, R. D., & Coyle, F. A. (1968b). Scoring error on the MMPI. *Journal of Clinical Psychology, 24,* 68–69.

Fowler, R. D., & Coyle, F. A. (1969). Collegiate normative data on MMPI content scales. *Journal of Clinical Psychology, 25,* 62–63.

Freeman, C., Calsyn, D., & Louks, J. (1976). The use of the MMPI with low back pain patients. *Journal of Clinical Psychology, 32,* 294–298.

Friberg, R. R. (1967). Measures of homosexuality:

Cross-validation of two MMPI scales and implications for usage. *Journal of Consulting Psychology, 31*, 88–91.

Fricke, B. G. (1956). Conversion hysterics and the MMPI. *Journal of Clinical Psychology, 12*, 322–326.

Friedman, A. F., Webb, J. T., & Lewak, R. (1989). *Psychological assessment with the MMPI*. Hillsdale, NJ: Erlbaum.

Friedrich, W. N. (1988). Child abuse and sexual abuse. In R. L. Greene (Ed.), *The MMPI: Use in specific populations* (pp. 246–258). San Antonio: Grune & Stratton.

Fry, F. D. (1949). A study of the personality traits of college students and of state prison inmates as measured by the MMPI. *Journal of Psychology, 28*, 439–449.

Gallucci, N. T. (1984). Prediction of dissimulation on the MMPI in a clinical field setting. *Journal of Consulting and Clinical Psychology, 52*, 917–918.

Gallucci, N. T. (1985). Influence of dissimulation on indexes of response consistency for the MMPI. *Psychological Reports, 57*, 1013–1014.

Gallucci, N. T., Kay, D. C., & Thornby, J. I. (1989). The sensitivity of 11 substance abuse scales from the MMPI to change in clinical status. *Psychology of Addictive Behaviors, 3*, 29–33.

Gauron, E., Severson, R., & Englehart, R. (1962). MMPI *F* scores and psychiatric diagnosis. *Journal of Consulting Psychology, 26*, 488.

Gayton, W. F., Burchstead, G. N., & Matthews, G. R. (1986). An investigation of the utility of an MMPI Posttraumatic Stress Disorder subscale. *Journal of Clinical Psychology, 42*, 916–917.

Gearing, M. L. (1979). The MMPI as a primary differentiator and predictor of behavior in prison: A methodological critique and review of the recent literature. *Psychological Bulletin, 86*, 929–963.

Genthner, R. W., & Graham, J. R. (1976). Effects of short-term public psychiatric hospitalization for both black and white patients. *Journal of Consulting and Clinical Psychology, 44*, 118–124.

Giannetti, R. A., Johnson, J. H., Klingler, D. E., & Williams, T. A. (1978). Comparison of linear and configural MMPI diagnostic methods with an uncontaminated criterion. *Journal of Consulting and Clinical Psychology, 46*, 1046–1052.

Gilberstadt, H. (1970). *Comprehensive MMPI code book for males*. Minneapolis: MMPI Research Laboratory, Veterans Administration Hospital.

Gilberstadt, H., & Duker, J. (1965). *A handbook for clinical and actuarial MMPI interpretation*. Philadelphia: Saunders.

Goldberg, L. R. (1965). Diagnosticians vs. diagnostic signs: The diagnosis of psychosis vs. neurosis from the MMPI. *Psychological Monographs, 79* (9, Whole No. 602).

Goldberg, L. R. (1969). The search for configural relationships in personality assessment: The diagnosis of psychosis vs. neurosis from the MMPI. *Multivariate Behavioral Research, 4*, 523–536.

Golden, C, J., Sweet, J. J., & Osmon, D. C. (1979). The diagnosis of brain-damage by the MMPI: A comprehensive evaluation. *Journal of Personality Assessment, 43*, 138–142.

Gonen, J. Y., & Lansky, L. M. (1968). Masculinity, femininity, and masculinity-femininity: A phenomenological study of the *Mf* scale of the MMPI. *Psychological Reports, 23*, 183–194.

Good, P. K., & Brantner, J. P. (1961). *The physician's guide to the MMPI*. Minneapolis: University of Minnesota Press.

Good, P. K., & Brantner, J. P. (1974). *A practical guide to the MMPI*. Minneapolis: University of Minnesota Press.

Goodstein, L. D. (1954). Regional differences in MMPI responses among male college students. *Journal of Consulting Psychology, 18*, 437–441.

Gordon, N. G., & Swart, E. C. (1973). A comparison of the Harris-Lingoes subscales between the original standardization population and an inpatient Veterans Administration hospital population. *VA Newsletter for Research in Mental Health and Behavioral Sciences, 15*, 28–31.

Gottesman, I. I., Hanson, D. R., Kroeker, T. A., & Briggs, P. F. (1987). New MMPI normative data and power-transformed T score tables for the Hathaway-Monachesi Minnesota cohort of 14,019 15-year-olds and 3,674 18-year-olds. In R. P. Archer (Ed.), *Using the MMPI with adolescents* (pp. 241–297). Hillsdale, NJ: Erlbaum.

Gottesman, I. I., & Prescott, C. A. (1989). Abuses of the MacAndrew alcoholism scale: A critical review. *Clinical Psychology Review, 9*, 223–242.

Gough, H. G. (1947). Simulated patterns on the MMPI. *Journal of Abnormal and Social Psychology, 42*, 215–225.

Gough, H. G. (1950). The *F* minus *K* dissimulation index for the MMPI. *Journal of Consulting Psychology, 14*, 408–413.

Gough, H. G. (1954). Some common misconceptions about neuroticism. *Journal of Consulting Psychology, 18*, 287–292.

Gough, H. G. (1957). *California Psychological Inventory manual*. Palo Alto, CA: Consulting Psychologists Press.

Gough, H. G., McClosky, H., & Meehl, P. E. (1951). A personality scale for dominance. *Journal of Abnormal and Social Psychology, 46*, 360–366.

Gough, H. G., McClosky, H., & Meehl, P. E. (1952). A personality scale for social responsibility. *Journal of Abnormal and Social Psychology, 47*, 73–80.

Graham, J. R. (1977). *The MMPI: A practical guide*. New York: Oxford.

Graham, J. R. (1978). Review of MMPI special scales. In P. McReynolds (Ed.), *Advances in psychological assessment* (Vol. IV, pp. 11–55). San Francisco: Jossey-Bass.

Graham, J. R. (1979). *Using the MMPI in counseling and psychotherapy. Clinical notes on the MMPI*. No. 1. Minneapolis: National Computer Systems.

Graham, J. R. (1987). *The MMPI: A practical guide* (2nd ed.). New York: Oxford.

Graham, J. R. (1990a). Congruence between MMPI and MMPI-2 codetypes. *MMPI-2 News and Profiles, 1*, 1–2, 12.

Graham, J. R. (1990b). *MMPI-2: Assessing personality and psychopathology*. New York: Oxford.

Graham, J. R., & Mayo, M. A. (1985, March). *A comparison of MMPI strategies for identifying black and white male alcoholic*. Paper presented at the 20th Annual Symposium on Recent Developments in the Use of the MMPI, Honolulu.

Graham, J. R., & Schroeder, H. E. (1972). Abbreviated *Mf* and *Si* scales for the MMPI. *Journal of Personality Assessment, 36*, 436–439.

Graham, J. R., Schroeder, H. E., & Lilly, R. S. (1971). Factor analysis of items on the Social Introversion and Masculinity-Femininity scales of the MMPI. *Journal of Clinical Psychology, 27*, 367–370.

Graham, J. R., Smith, R. L., & Schwartz, G. F. (1986). Stability of MMPI configurations for psychiatric inpatients. *Journal of Consulting and Clinical Psychology, 54*, 375–380.

Graham, J. R., & Strenger, V. E. (1988). MMPI characteristics of alcoholics: A review. *Journal of Consulting and Clinical Psychology, 56*, 197–205.

Graham, J. R., & Tisdale, M. J. (1983, April). *Interpretation of low Scale 5 scores for women of high educational levels*. Paper presented at the 18th Annual Symposium on Recent Developments in the Use of the MMPI, Minneapolis.

Gravitz, M. A. (1967). Frequency and content of test items normally omitted from MMPI scales. *Journal of Consulting Psychology, 31*, 642.

Gravitz, M. A. (1968). Normative findings for the frequency of MMPI critical items. *Journal of Clinical Psychology, 24*, 220.

Gravitz, M. A. (1970). Validity implications of normal adult MMPI "L" scale endorsement. *Journal of Clinical Psychology, 26*, 497–499.

Gravitz, M. A. (1971). Declination rates on the MMPI validity and clinical scales. *Journal of Clinical Psychology, 27*, 103.

Gravitz, M. A. (1987). An empirical study of MMPI *F* scale validity. *Psychological Reports, 60*, 389–390.

Gravitz, M. A., & Gerton, M. l. (1976). An empirical study of internal consistency in the MMPI. *Journal of Clinical Psychology, 32*, 567–568.

Gray, W. S., & Robinson, H. M. (1963). *Gray Oral Reading Test*. Indianapolis: Bobbs-Merrill.

Grayson, H. M. (1951). *A psychological admissions testing program and manual*. Los Angeles: Veterans Administration Center, Neuropsychiatric Hospital.

Grayson, H. M., & Olinger, L. B. (1957). Simulation of "normalcy" by psychiatric patients on the MMPI. *Journal of Consulting Psychology, 21*, 73–77.

Greene, R. L. (1977). Student acceptance of generalized personality interpretations: A reexamination. *Journal of Consulting and Clinical Psychology, 45*, 965–966.

Greene, R. L. (1978a). An empirically derived MMPI carelessness scale. *Journal of Clinical Psychology, 34*, 407–410.

Greene, R. L. (1978b). Can clients provide valuable feedback to clinicians about their personality interpretations? Greene replies. *Journal of Consulting and Clinical Psychology, 46*, 1496–1497.

Greene, R. L. (1979). Response consistency on the MMPI: The TR index. *Journal of Personality Assessment, 43*, 69–71.

Greene, R. L. (1980). *The MMPI: An interpretive manual*. New York: Grune & Stratton.

Greene, R. L. (1982). Some reflections on "MMPI short forms: A literature review." *Journal of Personality Assessment, 46,* 486–487.

Greene, R. L. (1986). [MMPI data research tape for normal adults and college students]. Unpublished raw data.

Greene, R. L. (1987). Ethnicity and MMPI performance: A review. *Journal of Consulting and Clinical Psychology, 55,* 497–512.

Greene, R. L. (1988a). Summary. In R. L. Greene (Ed.), *The MMPI: Use with specific populations* (pp. 316–321). San Antonio: Grune & Stratton.

Greene, R. L. (1988b). The relative efficacy of *F-K* and the obvious and subtle scales to detect overreporting of psychopathology on the MMPI. *Journal of Clinical Psychology, 44,* 152–159.

Greene, R. L. (Ed.). (1988c). *The MMPI: Use in specific populations*. San Antonio: Grune & Stratton.

Greene, R. L. (1989). *Assessing the validity of MMPI profiles in clinical settings. Clinical Notes on the MMPI,* No. 11. Minneapolis: National Computer Systems.

Greene, R. L. (1990). Stability of MMPI scale scores across four codetypes over four decades. *Journal of Personality Assessment, 55,* 1–6.

Greene, R. L. (1990, March). *The effects of age, education, gender, and specific MMPI codetypes on the MacAndrew Alcoholism Scale*. Paper presented at the annual meeting of the Society for Personality Assessment, San Diego.

Greene, R. L., Arredondo, R., & Davis, H. G. (1990, August). *The comparability between the MacAndrew Alcoholism Scale—Revised (MMPI-2) and the MacAndrew Alcoholism Scale (MMPI)*. Paper presented at the annual meeting of the American Psychological Association, Boston.

Greene, R. L., & Brown, R. C. (1988). *MMPI adult interpretive system*. Lutz, FL: Psychological Assessment Resources.

Greene, R. L., & Brown, R. C. (1990). *MMPI-2 adult interpretive system*. Lutz, FL: Psychological Assessment Resources.

Greene, R. L., Davis, H. G., & Welch, S. M. (1988, August). *Clinical correlates of self-deception and impression management on the MMPI*. Paper presented at the annual meet-

ing of the American Psychological Association, Atlanta.

Greene, R. L., & Garvin, R. D. (1988). Substance abuse/dependence. In R. L. Greene (Ed.), *The MMPI: Use in specific populations* (pp. 159–197). San Antonio: Grune & Stratton.

Griffith, A. V., & Fowler, R. D. (1960). Psychasthenic and Hypomanic scales of the MMPI and reaction to authority. *Journal of Counseling Psychology, 7,* 146–147.

Griffith, A. V., Upshaw, H. S., & Fowler, R. D. (1958). The Psychasthenic and Hypomanic scales of the MMPI and uncertainty in judgments. *Journal of Clinical Psychology, 14,* 385–386.

Gross, L. R. (1959). MMPI *L-F-K* relationships with criteria of behavioral disturbance and social adjustment in a schizophrenic population. *Journal of Consulting Psychology, 23,* 319–323.

Grossman, L. S., & Wasyliw, O. E. (1988). A psychometric study of stereotypes: Assessment of malingering in a criminal forensic group. *Journal of Personality Assessment, 52,* 549–563.

Gulas, L. (1974). MMPI low-point codes for a "normal" young adult population: A normative study. *Journal of Clinical Psychology, 30,* 77–78.

Gynther, M. D. (1961). The clinical utility of "invalid" MMPI *F* scores. *Journal of Consulting Psychology, 25,* 540–542.

Gynther, M. D. (1972). White norms and black MMPIs: A prescription for discrimination? *Psychological Bulletin, 78,* 386–402.

Gynther, M. D. (1979). Ethnicity and personality: An update. In J. N. Butcher (Ed.), *New developments in the use of the MMPI* (pp. 113–140). Minneapolis: University of Minnesota Press.

Gynther, M. D. (1983). MMPI interpretation: The effects of demographic variables. In C. D. Spielberger & J. N. Butcher (Eds.), *Advances in personality assessment* (Vol. 3, pp. 175–193). New York: Lawrence Erlbaum.

Gynther, M. D. (1989). MMPI comparisons of blacks and whites: A review and commentary. *Journal of Clinical Psychology, 45,* 878–883.

Gynther, M. D., Altman, H., & Sletten, I. W. (1973). Replicated correlates of MMPI two-point code types: The Missouri actuarial system. *Journal of Clinical Psychology, 29,* 263–289.

Gynther, M. D., Altman, H., & Warbin, R. (1973a). Behavioral correlates for the MMPI *4-9, 9-4* codetypes: A case of the emperor's new clothes? *Journal of Consulting and Clinical Psychology, 40*, 259–263.

Gynther, M. D., Altman, H., & Warbin, R. (1973b). Interpretation of uninterpretable MMPI profiles. *Journal of Consulting and Clinical Psychology, 40*, 78–83.

Gynther, M. D., & Brilliant, P. J. (1968). The MMPI K^+ profile: A reexamination. *Journal of Consulting and Clinical Psychology, 32*, 616–617.

Gynther, M. D., & Burkhart, B. R. (1983). Are subtle MMPI items expendable? In J. N. Butcher & C. D. Spielberger (Eds.), *Advances in personality assessment* (Vol. 2, pp. 115–132). Hillsdale NJ: Lawrence Erlbaum.

Gynther, M. D., Burkhart, B. R., & Hovanitz, C. (1979). Do face-valid items have more predictive validity than subtle items? The case of the MMPI *Pd* scale. *Journal of Consulting and Clinical Psychology, 47*, 295–300.

Gynther, M. D., Fowler, R. D., & Erdberg, P. (1971). False positives galore: The application of standard MMPI criteria to a rural, isolated, Negro sample. *Journal of Clinical Psychology, 27*, 234–237.

Gynther, M. D., & Green, S. B. (1980). Accuracy may make a difference, but does a difference make for accuracy?: A response to Pritchard and Rosenblatt. *Journal of Consulting and Clinical Psychology, 48*, 268–272.

Gynther, M. D., Lachar, D., & Dahlstrom, W. G. (1978). Are special norms for minorities needed? Development of an MMPI *F* scale for blacks. *Journal of Consulting and Clinical Psychology, 46*, 1403–1408.

Gynther, M. D., & Petzel, T. P. (1967). Differential endorsement of MMPI *F* scale items by psychotics and behavior disorders. *Journal of Clinical Psychology, 23*, 185–188.

Gynther, M. D., & Shimkunas, A. M. (1965a). Age, intelligence, and MMPI *F* scores. *Journal of Consulting Psychology, 29*, 383–388.

Gynther, M. D., & Shimkunas, A. M. (1965b). More data on MMPI *F* > 16 scores. *Journal of Clinical Psychology, 21*, 275–277.

Gynther, M. D., & Witt, P. H. (1976). Windstorms and important persons: Personality characteristics of black educators. *Journal of Clinical Psychology, 32*, 613–616.

Haertzen, C. A., & Hill, H. E. (1963). Assessing subjective effects of drugs: An index of carelessness and confusion for use with the Addiction Research Center Inventory (ARCI). *Journal of Clinical Psychology, 19*, 407–412.

Hale, G., Zimostrad, S., Duckworth, J., & Nicholas, D. (1986). *The abusive personality: MMPI profiles of male batterers.* Paper presented at the 21th Annual Symposium on Recent Advances in the Use of the MMPI, Clearwater, FL.

Hall, G. C. N., Mauiro, R. D., Vitaliano, P. P., & Proctor, W. C. (1986). The utility of the MMPI with men who have sexually assaulted children. *Journal of Consulting and Clinical Psychology, 54*, 493–496.

Hampton, P. J. (1953). The development of a personality questionnaire for drinkers. *Genetic Psychological Monographs, 48*, 55–115.

Hanvik, L. J. (1949). *Some psychological dimensions of low-back pain.* Unpublished doctoral dissertation, University of Minnesota, Minneapolis.

Hanvik, L. J. (1951). MMPI profiles in patients with low back pain. *Journal of Consulting Psychology, 15*, 350–353.

Harding, C. F., Holz, W. C., & Kawakami, D. (1958). The differentiation of schizophrenic and superficially similar reactions. *Journal of Clinical Psychology, 14*, 147–149.

Hare, R. D. (1985). Comparison of procedures for the assessment of psychopathy. *Journal of Consulting and Clinical Psychology, 53*, 7–16.

Harrell, T. H. (1990, August). *The MMPI-2: Do the old interpretations hold true?* Paper presented at the annual meeting of the American Psychological Association, Boston.

Harris, R. E., & Lingoes, J. C. (1955). *Subscales for the MMPI: An aid to profile interpretation.* Unpublished manuscript, University of California.

Harris, R. J., Wittner, W., Koppell, B., & Hilf, F. D. (1970). MMPI scales vs. interviewer ratings of paranoia. *Psychological Reports, 27*, 447–450.

Harrison, R. H., & Kass, E. H. (1967). Differences between Negro and white pregnant women on the MMPI. *Journal of Consulting Psychology, 31*, 454–463.

Harrison, R. H., & Kass, E. H. (1968). MMPI correlates of Negro acculturation in a northern city. *Journal of Personality and Social Psychology, 10*, 262–270.

Hartshorne, H., & May, M. A. (1928). *Studies in deceit.* New York: Macmillan.

Harvey, M. A., & Sipprelle, C. N. (1976). Demand characteristic effects on the subtle and obvious subscales of the MMPI. *Journal of Personality Assessment, 40*, 539–544.

Hathaway, S. R. (1956). Scales *5* (Masculinity-Femininity), *6* (Paranoia), and *8* (Schizophrenia). In G. S. Welsh & W. G. Dahlstrom (Eds.), *Basic readings on the MMPI in psychiology and medicine* (pp. 104–111). Minneapolis: University of Minnesota Press.

Hathaway, S. R. (1972). Where have we gone wrong? The mystery of the missing progress. In J. N. Butcher (Ed.), *Objective personality assessment: Changing perspectives* (pp. 21–43). New York: Academic.

Hathaway, S. R. (1980). Scales *5* (Masculinity-Femininity), *6* (Paranoia), and *8* (Schizophrenia). In W. G. Dahlstrom & L. Dahlstrom (Eds.), *Basic readings on the MMPI in psychology and medicine: A new selection on personality measurement* (pp. 65–75). Minneapolis: University of Minnesota Press.

Hathaway, S. R., & Briggs, P. F. (1957). Some normative data on new MMPI scales. *Journal of Clinical Psychology, 13*, 364–368.

Hathaway, S. R., & McKinley, J. C. (1940). A multiphasic personality schedule (Minnesota): I. Construction of the schedule. *Journal of Psychology, 10*, 249–254.

Hathaway, S. R., & McKinley, J. C. (1942). A multiphasic personality schedule (Minnesota): III. The measurement of symptomatic depression. *Journal of Psychology, 14*, 73–84.

Hathaway, S. R., & McKinley, J. C. (1951). *MMPI manual.* New York: Psychological Corporation.

Hathaway, S. R., & McKinley, J. C. (1967). *MMPI manual* (Rev. ed.). New York: Psychological Corporation.

Hathaway, S. R., & McKinley, J. C. (1983). *Manual for administration and scoring of the MMPI.* Minneapolis: National Computer Systems.

Hathaway, S. R., & Meehl, P. E. (1951). *An atlas for the clinical use of the MMPI.* Minneapolis: University of Minnesota Press.

Hathaway, S. R., & Monachesi, E. D. (1963). *Adolescent personality and behavior: MMPI patterns of normal, delinquent, dropout, and other outcomes.* Minneapolis: University of Minnesota Press.

Haven, G. A., & Cole, K. M. (1972). Psychological correlates of low-back pain syndrome and their relationship to the effectiveness of a low-back pain program. *Newsletter for Research in Psychology, 14*, 31–33.

Hedlund, J. L. (1977). MMPI clinical scale correlates. *Journal of Consulting and Clinical Psychology, 45*, 739–750.

Hedlund, J. L., & Won Cho, D. (1979). [MMPI data research tape for Missouri Department of Mental Health patients.] Unpublished raw data.

Hedlund, J. L., Won Cho, D., & Powell, B. J. (1975). Use of MMPI short forms with psychiatric patients. *Journal of Consulting and Clinical Psychology, 43*, 924.

Heilbrun, A. B. (1961). The psychological significance of the MMPI *K* scale in a normal population. *Journal of Consulting Psychology, 25*, 486–491.

Heilbrun, A. B. (1963). Revision of the MMPI *K* correction procedure for improved detection of maladjustment in a normal college population. *Journal of Consulting Psychology, 27*, 161–165.

Heilbrun, A. B. (1979). Psychopathy and violent crime. *Journal of Consulting and Clinical Psychology, 47*, 509–516.

Helmes, E., & McLaughlin, J. D. (1983). A comparison of three MMPI short forms: Limited clinical utility in classification. *Journal of Consulting and Clinical Psychology, 51*, 786–787.

Henrichs, T. F. (1964). Objective configural rules for disciminating MMPI profiles in a psychiatric population. *Journal of Clinical Psychology, 20*, 157–159.

Henrichs, T. F. (1966). A note on the extension of MMPI configural rules. *Journal of Clinical Psychology, 22*, 51–52.

Herreid, C. F., & Herreid, J. R. (1966). Differences in MMPI scores in native and nonnative Alaskans. *Journal of Social Psychology, 70*, 191–198.

Hibbs, B. J., Kobos, J. C., & Gonzalez, J. (1979). Effects of ethnicity, sex, and age on MMPI profiles. *Psychological Reports, 45*, 591–597.

Hill, H. E., Haertzen, C. A., & Glaser, R. (1960). Personality characteristics of narcotic addicts as indicated by the MMPI. *Journal of General Psychology, 62*, 127–139.

Hiner, D. L., Ogren, D. J., & Baxter, J. C. (1969). Ideal-self responding on the MMPI. *Journal of Projective Techniques and Personality Assessment, 33*, 389–396.

Hodo, G. L., & Fowler, R. D. (1976). Frequency

of MMPI two-point codes in a large alcoholic sample. *Journal of Clinical Psychology, 32,* 487–489.

Hoffmann, H., Loper, R. G., & Kammeier, M. L. (1974). Identifying future alcoholics with MMPI alcoholism scales. *Quarterly Journal of Studies on Alcohol, 35,* 490–498.

Hoffmann, N. G., & Butcher, J. N. (1975). Clinical limitations of three MMPI short forms. *Journal of Consulting and Clinical Psychology, 43,* 32–39.

Hokanson, J. E., & Calden, G. (1960). Negrowhite differences on the MMPI. *Journal of Clinical Psychology, 16,* 32–33.

Holcomb, W. R., & Adams, N. (1982). Racial influences on intelligence and personality measures of people who commit murder. *Journal of Clinical Psychology, 38,* 793–796.

Holcomb, W. R., Adams, N. A., & Ponder, H. M. (1984). Are separate black and white MMPI norms needed?: An IQ-controlled comparison of accused murderers. *Journal of Clinical Psychology, 40,* 189–193.

Holden, R. R., & Jackson, D. N. (1979). Item subtlety and face validity in personality assessment. *Journal of Consulting and Clinical Psychology, 47,* 459–468.

Holland, T. R. (1979). Ethnic group differences in MMPI profile pattern and factorial structure among adult offenders. *Journal of Personality Assessment, 43,* 72–77.

Holland, T. R., & Levi, M. (1983). Personality correlates of extent versus type of antisocial behavior among adult offenders: A multivariate analysis. *Multivariate Behavioral Research, 18,* 391–400.

Holmes, G. R., Sabalis, R. F., Chestnut, E., & Khoury, L. (1984). Parent MMPI critical item and clinical scale changes in the 1970s. *Journal of Clinical Psychology, 40,* 1194–1198.

Holmes, W. O. (1953). *The development of an empirical MMPI scale for alcoholism.* Unpublished Master's thesis, San Jose State College.

Honaker, L. M. (1988). The equivalency of computerized and conventional MMPI administration: A critical review. *Clinical Psychology Review, 8,* 561–577.

Honaker, L. M. (1990, August). *MMPI and MMPI-2: Alternate forms or different tests?* Paper presented at the annual meeting of the American Psychological Association, Boston.

Honaker, L. M., Harrell, T. M., & Buffaloe, J. D. (1989). Equivalency of microtest computer MMPI administration for standard and special scales. *Computers in Human Behavior, 4,* 323–337.

Hoppe, C. M., & Singer, R. D. (1976). Over-controlled hostility, empathy, and egocentric balance in violent and nonviolent psychiatric offenders. *Psychological Reports, 39,* 1303–1308.

Horowitz, L. M., Wright, J. C., Lowenstein, E., & Parad, H. W. (1981). The prototype as a construct in abnormal psychology: 1. A method for deriving prototypes. *Journal of Abnormal Psychology, 90,* 568–574.

Hovanitz, C. A., & Gynther, M. D. (1980). The prediction of impulsive behavior: Comparative validities of obvious versus subtle MMPI hypomania (*Ma*) items. *Journal of Clinical Psychology, 36,* 422–427.

Hovey, H. B., & Lewis, E. G. (1967). Semi-automatic interpretation of the MMPI. *Journal of Clinical Psychology, 23,* 123–134.

Hoyt, D. P., & Sedlacek, G. M. (1958). Differentiating alcoholics from normals and abnormals with the MMPI. *Journal of Clinical Psychology, 14,* 69–74.

Hryckowian, M. J., & Gynther, M. D. (1988). MMPI item subtlety: Another look. *Journal of Clinical Psychology, 44,* 148–152.

Hsu, L. M. (1984). MMPI *T* scores: Linear versus normalized. *Journal of Consulting and Clinical Psychology, 52,* 821–823.

Hsu, L. M., & Betman, J. A. (1986). MMPI T score conversion tables, 1957–1983. *Journal of Consulting and Clinical Psychology, 54,* 497–501.

Huber, N. A., & Danahy, S. (1975). Use of the MMPI in predicting completion and evaluating changes in a long-term alcoholism treatment program. *Journal of Studies on Alcohol, 36,* 1230–1237.

Huesmann, L. R., Lefkowitz, M. M., & Eron, L. D. (1978). Sum of MMPI Scales *F, 4,* and *9* as a measure of aggression. *Journal of Consulting and Clinical Psychology, 46,* 1071–1078.

Hunt, H. F. (1948). The effect of deliberate deception on MMPI performance. *Journal of Consulting Psychology, 12,* 396–402.

Hunt, H. F., Carp, A., Cass, Jr., W. A., Winder, C. L., & Kantor, R. E. (1948). A study of the differential diagnostic efficiency of the MMPI. *Journal of Consulting Psychology, 12,* 331–336.

Hyer, L., Boudewyns, P., Harrison, W. R., O'Leary, W. C., Bruno, R. D., Saucer, R. T., & Blount, J. B. (1988). Vietnam veterans: Overreporting versus acceptable reporting of symptoms. *Journal of Personality Assessment, 52,* 475–486.

Hyer, L., Harkey, B., & Harrison, W. R. (1986). MMPI scales and subscales: Patterns of older, middle-aged, and younger inpatients. *Journal of Clinical Psychology, 42,* 596–601.

Ingram, J. C., Marchioni, P., Hill, G., Caraveo-Ramos, E., & McNeil, B. (1985). Recidivism, perceived problem-solving abilities, MMPI characteristics, and violence: A study of black and white incarcerated male adult offenders. *Journal of Clinical Psychology, 41,* 425–432.

Jackson, D. N. (1967). Review of J. Block: The challenge of response sets. *Educational and Psychological Measurement, 27,* 207–219.

Jackson, D. N. (1968). *Personality Research Form manual.* Goshen, NY: Research Psychologists Press.

Jackson, D. N. (1971). The dynamics of structured personality tests: 1971. *Psychological Review, 78,* 229–248.

Jarnecke, R. W., & Chambers, E. D. (1977). MMPI content scales: Dimensional structure, construct validity, and interpretive norms in a psychiatric population. *Journal of Consulting and Clinical Psychology, 45,* 1126–1131.

Jenkins, G. (1984). *Response sets and personality measures: The K scale of the MMPI.* Unpublished doctoral dissertation, Texas Tech University, Lubbock.

Johnson, J. H., Klingler, D. E., & Williams, T. A. (1977). An external criterion study of the MMPI validity indices. *Journal of Clinical Psychology, 33,* 154–156.

Jones, E. E. (1978). Black-white personality differences: Another look. *Journal of Personality Assessment, 42,* 244–252.

Jones, F. W., Neuringer, C., & Patterson, T. W. (1976). An evaluation of an MMPI response consistency measure. *Journal of Personality Assessment, 40,* 419–421.

Kamerown, D. B., Pincus, H. A., & Macdonald, D. I. (1986). Alcohol abuse, other drug abuse, and mental disorders in medical practice. *Journal of the American Medical Association, 255,* 2054–2057.

Kammeier, M. L., Hoffmann, H., & Loper, R. G. (1973). Personality characteristics of alcoholics as college freshmen and at time of treatment. *Quarterly Journal of Studies on Alcohol, 34,* 390–399.

Karol, R. L. (1985). MMPI omitted items: A method for quickly determining individual scale impact. *Journal of Consulting and Clinical Psychology, 53,* 134–135.

Kazan, A. T., & Sheinberg, I. M. (1945). Clinical note on the significance of the validity score (*F*) in the MMPI. *American Journal of Psychiatry, 102,* 181–183.

Keane, T. M., Malloy, P. F., & Fairbank, J. A. (1984). Empirical development of an MMPI subscale for the assessment of combat-related posttraumatic stress disorder. *Journal of Consulting and Clinical Psychology, 52,* 888–891.

Kelley, C. K., & King, G. D. (1978). Behavioral correlates for within-normal-limit MMPI profiles with and without elevated *K* in students at a university mental health center. *Journal of Clinical Psychology, 34,* 695–699.

Kelley, C. K., & King, G. D. (1979a). Behavioral correlates of infrequent two-point MMPI code types at a university mental health center. *Journal of Clinical Psychology, 35,* 576–585.

Kelley, C. K., & King, G. D. (1979b). Behavioral correlates of the *2-7-8* MMPI profile type in students at a university mental health center. *Journal of Consulting and Clinical Psychology, 47,* 679–685.

Kelley, C. K., & King, G. D. (1979c). Cross-validation of the *2-8/8-2* MMPI code type for young adult psychiatric outpatients. *Journal of Personality Assessment, 43,* 143–149.

Kelley, C. K., & King, G. D. (1980). Two- and three-point classification of MMPI profiles in which Scales *2, 7,* and *8* are the highest elevations. *Journal of Personality Assessment, 44,* 25–33.

Kincannon, J. C. (1968). Prediction of the standard MMPI scale scores from 71 items: The Mini-Mult. *Journal of Consulting and Clinical Psychology, 32,* 319–325.

King, G. D., & Kelley, C. K. (1977a). Behavioral correlates for Spike-*4*, Spike-*9*, and *4-9/9-4* MMPI profiles in students at a university mental health center. *Journal of Clinical Psychology, 33,* 718–724.

King, G. D., & Kelley, C. K. (1977b). MMPI behavioral correlates of Spike-*5* and two-point code types with Scale *5* as one elevation. *Journal of Clinical Psychology, 33,* 180–185.

King, H. F., Carroll, J. L., & Fuller, G. B. (1977). Comparison of nonpsychiatric blacks and whites on the MMPI. *Journal of Clinical Psychology, 33*, 725-728.

Kirk, A. R., & Zucker, R. A. (1979). Some sociopsychological factors in attempted suicide among urban black males. *Suicide and Life Threatening Behavior, 9*, 76-86.

Kline, J. A., Rozynko, V. V., Flint, G., & Roberts, A. C. (1973). Personality characteristics of male native American alcoholic patients. *International Journal of the Addictions, 8*, 729-732.

Klinge, V., & Strauss, M. E. (1976). Effects of scoring norms on adolescent psychiatric patients' MMPI profiles. *Journal of Personality Assessment, 40*, 13-17.

Kleinmuntz, B. (1960). Identification of maladjusted college students. *Journal of Counseling Psychology, 7*, 209-211.

Kleinmuntz, B. (1961a). The college maladjustment scale (MT): Norms and predictive validity. *Educational and Psychological Measurement, 21*, 1029-1033.

Kleinmuntz, B. (1961b). Screening: Identification or prediction? *Journal of Counseling Psychology, 8*, 279-280.

Kleinmuntz, B. (1963). MMPI decision rules for the identification of college maladjustment: A digital computer approach. *Psychological Monographs, 77*, 14(Whole No. 577).

Knapp, R. R. (1960). A reevaluation of the validity of MMPI scales of dominance and social responsibility. *Educational and Psychological Measurement, 20*, 381-386.

Koss, M. P., & Butcher, J. N. (1973). A comparison of psychiatric patients' self-report with other sources of clinical information. *Journal of Research in Personality, 7*, 225-236.

Koss, M. P., Butcher, J. N., & Hoffmann, N. G. (1976). The MMPI critical items: How well do they work? *Journal of Consulting and Clinical Psychology, 44*, 921-928.

Kroger, R. O., & Turnbull, W. (1975). Invalidity of validity scales: The case of the MMPI. *Journal of Consulting and Clinical Psychology, 43*, 48-55.

Lachar, D. (1974). *The MMPI: Clinical assessment and automated interpretation.* Los Angeles: Western Psychological Services.

Lachar, D., & Alexander, R. S. (1978). Veridicality of self-report: Replicated correlates of the Wiggins MMPI content scales. *Journal of Consulting and Clinical Psychology, 46*, 1349-1356.

Lachar, D., Klinge, V., & Grisell, J. L. (1976). Relative accuracy of automated MMPI narratives generated from adult norm and adolescent norm profiles. *Journal of Consulting and Clinical Psychology, 44*, 20-24.

Lachar, D., & Wrobel, T. A. (1979). Validating clinicians' hunches: Construction of a new MMPI critical item set. *Journal of Consulting and Clinical Psychology, 47*, 277-284.

Lacks, P. B., Rothenberg, P. J., & Unger, B. L. (1970). MMPI scores and marital status in male schizophrenics. *Journal of Clinical Psychology, 26*, 221-222.

Lair, C. V., & Trapp, E. P. (1962). The differential diagnostic value of MMPI with somatically disturbed patients. *Journal of Clinical Psychology, 18*, 146-147.

Landis, C., & Katz, S. E. (1934). The validity of certain questions which purport to measure neurotic tendencies. *Journal of Applied Psychology, 18*, 343-356.

Lane, P. J., & Kling, J. S. (1979). Construct validation of the Overcontrolled Hostility scale of the MMPI. *Journal of Consulting and Clinical Psychology, 47*, 781-782.

Lanyon, R. I. (1967). Simulation of normal and psychopathic MMPI personality patterns. *Journal of Consulting Psychology, 31*, 94-97.

Lanyon, R. I. (1968). *A handbook of MMPI group profiles.* Minneapolis: University of Minnesota Press.

Lanyon, R. I., & Lutz, R. W. (1984). MMPI discrimination of defensive and nondefensive felony sex offenders. *Journal of Consulting and Clinical Psychology, 52*, 841-843.

Lavin, P. (1984). [Summary of Tennessee Valley Authority data on the MMPI used in nuclear power plant personnel screening.] Unpublished raw data.

Lawson, H. H., Kahn, M. W., & Heiman, E. M. (1982). Psychopathology, treatment outcome and attitude toward mental illness in Mexican American and European patients. *International Journal of Social Psychology, 28*, 20-26.

Lawton, M. P., & Kleban, M. H. (1965). Prisoners' faking on the MMPI. *Journal of Clinical Psychology, 21*, 269-271.

Leon, G. R., Gillum, B., Gillum, R., & Gouze, M. (1979). Personality stability and change over a 30-year period-middle age to old age. *Journal of Consulting and Clinical Psychology, 47*, 517-524.

Leonard, C. V. (1977). The MMPI as a suicide

predictor. *Journal of Consulting and Clinical Psychology*, *45*, 367–377.

Lester, D., & Clopton, J. R. (1979). Suicide and overcontrol. *Psychological Reports*, *44*, 758.

Levitt, E. E. (1978). A note on "MMPI scale development methodology." *Journal of Personality Assessment*, *42*, 503–504.

Levitt, E. E. (1989). *The clinical application of MMPI special scales*. Hillsdale, NJ: Erlbaum.

Levitt, E. E. (1990). A structural analysis of the impact of MMPI-2 on the MMPI-1. *Journal of Personality Assessment*, *55*, 562–577.

Levy, L. H. (1963). *Psychological interpretation*. New York: Holt, Rinehart, & Winston.

Lichenstein, E. & Bryan, J. H. (1966). Short-term stability of MMPI profiles. *Journal of Consulting Psychology*, *30*, 172–174.

Lingoes, J. C. (1960). MMPI factors of the Harris and the Wiener subscales. *Journal of Consulting Psychology*, *24*, 74–83.

Liske, R., & McCormick, R. (1976). MMPI profiles compared for black and white hospitalized veterans. *Newsletter for Research in Mental Health and Behavioral Sciences*, *18*, 30–32.

Listiak, R. L., & Stone, L. A. (1971). Psychophysical approach to clinical judgment of low *T* scores on the MMPI. *Journal of Consulting and Clinical Psychology*, *36*, 447.

Little, K. B., & Fisher, J. (1958). Two new experimental scales of the MMPI. *Journal of Consulting Psychology*, *22*, 305–306.

Loper, R. G., Kammeier, M. L., & Hoffmann, H. (1973). MMPI characteristics of college freshman males who later became alcoholics. *Journal of Abnormal Psychology*, *82*, 159–162.

Louks, J. L., Freeman, C. W., & Calsyn, D. A. (1978). Personality organization as an aspect of back pain in a medical setting. *Journal of Personality Assessment*, *42*, 152–158.

Lubin, B., Larsen, R. M., Matarazzo, J. D., & Seever, M. (1985). Psychological test usage patterns in five professional settings. *American Psychologist*, *40*, 857–861.

MacAndrew, C. (1965). The differentiation of male alcoholic outpatients from nonalcoholic psychiatric outpatients by means of the MMPI. *Quarterly Journal of Studies on Alcohol*, *26*, 238–246.

MacAndrew, C. (1981). What the *MAC* scale tells us about men alcoholics: An interpretive review. *Journal of Studies on Alcohol*, *42*, 604–625.

MacAndrew, C. (1986). Toward the psychometric detection of substance misuse in young men: The *SAP* scale. *Journal of Studies on Alcohol*, *47*, 161–166.

MacAndrew, C. (1987). An examination of the applicability of the Substance Abuse Proclivity scale to young adult males. *Psychology of Addictive Behaviors*, *1*, 140–145.

MacAndrew, C. (1988). Differences in the self-depictions of female alcoholics and psychiatric outpatients: Towards a depiction of the modal female alcoholic. *Journal of Studies on Alcohol*, *49*, 71–77.

MacAndrew, C., & Geertsma, R. H. (1964). A critique of alcoholism scales derived from the MMPI. *Quarterly Journal of Studies on Alcohol*, *25*, 68–76.

Mallory, C. H., & Walker, C. E. (1972). MMPI O-H scale responses of assaultive and nonassaultive prisoners and associated life history variables. *Educational and Psychological Measurement*, *32*, 1125–1128.

Maloney, M. P., Duvall, S. W., & Friesen, J. (1980). Evaluation of response consistency on the MMPI. *Psychological Reports*, *46*, 295–298.

Manosevitz, M. (1971). Education and MMPI *Mf* scores in homosexual and heterosexual males. *Journal of Consulting and Clinical Psychology*, *36*, 395–399.

Marks, P. A., & Seeman, W. (1963). *The actuarial description of personality: An atlas for use with the MMPI*. Baltimore: Williams & Wilkins.

Marks, P. A., Seeman, W., & Haller, D. L. (1974). *The actuarial use of the MMPI with adolescents and adults*. Baltimore: Williams & Wilkins.

Marsella, A. J., Sanborn, K. O., Kameoka, V., Shizuru, L., & Brennan, J. (1975). Cross-validation of self-report measures of depression among normal populations of Japanese, Chinese, and Caucasian ancestry. *Journal of Clinical Psychology*, *31*, 281–287.

Martin, P. W., & Greene, R. L. (1979, March). *A comparison of the Pepper and Strong and Serkownek subscales for the Masculinity-Femininity scale of the MMPI*. Paper presented at the meeting of the Society for Personality Assessment, Scottsdale, AZ.

Matarazzo, J. D. (1955). MMPI validity scores as a function of increasing levels of anxiety. *Journal of Consulting Psychology*, *19*, 213–217.

McAnulty, D. P., Rappaport, N. B., & McAnulty,

R. D. (1985). An a posteriori investigation of standard MMPI validity scales. *Psychological Reports, 57*, 95–98.

McCreary, C. (1975). Personality profiles of persons convicted of indecent exposure. *Journal of Clinical Psychology, 31*, 260–262.

McCreary, C., & Padilla, E. (1977). MMPI differences among Black, Mexican-American, and White male offenders. *Journal of Clinical Psychology, 33*, 171–177.

McDonald, R. L., & Gynther, M. D. (1962). MMPI norms for southern adolescent Negroes. *Journal of Social Psychology, 58*, 277–282.

McDonald, R. L., & Gynther, M. D. (1963). MMPI differences associated with sex, race, and class in two adolescent samples. *Journal of Consulting Psychology, 27*, 112–116.

McGill, J. C. (1980). MMPI score differences among Anglo, Black, and Mexican-American welfare recipients. *Journal of Clinical Psychology, 36*, 147–151.

McGrath, R. E., & O'Malley, W. B. (1986). The assessment of denial and physical complaints: The validity of the *Hy* scale and associated MMPI signs. *Journal of Clinical Psychology, 42*, 754–760.

McGrath, R. E., O'Malley, W. B., & Dura, J. R. (1986). Alternative scoring system of repeated items on the MMPI: *Caveat emptor*. *Journal of Personality Assessment, 50*, 182–185.

McKegney, F. P. (1965). An item analysis of the MMPI *F* scale in juvenile delinquents. *Journal of Clinical Psychology, 21*, 201–205.

McKinley, J. C., & Hathaway, S. R. (1940). A multiphasic personality schedule (Minnesota): II. A differential study of hypochondriasis. *Journal of Psychology, 10*, 255–268.

McKinley, J. C., & Hathaway, S. R. (1942). A multiphasic personality schedule (Minnesota): IV. Psychasthenia. *Journal of Applied Psychology, 26*, 614–624.

McKinley, J. C., & Hathaway, S. R. (1944). The MMPI: V. Hysteria, hypomania, and psychopathic deviate. *Journal of Applied Psychology, 28*, 153–174.

McKinley, J. C., Hathaway, S. R., & Meehl, P. E. (1948). The MMPI: VI. The *K* scale. *Journal of Consulting Psychology, 12*, 20–31.

McLaughlin, J. D., Helmes, E., & Howe, M. G. (1983). Note on the reliability of three MMPI short forms. *Journal of Personality Assessment, 47*, 357–358.

Meehl, P. E. (1945). An investigation of a general normality or control factor in personality testing. *Psychological Monographs, 4* (Whole No. 274).

Meehl, P. E. (1956). Wanted—A good cookbook. *American Psychologist, 11*, 263–272.

Meehl, P. E. (1959). A comparison of clinicians with five statistical methods of identifying psychotic MMPI profiles. *Journal of Counseling Psychology, 6*, 102–109.

Meehl, P. E., & Dahlstrom, W. G. (1960). Objective configural rules for discriminating psychotic from neurotic MMPI profiles. *Journal of Consulting Psychology, 24*, 375–387.

Meehl, P. E., & Hathaway, S. R. (1946). The *K* factor as a suppressor variable in the MMPI. *Journal of Applied Psychology, 30*, 525–564.

Megargee, E. I. (1972). *The California Psychological Inventory handbook*. San Francisco: Jossey-Bass.

Megargee, E. I. (1985). Assessing alcoholism and drug abuse with the MMPI: Implication for employment screening. In C. D. Spielberger & J. N. Butcher (Eds.), *Advances in personality assessment* (Vol. 5, pp. 1–39). Hillsdale, NJ: Erlbaum.

Megargee, E. I., & Cook, P. E. (1975). Negative response bias and the MMPI overcontrolled-hostility scale: A response to Deiker. *Journal of Consulting and Clinical Psychology, 43*, 725–729.

Megargee, E. I., Cook, P. E., & Mendelsohn, G. A. (1967). Development and validation of an MMPI scale of assaultiveness in overcontrolled individuals. *Journal of Abnormal Psychology, 72*, 519–528.

Megargee, E. I., & Mendelsohn, G. A. (1962). A cross-validation of twelve MMPI indices of hostility and control. *Journal of Abnormal and Social Psychology, 65*, 431–438.

Mehlman, B., & Rand, M. E. (1960). Face validity of the MMPI. *Journal of General Psychology, 63*, 171–178.

Meikle, S., & Gerritse, R. (1970). MMPI "cookbook" pattern frequencies in a psychiatric unit. *Journal of Clinical Psychology, 26*, 82–84.

Mezzich, J. E., Damarin, F. L., & Erickson, J. R. (1974). Comparative validity of strategies and indices for differential diagnosis of depressive states from other psychiatric conditions using the MMPI. *Journal of Consulting and Clinical Psychology, 42*, 691–698.

Miller, C., Knapp, S. C., & Daniels, C. W. (1968). MMPI study of Negro mental hygiene clinic patients. *Journal of Abnormal Psychology, 73*, 168–173.

Miller, C., Wertz, C., & Counts, S. (1961). Racial differences on the MMPI. *Journal of Clinical Psychology, 17,* 159–161.

Miller, H. R., & Streiner, D. L. (1985). The Harris-Lingoes subscales: Fact or fiction? *Journal of Clinical Psychology, 41,* 45–51.

Miller, H. R., & Streiner, D. L. (1986). Differences in MMPI profiles with the norms of Colligan et al. *Journal of Consulting and Clinical Psychology, 54,* 843–845.

Monroe, J. J., Miller, J. S., & Lyle, Jr., W. H. (1964). The extension of psychopathic deviancy scales for the screening of addict patients. *Educational and Psychological Measurement, 24,* 47–56.

Montgomery, G. T., & Orozco, S. (1985). Mexican Americans' performance on the MMPI as a function of level of acculturation. *Journal of Clinical Psychology, 41,* 203–212.

Moore, C. D., & Handal, P. J. (1980). Adolescents' MMPI performance, cynicism, estrangement, and personal adjustment as a function of race and sex. *Journal of Clinical Psychology, 36,* 932–936.

Moreland, K. L. (1984). Comparative validity of the MMPI and two short forms: Psychiatric ratings. *Journal of Personality Assessment, 48,* 265–270.

Morey, L. C., Blashfield, R. K., Webb, W. W., & Jewell, J. (1988). MMPI scales for DSM-III personality disorders: A preliminary validation study. *Journal of Clinical Psychology, 44,* 47–50.

Morey, L. C., & Smith, M. R. (1988). Personality disorders. In R. L. Greene (Ed.), *The MMPI: Use with specific populations* (pp. 110–158). Philadelphia: Grune & Stratton.

Morey, L. C., Waugh, M. H., & Blashfield, R. K. (1985). MMPI scales for DSM-III personality disorders: Their derivation and correlates. *Journal of Personality Assessment, 49,* 245–251.

Muller, B. P., & Bruno, L. N. (1988, March). *The effects of ethnicity on personality assessment in police candidates.* Paper presented at the 23rd Annual Symposium on Recent Developments in the Use of the MMPI, St. Petersburg, FL.

Muller, B. P. & Bruno, L. N. (1990, August). *The myth of ethnic effects on the MMPI/MMPI-2.* Paper presented at the annual meeting of the American Psychological Association, Boston.

Murphree, H. B., Karabelas, M. J., & Bryan, L. L. (1962). Scores of inmates of a federal penitentiary on two scales of the MMPI. *Journal of Clinical Psychology, 18,* 137–139.

Murray, J. B., Munley, M. J., & Gilbart, T. E. (1965). The *Pd* scale of the MMPI for college students. *Journal of Clinical Psychology, 21,* 48–51.

Nakamura, C. Y. (1960). Validity of *K* scale (MMPI) in college counseling. *Journal of Counseling Psychology, 7,* 108–115.

Navran, L. (1954). A rationally derived MMPI scale to measure dependence. *Journal of Consulting Psychology, 18,* 192.

Nelson, L. D. (1987). Measuring depression in a clinical population using the MMPI. *Journal of Consulting and Clinical Psychology, 55,* 788–790.

Newmark, C. S., Gentry, L., Simpson, M., & Jones, T. (1978). MMPI criteria for diagnosing schizophrenia. *Journal of Personality Assessment, 42,* 366–373.

Newmark, C. S., & Hutchins, T. C. (1980). Age and MMPI indices of schizophrenia. *Journal of Clinical Psychology, 36,* 768–769.

Newmark, C. S., Ziff, D. R., Finch, Jr., A. J., & Kendall, P. C. (1978). Comparing the empirical validity of the standard form with two abbreviated MMPIs. *Journal of Consulting and Clinical Psychology, 46,* 53–61.

Newton, J. R. (1968). Clinical normative data for MMPI special scales: Critical items, manifest anxiety, and repression-sensitiziation. *Journal of Clinical Psychology, 24,* 427–430.

Nichols, D. S. (1987). *Interpreting the Wiggins MMPI content scales. Clinical notes on the MMPI,* No. 10. Minneapolis: National Computer Systems.

Nichols, D. S. (1988). Mood disorders. In R. L. Greene (Ed.), *The MMPI: Use in specific populations* (pp. 74–109). San Antonio: Grune & Stratton.

Nichols, D. S., Greene, R. L., & Schmolck, P. (1989). Criteria for assessing inconsistent patterns of item endorsement on the MMPI: Rationale, development, and empirical trials. *Journal of Clinical Psychology, 45,* 239–250.

O'Connor, J. P., & Stefic, E. C. (1959). Some patterns of hypochondriasis. *Educational and Psychological Measurement, 19,* 363–371.

Olmsted, D. W., & Monachesi, E. D. (1956). A validity check on MMPI scales of responsibility and dominance. *Journal of Abnormal and Social Psychology, 53,* 140–141.

Osborne, D., & Colligan, R. C. (1986). Linear equations for the development of non-normalized T score tables based on the contemporary normative study of the MMPI. *Journal of Clinical Psychology*, *42*, 482–484.

Osborne, D., Colligan, R. C., & Offord, K. P. (1986). Normative tables for the *F - K* index of the MMPI based on a contemporary normal sample. *Journal of Clinical Psychology*, *42*, 593–595.

Otto, R. K., Lang, A. R., Megargee, E. I., & Rosenblatt, A. I. (1988). Ability of alcoholics to escape detection by the MMPI. *Journal of Consulting and Clinical Psychology*, *56*, 452–457.

Overall, J. E., & Gomez-Mont, F. (1974). The MMPI-168 for psychiatric screening. *Educational and Psychological Measurement*, *34*, 315–319.

Padilla, E. R., Olmedo, E. L., & Loya, F. (1982). Acculturation and the MMPI performance of Chicano and Anglo college students. *Journal of Behavioral Sciences*, *4*, 451–466.

Page, J., Landis, C., & Katz, S. E. (1934). Schizophrenic traits in the functional psychoses and in normal individuals. *American Journal of Psychiatry*, *90*, 1213–1225.

Page, R. D., & Bozlee, S. (1982). A cross-cultural MMPI comparison of alcoholics. *Psychological Reports*, *50*, 639–646.

Pancoast, D. L., & Archer, R. P. (1989). Original adult MMPI norms in normal samples: A review with implications for future developments. *Journal of Personality Assessment*, *53*, 376–395.

Panton, J. H. (1959a). Inmate personality differences related to recidivism, age, and race as measured by the MMPI. *Journal of Correctional Psychology*, *4*, 28–35.

Panton, J. H. (1959b). The response of prison inmates to MMPI subscales. *Journal of Social Therapy*, *5*, 233–237.

Patalano, F. (1978). Personality dimensions of drug abusers who enter a drug-free therapeutic community. *Psychological Reports*, *42*, 1063–1069.

Patterson, E. T., Charles, H. L., Woodward, W. A., Roberts, W. R., & Penk, W. E. (1981). Differences in measures of personality and family environment among black and white alcoholics. *Journal of Consulting and Clinical Psychology*, *49*, 1–9.

Pauker, J. D. (1966). Identification of MMPI profile types in a female, inpatient, psychiatric setting using the Marks and Seeman rules. *Journal of Consulting Psychology*, *30*, 90.

Paulhus, D. L. (1984). Two-component models of social desirable responding. *Journal of Personality and Social Psychology*, *46*, 598–609.

Paulhus, D. L. (1986). Self-deception and impression management in test responses. In A. Angleitner & J. S. Wiggins (Eds.), *Personality assessment via questionnaires: Current issues in theory and measurement* (pp. 143–165). Berlin: Springer-Verlag.

Paulson, M. J., Afifi, A. A., Thomason, M. L., & Chaleff, A. (1974). The MMPI: A descriptive measure of psychopathology in abusive parents. *Journal of Clinical Psychology*, *30*, 387–390.

Payne, F. D., & Wiggins, J. S. (1972). MMPI profile types and the self-report of psychiatric patients. *Journal of Abnormal Psychology*, *79*, 1–8.

Penk, W. E., Keane, T., Robinowitz, R., Fowler, D. R., Bell, W. E., & Finkelstein, A. (1988). Post-traumatic stress disorder. In R. L. Greene (Ed.), *The MMPI: Use in specific populations* (pp. 198–213). San Antonio: Grune & Stratton.

Penk, W. E., Roberts, W. R., Robinowitz, R., Dolan, M. P., Atkins, H. G., & Woodward, W. A. (1982). MMPI differences of black and white polydrug abusers seeking treatment. *Journal of Consulting and Clinical Psychology*, *50*, 463–465.

Penk, W. E., Robinowitz, R., Roberts, W. R., Dolan, M. P., & Atkins, H. G. (1981). MMPI differences of male Hispanic-American, black, and white heroin addicts. *Journal of Consulting and Clinical Psychology*, *49*, 488–490.

Penk, W. E., Woodward, W. A., Robinowitz, R., & Hess, J. L. (1978). Differences in MMPI scores of black and white compulsive heroin users. *Journal of Abnormal Psychology*, *87*, 505–513.

Pepper, L, J., & Strong, P. N. (1958). *Judgmental subscales for the Mf scale of the MMPI*. Unpublished manuscript.

Persons, R. W., & Marks, P. A. (1971). The violent *4-3* MMPI personality type. *Journal of Consulting and Clinical Psychology*, *36*, 189–196.

Peteroy, E. T., & Pirrello, P. E. (1982). Comparison of MMPI scales for black and white hospitalized samples. *Psychological Reports*, *50*, 662.

Peterson, C. D. (1989). *Masculinity and femininity as independent dimensions on the MMPI-2*. Unpublished doctoral dissertation, University of North Carolina, Chapel Hill.

Peterson, D. R. (1954). The diagnosis of subclinical schizophrenia. *Journal of Consulting Psychology, 18*, 198–200.

Pichot, P., Perse, J., Lebeaux, M. O., Dureau, J. L., Perez, C., & Rychewaert, A. (1972). La personalite des sujets presentant des douleurs dorsales fonctionnelles valeur de l'inventaire Multiphasique de Personalite du Minnesota. *Revue de Psychoiogie Applique, 22*, 145–172.

Plemons, G. (1977). A comparison of MMPI scores of Anglo- and Mexican-American psychiatric patients. *Journal of Consulting and Clinical Psychology, 45*, 149–150.

Pollack, D., & Shore, J. H. (1980). Validity of the MMPI with Native Americans. *American Journal of Psychiatry, 137*, 946–950.

Posey, C. D., & Hess, A. K. (1984). The fakability of subtle and obvious measures of aggression by male prisoners. *Journal of Personality Assessment, 48*, 137–144.

Posey, C. D., & Hess, A. K. (1985). Aggressive response sets and subtle-obvious MMPI scale distinctions in male offenders. *Journal of Personality Assessment, 49*, 235–239.

Post, R. D., Clopton, J. R., Keefer, G., Rosenberg, D., Blyth, L. S., & Stein, M. (1986). MMPI predictors of mania among psychiatric patients. *Journal of Personality Assessment, 50*, 248–256.

Post, R. D., & Gasparikova-Krasnec, M. (1979). MMPI validity scales and behavioral disturbance in psychiatric inpatients. *Journal of Personality Assessment, 43*, 155–159.

Poythress, N. G., & Blaney, P. H. (1978). The validity of MMPI interpretations based on the Mini-Mult and the FAM. *Journal of Personality Assessment, 42*, 143–147.

Pritchard, D. A., & Rosenblatt, A. (1980a). Racial bias in the MMPI: A methodological review. *Journal of Consulting and Clinical Psychology, 48*, 263–267.

Pritchard, D. A., & Rosenblatt, A. (1980b). Reply to Gynther and Green. *Journal of Consulting and Clinical Psychology, 48*, 273–274.

Prokop, C. K. (1986). Hysteria scale elevations in low back pain patients: A risk factor for misdiagnosis? *Journal of Consulting and Clinical Psychology, 54*, 558–562.

Prokop, C. K. (1988). Chronic pain. In R. L. Greene (Ed.), *The MMPI: Use with specific populations* (pp. 22–49). San Antonio: Grune & Stratton.

Pruitt, W. A., & Van de Castle, R. L. (1962). Dependency measures and welfare chronicity. *Journal of Consulting Psychology, 26*, 559–560.

Quay, H., & Rowell, J. T. (1955). The validity of a schizophrenic screening scale of the MMPI. *Journal of Clinical Psychology, 11*, 92–93.

Quinsey, V. L., Maguire, A., & Varney, G. W. (1983). Assertion and overcontrolled hostility among mentally disordered murderers. *Journal of Consulting and Clinical Psychology, 51*, 550–556.

Rader, C. M. (1977). MMPI profile types of exposers, rapists, and assaulters in a court services population. *Journal of Consulting and Clinical Psychology, 45*, 61–69.

Rand, S. W. (1979). Correspondence between psychological reports based on the Mini-Mult and the MMPI. *Journal of Personality Assessment, 43*, 160–163.

Reilley, R. R., & Knight, G. E. (1970). MMPI scores of Mexican-American college students. *Journal of College Student Personnel, 11*, 419–422.

Rich, C. C., & Davis, H. G. (1969). Concurrent validity of MMPI alcoholism scales. *Journal of Clinical Psychology, 25*, 425–426.

Ries, H. A. (1966). The MMPI *K* scale as a predictor of prognosis. *Journal of Clinical Psychology, 22*, 212–213.

Robins, L. N., Helzer, J. E., Weisman, M. M., Orvaschel, H., Gruenberg, E., Burke, Jr., J. D., & Regier, D. A. (1984). Lifetime prevalence rates of specific psychiatric disorders in three sites. *Archives of General Psychiatry, 41*, 949–958.

Rogers, R. (1983). Malingering or random? A research note on obvious vs. subtle subscales of the MMPI. *Journal of Clinical Psychology, 39*, 257–258.

Rogers, R., Dolmetsch, R., & Cavanaugh, Jr., J. L. (1983). Identification of random responders on MMPI protocols. *Journal of Personality Assessment, 47*, 364–368.

Rogers, R., Harris, M., & Thatcher, A. A. (1983). Identification of random responders on the MMPI: An actuarial approach. *Psychological Reports, 53*, 1171–1174.

Rohan, W. P., Tatro, R. L., & Rotman, S. R. (1969). MMPI changes in alcoholics during hospitalization. *Quarterly Journal of Studies on Alcohol, 30*, 389–400.

Rosen, A. (1952). Reliability of MMPI scales. *American Psychologist, 7*, 341.

Rosen, A. (1954). Detection of suicidal patients:

An example of some limitations in the prediction of infrequent events. *Journal of Consulting Psychology, 18,* 397–403.

Rosen, A. (1958). Differentiation of diagnostic groups by individual MMPI scales. *Journal of Consulting Psychology, 22,* 453–457.

Rosen, A. C. (1974). Brief report of MMPI characteristics of sexual deviation. *Psychological Reports, 35,* 73–74.

Rosenblatt, A. I., & Pritchard, D. A. (1978). Moderators of racial differences on the MMPI. *Journal of Consulting and Clinical Psychology, 46,* 1572–1573.

Rubin, H. (1954). Validity of a critical-item scale for schizophrenia on the MMPI. *Journal of Consulting Psychology, 18,* 219–220.

Ruch, F. L., & Ruch, W. W. (1967). The *K* factor as a (validity) suppressor variable in predicting success in selling. *Journal of Applied Psychology, 51,* 201–204.

Saunders, T. R., & Gravitz, M. A. (1974). Sex differences in the endorsement of MMPI critical items. *Journal of Clinical Psychology, 30,* 557–558.

Scagnelli, J. (1975). The significance of dependency in the paranoid syndrome. *Journal of Clinical Psychology, 31,* 29–34.

Schenkenberg, T., Gottfredson, D. K., & Christensen, P. (1984). Age differences in MMPI scale scores from 1,189 psychiatric patients. *Journal of Clinical Psychology, 40,* 1420–1426.

Schlenger, W. E., & Kulka, R. A. (1987, August). *Performance of the Keane-Fairbank MMPI scale and other self-report measures in identifying post-traumatic stress disorder.* Paper presented at the annual meeting of the American Psychological Association, New York.

Schmidt, H. O. (1948). Notes on the MMPI: The *K* factor. *Journal of Consulting Psychology, 12,* 337–342.

Schneck, J. M. (1948). Clinical evaluation of the *F* scale on the MMPI. *American Journal of Psychiatry, 104,* 440–442.

Schretlen, D. (1990). A limitation of using the Wiener and Harmon obvious and subtle scales to detect faking on the MMPI. *Journal of Clinical Psychology, 46,* 782–786.

Schwartz, M. F., & Graham, J. R. (1979). Construct validity of the MacAndrew alcoholism scale. *Journal of Consulting and Clinical Psychology, 47,* 1090–1095.

Schwartz, M. S. (1969). "Organicity" and the MMPI *1-3-9* and *2-9* codes. *Proceedings of the 77th Annual Convention of the APA, 4,* 519–520.

Schwartz, M. S., & Krupp, N. E. (1971). The MMPl "conversion V" among 50,000 medical patients: A study of incidence, criteria, and profile elevation. *Journal of Clinical Psychology, 27,* 89–95.

Schwartz, M. S., Osborne, D., & Krupp, N. E. (1972). Moderating effects of age and sex on the association of medical diagnoses and *1-3/3-1* MMPI profiles. *Journal of Clinical Psychology, 28,* 502–505.

Serkownek, K. (1975). *Subscales for Scales 5 and 0 of the MMPI.* Unpublished manuscript.

Sheppard, D., Smith, G. T., & Rosenbaum, G. (1988). Use of MMPI subtypes in predicting completion of a residential alcoholism treatment program. *Journal of Consulting and Clinical Psychology, 56,* 590–596.

Shore, R. E. (1976). A statistical note on "Differential misdiagnosis of blacks and whites by the MMPI." *Journal of Personality Assessment, 40,* 21–23.

Shultz, T. D., Gibeau, P. J., & Barry, S. M. (1968). Utility of MMPl "cookbooks." *Journal of Clinical Psychology, 24,* 430–433.

Shweder, R. A. (1977a). Illusory correlation and the MMPI controversy. *Journal of Consulting and Clinical Psychology, 45,* 917–924.

Shweder, R. A. (1977b). Illusory correlation and the MMPI controversy: Reply to some of the allusions and elusions in Block's and Edwards' commentaries. *Journal of Consulting and Clinical Psychology, 45,* 936–940.

Silver, R. J., & Sines, L. K. (1962). Diagnostic efficiency of the MMPI with and without the *K* correction. *Journal of Clinical Psychology, 18,* 312–314.

Simon, W., & Gilberstadt, H. (1958). Analysis of the personality structure of 26 actual suicides. *Journal of Nervous and Mental Disease, 127,* 555–557.

Sines, J. O. (1966). Actuarial methods in personality assessment. In B. A. Maher (Ed.), *Progress in experimental personality research* (pp. 133–193). New York: Academic Press.

Sines, J. O. (1977). M-F: Bipolar and probably multidimensional. *Journal of Clinical Psychology, 33,* 1038–1041.

Sines, L. K., Baucom, D. H., & Gruba, G. H. (1979). A validity scale sign calling for caution in the interpretation of MMPIs among psychiatric inpatients. *Journal of Personality Assessment, 43,* 604–607.

Singer, M. I. (1970). Comparison of indicators of homosexuality on the MMPI. *Journal of Consulting and Clinical Psychology, 34,* 15–18.

Smith, C. P., & Graham, J. R. (1981). Behavioral correlates for the MMPI standard *F* scale and for a modified *F* scale for black and white psychiatric patients. *Journal of Consulting and Clinical Psychology, 49,* 455–459.

Smith, E. E. (1959). Defensiveness, insight, and the *K* scale. *Journal of Consulting Psychology, 23,* 275–277.

Snyder, D. K. (1989). Assessing chronic pain with the MMPI. In T. W. Miller (Ed.), *Chronic pain: Clinical issues in health care management.* Madison, CT: International Universities Press.

Snyder, D. K., Kline, R. B., & Podany, E. C. (1985). Comparison of external correlates of MMPI substance abuse scales across sex and race. *Journal of Consulting and Clinical Psychology, 53,* 520–525.

Snyter, C. M., & Graham, J. R. (1984). The utility of subtle and obvious MMPI subscales based on scale-specific ratings. *Journal of Clinical Psychology, 40,* 981–985.

Spirito, A., Faust, D., Myers, B., & Bechtel, D. (1988). Clinical utility of the MMPI in the evaluation of adolescent suicide attempters. *Journal of Personality Assessment, 52,* 204–211.

Stanton, J. M. (1956). Group personality profile related to aspects of antisocial behavior. *Journal of Criminal Law, Criminology, and Police Science, 47,* 340–349.

Stein, K. B. (1968). The TSC scales: The outcome of a cluster analysis of the 550 MMPI items. In P. McReynolds (Ed,), *Advances in psychological assessment.* (Vol. I, pp. 80–104). Palo Alto CA: Science & Behavior Books.

Sternbach, R. A., Wolf, S. R., Murphy, R. W., & Akeson, W. H. (1973). Traits of pain patients: The low-back "loser." *Psychosomatics, 14,* 226–229.

Stevens, M. R., & Reilley, R. R. (1980). MMPI short forms: A literature review. *Journal of Personality Assessment, 44,* 368–376.

Strauss, M. E., Gynther, M. D., & Wallhermfechtel, J. (1974). Differential misdiagnosis of blacks and whites by the MMPI. *Journal of Personality Assessment, 38,* 55–60.

Streiner, D. L., & Miller, H. R. (1986). Can a good short form of the MMPI ever be developed? *Journal of Clinical Psychology, 42,* 109–113.

Sue, S., & Sue, D. W. (1974). MMPI comparisons between Asian-American and non-Asian students utilizing a student health psychiatric clinic. *Journal of Counseling Psychology, 21,* 423–427.

Super, D. E. (1942). The Bernreuter Personality Inventory: A review of research. *Psychological Bulletin, 39,* 94–125.

Sutker, P. B., Allain, A. N., & Geyer, S. (1978). Female criminal violence and differential MMPI characteristics. *Journal of Consulting and Clinical Psychology, 46,* 1141–1143.

Sutker, P. B., Archer, R. P., & Allain, A. N. (1978). Drug abuse patterns, personality characteristics, and relationships with sex, race, and sensation seeking. *Journal of Consulting and Clinical Psychology, 46,* 1374–1378.

Sutker, P. B., Archer, R. P., & Allain, A. N. (1980). Psychopathology of drug abusers: Sex and ethnic considerations. *The International Journal of the Addictions, 15,* 605–613.

Sutker, P. B., & Kilpatrick, D. G. (1973). Personality, biographical, and racial correlates of sexual attitudes and behavior. *Proceedings of the American Psychological Association, 8,* 261–262.

Sweetland, A., & Quay, H. (1953). A note on the *K* scale of the MMPI. *Journal of Consulting Psychology, 17,* 314–316.

Swenson, W. M. (1961). Structured personality testing in the aged: An MMPI study of the gerontic population. *Journal of Clinical Psychology, 17,* 302–304.

Swenson, W. M., Pearson, J. S., & Osborne, D. (1973). *An MMPI source book: Basic item, scale, and pattern data on 50,000 medical patients.* Minneapolis: University of Minnesota Press.

Tamkin, A. S., & Scherer, I. W. (1957). What is measured by the "Cannot Say" scale of the group MMPI? *Journal of Consulting Psychology, 21,* 370.

Tanner, B. A. (1990). Composite descriptions associated with rare MMPI two-point code types: Codes that involve Scale *5. Journal of Clinical Psychology, 46,* 425–431.

Tarter, R. E., & Perley, R. N. (1975). Clinical and perceptual characteristics of paranoids and paranoid schizophrenics. *Journal of Clinical Psychology, 31,* 42–44.

Taulbee, E. S., & Sisson, B. D. (1957). Configurational analysis of MMPI profiles of psychiatric groups. *Journal of Consulting Psychology, 21,* 413–417.

Terman, L. M., & Miles, C. C. (1938). *Manual of information and directions for use of Attitude-Interest Analysis Test*. New York: McGraw-Hill.

Towne, W. S., & Tsushima, W. T. (1978). The use of the low back and the dorsal scales in the identification of functional low back patients. *Journal of Clinical Psychology, 34*, 88–91.

Truscott, D. (1990). Assessment of Overcontrolled Hostility in adolescence. *Psychological Assessment: A Journal of Consulting and Clinical Psychology, 2*, 145–148.

Tsushima, W. T., & Onorato, V. A. (1982). Comparison of MMPI scores of white and Japanese-American medical patients. *Journal of Consulting and Clinical Psychology, 50*, 150–151.

Tyler, F. T. (1951). A factorial analysis of fifteen MMPI scales. *Journal of Consulting Psychology, 15*, 451–456.

Tyler, F. T., & Michaelis, J. U. (1953). *K*-scores applied to MMPI scales for college women. *Educational and Psychological Measurement, 13*, 459–466.

Uecker, A. E., Boutilier, L. R., & Richardson, E. H. (1980). "Indianism" and MMPI scores of men alcoholics. *Journal of Studies on Alcohol, 41*, 357–362.

Velasquez, R. J. (1984). *An atlas of MMPI group profiles on Mexican Americans*. Los Angeles: Spanish Speaking Mental Health Research Center.

Velasquez, R. J., & Callahan, W. J. (1987). MMPI differences among three diagnostic groups of Mexican-American state hospital patients. *Psychological Reports, 60*, 1071–1074.

Velasquez, R. J., & Callahan, W. J. (1990a). MMPI comparisons of Hispanic- and White-American veterans seeking treatment for alcoholism. *Psychological Reports, 67*, 95–98.

Velasquez, R. J., & Callahan, W. J. (1990b). MMPIs of Hispanic, black, and white DSM-III schizophrenics. *Psychological Reports, 66*, 819–822.

Velasquez, R. J., Callahan, W. J., & Carrillo, R. (1989). MMPI profiles of Hispanic-American inpatient and outpatient sex offenders. *Psychological Reports, 65*, 1055–1058.

Velasquez, R. J., & Gimenez, L. (1987). MMPI differences among three diagnostic groups of Mexican-American state hospital patients. *Psychological Reports, 60*, 1071–1074.

Vesprani, G. J., & Seeman, W. (1974). MMPI *X* and zero items in a psychiatric outpatient group. *Journal of Personality Assessment, 38*, 61–64.

Vestre, N. D., & Watson, C. G. (1972). Behavioral correlates of the MMPI Paranoia scale. *Psychological Reports, 31*, 851–854.

Vincent, K. R. (1984). *MMPI-168 codebook*. Norwood, NJ: Ablex.

Vincent, N. M. P., Linsz, N. L., & Greene, M. I. (1966). The *L* scale of the MMPI as an index of falsification. *Journal of Clinical Psychology, 22*, 214–215.

Wales, B., & Seeman, W. (1968). A new method for detecting the fake good response set on the MMPI. *Journal of Clinical Psychology, 24*, 211–216.

Wales, B., & Seeman, W. (1972). Instructional sets and MMPI items. *Journal of Personality Assessment, 36*, 282–286.

Walker, C. E., & Ward, J. (1969). Identification and elimination of offensive items from the MMPI. *Journal of Projective Techniques and Personality Assessment, 33*, 385–388.

Walters, G. D. (1984). Identifying schizophrenia by means of Scale *8 Sc* of the MMPI. *Journal of Personality Assessment, 48*, 390–391.

Walters, G. D. (1985). Scale *4 (Pd)* of the MMPI and the diagnosis Antisocial Personality. *Journal of Personality Assessment, 49*, 474–476.

Walters, G. D. (1986). Screening for psychopathology in groups of black and white prison inmates by means of the MMPI. *Journal of Personality Assessment, 50*, 257–264.

Walters, G. D. (1988a). Assessing dissimulation and denial on the MMPI in a sample of maxium security, male inmates. *Journal of Personality Assessment, 52*, 465–474.

Walters, G. D. (1988b). Schizophrenia. In R. L. Greene (Ed.), *The MMPI: Use in specific populations* (pp. 50–73). San Antonio: Grune & Stratton.

Walters, G. D., & Greene, R. L. (1988). Differentiating between schizophrenic and manic inpatients by means of the MMPI. *Journal of Personality Assessment, 52*, 91–95.

Walters, G. D., Greene, R. L., & Jeffrey, T. B. (1984). Discriminating between alcoholic and nonalcoholic blacks and whites on the MMPI. *Journal of Personality Assessment, 48*, 486–488.

Walters, G. D., Greene, R. L., Jeffrey, T. B., Kruzich, D. J., & Haskin, J. J. (1983). Racial variations on the MacAndrew Alcoholism scale of the MMPI. *Journal of Consulting and Clinical Psychology, 51*, 947–948.

Walters, G. D., White, T. W., & Greene, R. L. (1988). Use of the MMPI to identify malingering and exaggeration of psychiatric symptomatology in male prison inmates. *Journal of Consulting and Clinical Psychology, 56,* 111–117.

Ward, L. C. (1986). MMPI item subtlety research: Current issues and directions. *Journal of Personality Assessment, 50,* 73–79.

Ward, L. C., & Dillon, E. A. (1990). Psychiatric symptoms of the Minnesota Multiphasic Personality Inventory (MMPI) Masculinity-Femininity scale. *Psychological Assessment: A Journal of Consulting and Clinical Psychology, 2,* 286–288.

Ward, L. C., & Ward, J. W. (1980). MMPI readability reconsidered. *Journal of Personality Assessment, 44,* 387–389.

Warman, R. E. & Hannum, T. E. (1965). MMPI pattern changes in female prisoners. *Journal of Research in Crime and Delinquency, 2,* 72–76.

Wasyliw, O. E., Grossman, L. S., Haywood, T. W., & Cavanaugh, Jr., J. L. (1988). The detection of malingering in criminal forensic groups: MMPI validity scales. *Journal of Personality Assessment, 52,* 321–333.

Watson, C. G., Klett, W. G., Walters, C., & Vassar, P. (1984). Suicide and the MMPI: A cross-validation of predictors. *Journal of Clinical Psychology, 40,* 115–119.

Wauck, L. A. (1950). Schizophrenia and the MMPI. *Journal of Clinical Psychology, 6,* 279–282.

Webb, J. T. (1971). Regional and sex differences in MMPI scale high-point frequencies of psychiatric patients. *Journal of Clinical Psychology, 27,* 483–486.

Wechsler, D. (1980). *Wechsler Adult Intelligence Scale-Revised manual.* New York: Psychological Corporation.

Weed, N. C., Ben-Porath, Y. S, & Butcher, J. N. (1990). Failure of the Wiener and Harmon Minnesota Multiphasic Personality Inventory (MMPI) subtle scales as personality descriptors and as validity indicators. *Psychological Assessment: A Journal of Consulting and Clinical Psychology, 2,* 281–285.

Weinstein, J., Averill, J. R., Opton, Jr., E. M., & Lazarus, R. S. (1968). Defensive style and discrepancy between self-report and physiological indexes of stress. *Journal of Personality and Social Psychology, 10,* 406–413.

Weisenberg, M. (1977). Pain and pain control. *Psychological Bulletin, 84,* 1008–1044.

Weiss, R. W., & Russakoff, S. (1977). Relationship of MMPI scores of drug-abusers to personal variables and type of treatment program. *Journal of Psychology, 96,* 25–29.

Welsh, G. S. (1956). Factor dimensions *A* and *R.* In G. S. Welsh & W. G. Dahlstrom (Eds.), *Basic readings on the MMPI in psychology and medicine* (pp. 264–281). Minneapolis: University of Minnesota Press.

Welsh, G. S. (1965). MMPI profiles and factor scales *A* and *R. Journal of Clinical Psychology, 21,* 43–47.

Werner, P. D., Becker, J. M. T., & Yesavage, J. A. (1983). Concurrent validity of the Overcontrolled Hostility scale for psychotics. *Psychological Reports, 52,* 93–94.

Wiener, D. N. (1948). Subtle and obvious keys for the MMPI. *Journal of Consulting Psychology, 12,* 164–170.

Wiggins, J. S. (1959). Interrelationships among MMPI measures of dissimulation under standard and social desirability instructions. *Journal of Consulting Psychology, 23,* 419–427.

Wiggins, J. S. (1966). Substantive dimensions of self-report in the MMPI item pool. *Psychological Monographs, 80*(22, Whole No. 630).

Wiggins, J. S. (1973). *Personality and prediction: Principles of personality assessment.* Reading, MA: Addison-Wesley.

Wiggins, J. S., Goldberg, L. R., & Appelbaum, M. (1971). MMPI content scales: Interpretive norms and correlations with other scales. *Journal of Consulting and Clinical Psychology, 37,* 403–410.

Wiggins, N., & Hoffman, P. J. (1968). Three models of clinical judgment. *Journal of Abnormal Psychology, 73,* 70–77.

Wilcox, P., & Dawson, J. G. (1977). Role-played and hypnotically induced simulation of psychopathology on the MMPI. *Journal of Clinical Psychology, 33,* 743–745.

Williams, C. L. (1983). Further investigation of the *Si* scale of the MMPI: Reliabilities, correlates, and subscale utility. *Journal of Clinical Psychology, 39,* 951–957.

Williams, C. L. (1986). MMPI profiles from adolescents: Interpretive strategies and treatment considerations. *Journal of Child and Adolescent Psychotherapy, 3,* 179–193.

Williams, C. L., & Butcher, J. N. (1989a). An MMPI study of adolescents: I. Empirical validity of the standard scales. *Psychological Assessment: A Journal of Consulting and Clinical Psychology, 1,* 251–259.

Williams, C. L., & Butcher, J. N. (1989b). An MMPI study of adolescents: II. Verification and limitations of code type classifications. *Psychological Assessment: A Journal of Consulting and Clinical Psychology, 1,* 260–265.

Wilson, R. L. (1980). *A comparison of the predictive validities of subtle versus obvious MMPI items: Predicting the elusive neurosis.* Unpublished Master's thesis, Auburn University.

Wimbish, L. G. (1984). *The importance of appropriate norms for the computerized interpretations of adolescent MMPI profiles.* Unpublished doctoral dissertation, Ohio State University, Columbus.

Winter, W. D., & Stortroen, M. (1963). A comparison of several MMPI indices to differentiate psychotics from normals. *Journal of Clinical Psychology, 19,* 220–223.

Winters, K. D., Newmark, C. S., Lumry, A. E., Leach, K., & Weintraub, S. (1985). MMPI codetypes characteristic of DSM-III schizophrenics, depressives, and bipolars. *Journal of Clinical Psychology, 41,* 382–386.

Witt, P. H., & Gynther, M. D. (1975). Another explanation for black-white MMPI differences. *Journal of Clinical Psychology, 31,* 69–70

Wong, M. R. (1984). MMPI Scale Five: Its meaning, or lack thereof. *Journal of Personality Assessment, 48,* 279–284.

Woodworth, R. S. (1920). *Personal data sheet.* Chicago: Stoelting.

Wooten, A. J. (1984). Effectiveness of the *K* correction in the detection of psychopathology and its impact on profile height and configuration among young adult men. *Journal of Consulting and Clinical Psychology, 52,* 468–473.

Worthington, D. L., & Schlottmann, R. S. (1986). The predictive validity of subtle and obvious empirically derived psychological test items under faking conditions. *Journal of Personality Assessment, 50,* 171–181.

Wrobel, T. A., & Lachar, D. (1982). Validity of the Wiener subtle and obvious scales for the MMPI: Another example of the importance of inventory-item content. *Journal of Consulting and Clinical Psychology, 50,* 469–470.

Yonge, G. D. (1966). Certain consequences of applying the *K* factor to MMPI scores. *Educational and Psychological Measurement, 26,* 887–893.

Zager, L. D., & Megargee, E. I. (1981). Seven MMPI alcohol and drug abuse scales: An empirical investigation of their interrelationships, convergent and discriminant validity, and degree of racial bias. *Journal of Personality and Social Psychology, 40,* 532–544.

Zelin, M. L. (1971). Validity of the MMPI scales for measuring twenty psychiatric dimensions. *Journal of Consulting and Clinical Psychology, 37,* 286–290.

Zuckerman, M., Levitt, E. E., & Lubin, B. (1961). Concurrent and construct validity of direct and indirect measures of dependency. *Journal of Consulting Psychology, 25,* 316–323.

Author Index

Subject Index